Python Programming for Engineers and Scientists

Cengage

Australia • Brazil • Canada • Mexico • Singapore • United Kingdom • United States

Python Programming for Engineers and Scientists

SVP, Product: Cheryl Costantini

VP, Product: Thais Alencar

Portfolio Product Director: Rita Lombard

Senior Portfolio Product Manager: Tim Anderson

Product Assistant: Emily Smith

Learning Designer: MariCarmen Constable

Content Manager: Samantha Enders

Digital Project Manager: John Smigelski

VP, Product Marketing: Jason Sakos

Senior Director, Product Marketing: Danae April

Product Marketing Manager: Mackenzie Paine

Content Acquisition Analyst: Ann Hoffman

Production Service: Straive

Designer: Gaby McCracken

Cover Image Source: Jackie Niam/Shutterstock.com.

For product information and technology assistance, contact us at
**Cengage Customer & Sales Support, 1-800-354-9706
or support.cengage.com.**

For permission to use material from this text or product, submit all requests online at **www.copyright.com**.

Library of Congress Control Number: 2023921243

ISBN: 979-8-214-00244-6

Cengage
5191 Natorp Boulevard
Mason, OH 45040
USA

Cengage is a leading provider of customized learning solutions. Our employees reside in nearly 40 different countries and serve digital learners in 165 countries around the world. Find your local representative at: **www.cengage.com**.

To learn more about Cengage platforms and services, register or access your online learning solution, or purchase materials for your course, visit **www.cengage.com**.

Notice to the Reader

Printed at CLDPC, USA, 01-24

Brief Contents

Contents

Chapter 3

Loops and Selection Statements   57

Chapter 4

Strings and Text Files   93

Chapter 5

Lists and Dictionaries   125

Chapter 6

Design with Functions   159

Chapter 7

Design with Recursion **185**

Chapter 8

Simple Graphics and Image Processing **211**

Chapter 9

Graphical User Interfaces   253

Chapter 10

Design with Classes   295

Chapter 11

Data Analysis and Visualization **353**

Chapter 12

Multithreading, Networks, and Client/Server Programming **391**

Chapter 13

Searching, Sorting, and Complexity Analysis ... 431

Appendix A

Python Resources ... 469

Appendix B

Installing the `images` and `breezypythongui` Libraries ... 471

Appendix C

The API for Image Processing   **473**

Appendix D

Transition from Python to Java and C++   **475**

Appendix E

Suggestions for Further Reading   **477**

Preface

This Python programming language textbook and course have been adapted from Cengage's successful *Fundamentals of Python: First Programs, 3e*, © 2024 authored by Kenneth Lambert. For this version, we have added a new section in each chapter titled Lab Activities to give engineering and science students Python programming activities relevant to their future studies. The textbook and course are intended for a first course in Python programming and problem solving.

This textbook covers five major aspects of computing:

1. **Programming basics**—Data types, control structures, algorithm development, and program design with functions are basic ideas that you need to master in order to solve problems with computers. This textbook examines these core topics in detail and gives you practice employing your understanding of them to solve a wide range of problems.

2. **Object-oriented programming (OOP)**—Object-oriented programming is the dominant programming paradigm used to develop large software systems. This textbook introduces you to the fundamental principles of OOP and enables you to apply them successfully.

3. **Data and information processing**—Most useful programs rely on data structures to solve problems. These data structures include strings, arrays, files, lists, and dictionaries. This textbook introduces you to these commonly used data structures and includes examples that illustrate criteria for selecting the appropriate data structures for given problems.

4. **Software development life cycle**—Rather than isolate software development techniques in one or two chapters, this textbook deals with them throughout in the context of numerous case studies. Among other things, you'll learn that coding a program is often not the most difficult or challenging aspect of problem solving and software development.

5. **Contemporary applications of computing**—The best way to learn about programming and problem solving is to create interesting programs with real-world applications. In this textbook, you'll begin by creating applications that involve numerical problems and text processing. For example, you'll learn the basics of encryption techniques, such as those that are used to make your credit card number and other information secure on the Internet. But unlike many other introductory textbooks, this one does not restrict itself to problems involving numbers and text. Most contemporary applications involve graphical user interfaces, event-driven programming, graphics, image manipulation, network communications, and data analysis. These topics are not consigned to the margins but are presented in depth after you have mastered the basics of programming.

Why Python?

Computer technology and applications have become increasingly more sophisticated over the past three decades, and so has the computer science curriculum, especially at the introductory level. Today's students learn a bit of programming and problem solving and are then expected to move quickly into topics like software development, complexity analysis, and data structures that 35 years ago were relegated to advanced courses. In addition, the ascent of object-oriented programming as the dominant paradigm of problem solving has led instructors and textbook authors to implant powerful, industrial-strength programming languages such as

C++ and Java in the introductory curriculum. As a result, instead of experiencing the rewards and excitement of solving problems with computers, beginning computer programming students often become overwhelmed by the combined tasks of mastering advanced concepts as well as the syntax of a programming language.

This textbook uses the Python programming language as a way of making the first year of studying computer programming more manageable and attractive for students and instructors alike. Python has the following pedagogical benefits:

- Python has simple, conventional syntax. Python statements are very close to those of pseudocode algorithms, and Python expressions use the conventional notation found in algebra. Thus, students can spend less time learning the syntax of a programming language and more time learning to solve interesting problems.

- Python has safe semantics. Any expression or statement whose meaning violates the definition of the language produces an error message.

- Python scales well. It is very easy for beginners to write simple programs in Python. Python also includes all of the advanced features of a modern programming language, such as support for data structures and object-oriented software development, for use when they become necessary.

- Python is highly interactive. Expressions and statements can be entered at an interpreter's prompts to allow the programmer to try out experimental code and receive immediate feedback. Longer code segments can then be composed and saved in script files to be loaded and run as modules or standalone applications.

- Python is general purpose. In today's context, this means that the language includes resources for contemporary applications, including media computing and networks.

- Python is free and is in widespread use in industry. Students can download Python to run on a variety of devices. There is a large Python user community, and expertise in Python programming has great résumé value.

To summarize these benefits, Python is a comfortable and flexible vehicle for expressing ideas about computation, both for beginners and for experts. If students learn these ideas well in the first course, they should have no problems making a quick transition to other languages needed for courses later in the curriculum. Most importantly, beginning students will spend less time staring at a computer screen and more time thinking about interesting problems to solve.

Organization of the Textbook

The approach of this textbook is easygoing, with each new concept introduced only when it is needed.

Chapter 1 introduces computer programming by focusing on two fundamental ideas, algorithms and information processing. A brief overview of computer hardware and software, followed by an extended discussion of the history of computing, sets the context for computational problem solving.

Chapters 2 and 3 cover the basics of problem solving and algorithm development using the standard control structures of expression evaluation, sequencing, Boolean logic, selection, and iteration with the basic numeric data types. Emphasis in these chapters is on problem solving that is both systematic and experimental, involving algorithm design, testing, and documentation.

Chapters 4 and 5 introduce the use of the strings, text files, lists, and dictionaries. These data structures are both remarkably easy to manipulate in Python and support some interesting applications. Chapter 5 also introduces simple function definitions as a way of organizing algorithmic code.

Chapter 6 explores the technique and benefits of procedural abstraction with function definitions. Top-down design and stepwise refinement with functions are examined as means of structuring code to solve complex problems. Details of namespace organization (parameters, temporary variables, and module variables) and communication among software components are discussed.

Chapter 7 examines recursive design with functions. A section on functional programming with higher-order functions shows how to exploit functional design patterns to simplify solutions.

Chapter 8 focuses on the use of existing objects and classes to compose programs. Special attention is paid to the application programming interface (API), or set of methods, of a class of objects and the manner in which objects cooperate to solve problems. This chapter also introduces two contemporary applications of computing: graphics and image processing. These are areas in which object-based programming is particularly useful.

Chapter 9 introduces the definition of new classes to construct graphical user interfaces (GUIs). The chapter contrasts the event-driven model of GUI programs with the process-driven model of terminal-based programs. The chapter explores the creation and layout of GUI components, as well as the design of GUI-based applications using the model/view pattern. The initial approach to defining new classes in this chapter is unusual for an introductory textbook: students learn that the easiest way to define a new class is to customize an existing class using subclassing and inheritance.

Chapter 10 continues the exploration of object-oriented design with the definition of entirely new classes. Several examples of simple class definitions from different application domains are presented. Some of these are then integrated into more realistic applications to show how object-oriented software components can be used to build complex systems. Emphasis is on designing appropriate interfaces for classes that exploit polymorphism.

Chapter 11 introduces tools and techniques for performing data analysis, a fast-growing application area of computer programming. Topics include the acquisition and cleaning of data sets, applying functions to determine relationships among data, and deploying graphs, plots, and charts to visualize these relationships.

Chapter 12 covers advanced material related to several important areas of computing: concurrent programming, networks, and client/server applications. This chapter thus gives students challenging experiences near the end of the first course. This chapter introduces multithreaded programs and the construction of simple network-based client/server applications.

Chapter 13 covers some topics addressed at the beginning of a traditional CS2 course. This chapter introduces complexity analysis with big-O notation. Enough material is presented to enable you to perform simple analyses of the running time and memory usage of algorithms and data structures, using search and sort algorithms as examples.

Features of the Textbook

This textbook explains and develops concepts carefully, using frequent examples and diagrams. New concepts are then applied in complete programs to show how they aid in solving problems. The chapters place an early and consistent emphasis on good writing habits and neat, readable documentation.

The textbook includes several other important features:

- **Chapter Objectives:** Each chapter begins with a set of learning objectives which describe the skills and concepts you will acquire from a careful reading of the chapter.

- **Chapter Summary:** Each chapter ends with a summary of the major concepts covered in the chapter.

- **Key Terms:** When a technical term is introduced in the text, it appears in boldface. The list of terms appears after the chapter summary. Definitions of the key terms are provided in the glossary.

> ## Exercise

Exercises: Most major sections of each chapter end with exercise questions that reinforce the reading by asking basic questions about the material in the section.

Case Study

Case Studies: The Case Studies present complete Python programs ranging from the simple to the substantial. To emphasize the importance and usefulness of the software development life cycle, case studies are discussed in the framework of a user request, followed by analysis, design, implementation, and suggestions for testing, with well-defined tasks performed at each stage. Some case studies are extended in end-of-chapter programming exercises.

Fail-Safe Programming

Fail-Safe Programming: Fail-Safe Programming sections include a discussion of ways to make a program detect and respond gracefully to disturbances in its runtime environment.

Review Questions

Review Questions: Multiple-choice review questions allow you to revisit the concepts presented in each chapter.

Programming Exercises

Programming Exercises: Each chapter ends with a set of programming projects of varying difficulty. Each programming exercise is mapped to one or more relevant chapter learning objectives and gives you the opportunity to design and implement a complete program that utilizes major concepts presented in that chapter.

Debugging Exercises

Debugging Exercises: Debugging exercises illustrate a typical program error with suggestions for repairing it.

Lab Activities

Lab Activities: The group of activities found at the end of each chapter will build a number of skills useful in the Engineering and Science fields. From building and using methods, to branching logic, iteration, searching, sorting and filtering, common application development skills with Python, and potentially with other languages, will be developed.

- **A software toolkit for image processing:** This textbook comes with an open-source Python toolkit for the easy image processing discussed in Chapter 8. The toolkit can be obtained with the ancillaries at **www.cengage.com**

- **A software toolkit for GUI programming:** This textbook comes with an open-source Python toolkit for the easy GUI programming introduced in Chapter 9. The toolkit can be obtained with the ancillaries at **www.cengage.com**

- **Appendices:** Five appendices include information on obtaining Python resources, installing the toolkits, using the toolkits' interfaces, and suggestions for further reading.

- **Glossary:** Definitions of key terms are collected in a glossary.

Inclusivity and Diversity

Cengage is committed to providing educational content that is inclusive and welcoming to *all* learners. Research demonstrates that students who experience a sense of belonging in class more successfully make meaning out of, and find relevance in, what they encounter in learning content. To improve both the learning process and outcomes, our materials seek to affirm the fullness of human diversity with respect to ability, language, culture, gender, age, socio-economics, and other forms of human difference that students may bring to the classroom.

Across the computing industry, standard coding language, such as "Master" and "Slave" is being retired in favor of language that is more inclusive, such as "Controller/Responder," "Supervisor/Worker," "Primary/Replica," or "Leader/Follower." At this time, different software development and social media companies are adopting their own replacement language and currently there is no shared standard. In addition, the terms "Master" and "Slave" remain deeply embedded in legacy code and understanding this terminology remains necessary for new programmers. When required for understanding, Cengage will introduce the non-inclusive term in the first instance but will then provide an appropriate replacement terminology for the remainder of the discussion or example. We appreciate your feedback as we work to make our products more inclusive for all.

For more information about Cengage's commitment to inclusivity and diversity, please visit **https://www.cengage .com/inclusion-diversity/**

Course Solutions

Online Learning Platform: MindTap

Today's leading online learning platform, MindTap for *Python Programming for Engineers and Scientists* provides complete control to craft a personalized, engaging learning experience that challenges students, builds confidence, and elevates performance.

MindTap introduces students to core concepts from the beginning of the course, using a simplified learning path that progresses from understanding to application and delivers access to eTextbooks, study tools, interactive media, auto-graded assessments, and performance analytics.

MindTap activities for *Python Programming for Engineers and Scientists* are designed to help students build the skills needed in today's workforce. Research shows employers seek critical thinkers, troubleshooters, and creative problem-solvers to stay relevant in our fast-paced, technology-driven world. MindTap achieves this with assignments and activities that provide hands-on practice and real-life relevance. Students are guided through assignments that reinforce basic knowledge and understanding before moving on to more challenging problems.

All MindTap activities and assignments are tied to defined chapter learning objectives. Hands-on coding labs provide real-life application and practice. Readings and dynamic visualizations support the lecture, while a post-course assessment measures exactly how much a student has learned. MindTap provides the analytics and reporting to easily see where the class stands in terms of progress, engagement, and completion rates. The content and learning path can be used as provided, customized directly in the MindTap platform, or integrated into the Learning Management System (LMS) to meet the needs of a particular course . Instructors can control what students see and when they see it. Learn more at **https://www.cengage.com/mindtap**.

In addition to the readings, the MindTap for *Python Programming for Engineers and Scientists* includes the following:

- **Coding labs.** These supplemental assignments provide real-world application and encourage students to practice new programming concepts in a complete online IDE. New and improved Guided Feedback provides personalized and immediate feedback to students as they proceed through their coding assignments so that they can understand and correct errors in their code.

- **Gradeable assessments and activities.** All assessments and activities from the readings are available as gradeable assignments within MindTap, including Exercises and Review Questions.

- **Video quizzes.** These graded assessments provide a visual explanation of foundational programming concepts that can be applied across multiple languages. Questions accompany each video to confirm understanding of new material.

- **Interactive activities.** These embedded interactive flowcharts, tabbed explorations, and click-to-reveal experiences are designed to engage students and help them assess their understanding of introductory computer science concepts as they progress through their chapter readings.

- **Interactive study aids.** Flashcards and PowerPoint lectures help users review main concepts from the units.

- **IDE.** Integrated into the learning path, MindTap includes an educational IDE with auto-graded coding assignments where students learn to read, write, and run code into a single graphical user interface (GUI), allowing them to develop critical thinking and problem-solving skills.

Supplemental Package

Instructor and Student Resources

Additional instructor and student resources for this product are available online.

Instructor assets include an Instructor's Manual, Educator's Guide, PowerPoint® slides, and a test bank powered by Cognero®. Student assets include data sets. Sign up or sign in at **www.cengage.com** to search for and access this product and its online resources.

- **Instructor Manual.** The Instructor Manual that accompanies this textbook includes additional instructional material to assist in class preparation, including items such as Overviews, Chapter Objectives, Teaching Tips, Quick Quizzes, Class Discussion Topics, Additional Projects, Additional Resources, and Key Terms.

- **Test Bank.** Cengage Testing Powered by Cognero is a flexible, online system that allows you to:

  - Author, edit, and manage test bank content from multiple Cengage solutions.

  - Create multiple test versions in an instant.

  - Deliver tests from your LMS, your classroom, or wherever you want.

- **PowerPoint Presentations.** This textbook provides PowerPoint slides to accompany each chapter. Slides may be used to guide classroom presentations, to make available to students for chapter review, or to print as classroom handouts. Files are provided for every figure in the textbook. Instructors may use the files to customize PowerPoint slides, illustrate quizzes, or create handouts.

- **Solution and Answer Guide.** Solutions and rationales to review questions and exercises are provided to assist with grading and student understanding.

- **Solutions.** Solutions to all programming exercises and case studies are available. If an input file is needed to run a programming exercise, it is included with the solution file.

- **Data Files.** Data files necessary to complete some of the steps in the programming exercises are available. If an input file is needed to run a program, it is included with the source code.

- **Educator's Guide.** The Educator's Guide contains a detailed outline of the corresponding MindTap course.

Supplements can be found at **https://faculty.cengage.com/**. Sign In or create an account, then search for this title. You can save the title for easy access and then download the resources that you need.

Acknowledgments

Thank you to our partners at MRCC Group for their work on this textbook: Michael Wegerbauer, Vice President; Michael Plucinski, Dan Neal, and Maura Sateriale, Subject Matter Experts.

In addition, thank you to the following people for the time and effort they contributed to *Python Programming for Engineers and Scientists*: Eric Williamson, Liberty University; Jason Carman, Horry, Georgetown Technical College; and Martin Osborne, Western Washington University.

Thank you also to Danielle Shaw, who helped to assure that the content of all data and solution files used for this textbook were correct and accurate.

Finally, thanks to the individuals at Cengage who made this book possible: Tran Pham, Portfolio Product Manager; Tim Anderson, Senior Portfolio Product Manager; Mary Convertino, Learning Designer; MariCarmen Constable, Learning Designer; Michelle Ruelos Cannistraci, Senior Content Manager; Samantha Enders, Content Manager; Troy Dundas, Technical Content Developer; Spencer Peppet, Developmental Editor; Ann Shaffer, Developmental Editor; and Emily Smith, Product Assistant.

## Chapter 1

Introduction

Learning Objectives

When you complete this chapter, you will be able to:

1.1 Describe the basic features of an algorithm

1.2 Explain how hardware and software collaborate in a computer's architecture

1.3 Summarize a brief history of computing

1.4 Compose and run a simple Python program

As a reader of this book, you almost certainly have played a video game and listened to digital music. It's likely that you have watched a movie on Netflix after preparing a snack in a microwave. Chances are that today you will make a phone call, send or receive a text message, take a photo, or consult your favorite social network on a smartphone, which is a small computer. You and your friends have most likely used a desktop or laptop computer to do significant coursework in high school or college.

Computer technology is almost everywhere: in our homes, schools, and in the places where we work and play. Computer technology is essential to modern entertainment, education, medicine, manufacturing, communications, government, and commerce. We have digital lifestyles in an information-based economy. Some people even claim that nature itself performs computations on information structures present in DNA and in the relationships among subatomic particles.

In the following chapters you will learn about computer science, which is the study of computation that has made this new technology and this new world possible. You will also learn how to use computers effectively and appropriately to enhance your own life and the lives of others.

1.1 Two Fundamental Ideas of Computer Science: Algorithms and Information Processing

Like most areas of study, computer science focuses on a broad set of interrelated ideas. Two of the most basic ones are algorithms and information processing. In this section, these ideas are introduced in an informal way. You will examine them in more detail in later chapters.

Algorithms

People computed long before the invention of modern computing devices, and many continue to use devices that we might consider primitive. For example, consider how merchants made change for customers in marketplaces before the existence of credit cards, pocket calculators, or cash registers. Making change can be a complex activity. It takes some mental effort to get it right every time. Let's consider what's involved in this process.

According to one method, the first step is to compute the difference between the purchase price and the amount of money that the customer gives the merchant. The result of this calculation is the total amount that the merchant must return to the purchaser. For example, if you buy a dozen eggs at the farmers' market for $2.39 and you give the farmer a $10 bill, she should return $7.61 to you. To produce this amount, the merchant selects the appropriate coins and bills that add up to $7.61.

According to another method, the merchant starts with the purchase price and goes toward the amount given. First, coins are selected to bring the price to the next dollar amount (in this case, $0.61 = 2 quarters, 1 dime, and 1 penny), then dollars are selected to bring the price to the next five-dollar amount (in this case, $2), and then, in this case, a $5 bill completes the transaction. As you will see in this book, there can be many possible methods or algorithms that solve the same problem, and the choice of the best one is a skill you will acquire with practice.

Few people can subtract three-digit numbers without resorting to some manual aids, such as pencil and paper. As you learned in grade school, you can carry out subtraction with pencil and paper by following a sequence of well-defined steps. You have probably done this many times but never made a list of the specific steps involved. Making such lists to solve problems is something computer scientists do all the time. For example, the following list of steps describes the process of subtracting two numbers using a pencil and paper:

Step 1 Write down the two numbers, with the larger number above the smaller number and their digits aligned in columns from the right.

Step 2 Assume that you will start with the rightmost column of digits and work your way left through the various columns.

Step 3 Write down the difference between the two digits in the current column of digits, borrowing a 1 from the top number's next column to the left if necessary.

Step 4 If there is no next column to the left, stop. Otherwise, move to the next column to the left, and go back to Step 3.

If the **computing agent** (in this case a human being) follows each of these simple steps correctly, the entire process results in a correct solution to the given problem. We assume in Step 3 that the agent already knows how to compute the difference between the two digits in any given column, borrowing if necessary.

To make change, most people can select the combination of coins and bills that represent the correct change amount without any manual aids, other than the coins and bills. But the mental calculations involved can still be described in a manner similar to the preceding steps, and we can resort to writing them down on paper if there is a dispute about the correctness of the change.

The sequence of steps that describes each of these computational processes is called an **algorithm**. Informally, an algorithm is like a recipe. It provides a set of instructions that tells us how to do something, such as make change, bake bread, or put together a piece of furniture. More precisely, an algorithm describes a process that ends with a solution to a problem. The algorithm is also one of the fundamental ideas of computer science. An algorithm has the following features:

1. An algorithm consists of a finite number of instructions.
2. Each individual instruction in an algorithm is well defined. This means that the action described by the instruction can be performed effectively or be **executed** by a computing agent. For example,

any computing agent capable of arithmetic can compute the difference between two digits. So, an algorithmic step that says "compute the difference between two digits" would be well defined. On the other hand, a step that says "divide a number by 0" is not well defined, because no computing agent could carry it out.

3. An algorithm describes a process that eventually halts after arriving at a solution to a problem. For example, the process of subtraction halts after the computing agent writes down the difference between the two digits in the leftmost column of digits.

4. An algorithm solves a general class of problems. For example, an algorithm that describes how to make change should work for any two amounts of money whose difference is greater than or equal to $0.00.

Creating a list of steps that describe how to make change might not seem like a major accomplishment to you. But the ability to break a task down into its component parts is one of the main jobs of a computer programmer. Once you write an algorithm to describe a particular type of computation, you can build a machine to do the computing. Put another way, if you can develop an algorithm to solve a problem, you can automate the task of solving the problem. You might not feel compelled to write a computer program to automate the task of making change, because you can probably already make change yourself fairly easily. But suppose you needed to do a more complicated task—such as sorting a list of 100 names. In that case, a computer program would be very handy.

Computers can be designed to run a small set of algorithms for performing specialized tasks, such as operating a microwave. But we can also build computers, like the one on your desktop, that are capable of performing a task described by any algorithm. These computers are truly general-purpose problem-solving machines. They are unlike any machines that were built before, and they have formed the basis of the completely new world in which we live.

Later in this book, we introduce a notation for expressing algorithms and some suggestions for designing algorithms. You will see that algorithms and algorithmic thinking are critical underpinnings of any computer system.

Information Processing

Since people first learned to write several thousand years ago, they have processed information. Information itself has taken many forms in its history, from the marks impressed on clay tablets in ancient Mesopotamia; to the first written texts in ancient Greece; to the printed words in the books, newspapers, and magazines mass-produced since the European Renaissance; to the abstract symbols of modern mathematics and science used during the past 350 years. Only recently, however, have human beings developed the capacity to automate the processing of information by building computers. In the modern world of computers, information is also commonly referred to as **data**. But what is information?

Like mathematical calculations, **information processing** can be described with algorithms. In our earlier example of making change, the subtraction steps involved manipulating symbols used to represent numbers and money. In carrying out the instructions of any algorithm, a computing agent manipulates information. The computing agent starts with some given information (known as **input**), transforms this information according to well-defined rules, and produces new information, known as **output**.

It is important to recognize that the algorithms that describe information processing can also be represented as information. Computer scientists have been able to represent algorithms in a form that can be executed effectively and efficiently by machines. They have also designed real machines, called electronic digital computers, which are capable of executing algorithms.

Computer scientists more recently discovered how to represent many other things, such as images, music, human speech, and video, as information. Many of the media and communication devices that we now take for granted would be impossible without this new kind of information processing. We examine many of these achievements in more detail in later chapters.

> ## Exercise 1-1

These short end-of-section exercises are intended to stimulate your thinking about computing.

1. List three common types of computing agents.

2. Write an algorithm that describes the second part of the process of making change (counting out the coins and bills).

3. Write an algorithm that describes a common task, such as baking a cake.

4. Describe an instruction that is not well defined and thus could not be included as a step in an algorithm. Give an example of such an instruction.

5. In what sense is a laptop computer a general-purpose problem-solving machine?

6. List four devices that use computers and describe the information that they process. (*Hint*: Think of the inputs and outputs of the devices.)

1.2 The Structure of a Modern Computer System

We now give a brief overview of the structure of modern computer systems. A modern computer system consists of **hardware** and **software**. Hardware consists of the physical devices required to execute algorithms. Software is the set of these algorithms, represented as **programs**, in particular **programming languages**. In the discussion that follows, we focus on the hardware and software found in a typical desktop computer system, although similar components are also found in other computer systems, such as smartphones and automatic teller machines (ATMs).

Computer Hardware

The basic hardware components of a computer are **memory**, a **central processing unit (CPU)**, and a set of **input/output devices**, as shown in **Figure 1-1**.

Figure 1-1   Hardware components of a modern computer system

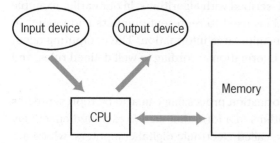

Human users primarily interact with the input and output devices. The input devices include a keyboard, a mouse, a trackpad, a microphone, and a touchscreen. Common output devices include a monitor and speakers. Computers can also communicate with the external world through various **ports** that connect them to **networks** and to other devices such as smartphones and digital cameras. The purpose of most input devices is to convert information that human beings deal with, such as text, images, and sounds, into information for computational processing. The purpose of most output devices is to convert the results of this processing back to human-usable form.

Computer memory is set up to represent and store information in electronic form. Specifically, information is stored as patterns of **binary digits** (1s and 0s). To understand how this works, consider a basic device such as a light switch, which can only be in one of two states, on or off. Now suppose there is a bank of switches that control 16 small lights in a row. By turning the switches off or on, we can represent any pattern of 16 binary digits (1s and 0s) as patterns of lights that are on or off. As you will see later in this book, computer scientists have discovered how to represent any information, including text, images, and sound, in binary form.

Now, suppose there are 8 of these groups of 16 lights. We can select any group of lights and examine or change the state of each light within that collection. We have just developed a tiny model of computer memory. The memory has 8 cells, each of which can store 16 **bits** of binary information. A diagram of this model, in which the memory cells are filled with binary digits, is shown in **Figure 1-2**. This memory is also sometimes called **primary memory** or internal or **random access memory (RAM)**.

Figure 1-2   A model of computer memory

Cell 7	1	1	0	1	1	1	1	0	1	1	1	1	1	1	0	1
Cell 6	1	0	1	1	0	1	1	1	1	1	1	0	1	1	1	1
Cell 5	1	1	1	1	1	1	1	1	0	1	1	1	1	0	1	1
Cell 4	1	0	1	1	1	0	1	1	1	1	1	1	0	1	1	1
Cell 3	1	1	1	0	1	1	1	1	1	0	1	1	1	1	1	1
Cell 2	0	0	1	1	1	1	0	1	1	1	0	1	1	1	0	1
Cell 1	1	1	1	0	1	1	1	1	1	1	1	1	1	0	1	1
Cell 0	1	1	1	0	1	1	0	1	1	1	1	1	1	1	1	0

The information stored in memory can represent any type of data, such as numbers, text, images, sound, or the instructions of a program. Once the information is stored in memory, we typically want to do something with it—that is, we want to process it. The part of a computer that is responsible for processing data is the central processing unit (CPU). This device, which is also sometimes called a **processor**, consists of electronic switches arranged to perform simple logical, arithmetic, and control operations. The CPU executes an algorithm by fetching its binary instructions from memory, decoding them, and executing them. Executing an instruction might involve fetching other binary information—the data—from memory as well.

The processor can locate data in a computer's primary memory very quickly. However, these data exist only as long as electric power comes into the computer. If the power fails or is turned off, the data in primary memory are lost. Clearly, a more permanent type of memory is needed to preserve data. This more permanent type of memory is called external or **secondary memory**, and it comes in several forms. **Magnetic storage media**, such as tapes and hard disks, allow bit patterns to be stored as patterns on a magnetic field. **Semiconductor storage media**, such as flash memory sticks and universal serial bus (USB) drives, perform much the same function with a different technology, as do **optical storage media**, such as compact disks (CDs) and digital video disks (DVDs). Some of these secondary storage media can hold much larger quantities of information than the internal memory of a computer.

Computer Software

You have learned that a computer is a general-purpose problem-solving machine. To solve any computable problem, a computer must be capable of executing any algorithm. Because it is impossible to anticipate all of the problems for which there are algorithmic solutions, there is no way to hardwire all potential algorithms into a computer's hardware. Instead, some basic operations are built into the hardware's processor and require any algorithm to use them. The algorithms are converted to binary form and then loaded, with their data, into the computer's memory. The processor can then execute the algorithms' instructions by running the hardware's more basic operations.

Any programs that are stored in memory so that they can be executed later are called software. A program stored in computer memory must be represented in binary digits, which is also known as **machine code**. Loading machine code into computer memory one digit at a time would be a tedious, error-prone task for human beings. It would be convenient if we could automate this process to get it right every time. For this reason, computer scientists have developed another program, called a **loader**, to perform this task. A loader takes a set of machine language instructions as input and loads them into the appropriate memory locations. When the loader is finished, the machine language program is ready to execute. Obviously, the loader cannot load itself into memory, so this is one of those algorithms that must be hardwired into the computer.

Now that a loader exists, you can load and execute other programs that make the development, execution, and management of programs easier. This type of software is called **system software**. The most important example of system software is a computer's **operating system**. You are probably already familiar with at least one of the most popular operating systems, such as Linux, Apple's macOS, and Microsoft's Windows. An operating system is responsible for managing and scheduling several concurrently running programs. It also manages the computer's memory, including the external storage, and manages communications between the CPU, the input/output devices, and other computers on a network. An important part of any operating system is its **file system**, which allows human users to organize their data and programs in permanent storage. Another important function of an operating system is to provide **user interfaces**—that is, ways for the human user to interact with the computer's software. A **terminal-based interface** accepts inputs from a keyboard and displays text output on a monitor screen. A **graphical user interface (GUI)** organizes the monitor screen around the metaphor of a desktop, with windows containing icons for folders, files, and applications. This type of user interface also allows the user to manipulate images with a pointing device such as a mouse. A **touchscreen interface** supports more direct manipulation of these visual elements with gestures such as pinches and swipes of the user's fingers. Devices that respond verbally and in other ways to verbal commands are also becoming widespread.

Another major type of software is called **applications software**, or simply **apps**. An application is a program that is designed for a specific task, such as editing a document or displaying a web page. Applications include web browsers, word processors, spreadsheets, database managers, graphic design packages, music production systems, and games, among millions of others. As you begin learning to write computer programs, you will focus on writing simple applications.

As you have learned, computer hardware can execute only instructions that are written in binary form—that is, in machine language. Writing a machine language program, however, would be an extremely tedious, error-prone task. To ease the process of writing computer programs, computer scientists have developed **high-level programming languages** for expressing algorithms. These languages resemble English and allow the author to express algorithms in a form that other people can understand.

A programmer typically starts by writing high-level language statements in a **text editor**. The programmer then runs another program called a **translator** to convert the high-level program code into executable code. Because it is possible for a programmer to make grammatical mistakes even when writing high-level code, the translator checks for **syntax errors** before it completes the translation process. If it detects any of these errors, the translator alerts the programmer via error messages. The programmer then has to revise the program. If the translation process succeeds without a syntax error, the program can be executed by the **run-time system**. The run-time system might execute the program directly on the hardware or run yet another program called an **interpreter** or **virtual machine** to execute the program. **Figure 1-3** shows the steps and software used in the coding process.

Figure 1-3 Software used in the coding process

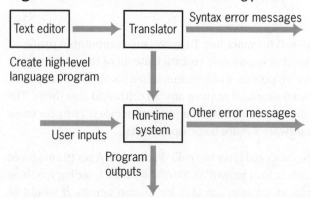

Exercise 1-2

1. List two examples of input devices and two examples of output devices.

2. What does the central processing unit (CPU) do?

3. How is information represented in hardware memory?

4. What is the difference between a terminal-based interface and a graphical user interface (GUI)?

5. What role do translators play in the programming process?

1.3 A Not-So-Brief History of Computing Systems

Now that you have in mind some of the basic ideas of computing and computer systems, let's take a moment to examine how they have taken shape in history. **Figure 1-4** summarizes some of the major developments in the history of computing. The discussion that follows provides more details about these developments.

Figure 1-4 Summary of major developments in the history of computing

Approximate Dates	Major Developments
Before 1800	• Mathematicians discover and use algorithms • Abacus used as a calculating aid • First mechanical calculators built by Pascal and Leibniz
Nineteenth century	• Jacquard's loom • Babbage's Analytical Engine • Boole's system of logic • Hollerith's punch-card machine
1930s	• Turing publishes results on computability • Shannon's theory of information and digital switching
1940s	• First electronic digital computers
1950s	• First symbolic programming languages • Transistors make computers smaller, faster, more durable, and less expensive • Emergence of data-processing applications
1960–1975	• Integrated circuits accelerate the miniaturization of hardware • First minicomputers • Time-sharing operating systems • Interactive user interfaces with keyboard and monitor • Proliferation of high-level programming languages • Emergence of a software industry and the academic study of computer science

(continues)

Figure 1-4   Summary of major developments in the history of computing (continued)

Approximate Dates	Major Developments
1975–1990	• First microcomputers and mass-produced personal computers • GUIs become widespread • Networks and the Internet
1990–2000	• Optical storage for multimedia applications, images, sound, and video • World Wide Web, web applications, and e-commerce • Laptops
2000–present	• Wireless computing, smartphones, and mobile applications • Computers embedded and networked in an enormous variety of cars, household appliances, and industrial equipment • Social networking and use of big data in finance and commerce • Digital streaming of music and video

Before Electronic Digital Computers

Ancient mathematicians developed the first algorithms. The word *algorithm* comes from the name of a Persian mathematician, Muhammad ibn Musa al-Khwarizmi, who wrote several mathematics textbooks in the ninth century. About 2300 years ago, the Greek mathematician Euclid, the inventor of geometry, developed an algorithm for computing the greatest common divisor of two numbers.

A device known as the abacus also appeared in ancient times. The abacus helped people perform simple arithmetic. Users calculated sums and differences by sliding beads on a grid of wires (see **Figure 1-5a**). The configuration of beads on the abacus served as the data.

In the seventeenth century, the French mathematician Blaise Pascal (1623–1662) built one of the first mechanical devices to automate the process of addition (see **Figure 1-5b**). The addition operation was embedded in the configuration of gears within the machine. The user entered the two numbers to be added by rotating some wheels. The sum or output number appeared on another rotating wheel. The German mathematician Gottfried Wilhelm Leibniz (1646–1716) built another mechanical calculator that included other arithmetic functions such as multiplication. Leibniz, who invented calculus concurrently with Newton, went on to propose the idea of computing with symbols as one of our most basic intellectual activities. He argued for a universal language in which one could solve any problem by calculating.

Early in the nineteenth century, the French engineer Joseph-Marie Jacquard (1752–1834) designed and constructed a machine that automated the process of weaving (see **Figure 1-5c**). Until then, each row in a weaving pattern had to be set up by hand, a quite tedious, error-prone process. Jacquard's loom was designed to accept input in the form of a set of punched cards. Each card described a row in a pattern of cloth. Although it was still an entirely mechanical device, Jacquard's loom possessed something that previous devices had lacked—the ability to execute an algorithm automatically. The set of cards expressed the algorithm or set of instructions that controlled the behavior of the loom. If the loom operator wanted to produce a different pattern, he just had to run the machine with a different set of cards.

The British mathematician Charles Babbage (1792–1871) took the concept of a programmable computer a step further by designing a model of a machine that, conceptually, bore a striking resemblance to a modern general-purpose computer. Babbage conceived his machine, which he called the Analytical Engine, as a mechanical device. His design called for four functional parts: a mill to perform arithmetic operations, a store to hold data and a program, an operator to run the instructions from punched cards, and an output to produce the results on punched cards. Sadly, Babbage's computer was never built. The project perished for lack of funds near the time when Babbage himself passed away.

Figure 1-5   Some early computing devices

(a) Abacus

(b) Pascal's Calculator

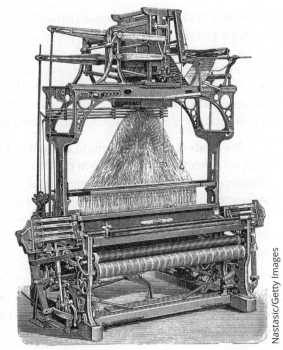

(c) Jacquard's Loom

In the last two decades of the nineteenth century, a U.S. Census Bureau statistician named Herman Hollerith (1860–1929) developed a machine that automated data processing for the U.S. Census. Hollerith's machine, which had the same component parts as Babbage's Analytical Engine, simply accepted a set of punched cards as input and then tallied and sorted the cards. His machine greatly shortened the time it took to produce statistical results on the U.S. population. Government and business organizations seeking to automate their data processing quickly adopted Hollerith's punched card machines. Hollerith was also one of the founders of a company that eventually became International Business Machines (IBM).

Also in the nineteenth century, the British secondary school teacher George Boole (1815–1864) developed a system of logic. This system consisted of a pair of values, TRUE and FALSE, and a set of three primitive operations on these values, AND, OR, and NOT. Boolean logic eventually became the basis for designing the electronic circuitry to process binary information.

A half century later, in the 1930s, the British mathematician Alan Turing (1912–1954) explored the theoretical foundations and limits of algorithms and computation. Turing's essential contributions were to develop the concept of a universal machine that could be specialized to solve any computable problems and to demonstrate that some problems are unsolvable by computers.

Human Beings as Computers (1940–1945)

The needs of the combatants in World War II expanded the practical applications of computing. Two significant examples were cryptanalysis, or the cracking of encoded messages, and the calculation of ballistics for artillery and bombing missions. The calculation of ballistics involved the creation and manipulation of complex tables of numerical information, while cryptanalysis required the discernment of significant patterns in chunks of text. Because machines were not yet available to automate these tasks, they were performed manually by human beings. These people, who numbered in the thousands, were primarily women highly skilled in mathematics and puzzle solving. They were known at the time as "computers," since computation is what they did. Major breakthroughs in this effort included the work of Agnes Meyer Driscoll and Genevieve Grotjan Feinstein, who cracked major Japanese codes for the U.S. Navy.

The First Electronic Digital Computers (1940–1950)

In the late 1930s, Claude Shannon (1916–2001), a mathematician and electrical engineer at Massachusetts Institute of Technology (MIT), wrote a classic paper titled "A Symbolic Analysis of Relay and Switching Circuits." In this paper, he showed how operations and information in other systems, such as arithmetic, could be reduced to Boolean logic and then to hardware. For example, if the Boolean values TRUE and FALSE were written as the binary digits 1 and 0, one could write a sequence of logical operations that computes the sum of two strings of binary digits. All that was required to build an electronic digital computer was the ability to represent binary digits as on/off switches and to represent the logical operations in other circuitry.

The needs of the combatants in World War II pushed the development of computer hardware into high gear. Several teams of scientists and engineers in the United States, England, and Germany independently created the first generation of general-purpose digital electronic computers during the 1940s. All of these scientists and engineers used Shannon's innovation of expressing binary digits and logical operations in terms of electronic switching devices. Among these groups was a team at Harvard University under the direction of Howard Aiken. Their computer, called the Mark I, became operational in 1944 and did mathematical work for the U.S. Navy during the war. The Mark I was considered an electromechanical device, because it used a combination of magnets, relays, and gears to store and process data.

Another team under J. Presper Eckert and John Mauchly, at the University of Pennsylvania, produced a computer called the Electronic Numerical Integrator and Calculator (ENIAC). The ENIAC calculated ballistics tables for the artillery of the U.S. Army toward the end of the war. Because the ENIAC used entirely electronic components, it was almost a thousand times faster than the Mark I.

Two other electronic digital computers were completed a bit earlier than the ENIAC. They were the Atanasoff–Berry Computer (ABC), built by John Atanasoff and Clifford Berry at Iowa State University in 1942, and the Colossus, constructed by a group working under Alan Turing in England in 1943. The ABC was created to solve systems of simultaneous linear equations. Although the ABC's function was much narrower than that of the ENIAC, the ABC is now regarded as the first electronic digital computer. The Colossus, whose existence had been top secret until recently, was used to crack the powerful German Enigma code during the war.

The first electronic digital computers, sometimes called **mainframe computers**, consisted of vacuum tubes, wires, and plugs, and they filled entire rooms. Although they were much faster than people at computing, by current standards they were extraordinarily slow and prone to breakdown. The early computers were also extremely difficult to program. To enter or modify a program, a team of workers had to rearrange the connections among the vacuum tubes by unplugging and replugging the wires. Each program was loaded by literally hardwiring it into the computer. With thousands of wires involved, it was easy to make a mistake.

The memory of these first computers stored only data, not the program that processed the data. As we have seen, the idea of a stored program first appeared 100 years earlier in Jacquard's loom and in Babbage's design for the Analytical Engine. In 1946, John von Neumann realized that the instructions of the programs could also be stored in binary form in an electronic digital computer's memory. His research group at Princeton developed one of the first modern stored-program computers.

Although the size, speed, and applications of computers have changed dramatically since those early days, the basic architecture and design of the electronic digital computer have remained remarkably stable.

The First Programming Languages (1950–1965)

The typical computer user now runs many programs, made up of millions of lines of code, that perform what would have seemed like magical tasks 30 or 40 years ago. But the first digital electronic computers had no software as we think of it today. The machine code for a few relatively simple and small applications had to be loaded by hand. As the demand for larger and more complex applications grew, so did the need for tools to expedite the programming process.

In the early 1950s, computer scientists realized that a symbolic notation could be used instead of machine code, and the first **assembly languages** appeared. The programmers would enter mnemonic codes for operations, such as ADD and OUTPUT, and for data variables, such as SALARY and RATE, at a **keypunch machine**. The keystrokes punched a set of holes in a small card for each instruction. The programmers then carried their stacks of cards to a system operator, who placed them in a device called a **card reader**. This device translated the holes in the cards to patterns in the computer's memory. A program called an **assembler** then translated the application programs in memory to machine code, and they were executed.

Programming in assembly language was an improvement over programming in machine code, since the symbolic notation used in assembly languages was easier for people to read and understand. Another advantage was that the assembler could catch some programming errors before the program was actually executed. However, the symbolic notation still appeared a bit arcane when compared with the notations of conventional mathematics. To remedy this problem, John Backus, a programmer working for IBM, developed FORTRAN (Formula Translation Language) in 1954. Programmers, many of whom were mathematicians, scientists, and engineers, could now use conventional algebraic notation. FORTRAN programmers still entered their programs on a keypunch machine, but the computer executed them after they were translated to machine code by a **compiler**.

FORTRAN was considered ideal for numerical and scientific applications. However, expressing the kind of data used in data processing—in particular, textual information—was difficult. For example, FORTRAN was not practical for processing information that included people's names, addresses, Social Security numbers, and the financial data of corporations and other institutions. In the early 1960s, a team led by Rear Admiral Grace Murray Hopper developed COBOL (Common Business Oriented Language) for data processing in the U.S. government. Banks, insurance companies, and other institutions were quick to adopt its use in data-processing applications.

Also in the late 1950s and early 1960s, John McCarthy, a computer scientist at MIT, developed a powerful and elegant notation called LISP (List Processing) for expressing computations. Based on a theory of recursive functions (a subject covered in Chapter 7), LISP captured the essence of symbolic information processing. A student of McCarthy, Steve "Slug" Russell, coded the first interpreter for LISP in 1960. The interpreter accepted LISP expressions directly as inputs, evaluated them, and printed their results. In its early days, LISP was used primarily for laboratory experiments in an area of research known as **artificial intelligence**. More recently, LISP has been touted as an ideal language for solving any difficult or complex problems.

Although they were among the first high-level programming languages, FORTRAN and LISP have survived for decades. They have undergone modifications to improve their capabilities and have served as models for the development of many other programming languages. COBOL, by contrast, is no longer in active use but has survived in the form of legacy programs that must still be maintained.

These new, high-level programming languages had one feature in common: **abstraction**. In science or any other area of enquiry, an abstraction allows humans to reduce complex ideas or entities to simpler ones. For example, a set of 10 assembly language instructions might be replaced with an equivalent algebraic expression that consists of only five symbols in FORTRAN. Any time you can say more with less, you are using an abstraction. The use of abstraction is also found in other areas of computing, such as hardware design and information architecture. The complexities do not actually go away, but the abstractions hide them from view. Abstraction allows computer scientists to conceptualize, design, and build ever more sophisticated and complex systems.

Integrated Circuits, Interaction, Time-Sharing, and Software Engineering (1965–1975)

In the late 1950s, the vacuum tube gave way to the transistor as the mechanism for implementing the electronic switches in computer hardware. As a solid-state device, the transistor was much smaller, more reliable, more durable, and less expensive to manufacture than a vacuum tube. Consequently, the hardware components of computers generally became smaller in physical size, more reliable, and less expensive. The smaller and more numerous the switches became, the faster the processing and the greater the capacity of memory to store information.

The development of the integrated circuit in the early 1960s allowed computer engineers to build ever smaller, faster, and less-expensive computer hardware components. They perfected a process of photographically etching transistors and other solid-state components onto very thin wafers of silicon, leaving an entire processor and memory on a single chip. In 1965, Gordon Moore, one of the founders of the computer chip manufacturer Intel, made a prediction that came to be known as Moore's Law. This prediction states that the processing speed and storage capacity of hardware will increase and its cost will decrease by approximately a factor of 2 every 18 months. This trend has held true for more than 50 years. For example, in 1965 there were about 50 electrical components on a chip, whereas by 2000, a chip could hold over 40 million components. Without the integrated circuit, human beings would not have gone to the moon in 1969, and we would not have the powerful and inexpensive handheld devices that we now use on a daily basis.

Minicomputers the size of a large office desk appeared in the 1960s, when the means of developing and running programs were changing. Until then, a computer was typically located in a restricted area with a single human operator. Programmers composed their programs on keypunch machines in another room or building. They then delivered their stacks of cards to the computer operator, who loaded them into a card reader and compiled and ran the programs in sequence on the computer. Programmers then returned to pick up the output results in the form of new stacks of cards or printouts. This mode of operation, also called batch processing, might cause a programmer to wait days for results, including error messages.

The increases in processing speed and memory capacity enabled computer scientists to develop the first time-sharing operating system. John McCarthy, the creator of the programming language LISP, recognized that a program could automate many of the functions performed by the human system operator. When memory, including magnetic secondary storage, became large enough to hold several users' programs at the same time, they could be scheduled for concurrent processing. Each process associated with a program would run for a slice of time and then yield the CPU to another process. All of the active processes would repeatedly cycle for a turn with the CPU until they finished.

Several users could now run their own programs simultaneously by entering commands at separate terminals connected to a single computer. As processor speeds continued to increase, each user gained the illusion that a time-sharing computer system belonged entirely to them.

By the late 1960s, programmers could enter program input at a terminal and also see program output immediately displayed on a cathode ray tube (CRT) screen. Compared to its predecessors, this new computer system was both highly interactive and much more accessible to its users. Interactive, multiuser computer systems could now support the development of large, complex software applications by teams of programmers. One such group, under the direction of Margaret Hamilton, constructed the programs that controlled the command and lunar landing modules for the Apollo Space Mission. She coined the term software engineering to refer to the construction of large software systems using a disciplined method of requirements analysis, design, coding, and testing that involves the coordination of a team of specialized developers.

Many relatively small- and medium-sized institutions, such as universities, were now able to afford computers. These machines were used not only for data processing and engineering applications but also for teaching and research in the new and rapidly growing field of computer science.

Personal Computing and Networks (1975–1990)

In the mid-1960s, Douglas Engelbart, a computer scientist working at the Stanford Research Institute (SRI), first saw one of the ultimate implications of Moore's Law: Eventually, perhaps within a generation, hardware components would become small enough and affordable enough to mass produce an individual computer for every person. What form would these personal computers take, and how would their owners use them? Two decades earlier, in 1945, Engelbart had read an article in *The Atlantic Monthly* titled "As We May Think" that had posed this question and offered some answers. The author, Vannevar Bush, a scientist at MIT, predicted that computing devices would serve as repositories of information and, ultimately, of all human knowledge. Owners of computing devices would consult this information by browsing through it with pointing devices, and they would contribute information to the knowledge base almost at will. Engelbart agreed that the primary purpose of the personal computer would be to augment the human intellect, and he spent the rest of his career designing computer systems that would accomplish this goal.

During the late 1960s, Engelbart built the first pointing device, or mouse. He also designed software to represent windows, icons, and pull-down menus on a **bit-mapped display screen**. He demonstrated that a computer user could not only enter text at the keyboard but could also directly manipulate the icons that represent files, folders, and computer applications on the screen.

But for Engelbart, personal computing did not mean computing in isolation. He participated in the first experiment to connect computers in a network, and he believed that soon people would use computers to communicate, share information, and collaborate on team projects.

Engelbart developed his first experimental system, which he called NLS (oNLine System) Augment, on a minicomputer at SRI. In the early 1970s, he moved to Xerox Palo Alto Research Center (PARC) and worked with a team under Alan Kay to develop the first desktop computer system. Called the Alto, this system had many of the features of Engelbart's Augment, as well as email and a functioning hypertext (a forerunner of the World Wide Web). Kay's group also developed a programming language called Smalltalk, which was designed to create programs for the new computer and to teach programming to children. Kay's goal was to develop a personal computer the size of a large notebook, which he called the Dynabook. Unfortunately for Xerox, the company's management had more interest in photocopy machines than in the work of Kay's visionary research group. However, a young entrepreneur named Steve Jobs visited the Xerox lab and saw the Alto in action. Almost a decade later, in 1984, Apple Computer, the now-famous company founded by Steve Jobs, brought forth the Macintosh, the first successful mass-produced personal computer with a GUI.

While Kay's group was busy building the computer system of the future in their research lab, dozens of hobbyists gathered near San Francisco to found the Homebrew Computer Club, the first personal computer users group. They met to share ideas, programs, hardware, and applications for personal computing. The first mass-produced personal computer, the Altair, appeared in 1975. The Altair contained Intel's 8080 processor, the first **microprocessor** chip. But from the outside, the Altair looked and behaved more like a miniature version of the early computers than the Alto. Programs and their input had to be entered by flipping switches, and output was displayed by a set of lights. However, the Altair was small enough for personal computing enthusiasts to carry home, and input/output devices eventually were invented to support the processing of text and sound.

The Osborne and the Kaypro were among the first mass-produced interactive personal computers. They boasted tiny display screens and keyboards, with floppy disk drives for loading system software, applications software, and users' data files. Early personal computing applications were word processors, spreadsheets, and games such as *Pac-Man* and *Spacewar!* These computers also ran CP/M (Control Program for Microcomputers), the first personal computer (PC)–based operating system.

In the early 1980s a college dropout named Bill Gates and his partner Paul Allen built their own operating system software, which they called Microsoft Disk Operating System (MS-DOS). They then arranged a deal with the giant computer manufacturer IBM to supply MS-DOS for the new line of PCs that the company intended to mass produce. This deal proved to be a very advantageous one for Gates's company, Microsoft. Not only did Microsoft receive a fee for each computer sold, it also got a head start on supplying applications software that would run on its operating system. Fast, high sales of the IBM PC and its clones to individuals and institutions quickly made MS-DOS the world's most widely used operating system. Within a few years, Gates and Allen had become billionaires, and within a decade, Gates had become the world's richest man, a position he held for 13 straight years.

Also in the 1970s, the U.S. government began to support the development of a network that would connect computers at military installations and research universities. The first such network, called Advanced Research Projects Agency Network (ARPANET), connected four computers at SRI, University of California at Los Angeles (UCLA), University of California Santa Barbara, and the University of Utah. Bob Metcalfe, a researcher associated with Kay's group at Xerox, developed a software protocol called Ethernet for operating a network of computers. Ethernet allowed computers to communicate in a local area network (LAN) within an organization and also with computers in other organizations via a wide area network (WAN). By the mid-1980s, the ARPANET had grown into what we now call the Internet, connecting computers owned by large institutions, small organizations, and individuals all over the world.

Consultation, Communication, and E-Commerce (1990–2000)

In the 1990s, computer hardware costs continued to plummet, and processing speed and memory capacity skyrocketed. Optical storage media, such as CDs and DVDs, were developed for mass storage. The digitizing and computational processing of images, sound, and video became feasible and widespread. By the end of the decade, entire movies were being shot or constructed and played back using digital devices. *Toy Story*, the first full-length animated feature film produced entirely by a computer, appeared in 1995. The capacity to create lifelike three-dimensional animations of whole environments led to a new technology called **virtual reality**. New devices appeared, such as flatbed scanners and digital cameras, which could be used along with the more traditional microphone and speakers to support the input, digitizing, and output of almost any type of information.

Desktop and laptop computers now not only performed useful work but also gave their users new means of personal expression. This decade saw the rise of computers as communication tools, with email, instant messaging, bulletin boards, chat rooms, and the World Wide Web.

Perhaps the most interesting story from this period concerns Tim Berners-Lee, the creator of the World Wide Web. In the late 1980s, Berners-Lee, a theoretical physicist doing research at the CERN Institute in Geneva, Switzerland, began to develop some ideas for using computers to share information. Computer engineers had been linking computers to networks for several years, and it was already common in research communities to exchange files and send and receive email around the world. However, the vast differences in hardware, operating systems, file formats, and applications still made it difficult for users who were not adept at programming to access and share this information. Berners-Lee was interested in creating a common medium for sharing information that would be easy to use, not only for scientists but also for any other person capable of manipulating a keyboard and mouse and viewing the information on a monitor.

Berners-Lee was familiar with Vannevar Bush's vision of a web-like consultation system, Engelbart's work on NLS Augment, and also with the first widely available hypertext systems. One of these systems, Apple Computer's HyperCard, broadened the scope of hypertext to **hypermedia**. HyperCard allowed authors to organize not just text but also images, sound, video, and executable applications into webs of linked information. However, a HyperCard database sat only on standalone computers; the links could not carry HyperCard data from one computer to another. Furthermore, the supporting software ran only on Apple's computers.

Berners-Lee realized that networks could extend the reach of a hypermedia system to any computers connected to the net, making their information available worldwide. To preserve its independence from particular operating systems, the new medium would need to have universal standards for distributing and presenting the information. To ensure this neutrality and independence, no private corporation or individual government could own the medium and dictate the standards.

Berners-Lee built the software for this new medium, which we now call the World Wide Web, in 1992. The software used many of the existing mechanisms for transmitting information over the Internet. People contribute information to the web by publishing files on computers known as **web servers**. The web server software on these computers is responsible for answering requests for viewing the information stored on the web server. To view information on the web, people use software called a **web browser**. In response to a user's commands, a web browser sends a request for information across the Internet to the appropriate web server. The server responds by sending the information back to the browser's computer, called a **web client**, where it is displayed or rendered in the browser.

Although Berners-Lee wrote the first web server and web browser software, he made two other even more important contributions. First, he designed a set of rules, called Hypertext Transfer Protocol (HTTP), which allows any server and browser to talk to each other. Second, he designed a language, Hypertext Markup Language (HTML), which allows browsers to structure the information to be displayed on web pages. He then made all of these resources available to anyone for free.

Berners-Lee's invention and gift of this universal information medium is a truly remarkable achievement. Today there are millions of web servers in operation around the world. Anyone with the appropriate training and resources—companies, government, nonprofit organizations, and private individuals—can start up a new web server or obtain space on one. Web browser software now runs not only on desktop and laptop computers but also on handheld devices such as cell phones.

The growth of the Internet, the web, and related software technologies also transformed manufacturing, retail sales, and finance in the latter half of this decade. Computer-supported automation dramatically increased productivity, while eliminating high-paying jobs for many people. Firms established and refined the chains of production and distribution of goods, from raw materials to finished products to retail sales, which were increasingly cost-effective and global in scope. Computer technology facilitated in large part the spread of giant big-box stores like Walmart and the rise of online stores like Amazon, while driving many local retailers out of business and creating a workforce of part-timers without benefits.

The technology that made online stores pervasive, called **web applications**, presented a revolution in the way in which software services were delivered to people. Instead of purchasing and running software for specific applications to run on one's own computer, one could obtain access to a specific service through a web browser. The web application providing this service ran on a remote computer or **server** located at the provider's place of business. The web browser played the role of the **client**, front end, or user interface for millions of users to access the same server application for a given service. **Client/server applications** had already been in use for email, bulletin boards, and chat rooms on the Internet, so this technology was simply deployed on the web when it became available.

The final major development of this decade took place in a computer lab at Stanford University, where two graduate students, Sergey Brin and Larry Page, developed algorithms for indexing and searching the web. The outcome of their work added a new verb to the dictionary: to google. Today, much of the world's economy and research relies upon Google's various search platforms.

Mobile Applications and Ubiquitous Computing (2000–present)

As the previous millennium drew to a close, computer hardware continued to shrink in size and cost and to provide more memory and greater processing speed. Laptop computers became smaller, faster, and more affordable to millions of people. The first handheld computing devices, called **personal digital assistants (PDAs)**, began to appear. Applications for these devices were limited to simple video games, address books, to-do lists, and note taking, and they had to be connected via cable to a laptop or desktop computer to transfer information.

Meanwhile, cellular technology became widespread, with millions of people beginning to use the first cell phones. These devices, which allowed calls to be made from a simple mechanical keypad, were "dumb" compared to today's smartphones. But cellular technology provided the basis for what was soon to come. At about the same time, wireless technology began to allow computers to communicate through the air to a base station with an Internet connection. The conditions for mobile and ubiquitous computing were now in place, awaiting only the kinds of devices and apps that would make them useful and popular.

No one foresaw the types of devices and applications that mobile computing would make possible better than Steve Jobs (the founder of Apple Computer, mentioned earlier). During the final dozen years of his life, Jobs brought forward from Apple several devices and technologies that revolutionized not only computing but also the way in which people engaged in cultural pursuits. The devices were the iPod, which began as a digital music player but evolved into a handheld general-purpose computing device; the iPhone, which added cellular phone technology to the iPod's capabilities; and the iPad, which realized Alan Kay's dreams of a personal notebook computer. All of these devices utilized touchscreen and voice recognition technology, which eliminated the need for bulky mechanical keypads.

The associated software technologies came in the form of Apple's iLife suite, a set of applications that allowed users to organize various types of media (music, photos, video, and books); and Apple's iTunes, iBooks, and App Stores, vendor sites that allowed developers to market mobile media and applications. The web browser that for a decade had given users access to web apps became just another type of app in the larger world of mobile computing.

The new millennium has seen another major addition to the digital landscape: social networking applications. Although various Internet forums, such as chatrooms and bulletin board systems, had been in use for a couple of decades, their use was not widespread. In 2004, Mark Zuckerberg, a student at Harvard University, changed all that when he launched Facebook from his college dorm room. The application allowed students to join a network to share their profiles; post messages, photos, and videos; and generally communicate as "friends." Participation in this network rapidly spread to include more than a billion users. Social networking technology now includes many other variations, as exemplified by LinkedIn, Twitter, Tumblr, Flickr, and Instagram.

During the past decade (2010–2020), as computing applications have migrated from standalone desktop machines to mobile devices, the storage of data has moved from individual devices to giant **server farms** to which these devices are wirelessly connected. Our data, including music, photos, text, financial assets, and geolocation, are now located in a **digital cloud**, which we can access from our phones, watches, TV sets, and automobiles, among other things. **Cloud computing** and wireless technology also underlie an even broader **Internet of Things (IOT)**, in which practically any physical objects (including my cat) containing the appropriate computer chips can send and receive digital information.

We conclude this not-so-brief overview by mentioning the rise of a technology known as **big data**. Governments, businesses, and hackers continually monitor Internet traffic for various purposes. This "clickstream" can be "mined" to learn users' preferences, interests, and behavior patterns to better serve them, exploit them, or spy on them. For example, an online store might advertise a product on a person's Facebook page immediately after that person viewed a similar product while shopping online or mentioned the product in the presence of a **virtual assistant** such as Alexa. Researchers in the field of **data science** have created algorithms that process massive amounts of data to discover trends and predict outcomes.

To summarize this history, one trend ties the last several decades of computing together: rapid technical progress. Processes and the things in which they are embedded have become automated, programmable, smaller, faster, highly interconnected, and easily visualized and interpreted.

If you want to learn more about the history of computing, consult the sources listed in Appendix E. We now turn to an introduction to programming in Python.

1.4 Getting Started with Python Programming

Guido van Rossum invented the Python programming language in the early 1990s. Python is a high-level, general-purpose programming language for solving problems on modern computer systems. The language and many supporting tools are free, and Python programs can run on any operating system. You can download Python, its documentation, and related materials from **www.python.org**. Instructions for downloading and installing Python are in Appendix A. In this section, we show you how to create and run simple Python programs.

Running Code in the Interactive Shell

Python is an interpreted language, and you can run simple Python expressions and statements in an interactive programming environment called the **shell**. The easiest way to open a Python shell is to launch the Integrated DeveLopment Environment (IDLE). This is an integrated program development environment that comes with the Python installation. When you do this, a window named **Python Shell** opens. **Figure 1-6** shows a shell window on macOS. A shell window running on a Windows system or a Linux system should look similar, if not identical, to this one. Note that the version of

Figure 1-6   Python shell window

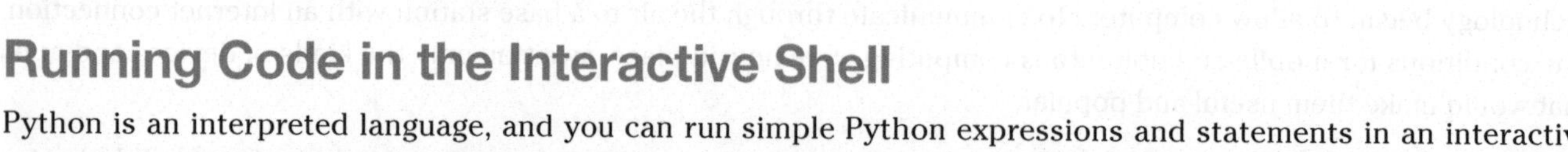

```
● ● ●                              IDLE Shell 3.10.4
      Python 3.10.4 (v3.10.4:9d38120e33, Mar 23 2022, 17:29:05) [Clang 13.0.0 (clang-1300.0.29.30)] on darwin
      Type "help", "copyright", "credits" or "license()" for more information.
>>> |



                                                                              Ln: 3  Col: 0
```

Python™

Python appearing in this screenshot is 3.10.4. This book assumes that you will use Python 3 rather than Python 2. There are substantial differences between the two versions, and many examples used in this book will not work with Python 2. A shell window contains an opening message followed by the special symbol >>>, called a shell prompt. The cursor at the shell prompt waits for you to enter a Python command. Note that you can get immediate help by entering **help** at the shell prompt or selecting **help** from the window's drop-down menu.

When you enter an expression or a statement, Python evaluates it and displays its result, if there is one, followed by a new prompt. The next few lines show the evaluation of several expressions and statements.

```
>>> 3 + 4                    # Simple arithmetic
7
>>> 3                        # The value of 3 is
3
>>> "Python is really cool!" # Use a string for text
'Python is really cool!'
>>> name = "Ken Lambert"     # Give a variable a value
>>> name                     # The value of name is
'Ken Lambert'
>>> "Hi there, " + name      # Create some new text
'Hi there, Ken Lambert'
>>> print('Hi there')        # Output some text
Hi there
>>> print("Hi there,", name) # Output two values
Hi there, Ken Lambert
```

Note the use of colors in the Python code. The IDLE programming environment uses color-coding to help the reader pick out different elements in the code. In this example, the items within quotation marks are in green, the names of standard functions are in purple, program comments are in red, and the responses of IDLE to user commands are in blue. The remaining code is in black. **Table 1-1** lists the color-coding scheme used in all program code in this book.

Table 1-1   Color-Coding of Python program elements in IDLE

Color	Type of Element	Examples
Black	Inputs in the IDLE shell Numbers Operator symbols Variable, function, and method references Punctuation marks	`67, +, name, y = factorial(x)`
Blue	Outputs in the IDLE shell Function, class, and method names in definitions	`'Ken Lambert'` `def factorial(n)`
Green	Strings	`"Ken Lambert", 'a'`
Orange	Keywords	`def, if, while`
Purple	Built-in function names	`abs, round, int`
Red	Program comments Error messages in the IDLE shell	`# Output the results` `ZeroDivisionError: division by zero`

The Python shell is useful for experimenting with short expressions or statements to learn new features of the language, as well as for consulting documentation on the language. To quit the Python shell, you can either select the window's close box or press the CTRL-D key combination.

The means of developing more complex and interesting programs are examined in the rest of this section.

Input, Processing, and Output

Most useful programs accept inputs from some source, process these inputs, and then finally output results to some destination. In terminal-based interactive programs, the input source is the keyboard, and the output destination is the terminal display. The Python shell itself is such a program; its inputs are Python expressions or statements. Its processing evaluates these items. Its outputs are the results displayed in the shell.

The programmer can also force the output of a value by using the **print** function. The simplest form for using this function looks like the following:

```
print(<expression>)
```

This example shows you the basic syntax (or grammatical rule) for using the **print** function. The angle brackets (the < and > symbols) enclose a type of phrase. In actual Python code, you would replace this syntactic form, including the angle brackets, with an example of that type of phrase. In this case, *<expression>* is shorthand for any Python expression, such as **3 + 4**.

When running the **print** function, Python first evaluates the expression and then displays its value. In the example shown earlier, **print** was used to display some text. The following is another example:

```
>>> print("Hi there")
Hi there
```

In this example, the text **"Hi there"** is the text that we want Python to display. In programming terminology, this piece of text is referred to as a string. In Python code, a string is always enclosed in quotation marks. However, the **print** function displays a string without the quotation marks.

You can also write a **print** function that includes two or more expressions separated by commas. In such a case, the **print** function evaluates the expressions and displays their results, separated by single spaces, on one line. The syntax for a **print** statement with two or more expressions looks like the following:

```
print(<expression>,…, <expression>)
```

Note the ellipsis (…) in this syntax example. The ellipsis indicates that you could include multiple expressions after the first one. Whether it outputs one or multiple expressions, the **print** function always ends its output with a newline. In other words, it displays the values of the expressions, and then it moves the cursor to the next line on the console window.

To begin the next output on the same line as the previous one, you can place the expression **end = ""**, which says "end the line with an empty string instead of a newline," at the end of the list of expressions, as follows:

```
print(<expression>, end = "")
```

As you create programs in Python, you'll often want your programs to ask the user for input. You can do this by using the **input** function. This function causes the program to stop and wait for the user to enter a value from the keyboard. When the user presses Return or Enter key, the function accepts the input value and makes it available to the program. A program that receives an input value in this manner typically saves it for further processing.

The following example receives an input string from the user and saves it for further processing. The user's input is in italics.

```
>>> name = input("Enter your name: ")
Enter your name: Ken Lambert
>>> name
'Ken Lambert'
>>> print(name)
Ken Lambert
>>>
```

The **input** function does the following:

1. Displays a prompt for the input. In this example, the prompt is **"Enter your name: "**.
2. Receives a string of keystrokes, called characters, entered at the keyboard and returns the string to the shell.

How does the **input** function know what to use as the prompt? The text in parentheses, **"Enter your name: "**, is an argument for the **input** function that tells it what to use for the prompt. An **argument** is a piece of information that a function needs to do its work.

The string returned by the function in our example is saved by assigning it to the variable **name**. The form of an assignment statement with the **input** function is the following:

```
<variable identifier> = input(<a string prompt>)
```

A **variable identifier**, or variable for short, is just a name for a value. When a variable receives its value in an input statement, the variable then refers to this value. If the user enters the name **"Ken Lambert"** in our last example, the value of the variable **name** can be viewed as follows:

```
>>> name
'Ken Lambert'
```

The **input** function always builds a string from the user's keystrokes and returns it to the program. After inputting strings that represent numbers, the programmer must convert them from strings to the appropriate numeric types. In Python, there are two **type conversion functions** for this purpose, called **int** (for integers) and **float** (for floating-point numbers). The next session inputs two integers and displays their sum:

```
>>> first = int(input("Enter the first number: "))
Enter the first number: 23
>>> second = int(input("Enter the second number: "))
Enter the second number: 44
>>> print("The sum is", first + second)
The sum is 67
```

Note that the **int** function is called with each result returned by the **input** function. The two numbers are added, and then their sum is output. **Table 1-2** summarizes the functions introduced in this subsection.

Table 1-2 Basic Python functions for input and output

Function	What it Does
`float(<a string of digits>)`	Converts a string of digits to a floating-point value
`int(<a string of digits>)`	Converts a string of digits to an integer value
`input(<a string prompt>)`	Displays the string prompt and waits for keyboard input; returns the string of characters entered by the user
`print(<expression>, ...,<expression>)`	Evaluates the expressions and displays them, separated by one space, in the console window
`<string 1> + <string 2>`	Glues the two strings together and returns the result

Editing, Saving, and Running a Script

While it is easy to try out short Python expressions and statements interactively at a shell prompt, it is more convenient to compose, edit, and save longer, more complex programs in files. We can then run these program files or scripts either within IDLE or from the operating system's command prompt without opening IDLE. Script files are also the means by which Python programs are distributed to others. Most important, as you know from writing term papers, files allow you to save, safely and permanently, many hours of work.

To compose and execute programs in this manner, you perform the following steps:

1. Select the option **New File** from the **File** menu of the shell window.
2. In the new window, enter Python expressions or statements on separate lines, in the order in which you want Python to execute them.
3. At any point, you may save the file by selecting File/Save. If you do this, you should use a **.py** extension. For example, your first program file might be named **myprogram.py**.
4. To run this file of code as a Python script, select **Run Module** from the **Run** menu or press the F5 key.

The command in Step 4 reads the code from the saved file and executes it. If Python executes any **print** functions in the code, you will see the outputs as usual in the shell window. If the code requests any inputs, the interpreter will pause to allow you to enter them. Otherwise, program execution continues invisibly behind the scenes. When the interpreter has finished executing the last instruction, it quits and returns you to the shell prompt.

Figure 1-7 shows an IDLE window containing a complete script that prompts the user for the width and height of a rectangle, computes its area, and outputs the result:

Figure 1-7   Python script in an IDLE window

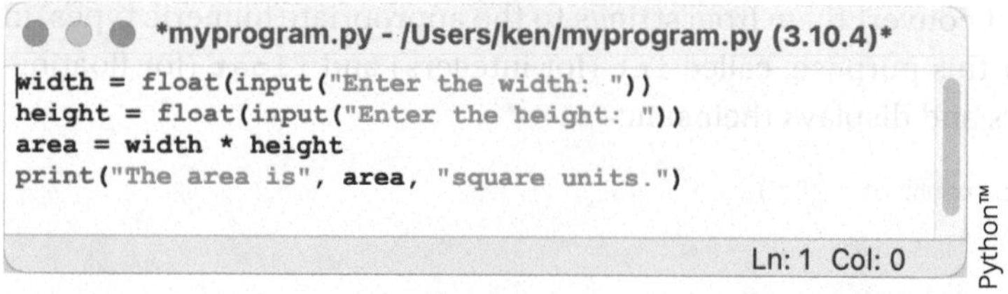

```
● ● ●   *myprogram.py - /Users/ken/myprogram.py (3.10.4)*
width = float(input("Enter the width: "))
height = float(input("Enter the height: "))
area = width * height
print("The area is", area, "square units.")


                                              Ln: 1  Col: 0
```

When the script is run from the IDLE window, it produces the interaction with the user in the shell window shown in **Figure 1-8**.

Figure 1-8   Interaction with a script in a shell window

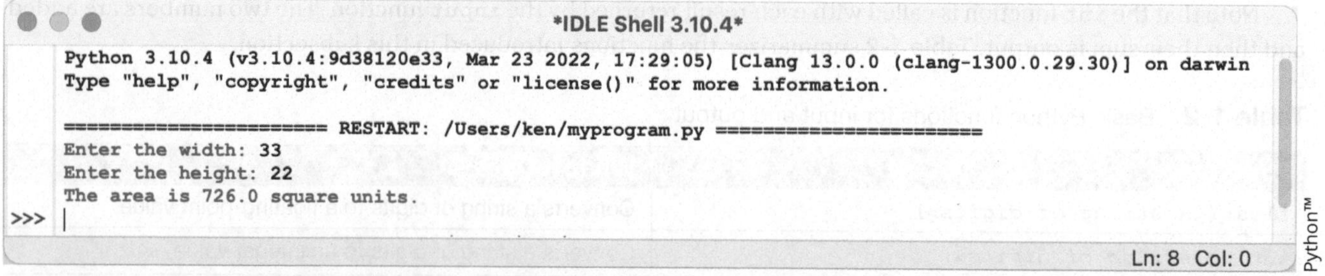

```
● ● ●                        *IDLE Shell 3.10.4*
  Python 3.10.4 (v3.10.4:9d38120e33, Mar 23 2022, 17:29:05) [Clang 13.0.0 (clang-1300.0.29.30)] on darwin
  Type "help", "copyright", "credits" or "license()" for more information.

  ===================== RESTART: /Users/ken/myprogram.py =====================
  Enter the width: 33
  Enter the height: 22
  The area is 726.0 square units.
>>> |
                                                                     Ln: 8  Col: 0
```

This can be a slightly less interactive way of executing programs than entering them directly at Python's interpreter prompt. However, running the script from the IDLE window will allow you to construct some complex programs, test them, and save them in program libraries that you can reuse or share with others.

Behind the Scenes: How Python Works

Whether you are running Python code as a script or interactively in a shell, the Python interpreter does a great deal of work to carry out the instructions in your program. This work can be broken into a series of steps, as shown in **Figure 1-9**.

1. The interpreter reads a Python expression or statement, also called the source code, and verifies that it is well formed. In this step, the interpreter behaves like a strict English teacher who rejects any sentence that

Figure 1-9   Steps in interpreting a Python program

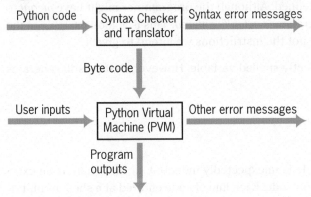

does not adhere to the grammar rules, or syntax, of the language. As soon as the interpreter encounters such an error, it halts translation with an error message.

2. If a Python expression is well formed, the interpreter then translates it to an equivalent form in a low-level language called **byte code**. When the interpreter runs a script, it completely translates it to byte code.

3. This byte code is next sent to another software component, called the **Python virtual machine (PVM)**, where it is executed. If another error occurs during this step, execution also halts with an error message.

Exercise 1-3

1. Describe what happens when the programmer enters the string **"Greetings!"** in the Python shell.

2. Write a line of code that prompts the user for his or her name and saves the user's input in a variable called **name**.

3. What is a Python script?

4. Explain what goes on behind the scenes when your computer runs a Python program.

Detecting and Correcting Syntax Errors

Programmers inevitably make typographical errors when editing programs, and the Python interpreter will nearly always detect them. Such errors are called syntax errors. The term *syntax* refers to the rules for forming sentences in a language. When Python encounters a syntax error in a program, it halts execution with an error message. The following sessions with the Python shell show several types of syntax errors and the corresponding error messages:

```
>>> length = int(input("Enter the length: "))
Enter the length: 44
>>> print(lenth)
Traceback (most recent call last):
  File "<pyshell#1>", line 1, in <module>
NameError: name 'lenth' is not defined
```

The first statement assigns an input value to the variable `length`. The next statement attempts to print the value of the variable `lenth`. Python responds that this name is not defined. Although the programmer might have *meant* to write the variable `length`, Python can read only what the programmer *actually entered*. This is a good example of the rule that a computer can read *only* the instructions it receives, not the instructions we intend to give it.

The next statement attempts to print the value of the correctly spelled variable. However, Python still generates an error message.

```
>>> print(length)
SyntaxError: unexpected indent
```

In this error message, Python explains that this line of code is unexpectedly indented. In fact, there is an extra space before the word `print`. Indentation is significant in Python code. Each line of code entered at a shell prompt or in a script must begin in the leftmost column, with no leading spaces. The only exception to this rule occurs in control statements and definitions, where nested statements must be indented one or more spaces.

You might think that it would be painful to keep track of indentation in a program. However, the Python language is much simpler than other programming languages. Consequently, there are fewer types of syntax errors to encounter and correct, and a lot less syntax for you to learn!

In our final example, the programmer attempts to add two numbers but forgets to include the second one:

```
>>> 3 +
SyntaxError: invalid syntax
```

In later chapters, you will learn more about other kinds of program errors and how to repair the code that generates them.

Summary

- One of the most fundamental ideas of computer science is the algorithm. An algorithm is a sequence of instructions for solving a problem. A computing agent can carry out these instructions to solve a problem in a finite amount of time.

- Another fundamental idea of computer science is information processing. Practically any relationship among real-world objects can be represented as information or data. Computing agents manipulate information and transform it by following the steps described in algorithms.

- Real computing agents can be constructed out of hardware devices. These consist of a CPU, memory, and input and output devices. The CPU contains circuitry that executes the instructions described by algorithms. The memory contains switches that represent binary digits. All information stored in memory is represented in binary form. Input devices such as a keyboard and flatbed scanner and output devices such as a monitor and speakers transmit information between the computer's memory and the external world. These devices also transfer information between a binary form and a form that human beings can use.

- Some real computers, such as those in fitness trackers and home thermostats, are specialized for a small set of tasks, whereas a desktop or laptop computer is a general-purpose problem-solving machine.

- Software provides the means whereby different algorithms can be run on a general-purpose hardware device. The term *software* can refer to editors and interpreters for developing programs; an operating system for managing hardware devices; user interfaces for communicating with human users; and applications such as word processors, spreadsheets, database managers, games, and media-processing programs.

- Software is written in programming languages. Languages such as Python are high level; they resemble English and allow authors to express their algorithms clearly to other people. A program called an interpreter translates a Python program to a lower-level form that can be executed on a real computer.

- The Python shell provides a command prompt for evaluating and viewing the results of Python expressions and statements. IDLE is an integrated development environment that allows the programmer to save programs in files and load them into a shell for testing.

- Python scripts are programs that are saved in files and run from a terminal command prompt. An interactive script consists of a set of input statements, statements that process these inputs, and statements that output the results.

- When a Python program is executed, it is translated into byte code. This byte code is then sent to the PVM for further interpretation and execution.

- Syntax is the set of rules for forming correct expressions and statements in a programming language. When the interpreter encounters a syntax error in a Python program, it halts execution with an error message. Two examples of syntax errors are a reference to a variable that does not yet have a value and an indentation that is unexpected.

Key Terms

abacus	data	networks
abstraction	data science	newline
algorithm	digital cloud	operating system
applications software	executed	optical storage media
argument	file system	output
artificial intelligence	graphical user interface (GUI)	personal digital assistants (PDAs)
assembler	hardware	ports
assembly languages	high-level programming languages	primary memory
batch processing	hypermedia	processor
big data	information processing	programs
binary digits	input	programming languages
bits	input/output devices	program libraries
bit-mapped display screen	integrated circuit	Python Shell
byte code	Internet of Things (IOT)	Python virtual machine (PVM)
card reader	interpreter	random access memory (RAM)
cathode ray tube (CRT) screen	keypunch machine	run-time system
central processing unit (CPU)	loader	secondary memory
client	machine code	semiconductor storage media
client/server applications	magnetic storage media	server
cloud computing	mainframe computers	server farms
compiler	memory	shell
computing agent	microprocessor	software
concurrent processing	Moore's Law	software engineering

solid-state device	text editor	virtual assistant
source code	touchscreen interface	virtual machine
string	transistor	virtual reality
syntax	translator	web applications
syntax errors	type conversion functions	web browser
system software	user interfaces	web client
terminal-based interface	variable identifier	web servers

Review Questions

1. Which of the following is an example of an algorithm?

   a. A dictionary

   b. A recipe

   c. A shopping list

   d. The spelling checker of a word processor

2. Which of the following contains information?

   a. An audio CD

   b. A refrigerator

   c. An automobile

   d. A stereo speaker

3. Which of the following is a general-purpose computing device?

   a. A cell phone

   b. A portable music player

   c. A microwave oven

   d. A programmable thermostat

4. Which of the following is an input device?

   a. Speaker

   b. Microphone

   c. Printer

   d. Display screen

5. Which of the following are output devices?

   a. A digital camera

   b. A keyboard

   c. A flatbed scanner

   d. A monitor

6. What is the purpose of the CPU?

   a. Store information

   b. Receive inputs from the human user

   c. Decode and execute instructions

   d. Send output to the human user

7. Which of the following translates and executes instructions in a programming language?

   a. A compiler

   b. A text editor

   c. A loader

   d. An interpreter

8. Which of the following outputs data in a Python program?

   a. The `input` function

   b. The assignment statement

   c. The `print` function

   d. The `main` function

9. What is IDLE used to do?

    a. Edit, compile, and run Python programs   **c.** Just compile Python programs

    b. Just edit Python programs   **d.** Just run Python programs

10. What is the set of rules for forming sentences in a language called?

    a. Semantics   **c.** Syntax

    b. Pragmatics   **d.** Logic

Programming Exercises

1. Write a Python program in a file named **myinfo.py** that prints (displays) your name, address, and telephone number. (LO: 1.4)

2. Open an IDLE window and enter the program from Figure 1-7 that computes the area of a rectangle. Save the program to a file named **rectangle.py** and load it into the shell by pressing the F5 key and correct any errors that occur. Test the program with different inputs by running it at least three times. (LO: 1.4)

3. Write a program in a file named **triangle.py** to compute the area of a triangle. Issue the appropriate prompts for the triangle's base and height. Then, use the formula `.5 * base * height` to compute the area. Test the program from an IDLE window. (LO: 1.4)

4. Write and test a program in a file named **circle.py** that computes the area of a circle. This program should request a number representing a radius as input from the user. It should use the formula `3.14 * radius ** 2` to compute the area and then output this result suitably labeled. (LO: 1.4)

5. A cuboid is a solid figure bounded by six rectangular faces. Its dimensions are its height, width, and depth. Write a Python program in a file named **cuboid.py** that computes and prints the volume of a cuboid, given its height, width, and depth as inputs. The volume is just the product of these three inputs. The output should be labeled as "cubic units." (LO: 1.4)

Debugging Exercise

Consider the following interaction at the Python shell:

```
>>> first = input("Enter the first integer: ")
Enter the first number: 23
>>> second = input("Enter the second integer: ")
Enter the second number: 44
>>> print("The sum is", first + second)
The sum of the two integers is 2344
```

The expected output is 67, but the output of this computation is 2344. Explain what causes this error and describe how to correct it.

1

Setup an Initial Testcode

Prompt

The startup that you work for has designated you, as a senior Python applications developer, to begin work on setting up the environment which will allow your development team to design and deploy applications to help setup various robot controls and automate our robotic hardware. As the organization's main product is a warehouse robot, these applications will provide a center piece for the marketing team to go out and sell our robots and their services.

For this first step, you will be setting up the Python command line development environment using the Idle shell. You will be working through not only the setup of it, but various settings like font size, edit window start and running your first script.

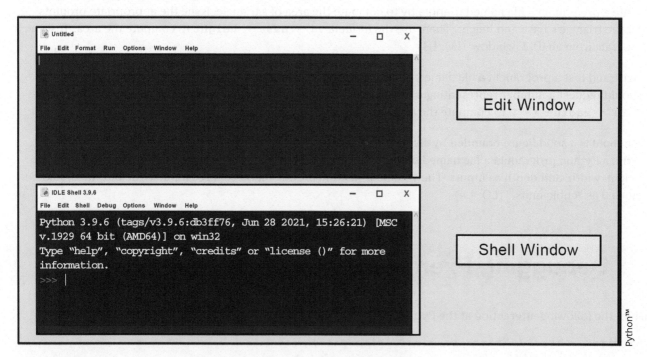

To begin, you will get Idle downloaded and setup, using this link:

1. Go to Python.org and download the latest version.
2. Once the wizard has finished running, you can startup Idle, which was installed as part of your Python download and setup.

Next, you will change the font settings and startup setting to:

1. Font size xxx

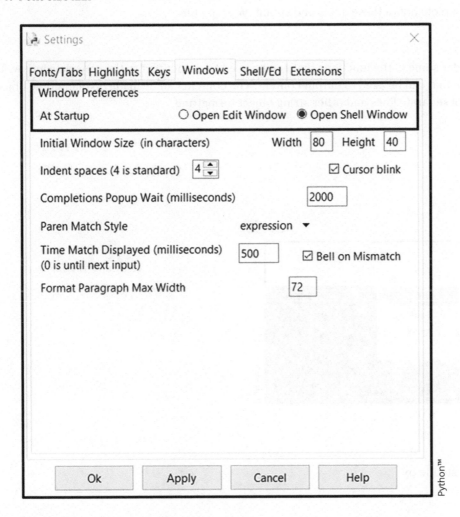

2. Python file startup

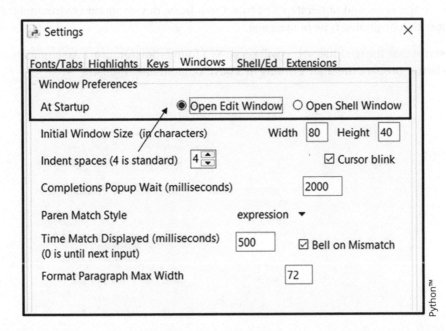

3. Finally, you will write and run your first hello world script

Congratulations, you have now completed your first assignment, the setup of your environment and the execution of your first application. Take a screenshot of these items and submit your .py file.

Hints

For output to the console, consider some of the functions that can be used to output text to the console window. The print method is one such method that can be used to output content. The content can be made up of multiple objects or string, in addition to the use of separate lines and other string object formatting.

Examples

```
print(object)
print(object, object)
print("My message")
```

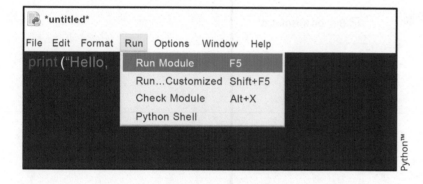

Answer

See Chapter 1_Setup an Initial Testcode.py

After Discussion

In this beginning assignment, the learner will have successfully setup their initial environment and been able to produce some basic output. This will showcase the skills and understanding to setup a basic development environment, IDE and ability to produce a basic script with a beginning type of message.

This assignment and the basic script that the user has setup will serve as a foundation for future assignments and the continuation of skill building to better prepare them for working in a development environment.

## Chapter 2

Software Development, Data Types, and Expressions

Learning Objectives

When you complete this chapter, you will be able to:

2.1 Describe the basic phases of software development: analysis, design, coding, and testing

2.2 Use strings for the terminal input and output of text

2.3 Use integers and floating-point numbers in arithmetic operations

2.4 Construct arithmetic expressions

2.5 Import functions from library modules

This chapter begins with a discussion of the software development process, followed by a case study in which you walk through the steps of program analysis, design, coding, and testing. The chapter also examines the basic elements that form programs. These include the data types for text and numbers and the expressions that manipulate them. The chapter concludes with an introduction to the use of functions and modules in simple programs.

2.1 The Software Development Process

There is much more to programming than writing lines of code, just as there is more to building houses than pounding nails. The other aspects of programming include organization and planning, and various conventions for diagramming those plans. Computer scientists refer to the process of planning and organizing a program as **software development**. There are several approaches to software development. One version is known as the **waterfall model**.

The waterfall model consists of several phases:

1. **Customer request:** In this phase, the programmers receive a broad statement of a problem that is potentially amenable to a computerized solution. This step is also called the user requirements phase.
2. **Analysis:** The programmers determine what the program will do. This is sometimes viewed as a process of clarifying the specifications for the problem.
3. **Design:** The programmers determine how the program will do its task.
4. **Implementation:** The programmers write the program. This step is also called the coding phase.
5. **Integration:** Large programs have many parts. In the integration phase, these parts are brought together into a smoothly functioning whole, usually not an easy task.
6. **Maintenance:** Programs usually have a long life; a lifespan of 5 to 15 years is common for software. During this time, requirements change, errors are detected, and minor or major modifications are made.

The phases of the waterfall model are shown in **Figure 2-1**. As you can see, the figure resembles a waterfall, in which the results of each phase flow down to the next. However, if a developer makes a mistake in an early phase, it may require them to back up and redo some of the work. Modifications made during maintenance also require backing up to earlier phases. Taken together, these phases are also called the **software development life cycle**.

Figure 2-1   The waterfall model of the software development process

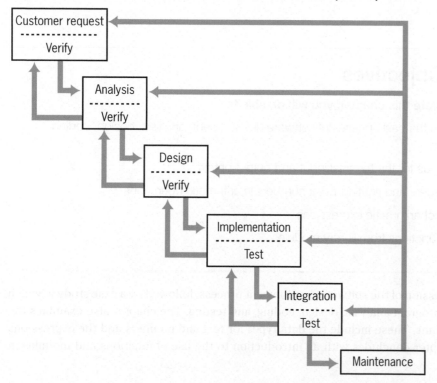

Although the diagram depicts distinct phases, this does not mean that developers must analyze and design a complete system before coding it. Modern software development is usually **incremental** and **iterative**. This means that analysis and design may produce a rough draft, skeletal version, or **prototype** of a system for coding, and then back up to earlier phases to fill in more details after some testing. For purposes of introducing this process, however, this chapter treats these phases as distinct.

Programs rarely work perfectly the first time they are run, which is why they should be subjected to extensive and careful testing. Many people think that testing is an activity that applies only to the implementation and integration phases; however, you should scrutinize the outputs of each phase carefully. Keep in mind that mistakes found early are much less expensive to correct than those found late. **Figure 2-2** illustrates some relative costs of repairing mistakes when found in different phases. These are not just financial costs but also costs in time and effort.

Figure 2-2 Relative costs of repairing mistakes that are found in different phases

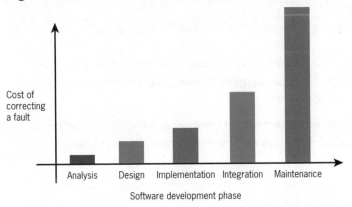

Keep in mind that the cost of developing software is not spread equally over the phases. The percentages shown in **Figure 2-3** are typical.

Figure 2-3 Percentage of total cost incurred in each phase of the development process

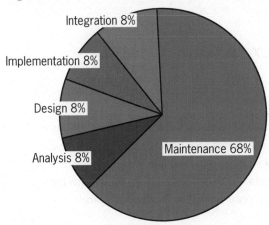

You might think that implementation takes the most time and therefore costs the most. However, as you can see in **Figure 2-3**, maintenance is the most expensive part of software development. The cost of maintenance can be reduced by careful analysis, design, and implementation.

As you read this book and begin to sharpen your programming skills, you should remember two points:

1. There is more to software development than writing code.
2. If you want to reduce the overall cost of software development, write programs that are easy to maintain. This requires thorough analysis, careful design, and a good coding style. You will learn more about coding styles throughout the book.

Exercise 2-1

1. List four phases of the software development process and explain what they accomplish.
2. Jack says that he will not bother with analysis and design but proceed directly to coding his programs. Why is that not a good idea?

Case Study 2-1 | Income Tax Calculator

Most of the chapters in this book include a case study that illustrates the software development process. This approach may seem overly elaborate for small programs, but it scales up well when programs become larger. The first case study develops a program that calculates income tax.

Each year, nearly everyone with an income faces the unpleasant task of computing their income tax return. If only it could be done as easily as suggested in this case study! Start with the customer request phase.

Request

The customer requests a program that computes a person's income tax.

Analysis

Analysis often requires the programmer to learn some things about the problem domain, in this case, the relevant tax law. For the sake of simplicity, let's assume the following tax laws:

- All taxpayers are charged a flat tax rate of 20%.

- All taxpayers are allowed a $10,000 standard deduction.

- For each dependent, a taxpayer is allowed an additional $3,000 deduction.

- Gross income must be entered to the nearest penny.

- The income tax is expressed as a decimal number.

Another part of analysis determines what information the user will have to provide. In this case, the user inputs are gross income and number of dependents. The program calculates the income tax based on the inputs and the tax law and then displays the income tax. Figure 2-4 shows the proposed terminal-based interface. Characters in italics indicate user inputs. The program prints the rest. The inclusion of an interface at this point is a good idea because it allows the customer and the programmer to discuss the intended program's behavior in a context understandable to both.

Figure 2-4 **The user interface for the income tax calculator**

```
Enter the gross income: 150000.00
Enter the number of dependents: 3
The income tax is $26200.0
```

Design

During analysis, you specify what a program is going to do. In the next phase, design, you describe how the program is going to do it. This usually involves writing an algorithm. In Chapter 1, you learned how to write algorithms in ordinary English. In fact, algorithms are more often written in a somewhat stylized version of English called **pseudocode**. Here is the pseudocode for our income tax program:

```
Input the gross income and number of dependents
Compute the taxable income using the formula
Taxable income = gross income - 10000 - (3000 * number of dependents)
Compute the income tax using the formula
Tax = taxable income * 0.20
Print the tax
```

Although there are no precise rules governing the syntax of pseudocode, in your pseudocode you should strive to describe the essential elements of the program in a clear and concise manner. Note that this pseudocode closely resembles Python code, so the transition to the coding step should be straightforward.

Implementation (Coding)

Given the preceding pseudocode, an experienced programmer would now find it easy to write the corresponding Python program. For a beginner, on the other hand, writing the code can be the most difficult part of the process. Although the program that follows is simple by most standards, do not expect to understand every bit of it at first. The rest of this chapter explains the elements that make it work, and much more.

```python
"""
Program: taxform.py
Author: Ken Lambert
Compute a person's income tax.
1. Significant constants
        tax rate
        standard deduction
        deduction per dependent
2. The inputs are
        gross income
        number of dependents
3. Computations:
        taxable income = gross income - the standard
            deduction - a deduction for each dependent
        income tax = is a fixed percentage of the taxable income
4. The outputs are
        the income tax
"""

# Initialize the constants
TAX_RATE = 0.20
STANDARD_DEDUCTION = 10000.0
DEPENDENT_DEDUCTION = 3000.0

# Request the inputs
grossIncome = float(input("Enter the gross income: "))
numDependents = int(input("Enter the number of dependents: "))

# Compute the income tax
taxableIncome = grossIncome - STANDARD_DEDUCTION - \
        DEPENDENT_DEDUCTION * numDependents
incomeTax = taxableIncome * TAX_RATE

# Display the income tax
print("The income tax is $" + str(incomeTax))
```

(continues)

Testing

The income tax program can run as a script from an IDLE window. If there are no syntax errors, you will be able to enter a set of inputs and view the results. However, a single run without syntax errors and with correct outputs provides just a slight indication of a program's correctness. Only thorough testing can build confidence that a program is working correctly. Testing is a deliberate process that requires some planning and discipline on the programmer's part. It would be much easier to turn the program in after the first successful run to meet a deadline or to move on to the next assignment. But your grade, your job, or people's lives might be affected by incomplete testing of software.

Testing can be performed easily from an IDLE window. The programmer loads the program repeatedly into the shell and enters different sets of inputs. The real challenge is coming up with sets of inputs that can reveal an error. An error at this point, also called a **logic error** or a **design error**, is an unexpected output.

A **correct program** produces the expected output for any legitimate input. The tax calculator's analysis does not provide a specification of what inputs are legitimate, but common sense indicates that they would be numbers greater than or equal to 0. Some of these inputs will produce outputs that are less than 0, but assume for now that these outputs are expected. Even though the range of the input numbers on a computer is finite, testing all of the possible combinations of inputs would be impractical. The challenge is to find a smaller set of inputs, called a **test suite**, from which you can conclude that the program will likely be correct for all inputs. In the tax program, try inputs of 0, 1, and 2 for the number of dependents. If the program works correctly with these, you can assume that it will work correctly with larger values. The test inputs for the gross income are a number equal to the standard deduction and a number twice that amount (10,000 and 20,000, respectively). These two values will show the cases of a minimum expected tax (0) and expected taxes that are less than or greater than 0. The program is run with each possible combination of the two inputs. Table 2-1 shows the possible combinations of inputs and the expected outputs in the test suite.

Table 2-1   The test suite for the tax calculator program

Number of Dependents	Gross Income	Expected Tax
0	10,000	0
1	10,000	−600
2	10,000	−1200
0	20,000	2000
1	20,000	1400
2	20,000	800

If there is a logic error in the code, it will almost certainly be caught using these data. Note that the negative outputs are not considered errors. You will see how to prevent such computations in the next chapter.

2.2 Strings, Assignment, and Comments

Text processing is by far the most common application of computing. Email, text messaging, web pages, and word processing all rely on and manipulate data consisting of strings of characters. This section introduces the use of strings for the output of text and the documentation of Python programs. It begins with an introduction to data types in general.

Data Types

In the real world, you use data all the time without bothering to consider what kind of data you're using. For example, consider this sentence: "In 2007, Micaela paid $120,000 for her house at 24 East Maple Street." This sentence includes at least four pieces of data—a name, a date, a price, and an address—but of course you don't have to stop to think about that before you utter the sentence. You certainly don't have to stop to consider that the name consists only of text characters, the date and house price are numbers, and so on. However, when you use data in a computer program, you do need to keep in mind the type of data you're using. You also need to keep in mind what you can do with (what operations can be performed on) particular data.

In programming, a **data type** consists of a set of values and a set of operations that can be performed on those values. A **literal** is the way a value of a data type looks to a programmer. The programmer can use a literal in a program to mention a data value. When the Python interpreter evaluates a literal, the value it returns is simply that literal. **Table 2-2** shows example literals of several Python data types.

Table 2-2   Literals for some Python data types

Type of Data	Python Type Name	Example Literals
Integers	`int`	`-1, 0, 1, 2`
Real numbers	`float`	`-0.55, .3333, 3.14, 6.0`
Character strings	`str`	`"Hi", "", 'A', "66"`

The first two data types listed in **Table 2-2**, `int` and `float`, are called **numeric data types**, because they represent numbers. You'll learn more about numeric data types later in this chapter. For now, focus on character strings—which are often referred to simply as strings.

String Literals

In Python, a string literal is a sequence of characters enclosed in single or double quotation marks. The following session with the Python shell shows some example strings:

```
>>> 'Hello there!'
'Hello there!'
>>> "Hello there!"
'Hello there!'
>>> ''
''
>>> ""
''
```

The last two string literals (" and "") represent the **empty string**. Although it contains no characters, the empty string is a string nonetheless. Note that the empty string is different from a string that contains a single blank space character, " ".

Double-quoted strings are handy for composing strings that contain single quotation marks or apostrophes. Here is a self-justifying example:

```
>>> "I'm using a single quote in this string!"
"I'm using a single quote in this string!"
>>> print("I'm using a single quote in this string!")
I'm using a single quote in this string!
```

Note that the `print` function displays the nested quotation mark but not the enclosing quotation marks. A double quotation mark can also be included in a string literal if one uses the single quotation marks to enclose the literal.

When you write a string literal in Python code that will be displayed on the screen as output, you need to determine whether you want to output the string as a single line or as a multiline paragraph. If you want to output the string as a single line, you have to include the entire string literal (including its opening and closing quotation marks) in the same line of code. Otherwise, a syntax error will occur. To output a paragraph of text that contains several lines, you could use a separate `print` function call for each line. However, it is more convenient to enclose the entire string literal, line breaks and all, within three consecutive quotation marks (either single or double) for printing. The next session shows how this is done:

```
>>> print("""This very long sentence extends
all the way to the next line.""")
This very long sentence extends
all the way to the next line.
```

Note that the first line in the output ends exactly where the first line ends in the code.

When you evaluate a string in the Python shell without the `print` function, you can see the literal for the **newline character**, `\n`, embedded in the result, as follows:

```
>>> """This very long sentence extends
all the way to the next line."""
'This very long sentence extends\nall the way to the next line.'
```

Escape Sequences

The newline character `\n` is called an **escape sequence**. Escape sequences are the way Python expresses special characters, such as the tab, the newline, and the backspace key, as literals. **Table 2-3** lists some escape sequences in Python.

Table 2-3   Some escape sequences in Python

Escape Sequence	Meaning
\b	Backspace
\n	Newline
\t	Horizontal tab
\\	The \ character
\'	Single quotation mark
\"	Double quotation mark

Because the backslash is used for escape sequences, it must be escaped to appear as a literal character in a string. Thus, `print('\\')` would display a single \ character.

String Concatenation

You can join two or more strings to form a new string using the concatenation operator **+**. Here is an example:

```
>>> "Hi " + "there, " + "Ken!"
'Hi there, Ken!'
```

The * operator allows you to build a string by repeating another string a given number of times. The left operand is a string, and the right operand is an integer. For example, if you want the string `"Python"` to be preceded by 10 spaces, it would be easier to use the * operator with 10 and one space than to enter the 10 spaces by hand. The next session shows the use of the * and + operators to achieve this result:

```
>>> " " * 10 + "Python"
'          Python'
```

Variables and the Assignment Statement

As you saw in Chapter 1, a **variable** associates a name with a value, making it easy to remember and use the value later in a program. You need to be mindful of a few rules when choosing names for your variables. For example, some names, such as `if`, `def`, and `import`, are reserved for other purposes and thus cannot be used for variable names. In general, a variable name must begin with either a letter or an underscore (_) and can contain any number of letters, digits, or other underscores. Python variable names are case sensitive; thus, the variable `WEIGHT` is a different name from the variable `weight`. Python programmers typically use lowercase letters for variable names, but in the case of variable names that consist of more than one word, it's common to begin each word in the variable name (except for the first one) with an uppercase letter. This makes the variable name easier to read. For example, the name `interestRate` is slightly easier to read than the name `interestrate`.

Programmers use all uppercase letters for the names of variables that contain values that the program never changes. Such variables are known as **symbolic constants**. Examples of symbolic constants in the tax calculator case study are `TAX_RATE` and `STANDARD_DEDUCTION`.

Variables receive their initial values and can be reset to new values with an **assignment statement**. The simplest form of an assignment statement is the following:

```
<variable name> = <expression>
```

As mentioned in Chapter 1, the terms enclosed in angle brackets name or describe a part of a Python code construct. Thus, the notation `<variable name>` stands for any Python variable name, such as `totalIncome` or `taxRate`. The notation `<expression>` stands for any Python expression, such as `" " * 10 + "Python"`.

The Python interpreter first evaluates the expression on the right side of the assignment symbol and then binds the variable name on the left side to this value. When this happens to the variable name for the first time, it is called **defining** or **initializing** the variable. Note that the = symbol means assignment, not equality. After you initialize a variable, subsequent uses of the variable name in expressions are known as **variable references**.

When the interpreter encounters a variable reference in any expression, it looks up the associated value. If a name is not yet bound to a value when it is referenced, Python signals an error. The next session shows some definitions of variables and their references:

```
>>> firstName = "Ken"
>>> secondName = "Lambert"
>>> fullName = firstName + " " + secondName
>>> fullName
'Ken Lambert'
```

The first two statements initialize the variables `firstName` and `secondName` to string values. The next statement references these variables, concatenates the values referenced by the variables to build a new string, and assigns the result to the variable `fullName` ("concatenate" means "glue together"). The last line of code is a simple reference to the variable `fullName`, which returns its value.

Variables serve two important purposes in a program. They help the programmer keep track of data that change over time. They also allow the programmer to refer to a complex piece of information with a simple name. Any time you can substitute a simple thing for a more complex one in a program, you make the program easier for programmers to understand and maintain. Such a process of simplification is called **abstraction**, and it is one of the fundamental ideas of computer science. Throughout this book, you'll learn about other abstractions used in computing, including functions, modules, and classes.

A wise programmer selects names that inform the human reader about the purpose of the data. This, in turn, makes the program easier to maintain and troubleshoot. A good program not only performs its task correctly but also reads like a carefully written essay in which each word conveys a specific and appropriate meaning. For example, a program that creates a payment schedule for a simple interest loan might use the variables `rate`, `initialAmount`, `currentBalance`, and `interest`.

Program Comments and Docstrings

This subsection on strings concludes with a discussion of **program comments** (sometimes also called block comments in other programming languages). A comment is a piece of program text that the computer ignores but that provides useful documentation to programmers. At the very least, the author of a program can include their name and a brief statement about the program's purpose at the beginning of the program file. This type of comment, called a **docstring**, is a multiline string of the form discussed earlier in this section. Here is a docstring that begins a typical program for a lab session:

```
"""
Program: circle.py
Author: Ken Lambert
Last date modified: 10/10/22

The purpose of this program is to compute the area of a circle. The input is an
integer or floating-point number representing the radius of the circle. The output
is a floating-point number labeled as the area of the circle.
"""
```

In addition to docstrings, **end-of-line comments** can document a program. These comments begin with the # symbol and extend to the end of a line. An end-of-line comment might explain the purpose of a variable or the strategy used by a piece of code, if it is not already obvious. Here is an example:

```
>>> RATE = 0.70 # Conversion rate for Canadian to US dollars
```

Throughout this book, docstrings appear in green and end-of-line comments appear in red.

In a program, good documentation can be as important as executable code. Ideally, program code is self-documenting, so a human reader can instantly understand it. However, a program is often read by people who are not its authors, and even the authors might find their own code difficult to read after months of not seeing it. The trick is to avoid documenting code that has an obvious meaning, but to aid the reader when the code alone might not provide sufficient understanding. With this end in mind, it's a good idea to do the following:

1. Begin a program with a statement of its purpose and other information that would help orient a programmer called on to modify the program at some future date.
2. Accompany a variable definition with a comment that explains the variable's purpose.
3. Precede major segments of code with brief comments that explain their purpose. The case study program presented earlier in this chapter does this.
4. Include comments to explain the workings of complex or tricky sections of code.

Exercise 2-2

1. Let the variable **x** be **"dog"** and the variable y be **"cat"**. Write the values returned by the following operations:

   a. x + y
   b. "the " + x + " chases the " + y
   c. x * 4

2. Write a string that contains your name and address on separate lines using embedded newline characters. Then write the same string literal without the newline characters.

3. How does one include an apostrophe as a character within a string literal?

4. What happens when the **print** function prints a string literal with embedded newline characters?

5. Which of the following are valid variable names?

   a. length
   b. _width
   c. firstBase
   d. 2MoreToGo
   e. halt!

6. List two of the purposes of program documentation.

2.3 Numeric Data Types and Character Sets

The first computer applications were created to crunch numbers. Although text and media processing have lately been of increasing importance, the use of numbers in many applications is still very important. This section gives a brief overview of numeric data types and their cousins, **character sets**.

Integers

As you learned in mathematics, the **integers** include 0, the positive whole numbers, and the negative whole numbers. Integer literals in a Python program are written without commas, and a leading negative sign indicates a negative value.

Although the range of integers is infinite, a real computer's memory places a limit on the magnitude of the largest positive and negative integers. The most common implementation of the **int** data type in many programming languages consists of the integers from $-2,147,483,648$ (-2^{31}) to $2,147,483,647$ $(2^{31} - 1)$. However, the magnitude of a Python integer is much larger and is limited only by the memory of your computer. As an experiment, try evaluating the expression **2147483647 ** 100**, which raises the largest positive **int** value to the 100th power. You will see a number that contains many lines of digits!

Floating-Point Numbers

A real number in mathematics, such as the value of π (3.1416…), consists of a whole number, a decimal point, and a fractional part. Real numbers have **infinite precision**, which means that the digits in the fractional part can continue forever. Like the integers, real numbers also have an infinite range. However, because a computer's memory is not infinitely large, a computer's memory limits not only the range but also the precision that can be represented for real numbers. Python uses **floating-point** numbers to represent real numbers. Values of the most common implementation of Python's **float** type range from approximately -10^{308} to 10^{308} and have 16 digits of precision.

A floating-point number can be written using either ordinary **decimal notation** or **scientific notation**. Scientific notation is often useful for mentioning very large numbers. **Table 2-4** shows some equivalent values in both notations.

Table 2-4 Decimal and scientific notations for floating-point numbers

Decimal Notation	Scientific Notation	Meaning
3.78	3.78e0	3.78×10^0
37.8	3.78e1	3.78×10^1
3780.0	3.78e3	3.78×10^3
0.378	3.78e-1	3.78×10^{-1}
0.00378	3.78e-3	3.78×10^{-3}

Character Sets

Some programming languages use different data types for strings and individual characters. In Python, character literals look just like string literals and are of the string type. To mark the difference, this book uses single quotes to enclose single-character strings and double quotes to enclose multicharacter strings. Thus, it refers to `'H'` as a character and `"Hi!"` as a string, even though they are both technically Python strings and both are color coded in green in this text.

As you learned in Chapter 1, all data and instructions in a program are translated to binary numbers before being run on a real computer. To support this translation, the characters in a string each map to an integer value. This mapping is defined in character sets, among them the **ASCII set** and the **Unicode set**. (The term ASCII stands for American Standard Code for Information Interchange.) In the 1960s, the original ASCII set encoded each keyboard character and several control characters using the integers from 0 through 127. An example of a control character is Ctrl + D, which is the command to terminate a shell window. As new function keys and some international characters were added to keyboards, the ASCII set doubled in size to 256 distinct values in the mid-1980s. Then, when characters and symbols were added from languages other than English, the Unicode set was created to support 65,536 values in the early 1990s. Unicode supports more than 128,000 values at the present time.

Table 2-5 shows the mapping of character values to the first 128 ASCII codes. The digits in the left column represent the leftmost digits of an ASCII code, and the digits in the top row are the rightmost digits. Thus, the ASCII code of the character `'R'` at row 8, column 2 is 82.

Table 2-5 The original ASCII character set

	0	1	2	3	4	5	6	7	8	9
0	NUL	SOH	STX	ETX	EOT	ENQ	ACK	BEL	BS	HT
1	LF	VT	FF	CR	SO	SI	DLE	DCI	DC2	DC3
2	DC4	NAK	SYN	ETB	CAN	EM	SUB	ESC	FS	GS
3	RS	US	SP	!	"	#	$	%	&	`
4	(	)	*	1	,	-	.	/	0	1
5	2	3	4	5	6	7	8	9	:	;
6	<	5	>	?	@	A	B	C	D	E
7	F	G	H	I	J	K	L	M	N	O
8	P	Q	R	S	T	U	V	W	X	Y
9	Z	[	\	]	^	_	`	a	b	c
10	d	e	f	g	h	I	j	k	l	m
11	n	o	P	q	r	S	t	u	v	w
12	X	y	z	{			}	~		DEL		

Some might think it odd to include characters in a discussion of numeric types. However, as you can see, the ASCII character set maps to a set of integers. Python's `ord` and `chr` functions convert characters to their numeric ASCII codes and back again, respectively. The next session uses these functions to explore the ASCII system:

```
>>> ord('a')
97
>>> ord('A')
65
>>> chr(65)
'A'
>>> chr(66)
'B'
```

Note that the ASCII code for `'B'` is the next number in the sequence after the code for `'A'`. These two functions provide a handy way to shift letters by a fixed amount. For example, if you want to shift three places to the right of the letter `'A'`, you can write `chr(ord('A') + 3)`.

Exercise 2-3

1. Which data type would most appropriately be used to represent the following data values?

    a. The number of months in a year
    b. The area of a circle
    c. The current minimum wage
    d. The approximate age of the universe (12,000,000,000 years)
    e. Your name

2. Explain the differences between the data types `int` and `float`.

3. Write the values of the following floating-point numbers in Python's scientific notation:

    a. 355.76
    b. 0.007832
    c. 4.3212

4. Consult Table 2-5 to write the ASCII values of the characters `'$'` and `'&'`.

2.4 Expressions

As you have seen, a literal evaluates to itself, whereas a variable reference evaluates to the variable's current value. Expressions provide an easy way to perform operations on data values to produce other data values. You saw strings used in expressions earlier. When entered at the Python shell prompt, an expression's operands are evaluated, and its operator is then applied to these values to compute the value of the expression. This section examines arithmetic expressions in more detail.

Arithmetic Expressions

An arithmetic expression consists of operands and operators combined in a manner that is already familiar to you from learning algebra. **Table 2-6** shows several arithmetic operators and gives examples of how you might use them in Python code.

Table 2-6 Arithmetic operators

Operator	Meaning	Syntax
–	Negation	`-a`
`**`	Exponentiation	`a ** b`
`*`	Multiplication	`a * b`
`/`	Division	`a / b`
`//`	Quotient	`a // b`
`%`	Remainder or modulus	`a % b`
`+`	Addition	`a + b`
–	Subtraction	`a – b`

In algebra, you are probably used to indicating multiplication like this: **ab**. However, in Python, you must indicate multiplication explicitly, using the multiplication operator (`*`), like this: **a * b**. Binary operators are placed between their operands (**a * b**, for example), whereas unary operators are placed before their operands (**- a**, for example).

The **precedence rules** you learned in algebra apply during the evaluation of arithmetic expressions in Python:

- Exponentiation has the highest precedence and is evaluated first.
- Unary negation is evaluated next, before multiplication, division, and remainder.
- Multiplication, both types of division, and remainder are evaluated before addition and subtraction.
- Addition and subtraction are evaluated before assignment.
- With two exceptions, operations of equal precedence are left associative, so they are evaluated from left to right. Exponentiation and assignment operations are right associative, so consecutive instances of these are evaluated from right to left.
- You can use parentheses to change the order of evaluation.

Table 2-7 shows some arithmetic expressions and their values.

Table 2-7 Some arithmetic expressions and their values

Expression	Evaluation	Value
`5 + 3 * 2`	`5 + 6`	`11`
`(5 + 3) * 2`	`8 * 2`	`16`
`6 % 2`	`0`	`0`
`2 * 3 ** 2`	`2 * 9`	`18`
`-3 ** 2`	`-(3 ** 2)`	`- 9`
`(3) ** 2`	`9`	`9`
`2 ** 3 ** 2`	`2 ** 9`	`512`
`(2 ** 3) ** 2`	`8 ** 2`	`64`
`45 / 0`	`Error: cannot divide by 0`	
`45 % 0`	`Error: cannot divide by 0`	

The last two lines of Table 2-7 show attempts to divide by 0, which result in an error. These expressions are good illustrations of the difference between syntax and **semantics**. Syntax is the set of rules for constructing well-formed expressions or sentences in a language. Semantics is the set of rules that allow an agent to interpret the meaning of those expressions or sentences. A computer generates a syntax error when an expression or a sentence is not well formed. A **semantic error** is detected when the action that an expression describes cannot be carried out, even though that expression is syntactically correct. Although the expressions `45 / 0` and `45 % 0` are syntactically correct, they are meaningless, because a computing agent cannot carry them out. Human beings can tolerate all kinds of syntax errors and semantic errors when they converse in natural languages. Computing agents, however, can tolerate none of these errors.

With the exception of exact division, when both operands of an arithmetic expression are of the same numeric type (`int` or `float`), the resulting value is also of that type. When each operand is of a different type, the resulting value is of the more general type. Note that the `float` type is more general than the `int` type. The quotient operator `//` produces an integer quotient, whereas the exact division operator `/` always produces a `float`. Thus, `3 // 4` produces `0`, whereas `3 / 4` produces `.75`.

Although spacing within an expression is not important to the Python interpreter, programmers usually insert a single space before and after each operator to make the code easier for people to read. Normally, an expression must be completed on a single line of Python code. When an expression becomes long or complex, you can move to a new line by placing a backslash character \ at the end of the current line. The next example shows this technique:

```
>>> 3 + 4 * \
2 ** 5
131
```

Make sure to insert the backslash before or after an operator. If you break lines in this manner in IDLE, the editor automatically indents the code properly.

As you will see shortly, you can also break a long line of code immediately after a comma. Examples include function calls with several arguments.

Mixed-Mode Arithmetic and Type Conversions

You have seen how the `//` operator produces an integer result and the `/` operator produces a floating-point result with two integers. What happens when one operand is an `int` and the other is a `float`? When working with a handheld calculator, you do not give much thought to the fact that you intermix integers and floating-point numbers. Performing calculations involving both integers and floating-point numbers is called **mixed-mode arithmetic**. For instance, if a circle has radius 3, you compute the area as follows:

```
>>> 3.14 * 3 ** 2
28.26
```

How does Python perform this type of calculation? In a binary operation on operands of different numeric types, the less general type (`int`) is temporarily and automatically converted to the more general type (`float`) before the operation is performed. Thus, in the example expression, the value 9 is converted to 9.0 before the multiplication.

You must use a **type conversion function** when working with the input of numbers. A type conversion function is a function with the same name as the data type to which it converts. Because the `input` function returns a string as its value, you must use the function `int` or `float` to convert the string to a number before performing arithmetic, as in the following example:

```
>>> radius = input("Enter the radius: ")
Enter the radius: 3.2
>>> radius
'3.2'
>>> float(radius)
3.2
>>> float(radius) ** 2 * 3.14
32.153600000000004
```

Table 2-8 lists some common type conversion functions and their uses.

Note that the **int** function converts a **float** to an **int** by truncation, not by rounding to the nearest whole number. Truncation simply chops off the number's fractional part. The **round** function rounds a **float** to the nearest **int** as in the next example:

```
>>> int(6.75)
6
>>> round(6.75)
7
```

Table 2-8 Type conversion functions

Conversion Function	Example Use	Value Returned
`int(<a number or a string>)`	`int(3.77)`	3
	`int("33")`	33
`float(<a number or a string>)`	`float(22)`	22.0
`str(<any value>)`	`str(99)`	'99'

Another use of type conversion occurs in the construction of strings from numbers and other strings. For instance, assume that the variable **profit** refers to a floating-point number that represents an amount of money in dollars and cents. Suppose that, to build a string that represents this value for output, you need to concatenate the $ symbol to the value of **profit**. However, Python does not allow the use of the + operator with a string and a number:

```
>>> profit = 1000.55
>>> print('$' + profit)

Traceback (most recent call last):
   File "<stdin>", line 1, in <module>
TypeError: cannot concatenate 'str' and 'float' objects
```

To solve this problem, use the **str** function to convert the value of **profit** to a string and then concatenate this string to the $ symbol, as follows:

```
>>> print('$' + str(profit))
$1000.55
```

Python is a **strongly typed programming language**. The interpreter checks data types of all operands before operators are applied to those operands. If the type of an operand is not appropriate, the interpreter halts execution with an error message. This error checking prevents a program from attempting to do something that it cannot do.

Exercise 2-4

1. Let **x** = 8 and **y** = 2. Write the values of the following expressions:

    a. `x + y * 3`
    b. `(x + y) * 3`
    c. `x ** y`
    d. `x % y`
    e. `x / 12.0`
    f. `x // 6`

  2. Let **x** = 4.66. Write the values of the following expressions:

   a. round(x)
   b. int(x)

  3. How does a Python programmer round a **float** value to the nearest **int** value?

  4. How does a Python programmer concatenate a numeric value to a string value?

  5. Assume that the variable **x** has the value 55. Use an assignment statement to increment the value of **x** by 1.

2.5 Using Functions and Modules

So far this chapter has examined two ways to manipulate data within expressions. You can apply an operator such as + to one or more operands to produce a new data value. Alternatively, you can call a function such as **round** with one or more data values to produce a new data value. Python includes many useful functions, which are organized in libraries of code called **modules**. This section examines the use of functions and modules.

Calling Functions: Arguments and Return Values

A **function** is a chunk of code that can be called by name to perform a task. Functions often require **arguments**, that is, specific data values, to perform their tasks. Names that refer to arguments are also known as **parameters**. When a function completes its task (which is usually some kind of computation), the function may send a result back to the part of the program that called that function in the first place. The process of sending a result back to another part of a program is known as **returning a value**.

For example, the argument in the function call **round(6.5)** is the value **6.5**, and the value returned is **7**. When an argument is an expression, it is first evaluated, and then its value is passed to the function for further processing. For instance, the function call **abs(4 - 5)** first evaluates the expression **4 - 5** and then passes the result, **-1**, to **abs**. Finally, **abs** returns **1**.

The values returned by function calls can be used in expressions and statements. For example, the function call **print(abs(4 - 5) + 3)** prints the value **4**.

Some functions have only **optional arguments**, some have **required arguments**, and some have both required and optional arguments. For example, the **round** function has one required argument, the number to be rounded. When called with just one argument, the **round** function exhibits its **default behavior**, which is to return the nearest whole number with a fractional part of 0. However, when a second, optional argument is supplied, this argument, a number, indicates the number of places of precision to which the first argument should be rounded. For example, **round(7.563, 2)** returns **7.56**.

To learn how to use a function's arguments, consult the documentation on functions in the shell. For example, Python's **help** function displays information about **round**, as follows:

```
>>> help(round)
Help on built-in function round in module builtin:

round(...)
    round(number[, ndigits]) -> floating point number

    Round a number to a given precision in decimal digits(default 0 digits).
    This returns an int when called with one argument, otherwise the same type
    as number, ndigits may be negative.
```

Each argument passed to a function has a specific data type. When writing code that involves functions and their arguments, you need to keep these data types in mind. A program that attempts to pass an argument of the wrong data type to a function will usually generate an error. For example, one cannot take the square root of a string, but only of a number. Likewise, if a function call is placed in an expression that expects a different type of operand than that returned by the function, an error will be raised. If you're not sure of the data type associated with a particular function's arguments, read the documentation.

The `math` Module

Functions and other resources are coded in components called modules. Functions like **abs** and **round** from the `__builtin__` module are always available for use, whereas the programmer must explicitly import other functions from the modules where they are defined.

The **math** module includes several functions that perform basic mathematical operations. The next code session imports the **math** module and lists a directory of its resources:

```
>>> import math
>>> dir(math)
['__doc__', '__file__', '__loader__', '__name__',
 '__package__', '__spec__', 'acos', 'acosh', 'asin',
 'asinh', 'atan', 'atan2', 'atanh', 'ceil', 'copysign',
 'cos', 'cosh', 'degrees', 'e', 'erf', 'erfc', 'exp',
 'expm1', 'fabs', 'factorial', 'floor', 'fmod', 'frexp',
 'fsum', 'gamma', 'gcd', 'hypot', 'inf', 'isclose',
 'isfinite', 'isinf', 'isnan', 'ldexp', 'lgamma', 'log',
 'log10', 'log1p', 'log2', 'modf', 'nan', 'pi', 'pow',
 'radians', 'sin', 'sinh', 'sqrt', 'tan', 'tanh', 'tau',
 'trunc']
```

This list of function names includes some familiar trigonometric functions as well as Python's most exact estimates of the constants π and **e**.

To use a resource from a module, you write the name of a module as a qualifier, followed by a dot (.) and the name of the resource. For example, to use the value of **pi** from the **math** module, you would write the following code: **math.pi**. The next session uses this technique to display the value of π and the square root of 2:

```
>>> math.pi
3.1415926535897931
>>> math.sqrt(2)
1.4142135623730951
```

Once again, help is available if needed:

```
>>> help(math.cos)
Help on built-in function cos in module math:
cos(...)
    cos(x)

    Return the cosine of x (measured in radians).
```

Alternatively, you can browse through the documentation for the entire module by entering **help(math)**. The function **help** uses a module's own docstring and the docstrings of all its functions to print the documentation.

If you are going to use only a couple of a module's resources frequently, you can avoid the use of the qualifier with each reference by importing the individual resources, as follows:

```
>>> from math import pi, sqrt
>>> print(pi, sqrt(2))
3.14159265359 1.41421356237
```

Programmers occasionally import all of a module's resources to use without the qualifier. For example, the statement **from math import** * would import all of the **math** module's resources.

Generally, the first technique of importing resources (i.e., importing just the module's name) is preferred. The use of a module qualifier not only reminds the reader of a function's purpose but also helps the computer to discriminate between different functions that have the same name.

The Main Module

The case study presented earlier in this chapter showed how to write documentation for a Python script. To differentiate this script from the other modules in a program (and there could be many), programmers call it the **main module**. Like any module, the main module can also be imported. Instead of launching the script from a terminal prompt or loading it into the shell from IDLE, you can start IDLE from the terminal prompt and import the script as a module. Let's do that with the **taxform.py** script, as follows:

```
>>> import taxform
Enter the gross income: 120000
Enter the number of dependents: 2
The income tax is $20800.0
```

After importing a main module, you can view its documentation by running the **help** function:

```
>>> help(taxform)
DESCRIPTION
Program: taxform.py
Author: Ken
Compute a person's income tax.
Significant constants
    tax rate
    standard deduction
    deduction per dependent
The inputs are
    gross income
    number of dependents
Computations:
    net income = gross income - the standard deduction -
                 a deduction for each dependent
    income tax = is a fixed percentage of the net income
The outputs are
    the income tax
```

Program Format and Structure

This is a good time to step back and get a sense of the overall format and structure of simple Python programs. It's a good idea to structure your programs as follows:

- Start with an introductory comment stating the author's name, the purpose of the program, and other relevant information. This information should be in the form of a docstring.

- Then, include statements that do the following:

- Import any modules needed by the program.

- Initialize important variables, suitably commented.

- Prompt the user for input data and save the input data in variables.

- Process the inputs to produce the results.

- Display the results.

Take a moment to review the income tax program presented in the case study at the beginning of this chapter. Notice how the program conforms to this basic organization. Also, notice that the various sections of the program are separated by white space (blank lines). Remember, programs should be easy for other programmers to read and understand. They should read like essays!

Running a Script from a Terminal Command Prompt

Thus far in this book, you have been developing and running Python programs experimentally in IDLE. When a program's development and testing are finished, the program can be released to others to run on their computers. Python must be installed on a user's computer, but the user need not run IDLE to run a Python script.

One way to run a Python script is to open a terminal command prompt window. On a computer running Windows 10, click in the "**Type here to search**" box on the Taskbar, type **Command Prompt**, and click **Command Prompt** in the list. In earlier versions of Windows, select the **Start** button, select **All Programs**, select **Accessories**, and then select **Command Prompt**. On a Macintosh or UNIX-based system, this is a terminal window. A terminal window on a Macintosh is shown in **Figure 2-5**.

Figure 2-5 A terminal window on a Macintosh

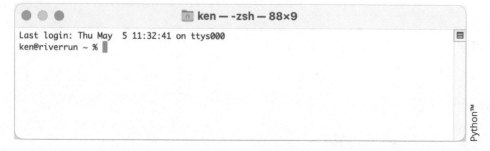

After the user has opened a terminal window, they must navigate or change directories until the prompt shows that they are attached to the directory that contains the Python script. For example, assuming that the script named **taxform.py** is in the **pythonfiles** directory under the terminal's current directory, **Figure 2-6** shows the commands to change to this directory and list its contents.

Figure 2-6 Changing to another directory and listing its contents

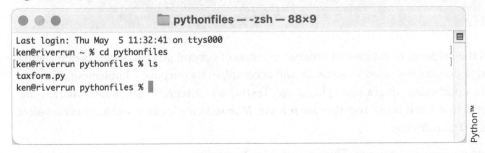

```
●  ●  ●                        📁 pythonfiles — -zsh — 88×9
Last login: Thu May  5 11:32:41 on ttys000
[ken@riverrun ~ % cd pythonfiles
[ken@riverrun pythonfiles % ls
taxform.py
ken@riverrun pythonfiles % █
```

When the user is attached to the appropriate directory, they can run the script by entering the command **python3 scriptname.py** at the command prompt (be careful: if you run **python** instead of **python3**, you might launch the interpreter for Python 2, which will not run all of the programs in this book). **Figure 2-7** shows this step and a run of the **taxform** script.

Figure 2-7 Running a Python script in a terminal window

```
●  ●  ●                        📁 pythonfiles — -zsh — 88×9
Last login: Thu May  5 11:32:41 on ttys000
[ken@riverrun ~ % cd pythonfiles
[ken@riverrun pythonfiles % ls
taxform.py
[ken@riverrun pythonfiles % python3 taxform.py
Enter the gross income: 42000
Enter the number of dependents: 2
The income tax is $5200.0
ken@riverrun pythonfiles % █
```

All Python installations also provide the capability of launching Python scripts by double-clicking the files from the operating system's file browser. On Windows systems, this feature is automatic, whereas on Macintosh and UNIX-based systems, the **.py** file type must be set to launch with the Python launcher application. When you launch a script in this manner, however, the command prompt window opens, shows the output of the script, and closes. To prevent this fly-by-window problem, you can add an input statement at the end of the script that pauses until the user presses the enter or return key, as follows:

```
input("Please press enter or return to quit the program. ")
```

Exercise 2-5

1. Explain the relationship between a function and its arguments.

2. The **math** module includes a **pow** function that raises a number to a given power. The first argument is the number, and the second argument is the exponent. Write a code segment that imports this function and calls it to print the values 8^2 and 5^4.

3. Explain how to display a directory of all of the functions in a given module.

4. Explain how to display help information on a particular function in a given module.

Summary

- The waterfall model describes the software development process in terms of several phases. Analysis determines what the software will do. Design determines how the software will accomplish its purposes. Implementation involves coding the software in a particular programming language. Testing and integration demonstrate that the software does what it is intended to do as it is put together for release. Maintenance locates and fixes errors after release and adds new features to the software.

- Literals are data values that can appear in a program. They evaluate to themselves.

- The string data type is used to represent text for input and output. Strings are sequences of characters. String literals are enclosed in pairs of single or double quotation marks. Two strings can be combined by concatenation to form a new string.

- Escape characters begin with a backslash and represent special characters such as the delete key and the newline.

- A docstring is a string enclosed by triple quotation marks and provides program documentation.

- Comments are pieces of code that are not evaluated by the interpreter but can be read by programmers to obtain information about a program.

- Variables are names that refer to values. The value of a variable is initialized and can be reset by an assignment statement. In Python a variable names a value, and there are no restrictions on which variables can name which values.

- The `int` data type represents integers. The `float` data type represents floating-point numbers. The magnitude of an integer or a floating-point number is limited by the memory of the computer, as is the number's precision in the case of floating-point numbers.

- Arithmetic operators are used to form arithmetic expressions. Operands can be numeric literals, variables, function calls, or other expressions.

- The operators are ranked in precedence. In descending order, they are exponentiation, negation, multiplication (`*`, `/`, and `%` are the same), addition (`+` and `–` are the same), and assignment. Operators with a higher precedence are evaluated before those with a lower precedence. Normal precedence can be overridden by parentheses.

- Mixed-mode operations involve operands of different numeric data types. They result in a value of the more inclusive data type.

- The type conversion functions can be used to convert a value of one type to a value of another type after input.

- A function call consists of a function's name and its arguments or parameters. When it is called, the function's arguments are evaluated, and these values are passed to the function's code for processing. When the function completes its work, it may return a result value to the caller.

- Python is a strongly typed language. The interpreter checks the types of all operands within expressions and halts execution with an error if they are not as expected for the given operators.

- A module is a set of resources, such as function definitions. Programmers access these resources by importing them from their modules.

- A semantic error occurs when the computer cannot perform the requested operation, such as an attempt to divide by 0. Python programs with semantic errors halt with an error message.

- A logic error occurs when a program runs to a normal termination but produces incorrect results.

Key Terms

abstraction	floating-point	program comments
analysis	function	prototype
arguments	implementation	pseudocode
arithmetic expression	incremental	required arguments
ASCII set	infinite precision	returning a value
assignment statement	initializing	scientific notation
character sets	integers	semantic error
correct program	integration	semantics
customer request	iterative	software development
data type	literal	software development life cycle
decimal notation	logic error	strongly typed programming
default behavior	maintenance	language
defining	main module	symbolic constants
design	mixed-mode arithmetic	test suite
design error	modules	type conversion function
docstring	newline character	Unicode set
empty string	numeric data types	variable
end-of-line comments	optional arguments	variable references
escape sequence	parameters	waterfall model
expressions	precedence rules	

Review Questions

1. What does a programmer do during the analysis phase of software development?

   a. Codes the program in a particular programming language
   b. Writes the algorithms for solving a problem
   c. Decides what the program will do and determines its user interface
   d. Tests the program to verify its correctness

2. What must a programmer use to test a program?

   a. All possible sets of legitimate inputs
   b. All possible sets of inputs
   c. A single set of legitimate inputs
   d. A reasonable set of legitimate inputs

3. What must you use to create a multiline string?

   a. A single pair of double quotation marks
   b. A single pair of single quotation marks
   c. A single pair of three consecutive double quotation marks
   d. Embedded newline characters

4. What is used to begin an end-of-line comment?

   a. / symbol
   b. # symbol
   c. % symbol
   d. * symbol

5. Which of the following lists of operators is ordered by decreasing precedence?

   a. +, *, **

   b. *, /, %

   c. **, *, +

   d. +, -

6. The expression 2 ** 3 ** 2 evaluates to which of the following values?

   a. 64

   b. 512

   c. 8

   d. 12

7. The expression round(23.67) evaluates to which of the following values?

   a. 23

   b. 23.7

   c. 24.0

   d. 24

8. Assume that the variable name has the value 33. What is the value of name after the assignment name = name * 2 executes?

   a. 35

   b. 33

   c. 66

   d. 1089

9. Write an import statement that imports just the functions sqrt and log from the math module.

10. What are the purposes of the dir function and the help function?

Programming Exercises

In each of the exercises that follow, you should write a program that contains an introductory docstring. This documentation should describe what the program will do (analysis) and how it will do it (design the program in the form of a pseudocode algorithm). Include suitable prompts for all inputs, and label all outputs appropriately. After you have coded a program, be sure to test it with a reasonable set of legitimate inputs.

1. The tax calculator program of the case study outputs a floating-point number that might show more than two digits of precision. Use the **round** function to modify the program in the file **taxform.py** to display at most two digits of precision in the output number. (LO: 2.4)

2. You can calculate the surface area of a cube if you know the length of an edge. Write a program in the file **cube.py** that takes the length of an edge (an integer) as input and prints the cube's surface area as output. (LO: 2.4)

3. Five Star Retro Video rents DVDs to the same connoisseurs who like to buy vinyl records. The store rents new videos for $3.00 a night, and oldies for $2.00 a night. Write a program in the file **fivestar.py** that the clerks at Five Star Retro Video can use to calculate the total charge for a customer's video rentals. The program should prompt the user for the number of each type of video and output the total cost. (LO: 2.3, 2.4)

4. Write a program in the file **sphere.py** that takes the radius of a sphere (a floating-point number) as input and then outputs the sphere's diameter, circumference, surface area, and volume. (LO: 2.3, 2.4, 2.5)

5. An object's momentum is its mass multiplied by its velocity. Write a program in the file **momentum.py** that accepts an object's mass (in kilograms) and velocity (in meters per second) as inputs and then outputs its momentum. (LO: 2.3, 2.4)

6. The kinetic energy of a moving object is given by the formula $KE = (1/2) \, mv^2$, where m is the object's mass and v is its velocity. Modify the program you created in Programming Exercise 5 so that it prints the object's kinetic energy as well as its momentum. (LO: 2.3, 2.4)

7. Write a program in the file **minutes.py** that takes as input a number of years and calculates and prints the number of minutes in that period of time. (LO: 2.4)

8. Light travels at 3 * 10⁸ meters per second. A light-year is the distance a light beam travels in one year. Write a program in the file **lightyear.py** that expects a number of years as input and calculates and displays the value of the distance traveled in meters. (LO: 2.4)

9. Write a program in the file **klickstonauts.py** that takes as input a number of kilometers and prints the corresponding number of nautical miles. Use the following approximations:

   - A kilometer represents 1/10,000 of the distance between the North Pole and the equator.

   - There are 90 degrees, containing 60 minutes of arc each, between the North Pole and the equator.

   - A nautical mile is 1 minute of an arc. (LO: 2.4)

10. An employee's total weekly pay equals the hourly wage multiplied by the total number of regular hours plus any overtime pay. Overtime pay equals the total overtime hours multiplied by 1.5 times the hourly wage. Write a program in the file **employeepay.py** that takes as inputs the hourly wage, total regular hours, and total overtime hours and displays an employee's total weekly pay. (LO: 2.3, 2.4)

Debugging Exercise

Jill has written a program that computes the sales tax on the purchase of an item, given the price of the item (a floating-point number) and the percent tax rate (an integer). The output of the program is the purchase price, the tax, and the total amount to be paid. Here is her code:

```
purchasePrice = float(input("Enter the purchase price as $: "))
taxRate = int(input("Enter the tax rate as %: "))
tax = purchasePrice * taxRate
totalOwed = purchasePrice + tax
print("Purchase price: ", purchasePrice)
print("Tax:            ", tax)
print("Total owed:     ", totalOwed)
```

When she tested his program with a purchase price of $5.50 and a sales tax of 5%, Jill observed the following unexpected output:

```
Enter the purchase price as $: 5.50
Enter the tax rate as %: 5
Purchase price:  5.5
Tax:             27.5
Total owed:      33.0
```

Describe the error, explain why it happened, and suggest a correction.

2

Initial Robot Pseudocode

Prompt

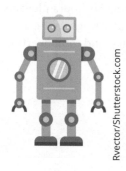

Rvector/Shutterstock.com

Ira Yapanda/Shutterstock.com

tele52/Shutterstock.com

Now that you have set up your environment, you are going to begin to spec out the various parameters for our robot's software. Remember, this robot is going to be working in a warehouse type environment, fulfilling various procedures such as filling boxes, creating pallets, and other tasks of getting our products sorted and ready to ship to the organization's various customers.

We are building toward making functions and methods. Functions are exactly what they sound like: they are things that you can do. We will cover them in more depth in Chapter 6, but for now, consider one of the most common functions, print(). If you want to print a string, you can enter print("Hello World!") into your IDLE. There are 71 built-in functions built into Python 3.11, with thousands, across the various libraries. You can even build your own!

When you create a function, you need to consider the things you need. For example, you may create a function to divide two numbers, so it would take a variable "dividend" and a variable "divisor" so it would look like "divide(dividend, divisor)". Keep this in mind when writing out your pseudocode.

With that in mind, you will be creating some pseudocode for a product picking operation and for a palletizing operation which will help guide the robot as it performs these operations. Consider the following examples:

Examples:

1. *If the box is greater than or equal to 60*
      Print "Filled"
   else
      Print "Continue adding items"
2. *Set total to zero*
   Set number of products to one

> *While number of products is less than or equal to ten*
> > *Input the next product*
> > *Add the product into the total*
> > *Set the weight to the total multiplied by ten*
> > *Print the total weight.*

Your pseudocode will include methods which are called fillBox and createPallet. Those two methods will contain your pseudocode for performing the actions. Remember formatting considerations like indenting and spacing.

Part 2:

Now that you have created your pseudocode, you will begin to translate that into a script. For this portion of the script, you are going to declare some variables and to get started, print them out. Using the above scenario, you are going to declare several variables and types:

1. A robot name stored in a string variable
2. The robot's battery charge is stored as a whole number

Print out those variable types in a sentence that looks like:
Herby the robot's current charge is 89%

Hints

Pseudocode is a high-level programming language that cannot be used as actual source code and compilation/execution but can be used to create the flow and direction that could eventually be translated into usable source code that can be turned into an application.

Pseudocode is a type of writing which is close to code but more human language-based: something a person could read and understand. Consider the following:

This program will allow the user to check if a number entered is even or odd.

if number/2 produces no remainder
> *print output*
> > *"This number is even"*

if number/2 produces a remainder
> *print output*
> > *"This number is odd"*

Answer

Pseudocode does not have an official syntax, can vary from programmer to programmer, and can sometimes take on more of the syntax of the future program if the language being used is known.

After Discussion

In this assignment, learners are now being asked to develop an application which will start to perform various activities, of which new activities will be added to the application each week. In this initial stage of the project, learners will be writing pseudocode to start to create the general flow and direction for how the application will be developed.

In addition, users will be creating a general Python project pseudocode which will include a couple of methods for eventual activities that the robot will engage in while working in the warehouse. Learners will write the pseudocode to allow for various methods to be called to fulfill certain activities, like filling a box or creating a pallet in this week's script.

Referring to the example above, this pseudocode will be written to determine the robot's charge and output for the user to review and keep track of. This shows users what the activity is and that those activities can then be translated into actual Python code.

## Chapter 3

Loops and Selection Statements

Learning Objectives

When you complete this chapter, you will be able to:

3.1 Write a loop to repeat a sequence of actions a fixed number of times

3.2 Format text for output

3.3 Use selection statements with Boolean expressions to make choices in a program

3.4 Write loops that continue when a Boolean expression is true and halt when it becomes false

All the programs you have studied so far in this book have consisted of short sequences of instructions that are executed one after the other. Even if we allowed the sequence of instructions to be quite long, this type of program would not be very useful. Like people, computers must be able to repeat a set of actions. They also must be able to select an action to perform in a particular situation. This chapter focuses on **control statements**—statements that allow the computer to select or repeat an action.

3.1 Definite Iteration: The `for` Loop

We begin our study of control statements with repetition statements, also known as **loops**, which repeat an action. Each repetition of the action is known as a **pass** or an **iteration**. There are two types of loops—those that repeat an action a predefined number of times (**definite iteration**) and those that perform the action until the program determines that it needs to stop (**indefinite iteration**). In this section, we examine Python's `for` loop, the control statement that most easily supports definite iteration.

Executing a Statement a Given Number of Times

As related in Mary Shelley's nineteenth-century novel, *Frankenstein; or, The Modern Prometheus*, when Dr. Frankenstein's monster came to life, the doctor exclaimed, "It's alive! It's alive!" If Dr. Frankenstein were trying to print those exclamations with a computer, he would be able to do so easily. A computer can print exclamations like these not just twice, but a dozen or a hundred times, and you do not have to write two, a dozen, or one hundred output statements to accomplish this. Here is a **for** loop that runs the same output statement four times:

```
>>> for eachPass in range(4):
        print("It's alive!", end = " ")
It's alive! It's alive! It's alive! It's alive!
```

This loop repeatedly calls one function—the **print** function. The constant 4 on the first line tells the loop how many times to call this function. If we want to print 10 or 100 exclamations, we just change the 4 to 10 or to 100. The form of this type of **for** loop is

```
for <variable> in range(<an integer expression>):
    <statement-1>
    .
    .
    <statement-n>
```

The first line of code in a loop is sometimes called the **loop header**. For now, the only relevant information in the header is the integer expression, which denotes the number of iterations that the loop performs. The colon (:) ends the loop header. The **loop body** comprises the statements in the remaining lines of code, below the header. These statements are executed in sequence on each pass through the loop. Note that the statements in the loop body *must be indented and aligned in the same column*. The IDLE shell or script window will automatically indent lines under a loop header, but you may see syntax errors if this indentation is off by even one space. It is best to indent four spaces if the indentation does not automatically occur when you move to the next line of code.

Now let's explore how Python's exponentiation operator might be implemented in a loop. Recall that this operator raises a number to a given power. For instance, the expression **2 ** 3** computes the value of 2^3, or **2 * 2 * 2**. The following session uses a loop to compute an exponentiation for a nonnegative exponent. We use three variables to designate the number, the exponent, and the product. The product is initially 1. On each pass through the loop, the product is multiplied by the number and reset to the result. To allow us to trace this process, the value of the product is also printed on each pass.

```
>>> number = 2
>>> exponent = 3
>>> product = 1
>>> for eachPass in range(exponent):
        product = product * number
        print(product, end = " ")
2 4 8
>>> product
8
```

As you can see, if the exponent were 0, the loop body would not execute, and the value of **product** would remain as 1, which is the value of any number raised to the zero power.

The use of variables in the preceding example demonstrates that our exponentiation loop is an algorithm that solves a *general class* of problems. The user of this particular loop not only can raise two to the third power but also can raise any number to any nonnegative power, just by substituting different values for the variables **number** and **exponent**.

Count-Controlled Loops

When Python executes the type of **for** loop just discussed, it counts from 0 to the value of the header's integer expression minus 1. On each pass through the loop, the header's variable is bound to the current value of this count. The next code segment demonstrates this fact:

```
>>> for count in range(4):
        print(count, end = " ")

0 1 2 3
```

Loops that count through a range of numbers are also called **count-controlled loops**. The value of the count on each pass is often used in computations. For example, consider the factorial of 4, which is 1 * 2 * 3 * 4 = 24. A code segment to compute this value starts with a product of 1 and resets this variable to the result of multiplying it and the loop's count plus 1 on each pass, as follows:

```
>>> product = 1
>>> for count in range(4):
        product = product * (count + 1)

>>> product
24
```

Note that the value of **count + 1** is used on each pass to ensure that the numbers used are 1 through 4 rather than 0 through 3.

To count from an explicit lower bound, the programmer can supply a second integer expression in the loop header. When two arguments are supplied to **range**, the count ranges from the first argument to the second argument minus 1. The next code segment uses this variation to simplify the code in the loop body:

```
>>> product = 1
>>> for count in range(1, 5):
        product = product * count

>>> product
24
```

The only thing in this version to be careful about is the second argument of **range**, which should specify an integer greater by 1 than the desired upper bound of the count. Here is the form of this version of the **for** loop:

```
for <variable> in range(<lower bound>, <upper bound + 1>):   <loop body>
```

Accumulating a single result value from a series of values is a common operation in computing. Here is an example of a **summation**, which accumulates the sum of a sequence of numbers from a lower bound through an upper bound:

```
>>> lower = int(input("Enter the lower bound: "))
Enter the lower bound: 1
>>> upper = int(input("Enter the upper bound: "))
Enter the upper bound: 10
>>> theSum = 0
```

```
>>> for number in range(lower, upper + 1):
        theSum = theSum + number
>>> theSum
55
```

Note that we use the variable **theSum** rather than **sum** to accumulate the sum of the numbers in this code. This is because **sum** is the name of a built-in Python function, and it's a good idea to avoid using such names for other purposes in our code.

Augmented Assignment

Expressions such as $x = x + 1$ or $x = x - 2$ occur so frequently in loops that Python includes abbreviated forms for them. The assignment symbol can be combined with the arithmetic and concatenation operators to provide **augmented assignment operations**. Following are several examples:

```
a = 17
s = "hi"
a += 3                  # Equivalent to a = a + 3
a -= 3                  # Equivalent to a = a - 3
a *= 3                  # Equivalent to a = a * 3
a /= 3                  # Equivalent to a = a / 3
a %= 3                  # Equivalent to a = a % 3
s += " there"           # Equivalent to s = s + " there"
```

All these examples have the format

```
<variable> <operator>= <expression>
```

which is equivalent to

```
<variable> = <variable> <operator> <expression>
```

Note that there is no space between **<operator>** and **=**. The augmented assignment operations and the standard assignment operations have the same precedence.

Loop Errors: Off-by-One Error

The **for** loop is not only easy to write but also fairly easy to write correctly. Once we get the syntax correct, we need to be concerned about only one other possible error: the loop fails to perform the expected number of iterations. Because this number is typically off by one, the error is called an **off-by-one error**. For the most part, off-by-one errors result when the programmer incorrectly specifies the upper bound of the loop. The programmer might intend the following loop to count from 1 through 4, but it counts from 1 through 3:

```
# Count from 1 through 4, we think
>>> for count in range(1,4):
        print(count)

1
2
3
```

Note that this is not a syntax error, but rather a logic error. Unlike syntax errors, logic errors are not detected by the Python interpreter, but only by the eyes of a programmer who carefully inspects a program's output.

Traversing the Contents of a Data Sequence

Although we have been using the **for** loop as a simple count-controlled loop, the loop itself visits each number in a sequence of numbers generated by the **range** function. The next code segment shows what these sequences look like:

```
>>> list(range(4))
[0, 1, 2, 3]
>>> list(range(1, 5))
[1, 2, 3, 4]
```

In this example, the sequence of numbers generated by the function **range** is fed to Python's **list** function, which returns a special type of sequence called a list. Strings are also sequences of characters. The values contained in any sequence can be visited by running a **for** loop, as follows:

```
for <variable> in <sequence>:
    <do something with variable>
```

On each pass through the loop, the variable is bound to or assigned the next value in the sequence, starting with the first one and ending with the last one. The following code segment traverses or visits all the elements in two sequences and prints the values contained in them, separated by spaces:

```
>>> for number in [6, 4, 8]:
        print(number, end = " ")
6 4 8
>>> for character in "Hi there!":
        print(character, end = " ")
H i   t h e r e !
```

Specifying the Steps in the Range

The count-controlled loops we have seen thus far count through consecutive numbers in a series. However, in some programs we might want a loop to skip some numbers, perhaps visiting every other one or every third one. A variant of Python's **range** function expects a third argument that allows you to nicely skip some numbers. The third argument specifies a **step value**, or the interval between the numbers used in the range, as shown in the examples that follow:

```
>>> list(range(1, 6, 1))      # Same as using two arguments
[1, 2, 3, 4, 5]
>>> list(range(1, 6, 2))      # Use every other number
[1, 3, 5]
>>> list(range(1, 6, 3))      # Use every third number
[1, 4]
```

Now, suppose you had to compute the sum of the even numbers between 1 and 10. Here is the code that solves this problem:

```
>>> theSum = 0
>>> for count in range(2, 11, 2):
        theSum += count
>>> theSum
```

Loops That Count Down

All of our loops until now have counted up from a lower bound to an upper bound. Once in a while, a problem calls for counting in the opposite direction, from the upper bound down to the lower bound. For example, when the top-10 singles tunes are released, they might be presented in order from lowest (10th) to highest (1st) rank. In the next session, a loop displays the count from 10 down to 1 to show how this would be done:

```
>>> for count in range(10, 0, -1):
        print(count, end = " ")
10 9 8 7 6 5 4 3 2 1
>>> list(range(10, 0, -1))
[10, 9, 8, 7, 6, 5, 4, 3, 2, 1]
```

When the step argument is a negative number, the **range** function generates a sequence of numbers from the first argument down to the second argument plus 1. Thus, in this case, the first argument should express the upper bound, and the second argument should express the lower bound minus 1.

Exercise 3-1

1. Write the outputs of the following loops:

   a. ```
   for count in range(5):
       print(count + 1, end = " ")
   ```

   b. ```
   for count in range(1, 4):
       print(count, end = " ")
   ```

   c. ```
   for count in range(1, 6, 2):
       print(count, end = " ")
   ```

   d. ```
   for count in range(6, 1, -1):
       print(count, end = " ")
   ```

2. Write a loop that prints your name 100 times. Each output should begin on a new line.

3. Explain the role of the variable in the header of a **for** loop.

4. Write a loop that prints the first 128 ASCII values followed by the corresponding characters (see the section on characters in Chapter 2). Be aware that most of the ASCII values in the range "0…31" belong to special control characters with no standard print representation, so you might see strange symbols in the output for these values.

5. Assume that the variable **testString** refers to a string. Write a loop that prints each character in this string, followed by its ASCII value.

3.2 Formatting Text for Output

Before turning to our next case study, we need to examine more closely the format of text for output. Many data-processing applications require output that has a **tabular format**, like in spreadsheets or tables of numeric data. In this format, numbers and other information are aligned in columns that can be either left-justified or right-justified.

A column of data is left-justified if its values are vertically aligned beginning with their leftmost characters. A column of data is right-justified if its values are vertically aligned beginning with their rightmost characters. To maintain the margins between columns of data, left-justification requires the addition of spaces to the right of the datum, whereas right-justification requires adding spaces to the left of the datum. A column of data is centered if there are an equal number of spaces on either side of the data within that column.

The total number of data characters and additional spaces for a given datum in a formatted string is called its **field width**.

The **print** function automatically begins printing an output datum in the first available column. The next example, which displays the exponents 7 through 10 and the values of 10^7 through 10^{10}, shows the format of two columns produced by the **print** function:

```
>>> for exponent in range(7, 11):
        print(exponent, 10 ** exponent)
7 10000000
8 100000000
9 1000000000
10 10000000000
```

Note that when the exponent reaches 10, the output of the second column shifts over by a space and looks messy. The output would look neater if the left column were left-justified and the right column were right-justified. When we format floating-point numbers for output, we often would like to specify the number of digits of precision to be displayed as well as the field width. This is especially important when displaying financial data in which exactly two digits of precision are required.

Python includes a general formatting mechanism that allows the programmer to specify field widths for different types of data. The next session shows how to right-justify and left-justify the string **"four"** within a field width of 6:

```
>>> "%6s" % "four"    # Right justify in 6 columns
'  four'
>>> "%-6s" % "four"   # Left justify in 6 columns
'four  '
```

The first line of code right-justifies the string by padding it with two spaces to its left. The next line of code left-justifies by placing two spaces to the string's right.

The simplest form of this operation is the following:

<format string> **%** *<datum>*

This version contains a **format string**, the **format operator %**, and a single data value to be formatted. The format string can contain string data and other information about the format of the datum. To format the string data value in our example, we used the notation **%<*field width*>s** in the format string. When the field width is positive, the datum is right-justified; when the field width is negative, the datum is left-justified. If the field width is less than or equal to the datum's print length in characters, no justification is added. The **%** operator works with this information to build and return a formatted string.

To format integers, you use the letter **d** instead of **s**. To format a sequence of data values, you construct a format string that includes a format code for each datum and place the data values in a tuple following the **%** operator. The form of the second version of this operation follows:

<format string> **%** **(***<datum-1>***, …,** *<datum-n>***)**

Armed with the format operation, our powers of 10 loop can now display the numbers in nicely aligned columns. The first column is left-justified in a field width of 3, and the second column is right-justified in a field width of 12.

```
>>> for exponent in range(7, 11):
        print("%-3d%12d" % (exponent, 10 ** exponent))
7        10000000
8       100000000
9      1000000000
10    10000000000
```

The format information for a data value of type `float` has the form

`%<field width>.<precision>f`

where `.<precision>` is optional. The next session shows the output of a floating-point number without, and then with, a format string:

```
>>> salary = 100.00
>>> print("Your salary is $" + str(salary))
Your salary is $100.0
>>> print("Your salary is $%0.2f" % salary)
Your salary is $100.00
```

Here is another, minimal, example of the use of a format string, which says to use a field width of 6 and a precision of 3 to format the `float` value 3.14:

```
>>> "%6.3f" % 3.14
' 3.140'
```

Note that Python adds a digit of precision to the string and pads it with a space to the left to achieve the field width of 6. This width includes the place occupied by the decimal point.

Exercise 3-2

1. Assume that the variable **amount** refers to 24.325. Write the outputs of the following statements:

   a. `print ("Your salary is $%0.2f" % amount)`

   b. `print ("The area is %0.1f" % amount)`

   c. `print ("%7f" % amount)`

2. Write a code segment that displays the values of the integers **x**, **y**, and **z** on a single line, such that each value is right-justified with a field width of 6.

3. Write a format operation that builds a string for the **float** variable **amount** that has exactly two digits of precision and a field width of zero.

4. Write a loop that outputs the numbers in a list named **salaries**. The outputs should be formatted in a column that is right-justified, with a field width of 12 and a precision of 2.

Case Study 3-1 | An Investment Report

Albert Einstein once said that "Compound interest is the eighth wonder of the world. He who understands it, earns it; he who doesn't, pays it." Our next case study, which computes an investment report, shows why.

Request

Write a program that computes an investment report.

Analysis

The inputs to this program are the following:

- An initial amount to be invested (a floating-point number)

- A period of years (an integer)

- An interest rate (a percentage expressed as an integer)

The program uses a simplified form of compound interest, in which the interest is computed once each year and added to the total amount invested. The output of the program is a report in tabular form that shows, for each year in the term of the investment, the year number, the initial balance in the account, the interest earned, and the ending balance, all for that year. The columns of the table are suitably labeled with a header in the first row. Following the output of the table, the program prints the total amount of the investment balance and the total amount of interest earned for the period. The proposed user interface is shown in Figure 3-1.

Figure 3-1   **The user interface for the investment report program**

```
Enter the investment amount: 10000.00
Enter the number of years: 5
Enter the rate as a %: 5
Year   Starting balance   Interest   Ending balance
  1            10000.00    500.00          10500.00
  2            10500.00    525.00          11025.00
  3            11025.00    551.25          11576.25
  4            11576.25    578.81          12155.06
  5            12155.06    607.75          12762.82
Ending balance: $12762.82
Total interest earned: $2762.82
```

Design

The four principal parts of the program perform the following tasks:

1. Receive the user's inputs and initialize data.

2. Display the table's header.

3. Compute the results for each year and display them as a row in the table.

4. Display the totals.

(continues)

The third part of the program, which computes and displays the results, is a loop. The following is a slightly simplified version of the pseudocode for the program, without the details related to formatting the outputs:

```
Input the starting balance, number of years, and interest rate
Set the total interest to 0.0
Print the table's heading
For each year
    compute the interest
    compute the ending balance
    print the year, starting balance, interest, and ending balance
    update the starting balance
    update the total interest
print the ending balance and the total interest
```

Note that **starting balance** refers to the original input balance and also to the balance that begins each year of the term. Ignoring the details of the output at this point allows us to focus on getting the computations correct. We can translate this pseudocode to a Python program to check our computations. A rough draft of a program is called a **prototype**. Once we are confident that the prototype is producing the correct numbers, we can return to the design and work out the details of formatting the outputs.

The format of the outputs is guided by the requirement that they be aligned nicely in columns. We use a format string to right-justify all of the numbers on each row of output. We also use a format string for the string labels in the table's header. After some trial and error, we come up with field widths of 4, 18, 10, and 16 for the year, starting balance, interest, and ending balance, respectively. We can also use these widths in the format string for the header.

Implementation (Coding)

The code for this program shows each of the major parts described in the design, set off by end-of-line comments. Note the use of the many variables to track the various amounts of money used by the program. Wisely, we have chosen names for these variables that clearly describe their purpose. The format strings in the **print** statements are rather complex, but we have made an effort to format them so the information they contain is still fairly readable.

```
"""
Program: investment.py
Author: Ken
Compute an investment report.
1. The inputs are
        starting investment amount
        number of years
        interest rate (an integer percent)
2. The report is displayed in tabular form with a header.
3. Computations and outputs:
        for each year
            compute the interest and add it to the investment
            print a formatted row of results for that year
4. The ending investment and interest earned are also displayed.
"""

# Accept the inputs
startBalance = float(input("Enter the investment amount: "))
```

```
years = int(input("Enter the number of years: "))
rate = int(input("Enter the rate as a %: "))
# Convert the rate to a decimal number
rate = rate / 100
# Initialize the accumulator for the interest
totalInterest = 0.0
# Display the header for the table
print("%4s%18s%10s%16s" % \
        ("Year", "Starting balance",
         "Interest", "Ending balance"))
# Compute and display the results for each year
for year in range(1, years + 1):
    interest = startBalance * rate
    endBalance = startBalance + interest
    print("%4d%18.2f%10.2f%16.2f" % \
            (year, startBalance, interest, endBalance))
    startBalance = endBalance
    totalInterest += interest
# Display the totals for the period
print("Ending balance: $%0.2f" % endBalance)
print("Total interest earned: $%0.2f" % totalInterest)
```

Testing

When testing a program that contains a loop, we should focus first on the input that determines the number of iterations. In our program, this value is the number of years. We enter a value that yields the smallest possible number of iterations, then increase this number by 1, then use a slightly larger number, such as 5, and finally we use a number close to the maximum expected, such as 50 (in our problem domain, probably the largest realistic period of an investment). The values of the other inputs, such as the investment amount and the rate in our program, should be reasonably small and stay fixed for this phase of the testing. If the program produces correct outputs for all of these inputs, we can be confident that the loop is working correctly.

In the next phase of testing, we examine the effects of the other inputs on the results, including their format. We know that the other two inputs to our programs, the investment and the rate, already produce correct results for small values. A reasonable strategy might be to test a large investment amount with the smallest and largest number of years and a small rate, and then with the largest number of years and the largest reasonable rate. Table 3-1 organizes these sets of test data for the program.

Table 3-1   The data sets for testing the investment program

Investment	Years	Rate
100.00	1	5
100.00	2	5
100.00	5	5
100.00	50	5
10000.00	1	5
10000.00	50	5
10000.00	50	20

3.3 Selection: `if` and `if-else` Statements

We have seen that computers can plow through long sequences of instructions, once or repeatedly. However, not all problems can be solved in this manner. In some cases, instead of moving straight ahead to execute the next instruction, the computer might be faced with two alternative courses of action. The computer must pause to examine or test a **condition**, which expresses a hypothesis about the state of its world at that point in time. If the condition is true, the computer executes the first alternative action and skips the second alternative. If the condition is false, the computer skips the first alternative action and executes the second alternative.

In other words, instead of moving blindly ahead, the computer exercises some intelligence by responding to conditions in its environment. In this section, we explore several types of **selection statements**, or control statements, that allow a computer to make choices. But first, we need to examine how a computer can test conditions.

The Boolean Type, Comparisons, and Boolean Expressions

Before you can test conditions in a Python program, you need to understand the **Boolean data type**, which is named for the nineteenth-century British mathematician George Boole. The Boolean data type consists of only two data values—true and false. In Python, the two Boolean literals are written as **True** and **False**.

Simple Boolean expressions consist of the Boolean values **True** or **False**, variables bound to those values, function calls that return Boolean values, or comparisons. The condition in a selection statement often takes the form of a comparison. For example, you might compare value A to value B to see which one is greater. The result of the comparison is a Boolean value. It is either true or false that value A is greater than value B. To write expressions that make comparisons, you have to be familiar with Python's comparison operators, which are listed in **Table 3-2**.

Table 3-2   The comparison operators

Comparison Operator	Meaning
==	Equals
!=	Not equals
<	Less than
>	Greater than
<=	Less than or equal
>=	Greater than or equal

The following session shows some example comparisons and their values:

```
>>> 4 == 4
True
>>> 4 != 4
False
>>> 4 < 5
True
>>> 4 >= 3
True
>>> 'A' < 'B'
True
```

Note that `==` means equals, whereas `=` means assignment. As you learned in Chapter 2, when evaluating expressions in Python, you need to be aware of precedence—that is, the order in which operators are applied in complex expressions. The comparison operators are applied after addition but before assignment.

`if-else` Statements

The `if-else` **statement** is the most common type of selection statement. It is also called a **two-way selection statement**, because it directs the computer to make a choice between two alternative courses of action.

The `if-else` statement is often used to check inputs for errors and to respond with error messages if necessary. The alternative is to go ahead and perform the computation if the inputs are valid.

For example, suppose a program inputs the area of a circle and computes and outputs its radius. Legitimate inputs for this program would be positive numbers. But, by mistake, the user could still enter a zero or a negative number. Because the program has no choice but to use this value to compute the radius, it might crash (stop running) or produce a meaningless output. The next code segment shows how to use an `if-else` statement to locate (trap) this error and respond to it:

```python
import math
area = float(input("Enter the area: "))
if area > 0:
    radius = math.sqrt(area / math.pi)
    print("The radius is", radius)
else:
    print("Error: the area must be a positive number")
```

Here is the Python syntax for the `if-else` statement:

```python
if <condition>:
    <sequence of statements-1>
else:
    <sequence of statements-2>
```

The condition in the `if-else` statement must be a **Boolean expression**—that is, an expression that evaluates to either true or false. The two possible actions each consist of a sequence of statements. Note that each sequence *must be indented at least one space* beyond the symbols `if` and `else`. Finally, note the use of the colon (`:`) following the condition and the word `else`. **Figure 3-2** shows a flow diagram of the semantics of the `if-else` statement. In that diagram, the diamond containing the question mark indicates the condition.

Figure 3-2 The semantics of the `if-else` statement

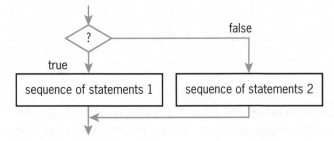

Our next example prints the maximum and minimum of two input numbers.

```python
first = int(input("Enter the first number: "))
second = int(input("Enter the second number: "))
if first > second:
    maximum = first
    minimum = second
else:
    maximum = second
    minimum = first
print("Maximum:", maximum)
print("Minimum:", minimum)
```

Python includes two functions, **max** and **min**, that make the **if-else** statement in this example unnecessary. In the following example, the function **max** returns the largest of its arguments, whereas **min** returns the smallest of its arguments:

```python
first = int(input("Enter the first number: "))
second = int(input("Enter the second number: "))
print("Maximum:", max(first, second))
print("Minimum:", min(first, second))
```

One-Way Selection Statements

The simplest form of selection is the **if** statement. This type of control statement is also called a **one-way selection statement** because it consists of a condition and just a single sequence of statements. If the condition is **True**, the sequence of statements is run. Otherwise, control proceeds to the next statement following the entire selection statement. Here is the syntax for the **if** statement:

```
if <condition>:
    <sequence of statements>
```

Figure 3-3 shows a flow diagram of the semantics of the **if** statement.

Figure 3-3 The semantics of the **if** statement

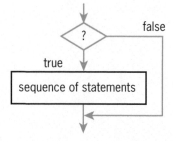

Simple **if** statements are often used to prevent an action from being performed if a condition is not right. For example, the absolute value of a negative number is the arithmetic negation of that number; otherwise it is just that number. The next session uses a simple **if** statement to reset the value of a variable to its absolute value:

```python
>>> if x < 0:
        x = -x
```

Multiway `if` Statements

Occasionally, a program is faced with testing several conditions that include more than two alternative courses of action. For example, consider the problem of converting numeric grades to letter grades. **Table 3-3** shows a simple grading scheme that is based on three assumptions: that numeric grades can range from 0 to 100, that they are integers, and that the letter grades are A, B, C, and F.

Table 3-3   A simple grading scheme

Letter Grade	Range of Numeric Grades
A	All grades above 89
B	All grades above 79 and below 90
C	All grades above 69 and below 80
F	All grades below 70

Expressed in English, an algorithm that uses this scheme would state that if the numeric grade is greater than 89, then the letter grade is A, else if the numeric grade is greater than 79, then the letter grade is B, ..., else (as a default case) the letter grade is F.

The process of testing several conditions and responding accordingly can be described in code by a **multiway selection statement**. Here is a short Python script that uses such a statement to determine and print the letter grade corresponding to an input numeric grade:

```python
number = int(input("Enter the numeric grade: "))
if number > 89:
    letter = 'A'
elif number > 79:
    letter = 'B'
elif number > 69:
    letter = 'C'
else:
    letter = 'F'
print("The letter grade is", letter)
```

Note that `elif` is short for `else if`, since `else if` is not legal Python syntax. The multiway `if` statement considers each condition until one evaluates to `True` or they all evaluate to `False`. When a condition evaluates to `True`, the corresponding action is performed and control skips to the end of the entire selection statement. If no condition evaluates to `True`, then the action after the trailing `else` is performed.

The syntax of the multiway `if` statement is the following:

```python
if <condition-1>:
    <sequence of statements-1>
elif <condition-n>:
    <sequence of statements-n>
else:
    <default sequence of statements>
```

Once again, indentation helps the human reader and the Python interpreter to see the logical structure of this control statement. **Figure 3-4** shows a flow diagram of the semantics of a multiway `if` statement with two conditions and a trailing `else` clause.

Figure 3-4   The semantics of the multiway `if` statement

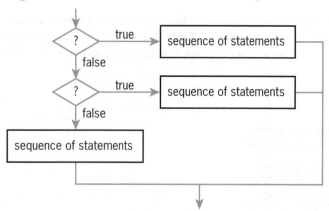

Logical Operators and Compound Boolean Expressions

Often a course of action must be taken if either of two conditions is true. For example, valid inputs to a program often lie within a given range of values. Any input above this range should be rejected with an error message, and any input below this range should be dealt with in a similar fashion. The next code segment accepts only valid inputs for our grade conversion script and displays an error message otherwise:

```
number = int(input("Enter the numeric grade: "))
if number > 100:
    print("Error: grade must be between 100 and 0")
elif number < 0:
    print("Error: grade must be between 100 and 0")
else:
    # The code to compute and print the result goes here
```

Note that the first two conditions are associated with identical actions. If either the first condition is true or the second condition is true, the program outputs the same error message. The two conditions can be combined in a Boolean expression that uses the **logical operator or**. The resulting **compound Boolean expression** simplifies the code somewhat, as follows:

```
number = int(input("Enter the numeric grade: "))
if number > 100 or number < 0:
    print("Error: grade must be between 100 and 0")
else:
    # The code to compute and print the result goes here
```

Yet another way to describe this situation is to say that if the number is greater than or equal to 0 and less than or equal to 100, then we want the program to perform the computations and output the result; otherwise, it should output an error message. The logical operator **and** can be used to construct a different compound Boolean expression to express this logic:

```
number = int(input("Enter the numeric grade: "))
if number >= 0 and number <= 100:
    # The code to compute and print the result goes here
else:
    print("Error: grade must be between 100 and 0")
```

Python includes all three Boolean or logical operators, **and**, **or**, and **not**. Both the **and** operator and the **or** operator expect two operands. The **and** operator returns **True** if and only if both of its operands are true, and returns **False** otherwise. The **or** operator returns **False** if and only if both of its operands are false, and returns **True** otherwise. The **not** operator expects a single operand and returns its logical negation, **True** if it's false, and **False** if it's true.

The behavior of each operator can be completely specified in a truth table for that operator. Each row below the first one in a truth table contains one possible combination of values for the operands and the value resulting from applying the operator to them. The first row contains labels for the operands and the expression being computed. **Figure 3-5** shows the truth tables for **and**, **or**, and **not**.

Figure 3-5   The truth tables for `and`, `or`, and `not`

A	B	A and B
True	True	True
True	False	False
False	True	False
False	False	False

A	B	A or B
True	True	True
True	False	True
False	True	True
False	False	False

A	not A
True	False
False	True

The next example verifies some of the claims made in the truth tables in Figure 3-5:

```
>>> A = True
>>> B = False
>>> A and B
False
>>> A or B
True
>>> not A
False
```

In Chapter 2, you saw that multiplication and division have a higher precedence than addition and subtraction. This means that operators with a higher precedence are evaluated first, even if they appear to the right of operators of lower precedence. The same idea applies to the comparison, logical, and assignment operators. The logical operators are evaluated after comparisons but before the assignment operator. The **not** operator has a higher precedence than the **and** operator, which has a higher precedence than the **or** operator. Thus, in our example, **not A and B** evaluates to `False`, whereas `not (A and B)` evaluates to `True`. While you will not usually have to worry about operator precedence in most code, you might see code like the following, which shows all the different types of operators in action:

```
>>> A = 2
>>> B = 3
>>> result = A + B * 2 < 10 or B == 2
>>> result
True
```

Table 3-4 summarizes the precedence of the operators discussed thus far in this book.

Table 3-4   Operator precedence, from highest to lowest

Type of Operator	Operator Symbol
Exponentiation	**
Arithmetic negation	-
Multiplication, division, remainder	*, /, %
Addition, subtraction	+, -
Comparison	==, !=, <, >, <=, >=
Logical negation	not
Logical conjunction	and
Logical disjunction	or
Assignment	=

Short-Circuit Evaluation

The Python virtual machine sometimes knows the value of a Boolean expression before it has evaluated all of its operands. For instance, in the expression `A and B`, if `A` is false, then so is the expression, and there is no need to evaluate `B`.

Likewise, in the expression `A or B`, if `A` is true, then so is the expression, and again there is no need to evaluate `B`. This approach, in which evaluation stops as soon as possible, is called **short-circuit evaluation**.

There are times when short-circuit evaluation is advantageous. Consider the following example:

```
count = int(input("Enter the count: "))
theSum = int(input("Enter the sum: "))
if count > 0 and theSum // count > 10:
    print("average > 10")
else:
    print("count = 0 or average <= 10")
```

If the user enters 0 for the count, the condition contains a potential division by zero; however, because of short-circuit evaluation the division by zero is avoided.

Testing Selection Statements

Because selection statements add extra logic to a program, they open the door for extra logic errors. Take special care when testing programs that contain selection statements.

The first rule of thumb is to make sure that all of the possible branches or alternatives in a selection statement are exercised. This will happen if the test data include values that make each condition true and also each condition false. In our grade-conversion example, the test data should definitely include numbers that produce each of the letter grades.

After testing all of the actions, you should also examine all of the conditions. For example, when a condition contains a single comparison of two numbers, try testing the program with operands that are equal, with a left operand that is less by one, and with a left operand that is greater by one, to catch errors in the boundary cases.

Finally, you need to test conditions that contain compound Boolean expressions using data that produce all of the possible combinations of values of the operands. As a blueprint for testing a compound Boolean expression, use the truth table for that expression.

Exercise 3-3

1. Assume that **x** is 3 and **y** is 5. Write the values of the following expressions:

   a. x == y
   b. x > y - 3
   c. x <= y - 2
   d. x == y or x > 2
   e. x != 6 and y > 10
   f. x > 0 and x < 100

2. Assume that **x** refers to an integer. Write a code segment that prints the integer's absolute value without using Python's **abs** function.

3. Write a loop that counts the number of space characters in a string. Recall that the space character is represented as **' '**.

4. Assume that the variables **x** and **y** refer to strings. Write a code segment that prints these strings in alphabetical order. You should assume that they are not equal.

5. Explain how to check for an invalid input number and prevent it being used in a program. You may assume that the user enters a number.

6. Construct truth tables for the following Boolean expressions:
   a. not (A or B)
   b. not A and not B

7. Explain the role of the trailing **else** part of an extended **if** statement.

8. The variables **x** and **y** refer to numbers. Write a code segment that prompts the user for an arithmetic operator and prints the value obtained by applying that operator to **x** and **y**.

9. Does the Boolean expression **count > 0 and total // count > 0** contain a potential error? If not, why not?

3.4 Conditional Iteration: The while Loop

Earlier we examined the **for** loop, which executes a set of statements a definite number of times specified by the programmer. In many situations, however, the number of iterations in a loop is unpredictable. The loop eventually completes its work, but only when a condition changes. For example, the user might be asked for a set of input values. In that case, only the user knows the number they will enter. The program's input loop accepts these values until they enter a special value or **sentinel** that terminates the input. This type of process is called **conditional iteration**, meaning that the process continues to repeat as long as a condition remains true. In this section, we explore the use of the `while` loop to describe conditional iteration.

The Structure and Behavior of a `while` Loop

Conditional iteration requires that a condition be tested within the loop to determine whether the loop should continue. Such a condition is called the loop's **continuation condition**. If the continuation condition is false, the loop ends. If the continuation condition is true, the statements within the loop are executed again. The `while loop` is tailor-made for this type of control logic. Here is its syntax:

```
while <condition>:
    <sequence of statements>
```

The form of this statement is almost identical to that of the one-way selection statement. However, the use of the reserved word `while` instead of `if` indicates that the sequence of statements might be executed many times, as long as the condition remains true.

Clearly, something eventually has to happen within the body of the loop to make the loop's continuation condition become false. Otherwise, the loop will continue forever, an error known as an **infinite loop**. At least one statement in the body of the loop must update a variable that affects the value of the condition. **Figure 3-6** shows a flow diagram for the semantics of a `while` loop.

Figure 3-6   The semantics of a `while` loop

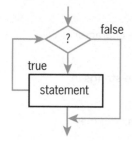

The following example is a short script that prompts the user for a series of numbers, computes their sum, and outputs the result. Instead of forcing the user to enter a definite number of values, the program stops the input process when the user simply presses the return or enter key. The program recognizes this value as the empty string. We first present a rough draft in the form of a pseudocode algorithm:

```
set the sum to 0.0
input a string
while the string is not the empty string
    convert the string to a float
    add the float to the sum
    input a string
print the sum
```

Note that there are two input statements, one just before the loop header and one at the bottom of the loop body. The first input statement initializes a variable to a value that the loop condition can test. This variable is also called the **loop control variable**. The second input statement obtains the other input values, including one that will terminate the loop. Note also that the input must be received as a string, not a number, so the program can test for an empty string.

If the string is not empty, we assume that it represents a number, and we convert it to a **float**. Here is the Python code for this script, followed by a trace of a sample run:

```
theSum = 0.0
data = input("Enter a number or just enter to quit: ")
while data != "":
    number = float(data)
    theSum += number
    data = input("Enter a number or just enter to quit: ")
print("The sum is", theSum)
Enter a number or just enter to quit: 3
Enter a number or just enter to quit: 4
Enter a number or just enter to quit: 5
Enter a number or just enter to quit:
The sum is 12.0
```

On this run, there are four inputs, including the empty string. Now, suppose we run the script again, and the user enters the empty string at the first prompt. The **while** loop's condition is immediately false, and its body does not execute at all! The sum prints as 0.0, which is just fine.

The **while** loop is also called an **entry-control loop** because its condition is tested at the top of the loop. This implies that the statements within the loop can execute zero or more times.

Count Control with a `while` Loop

You can also use a **while** loop for a count-controlled loop. The next two code segments show the same summations with a **for** loop and a **while** loop, respectively.

```
# Summation with a for loop
theSum = 0
for count in range(1, 100001):
    theSum += count
print(theSum)
# Summation with a while loop
theSum = 0
count = 1
while count <= 100000:
    theSum += count
    count += 1
print(theSum)
```

Although both loops produce the same result, there is a trade-off. The second code segment is noticeably more complex. It includes a Boolean expression and two extra statements that refer to the **count** variable. This loop control variable must be explicitly initialized before the loop header and incremented in the loop body. The **count** variable must also be examined in the explicit continuation condition. This extra manual labor for the programmer is not only time-consuming but also potentially a source of new errors in loop logic.

By contrast, a **for** loop specifies the control information concisely in the header and automates its manipulation behind the scenes. However, we will soon see problems for which a **while** loop is the only solution. Therefore, you must master the logic of **while** loops and also be aware of the logic errors that they could produce.

The next example shows two versions of a script that counts down from an upper bound of 10 to a lower bound of 1. It's up to you to decide which one is easier to understand and write correctly.

```
# Counting down with a for loop
for count in range(10, 0, -1):
    print(count, end = " ")
# Counting down with a while loop
count = 10
while count >= 1:
    print(count, end = " ")
    count -= 1
```

The `while True` Loop and the `break` Statement

Although the `while` loop can be complicated to write correctly, it is possible to simplify its structure and improve its readability. The first example script of this section, which contained two input statements, is a good candidate for such improvement. This loop's structure can be simplified if we receive the first input inside the loop and break out of the loop if a test shows that the continuation condition is false. This implies postponing the actual test until the middle of the loop. Python includes a `break` statement that will allow us to make this change in the program. Here is the modified script:

```
theSum = 0.0
while True:
    data = input("Enter a number or just enter to quit: ")
    if data == "":
        break
    number = float(data)
    theSum += number
print("The sum is", theSum)
```

The first thing to note is that the loop's entry condition is the Boolean value `True`. Some beginning programmers may become alarmed at this condition, which seems to imply that the loop will never exit. However, this condition is extremely easy to write and guarantees that the body of the loop will execute at least once. Within this body, the input datum is received. It is then tested for the loop's termination condition in a one-way selection statement. If the user wants to quit, the input will equal the empty string, and the `break` statement will cause an exit from the loop. Otherwise, control continues beyond the selection statement to the next two statements that process the input.

Our next example modifies the input section of the grade-conversion program to continue taking input numbers from the user until they enter an acceptable value. The logic of this loop is similar to that of the previous example.

```
while True:
    number = int(input("Enter the numeric grade: "))
    if number >= 0 and number <= 100:
        break
    else:
        print("Error: grade must be between 100 and 0")
print(number)  # Just echo the valid input
```

A trial run with just this segment shows the following interaction:

```
Enter the numeric grade: 101
Error: grade must be between 100 and 0
```

```
Enter the numeric grade: -1
Error: grade must be between 100 and 0
Enter the numeric grade: 45
45
```

Some computer scientists argue that a `while True` loop with a delayed exit violates the entry-control spirit of the `while` loop. However, in cases where the body of the loop must execute at least once, this technique simplifies the code and actually makes the program's logic clearer. If you are not persuaded by this reasoning and still want to test for the continuation and exit at the top of the loop, you can use a Boolean variable to control the loop. Here is a version of the numeric input loop that uses a Boolean variable:

```python
done = False
while not done:
    number = int(input("Enter the numeric grade: "))
    if number >= 0 and number <= 100:
        done = True
    else:
        print("Error: grade must be between 100 and 0")
print(number) # Just echo the valid input
```

For a classic discussion of this issue, see Eric Roberts's article "Loop Exits and Structured Programming: Reopening the Debate," *ACM SIGCSE Bulletin*, Volume 27, Number 1, March 1995, pp. 268–272.

Although the **break** statement is quite useful when it controls a loop with at least one iteration, you should primarily use it for just a single exit point from such loops.

Random Numbers

The choices our algorithms have made thus far have been completely determined by given conditions that are either true or false. Many situations, such as games, include some randomness in the choices that are made. For example, we might toss a coin to see who kicks off in a football game. There is an equal probability of a coin landing heads-up or tails-up. Likewise, the roll of a die in many games entails an equal probability of the numbers 1 through 6 landing face-up. To simulate this type of randomness in computer applications, programming languages include resources for generating **random numbers**. Python's **random** module supports several ways to do this, but the easiest is to call the function **random.randint** with two integer arguments. The function **random.randint** returns a random number from among the numbers between the two arguments and including those numbers. The next session simulates the roll of a die 10 times:

```python
>>> import random
>>> for roll in range(10):
        print(random.randint(1, 6), end = " ")
2 4 6 4 3 2 3 6 2 2
```

Although some values are repeated in this small set of calls, over the course of a large number of calls, the distribution of values approaches true randomness.

We can now use **random.randint**, selection, and a loop to develop a simple guessing game. At start-up, the user enters the smallest number and the largest number in the range. The computer then selects a number from this range. On each pass through the loop, the user enters a number to attempt to guess the number selected by the computer. The program responds by saying "You've got it," "Too large!," or "Too small!" When the user finally guesses the correct number, the program congratulates them and tells them the total number of guesses. Here is the code, followed by a sample run:

```python
import random
smaller = int(input("Enter the smaller number: "))
```

```
larger = int(input("Enter the larger number: "))
myNumber = random.randint(smaller, larger)
count = 0
while True:
    count += 1
    userNumber = int(input("Enter your guess: "))
    if userNumber < myNumber:
        print("Too small!")
    elif userNumber > myNumber:
        print("Too large!")
    else:
        print("Congratulations! You've got it in", count, "tries!")
        break
Enter the smaller number: 1
Enter the larger number: 100
Enter your guess: 50
Too small!
Enter your guess: 75
Too large!
Enter your guess: 63
Too small!
Enter your guess: 69
Too large!
Enter your guess: 66
Too large!
Enter your guess: 65
You've got it in 6 tries!
```

Note that our code is designed to allow the user to guess the number intelligently by starting at the midpoint between the two initial numbers and eliminating half the remaining numbers with each incorrect guess. Ideally, the user should be able to guess the correct number in no more than $\log_2 (upper - lower + 1)$ attempts. You will explore the concept of $\log_2$ in the exercises and projects.

Loop Logic, Errors, and Testing

You have seen that the **while** loop is typically a **condition-controlled loop**, meaning that its continuation depends on the truth or falsity of a given condition. Since **while** loops can be the most complex control statements, careful design and testing are needed to ensure their correct behavior. Testing a **while** loop must combine elements of testing used with **for** loops and with selection statements. Errors to rule out during testing the **while** loop include an incorrectly initialized loop control variable, failure to update this variable correctly within the loop, and failure to test the variable correctly in the continuation condition. Moreover, if one simply forgets to update the control variable, the result is an infinite loop, which does not even qualify as an algorithm! To halt a loop that appears to be hung during testing, type **Control-c** in the terminal window or in the IDLE shell.

Genuine condition-controlled loops can be easy to design and test. If the continuation condition is already available for examination at loop entry, check it there and provide test data that produce 0, 1, and at least 5 iterations.

If the loop must run at least once, use a **while True** loop and delay the examination of the termination condition until it becomes available in the body of the loop. Ensure that something occurs in the loop to allow the condition to be checked and a **break** statement to be reached eventually.

Exercise 3-4

1. Translate the following **for** loops to equivalent **while** loops:

    a. `for count in range(100):`
          `print(count)`

    b. `for count in range(1, 101):`
          `print(count)`

    c. `for count in range(100, 0, -1):`
          `print(count)`

2. The factorial of an integer N is the product of the integers between 1 and N, inclusive. Write a **while** loop that computes the factorial of a given integer N.

3. The log$_2$ of a given number N is given by M in the equation $N = 2^M$. Using integer arithmetic, the value of M is approximately equal to the number of times N can be evenly divided by 2 until it becomes 0. Write a loop that computes this approximation of the log$_2$ of a given number N. You can check your code by importing the **math.log** function and evaluating the expression **round(math.log(N, 2))** (note that the **math.log** function returns a floating-point value).

4. Describe the purpose of the **break** statement and the type of problem for which it is well suited.

5. What is the maximum number of guesses necessary to guess correctly a given number between the numbers N and M?

6. What happens when the programmer forgets to update the loop control variable in a **while** loop?

Case Study 3-2 | Approximating Square Roots

Users of pocket calculators or Python's **math** module do not have to think about how to compute square roots, but the people who built those calculators or wrote the code for that module certainly did. In this case study, we open the hood and see how this might be done.

Request

Write a program that computes square roots.

Analysis

The input to this program is a positive floating-point number or an integer. The output is a floating-point number representing the square root of the input number. For purposes of comparison, we also output Python's estimate of the square root using **math.sqrt**. Here is the proposed user interface:

```
Enter a positive number:     3
The program's estimate:      1.73205081001
Python's estimate:           1.73205080757
```

(continues)

Design

In the seventeenth century, Sir Isaac Newton discovered an algorithm for approximating the square root of a positive number. Recall that the square root y of a positive number x is the number y such that $y^2 = x$. Newton discovered that if one's initial estimate of y is z, then a better estimate of y can be obtained by taking the average of z together with x / z. The estimate can be transformed by this rule again and again, until a satisfactory estimate is reached.

A quick session with the Python interpreter shows this method of successive approximations in action. We let **x** be 25 and our initial estimate, **z**, be 1. We then use Newton's method to reset **z** to a better estimate and examine **z** to check it for closeness to the actual square root, 5. Here is a transcript of our interaction:

```
>>> x = 25
>>> z = 1                  # Our initial approximation
>>> z = (z + x / z) / 2 # Our first improvement
>>> z
13.0
>>> z = (z + x / z) / 2 # Our second improvement
>>> z
7.0
>>> z = (z + x / z) / 2 # Our third improvement - got it!
>>> z
5.0
```

After three transformations, the value of **z** is exactly equal to 5, the square root of 25. To include cases of numbers, such as 2 and 10, with irrational square roots, we can use an initial guess of 1.0 to produce floating-point results.

We now develop an algorithm to automate the process of successive transformations, because there might be many of them, and we don't want to write them all. Exactly how many of these operations are required depends on how close we want our final approximation to be to the actual square root. This closeness value, called the tolerance, can be compared to the difference between the value of **x** and the square of our estimate at any given time. While this difference is greater than the tolerance, the process continues; otherwise, it stops. The tolerance is typically a small value, such as 0.000001.

Our algorithm allows the user to input the number, uses a loop to apply Newton's method to compute the square root, and prints this value. Here is the pseudocode, followed by an explanation:

```
set x to the user's input value
set tolerance to 0.000001
set estimate to 1.0
while True
    set estimate to (estimate + x / estimate) / 2
    set difference to abs(x - estimate ** 2)
    if difference <= tolerance:
        break
output the estimate
```

Because our initial estimate is 1.0, the loop must compute at least one new estimate. Therefore, we use a **while True** loop. This loop transforms the estimate before determining whether it is close enough to the tolerance value to stop the process. The process should stop when the difference between the square of our estimate and the original number becomes less than or equal to the tolerance value. Note that this difference may be positive or negative, so we use the **abs** function to obtain its absolute value before examining it.

A more orthodox use of the **while** loop would compare the difference to the tolerance in the loop header. However, the difference must then be initialized before the loop to a large and rather meaningless value. The algorithm presented here captures the logic of the method of successive approximations more cleanly and simply.

Implementation (Coding)

The code for this program is straightforward.

```
"""
Program: newton.py
Author: Ken
Compute the square root of a number.
1. The input is a number.
2. The outputs are the program's estimate of the square root using Newton's
   method of successive approximations and Python's own estimate using math.sqrt.
"""

import math

# Receive the input number from the user
x = float(input("Enter a positive number: "))

# Initialize the tolerance and estimate
tolerance = 0.000001
estimate = 1.0

# Perform the successive approximations
while True:
    estimate = (estimate + x / estimate) / 2
    difference = abs(x - estimate ** 2)
    if difference <= tolerance:
        break

# Output the result
print("The program's estimate: ", ", estimate)
print("Python's estimate: ", math.sqrt(x))
```

Testing

The valid inputs to this program are positive integers and floating-point numbers. The display of Python's own most accurate estimate of the square root provides a benchmark for assessing the correctness of our own algorithm. We should at least provide a couple of perfect squares, such as 4 and 9, as well as numbers whose square roots are inexact, such as 2 and 3. A number between 1 and 0, such as .25, should also be included. Because the accuracy of our algorithm also depends on the size of the tolerance, we might alter this value during testing as well.

Fail-Safe Programming

You have seen several types of program errors so far in this book. They are classified in terms of three broad categories:

1. **Syntax errors.** These occur when an item of program code is not grammatically well-formed. For example, an arithmetic expression might omit one of its operands. Syntax errors in Python are caught before the program is run, at compile time.

2. **Semantic errors.** These occur when an item of program code is well-formed but the computer cannot carry out the specified operation. For example, a syntactically correct arithmetic expression might attempt to divide a number by 0. Semantic errors in Python are caught during program execution at runtime.

3. **Logic errors.** These occur when a program runs to a normal termination (no syntax or semantic errors) but does not produce the expected outputs. For example, a loop that sums a sequence of numbers might be off by one, so the program's output does not show the correct sum of that sequence.

A program that is free of these three types of errors is considered **correct** in a narrow, technical sense. For example, a program with a logically sound summation loop will guarantee a correct sum for any legitimate lower bound and upper bound of a sequence of numbers; and a program with a logically sound expression to compute the radius of a circle will guarantee the correct radius for any legitimate area.

However, many programs operate in an environment where the inputs to the computations might not be legitimate, especially in cases where human users might enter them. In these cases, a program must be able to detect, trap, and recover from user errors. Such programs are considered not just correct in the narrow sense but also **robust**. The discipline of creating robust programs that can gracefully avoid or trap and recover from such errors is called **fail-safe programming**.

As an example of illegitimate input, consider a program that computes the radius of a circle, given its area as an input. This program will only work correctly for an area that is greater than or equal to 0. But suppose that a user enters a negative number as input. The program cannot in that case even produce an incorrect output; it will halt with a runtime error, because it cannot take the square root of a negative number.

A fail-safe program handles this possibility by checking the input for validity before performing the computation or informing the user with an error message otherwise. Moreover, the program can continue to prompt the user for inputs until she enters a value within the expected range. Here is the code for a Python script that exhibits a fail-safe discipline:

```python
import math
while True:
    area = float(input("Enter the area of the circle: "))
    if area < 0:
        print("Error: the area must be greater than 0; please try again.")
    else:
        break
print("The radius of the circle is",
    math.sqrt(area) / math.pi)
```

The control statements for selection and iteration provide powerful tools for creating fail-safe programs. You will see other tools for detecting and handling exceptional conditions in later chapters of this book.

Summary

- Control statements determine the order in which other statements are executed in a program.

- Definite iteration is the process of executing a set of statements a fixed, predictable number of times. The `for` loop is an easy and convenient control statement for describing a definite iteration.

- The `for` loop consists of a header and a set of statements called the body. The header contains information that controls the number of times that the body executes.

- The `for` loop can count through a series of integers. Such a loop is called a count-controlled loop.

- During the execution of a count-controlled `for` loop, the statements in the loop's body can reference the current value of the count using the loop header's variable.

- Python's `range` function generates the sequence of numbers in a count-controlled `for` loop. This function can receive one, two, or three arguments. A single argument M specifies a sequence of numbers 0 through $M-1$. Two arguments M and N specify a sequence of numbers M through $N-1$. Three arguments M, N, and S specify a sequence of numbers M up through $N-1$, stepping by S, when S is positive, or M down through $N+1$, stepping by S, when S is negative.

- The `for` loop can traverse and visit the values in a sequence. Example sequences are a string of characters and a list of numbers.

- A format string and its operator `%` allow the programmer to format data using a field width and a precision.

- An off-by-one error occurs when a loop does not perform the intended number of iterations, there being one too many or one too few. This error can be caused by an incorrect lower bound or upper bound in a count-controlled loop.

- Boolean expressions contain the values `True` or `False`, variables bound to these values, comparisons using the relational operators, or other Boolean expressions using the logical operators. Boolean expressions evaluate to `True` or `False` and are used to form conditions in programs.

- The logical operators `and`, `or`, and `not` are used to construct compound Boolean expressions. The values of these expressions can be determined by constructing truth tables.

- Python uses short-circuit evaluation in compound Boolean expressions. The evaluation of the operands of `or` stops at the first true value, whereas the evaluation of the operands of `and` stops at the first false value.

- Selection statements are control statements that enable a program to make choices. A selection statement contains one or more conditions and the corresponding actions. Instead of moving straight ahead to the next action, the computer examines a condition. If the condition is true, the computer performs the corresponding action and then moves to the action following the selection statement. Otherwise, the computer moves to the next condition, if there is one, or to the action following the selection statement.

- A two-way selection statement, also called an `if-else` statement, has a single condition and two alternative courses of action. A one-way selection statement, also called an `if` statement, has a single condition and a single course of action. A multiway selection statement, also called an extended `if` statement, has at least two conditions and three alternative courses of action.

- Conditional iteration is the process of executing a set of statements while a condition is true. The iteration stops when the condition becomes false. Because it cannot always be anticipated when this will occur, the number of iterations usually cannot be predicted.

- A `while` loop is used to describe conditional iteration. This loop consists of a header and a set of statements called the body. The header contains the loop's continuation condition. The body executes as long as the continuation condition is true.

- The **while** loop is an entry-control loop. This means that the continuation condition is tested at loop entry, and if it is false, the loop's body will not execute. Thus, the **while** loop can describe zero or more iterations.

- The **break** statement can be used to exit a **while** loop from its body. The **break** statement is usually used when the loop must perform at least one iteration. The loop header's condition in that case is the value **True**. The **break** statement is nested in an **if** statement that tests for a termination condition.

- Any **for** loop can be converted to an equivalent **while** loop. In a count-controlled **while** loop, the programmer must initialize and update a loop control variable.

- An infinite loop occurs when the loop's continuation condition never becomes false and no other exit points are provided. The primary cause of infinite loops is the programmer's failure to update a loop control variable properly.

- The function **random.randint** returns a random number in the range specified by its two arguments.

Key Terms

augmented assignment operations	format operator	pass
Boolean data type	format string	prototype
Boolean expression	**if** statement	random numbers
break statement	**if-else** statement	robust
compound Boolean expression	indefinite iteration	selection statements
condition	infinite loop	sentinel (or sentinel value)
condition-controlled loop	iteration	short-circuit evaluation
conditional iteration	list	simple Boolean expressions
continuation condition	logical negation	step value
control statements	logical operator	summation
correct	loops	tabular format
count-controlled loops	loop body	termination condition
definite iteration	loop control variable	truth table
entry-control loop	loop header	two-way selection statement
fail-safe programming	multiway selection statement	**while** loop
field width	off-by-one error	
for loop	one-way selection statement	

Review Questions

1. How many times does a loop with the header **for count in range (10):** execute the statements in its body?

   a. 9 times

   b. 10 times

   c. 11 times

   d. 12 times

2. A `for` loop is convenient for

   a. making choices in a program.
   b. running a set of statements a predictable number of times.
   c. counting through a sequence of numbers.
   d. describing conditional iteration.

3. What is the output of the loop `for count in range(5): print(count, end = " ")`?

   a. 1 2 3 4 5
   b. 1 2 3 4
   c. 0 1 2 3 4
   d. 0 1 2 3 4 5

4. When the function `range` receives two arguments, what does the second argument specify?

   a. The last value of a sequence of integers
   b. The last value of a sequence of integers plus 1
   c. The last value of a sequence of integers minus 1
   d. The step value for the loop

5. Consider the following code segment:

```
x = 5
y = 4
if x > y:
    print(y)
else:
    print(x)
```

   What value does this code segment print?

   a. 4
   b. 5
   c. 9
   d. 20

6. A Boolean expression using the **and** operator returns **True** when

   a. both operands are true.
   b. one operand is true.
   c. neither operand is true.
   d. one operand is false

7. By default, the `while` loop is a(n)

   a. entry-controlled loop.
   b. exit-controlled loop.
   c. count-controlled loop.
   d. loop that iterates a definite, preestablished number of times.

8. Consider the following code segment:

```
count = 5
while count > 1:
    print(count, end = " ")
    count -= 1
```

   What is the output produced by this code?

   a. 1 2 3 4 5
   b. 2 3 4 5
   c. 5 4 3 2 1
   d. 5 4 3 2

9. Consider the following code segment, which is intended to print the integers 1 through 10:

```
count = 1
while count <= 10:
    print(count, end = " ")
```

Which of the following describes the error in this code?

a. The loop is off by 1.

b. The loop control variable is not properly initialized.

c. The comparison points the wrong way.

d. The loop is infinite.

10. Consider the following code segment:

```
theSum = 0.0
while True:
    number = input("Enter a number: ")
    if number == "":
        break
    theSum += float(number)
```

How many iterations does this loop perform?

a. None

b. At least one

c. Zero or more

d. Ten

Programming Exercises

1. Write a program in the file **equilateral.py** that accepts the lengths of three sides of a triangle as inputs. The program output should indicate whether or not the triangle is an equilateral triangle. (LO: 3.3)

2. Write a program in the file **right.py** that accepts the lengths of three sides of a triangle as inputs. The program output should indicate whether or not the triangle is a right triangle. Recall from the Pythagorean theorem that in a right triangle, the square of one side equals the sum of the squares of the other two sides. (LO: 3.3)

3. Modify the guessing-game program of Section 3.5 in the file **guess.py** so that the user thinks of a number that the computer must guess. The computer must make no more than the minimum number of guesses, and it must prevent the user from cheating by entering misleading hints. (*Hint*: Use the **math.log** function to compute the minimum number of guesses needed after the lower and upper bounds are entered.) (LO: 3.3, 3.4)

4. A standard science experiment is to drop a ball and see how high it bounces. Once the "bounciness" of the ball has been determined, the ratio gives a bounciness index. For example, if a ball dropped from a height of 10 feet bounces 6 feet high, the index is 0.6, and the total distance traveled by the ball is 16 feet after one bounce. If the ball were to continue bouncing, the distance after two bounces would be 10 ft + 6 ft + 6 ft + 3.6 ft = 25.6 ft. Note that the distance traveled for each successive bounce is the distance to the floor plus 0.6 of that distance as the ball comes back up. Write a program in the file **bouncy.py** that lets the user enter the initial height from which the ball is dropped and the number of times the ball is allowed to continue bouncing. Output should be the total distance traveled by the ball. (LO: 3.1)

5. A local biologist needs a program to predict population growth. The inputs would be the initial number of organisms, the rate of growth (a real number greater than 0), the number of hours it takes to achieve this rate, and a number of hours during which the population grows. For example, one might start with a population of 500 organisms, a growth rate of 2, and a growth period to achieve this rate of 6 hours. Assuming that none of the organisms die, this would imply that this population would double in size every 6 hours. Thus, after allowing 6 hours for growth, we would have 1000 organisms, and after 12 hours, we would have 2000 organisms. Write a program in the file **population.py** that takes these inputs and displays a prediction of the total population. (LO: 3.1)

6. The German mathematician Gottfried Leibniz developed the following method to approximate the value of π:
   $$\pi/4 = 1 - 1/3 + 1/5 - 1/7 + \cdots$$
   Write a program in the file **leibniz.py** that allows the user to specify the number of iterations used in this approximation and that displays the resulting value. (LO: 3.1)

7. Teachers in most school districts are paid on a schedule that provides a salary based on their number of years of teaching experience. For example, a beginning teacher in the Lexington School District might be paid $30,000 the first year. For each year of experience after this first year, up to 10 years, the teacher receives a 2% increase over the preceding value. Write a program in the file **salary.py** that displays a salary schedule, in tabular format, for teachers in a school district. The inputs are the starting salary, the percentage increase, and the number of years in the schedule. Each row in the schedule should contain the year number and the salary for that year. (LO: 3.1, 3.2)

8. The greatest common divisor of two positive integers, A and B, is the largest number that can be evenly divided into both of them. Euclid's algorithm can be used to find the greatest common divisor (GCD) of two positive integers. You can implement this algorithm in the following manner:

   a. Compute the remainder of dividing the larger number by the smaller number.

   b. Replace the larger number with the smaller number and the smaller number with the remainder.

   c. Repeat this process until the smaller number is zero.

   d. The larger number at this point is the GCD of A and B. Write a program in the file **gcd.py** that lets the user enter two integers and then prints each step in the process of using the Euclidean algorithm to find their GCD. (LO: 3.4)

9. Write a program in the file **sum.py** that receives a series of numbers from the user and allows the user to press the enter key to indicate that he or she is finished providing inputs. After the user presses the enter key, the program should print the sum of the numbers and their average. (LO: 3.3, 3.4)

10. The credit plan at TidBit Computer Store specifies a 10% down payment and an annual interest rate of 12%. Monthly payments are 5% of the listed purchase price, minus the down payment. Write a program in the file **tidbit.py** that takes the purchase price as input. The program should display a table, with appropriate headers, of a payment schedule for the lifetime of the loan. Each row of the table should contain the following items:

   - the month number (beginning with 1)

   - the current total balance owed

   - the interest owed for that month

   - the amount of principal owed for that month

   - the payment for that month

   - the balance remaining after payment

   The amount of interest for a month is equal to balance * rate / 12. The amount of principal for a month is equal to the monthly payment minus the interest owed. (LO: 3.2, 3.3, 3.4)

11. In the game of Lucky Sevens, the player rolls a pair of dice. If the dots add up to 7, the player wins $4; otherwise, the player loses $1. Suppose that, to entice the gullible, a casino tells players that there are lots of ways to win: (1, 6), (2, 5), and so on. A little mathematical analysis reveals that there are not enough ways to win to make the game worthwhile; however, because many people's eyes glaze over at the first mention of mathematics, your challenge is to write a program in the file **sevens.py** that demonstrates the futility of playing the game. Your program should take as input the amount of money that the player wants to put into the pot, and play the game until the pot is empty. At that point, the program should print the number of rolls it took to break the player, as well as maximum amount of money in the pot. (LO: 3.3, 3.4)

Debugging Exercise

Jack has written a program that computes and prints the average of 10 test scores. The program prompts the user for each input score. Here is the code for this program:

```
count = 1
while count < 10:
    score = int(input("Enter test score number " + str(count) + ": ")
    total = total + score
    count = count + 1
average = total / count
print("The average test score is", average)
```

This program contains an error. State what type of error this is, describe how it is detected, and explain how to correct it.

Loops and Branching Logic

Prompt

Rvector/Shutterstock.com

Ira Yapanda/Shutterstock.com

tele52/Shutterstock.com

With your pseudocode written and a basic script for creating, setting and outputting variables in place, you're going to continue pickItems to add to your script other features like loops and branching logic to help to define how, when, and how much your robot performs some of these actions.

Your script is going to have several additional items now:

1. Methods
2. Branching Logic
3. Loops

You are familiar with loops, which execute the same instructions as long as certain criteria is let. You understand that branching logic are things like "if else" statements. Methods, however, are new. A method is like a function that "belongs" to an object. For instance, if you have a string, you can use the ".lowercase()" method to make sure all characters in the string are lowercase. This method does not apply to floats or integers.

With these new options in place, you're going to allow your robot to make certain decisions based on user requests. For instance, create a method named "pickItems," which will allow users to select a type of item to get. Users will be able to choose from the following options:

1. Hardware
2. Lumber
3. Paint

Depending on which item the user selected, you will add one to that type of item. Allow the users to continue adding items until they decide to stop. Typically, a while loop would be a good option for doing so.

Next, you're going to have an outputOrder method which will output the number of hardware, lumber, and paint items that the user had our robot select.

Herby the robot picked # of hardware items.

Herby the robot picked # of lumber items.

Herby the robot picked # of paint items.

Examples:

```
def functionExample(pName):
 print("Hello "+pName)
functionExample("Dan")
```

Branching:

```
userAge = 10
if(userAge > 10)
        print("You are old enough to ride this ride")
```

Loops:

```
lumber = ["2x4", "2x8", "plywood"]
for x in lumber:
  print(x)
```

Hints

When you are putting together application content, it is best to break the logic and the pieces down into small parts; only as large they would be useful not only for this application, but others as well. By creating methods, this will help you to create specific tools and those tools can then be used to solve application objectives but also objectives in other applications. You will create a method in Python using the def statement and then the statements in that method will be indented underneath.

For branching and looping, you have the if statement for branching logic. You can compare things, test for NULL values, all manner of tests. For looping, you can iterate through a number of user-supplied needs, like the number of lines in a file or a user defined number of times, etc... Consider a for or while loop for your looping needs. Consider the use of the if, else, and elif statements for the branching logic portion.

Answer

See Chapter 3_Loops and Branching Logic.py

After Discussion

As you are progressing along and building out your application, adding more tools and features as you go, you can now begin to add in methods, branching, and iteration. These are some of the basic underpinnings of application development.

With iteration, you are allowing users to perform a repetitive action as many times as they wish. Whether that is user supplied or coming from another source, looping/iteration can help to automate and perform actions which will reduce errors. Adding users, deleting users, creating new data records, the list of activities that can be controlled through iteration are numerous.

With branching, users can implement business logic into the applications they are creating. Greater than 10, do this. Less than 0, do that. There are many comparisons that can be made and issues that might crop up on an application that can be planned for and handled using branching. This would consist of using the if and elif statements to help with determining what a user entered and subsequently, what action to take.

Finally, with the use of methods, the above activities can be packaged into certain functionality. Maybe you create an add user method, or a modify user method. These methods, as their name might imply, will handle certain, specific functionality.

With these three components, the ability to create basic applications which can work with user input, connect to databases, service other applications, all of these can be worked with through use of these components. As you continue along, you will add more elements to your application. Well done!

## Chapter 4

Strings and Text Files

Learning Objectives

When you complete this chapter, you will be able to:

4.1 Access individual characters in a string, retrieve a substring from a string, and search for a substring in a string

4.2 Encrypt the data in a string

4.3 Convert a string representation of a number from one base to another base

4.4 Use string methods to manipulate strings

4.5 Open a text file for output and write strings or numbers to the file, open a text file for input and read strings or numbers from the file, and use library functions to access and navigate a file system

Computation is often concerned with manipulating text. Word processing and program editing are obvious examples, but text also forms the basis of email, web pages, and text messaging. In this chapter, we explore strings and text files, which are useful data structures for organizing and processing text.

4.1 Accessing Characters and Substrings in Strings

In Chapters 1 and 2 we used strings for input and output. We also combined strings via concatenation to form new strings. In Chapter 3, you learned how to format a string and to visit each of its characters with a **for** loop. In this section, we examine the internal structure of a string more closely, and you will learn how to extract portions of a string called **substrings**.

The Structure of Strings

Unlike an integer, which cannot be decomposed into more primitive parts, a string is a **data structure**. A data structure is a compound unit that consists of several other pieces of data. A string is a sequence of zero or more characters. Recall that you can mention a Python string using either single quote marks or double quote marks. Here are some examples:

```
>>> "Hi there!"
'Hi there!'
>>> ""
''
>>> 'R'
'R'
```

Note that the shell prints a string using single quotes, even when you enter it using double quotes. In this book, we use single quotes with single-character strings and double quotes with the empty string or with multicharacter strings.

When working with strings, the programmer sometimes must be aware of a string's length and the positions of the individual characters within the string. A string's length is the number of characters it contains. Python's **len** function returns this value when it is passed a string, as shown in the following session:

```
>>> len("Hi there!")
9
>>> len("")
0
```

The positions of a string's characters are numbered from 0, on the left, to the length of the string minus 1, on the right. **Figure 4-1** illustrates the sequence of characters and their positions in the string **"Hi there!"**. Note that the ninth and last character, **'!'**, is at position 8.

Figure 4-1 Characters and their positions in a string

```
H  i     t  h  e  r  e  !
0  1  2  3  4  5  6  7  8
```

The string is an **immutable data structure**. This means that its internal data elements, the characters, can be accessed but cannot be replaced, inserted, or removed.

The Subscript Operator

Although a simple **for** loop can access any of the characters in a string, sometimes you just want to inspect one character at a given position without visiting them all. The **subscript operator** **[]** makes this possible. The simplest form of the subscript operation is the following:

```
<a string>[<an integer expression>]
```

The first part of this operation is the string you want to inspect. The integer expression in brackets indicates the position of a particular character in that string. The integer expression is also called an **index**. In the following examples, the subscript operator is used to access characters in the string **"Alan Turing"**:

```
>>> name = "Alan Turing"
>>> name[0]                   # Examine the first character
'A'
>>> name[3]                   # Examine the fourth character
'n'
>>> name[len(name)]           # Oops! An index error!
```

```
Traceback (most recent call last):
  File "<stdin>", line 1, in <module>
IndexError: string index out of range
>>> name[len(name) - 1]     # Examine the last character
'g'
>>> name[-1]                # Shorthand for the last character
'g'
>>> name[-2]                # Shorthand for next to last character
'n'
```

Note that attempting to access a character using a position that equals the string's length results in an error. The positions usually range from 0 to the length minus 1. However, Python allows negative subscript values to access characters at or near the end of a string. The programmer counts backward from –1 to access characters from the right end of the string.

The subscript operator is also useful in loops where you want to use the positions as well as the characters in a string. The next code segment uses a count-controlled loop to display the characters and their positions:

```
>>> data = "Hi there!"
>>> for index in range(len(data)):
        print(index, data[index])

0 H
1 i
2
3 t
4 h
5 e
6 r
7 e
8 !
```

Slicing for Substrings

Some applications extract portions of strings called substrings. For example, an application that sorts filenames according to type might use the last three characters in a filename, called its **extension**, to determine the file's type (exceptions to this rule, such as the extensions ".py" and ".html", will be considered later in this chapter). On a Windows file system, a filename ending in ".txt" denotes a human-readable text file, whereas a filename ending in ".exe" denotes an executable file of machine code. You can use Python's subscript operator to obtain a substring through a process called **slicing**. To extract a substring, the programmer places a colon (:) in the subscript. An integer value can appear on either side of the colon. Here are some examples that show how slicing is used:

```
>>> name = "myfile.txt"    # The entire string
>>> name[0:]
'myfile.txt'
>>> name[0:1]              # The first character
'm'
>>> name[0:2]              # The first two characters
'my'
>>> name[:len(name)]      # The entire string
```

```
'myfile.txt'
>>> name[2:6]                    # Drill to extract 'file'
'file'
>>> name[-3:]                    # The last three characters
'txt'
```

Generally, when two integer positions are included in the slice, the range of characters in the substring extends from the first position up to but not including the second position. When the integer is omitted on either side of the colon, all of the characters extending to the end or the beginning are included in the substring. Note that the last line of code provides the correct range to obtain the filename's three-character extension.

Testing for a Substring with `in` Operator

Another problem involves picking out strings that contain known substrings. For example, you might want to pick out filenames with a `.txt` extension. A slice would work for this, but using Python's `in` operator is much simpler. When used with strings, the left operand of `in` is a target substring, and the right operand is the string to be searched. The operator `in` returns `True` if the target string is somewhere in the search string, or `False` otherwise. The next code segment traverses a list of filenames and prints just the filenames that have a `.txt` extension:

```
>>> fileList = ["myfile.txt", "myprogram.exe",   "yourfile.txt"]
>>> for fileName in fileList:
        if ".txt" in fileName:
            print(fileName)
myfile.txt
yourfile.txt
```

Exercise 4-1

1. Assume that the variable **data** refers to the string **"myprogram.exe"**. Write the values of the following expressions:

   a. `data[2]`
   b. `data[-1]`
   c. `len(data)`
   d. `data[0:8]`

2. Assume that the variable **data** refers to the string **"myprogram.exe"**. Write the expressions that perform the following tasks:

   a. Extract the substring **"gram"** from **data**.
   b. Remove the extension **".exe"** from **data**.
   c. Extract the character at the middle position from **data**.

3. Assume that the variable **myString** refers to a string. Write a code segment that uses a loop to print the characters of the string in reverse order.

4. Assume that the variable **myString** refers to a string, and the variable **reversedString** refers to an empty string. Write a loop that adds the characters from **myString** to **reversedString** in reverse order.

4.2 Data Encryption

As you might imagine, data traveling on the Internet is vulnerable to potential spies and thieves. It is easy to observe data crossing a network, particularly now that more and more forms of communication involve wireless transmissions. For example, a person can sit in a car in the parking lot outside any major hotel and pick up transmissions between almost any two computers if that person runs the right **sniffing software**. For this reason, most applications now use **data encryption** to protect information transmitted on networks. Some application protocols include secure versions that use data encryption. Examples of such versions are FTPS and HTTPS, which are secure versions of FTP and HTTP for file transfer and web page transfer, respectively.

Encryption techniques are as old as the practice of sending and receiving messages. The sender encrypts a message by translating it to a secret code, called a **cipher text**. At the other end, the receiver **decrypts** the cipher text back to its original **plaintext** form. Both parties to this transaction must have at their disposal one or more **keys** that allow them to encrypt and decrypt messages. To give you a taste of this process, let us examine an encryption strategy in detail.

A simple encryption method that has been in use for thousands of years is called a **Caesar cipher**. Recall that the character set for text is ordered as a sequence of distinct values. This encryption strategy replaces each character in the plaintext with the character that occurs a given distance away in the sequence. For positive distances, the method wraps around to the beginning of the sequence to locate the replacement characters for those characters near its end. For example, if the distance value of a Caesar cipher equals three characters, the string **"invaders"** would be encrypted as **"lqydghuv"**. To decrypt this cipher text back to plaintext, you apply a method that uses the same distance value but looks to the left of each character for its replacement. This decryption method wraps around to the end of the sequence to find a replacement character for one near its beginning. **Figure 4-2** shows the first five and the last five plaintext characters of the lowercase alphabet and the corresponding cipher text characters for a Caesar cipher with a distance of +3. The numeric ASCII values are listed above and below the characters.

Figure 4-2   A Caesar cipher with distance +3 for the lowercase alphabet

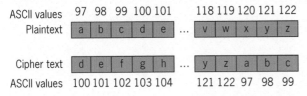

Note the wraparound effect for the last three plaintext characters, whose cipher text characters start at the beginning of the alphabet. For example, the plaintext character "x" with ASCII 120 maps to the cipher character "a" with ASCII 97, because ASCII 120 is less than three characters from the end of the plaintext sequence.

The next two Python scripts implement Caesar cipher methods for any strings that contain the lowercase letters of the alphabet and for any distance values between 0 and 26. Recall that the **ord** function returns the ordinal position of a character value in the ASCII sequence, whereas **chr** is the inverse function.

```
"""
File: encrypt.py
Encrypts an input string of lowercase letters and prints the result. The other input
is the distance value.
"""

plainText = input("Enter a one-word, lowercase message: ")
distance = int(input("Enter the distance value: "))
code = ""
for ch in plainText:
    ordvalue = ord(ch)
```

```
        cipherValue = ordvalue + distance
        if cipherValue > ord('z'):
            cipherValue = ord('a') + distance - \
                          (ord('z') - ordvalue + 1)
        code += chr(cipherValue)
print(code)
"""

File: decrypt.py
Decrypts an input string of lowercase letters and prints the result. The other input
is the distance value.
"""
code = input("Enter the coded text: ")
distance = int(input("Enter the distance value: "))
plainText = ""
for ch in code:
    ordvalue = ord(ch)
    cipherValue = ordvalue - distance
    if cipherValue < ord('a'):
        cipherValue = ord('z') - \
                      (distance - (ord('a') - ordvalue - 1))
    plainText += chr(cipherValue)
print(plainText)
```

Here are some executions of the two scripts in the IDLE shell:

```
Enter a one-word, lowercase message: invaders
Enter the distance value: 3
lqydghuv
Enter the coded text: lqydghuv
Enter the distance value: 3
invaders
```

These scripts could easily be extended to cover all of the characters, including spaces and punctuation marks.

Although it worked reasonably well in ancient times, a Caesar cipher would be no match for a competent spy with a computer. Assuming that there are 128 ASCII characters, all you would have to do is write a program that would run the same line of text through the extended **decrypt** script with the values 0 through 127 until a meaningful plaintext is returned. It would take less than a second to do that on most modern computers. The main shortcoming of this encryption strategy is that the plaintext is encrypted one character at a time, and each encrypted character depends on that single character and a fixed distance value. In a sense, the structure of the original text is preserved in the cipher text, so it might not be hard to discover a key by visual inspection.

A more sophisticated encryption scheme is called a **block cipher**. A block cipher uses plaintext characters to compute two or more encrypted characters. This is accomplished by using a mathematical structure known as an **invertible matrix** to determine the values of the encrypted characters. The matrix provides the key in this method. The receiver uses the same matrix to decrypt the cipher text. The fact that information used to determine each character comes from a block of data makes it more difficult to determine the key. We will explore the use of a block cipher to encrypt text in Chapter 9, where we introduce a grid data type.

Exercise 4-2

1. Write the encrypted text of each of the following words using a Caesar cipher with a distance value of +3:

   a. python
   b. hacker
   c. wow

2. Consult the Table of ASCII values (Table 2-5) in Chapter 2 and suggest how you would modify the encryption and decryption scripts in this section to work with strings containing all of the printable characters.

3. You are given a string that was encoded by a Caesar cipher with an unknown distance value. The text can contain any of the printable ASCII characters. Suggest an algorithm for cracking this code.

4.3 Strings and Number Systems

When you perform arithmetic operations, you use the **decimal number system**. This system, also called the **base 10 number system**, uses the 10 characters 0, 1, 2, 3, 4, 5, 6, 7, 8, and 9 as digits. As we saw in Chapter 1, the **binary number system** is used to represent all information in a digital computer. The two digits in this **base 2 number system** are 0 and 1. Because binary numbers can be long strings of 0s and 1s, computer scientists often use other number systems, such as **octal** (base 8) and **hexadecimal** (base 16) as shorthand for these numbers.

To identify the system being used, you attach the base as a subscript to the number. For example, the following numbers represent the quantity 415_{10} in the binary, octal, decimal, and hexadecimal systems:

415 in binary notation	110011111_2
415 in octal notation	637_8
415 in decimal notation	415_{10}
415 in hexadecimal notation	$19F_{16}$

The digits used in each system are counted from 0 to $n-1$, where n is the system's base. Thus, the digits 8 and 9 do not appear in the octal system. To represent digits with values larger than 9_{10}, systems such as base 16 use letters. Thus, A_{16} represents the quantity 10_{10}, whereas 10_{16} represents the quantity 16_{10}. In this section, we examine how these systems represent numeric quantities and how to translate from one notation to another.

The Positional System for Representing Numbers

All of the number systems we have examined use **positional notation**—that is, the value of each digit in a number is determined by the digit's position in the number. In other words, each digit has a **positional value**. The positional value of a digit is determined by raising the base of the system to the power specified by the position ($base^{position}$). For an n-digit number, the positions (and exponents) are numbered from $n-1$ down to 0, starting with the leftmost digit and moving to the right. For example, as **Figure 4-3** illustrates, the positional values of the three-digit number 415_{10} are $100(10^2)$, $10(10^1)$, and $1(10^0)$, moving from left to right in the number.

Figure 4-3   The first three positional values in the base 10 number system

```
Positional values  100  10   1
Positions            2   1   0
```

To determine the quantity represented by a number in any system from base 2 through base 10, you multiply each digit (as a decimal number) by its positional value and add the results. The following example shows how this is done for a three-digit number in base 10:

$$415_{10} =$$

$$4 * 10^2 + 1 * 10^1 + 5 * 10^0 =$$

$$4 * 100 + 1 * 10 + 5 * 1 \quad =$$

$$400 \quad + 10 \quad + 5 \quad = 415$$

Converting Binary to Decimal

Like the decimal system, the binary system also uses positional notation. However, each digit or bit in a binary number has a positional value that is a power of 2. In the discussion that follows, we occasionally refer to a binary number as a string of bits or a **bit string**. You determine the integer quantity that a string of bits represents in the usual manner: Multiply the value of each bit (0 or 1) by its positional value and add the results. Let's do that for the number 1100111_2:

$$1100111_2 =$$

$$1 * 2^6 + 1 * 2^5 + 0 * 2^4 + 0 * 2^3 + 1 * 2^2 + 1 * 2^1 + 1 * 2^0 =$$

$$1 * 64 + 1 * 32 + 0 * 16 + 0 * 8 + 1 * 4 + 1 * 2 + 1 * 1 \quad =$$

$$64 \quad + 32 \qquad\qquad\qquad + 4 \quad + 2 \quad + 1 \quad = 103$$

Not only have we determined the integer value of this binary number, but we have also converted it to decimal in the process! In computing the value of a binary number, we can ignore the values of the positions occupied by 0s and simply add the positional values of the positions occupied by 1s.

We can code an algorithm for the conversion of a binary number to the equivalent decimal number as a Python script. The input to the script is a string of bits, and its output is the integer that the string represents. The algorithm uses a loop that accumulates the sum of a set of integers. The sum is initially 0. The exponent that corresponds to the position of the string's leftmost bit is the length of the bit string minus 1. The loop visits the digits in the string from the first to the last (left to right) but counts from the largest exponent of 2 down to 0 as it goes. Each digit is converted to its integer value (1 or 0), multiplied by its positional value, and the result is added to the ongoing total. A positional value is computed by using the ** operator. Here is the code for the script, followed by some example sessions in the shell:

```
"""
File: binarytodecimal.py
Converts a string of bits to a decimal integer.
"""

bitString = input("Enter a string of bits: ")
decimal = 0
exponent = len(bitString) - 1
for digit in bitString:
    decimal = decimal + int(digit) * 2 ** exponent
    exponent = exponent - 1
print("The integer value is", decimal)
Enter a string of bits: 1111
The integer value is 15
Enter a string of bits: 101
The integer value is 5
```

Converting Decimal to Binary

How are integers converted from decimal to binary? One algorithm uses division and subtraction instead of multiplication and addition. This algorithm repeatedly divides the decimal number by 2. After each division, the remainder (either a 0 or a 1) is placed at the beginning of a string of bits. The quotient becomes the next dividend in the process. The string of bits is initially empty, and the process continues while the decimal number is greater than 0.

Let's code this algorithm as a Python script and run it to display the intermediate results in the process. The script expects a nonnegative decimal integer as an input and prints the equivalent bit string. The script checks first for a 0 and prints the string '0' as a special case. Otherwise, the script uses the algorithm just described. On each pass through the loop, the values of the quotient, remainder, and result string are displayed. Here is the code for the script, followed by a session to convert the number 34:

```
"""
File: decimaltobinary.py
Converts a decimal integer to a string of bits.
"""
decimal = int(input("Enter a decimal integer: "))
if decimal == 0:
    print(0)
else:
    print("Quotient Remainder Binary")
    bitString = ""
    while decimal > 0:
        remainder = decimal % 2
        decimal = decimal // 2
        bitString = str(remainder) + bitString
        print("%5d%8d%12s" % (decimal, remainder, bitString))
print("The binary representation is", bitString)
Enter a decimal integer: 34
Quotient Remainder Binary

   17      0           0
    8      1          10
    4      0         010
    2      0        0010
    1      0       00010
    0      1      100010

The binary representation is 100010
```

Conversion Shortcuts

There are various shortcuts for determining the decimal integer values of some binary numbers. One useful method involves learning to count through the numbers corresponding to the decimal values 0 through 8, as shown in **Table 4-1**.

Note the rows that contain exact powers of 2 (2, 4, and 8 in decimal). Each of the corresponding binary numbers in that row contains a 1 followed by a number of zeroes that equal the exponent used to compute that power of 2. Thus, a quick way to compute the decimal value of the number 10000_2 is 2^4 or 16_{10}.

Table 4-1 The numbers 0 through 8 in binary

Decimal	Binary
0	0
1	1
2	10
3	11
4	100
5	101
6	110
7	111
8	1000

The rows whose binary numbers contain all 1s correspond to decimal numbers that are one less than the next exact power of 2. For example, the number 111_2 equals $2^3 - 1$ or 7_{10}. Thus, a quick way to compute the decimal value of the number 11111_2 is $2^5 - 1$, or 31_{10}.

Octal and Hexadecimal Numbers

The octal system uses a base of eight and the digits 0 ... 7. Conversions of octal to decimal and decimal to octal use algorithms similar to those discussed thus far (using powers of 8 and multiplying or dividing by 8, instead of 2). But the real benefit of the octal system is the ease of converting octal numbers to and from binary. With practice, you can learn to do these conversions quite easily by hand, and in many cases by eye. To convert from octal to binary, you start by assuming that each digit in the octal number represents three digits in the corresponding binary number. You then start with the leftmost octal digit and write down the corresponding binary digits, padding these to the left with 0s to the count of 3, if necessary. You proceed in this manner until you have converted all of the octal digits. **Figure 4-4** shows such a conversion.

Figure 4-4 The conversion of octal to binary

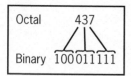

To convert binary to octal, you begin at the right and factor the bits into groups of three bits each. You then convert each group of three bits to the octal digit they represent.

As the size of a number system's base increases, so does the system's expressive power, its ability to say more with less. As bit strings get longer, the octal system becomes a less useful shorthand for expressing them. The hexadecimal or base-16 system (called "hex" for short), which uses 16 different digits, provides a more concise notation than octal for larger numbers. Base 16 uses the digits 0 ... 9 for the corresponding integer quantities and the letters A ... F for the integer quantities 10 ... 15.

The conversion between numbers in the two systems works as follows. Each digit in the hexadecimal number is equivalent to four digits in the binary number. Thus, to convert from hexadecimal to binary, you replace each hexadecimal digit with the corresponding 4-bit binary number. To convert from binary to hexadecimal, you factor the bits into groups of four and look up the corresponding hex digits. (This is the kind of stuff that hackers memorize.) **Figure 4-5** shows a mapping of hexadecimal digits to binary digits.

Figure 4-5   The conversion of hexadecimal to binary

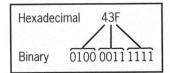

> ## Exercise 4-3

1. Translate each of the following numbers to decimal numbers:

    a. 11001_2
    b. 100000_2
    c. 11111_2

2. Translate each of the following numbers to binary numbers:

    a. 47_{10}
    b. 127_{10}
    c. 64_{10}

3. Translate each of the following numbers to binary numbers:

    a. 47_8
    b. 127_8
    c. 64_8

4. Translate each of the following numbers to decimal numbers:

    a. 47_8
    b. 127_8
    c. 64_8

5. Translate each of the following numbers to decimal numbers:

    a. 47_{16}
    b. 27_{16}
    c. AA_{16}

4.4 String Methods

Text processing involves many different operations on strings. For example, consider the problem of analyzing someone's writing style. Short sentences containing short words are generally considered more readable than long sentences containing long words. A program to compute a text's average sentence length and the average word length might provide a rough analysis of style.

Let's start with counting the words in a single sentence and finding the average word length. This task requires locating the words in a string. Fortunately, Python includes a set of string operations called **methods** that make tasks like this one easy. In the next session, we use the string method **split** to obtain a list of the words contained in an input string. We then print the length of the list, which equals the number of words, and compute and print the average of the lengths of the words in the list.

```
>>> sentence = input("Enter a sentence: ")
Enter a sentence: This sentence has no long words.
```

```
>>> listOfWords = sentence.split()
>>> print("There are", len(listOfWords), "words.")
There are 6 words.
>>> sum = 0
>>> for word in listOfWords:
        sum += len(word)
>>> print("The average word length is", sum / len(listOfWords))
The average word length is 4.5
```

A method behaves like a function but has a slightly different syntax. Unlike a function, a method is always called with a given data value called an **object**, which is placed before the method name in the call. The syntax of a method call is the following:

<an object>.<method name>(<argument-1>,..., <argument-n>)

Methods can also expect arguments and return values. A method knows about the internal state of the object with which it is called. Thus, the method **split** in our example builds a list of the words in the string object to which **sentence** refers and returns it.

In short, methods are as useful as functions, but you need to get used to the dot notation, which you have already seen when using a function associated with a module. In Python, all data values are in fact objects, and every data type includes a set of methods to use with objects of that type.

Table 4-2 lists some useful string methods. You can view the complete list and the documentation of the string methods by entering **dir(str)** at a shell prompt; you enter **help(str.<method-name>)** to receive documentation

Table 4-2 Some useful string methods, with the variable **s** used to refer to any string

String Method	What it Does
s.center(width)	Returns a copy of s centered within the given number of columns.
s.count(sub [, start [, end]])	Returns the number of nonoverlapping occurrences of substring sub in s. Optional arguments start and end are interpreted as in slice notation.
s.endswith(sub)	Returns True if s ends with sub or False otherwise.
s.find(sub [, start [, end]])	Returns the lowest index in s where substring sub is found. Optional arguments start and end are interpreted as in slice notation.
s.isalpha()	Returns True if s contains only letters or False otherwise.
s.isdigit()	Returns True if s contains only digits or False otherwise.
s.join(sequence)	Returns a string that is the concatenation of the strings in the sequence. The separator between elements is s.
s.lower()	Returns a copy of s converted to lowercase.
s.replace(old, new [, count])	Returns a copy of s with all occurrences of substring old replaced by new. If the optional argument count is given, only the first count occurrences are replaced.
s.split([sep])	Returns a list of the words in s, using sep as the delimiter string. If sep is not specified, any whitespace string is a separator.
s.startswith(sub)	Returns True if s starts with sub or False otherwise.
s.strip([aString])	Returns a copy of s with leading and trailing whitespace (tabs, spaces, newlines) removed. If aString is given, remove characters in aString instead.
s.upper()	Returns a copy of s converted to uppercase.

on the use of an individual method. Note that some arguments in this documentation might be enclosed in square brackets ([]). These indicate that the arguments are optional and may be omitted when the method is called.

The next session shows some string methods in action:

```
>>> s = "Hi there!"
>>> len(s)
9
>>> s.center(11)
' Hi there! '
>>> s.count('e')
2
>>> s.endswith("there!")
True
>>> s.startswith("Hi")
True
>>> s.find("the")
3
>>> s.isalpha()
False
>>> "abc".isalpha()
True
>>> "326".isdigit()
True
>>> words = s.split()
>>> words
['Hi', 'there!']
>>> "".join(words)
'Hithere!'
>>> " ". join(words)
'Hi there!'
>>> s.lower()
'hi there!'
>>> s.upper()
'HI THERE!'
>>> s.replace('i', 'o')
'Ho there!'
>>> " Hi there! ".strip()
'Hi there!'
```

Now that you know about the string method **split**, you are in a position to use a more general strategy for extracting a filename's extension than the one used earlier in this chapter. The method **split** returns a list of words in the string upon which it is called. This method assumes that the default separator character between the words is a space. You can override this assumption by passing a period as an argument to **split**, as shown in the next session:

```
>>> "myfile.txt".split('.')
['myfile', 'txt']
>>> "myfile.py".split('.')
```

```
['myfile', 'py']
>>> "myfile.html".split('.')
['myfile', 'html']
```

Note that the extension, regardless of its length, is the last string in each list. You can now use the subscript `[-1]`, which also extracts the last element in a list, to write a general expression for obtaining any filename's extension, as follows:

```
filename.split('.')[-1]
```

Exercise 4-4

1. Assume that the variable **data** refers to the string **"Python rules!"**. Use a string method from Table 4-2 to perform the following tasks:

   a. Obtain a list of the words in the string.
   b. Convert the string to uppercase.
   c. Locate the position of the string **"rules"**.
   d. Replace the exclamation point with a question mark.

2. Using the value of **data** from Exercise 1, write the values of the following expressions:

   a. `data.endswith('i')`
   b. `"totally ".join(data.split())`

4.5 Text Files

So far in this book, you have seen examples of programs that have taken input data from users at the keyboard. Most of these programs can receive their input from text files as well. A **text file** is a software object that stores data on a permanent medium such as a disk, CD, or flash memory. When compared to keyboard input from a human user, the main advantages of taking input data from a file are the following:

- The data set can be much larger.

- The data can be input much more quickly and with less chance of error.

- The data can be used repeatedly with the same program or with different programs.

Text Files and Their Format

Using a text editor such as Notepad or TextEdit, you can create, view, and save data in a text file (but be careful: some text editors use RTF as a default format for text, so you should make sure to change this to "Plain text" in your editor's preferences if that is the case). Your Python programs can output data to a text file, a procedure explained later in this section. The data in a text file can be viewed as characters, words, numbers, or lines of text, depending on the text file's format and on the purposes for which the data are used. When the data are numbers (either integers or floats), they must be separated by white space characters—spaces, tabs, and newlines—in the file. For example, a text file containing six floating-point numbers might look like

34.6   22.33   66.75

77.12   21.44   99.01

when examined with a text editor. Note that this format includes a space or a newline as a separator of items in the text.

All data output to or input from a text file must be strings. Thus, numbers must be converted to strings before output, and these strings must be converted back to numbers after input.

Writing Text to a File

Data can be output to a text file using a file object. Python's open function, which expects a file name and a **mode string** as arguments, opens a connection to the file on disk and returns a file object.

The mode string is **'r'** for input files and **'w'** for output files. Thus, the following code opens a file object on a file named **myfile.txt** for output:

```
>>> f = open("myfile.txt", 'w')
```

If the file does not exist, it is created with the given filename. If the file already exists, Python opens it. When an existing file is opened for output, any data already in it are erased.

String data are written (or output) to a file using the method **write** with the file object. The **write** method expects a single string argument. If you want the output text to end with a newline, you must include the escape character **'\n'** in the string. The next statement writes two lines of text to the file:

```
>>> f.write("First line.\nSecond line.\n")
```

When all of the outputs are finished, the file should be closed using the method **close**, as follows:

```
>>> f.close()
```

Failure to close an output file can result in data being lost. The reason for this is that many systems accumulate data values in a **buffer** before writing them out as large chunks; the **close** operation guarantees that data in the final chunk are output successfully.

Writing Numbers to a File

The file method **write** expects a string as an argument. Therefore, other types of data, such as integers or floating-point numbers, must first be converted to strings before being written to an output file. In Python, the values of most data types can be converted to strings by using the **str** function. The resulting strings are then written to a file with a space or a newline as a separator character.

The next code segment illustrates the output of integers to a text file. Five hundred random integers between 1 and 500 are generated and written to a text file named **integers.txt**. The newline character is the separator.

```
import random
f = open("integers.txt", 'w')
for count in range(500):
    number = random.randint(1, 500)
    f.write(str(number) + '\n')
f.close()
```

Reading Text from a File

You open a file for input in a similar manner to opening a file for output. The only thing that changes is the mode string, which, in the case of opening a file for input, is **'r'**. However, if a file with that name is not accessible, Python raises an error. Here is the code for opening **myfile.txt** for input:

```
>>> f = open("myfile.txt", 'r')
```

There are several ways to read data from an input file. The simplest way is to use the file method **read** to input the entire contents of the file as a single string. If the file contains multiple lines of text, the newline characters will be embedded in this string. The next session shows how to use the method **read**:

```
>>> text = f.read()
>>> text
'First line.\nSecond line.\n'
>>> print(text)
First line.
Second line.
```

After input is finished, another call to **read** would return an empty string to indicate that the end of the file has been reached. To repeat an input, the file must be reopened in order to "rewind" it for another input process. It is not necessary to close the file. Alternatively, an application might read and process the text one line at a time. A **for** loop accomplishes this nicely. The **for** loop views a file object as a sequence of lines of text. On each pass through the loop, the loop variable is bound to the next line of text in the sequence. Here is a session that reopens our example file and visits the lines of text in it:

```
>>> f = open("myfile.txt", 'r')
>>> for line in f:
        print(line)
First line.
Second line.
```

Note that **print** appears to output an extra newline. This is because each line of text input from the file retains its newline character.

In cases where you might want to read a specified number of lines from a file (say, the first line only), you can use the file method **readline**. The **readline** method consumes a line of input and returns this string, including the newline. If **readline** encounters the end of the file, it returns the empty string. The next code segment uses our old friend, the **while True** loop, to input all of the lines of text with **readline**:

```
>>> f = open("myfile.txt", 'r')
>>> while True:
        line = f.readline()
        if line == "":
            break
        print(line)
First line.
Second line.
```

Reading Numbers from a File

All of the file input operations return data to the program as strings. If these strings represent other types of data, such as integers or floating-point numbers, the programmer must convert them to the appropriate types before manipulating them further. In Python, the string representations of integers and floating-point numbers can be converted to the numbers themselves by using the functions **int** and **float**, respectively.

When reading data from a file, another important consideration is the format of the data items in the file. Earlier, we showed an example code segment that output integers separated by newlines to a text file. During input, these data can be read with a simple **for** loop. This loop accesses a line of text on each pass. To convert this line to the integer contained in it, the programmer runs the string method **strip** to remove the newline and then runs the **int** function to obtain the integer value.

The next code segment illustrates this technique. It opens the file of random integers written earlier, reads them, and prints their sum.

```
f = open("integers.txt", 'r')
theSum = 0
for line in f:
    line = line.strip()
    number = int(line)
    theSum += number
print("The sum is", theSum)
```

Obtaining numbers from a text file in which they are separated by spaces is a bit trickier. One method proceeds by reading lines in a **for** loop, as before. But each line now can contain several integers separated by spaces. You can use the string method **split** to obtain a list of the strings representing these integers and then process each string in this list with another **for** loop.

The next code segment modifies the previous one to handle integers separated by spaces and/or newlines.

```
f = open("integers.txt", 'r')
theSum = 0
for line in f:
    wordlist = line.split()
    for word in wordlist:
        number = int(word)
        theSum += number
print("The sum is", theSum)
```

Note that the line does not have to be stripped of the newline, because **split** takes care of that automatically.

Table 4-3 summarizes the file operations discussed in this section. Note that the dot notation is not used with **open** function, which returns a new file object.

Table 4-3   Some file operations

Method	What it Does
open(filename, mode)	Opens a file at the given filename and returns a file object. The **mode** can be 'r', 'w', 'rw', or 'a'. The last two values, 'rw' and 'a', mean read/write and append, respectively.
f.close()	Closes an output file. Not needed for input files.
f.write(aString)	Outputs **aString** to a file.
f.read()	Inputs the contents of a file and returns them as a single string. Returns "" if the end of file is reached.
f.readline()	Inputs a line of text and returns it as a string, including the newline. Returns "" if the end of file is reached.

Accessing and Manipulating Files and Directories on Disk

As you probably know, the file system of a computer allows you to create folders or directories, within which you can organize files and other directories. The complete set of directories and files forms a tree-like structure, with a single **root directory** at the top and branches down to nested files and subdirectories. **Figure 4-6** shows a portion of a file system, with directories named `lambertk`, `parent`, `current`, `sibling`, and `child`. Each of the last four directories contains a distinct file named `myfile.txt`.

When you launch Python, either from the terminal or from IDLE, the shell is connected to a **current working directory**. At any point during the execution of a program, you can open a file in this directory just by using the file's name. However, you can also access any other file or directory within the computer's file system by using a **pathname**. A file's pathname specifies the chain of directories needed to access a file or directory. When the chain starts with the root directory, it's called an **absolute pathname**. When the chain starts from the current working directory, it's called a **relative pathname**.

An absolute pathname consists of one or more directory names, separated by the `'/'` character (for a Unix-based system and macOS) or the `'\'` character (for a Windows-based system). The root directory is the leftmost name and the target directory or file name is the rightmost name. The `'/'` character must begin an absolute pathname on Unix-based systems, and a disk drive letter must begin an absolute pathname on Windows-based systems. If you are mentioning a pathname in a Python string, you must escape each `'\'` character with another `'\'` character.

For example, on a macOS file system, if `Users` is the root directory above `lambertk` in Figure 4-6, then

Figure 4-6 A portion of a file system

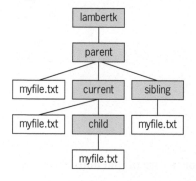

/Users/lambertk/parent/current/child/myfile.txt

is the absolute path to the file named **myfile.txt** in the `child` directory. On the `c:` drive of a Windows file system, the same pathname would be

C:\Users\lambertk\parent\current\child\myfile.txt

In the previous section, we used a filename to open a file in the current working directory for input or output. Now we can use an absolute pathname to open a file anywhere in the file system. Returning to Figure 4-6, to open the file **myfile.txt** in the `child` directory from the `current` directory, you can run the statement

```
f = open("/Users/lambertk/parent/current/child/myfile.txt", 'r')
```

Because absolute pathnames can become unwieldy, you can abbreviate a path by providing a relative pathname. Pathnames to files in directories below the current working directory begin with a subdirectory name and are completed with names and separator symbols on the way to the target filename. Paths to items in the other parts of the file system require you to specify a move "up" to one or more ancestor directories by using the .. symbol between the separators. **Table 4-4** lists the relative Unix pathnames for each instance of a file named **myfile.txt** from the `current` directory in Figure 4-6.

Table 4-4   Relative pathnames from current directory to myfile.txt in Figure 4-6

Pathname	Target Directory
myfile.txt	current
child/myfile.txt	child
../myfile.txt	parent
../sibling/myfile.txt	sibling

Note that relative pathnames do not begin with the separator symbol. To open the files named **myfile.txt** in the `child`, `parent`, and `sibling` directories, where `current` is the current working directory, you could use relative pathnames as follows:

```
childFile = open("child/myfile.txt", 'r')
parentFile = open("../myfile.txt", 'r')
siblingFile = open("../sibling/myfile.txt", 'r')
```

When designing Python programs that interact with files, it's a good idea to include error recovery. For example, before attempting to open a file for input, the programmer should check to see if a file with the given pathname exists on the disk. Tables 4-5 and 4-6 explain some file system functions, including a function (`os.path.exists`) that supports this checking. They also list some functions that allow your programs to navigate to a given directory in the file system, as well as to perform some disk housekeeping. The functions listed in Tables 4-5 and 4-6 are self-explanatory, and you are encouraged to experiment. For example, the following code segment will print all of the names of files in the current working directory that have a **.py** extension:

Table 4-5   Some file system functions

`os` Module Function	What it Does
`chdir(path)`	Changes the current working directory to `path`
`getcwd()`	Returns the path of the current working directory
`listdir(path)`	Returns a list of the names in the directory named `path`
`mkdir(path)`	Creates a new directory named `path` and places it in the current working directory
`remove(path)`	Removes the file named `path` from the current working directory
`rename(old, new)`	Renames the file or directory named `old` to `new`
`rmdir(path)`	Removes the directory named `path` from the current working directory
`sep`	A variable that holds the separator character (`'/'` or `'\'`) of the current file system

Table 4-6   More file system functions

`os.path` Module Function	What it Does
`exists(path)`	Returns `True` if `path` exists and `False` otherwise
`isdir(path)`	Returns `True` if `path` names a directory and `False` otherwise
`isfile(path)`	Returns `True` if `path` names a file and `False` otherwise
`getsize(path)`	Returns the size of the object names by `path` in bytes
`normcase(path)`	Converts path to a pathname appropriate for the current file system; for example, converts forward slashes to backslashes and letters to lowercase on a Windows system

```
import os
currentDirectoryPath = os.getcwd()
listOfFileNames = os.listdir(currentDirectoryPath)
for name in listOfFileNames:
    if ".py" in name:
        print(name)
```

Note that the operations listed in Tables 4-5 and 4-6 are functions, not methods. Thus, the call

```
os.rename("oldname.txt", "newname.txt")
```

is a function called on its defining module, not a method called on an object.

Exercise 4-5

1. Write a code segment that opens a file named **myfile.txt** for input and prints the number of lines in the file.

2. Write a code segment that opens a file for input and prints the number of four-letter words in the file.

3. Assume that a file contains integers separated by newlines. Write a code segment that opens the file and prints the average value of the integers.

4. Write a code segment that prints the names of all of the items in the current working directory.

5. Write a code segment that prompts the user for a filename. If the file exists, the program should print its contents on the terminal. Otherwise, it should print an error message.

Case Study 4-1 | Text Analysis

In 1949, Dr. Rudolf Flesch published *The Art of Readable Writing*, in which he proposed a measure of text readability known as the Flesch Index. This index is based on the average number of syllables per word and the average number of words per sentence in a piece of text. Index scores usually range from 0 to 100, and they indicate readable prose for the following grade levels:

Flesch Index	Grade Level of Readability
0–30	College
50–60	High school
90–100	Fourth grade

In this case study, we develop a program that computes the Flesch Index for a text file.

Request

Write a program that computes the Flesch Index and grade level for text stored in a text file.

Analysis

The input to this program is the name of a text file. The outputs are the number of sentences, words, and syllables in the file, as well as the file's Flesch Index and grade level equivalent.

During analysis, we consult experts in the problem domain to learn any information that might be relevant in solving the problem. For our problem, this information includes the definitions of *sentence*, *word*, and *syllable*. For the purposes of this program, these terms are defined in Table 4-7.

Table 4-7 Definitions of items used in the text analysis program

Word	Any sequence of non-whitespace characters.
Sentence	Any sequence of words ending in a period, question mark, exclamation point, colon, or semicolon.
Syllable	Any word of three characters or less; or any vowel (a, e, i, o, u) or pair of consecutive vowels, except for a final -es, -ed, or -e that is not -le.

Note that the definitions of *word* and *sentence* are approximations. Some words, such as *doubles* and *kettles*, end in *-es* but will be counted as having one syllable, and an ellipsis (…) will be counted as three syllables.

Flesch's formula to calculate the index F is the following:

$$F = 206.835 - 1.015 \times (words / sentences) - 84.6 \times (syllables / words)$$

The Flesch–Kincaid Grade Level Formula is used to compute the equivalent grade level G:

$$G = 0.39 \times (words / sentences) + 11.8 \times (syllables / words) - 15.59$$

Design

This program will perform the following tasks:

1. Receive the filename from the user, open the file for input, and input the text.

2. Count the sentences in the text.

3. Count the words in the text.

4. Count the syllables in the text.

5. Compute the Flesch Index.

6. Compute the grade level equivalent.

7. Print these two values with the appropriate labels, as well as the counts from tasks 2–4.

The first and last tasks require no design. Let's assume that the text is input as a single string from the file and is then processed in tasks 2–4. These three tasks can be designed as code segments that use the input string and produce an integer value. Task 5, computing the Flesch Index, uses the three integer results of tasks 2–4 to compute the Flesch Index. Finally, task 6 is a code segment that uses the same integers and computes the grade level equivalent. The five tasks are listed in Table 4-8, where **text** is a variable that refers to the string read from the file.

All the real work is done in the tasks that count the items:

- Add the number of characters in **text** that end the sentences. These characters were specified in analysis, and the string method **count** is used to count them in the algorithm.

(continues)

- Split **text** into a list of words and determine the **text** length.
- Count the syllables in each word in **text**.

Table 4-8 The tasks defined in the text analysis program

Task	What it Does
count the sentences	Counts the number of sentences in **text**.
count the words	Counts the number of words in **text**.
count the syllables	Counts the number of syllables in **text**.
compute the Flesch Index	Computes the Flesch Index for the given numbers of sentences, words, and syllables.
compute the grade level	Computes the grade level equivalent, to the nearest whole number, for the given numbers of sentences, words, and syllables.

The third task is the most complex. For each word in the text, we must count the syllables in that word. From analysis, we know that each distinct vowel counts as a syllable, unless it is in the endings *-ed*, *-es*, or *-e* (but not *-le*). For now, we ignore the possibility of consecutive vowels.

Implementation (Coding)

The main tasks are marked off in the program code with a blank line and a comment.

```
"""
Program: textanalysis.py
Author: Ken
Computes and displays the Flesch Index and the Grade Level Equivalent for the
readability of a text file.
"""
# Take the inputs
fileName = input("Enter the file name: ")
inputFile = open(fileName, 'r')
text = inputFile.read()
# Count the sentences
 sentences = text.count('.') + text.count('?') + \
             text.count(':') + text.count(';') + \
             text.count('!')
# Count the words
words = len(text.split())
# Count the syllables
syllables = 0
vowels = "aeiouAEIOU"
for word in text.split():
    for vowel in vowels:
        syllables += word.count(vowel)
    for ending in ['es', 'ed', 'e']:
        if word.endswith(ending):
```

```
                syllables -= 1
            if word.endswith('le'):
                syllables += 1
# Compute the Flesch Index and Grade Level
index = 206.835 - 1.015 * (words / sentences) - \
        84.6 * (syllables / words)
level = round (0.39 * (words / sentences) + 11.8 * \
        (syllables / words) - 15.59)
# Output the results
print("The Flesch Index is", index)
print("The Grade Level Equivalent is", level)
print(sentences, "sentences")
print(words, "words")
print(syllables, "syllables")
```

Testing

Although the main tasks all collaborate in the text analysis program, they can be tested more or less independently before the entire program is tested. After all, there is no point in running the complete program if you are unsure that even one of the tasks works correctly.

This kind of procedure is called **bottom-up testing**. Each task is coded and tested before it is integrated into the overall program. After you have written code for one or two tasks, you can test them in a short script. This script is called a **driver**. For example, here is a driver that tests the code for computing the Flesch Index and the grade level equivalent without using a text file:

```
"""
Program: fleschdriver.py
Author: Ken
Test driver for Flesch Index and Grade level.
"""
sentences = int(input("Sentences: "))
words = int(input("Words: "))
syllables = int(input("Syllables: "))
index = 206.835 - 1.015 * (words / sentences) - \
        84.6 * (syllables / words)
print("Flesch Index:", index)
level = round(0.39 * (words / sentences) + 11.8 * \
        (syllables / words) - 15.59)
print("Grade Level:", level)
```

This driver allows the programmer not only to verify the two tasks but also to obtain some data to use when testing the complete program later on. For example, the programmer can supply a text file that contains the number of sentences, words, and syllables already tested in the driver, and then compare the two test results.

In bottom-up testing, the lower-level tasks must be developed and tested before those tasks that depend on the lower-level tasks.

When you have tested all of the parts, you can integrate them into the complete program. The test data at that point should be short files that produce the expected results. Then, you should use longer files. For example, you might see if plaintext versions of Dr. Seuss's *Green Eggs and Ham* and Shakespeare's *Hamlet* produce grade levels of 5th grade and 12th grade, respectively. Or you could test the program with its own source program file—but we predict that its readability will seem quite low, because it lacks most of the standard end-of-sentence marks!

Fail-Safe Programming

Programs that work with text files face challenges dealing with conditions in the "outside world" that could cause errors. For example, a program might attempt to open an input file that does not exist in external storage, or, if the file does exist, it might contain data that are not in the expected format. These two types or errors, among others, can be caught and dealt with at runtime, thus allowing the program to recover gracefully.

Earlier in this chapter, you saw a short program that prints the sum of the integers in a text file. This program makes two critical assumptions about the input file:

1. That it exists in external storage.

2. That it contains words that consist of decimal digits.

The program will run correctly if both conditions are true, but what happens when the file is unavailable or it contains a word with letters or punctuation marks? In the case of a missing input file, we see a **FileNotFoundError** at runtime:

```
Traceback (most recent call last):
  File "/Users/lambertk/pythonfiles/sumintegers.py", line 1, in <module>
    f = open("integers.txt", 'r')
FileNotFoundError: [Errno 2] No such file or directory: 'integers.txt'
```

In the case where the input file does exist but at least one word, such as "Ken," does not consist of digits, we see a **ValueError** at runtime:

```
Traceback (most recent call last):
  File "/Users/lambertk/pythonfiles/sumintegers.py", line 11, in <module>
    number = int(word)
ValueError: invalid literal for int() with base 10: 'Ken'
```

To handle these possible errors and recover from them, the program can check the conditions and print the appropriate error messages if they are not satisfied. Here is a revised program that performs these tests and responds in a robust manner:

```
import os.path
fileName = "integers.txt"
if os.path.exists(fileName):  # Check for missing file
```

```
f = open(fileName, 'r')
theSum = 0
invalidInteger = False
for line in f:
    wordlist = line.split()
    for word in wordlist:
        if word.isdigit():  # Check for valid integer
            number = int(word)
            theSum += number
        else:
            invalidInteger = True
            print("Invalid integer in file: ", word)
            break
if not invalidInteger:
    print("The sum is", theSum)
else:
    print("The file", fileName, "does not exist")
```

Although the logic of the nested **if-else** statements is somewhat convoluted in this code, the extra effort to produce a robust program when working with text files is well worth it.

Summary

- A string is a sequence of zero or more characters. The **len** function returns the number of characters in its string argument. Each character occupies a position in the string. The positions range from 0 to the length of the string minus 1.

- A string is an immutable data structure. Its contents can be accessed, but its structure cannot be modified.

- The subscript operator [] can be used to access a character at a given position in a string. The operand or index inside the subscript operator must be an integer expression whose value is less than the string's length. A negative index can be used to access a character at or near the end of the string, starting with –1.

- A subscript operator can also be used for slicing—to fetch a substring from a string. When the subscript has the form [*<start>*:], the substring contains the characters from the **start** position to the end of the string. When the form is [:*<end>*], the positions range from the first one to **end - 1**. When the form is [*<start>*:*<end>*], the positions range from **start** to **end - 1**.

- The **in** operator is used to detect the presence or absence of a substring in a string. Its usage is *<substring>* **in** *<a string>*.

- A method is an operation that is used with an object. A method can expect arguments and return a value.

- The string type includes many useful methods for use with string objects.

- A text file is a software object that allows a program to transfer data to and from permanent storage on disk, CDs, or flash memory.

- A file object is used to open a connection to a text file for input or output.

- The file method `write` is used to output a string to a text file.

- The file method `read` inputs the entire contents of a text file as a single string.

- The file method `readline` inputs a line of text from a text file as a string.

- The `for` loop treats an input file as a sequence of lines. On each pass through the loop, the loop's variable is bound to a line of text read from the file.

Key Terms

absolute pathname	data encryption	octal
base 10 number system	data structure	pathname
base 2 number system	decimal number system	plaintext
binary number system	driver	positional notation
bit shift	extension	positional value
bit string	hexadecimal	relative pathname
block cipher	immutable data structure	root directory
bottom-up testing	index	slicing
buffer	invertible matrix	sniffing software
Caesar cipher	keys	subscript operator
cipher text	methods	substrings
current working directory	mode string	text file
decrypt	object	

Review Questions

For Questions 1–6, assume that the variable `data` refers to the string `"No way!"`.

1. The expression `len(data)` evaluates to

   a. 8   **c.** 6

   b. 7   **d.** 10

2. The expression `data[1]` evaluates to

   a. 'N'   **c.** 'p'

   b. 'o'   **d.** 'e'

3. The expression `data[-1]` evaluates to

   a. '!'   **c.** 'o'

   b. 'y'   **d.** 'u'

4. The expression `data[3:6]` evaluates to

   a. `'way!'`

   b. `'way'`

   c. `' wa'`

   d. `'w'`

5. The expression `data.replace("No", "Yes")` evaluates to

   a. `'No way!'`

   b. `'Yo way!'`

   c. `'Yes way!'`

   d. `'My way!'`

6. The expression `data.find("way!")` evaluates to

   a. 2

   b. 3

   c. True

   d. False

7. A Caesar cipher locates the coded text of a plaintext character

   a. a given distance to the left or to the right in the sequence of characters

   b. in an inversion matrix

   c. by converting it to its ASCII integer value

   d. by replacing it with its binary representation

8. The binary number 111 represents the decimal integer

   a. 111

   b. 3

   c. 7

   d. 8

9. Which of the following binary numbers represents the decimal integer value 8?

   a. 11111111

   b. 100

   c. 1000

   d. 10000

10. Which file method is used to read the entire contents of a file in a single operation?

   a. `readline`

   b. `read`

   c. a `for` loop

   d. `input`

Programming Exercises

1. Write a script in the file **encrypt.py** that inputs a line of plaintext and a distance value and outputs an encrypted text using a Caesar cipher. The script should work for any printable characters. (LO: 4.1, 4.2)

2. Write a script in the file **decrypt.py** that inputs a line of encrypted text and a distance value and outputs plaintext using a Caesar cipher. The script should work for any printable characters. (LO: 4.1, 4.2)

3. Modify the scripts of Programming Exercises 1 and 2 to encrypt and decrypt entire files of text. (LO: 4.1, 4.5)

4. Octal numbers have a base of eight and the digits 0–7. Write the scripts **octaltodecimal.py** and **decimaltooctal.py**, which convert numbers between the octal and decimal representations of integers. These scripts use algorithms that are similar to those of the `binaryToDecimal` and `decimalToBinary` scripts developed in Section 4-3. (LO: 4.1, 4.3)

5. A `bit shift` is a procedure whereby the bits in a bit string are moved to the left or to the right. For example, we can shift the bits in the string `1011` two places to the left to produce the string `1110`. Note that the leftmost two bits are wrapped around to the right side of the string in this operation. Define two scripts, **shiftleft.py** and **shiftright.py**, that expect a bit string as an input. The script `shiftLeft` shifts the bits in its input one place to the

left, wrapping the leftmost bit to the rightmost position. The script `shiftRight` performs the inverse operation. Each script prints the resulting string. (LO: 4.1, 4.4)

6. Use the strategy of the decimal to binary conversion and the bit shift left operation defined in Programming Exercise 5 to code a new encryption algorithm in the file **encrypt.py**. The algorithm should add 1 to each character's numeric ASCII value, convert it to a bit string, and shift the bits of this string one place to the left. A single-space character in the encrypted string separates the resulting bit strings. (LO: 4.1, 4.4)

7. Write a script in the file **decrypt.py** that decrypts a message coded by the method used in Programming Exercise 6. (LO: 4.1, 4.2, 4.4)

8. Write a script named **copyfile.py**. This script should prompt the user for the names of two text files. The contents of the first file should be input and written to the second file. (LO: 4.5)

9. Write a script named **numberlines.py**. This script creates a program listing from a source program. This script should prompt the user for the names of two files. The input filename could be the name of the script itself, but be careful to use a different output filename! The script copies the lines of text from the input file to the output file, numbering each line as it goes. The line numbers should be right-justified in four columns, so that the format of a line in the output file looks like this example: (LO: 4.5)

```
   1> This is the first line of text.
```

10. Write a script named **dif.py**. This script should prompt the user for the names of two text files and compare the contents of the two files to see if they are the same. If they are, the script should simply output **"Yes"**. If they are not, the script should output **"No"**, followed by the first lines of each file that differ from each other. The input loop should read and compare lines from each file. The loop should break as soon as a pair of different lines is found. (LO: 4.1, 4.5)

Debugging Exercise

Jack just completed the program for the Flesch text analysis from this chapter's case study. His supervisor, Jill, has discovered an error in his code. The error causes the program to count a syllable containing consecutive vowels as multiple syllables. Suggest a solution to this problem in Jack's code and modify the program so that it handles these cases correctly.

Files and Data Management

Prompt

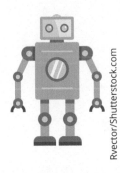

Rvector/Shutterstock.com

Ira Yapanda/Shutterstock.com

tele52/Shutterstock.com

You've been able to simulate some output, added methods, loops, and branching statements to help your robot perform the required actions of the organizations, its vendors, employees, and customers. One area that could continue to help your robot perform actions in bulk is to create a flat data file which would allow it to be automated. With that in mind, you're going to take the supplied csv file here and work with that file to perform the actions of getting the hardware, lumber, and paint, all of which will be supplied in the text file.

You will open the file, read each line, get the number of items for the robot to acquire in the order, and output that to the console. Upon reaching the end of the file, your method, outputOrderAuto, will output statements to reflect the items listed in the file:

Herby the robot added x # of hardware items to the order.

Herby the robot added x # of lumber items to the order.

Herby the robot added x # of paint items to the order.

At the end of the modification of this script, your robot controller script will have three methods:

pickItems

outputOrder

ourputOrderAuto

Examples:

Method Example:

```
def functionExample(pName):
 print("Hello "+pName)

functionExample("Dan")
```

121

Branching Example:

```
userAge = 10
if(userAge > 10)
        print("You are old enough to ride this ride")
```

Loops Example:

```
lumber = ["2x4", "2x8", "plywood"]
for x in lumber:
  print(x)
```

File handling:

```
# import the csv module


# file name
fName = "robotOrder.csv"


# initializing the container variables
field = []
row = []
# read file
with open(file_name, mode='r') as file:
        # Read the file lines
        lines = file.readlines()


        # Remove the header row
        lines.pop(0)


        # Initialize a dictionary to store the items
        items = {"Hardware": 0, "Lumber": 0, "Paint": 0}



    # get field names
    field = next(fReader)

    # get data row
    for nRow in fReader:
        row.append(nRow)
```

Hints

As you continue along in the development of your robot controller application, you've been asked to work with files. A common activity in the development of applications is the ability to work with files. Middleware applications can often serve as a bridge from one application to the next. In this case, our robot can source data files it can use to pick the order for the various customers. When working with a data file, usually a csv, xml, or json file, there are tools that exist in Python for working with that file type. So, in this script addition, you'll make use of the Python import csv tool and the open function to open the csv file supplied with this assignment.

You'll continue to loop through the file until you get to the end, keeping track of the various elements, which will be used to output at the end. You'll be making use of a couple of arrays to store the rows and the fields.

Answer

See Chapter 4_Files and Data Management.py

After Discussion

With this assignment, you've added an important component to the development of your robot controller, and this is the ability to keep track of data and the ability to output that data. Also, by keeping track of the data, you could perform any number of updates as a result, whether that is updating a database, filling a box, or whatever other actions could be driven by the data. In this assignment, you have now started working with Python imports, which can greatly expand your abilities and tools that you can work with in your applications. Well done!

## Chapter 5

Lists and Dictionaries

Learning Objectives

When you complete this chapter, you will be able to:

5.1 Construct lists and access items in those lists, use methods to manipulate lists, and perform traversals of lists to process items in the lists

5.2 Define simple functions that expect parameters and return values

5.3 Construct dictionaries and access entries in those dictionaries and use methods to manipulate dictionaries

---

As data-processing problems have become more complex, computer scientists have developed data structures to help solve them. A data structure combines several data values into a unit so they can be treated as one thing. The data elements within a data structure are usually organized in a special way that allows the programmer to access and manipulate them. As you saw in Chapter 4, a string is a data structure that organizes text as a sequence of characters. In this chapter, we explore the use of two other common data structures: the list and the dictionary. A **list** allows the programmer to manipulate a sequence of data values of any types. A **dictionary** organizes data values by association with other data values rather than by sequential position.

Lists and dictionaries provide powerful ways to organize data in useful and interesting applications. In addition to exploring the use of lists and dictionaries, this chapter also introduces the definition of simple functions. These functions help to organize program instructions, in much the same manner as data structures help to organize data.

5.1 Lists

A list is a sequence of data values called **items** or **elements**. An item can be of any type. Here are some real-world examples of lists:

- A shopping list for the grocery store
- A to-do list

- A roster for an athletic team
- A guest list for a wedding
- A recipe, which is a list of instructions
- A text document, which is a list of lines

The logical structure of a list resembles the structure of a string. Each of the items in a list is ordered by position. Like a character in a string, each item in a list has a unique index that specifies its position. The index of the first item is 0, and the index of the last item is the length of the list minus 1. As sequences, lists and strings share many of the same operators, but they include different sets of methods, which are examined in detail in the following sections.

List Literals and Basic Operators

As you have seen, literal string values are written as sequences of characters enclosed in quote marks. In Python, a list literal is written as a sequence of data values separated by commas. The entire sequence is enclosed in square brackets ([and]). Here are some example list literals:

```
[1951, 1969, 1984]                 # A list of integers
["apples", "oranges", "cherries"]  # A list of strings
[]                                 # An empty list
```

You can also use other lists as elements in a list, thereby creating a list of lists. Here is one example of such a list:

```
[[5, 9], [541, 78]]
```

It is interesting that when the Python interpreter evaluates a list literal, each of the elements is evaluated as well. When an element is a number or a string, that literal is included in the resulting list. However, when the element is a variable or any other expression, its value is included in the list, as shown in the following session:

```
>>> import math
>>> x = 2
>>> [x, math.sqrt(x)]
[2, 1.4142135623730951]
>>> [x + 1]
[3]
```

Thus, you can think of the [] delimiters as a kind of function, like **print**, which evaluates its arguments before using their values.

You can also build lists of integers using the **range** and **list** functions introduced in Chapter 3. The next session shows the construction of two lists and their assignment to variables:

```
>>> first = [1, 2, 3, 4]
>>> second = list(range(1, 5))
>>> first
[1, 2, 3, 4]
```

```
>>> second
[1, 2, 3, 4]
```

The **list** function can build a list from any iterable sequence of elements, such as a string:

```
>>> third = list("Hi there!")
>>> third
['H', 'i', ' ', 't', 'h', 'e', 'r', 'e', '!']
```

The function **len** and the subscript operator [] work just as they do for strings:

```
>>> len(first)
4
>>> first[0]
1
>>> first[2:4]
[3, 4]
```

Concatenation (+) and equality (==) also work as expected for lists:

```
>>> first + [5, 6]
[1, 2, 3, 4, 5, 6]
>>> first == second
True
```

The **print** function strips the quotation marks from a string, but it does not alter the look of a list:

```
>>> print("1234")
1234
>>> print([1, 2, 3, 4])
[1, 2, 3, 4]
```

To print the contents of a list without the brackets and commas, you can use a **for** loop, as follows:

```
>>> for number in [1, 2, 3, 4]:
        print(number, end = " ")
1 2 3 4
```

Finally, you can use the **in** operator to detect the presence or absence of a given element:

```
>>> 3 in [1, 2, 3]
True
>>> 0 in [1, 2, 3]
False
```

Table 5-1 summarizes these operators and functions, where **L** refers to a list.

Table 5-1 Some operators and functions used with lists

Operator or Function	What it Does
L[<*an integer expression*>]	Subscript used to access an element at the given index position
L[<*start*>:<*end*>]	Slices for a sublist; returns a new list
L1 + L2	List concatenation; returns a new list consisting of the elements of the two operands
print(L)	Prints the literal representation of the list
len(L)	Returns the number of elements in the list
list(range(<*upper*>))	Returns a list containing the integers in the range 0 through upper - 1
==, !=, <, >, <=, >=	Compares the elements at the corresponding positions in the operand lists; returns **True** if all the results are true, or **False** otherwise
for <*variable*> in L: <*statement*>	Iterates through the list, binding the variable to each element
<*any value*> in L	Returns **True** if the value is in the list or **False** otherwise

Replacing an Element in a List

The examples discussed thus far might lead you to think that a list behaves exactly like a string. However, there is one huge difference. Because a string is immutable, its structure and contents cannot be changed. But a list is changeable—that is, it is mutable. At any point in a list's lifetime, elements can be inserted, removed, or replaced. The list itself maintains its identity, but its internal state—its length and its contents—can change.

The subscript operator is used to replace an element at a given position, as shown in the next session:

```
>>> example = [1, 2, 3, 4]
>>> example
[1, 2, 3, 4]
>>> example[3] = 0
>>> example
[1, 2, 3, 0]
```

Note that the subscript operation refers to the target of the assignment statement, which is not the list but an element's position within it. Much of list processing involves replacing each element with the result of applying some operation to that element. The following discussion presents two examples of how this is done.

The first session shows how to replace each number in a list with its square:

```
>>> numbers = [2, 3, 4, 5]
>>> numbers
[2, 3, 4, 5]
>>> for index in range(len(numbers)):
        numbers[index] = numbers[index] ** 2
>>> numbers
[4, 9, 16, 25]
```

Note that the code uses a **for** loop over an index rather than a **for** loop over the list elements, because the index is needed to access the positions for the replacements. The next session uses the string method **split** to extract a list of the words in a sentence. These words are then converted to uppercase letters within the list:

```
>>> sentence = "This example has five words."
>>> words = sentence.split()
>>> words
['This', 'example', 'has', 'five', 'words.']
>>> for index in range(len(words)):
        words[index] = words[index].upper()
>>> words
['THIS', 'EXAMPLE', 'HAS', 'FIVE', 'WORDS.']
```

List Methods for Inserting and Removing Elements

The **list** type includes several methods for inserting and removing elements. These methods are summarized in **Table 5-2**, where **L** refers to a list. To learn more about each method, enter **help(list.<method name>)** in a Python shell.

Table 5-2 **list** methods for inserting and removing elements

list Method	What it Does
L.append(element)	Adds element to the end of L.
L.extend(aList)	Adds the elements of aList to the end of L.
L.insert(index, element)	Inserts element at index if index is less than the length of L. Otherwise, inserts element at the end of L.
L.pop()	Removes and returns the element at the end of L.
L.pop(index)	Removes and returns the element at index.

The method **insert** expects an integer index and the new element as arguments. When the index is less than the length of the list, this method places the new element before the existing element at that index, after shifting elements to the right by one position. At the end of the operation, the new element occupies the given index position. When the index is greater than or equal to the length of the list, the new element is added to the end of the list. The next session shows **insert** in action:

```
>>> example = [1, 2]
>>> example
[1, 2]
>>> example.insert(1, 10)
>>> example
[1, 10, 2]
>>> example.insert(3, 25)
>>> example
[1, 10, 2, 25]
```

The method **append** is a simplified version of **insert**. The method **append** expects just the new element as an argument and adds the new element to the end of the list. The method **extend** performs a similar operation but adds the elements of its list argument to the end of the list. The next session shows the differences between **append**, **extend**, and the **+** operator

```
>>> example = [1, 2]
>>> example
[1, 2]
>>> example.append(3)
>>> example
[1, 2, 3]
>>> example.extend([11, 12, 13])
>>> example
[1, 2, 3, 11, 12, 13]
>>> example + [14, 15]
[1, 2, 3, 11, 12, 13, 14, 15]
>>> example
[1, 2, 3, 11, 12, 13]
```

Note that the **+** operator builds and returns a new list containing the elements of the two operands, whereas **append** and **extend** modify the list object on which the methods are called.

The method **pop** is used to remove an element at a given position. If the position is not specified, **pop** removes and returns the last element. If the position is specified, **pop** removes the element at that position and returns it. In that case, the elements that followed the removed element are shifted one position to the left. The next session removes the last and first elements from the example list:

```
>>> example
[1, 2, 10, 11, 12, 13]
>>> example.pop()          # Remove the last element
13
>>> example
[1, 2, 10, 11, 12]
>>> example.pop(0)         # Remove the first element
1
>>> example
[2, 10, 11, 12]
```

Note that the method **pop** and the subscript operator expect the index argument to be within the range of positions currently in the list. If that is not the case, Python raises an exception.

Searching a List

After elements have been added to a list, a program can search for a given element. The **in** operator determines an element's presence or absence, but programmers often are more interested in the position of an element if it is found (for replacement, removal, or other use). Unfortunately, the **list** type does not include the convenient **find** method that is used with strings. Recall that **find** returns either the index of the given substring in a string or –1 if the substring is not found. Instead of **find**, you must use the method **index** to locate an element's position in a list. It is unfortunate that **index** raises an exception when the target element is not found. To guard against this unpleasant consequence, you must first use the **in** operator to test for presence and then the `index` method if this test returns `True`. The next code segment shows how this is done for an example list and target element:

```
aList = [34, 45, 67]
target = 45
if target in aList:
    print(aList.index(target))
else:
    print(-1)
```

Sorting a List

Although a list's elements are always ordered by position, it is possible to impose a **natural ordering** on them as well. In other words, you can arrange some elements in numeric or alphabetical order. A list of numbers in ascending order and a list of names in alphabetical order are sorted lists. When the elements can be related by comparing them for less than and greater than as well as equality, they can be sorted. The `list` method `sort` mutates a list by arranging its elements in ascending order. Here is an example of its use:

```
>>> example = [4, 2, 10, 8]
>>> example
[4, 2, 10, 8]
>>> example.sort()
>>> example
[2, 4, 8, 10]
```

Mutator Methods and the Value None

The functions and methods examined in previous chapters return a value that the caller can then use to complete its work. Mutable objects (such as lists) have some methods devoted entirely to modifying the internal state of the object. Such methods are called **mutators**. Examples are the `list` methods `insert`, `append`, `extend`, `pop`, and `sort`. Because a change of state is all that is desired, a mutator method usually returns no value of interest to the caller (but note that `pop` is an exception to this rule). Python nevertheless automatically returns the special value `None` even when a method does not explicitly return a value. We mention this now only as a warning against the following type of error. Suppose you forget that `sort` mutates a list, and instead you mistakenly think that it builds and returns a new, sorted list and leaves the original list unsorted. Then you might write code like the following to obtain what you think is the desired result:

```
>>> aList = aList.sort()
```

Unfortunately, after the list object is sorted, this assignment has the result of setting the variable `aList` to the value `None`. The next `print` statement shows that the reference to the list object is lost:

```
>>> print(aList)
None
```

Later in this book, you will learn how to make something useful out of `None`.

Aliasing and Side Effects

As you learned earlier, numbers and strings are immutable. That is, you cannot change their internal structure. However, because lists are mutable, you can replace, insert, or remove elements. The mutable property of lists leads to some interesting phenomena, as shown in the following session:

```
>>> first = [10, 20, 30]
>>> second = first
>>> first
[10, 20, 30]
>>> second
[10, 20, 30]
>>> first[1] = 99
>>> first
[10, 99, 30]
>>> second
[10, 99, 30]
```

In this example, a single list object is created and modified using the subscript operator. When the second element of the list named **first** is replaced, the second element of the list named **second** is replaced also. This type of change is what is known as a **side effect**. This happens because after the assignment **second = first**, the variables **first** and **second** refer to the exact same list object. They are **aliases** for the same object, as shown in **Figure 5-1**. This phenomenon is known as **aliasing**.

Figure 5-1   Two variables refer to the same list object

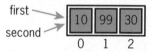

If the data are immutable strings, aliasing can save on memory. But as you might imagine, aliasing is not always a good thing when side effects are possible. Assignment creates an alias to the same object rather than a reference to a copy of the object. To prevent aliasing, you can create a new object and copy the contents of the original to it, as shown in the next session:

```
>>> third = []
>>> for element in first:
        third.append(element)
>>> first
[10, 99, 30]
>>> third
[10, 99, 30]
>>> first[1] = 100
>>> first
[10, 100, 30]
>>> third
[10, 99, 30]
```

The variables **first** and **third** refer to two different list objects, although their contents are initially the same, as shown in **Figure 5-2**. The important point is that they are not aliases, so you don't have to be concerned about side effects.

Figure 5-2   Two variables refer to different list objects

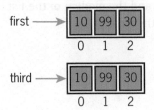

A simpler way to copy a list is to pass the source list to a call of the `list` function, as follows:

```
>>> third = list(first)
```

Equality: Object Identity and Structural Equivalence

Occasionally, programmers need to see whether two variables refer to the exact same object or to different objects. For example, you might want to determine whether one variable is an alias for another. The `==` operator returns `True` if the variables are aliases for the same object. Unfortunately, `==` also returns `True` if the contents of two different objects are the same. The first relation is called **object identity**, whereas the second relation is called **structural equivalence**. The `==` operator has no way of distinguishing between these two types of relations.

Python's `is` operator can be used to test for object identity. It returns `True` if the two operands refer to the exact same object, and it returns `False` if the operands refer to distinct objects (even if they are structurally equivalent). The next session shows the difference between `==` and `is`, and **Figure 5-3** depicts the objects in question.

```
>>> first = [20, 30, 40]
>>> second = first
>>> third = list(first)          # Or first[:]
>>> first == second
True
>>> first == third
True
>>> first is second
True
>>> first is third
False
```

Figure 5-3   Three variables and two distinct list objects

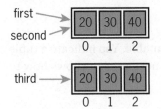

Example: Using a List to Find the Median of a Set of Numbers

Researchers who do quantitative analysis are often interested in the median of a set of numbers. For example, the U.S. government often gathers data to determine the median family income. Roughly speaking, the median is the value that is less than half the numbers in the set and greater than the other half. If the number of values in a list is odd, the median of the list is the value at the midpoint when the set of numbers is sorted; otherwise, the median is the average of the two values surrounding the midpoint. Thus, the median of the list [1, 3, 3, 5, 7] is 3, and the median of the list [1, 2, 4, 4] is also 3. The following script inputs a set of numbers from a text file and prints their median:

```
"""
File: median.py
Prints the median of a set of numbers in a file.
"""

fileName = input("Enter the filename: ")
f = open(fileName, 'r')
# Input the text, convert it to numbers, and
# add the numbers to a list
numbers = []
for line in f:
    words = line.split()
    for word in words:
        numbers.append(float(word))
# Sort the list and print the number at its midpoint
numbers.sort()
midpoint = len(numbers) // 2
print("The median is", end = " ")
if len(numbers) % 2 == 1:
    print(numbers[midpoint])
else:
    print((numbers[midpoint] + numbers[midpoint - 1]) / 2)
```

Note that the input process is the most complex part of this script. An accumulator list, **numbers**, is set to the empty list. The **for** loop reads each line of text and extracts a list of words from that line. The nested **for** loop traverses this list to convert each word to a number. The **list** method **append** then adds each number to the end of **numbers**, the accumulator list. The remaining lines of code locate the median value. When run with an input file whose contents are

```
3 2 7
8 2 1
5
```

the script produces the following output:

```
The median is 3.0
```

Tuples

A **tuple** is a type of sequence that resembles a list, except that, unlike a list, a tuple is immutable. You indicate a tuple literal in Python by enclosing its elements in parentheses instead of square brackets. The next session shows how to create several tuples:

```
>>> fruits = ("apple", "banana")
>>> fruits
('apple', 'banana')
>>> meats = ("fish", "poultry")
>>> meats
('fish', 'poultry')
>>> food = meats + fruits
```

```
>>> food
('fish', 'poultry', 'apple', 'banana')
>>> veggies = ["celery", "beans"]
>>> tuple(veggies)
('celery', 'beans')
```

Most of the operators and functions used with lists also apply to tuples. For the most part, anytime you foresee using a list whose structure will not change, you can, and should, use a tuple instead. For example, the set of vowels and the set of punctuation marks in a text-processing application could be represented as tuples of strings. You must be careful when using a tuple of one element. When that is the case, you place a comma after the expression within the parentheses, as shown in the following session:

```
>>> badSingleton = (3)
>>> badSingleton
3
>>> goodSingleton = (3,)
>>> goodSingleton
(3,)
```

Exercise 5-1

1. Assume that the variable **data** refers to the list [5, 3, 7]. Write the values of the following expressions:
   a. data[2]
   b. data[-1]
   c. len(data)
   d. data[0:2]
   e. 0 in data
   f. data + [2, 10, 5]
   g. tuple(data)

2. Assume that the variable data refers to the list [5, 3, 7]. Write the expressions that perform the following tasks:
   a. Replace the value at position 0 in **data** with that value's negation.
   b. Add the value 10 to the end of **data**.
   c. Insert the value 22 at position 2 in **data**.
   d. Remove the value at position 1 in **data**.
   e. Add the values in the list **newData** to the end of **data**.
   f. Locate the index of the value 7 in **data**, safely.
   g. Sort the values in **data**.

3. What is a mutator method? Explain why mutator methods usually return the value **None**.

4. Write a loop that accumulates the sum of the numbers in a list named **data**.

5. Assume that **data** refers to a list of numbers, and **result** refers to an empty list. Write a loop that adds the nonzero values in **data** to the **result** list, keeping them in their relative positions.

6. Write a loop that replaces each number in a list named **data** with its absolute value.

7. Describe the costs and benefits of aliasing, and explain how it can be avoided.

8. Explain the difference between structural equivalence and object identity.

5.2 Defining Simple Functions

Thus far, our programs have consisted of short code segments or scripts. Some of these have used built-in functions to do useful work. Some of our scripts might also be useful enough to package as functions to be used in other scripts. Moreover, defining our own functions allows us to organize our code in existing scripts more effectively. This section provides a brief overview of how to do this. We'll examine program design with functions in more detail in Chapter 6.

The Syntax of Simple Function Definitions

Most of the functions used thus far expect one or more arguments and return a value. Let's define a function that expects a number as an argument and returns the square of that number. First, we consider how the function will be used. Its name is **square**, so you can call it like this:

```
>>> square(2)
4
>>> square(6)
36
>>> square(2.5)
6.25
```

The definition of this function consists of a **header** and a **body**. Here is the code:

```
def square(x):
    """Returns the square of x."""
    return x * x
```

The header includes the keyword **def** as well as the function name and list of parameters. The function's body contains one or more statements, indented below the function header. Here is the syntax:

```
def <function name>(<parameter-1>, ..., <parameter-n>):
    <body>
```

The function's body contains the statements that execute when the function is called. Our function contains a single **return** statement, which simply returns the result of multiplying its argument, named **x**, by itself. Note that the argument name, also called a parameter, behaves just like a variable in the body of the function. This variable does not receive an initial value until the function is called. For example, when the function **square** is called with the argument 6, the parameter **x** will have the value 6 in the function's body.

Our function also contains a docstring. This string contains information about what the function does. It is displayed in the shell when the programmer enters **help(square)**.

A function can be defined in a Python shell, but it is more convenient to define it in an IDLE window, where it can be saved to a file. Loading the window into the shell then loads the function definition as well. Like variables, functions generally must be defined in a script before they are called in that same script.

Our next example function computes the average value in a list of numbers. The function might be used as follows:

```
>>> average([1, 3, 5, 7])
4.0
```

Here is the code for the function's definition:

```
def average(lyst):
    """Returns the average of the numbers in lyst."""
```

```
    theSum = 0
    for number in lyst:
        theSum += number
    return theSum / len(lyst)
```

Parameters and Arguments

A parameter is the name used in the function definition for an argument that is passed to the function when it is called. For now, the number and positions of the arguments of a function call should match the number and positions of the parameters in that function's definition. Some functions expect no arguments, so they are defined with no parameters.

The `return` Statement

The programmer places a **return** statement at each exit point of a function when that function should explicitly return a value. The syntax of the **return** statement for these cases is the following:

```
return <expression>
```

Upon encountering a **return** statement, Python evaluates the expression and immediately transfers control back to the caller of the function. The value of the expression is also sent back to the caller. If a function contains no **return** statement, Python transfers control to the caller after the last statement in the function's body is executed, and the special value **None** is automatically returned.

Boolean Functions

A Boolean function usually tests its argument for the presence or absence of some property. The function returns **True** if the property is present, or **False** otherwise. The next example shows the use and definition of the Boolean function odd, which tests a number to see whether it is odd.

```
>>> odd(5)
True
>>> odd(6)
False
def odd(x):
    """Returns True if x is odd or False otherwise."""
    if x % 2 == 1:
        return True
    else:
        return False
```

Note that this function has two possible exit points, in either of the alternatives within the **if/else** statement.

Defining a `main` Function

In scripts that include the definitions of several cooperating functions, it is often useful to define a special function named **main** that serves as the entry point for the script. This function usually expects no arguments and returns no value. Its purpose might be to take inputs, process them by calling other functions, and print the results. The definition of the **main** function and the other function definitions need appear in no particular order in the script, as long as **main** is called at the very end of the script. The next example shows a complete script that is organized in the manner just described. The **main** function prompts the user for a number, calls the **square** function to compute its square, and prints the result. You can define the **main** and the **square** functions in any order. When Python loads this module, the code for both function definitions is loaded and compiled, but not executed. Note that **main** is then called within an **if** statement as the last step in the script. This has the effect of transferring control to the first instruction in the **main** function's definition. When **square** is called from **main**, control is transferred from **main** to the first instruction in **square**. When a function completes execution, control returns to the next instruction in the caller's code.

```
"""
File: computesquare.py
Illustrates the definition of a main function.
"""

def main():
    """The main function for this script."""
    number = float(input("Enter a number: "))
    result = square(number)
    print("The square of", number, "is", result)

def square(x):
    """Returns the square of x."""
    return x * x

# The entry point for program execution
if __name__ == "__main__":
    main()
```

Like all scripts, the preceding script can be run from IDLE, run from a terminal command prompt, or imported as a module. When the script is imported as a module, the value of the module variable __name__ will be the name of the module, **"computeSquare"**. In that case, the **main** function is not called, but the script's functions become available to be called by other code. When the script is launched from IDLE or a terminal prompt, the value of the module variable __name__ will be **"__main__"**. In that case, the **main** function is called and the script runs as a standalone program. This mechanism aids in testing, as the script can be run repeatedly in the shell by calling **main()**, rather than reloading it from the editor's window. We will start defining and using a **main** function in our case studies from this point forward.

Exercise 5-2

1. What roles do the parameters and the **return** statement play in a function definition?

2. Define a function named **even**. This function expects a number as an argument and returns **True** if the number is divisible by 2, or it returns **False** otherwise. (*Hint:* A number is evenly divisible by 2 if the remainder is 0.)

3. Use the function **even** to simplify the definition of the function **odd** presented in this section.

4. Define a function named **summation**. This function expects two numbers, named **low** and **high**, as arguments. The function computes and returns the sum of the numbers between **low** and **high**, inclusive.

5. What is the purpose of a **main** function?

Case Study 5-1 | Generating Sentences

Can computers write poetry? We'll attempt to answer that question in this case study by giving a program a few words to play with.

Request

Write a program that generates sentences.

Analysis

Sentences in any language have a structure defined by a **grammar**. They also include a set of words from the **vocabulary** of the language. The vocabulary of a language like English consists of many thousands of words, and the grammar rules are quite complex. For the sake of simplicity this program will generate sentences from a simplified subset of English. The vocabulary will consist of sample words from several parts of speech, including nouns, verbs, articles, and prepositions. From these words, you can build noun phrases, prepositional phrases, and verb phrases. From these constituent phrases, you can build sentences. For example, the sentence "The girl hit the ball with the bat" contains three noun phrases, one verb phrase, and one prepositional phrase. Table 5-3 summarizes the grammar rules for this subset of English.

Table 5-3   The grammar rules for the sentence generator

Phrase	Its Constituents
Sentence	Noun phrase + Verb phrase
Noun phrase	Article + Noun
Verb phrase	Verb + Noun phrase + Prepositional phrase
Prepositional phrase	Preposition + Noun phrase

The rule for **Noun phrase** says that it is an **Article** followed by (+) a **Noun**. Thus, a possible noun phrase is "the bat." Note that some of the phrases in the left column of Table 5-3 also appear in the right column as constituents of other phrases. Although this grammar is much simpler than the complete set of rules for English grammar, you should still be able to generate sentences with quite a bit of structure.

The program will prompt the user for the number of sentences to generate. The proposed user interface follows:

```
Enter the number of sentences: 3
THE BOY HIT THE BAT WITH A BOY
THE BOY HIT THE BALL BY A BAT
THE BOY SAW THE GIRL WITH THE GIRL

Enter the number of sentences: 2
A BALL HIT A GIRL WITH THE BAT
A GIRL SAW THE BAT BY A BOY
```

Design

Of the many ways to solve the problem in this case study, perhaps the simplest is to assign the task of generating each phrase to a separate function. Each function builds and returns a string that represents its

(continues)

phrase. This string contains words drawn from the parts of speech and from other phrases. When a function needs an individual word, it is selected at random from the words in that part of speech. When a function needs another phrase, it calls another function to build that phrase. The results, all strings, are concatenated with spaces and returned.

The function for **Sentence** is the easiest. It just calls the functions for **Noun phrase** and **Verb phrase** and concatenates the results, as in the following:

```
def sentence():
    """Builds and returns a sentence."""
    return nounPhrase() + " " + verbPhrase() + "."
```

The function for **Noun phrase** picks an article and a noun at random from the vocabulary, concatenates them, and returns the result. We assume that the variables **articles** and **nouns** refer to collections of these parts of speech and develop these later in the design. The function **random.choice** returns a random element from such a collection.

```
def nounPhrase():
    """Builds and returns a noun phrase."""
    return random.choice(articles) + " " + random.choice(nouns)
```

The design of the remaining two phrase-structure functions is similar.

The **main** function drives the program with a count-controlled loop:

```
def main():
    """Allows the user to input the number of sentences to generate."""
    number = int(input("Enter the number of sentences: "))
    for count in range(number):
        print(sentence())
```

The variables **articles** and **nouns** used in the program's functions refer to the collections of actual words belonging to these two parts of speech. Two other collections, named **verbs** and **prepositions**, also will be used. The data structure used to represent a collection of words should allow the program to pick one word at random. Because the data structure does not change during the course of the program, you can use a tuple of strings. Four tuples serve as a common pool of data for the functions in the program and are initialized before the functions are defined.

Implementation (Coding)

When functions use a common pool of data, you should define or initialize the data before the functions are defined. Thus, the variables for the data are initialized just below the **import** statement.

```
"""
Program: generator.py
Author: Ken
Generates and displays sentences using simple grammar
and vocabulary. Words are chosen at random.
"""

import random
```

```
# Vocabulary: words in 4 different parts of speech
articles     =   ("A", "THE")
nouns        =   ("BOY", "GIRL", "BAT", "BALL")
verbs        =   ("HIT", "SAW", "LIKED")
prepositions =   ("WITH", "BY")

def sentence():
    """Builds and returns a sentence."""
    return nounPhrase() + " " + verbPhrase()

def nounPhrase():
    """Builds and returns a noun phrase."""
    return random.choice(articles) + " " + random.choice(nouns)

def verbPhrase():
    """Builds and returns a verb phrase."""
    return random.choice(verbs) + " " + nounPhrase() + " " + \
           prepositionalPhrase()

def prepositionalPhrase():
    """Builds and returns a prepositional phrase."""
    return random.choice(prepositions) + " " + nounPhrase()

def main():
    """Allows the user to input the number of sentences
    to generate."""
    number = int(input("Enter the number of sentences: "))
    for count in range(number):
        print(sentence())

# The entry point for program execution
if __name__ == "__main__":
    main()
```

Testing

It may not be poetry, but testing is still important. The functions developed in this case study can be tested in a bottom-up manner. To do so, you must initialize the data first. Then you can run the lowest-level function, **nounPhrase**, immediately to check its results, and you can work up to sentences from there.

On the other hand, testing can also follow the design, which took a top-down path. You might start by writing headers for all of the functions and simple **return** statements that return the functions' names. Then you can complete the code for the **sentence** function first, test it, and proceed downward from there. The wise programmer can also mix bottom-up and top-down testing as needed.

5.3 Dictionaries

Lists organize their elements by position. This mode of organization is useful when you want to locate the first element, the last element, or visit each element in a sequence. However, in some situations, the position of a datum in a structure is irrelevant because we're interested in its association with some other element in the structure. For example, you might want to look up Ethan's phone number but don't care where that number is in your contacts.

A dictionary organizes information by **association**, not position. For example, when you use a dictionary to look up the definition of "mammal," you don't start at page 1; instead, you turn directly to the words beginning with "M." Phone contacts, address books, encyclopedias, and other reference sources also organize information by association. In computer science, data structures organized by association are also called **tables** or **association lists**. In Python, a dictionary associates a set of **keys** with **values**. For example, the keys in *Webster's Dictionary* comprise the set of words, whereas the associated data values are their definitions. In this section, you examine the use of dictionaries in data processing.

Dictionary Literals

A Python dictionary is written as a sequence of key/value pairs separated by commas. These pairs are sometimes called **entries**. The entire sequence of entries is enclosed in curly braces ({ and }). A colon (:) separates a key and its value. Here are some example dictionaries:

A phone book: `{"Savannah":"476-3321", "Nathaniel":"351-7743"}`
Personal information: `{"Name":"Molly", "Age":18}`

You can even create an empty dictionary—that is, a dictionary that contains no entries. You would create an empty dictionary in a program that builds a dictionary from scratch. Here is an example of an empty dictionary:

`{}`

The keys in a dictionary can be data of any immutable types, including tuples, although keys normally are strings or integers. The associated values can be of any types. Although the entries may appear to be ordered in a dictionary, this ordering is not significant, and the programmer should not rely on it.

Adding Keys and Replacing Values

You add a new key/value pair to a dictionary by using the subscript operator `[]`. The form of this operation is the following:

```
<a dictionary>[<a key>] = <a value>
```

The next code segment creates an empty dictionary and adds two new entries:

```
>>> info = {}
>>> info["name"] = "Sandy"
>>> info["occupation"] = "hacker"
>>> info
{'name':'Sandy', 'occupation':'hacker'}
```

The subscript is also used to replace a value at an existing key, as follows:

```
>>> info["occupation"] = "manager"
>>> info
{'name':'Sandy', 'occupation':'manager'}
```

Here is a case of the same operation used for two different purposes: insertion of a new entry and modification of an existing entry. As a rule, when the key is absent in the dictionary, the key and its value are inserted; when the key already exists, its associated value is replaced.

Accessing Values

You can also use the subscript to obtain the value associated with a key. However, if the key is not present in the dictionary, Python raises an exception. Here are some examples, using the **info** dictionary, which was set up earlier:

```
>>> info["name"]
'Sandy'
>>> info["job"]
Traceback (most recent call last):
    File "<pyshell#1>", line 1, in <module>
        info["job"]
KeyError: 'job'
```

If the existence of a key is uncertain, the programmer can test for it using the operator **in**, as follows:

```
>>> if "job" in info:
        print(info["job"])
```

A far easier strategy is to use the method **get**. This method expects two arguments, a possible key and a default value. If the key is in the dictionary, the associated value is returned. However, if the key is absent, the default value passed to **get** is returned. Here is an example of the use of **get** with a default value of **None**:

```
>>> print(info.get("job", None))
None
```

Removing Keys

To delete an entry from a dictionary, one removes its key using the method **pop**. This method expects a key and an optional default value as arguments. If the key is in the dictionary, it is removed, and its associated value is returned. Otherwise, the default value is returned. If **pop** is used with just one argument, and this key is absent from the dictionary, Python raises an exception. The next session attempts to remove two keys and prints the values returned:

```
>>> print(info.pop("job", None))
None
>>> print(info.pop("occupation"))
manager
>>> info
{'name':'Sandy'}
```

Traversing a Dictionary

When a **for** loop is used with a dictionary, the loop's variable is bound to each key in an unspecified order. The next code segment prints all of the keys and their values in our **info** dictionary:

```
for key in info:
    print(key, info[key])
```

Alternatively, you could use the dictionary method `items()` to access the dictionary's entries. The next session shows a run of this method with a dictionary of grades:

```
>>> grades = {90:'A', 80:'B', 70:'C'}
>>> list(grades.items())
[(80,'B'), (90,'A'), (70,'C')]
```

Note that the entries are represented as tuples within the list. A tuple of variables can then access the key and value of each entry in this list within a `for` loop:

```
for (key, value) in grades.items():
    print(key, value)
```

The use of a tuple of variables rather than a simple variable in the `for` loop is a powerful way to implement this traversal. On each pass through the loop, the variables `key` and `value` within the tuple are assigned the key and value of the current entry in the list. The use of a structure containing variables to access data within another structure is called **pattern matching**.

If a special ordering of the keys is needed, you can obtain a list of keys using the `keys` method and process this list to rearrange the keys. For example, you can sort the list and then traverse it to print the entries of the dictionary in alphabetical order:

```
theKeys = list(info.keys())
theKeys.sort()
for key in theKeys:
    print(key, info[key])
```

To see the complete documentation for dictionaries, you can run `help(dict)` at a shell prompt. **Table 5-4** summarizes the commonly used dictionary operations, where `d` refers to a dictionary.

Table 5-4 Some commonly used dictionary operations

Dictionary Operation	What it Does
`len(d)`	Returns the number of entries in `d`
`d[key]`	Used for inserting a new key, replacing a value, or obtaining a value at an existing key
`d.get(key [, default])`	Returns the value if the key exists or returns the default if the key does not exist; raises an error if the default is omitted and the key does not exist
`d.pop(key [, default])`	Removes the key and returns the value if the key exists or returns the default if the key does not exist; raises an error if the default is omitted and the key does not exist
`list(d.keys())`	Returns a list of the keys
`list(d.values())`	Returns a list of the values
`list(d.items())`	Returns a list of tuples containing the keys and values for each entry
`d.clear()`	Removes all the keys
`for key in d:`	`key` is bound to each key in `d` in an unspecified order

Example: The Hexadecimal System Revisited

In Chapter 4, we discussed a method for converting numbers quickly between the binary and the hexadecimal systems. Now let's develop a Python function that uses that method to convert a hexadecimal number to a binary number. The algorithm visits each digit in the hexadecimal number, selects the corresponding four bits that represent that digit in binary, and adds these bits to a result string. You could express this selection process with a complex `if/else` statement, but there is an easier way. If you maintain the set of associations between hexadecimal digits and binary digits in a dictionary, then you can just look up each hexadecimal digit's binary equivalent with a subscript operation. Such a dictionary is sometimes called a lookup table. Here is the definition of the lookup table required for hex-to-binary conversions:

```
hexToBinaryTable = {'0':'0000', '1':'0001', '2':'0010',
                    '3':'0011', '4':'0100', '5':'0101',
                    '6':'0110', '7':'0111', '8':'1000',
                    '9':'1001', 'A':'1010', 'B':'1011',
                    'C':'1100', 'D':'1101', 'E':'1110',
                    'F':'1111'}
```

The function itself, named **convert**, is simple. It expects two parameters: a string representing the number to be converted and a table of associations of digits. Here is the code for the function, followed by a sample session:

```
def convert(number, table):
    """Builds and returns the base two representation of number."""
    binary = ""
    for digit in number:
        binary = binary + table[digit]
    return binary
>>> convert("35A", hexToBinaryTable)
'001101011010'
```

Note that you pass **hexToBinaryTable** as an argument to the function. The function then uses the associations in this particular table to perform the conversion. The function would serve equally well for conversions from octal to binary, provided that you set up and pass it an appropriate lookup table.

Example: Finding the Mode of a List of Values

The **mode** of a list of values is the value that occurs most frequently. The following script inputs a list of words from a text file and prints their mode. The script uses a list and a dictionary. The list is used to obtain the words from the file, as in earlier examples. The dictionary associates each unique word with the number of its occurrences in the list. The script also uses the function **max**, first introduced in Chapter 3, to compute the maximum of two values. When used with a single iterable argument, **max** returns the largest value contained therein. Here is the code for the script:

```
fileName = input("Enter the filename: ")
f = open(fileName, 'r')
# Input the text, convert its words to uppercase, and
# add the words to a list
words = []
for line in f:
    for word in line.split():
        words.append(word.upper())
# Obtain the set of unique words and their
# frequencies, saving these associations in
# a dictionary
theDictionary = {}
for word in words:
```

```
    number = theDictionary.get(word, None)
  if number == None:
      # word entered for the first time
      theDictionary[word] = 1
  else:
     # word already seen, increment its number
     theDictionary[word] = number + 1
# Find the mode by obtaining the maximum value
# in the dictionary and determining its key
theMaximum = max(theDictionary.values())
for key in theDictionary:
    if theDictionary[key] == theMaximum:
        print("The mode is", key)
        break
```

Exercise 5-3

1. Give three examples of real-world objects that behave like a dictionary.

2. Assume that the variable **data** refers to the dictionary **{'b':20, 'a':35}**. Write the values of the following expressions:

   a. data['a']
   b. data.get('c', None)
   c. len(data)
   d. data.keys()
   e. data.values()
   f. data.pop('b')
   g. data # After the pop above

3. Assume that the variable **data** refers to the dictionary **{'b':20, 'a':35}**. Write the expressions that perform the following tasks:

   a. Replace the value at the key **'b'** in **data** with that value's negation.
   b. Add the key/value pair **'c':40** to **data**.
   c. Remove the value at key **'b'** in **data**, safely.
   d. Print the keys in **data** in alphabetical order.

Case Study 5-2 | Nondirective Psychotherapy

In the early 1960s, the MIT computer scientist Joseph Weizenbaum developed a famous program called ELIZA that could converse with the computer user, mimicking a nondirective style of psychotherapy. The doctor in this kind of therapy is essentially a good listener who responds to the patient's statements by rephrasing them or indirectly asking for more information. To illustrate the use of data structures, we can develop a drastically simplified version of this program.

Request

Write a program that emulates a nondirective psychotherapist.

Analysis

Figure 5-4 shows the program's interface as it changes throughout a sequence of exchanges with the user.

Figure 5-4   A session with the doctor program

```
Good morning, I hope you are well today.
What can I do for you?

>> My mother and I don't get along
Why do you say that your mother and you don't get along

>> she always favors my sister
You seem to think that she always favors your sister

>> my dad and I get along fine
Can you explain why your dad and you get along fine

>> he helps me with my homework
Please tell me more

>> quit
Have a nice day!
```

When the user enters a statement, the program responds in one of two ways:

1. With a randomly chosen hedge, such as "Please tell me more."

2. By changing some key words in the user's input string and appending this string to a randomly chosen qualifier. Thus, to "My teacher always plays favorites," the program might reply, "Why do you say that your teacher always plays favorites?"

Design

The program consists of a set of collaborating functions that share a common data pool.

Two of the data sets are the hedges and the qualifiers. Because these collections do not change and their elements must be selected at random, you can use tuples to represent them. Their names, of course, are **hedges** and **qualifiers**.

The other set of data consists of mappings between first-person pronouns and second-person pronouns. For example, when the program sees "I" in a patient's input, it should respond with a sentence containing "you." The best type of data structure to hold these correlations is a dictionary. This dictionary is named **replacements**.

The **main** function displays a greeting, displays a prompt, and waits for user input. The following is pseudocode for the main loop:

```
output a greeting to the patient
while True
    prompt for and input a string from the patient
    if the string equals "Quit"
```

(continues)

```
        output a sign-off message to the patient
        break
    call another function to obtain a reply to this string
    output the reply to the patient
```

Our therapist might not be an expert, but it seems willing to go on forever. If the patient must quit to do something else, they can do so by typing "quit" to end the program.

The **reply** function expects the patient's string as an argument and returns another string as the reply. This function implements the two strategies for making replies suggested in the analysis phase. A quarter of the time a hedge is warranted. Otherwise, the function constructs its reply by changing the persons in the patient's input and appending the result to a randomly selected qualifier. The **reply** function calls yet another function, **changePerson**, to perform the complex task of changing persons.

```
def reply(sentence):
    """Builds and returns a reply to the sentence."""
    probability = random.randint(1, 4)
    if probability == 1:
        return random.choice(hedges)
    else:
        return random.choice(qualifiers) + changePerson(sentence)
```

The **changePerson** function extracts a list of words from the patient's string. It then builds a new list wherein any pronoun key in the replacements dictionary is replaced by its pronoun/value. This list is then converted back to a string and returned.

```
def changePerson(sentence):
    """Replaces first person pronouns with second person pronouns."""
    words = sentence.split()
    replyWords = []
    for word in words:
        replyWords.append(replacements.get(word, word))
    return " ".join(replyWords)
```

Note that the attempt to get a replacement from the **replacements** dictionary either succeeds and returns an actual replacement pronoun, or the attempt fails and returns the original word. The string method **join** glues together the words from the **replyWords** list with a space character as a separator.

Implementation (Coding)

The structure of this program resembles that of the sentence generator developed in the first case study of this chapter. The three data structures are initialized near the beginning of the program, and they never change. The three functions collaborate in a straightforward manner. Here is the code:

```
"""
Program: doctor.py
Author: Ken
Conducts an interactive session of nondirective
psychotherapy.
"""
```

```
import random

hedges = ("Please tell me more.",
          "Many of my patients tell me the same thing.",
          "Please continue.")

qualifiers = ("Why do you say that ",
              "You seem to think that ",
              "Can you explain why ")

replacements = {"I":"you", "me":"you", "my":"your",
                "we":"you", "us":"you", "mine":"yours"}

def reply(sentence):
    """Builds and returns a reply to the sentence."""
    probability = random.randint(1, 4)
    if probability == 1:
        return random.choice(hedges)
    else:
        return random.choice(qualifiers) + changePerson(sentence)

def changePerson(sentence):
    """Replaces first person pronouns with second person pronouns."""
    words = sentence.split()
    replyWords = []
    for word in words:
        replyWords.append(replacements.get(word, word))
    return " ".join(replyWords)

def main():
    """Handles the interaction between patient and doctor."""
    print("Good morning, I hope you are well today.")
    print("What can I do for you?")
    while True:
        sentence = input("\n>> ")
        if sentence.upper() == "QUIT":
            print("Have a nice day!")
            break
        print(reply(sentence))

# The entry point for program execution
if __name__ == "__main__":
    main()
```

(continues)

Testing

As in the sentence-generator program, the functions in this program can be tested in a bottom-up or a top-down manner. As you will see, the program's replies break down when the user addresses the therapist in the second person, when the user inputs contractions (e.g., "I'm" and "I'll"), when the user addresses the doctor directly with sentences like "You are not listening to me," and in many other ways. As you'll see in the Programming Exercises at the end of this chapter, with a little work you can make the replies more realistic.

Fail-Safe Programming

In Chapter 4, we examined the detection of and response to a type of error that can occur when a program processes data in text files—the data in that example are intended to represent integers but might not be in the proper format (words consisting of digits only). A similar situation can occur in cases of interactive input of numbers, where either integers or floating-point numbers are expected from the human user. For example, consider the two inputs from the tax calculator Case Study of Chapter 2:

```
grossIncome = float(input("Enter the gross income: "))
numDependents = int(input("Enter the number of dependents: "))
```

The **input** function returns a string in each case, which is then converted to a **float** or an **int**. The **float** function expects as an argument a string consisting of digits only or a string consisting of digits and a single decimal point. If this string contains any other character, Python raises a **ValueError** and halts the program at runtime. Likewise, the **int** function expects as an argument a string consisting of digits only, and if any other character is present, Python responds with a **ValueError**.

Clearly, interactive programs with numeric inputs can perform in a robust or fail-safe manner only if you add machinery that can detect and recover from such errors. This machinery could be provided in the form of two new functions, named **inputInt** and **inputFloat**. These functions would apply the type conversion functions to input strings only after users have successfully entered strings of the proper format. Each function would display error messages until the user enters a properly formed string. Our new functions could be used in any application requiring numeric inputs.

The next session shows the use of the **inputInt** function with two error cases:

```
>>> numDependents = inputInt("Enter the number of dependents: "))
Enter the number of dependents: 2.5
Error: the input must consist only of digits
Enter the number of dependents: Ken
Error: the input must consist only of digits
Enter the number of dependents: 2
2
>>>
```

We will explore how to develop such functions in Chapter 6.

Summary

- A list is a sequence of zero or more elements. The elements can be of any type. The `len` function returns the number of elements in its list argument. Each element occupies a position in the list. The positions range from 0 to the length of the list minus 1.

- Lists can be manipulated with many of the operators used with strings, such as the subscript, concatenation, comparison, and `in` operators. Slicing a list returns a sublist.

- The list is a mutable data structure. An element can be replaced with a new element, added to the list, or removed from the list. Replacement uses the subscript operator. The `list` type includes several methods for insertion and removal of elements.

- The method `index` returns the position of a target element in a list. If the element is not in the list, an error is raised.

- The elements of a list can be arranged in ascending order by calling the `sort` method.

- Mutator methods are called to change the state of an object. These methods usually return the value `None`. This value is automatically returned by any function or method that does not have a `return` statement.

- Assignment of one variable to another variable causes both variables to refer to the same data object. When two or more variables refer to the same data object, they are aliases. When that data value is a mutable object such as a list, side effects can occur. A side effect is an unexpected change to the contents of a data object. To prevent side effects, avoid aliasing by assigning a copy of the original data object to the new variable.

- A tuple is quite similar to a list, but it has an immutable structure.

- A function definition consists of a header and a body. The header contains the function's name and a parenthesized list of argument names. The body consists of a set of statements.

- The `return` statement returns a value from a function definition.

- The number and positions of arguments in a function call must match the number and positions of required parameters specified in the function's definition.

- A dictionary associates a set of keys with values. Dictionaries organize data by content rather than position.

- The subscript operator is used to add a new key/value pair to a dictionary or to replace a value associated with an existing key.

- The `dict` type includes methods to access and remove data in a dictionary.

- The `for` loop can traverse the keys of a dictionary. The methods `keys` and `values` return access to a dictionary's keys and values, respectively.

- Bottom-up testing of a program begins by testing its lower-level functions and then testing the functions that depend on those lower-level functions. Top-down testing begins by testing the program's `main` function and then testing the functions on which the `main` function depends. These lower-level functions are initially defined to return their names.

Key Terms

alias	header	pattern matching
association	item	side effect
association list	keys	structural equivalence
body	list	table
Boolean function	median	tuple
dictionary	mode	values
element	mutator	vocabulary
entries	natural ordering	
grammar	object identity	

Review Questions

For Questions 1–6, assume that the variable `data` refers to the list `[10, 20, 30]`.

1. The expression `data[1]` evaluates to

   a. `10`

   b. `20`

   c. `30`

   d. `0`

2. The expression `data[1:3]` evaluates to

   a. `[10, 20, 30]`

   b. `[20, 30]`

   c. `[10, 30]`

   d. `[30]`

3. The expression `data.index(20)` evaluates to

   a. `1`

   b. `2`

   c. `True`

   d. `False`

4. The expression `data + [40, 50]` evaluates to

   a. `[10, 60, 80]`

   b. `[10, 20, 30, 40, 50]`

   c. `[50, 70]`

   d. `[0]`

5. After the statement `data[1] = 5,` `data` evaluates to

   a. `[5, 20, 30]`

   b. `[10, 5, 30]`

   c. `5`

   d. `[10, 20, 5]`

6. After the statement `data.insert(1, 15)`, the original `data` evaluates to

   a. `[15, 10, 20, 30]`

   b. `[10, 15, 30]`

   c. `[10, 15, 20, 30]`

   d. `[10, 20, 30, 15]`

For Questions 7–9, assume that the variable `info` refers to the dictionary `{"name":"Sandy", "age":17}`.

7. The expression `list(info.keys())` evaluates to

   a. `("name", "age")`

   b. `["name", "age"]`

   c. `("Sandy", 17)`

   d. `(17, "Sandy")`

8. The expression `info.get("hobbies", None)` evaluates to

   a. `"knitting"`

   b. `None`

   c. `1000`

   d. `2000`

9. The method to remove an entry from a dictionary is named

   a. `delete`

   b. `pop`

   c. `remove`

   d. `insert`

10. Which of the following are immutable data structures?

   a. dictionaries and lists

   b. strings and tuples

   c. integers and floats

   d. menus and buttons

Programming Exercises

1. A group of statisticians at a local college has asked you to create a set of functions that compute the median and mode of a set of numbers, as defined in Section 5.4. Define these functions in a module named **stats.py**. Also include a function named **mean**, which computes the average of a set of numbers. Each function should expect a list of numbers as an argument and return a single number. Each function should return 0 if the list is empty. Include a **main** function that tests the three statistical functions with a given list. (LO: 5.1, 5.2)

2. Write a program in the file **navigate.py** that allows the user to navigate the lines of text in a file. The program should prompt the user for a filename and input the lines of text into a list. The program then enters a loop in which it prints the number of lines in the file and prompts the user for a line number. Actual line numbers range from 1 to the number of lines in the file. If the input is 0, the program quits. Otherwise, the program prints the line associated with that number. (LO: 5.1)

3. Modify the sentence-generator program of Case Study 5-1 (in the file **generator.py**) so that it inputs its vocabulary from a set of text files at startup. The filenames are **nouns.txt**, **verbs.txt**, **articles.txt**, and **prepositions.txt**. (*Hint:* Define a single new function, `getWords`. This function should expect a filename as an argument. The function should open an input file with this name, define a temporary list, read words from the file, and add them to the list. The function should then convert the list to a tuple and return this tuple. Call the function with an actual filename to initialize each of the four variables for the vocabulary.) (LO: 5.1, 5.2)

4. Make the following modifications to the original sentence-generator program in the file **generator.py**:

   a. The prepositional phrase is optional. (It can appear with a certain probability.)

   b. A conjunction and a second independent clause are optional: The boy took a drink, and the girl played baseball.

   c. An adjective is optional: The girl kicked the red ball with a sore foot.

   You should add new variables for the sets of adjectives and conjunctions. (LO: 5.1, 5.2)

5. Chapter 4 presented an algorithm for converting from binary to decimal. You can generalize this algorithm to work for a representation in any base. Instead of using a power of 2, this time you use a power of the base.

Also, you use digits greater than 9, such as A ... F, when they occur. Define a function named `repToDecimal` in the file **convert.py** that expects two arguments, a string and an integer. The second argument should be the base. For example, `repToDecimal("10", 8)` returns 8, whereas `repToDecimal("10", 16)` returns 16. The function should use a lookup table to find the value of any digit. Make sure that this table (it is actually a dictionary) is initialized before the function is defined. For its keys, use the 10 decimal digits (all strings) and the letters A ... F (all uppercase). The value stored with each key should be the integer that the digit represents. (The letter `'A'` associates with the integer value 10, and so on.) The main loop of the function should convert each digit to uppercase, look up its value in the table, and use this value in the computation. Include a `main` function that tests the conversion function with numbers in several bases. (LO: 5.2, 5.3)

6. Define a function `decimalToRep` in the file **convert.py** that returns the representation of an integer in a given base. The two arguments should be the integer and the base. The function should return a string. It should use a lookup table that associates integers with digits. Include a main function that tests the conversion function with numbers in several bases. (LO: 5.2, 5.3)

7. Write a program in the file **unique.py** that inputs a text file. The program should print the unique words in the file in alphabetical order. (LO: 5.1)

8. A file concordance tracks the unique words in a file and their frequencies. Write a program in the file **concordance.py** that displays a concordance for a file. The program should output the unique words and their frequencies in alphabetical order. Variations are to track sequences of two words and their frequencies, or *n* words and their frequencies. (LO: 5.3)

9. In the therapist program, when the patient addresses the therapist personally, the therapist's reply does not change persons appropriately. To see an example of this problem, test the program with "you are not a helpful therapist." Fix this problem by repairing the dictionary of replacements in the file **doctor.py**. (LO: 5.3)

10. Conversations often shift focus to earlier topics. Modify the therapist program in the file **doctor.py** to support this capability. Add each patient input to a history list. Then occasionally choose an element at random from this list, change persons, and prepend (add at the beginning) the qualifier "Earlier you said that" to this reply. Make sure that this option is triggered only after several exchanges have occurred. (LO: 5.1, 5.2)

Debugging Exercise

Jack is developing a program that calls for converting a list of words to uppercase. He tries out a strategy for this task in the Python shell, as follows:

```
>>> listOfWords = ["Apple", "orange", "banana"]
>>> for word in listOfWords:
        word = word.upper()
>>> listOfWords
['Apple', 'orange', 'banana']
```

Jack's strategy does not appear to produce the expected result. Describe the error, explain why it happened, and suggest a correction.

Lists and Dictionaries

Prompt

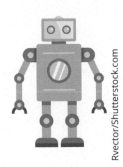

Rvector/Shutterstock.com

Ira Yapanda/Shutterstock.com

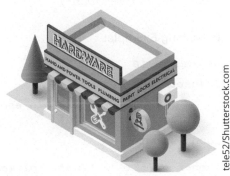

tele52/Shutterstock.com

Now that you have successfully completed reading the file, we want to take that one step forward. You kept track of some data points for output purposes in your script. Those more primitive data types can be somewhat limiting in the ability to be used, passed around, and worked with. With all of the skills that you've added scripting-wise during the course of our robotic journey together, you've acquired a good fledgling set of skills.

With that in mind, the next step is to start working out how to make use of both lists and dictionaries in Python for storage purposes. You're going to create a couple of lists and a dictionary for storing the items that you read in from the file. You could only use one or the other but note how different and in what situations that you might use both.

At the end, you're going to produce the same output but again, note how this is different than using the primitive data types like strings and numbers. How would using a list or a dictionary be better than using single data points?

Remember,
You will open the file, read each line, get the number of items for the robot to acquire in the order, and output that to the console. Upon reaching the end of the file, your method, outputOrderAuto, will output statements to reflect the items listed in the file:

Herby the robot added x # of hardware items to the order.

Herby the robot added y # of lumber items to the order.

Herby the robot added z # of paint items to the order.

At the end of the modification of this script, your robot controller script will have three methods:

pickItems

outputOrder

ourputOrderAuto

Examples:

Method Example:

```
def functionExample(pName):
 print("Hello "+pName)


functionExample("Dan")
```

Branching Example:

```
userAge = 10
if(userAge > 10)
        print("You are old enough to ride this ride")
```

Loops Example:

```
lumber = ["2x4", "2x8", "plywood"]
for x in lumber:
  print(x)
```

File handling:

```
# import the csv module


# file name
fName = "robotOrder.csv"


# initializing the container variables
field = []
row = []


# read file
with open(file_name, m with open(file_name, mode='r') as file:
        # Read the file lines
        lines = file.readlines()

        # Remove the header row
        lines.pop(0)

        # Initialize a dictionary to store the items
        items = {"Hardware": 0, "Lumber": 0, "Paint": 0}
```

```
ode='r') as file:
        # Read the file lines
        lines = file.readlines()


        # Remove the header row
        lines.pop(0)


        # Initialize a dictionary to store the items
        items = {"Hardware": 0, "Lumber": 0, "Paint": 0}



with open(fName, 'r') as fFile:
    # create csv reader object
    fReader = csv.reader(fFile)

    # get field names
    field = next(fReader)

    # get data row
    for nRow in fReader:
        row.append(nRow)
```

List:

```
inventory = [item1, item2, item3, ...]
print(inventory) # ['item1', 'item2', 'item3']
print(inventory[0]) # item1
inventory.append('item4') # adds 'inventory4' at the end of the list

del inventory[0 #removes the first item from the list]
inventory.remove('item2') # removes item2 from the list
```

Dictionary:

```
inventory={
    'type':'Lumber',
    'descrip':'2x4'
}
print(inventory) # {'type': 'Lumber', 'descrip': '2x4'}
```

Hints

In the last assignment, you were exposed to some new tools like arrays, imports, and file handling, all of which can be invaluable tools for building applications. However, working with components like arrays can be less effective than other variable types like dictionaries or lists. In this assignment, you'll be switching over your arrays to work with those other types. Lists work with square brackets and dictionaries work with squiggly brackets.

In addition, you'll continue to work with files, but storing them in different variable types. This will give you good exposure for working with a number of different data types, as having a basic understanding of working with a number of different data types is important. With the dictionary, you'll be using the key/pair combination to store information. With the List, you'll be working with the delete, remove, and other methods that are included with this variable type.

Answer

See Chapter 5_Lists and Dictionaries.py

After Discussion

In this assignment, you're continuing to work with data but using new variable types and also performing different operations on the data. Being able to manipulate and work with data is extremely important, as this can be used to continue to refine and eventually analyze your data. While the primary goal of working with data is to complete various objectives, there are also many supporting activities that can be engaged with as it relates to data to better forecast and understand the needs of an organization. This in turn makes the primary objectives easier to fulfill.

Working with files, dictionaries, lists, and other components of data handling, to include branching and looping, forms a great set of tools that a developer can use to solve many problems. Good work!

## Chapter 6

Design with Functions

Learning Objectives

When you complete this chapter, you will be able to:

- **6.1** Explain why functions are useful in structuring code in a program
- **6.2** Employ top-down design to assign tasks to functions
- **6.3** Explain the use of the namespace in a program and exploit it effectively and define a function with required and optional parameters

Design is important in many fields. The architect who designs a building; the engineer who designs a bridge or a new automobile; and the politician, advertising executive, or army general who designs the next campaign must organize the structure of a system and coordinate the actors within it to achieve its purpose. Design is equally important in constructing software systems, some of which are the most complex artifacts ever built by human beings. In this chapter, we explore the use of functions to design software systems.

6.1 A Quick Review of What Functions Are and How They Work

You have been using built-in functions since Chapter 2, and Chapter 5 briefly discussed how to define functions so you could use them in case studies. Before delving into the use of functions in designing programs, it will be a good idea to review what you have learned about functions thus far.

1. A function packages an algorithm in a chunk of code that you can call by name. For example, the **reply** function in the doctor program of Chapter 5 builds and returns a doctor's reply to a patient's sentence.

2. A function can be called from anywhere in a program's code, including code within other functions. During program execution, there may be a complex chain of function calls, where one function calls another and waits for its results to be returned, and so on. For example, in the doctor program, the **main** function calls the **reply** function, which in turn calls the **changePerson** function. The result of **changePerson** is returned to **reply**, whose result is returned to **main**.

3. A function can receive data from its caller via arguments. For example, the doctor program's **reply** function expects one argument—a string representing the patient's sentence. However, some functions, like those of the sentence generator program of Chapter 5, need no arguments to do their work.

4. When a function is called, any expressions supplied as arguments are first evaluated. Their values are copied to temporary storage locations named by the parameters in the function's definition. The parameters play the same role as variables in the code that the function then executes.

5. A function may have one or more **return** statements, whose purpose is to terminate the execution of the function and return control to its caller. A **return** statement may be followed by an expression. In that case, Python evaluates the expression and makes its value available to the caller when the function stops execution. For example, the doctor program's **reply** function returns either the value returned by the **random.choice** function or the value returned by the **changePerson** function. If a function does not include a **return** statement, Python automatically returns the value **None** to the caller.

With these reminders about the use and behavior of functions under your belt, you are now ready to tackle the finer points of program design with functions.

Functions as Abstraction Mechanisms

Thus far in this book, programs have consisted of algorithms and data structures expressed in the Python programming language. The algorithms, in turn, are composed of built-in operators, control statements, calls to built-in functions, and programmer-defined functions, which were introduced in Chapter 5.

Strictly speaking, functions are not necessary. It is possible to construct any algorithm using only Python's built-in operators and control statements. However, in any significant program, the resulting code would be extremely complex, difficult to prove correct, and almost impossible to maintain.

The problem is that the human brain can wrap itself around just a few things at once (psychologists say three things comfortably, and at most seven). People cope with complexity by developing a mechanism to simplify or hide it. This mechanism is called an **abstraction**. Put most plainly, an abstraction hides detail and thus allows a person to view many things as just one thing. You use abstractions to refer to the most common tasks in everyday life. For example, consider the expression "doing my laundry." This expression is simple, but it refers to a complex process that involves fetching dirty clothes from the hamper, separating them into whites and colors, loading them into the washer, transferring them to the dryer, and folding them and putting them into the dresser. Indeed, without abstractions, most everyday activities would be impossible to discuss, plan, or carry out. Likewise, effective designers must invent useful abstractions to control complexity. In this section, you examine the various ways in which functions serve as abstraction mechanisms in a program.

Functions Eliminate Redundancy

The first way that functions serve as abstraction mechanisms is by eliminating redundant, or repetitious, code. To explore the concept of redundancy, let's look at a function named **summation**, which returns the sum of the numbers within a given range of numbers. Here is the definition of **summation**, followed by a session showing its use:

```
def summation(lower, upper):
    """Arguments: A lower bound and an upper bound
    Returns: the sum of the numbers from lower through upper
    """
    result = 0
    while lower <= upper:
        result += lower
        lower += 1
    return result
>>> summation(1,4) # The summation of the numbers 1..4
```

```
10

>>> summation(50,100) # The summation of the numbers 50..100
3825
```

If the **summation** function didn't exist, the programmer would have to write the entire algorithm every time a summation is computed. In a program that must calculate multiple summations, the same code would appear multiple times. In other words, redundant code would be included in the program. Code redundancy is bad for several reasons. For one thing, it requires programmers to laboriously enter or copy the same code over and over, and to get it correct every time. Then, if programmers decide to improve the algorithm by adding a new feature or making it more efficient, they must revise each instance of the redundant code throughout the entire program. As you can imagine, this would be a maintenance nightmare.

By relying on a single function definition instead of multiple instances of redundant code, programmers free themselves to write only a single algorithm in just one place—say, in a library module. Any other module or program can then import the function for its use. Once imported, the function can be called as many times as necessary. When the programmers need to debug, repair, or improve the function, they need to edit and test only the single function definition. There is no need to edit the parts of the program that call the function.

Functions Hide Complexity

Another way that functions serve as abstraction mechanisms is by hiding complicated details. To understand why this is true, let's return to the **summation** function. Although the idea of summing a range of numbers is simple, the code for computing a summation is not. This is not only about the amount or length of the code but also about the number of interacting components. There are three variables to manipulate, as well as count-controlled loop logic to construct.

Now suppose, somewhat unrealistically, that only one summation is performed in a program, and it is performed in no other program. Who needs a function now? It all depends on the complexity of the surrounding code. Remember that the programmers responsible for maintaining a program can wrap their brains around just a few things at a time. If the code for the summation is placed in a context of code that is even slightly complex, the increase in complexity might be enough to result in conceptual overload for the poor programmers.

A function call expresses the idea of a process to the programmer without forcing them to wade through the complex code that realizes that idea. As in other areas of science and engineering, the simplest accounts and descriptions are generally the best.

Functions Support General Methods with Systematic Variations

An algorithm is a **general method** for solving a class of problems. The individual problems that make up a class of problems are known as **problem instances**. The problem instances for our summation algorithm are the pairs of numbers that specify the lower and upper bounds of the range of numbers to be summed. The problem instances of a given algorithm can vary from program to program or even within different parts of the same program. When you design an algorithm, it should be general enough to provide a solution to many problem instances, not just one or a few of them. In other words, a function should provide a general method with systematic variations.

The **summation** function contains both the code for the summation algorithm and the means of supplying problem instances to this algorithm. The problem instances are the data sent as arguments to the function. The parameters or argument names in the function's header behave like variables waiting to be assigned data whenever the function is called.

If designed properly, a function's code captures an algorithm as a general method for solving a class of problems. The function's arguments provide the means for systematically varying the problem instances that its algorithm solves. Additional arguments can broaden the range of problems that are solvable. For example, the **summation** function could take a third argument that specifies the step to take between numbers in the range. You will examine shortly how to provide additional arguments that do not add complexity to a function's default uses.

Functions Support the Division of Labor

In a well-organized system, whether it is human-made or not, each part does its own job or plays its own role in collaborating to achieve a common goal. Specialized tasks get divided up and assigned to specialized agents. Some agents might assume the role of managing the tasks of others or coordinating them in some way. But, regardless of the task, good agents mind their own business and do not try to do the jobs of others.

In contrast, a poorly organized system suffers from agents performing tasks for which they are not trained or designed, or from busybody agents who do not mind their own business. Division of labor breaks down.

In a computer program, functions can enforce a division of labor. Ideally, each function performs a single coherent task, such as computing a summation or formatting a table of data for output. Each function is responsible for using certain data, computing certain results, and returning these to the parts of the program that requested them. Each of the tasks required by a system can be assigned to a function, including the tasks of managing or coordinating the use of other functions. In the sections that follow, we examine several design strategies that employ functions to enforce a division of labor in programs.

> ## Exercise 6-1

1. Anne complains that defining functions to use in her programs is a lot of extra work. She says she can finish her programs much more quickly if she just writes them using the basic operators and control statements. State three reasons why her view is shortsighted.

2. Explain how an algorithm solves a general class of problems and how a function definition can support this property of an algorithm.

6.2 Problem Solving with Top-Down Design

One popular design strategy for programs of any significant size and complexity is called top-down design. This strategy starts with a global view of the entire problem and breaks the problem into smaller, more manageable subproblems—a process known as problem decomposition. As each subproblem is isolated, its solution is assigned to a function. Problem decomposition may continue down to lower levels, because a subproblem might in turn contain two or more lower-level problems to solve. As functions are developed to solve each subproblem, the solution to the overall problem is gradually filled out in detail. This process is also called stepwise refinement.

The early program examples in Chapters 1–4 were simple enough that they could be decomposed into three parts—the input of data, its processing, and the output of results. None of these parts required more than one or two statements of code, and they all appeared in a single sequence of statements.

However, beginning with the text analysis program of Chapter 4, the case study problems became complicated enough to warrant decomposition and assignment to additional programmer-defined functions. Because each problem had a different structure, the design of the solution took a slightly different path. This section revisits each program to explore how their designs took shape.

The Design of the Text Analysis Program

Although the text analysis program (Case Study 4-1.) is not actually structured in terms of programmer-defined functions, we can now explore how that could have been done. The program requires simple input and output components, so these can be expressed as statements within a `main` function. However, the processing of the input is complex enough to decompose into smaller subprocesses, such as obtaining the counts of the sentences, words, and syllables and calculating the readability scores. Generally, you develop a new function for each of these computational tasks. The relationships among the functions in this design are expressed in the structure chart shown in **Figure 6-1**. A structure chart is a diagram that shows the relationships among a program's functions and the passage of data between them.

Figure 6-1   A structure chart for the text analysis program

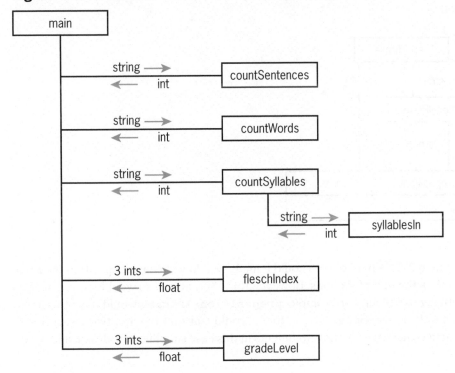

Each box in the structure chart is labeled with a function name. The **main** function at the top is where the design begins, and decomposition leads us to the lower-level functions on which **main** depends. The lines connecting the boxes are labeled with data type names, and arrows indicate the flow of data between them. For example, the function **countSentences** takes a string as an argument and returns the number of sentences in that string. Note that all functions except one are just one level below **main**. Because this program does not have a deep structure, the programmer can develop it quickly just by thinking of the results that **main** needs to obtain from its collaborators.

The Design of the Sentence Generator Program

From a global perspective, the sentence generator program (Case Study 5-1) consists of a main loop in which sentences are generated a user-specified number of times. The I/O and loop logic are simple enough to place in the **main** function. The rest of the design involves generating a sentence. Here, you decompose the problem by simply following the grammar rules for phrases. To generate a sentence, you generate a noun phrase followed by a verb phrase, and so on. Each of the grammar rules poses a problem that is solved by a single function. The top-down design flows out of the top-down structure of the grammar. The structure chart for the sentence generator is shown in **Figure 6-2**.

The structure of a problem can often give you a pattern for designing the structure of the program to solve it. In the case of the sentence generator, the structure of the problem comes from the grammar rules, although they are not explicit data structures in the program. In later chapters, you will see many examples of program designs that also mirror the structure of the data being processed.

The design of the sentence generator differs from the design of the text analyzer in one other important way. The functions in the text analyzer all receive data from the **main** function via parameters or arguments. By contrast, the functions in the sentence generator receive their data from a common pool of data defined at the beginning of the

Figure 6-2 A structure chart for the sentence generator program

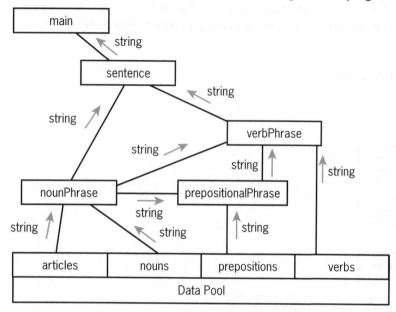

module and shown at the bottom of Figure 6-2. This pool of data could equally well have been set up within the **main** function and passed as arguments to each of the other functions. However, this alternative also would require passing arguments to functions that do not actually use them. For example, **prepositionalPhrase** would have to receive arguments for **articles** and **nouns** as well as **prepositions**, so that it could transmit the first two structures to **nounPhrase**. Using a common pool of data rather than function arguments in this case simplifies the design and makes program maintenance easier.

The Design of the Doctor Program

At the top level, the designs of the doctor program (Case Study 5-2) and the sentence generator program are similar. Both programs have main loops that take a single user input and print a result. The structure chart for the doctor program is shown in **Figure 6-3**.

Figure 6-3 A structure chart for the doctor program

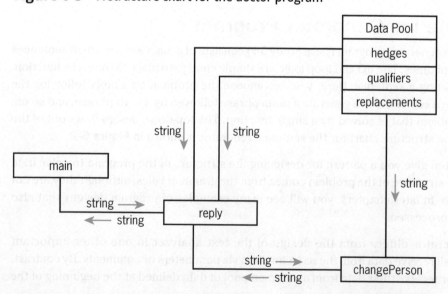

The doctor program processes the input by responding to it as an agent would in a conversation. Thus, the responsibility for responding is delegated to the **reply** function. Note that the two functions **main** and **reply** have distinct responsibilities. The job of **main** is to handle user interaction with the program, whereas **reply** is responsible for implementing the "doctor logic" of generating an appropriate reply. The assignment of roles and responsibilities to different actors in a program is also called responsibility-driven design. The division of responsibility between functions that handle user interaction and functions that handle data processing is one that we will see again and again in the coming chapters.

If there were only one way to reply to the user, the problem of how to reply would not be further decomposed. However, because there are at least two options, **reply** is given the task of implementing the logic of choosing one of them, and it asks for help from other functions, such as **changePerson**, to carry out each option.

Separating the logic of choosing a task from the process of carrying out a task makes the program more maintainable. To add a new strategy for replying, you add a new choice to the logic of **reply** and then add the function that carries out this option. If you want to alter the likelihood of a given option, you just modify a line of code in **reply**.

The data flow scheme used in the doctor program combines the strategies used in the text analyzer and the sentence generator. The doctor program's functions receive their data from two sources. The patient's input string is passed as an argument to **reply** and **changePerson**, whereas the qualifiers, hedges, and pronoun replacements are looked up in a common pool of data defined at the beginning of the module. Once again, the use of a common pool of data allows the program to grow easily as new data sources, such as the history list suggested in Programming Exercise 10 in Chapter 5, are added to the program.

An adage captures the essence of top-down design: When in doubt about the solution to a problem, pass the task to someone else. If you choose the right agents, the task ultimately stops at an agent who has no doubt about how to solve the problem.

Exercise 6-2

1. Draw a structure chart for one of the solutions to the programming exercises of Chapters 4 and 5. The program should include at least two function definitions other than the **main** function.

2. Describe the processes of top-down design and stepwise refinement. Where does the design start, and how does it proceed?

Case Study 6-1 | Recognizing Sentences

Early word processing applications included a menu option to check the spelling and grammar within a document. These functions are now performed in real time while the author is typing. An author is alerted to potential errors with suggested changes offered for acceptance or refusal, and the menu option is now to *disable* these functions. In this case study, we employ top-down design to develop a simple grammar checker.

Request

Write a program to check the grammar of sentences in English.

Analysis

To make the problem manageable, the grammar and vocabulary of English sentences are the same as those used by the sentence generator program of Chapter 5 (see Table 5-3). The inputs to the new program

(continues)

are strings that purport to be sentences, and the output is either "Ok, grammatically correct" or "Not ok, grammatically incorrect." To qualify as a grammatically correct sentence, an input string must contain words that

- are in the vocabulary of the language
- go together to make properly formed noun phrases, verb phrases, and prepositional phrases as specified by the grammar rules.

Note that no attempt is made to check a word's spelling, and no attempt is made to determine whether a grammatically correct sentence is also a meaningful sentence. The program prompts the user for inputs until the user presses the return key to quit. Here is a sample session with the program:

```
>>> main()
Enter a sentence or press return to quit: The boy saw a gril with a bat
Not ok, grammatically incorrect
Enter a sentence or press return to quit: The boy saw a girl with a bat
Ok, grammatically correct
Enter a sentence or press return to quit: Saw boy girl a bat with
Not ok, grammatically incorrect
Enter a sentence or press return to quit: The bat threw a boy at a girl
Not ok, grammatically incorrect
Enter a sentence or press return to quit:
>>>
```

Design

Because the vocabulary of our English subset is the same as the one used in the sentence generator program, you can place words belonging to the four parts of speech in the same set of data structures, named **nouns**, **verbs**, **prepositions**, and **articles**, in the new program.

As mentioned earlier in this chapter, the design of the sentence generator program proceeded in top-down fashion by following the structure specified in the grammar rules for constructing sentences. For example, to construct a sentence, you called the **sentence** function, which in turn called the **nounPhrase** and **verbPhrase** functions to generate a noun phrase and a verb phrase to concatenate to form a sentence.

You can employ a similar strategy in the design of our grammar checker. Beginning with the top-level rule, you will now assign to a function the task of recognizing the phrase specified by each grammar rule. Thus, to enforce the grammar rule

```
sentence = nounphrase verbphrase
```

which says that a sentence is a noun phrase followed by a verb phrase, the **sentence** function still calls the **nounPhrase** and **verbPhrase** functions. However, in this case, you will not build a new sentence from these phrases, but instead attempt to recognize a given sequence of words as forming these two types of phrases. It follows that a sequence of words must be supplied as an argument to each function, and each function must return a Boolean value. The value **True** is returned when a phrase is grammatically correct, and the value **False** is returned when the phrase is not grammatically correct. If you assume that the parameter **words** names a list of words in the input string, then the pseudocode design of the top-level **sentence** function follows:

```
Function sentence(words)
    Return nounPhrase(words) and verbPhrase(words)
```

This function essentially says that the list of words forms a grammatically correct sentence if and only if the first part of that list forms a grammatically correct noun phrase and the second part forms a grammatically correct verb phrase.

Working your way down in the design process, the function to recognize a noun phrase must determine whether the first two words in the list of words are an article and a noun, according to the following grammar rule:

```
nounphrase = article noun
```

The function recognizes a noun phrase if and only if the first word in the **words** list is in the set of articles and the second word in the **words** list is in the set of nouns. But you cannot just assume that there are at least two words in the **words** list at this point, because the string may be empty or have just one word (these would be cases of grammatical errors). So, you must check first and return **False** if the length of the **words** list is less than 2. Moreover, because the entire recognition process must then move on to the next phrase in the **words** list after the noun phrase, the function must remove the two words just examined from this list. Here is the design for the **nounPhrase** function:

```
Function nounPhrase(words)
    If length of words is less than 2
        Return False
    Else
        Set article to the first word in words and remove this word
        Set noun to the first word in words and remove this word
        Return article in articles and noun in nouns
```

As you can see, the **words** list will get shorter and shorter as the processing continues. Note also that when we get to the point where you must deal with an individual word, it is not selected at random from the vocabulary to add to a new sentence but instead is queried about its membership in the appropriate lexical category at that point. The design of the functions for **verbPhrase** and **prepositionalPhrase** follows a similar pattern.

Implementation (Coding)

The data structures for the sentence recognizer can be copied from the sentence generator. The **main** function uses a standard sentinel-based loop to take inputs, test them for "sentencehood," and print the results. The remaining functions come directly out of the design phase. Here is the code:

```
"""
File: recognizer.py

A grammar checker for sentences in a subset of English
defined by the following grammar rules:

sentence = nounphrase verbphrase
nounphrase = article noun
verbphrase = verb nounphrase prepositionalphrase
prepositionalphrase = preposition nounphrase

The parts of speech are nouns, verbs, articles,
and prepositions.
```

(continues)

```
Inputs: purported sentences
Outputs: Ok, grammatically correct or
Not ok, grammatically incorrect
"""

articles = ("A", "THE")

nouns = ("BOY", "GIRL", "BAT", "BALL")

verbs = ("HIT", "SAW", "LIKED")

prepositions = ("WITH", "BY")

# sentence = nounphrase verbphrase
def sentence(words):
    """Returns True if the words form
    a sentence or False otherwise."""
    return nounPhrase(words) and verbPhrase(words)

# nounphrase = article noun
def nounPhrase(words):
    """Returns True if the first two words
    form a noun phrase or False otherwise."""
    if len(words) < 2:
        return False
    else:
        article = words.pop(0)
        noun = words.pop(0)
        return article in articles and noun in nouns

# verbphrase = verb nounphrase prepositionalphrase
def verbPhrase(words):
    """Returns True if the words form
    a verb phrase or False otherwise."""
    if len(words) == 0:
        return False
    else:
        verb = words.pop(0)
        return verb in verbs and nounPhrase(words) and \
                prepositionalPhrase(words)

# prepositionalphrase = preposition nounphrase
def prepositionalPhrase(words):
    """Returns True if the words form
    a prepositional phrase or False otherwise."""
    if len(words) == 0:
        return False
```

```
        else:
            preposition = words.pop(0)
            return preposition in prepositions and nounPhrase(words)

def main():
    """Tests inputs for grammatical correctness until the
    user presses return."""
    while True:
        userInput = input("Enter a sentence or press return to quit: ")
        if userInput == "":
            return
        else:
            words = userInput.upper().split()
            if sentence(words):
                print("Ok, grammatically correct")
            else:
                print("Not ok, grammatically incorrect")
if __name__ == "__main__":
    main()
```

Testing

Although we used top-down design to develop this program, testing can be simplified if we work bottom up. To do this, you comment out the final two lines of code that launch the program before loading the code into the Python shell. At that point, you begin by running the most basic bottom-level function **nounPhrase** with several lists of words that explore the following situations:

1. Two words that form a grammatically correct noun phrase

2. One word

3. Zero words

4. Two words that include a valid article and an invalid noun

5. Two words that include an invalid article and a valid noun

6. Two words that include an invalid article and an invalid noun

Here is a session showing these options, which exhaust the types of possibilities that this function could encounter:

```
>>> nounPhrase("the ball".upper().split())      #1
True
>>> nounPhrase("Python".upper().split())        #2
False
>>> nounPhrase("".upper().split())              #3
False
>>> nounPhrase("the hear".upper().split())      #4
False
>>> nounPhrase("throw ball".upper().split())    #5
```

(continues)

```
False
>>> nounPhrase("that Python".upper().split()) #6
False
```

Moving up one level in the design, you then test the function **prepositionalPhrase**. Data options include a grammatically correct prepositional phrase, a phrase with an invalid preposition and a valid noun phrase, and a phrase with a valid preposition and an invalid noun phrase. Testing then continues with **verbPhrase**, followed by **sentence**, before running the program with its **main** function. Bottom-up testing tends to narrow the search space for errors by testing each function only after the functions on which it depends have been verified to be correct.

6.3 Managing a Program's Namespace

Throughout this book, you have tried to behave like good authors by choosing your words (and the code used in your programs) carefully. You have taken care to select variable names that reflect their purpose in a program or the character of the objects in a given problem domain. Of course, these variable names are meaningful only to you, the human programmer. To the computer, the only meaning of a variable name is the value to which it happens to refer at any given point in program execution. The computer can keep track of these values easily. However, a programmer charged with editing and maintaining code can occasionally get lost as a program gets larger and more complex. In this section, you learn more about how a program's namespace—that is, the set of its variables and their values—is structured and how you can control it via good design principles.

Module Variables, Parameters, and Temporary Variables

Begin by analyzing the namespace of the doctor program of Case Study 5-2. This program includes many variable names; for the purposes of this example, focus on the code for the variable **replacements** and the function **changePerson**.

```
replacements = {"I":"you", "me":"you", "my":"your",
                "we":"you", "us":"you", "mine":"yours"}
def changePerson(sentence):
    """Replaces first person pronouns with second person
    pronouns."""
    words = sentence.split( )
    replyWords = []
    for word in words:
        replyWords.append(replacements.get(word, word))
    return " ".join(replyWords)
```

This code appears in the file **doctor.py**, so its module name is **doctor**. The names in this code fall into four categories, depending on where they are introduced:

1. **Module variables.** The names **replacements** and **changePerson** are introduced at the level of the module. Although **replacements** names a dictionary and **changePerson** names a function, they are both considered variables. You can see the module variables of the **doctor** module by importing it and entering **dir(doctor)** at a shell prompt. When module variables are introduced in a program, they are immediately given a value.

2. **Parameters.** The name **sentence** is a parameter of the function **changePerson**. A parameter name behaves like a variable and is introduced in a function or method header. The parameter does not receive a value until the function is called.

3. **Temporary variables.** The names `words`, `replyWords`, and `word` are introduced in the body of the function `changePerson`. Like module variables, temporary variables receive their values as soon as they are introduced.

4. **Method names.** The names `split` and `join` are introduced or defined in the `str` type. As mentioned earlier, a method reference always uses an object, in this case, a string, followed by a dot and the method name.

Your first simple programs contained module variables only. The use of function definitions brought parameters and temporary variables into play. You will now explore the significance of these distinctions.

Scope

In ordinary writing, the meaning of a word often depends on its surrounding context. For example, in the sports section of the newspaper, the word "bat" means a stick for hitting baseballs, whereas in a story about vampires it means a flying mammal. In a program, the context that gives a name a meaning is called its scope. In Python, a name's scope is the area of program text in which the name refers to a given value.

Return to the example from the doctor program to determine the scope of each variable. For reasons that will become clear in a moment, it will be easiest if you work outward, starting with temporary variables first.

The scope of the temporary variables `words`, `replyWords`, and `word` is the area of code in the body of the function `changePerson`, just below where each variable is introduced. In general, the meanings of temporary variables are restricted to the body of the functions in which they are introduced, and they are invisible elsewhere in a module. The restricted visibility of temporary variables befits their role as temporary working storage for a function.

The scope of the parameter `sentence` is the entire body of the function `changePerson`. Like temporary variables, parameters are invisible outside the function definitions where they are introduced.

The scope of the module variables `replacements` and `changePerson` includes the entire module below the point where the variables are introduced. This includes the code nested in the body of the function `changePerson`. The scope of these variables also includes the nested bodies of other function definitions that occur *earlier*. This allows these variables to be referenced by any functions, regardless of where they are defined in the module. For example, the `reply` function, which calls `changePerson`, might be defined before `changePerson` in the doctor module.

Although a Python function can reference a module variable for its value, it cannot under normal circumstances assign a new value to a module variable. When such an attempt is made, the Python Virtual Machine (PVM) creates a new, temporary variable of the same name within the function. The following script shows how this works:

```
x = 5
def f():
    x = 10          # Attempt to reset x
f()                 # Does the top-level x change?
print (x)           # No, this displays 5
```

When the function `f` is called, it does not assign 10 to the module variable `x`; instead, it assigns 10 to a temporary variable `x`. In fact, once the temporary variable is introduced, the module variable is no longer visible within function `f`. In any case, the module variable's value remains unchanged by the call. There is a way to allow a function to modify a module variable, but in Chapter 10 we explore a better way to manage common pools of data that require changes.

Lifetime

A computer program has two natures. On the one hand, a program is a piece of text containing names that a human being can read for a meaning. Viewed from this perspective, variables in a program have a scope that determines their visibility. On the other hand, a program describes a process that exists for a period of time on a real computer. Viewed from this other perspective, a program's variables have another important property called a lifetime. A variable's lifetime is the period of time during program execution when the variable has memory storage associated with it. When a variable comes into existence, storage is allocated for it; when it goes out of existence, storage is reclaimed by the PVM.

Module variables come into existence when they are introduced via assignment and generally exist for the lifetime of the program that introduces or imports those module variables. Parameters and temporary variables come into existence when they are bound to values during a function call but go out of existence when the function call terminates.

The concept of lifetime explains the existence of two variables called **x** in our last example session. The module variable **x** comes into existence before the temporary variable **x** and survives the call of function **f**. During the call of **f**, storage exists for both variables, so their values remain distinct.

Using Keywords for Default and Optional Arguments

A function's arguments are one of its most important features. Arguments provide the function's caller with the means of transmitting information to the function. Adding an argument or two to a function can increase its generality by extending the range of situations in which the function can be used. However, programmers often use a function in a restricted set of "essential" situations, in which the extra arguments might be an annoyance. In these cases, the use of the extra arguments should be optional for the caller of the function. When the function is called without the extra arguments, it provides reasonable default values for those arguments that produce the expected results.

For example, Python's **range** function can be called with one, two, or three arguments. When all three arguments are supplied, they indicate a lower bound, an upper bound, and a step value. When only two arguments are given, the step value defaults to 1. When a single argument is given, the step is assumed to be 1, and the lower bound automatically is 0.

The programmer can also specify optional arguments with default values in any function definition. Here is the syntax:

```
def <function name>(<required arguments>,
                    <key-1> = <val-1>, ... <key-n> = <val-n>)
```

The required arguments are listed first in the function header. These are the ones that are essential for the use of the function by any caller. Following the required arguments are one or more default arguments or keyword arguments. These are assignments of values to the argument names. When the function is called without these arguments, their default values are automatically assigned to them. When the function is called with these arguments, the default values are overridden by the caller's values.

For example, suppose you define a function, **repToInt**, to convert string representations of numbers in a given base to their integer values (see Chapter 4). The function expects a string representation of the number and an integer base as arguments. Here is the code:

```
def repToInt(repString, base):
    """Converts the repString to an int in the base
    and returns this int."""
    decimal = 0
    exponent = len(repString) - 1
    for digit in repString:
        decimal = decimal + int(digit) * base ** exponent
        exponent -= 1
    return decimal
```

As written, this function can be used to convert string representations in bases 2 through 10 to integers. But suppose that 75% of the time programmers use the **repToInt** function to convert binary numbers to decimal form. If you alter the function header to provide a default of 2 for **base**, those programmers will be grateful. Here is the proposed change to the function header, followed by a session that shows its impact:

```
def repToInt(repString, base = 2):
>>> repToInt("10", 10)        # Override the default to 10
10
>>> repToInt("10", 8)         # Override the default to 8
8
>>> repToInt("10", 2)         # Same as the default, not necessary
2
>>> repToInt("10")            # Base 2 by default
2
```

When using functions that have default arguments, you must provide the required arguments and place them in the same positions as they are in the function definition's header. The default arguments that follow can be supplied in two ways:

1. **By position**. In this case, the values are supplied in the order in which the arguments occur in the function header. Defaults are used for any arguments that are omitted.

2. **By keyword**. In this case, one or more values can be supplied in any order, using the syntax *<key>* = *<value>* in the function call.

Here is an example of a function with one required argument and two default arguments and a session that shows these options:

```
>>> def example(required, option1 = 2, option2 = 3):
        print(required, option1, option2)
>>> example(1)                      # Use all the defaults
1 2 3
>>> example(1, 10)                  # Override the first default
1 10 3
>>> example(1, 10, 20)             # Override all the defaults
1 10 20
>>> example(1, option2 = 20)       # Override the second default
1 2 20
>>> example(1, option2 = 20, option1 = 10)      # In any order
1 10 20
```

Default arguments are a powerful way to simplify design and make functions more general.

Exercise 6-3

1. Where are module variables, parameters, and temporary variables introduced and initialized in a program?

2. What is the scope of a variable? Give an example.

3. What is the lifetime of a variable? Give an example.

Fail-Safe Programming

Chapter 5 discussed the use of two functions for robust numeric input, named **inputInt** and **inputFloat**. Unlike Python's built-in **input** function, these two functions check the user's input string to verify that it conforms to the format of an integer or a floating-point number. If no error occurs, the string is converted to a value of the appropriate numeric type (**int** or **float**) and this value is returned to the caller. Otherwise, an error message is output and the input process continues. Each of these functions performs quite a bit of useful work, and you are now in a position to define them. Begin with the **inputInt** function; the development of the **inputFloat** function is left as a programming exercise for you.

Recall that **inputInt** expects a string prompt as an argument and returns an integer. The design calls for the function to use a loop that takes at least one input. Following this input, the function verifies that the string contains only digits before returning the corresponding integer value. If the string does not pass muster as an integer, the function outputs an error message and continues in the loop. The string method **isdigit** returns **True** if the string contains only digits or **False** otherwise. Here is the design, followed by the Python implementation:

```
Function inputInt(prompt)
    While true
        Prompt the user for and input theString
        If theString.isdigit()
            Return int(theString)
        Else
            Print an error message
```

```python
def inputInt(prompt):
    """Guarantees that the user inputs an integer,
    using the given prompt. Returns the integer."""
    while True:
        theString = input(prompt)
        if theString.isdigit():
            return int(theString)
        else:
            print("Error: the input must consist only of digits")
```

Note that you can use a **return** statement to exit both the **while** loop and the function with the return value.

Summary

- A function serves as an abstraction mechanism by allowing the programmer to view many things as one thing.

- A function eliminates redundant patterns of code by specifying a single place where the pattern is defined.

- A function hides a complex chunk of code in a single named entity.

- A function allows a general method to be applied in varying situations. The variations are specified by the function's arguments.

- Functions support the division of labor when a complex task is factored into simpler subtasks.

- Top-down design is a strategy that decomposes a complex problem into simpler subproblems and assigns their solutions to functions. In top-down design, you begin with a top-level `main` function and gradually fill in the details of lower-level functions in a process of stepwise refinement.

- Cooperating functions communicate information by passing arguments and receiving return values. They also can receive information directly from common pools of data.

- A structure chart is a diagram of the relationships among cooperating functions. The chart shows the dependency relationships in a top-down design, as well as data flows among the functions and common pools of data.

- The namespace of a program is structured in terms of module variables, parameters, and temporary variables. A module variable, whether it names a function or a datum, is introduced and receives its initial value at the top level of the module. A parameter is introduced in a function header and receives its initial value when the function is called. A temporary variable is introduced in an assignment statement within the body of a function definition.

- The scope of a variable is the area of program text within which it has a given value. The scope of a module variable is the text of the module below the variable's introduction and the bodies of any function definitions. The scope of a parameter is the body of its function definition. The scope of a temporary variable is the text of the function body below its introduction.

- Scope can be used to control the visibility of names in a namespace. When two variables with different scopes have the same name, a variable's value is found by looking outward from the innermost enclosing scope. In other words, a temporary variable's value takes precedence over a parameter's value and a module variable's value when all three have the same name.

- The lifetime of a variable is the duration of program execution during which it uses memory storage. Module variables exist for the lifetime of the program that uses them. Parameters and temporary variables exist for the lifetime of a particular function call.

Key Terms

abstraction	namespace	scope
default arguments	optional arguments	stepwise refinement
general method	parameters	structure chart
keyword arguments	problem decomposition	temporary variable
lifetime	problem instances	top-down design
method names	required arguments	
module variables	responsibility-driven design	

Review Questions

1. The type of statement that returns a value from a function is the

   a. `if-else` statement
   b. `break` statement
   c. `while` statement
   d. `return` statement

2. When a function does not include a return statement, that function returns the value

   a. `False`
   b. 0
   c. `None`
   d. nothing at all

3. The part of the function that can vary with the context of its call is (are) its

   a. `return` statement
   b. docstring
   c. name
   d. arguments

4. The part(s) of a function that provides information about its use is (are) its

   a. `return` statement
   b. docstring
   c. set of statements in its body
   d. arguments

5. A function's parameters

   a. name variables whose values are the values of the function's arguments when it is called
   b. are synonymous with the function's arguments
   c. are always required
   d. are synonymous with the function's temporary variables

6. Top-down design is a strategy that

   a. develops lower-level functions before the functions that depend on those lower-level functions
   b. starts with the `main` function and develops the functions on each successive level beneath the `main` function
   c. develops the functions for a program in a random order
   d. develops the functions for a program in alphabetical order by function name

7. The relationships among functions in a top-down design are shown in a

   a. syntax diagram
   b. flow diagram
   c. structure chart
   d. table of contents

8. The scope of a temporary variable is

   a. the statements in the body of the function where the variable is introduced
   b. the entire module in which the variable is introduced
   c. the statements in the body of the function after the statement where the variable is introduced
   d. the time during which storage for the variable is available

9. The lifetime of a parameter is

   a. the duration of program execution
   b. the duration of its function's execution
   c. approximately one hour
   d. a few microseconds

10. The required arguments to a function must appear

    a. before the optional arguments
    b. after the optional arguments
    c. in any order
    d. either before or after the optional arguments

Programming Exercises

1. Package Newton's method for approximating square roots (Case Study 3-2) in a function named **newton**. This function expects the input number as an argument and returns the estimate of its square root. The script in the file named **newton.py** should also include a **main** function that allows the user to compute square roots of inputs until she presses the enter/return key. (LO: 6.2)

2. Restructure Newton's method (Case Study 3-2) by decomposing it into three cooperating functions. The task of testing for the limit is assigned to a function named **limitReached**, whereas the task of computing a new approximation is assigned to a function named **improveEstimate**. Each function, in the file named **newton.py**, expects the relevant arguments and returns an appropriate value. (LO: 6.2)

3. A list is sorted in ascending order if it is empty or each item except the last one is less than or equal to its successor. Define a predicate **isSorted** that expects a list as an argument and returns **True** if the list is sorted or returns **False** otherwise. (*Hint:* For a list of length 2 or greater, loop through the list and compare pairs of items, from left to right, and return **False** if the first item in a pair is greater.) Include the function in a short tester program in the file named **testsort.py**. (LO: 6.2)

4. Modify the grammar checker of this chapter's Case Study, in the file **recognizer.py**, so that it recognizes the following additional types of variations in phrases:

    a. A verb phrase with no prepositional phrase (example: "The boy saw the girl").
    b. A noun phrase in which the noun is modified by an adjective (example: "The girl hit the red ball with a bat").
    c. A sentence that connects two independent clauses with a conjunction (example: "The boy threw the ball and the girl hit the ball").

    You should add new variables for the sets of adjectives and conjunctions. (LO: 6.2)

5. Design, implement, and test a program in the file named **commandinterpreter.py** that uses a simple text-based command interpreter. Here is a sample session with the program:

```
1 Open
2 Save
3 Compile
4 Run
5 Quit
Enter a number: 2
Command = Save
1 Open
2 Save
3 Compile
4 Run
5 Quit
Enter a number: 3
Command = Compile
1 Open
2 Save
3 Compile
4 Run
5 Quit
```

```
Enter a number: 5
Command = Quit
Have a nice day!
```

The program's **main** function

a. Displays a menu of commands.

b. Accepts an input command from the user.

c. Calls a function to perform the command.

d. Repeats steps a through c until the user selects the **"Quit"** command.

The program should define three other functions, named **printMenu**, **acceptCommand**, and **performCommand**, to carry out steps a, b, and c, respectively. The function to display the menu expects a list of menu options as an argument and displays these options prefixed with numbers. The function to accept an input command expects the length of the menu list as an argument. The function repeatedly prompts the user for a number in the range of options and takes inputs until the user enters a number within the range. The function either displays an error message for an invalid input or returns a valid input. The function to perform a command takes a command number and the menu as arguments and displays the selected command in the menu. Test your program with the menu **["Open", "Save", "Compile", "Run", "Quit"]** and at least one other menu. Note that all menus must include a **"Quit"** command as the last item in the menu. (LO: 6.2)

6. Define and test a function **myRange** in the file named **testmyrange.py**. This function should behave like Python's standard **range** function, with the required and optional arguments, but it should return a list. Do not use the **range** function in your implementation! (*Hints:* Study Python's help on **range** to determine the names, positions, and what to do with your function's parameters. Use a default value of **None** for the two optional parameters. If these parameters both equal **None**, then the function has been called with just the stop value. If just the third parameter equals **None**, then the function has been called with a start value as well. Thus, the first part of the function's code establishes what the values of the parameters are or should be. The rest of the code uses those values to build a list by counting up or down.) (LO: 6.3)

7. Add a function named **inputFloat** to the module **testinputfunctions** (available in the file named **testinputfunctions.py** in the Data Files for this chapter). This function behaves like the function **inputInt** developed in this chapter but provides for the robust input of floating-point numbers. This function allows digits only or digits and a single decimal point in the input string. Test your new function in this module. (LO: 6.2)

Debugging Exercise

Jack is developing a function named **shuffleString**, which rearranges the characters is a given string in random positions. He reasons that he can split the string into a list of its characters, then shuffle this list, and finally join the resulting list back into a string. He tries out his strategy for this task in the Python shell, as follows:

```
>>> import random
>>> def shuffleString(theString):
        return "".join(random.shuffle(list(theString)))
>>> shuffleString("Apples are red")
Traceback (most recent call last):
  File "<pyshell#4>", line 1, in <module>
    shuffleString("Apples are red")
  File "<pyshell#2>", line 2, in shuffleString
    return "".join(random.shuffle(list(theString)))
TypeError: can only join an iterable
```

Jack's strategy does not appear to produce the expected result. Determine the cause of the error and correct it.

6A

Palindrome Checker

Prompt

According to Merriam-Webster, a palindrome "is a word, verse, or sentence (such as Able was I ere I saw Elba) or a number (such as 1881) that reads the same backward or forward."

Write a function that outputs True or False based on if the input was a palindrome or not. You can output via printing True/False, or by returning True/False. You may disregard punctuation and whitespace.

Hints

To a computer, an uppercase letter ("A") is not equal to a lowercase version ("a"). Use the .lower() method on a string to convert it to all lowercase letters to make this lab easier.

We also do not want to count spaces or punctuation at all. You will need to find a way to skip these in your program.

Examples

>>> "Hello, World!".lower()

'hello, world!'

Answer

See Chapter 6_Palindrome Checker.py

After Discussion

There are a few different ways to solve this lab. We solved this lab by iterating through the characters of the given string. If a given character was in our list of characters to not worry about, we skipped and went on to the next character. Because our for loop is handling going from right to left in the checkString, we have a temporary variable tracking the index from right to left. We need to move this value ourselves and take into account continuing to move our index left as long as the current value is in our skip list.

Once we find a mismatch, we can fail out as there is no need to continue checking, we have broken the conditions and we know we do not have a palindrome. If our left-to-right index is greater than our right-to-left index, we are double checking values and wasting resources, we can return. If our two indexes are pointing to the same character, there is no need to continue checking either as that character will always be equal to itself.

When testing your code, remember to test the positive but also in the negative. Make sure things that should be getting flagged as positive are, but also things that should be returning negative are as well!

6B

String Reverse

Prompt

Rvector/Shutterstock.com

Ira Yapanda/Shutterstock.com

tele52/Shutterstock.com

Write a function that takes a string as a parameter, and returns that string reversed.

Bonus: Think of at least 2 ways to reverse a string in Python.

Examples

"123" becomes "321"

"STEM" becomes "METS"

"Reverse me!" becomes "!em esreveR"

Answer

Refer to string_reverse.py

After Discussion

string_reverse_way1() iterates through the given string, in reverse order, appending each character onto the back of a new string that will get returned.

string_reverse_way2() takes a string object and turns it into a list object. It then uses the .reverse() function built into Python lists to reverse the order of the list. It then turns that list back into a string and returns the answer. Remember that Python strings are immutable, whereas lists are mutable.

Custom Multiply

Prompt

If we go back to elementary school, we remember multiplication is just repeated addition. That is, when you multiply a number by 2, you add it to itself. Multiplying a number by 3 means you add it to itself, and then add it to itself again.

Write a function that "manually" multiplies two numbers together. Make sure you account for inputs that are 0 or negative! Do not worry about fractions or decimals, only handle integers.

Hints

> Remember, adding a negative number is the same as subtracting a positive one!

> Multiplying two positive numbers results in a positive number. Multiplying a positive number by a negative number will result in a negative number. Multiplying two negative numbers cancels out the negative.

Examples

```
5 * 2 = 5 + 5 = 10

4 * 3 = 4 + 4 + 4 = 12

12 * -2 = -12 + -12 = -24
```

Answer

See custom_multipler.py

After Discussion

Because we use "range(0,x)" we first make sure that x is positive. If x is negative, we do some basic algebra:

```
-x * y = (-1)*x * y = x * (-1)*y = x * -y
```

This preserves the sign of x in the equation, while making the range() statement work as well. From here, we just perform repeated addition (if y is negative, it will be subtraction) the needed number of times. Python handles the rest!

As always, there are multiple solutions to this exercise.

Prompt

Often in STEM we will have to implement algorithms and define constraints on a system. Here is a simple algorithm that has several real life use cases, such as determining if a credit card number is valid or not. There are multiple ways to complete this, some will be more "pythonic" than others. First, get your code working. Then go back and see if there are any optimizations you can make, or anywhere you can "clean it up." Your code should indicate somehow if a number is a Luhn number or not—it may return True/False, print True/False, or some other clear way.

The Luhn Algorithm has four steps:

1. Drop the last digit. This is a checksum digit we will use later.
2. Starting with digits on the rightmost position (after you did step 1), move left. Double the value of every other digit, starting with the first digit. If the resulting value is above 10, add the 2 digits of the result. Example: 6 doubled would equal 12. Then you would add 1 with 2 to result in 3.
3. Keep track of the total sum of the digits as you move across, using either the doubled value or the original digit where you do not perform step 2.
4. Perform the following equation. If the result is zero, you have a valid Luhn number.
   (TotalSum + Checksum) % 10

Examples

Example: 679

1. Payload = 67, checksum = 9
2. 7*2 = 14. 1 + 4 = 5

   6 is not every other digit, do not double, but add it to the total sum.
3. Total Sum = 1 + 4 + 6 = 11.

   Add back in the checksum. 11 + 9 = 20.
4. 20%10 == 0. 679 is a Luhn number.

Example: 12344

1. Payload = 1234, checksum = 4
2. 4*2 = 8.

   3

   2*2 = 4.

   1

3. Total Sum = 1 + 4 + 3 + 8 = 16.

   Add back in the checksum. 16 + 4 = 20.

4. 20%10 == 0. 12344 is a Luhn number.

Example: 26219

1. Payload = 2621 checksum = 9

2. 1*2 = 2

   2

   6*2 = 12, 1 + 2 = 3

   2

3. 2 + 2 + 3 + 2 = 9

   9 + 9 = 18

   18%10 is not equal to 0, 26219 is NOT a valid Luhn number.

Hints

sum() is a function that takes a list of numbers and returns the result of that list added up. Keeping in mind how map works, this may help shortening up your code.

Answer

See Chapter 6_Luhn Algorithm.py

After Discussion

Our main function applies the luhn() to every value in our list of values to try.

In Python, it is possible to overwrite function names like sum or len. This will break calls to these functions later in the code. One of the possible solutions you might see is to use another spelling, such as some for a sum. Another possible way around this is to use a more descriptive variable name, such as "finalSum" or "totalSum".

The range() statement loops from right to left, skipping past the very last digit, per part 1 of the algorithm steps. If we need to double the digit, we do, and if the result is multiple digits (which is the same as being greater than 9), we convert the whole number into a string of digits, and then convert each digit an int, and sum them together. Any 2 single digit numbers will at most result in a 2 digit number, but our code is quick, clear, and would apply to any length number to start with.

After our loop we add it to the initially dropped digit, and check to see if our result ends in 0!

## Chapter 7

Design with Recursion

Learning Objectives

After you complete this chapter, you will be able to:

7.1 Define a recursive function

7.2 Use higher-order functions for mapping, filtering, and reducing

---

In Chapter 6, you learned about the many benefits of defining and using functions in programs. These advantages include the following:

- Providing an abstraction mechanism that hides complex code (by using one name to stand for a complex process)

- Eliminating redundant code (by writing a commonly used chunk of code in just one place but being able to call it from many places in many programs)

- Supporting the development of general methods (algorithms) with systematic variations tailored to particular situations (parameters)

- Fostering the decomposition of complex problems into simpler subproblems that can be solved incrementally (top-down design and stepwise refinement)

In this chapter, we take these benefits a step further and explore the design and use of recursive functions.

7.1 Design with Recursive Functions

In top-down design, you decompose a complex problem into a set of simpler problems and solve these with different functions. In some cases, you can decompose a complex problem into smaller problems of the same form. The subproblems then can all be solved by using the same function. This design strategy is called **recursive design**, and the resulting functions are called recursive functions.

Defining a Recursive Function

A **recursive function** is a function that calls itself. To prevent a function from repeating itself indefinitely, it must contain at least one selection statement. This statement examines a condition called a **base case** to determine whether to stop or to continue with another **recursive step**.

Let's examine how to convert an iterative algorithm to a recursive function. Here is a definition of a function `displayRange` that prints the numbers from a lower bound to an upper bound:

```
def displayRange(lower, upper):
    """Outputs the numbers from lower through upper."""
    while lower <= upper:
        print(lower)
        lower = lower + 1
```

How would we go about converting this function to a recursive one? First, you should note two important facts:

1. The loop's body continues execution while `lower <= upper`.

2. When the function executes, `lower` is incremented by 1, but `upper` never changes.

The equivalent recursive function performs similar primitive operations, but the loop is replaced with a selection statement, and the assignment statement is replaced with a **recursive call** of the function. Here is the code with these changes:

```
def displayRange(lower, upper):
    """Outputs the numbers from lower through upper."""
    if lower <= upper:
        print(lower)
        displayRange(lower + 1, upper)
```

Although the syntax and design of the two functions are different, the same algorithmic process is executed. Each call of the recursive function visits the next number in the sequence, just as the loop does in the iterative version of the function.

Most recursive functions expect at least one argument. This data value is used to test for the base case that ends the recursive process, and it is modified in some way before each recursive step. The modification of the data value should produce a new data value that allows the function to reach the base case eventually. In the case of `displayRange`, the value of the argument `lower` is incremented before each recursive call so that it eventually exceeds the value of the argument `upper`.

Our next example is a recursive function that builds and returns a value. In Chapter 6, we defined an iterative version of the `summation` function that expects two arguments named `lower` and `upper`. The `summation` function computes and returns the sum of the numbers between these two values. In the recursive version, `summation` returns 0 if `lower` exceeds `upper` (the base case). Otherwise, the function adds `lower` to the `summation` of `lower + 1` and `upper` and returns this result. Here is the code for this function:

```
def summation(lower, upper):
    """Returns the sum of the numbers from lower through
    upper."""
    if lower > upper:
        return 0
    else:
        return lower + summation(lower + 1, upper)
```

The recursive call of `summation` adds the numbers from `lower + 1` through `upper`. The function then adds `lower` to this result and returns it.

It takes a certain amount of faith to buy into the notion that a recursive call of `summation` will work as expected. As we explain how recursion works and how it can simplify solutions to problems, the mystery surrounding it will fade away.

Recursive Algorithms

Although recursive algorithms generally describe the same processes as their iterative counterparts, recursion allows the programmer to think about them in a simpler manner. For example, when given a range of numbers to print, the recursive algorithm for `printRange` says

```
If there are more numbers to print in the range
    Print the next number
    Print the range of numbers after this one
```

Likewise, when given a range of numbers to sum, the recursive algorithm for summation says

```
If there are no more numbers to add in the range
    Return 0
Else
    Return the sum of the next number and the summation
    of the range of numbers after this one
```

Spotting situations where you can express a recursive solution to a problem is an acquired art that comes with seeing many examples in practice. But understanding a bit more about the mechanics of recursion will help clear up any mystery.

Tracing a Recursive Function

To get a better understanding of how a recursive function works, it is helpful to trace its calls. Let's do that for the recursive version of the `summation` function. You add an argument for a margin of indentation and `print` statements to trace the two arguments and the value returned on each call. The first statement on each call computes the indentation, which is then used in printing the two arguments. The value computed is also printed with this indentation just before each call returns. Here is the code, followed by a session showing its use:

```python
def summation(lower, upper, margin):
    """Returns the sum of the numbers from lower through upper,
    and outputs a trace of the arguments and return values
    on each call."""
    blanks = " " * margin
    print(blanks, lower, upper)
    if lower > upper:
        print(blanks, 0)
        return 0
    else:
        result = lower + summation(lower + 1, upper,
                                   margin + 4)
        print(blanks, result)
        return result
```

```
>>> summation(1, 4, 0)
1 4
    2 4
        3 4
            4 4
                5 4
                0
            4
        7
    9
10
10
```

The displayed pairs of arguments are indented further to the right as the calls of **summation** proceed. Note that the value of **lower** increases by 1 on each call, whereas the value of **upper** stays the same. The final call of **summation** returns 0. As the recursion unwinds, each value returned is aligned with the arguments above it and increases by the current value of **lower**. This type of tracing can be a useful debugging tool for recursive functions.

Using Recursive Definitions to Construct Recursive Functions

Recursive functions are frequently used to design algorithms for computing values that have a **recursive definition**. A recursive definition consists of equations that state what a value is for one or more base cases and one or more recursive cases. For example, the Fibonacci sequence is a series of values with a recursive definition. The first and second numbers in the Fibonacci sequence are 1. Thereafter, each number in the sequence is the sum of its two predecessors, as follows:

1 1 2 3 5 8 13 . . .

More formally, a recursive definition of the nth **Fibonacci number** is the following:

```
Fib(n) = 1, when n = 1 or n = 2
Fib(n) = Fib(n - 1) + Fib(n - 2), for all n > 2
```

Given this definition, you can construct a recursive function that computes and returns the nth Fibonacci number. Here it is:

```
def fib(n):
    """Returns the nth Fibonacci number."""
    if n < 3:
        return 1
    else:
        return fib(n - 1) + fib(n - 2)
```

Note that the base case as well as the two recursive steps return values to the caller.

Recursion in Sentence Structure

Recursive solutions can often flow from the structure of a problem. For example, the grammatical structure of sentences in a language can be highly recursive. A noun phrase (such as "the ball") can be modified by a prepositional phrase (such as "on the bench"), which also contains another noun phrase. The structure of these two phrases is expressed in the following two grammar rules:

```
nounphrase = article noun [prepositionalphrase]
prepositionalphrase = preposition nounphrase
```

Note that the square brackets [] enclose an optional item in the rule for `nounphrase`.

If you use this modified version of the noun phrase rule in the sentence generator (Case Study 5-1), the `nounPhrase` function could call the `prepositionalPhrase` function, which in turn calls `nounPhrase` again. This phenomenon is known as **indirect recursion**. To keep this process from going on forever, `nounPhrase` must also have the option to not generate a prepositional phrase. The code for a revised `nounPhrase` function generates a modifying prepositional phrase approximately 25 percent of the time:

```python
def nounPhrase():
    """Returns a noun phrase, which is an article followed
    by a noun, and an optional prepositional phrase."""
    phrase = random.choice(articles) + " " + random.choice(nouns)
    prob = random.randint(1, 4)  # 25% probability
    if prob == 1:
        return phrase + " " + prepositionalPhrase()
    else:
        return phrase

# prepositionalphrase = preposition nounphrase
def prepositionalPhrase():
    """Builds and returns a prepositional phrase."""
    return random.choice(prepositions) + " " + nounPhrase()
```

You can use a similar strategy to generate sentences that consist of two or more independent clauses connected by conjunctions, such as "One programmer uses recursion, and another programmer uses loops." A modified grammar rule that allows at most two independent clauses in a sentence would be

sentence = nounphrase verbphrase [conjunction nounphrase verbphrase]

But once you realize that a noun phrase followed by a verb phrase is just another sentence, you can substitute the term **sentence** for the terms that follow the conjunction:

sentence = nounphrase verbphrase [conjunction sentence]

This rule says that a sentence is at least a noun phrase followed by a verb phrase (the base case) followed by an optional conjunction and another sentence (the recursive step). The resulting function to generate sentences would employ a direct recursive call to process this option, as follows:

```python
# sentence = nounphrase verbphrase [conjunction sentence]
def sentence():
    """Builds and returns a prepositional phrase."""
    phrase = nounPhrase() + " " + verbPhrase()
    prob = random.randint(1, 4)    # 25% probability
    if prob == 1:
        return phrase + " " + random.choice(conjunctions) + " " + sentence()
    else:
        return phrase
```

The recursive structure of the grammar makes possible the generation of sentences containing arbitrarily many independent clauses, depending on the probability of selecting this option in the grammar rule.

As you saw in Case Study 6-1: Recognizing Sentences, the structure of a grammar checker for sentences also flows from the grammar of those sentences. The Programming Exercises will give you an opportunity to explore the use of recursion in the grammar checker.

Infinite Recursion

Recursive functions tend to be simpler than the corresponding loops, but they still require thorough testing. One design error that might trip up a programmer occurs when the function can (theoretically) continue executing forever, a situation known as **infinite recursion**. Infinite recursion arises when the programmer fails to specify the base case or to reduce the size of the problem in a way that terminates the recursive process. In fact, the Python virtual machine (PVM) eventually runs out of memory resources to manage the process, so it halts execution with a message indicating a **stack overflow error**. The next session defines a function that leads to this result:

```
>>> def runForever(n):
        if n > 0:
            runForever(n)
        else:
            runForever(n - 1)
>>> runForever(1)
Traceback (most recent call last):
  File "<pyshell#6>", line 1, in <module>
    runForever(1)
  File "<pyshell#5>", line 3, in runForever
    runForever(n)
  File "<pyshell#5>", line 3, in runForever
    runForever(n)
  File "<pyshell#5>", line 3, in runForever
    runForever(n)
  [Previous line repeated 989 more times]
  File "<pyshell#5>", line 2, in runForever
    if n > 0:
RecursionError: maximum recursion depth exceeded in comparison
```

The PVM keeps calling **runForever(1)** until there is no memory left to support another recursive call. Unlike an infinite loop, an infinite recursion eventually halts execution with an error message.

The Costs and Benefits of Recursion

Although recursive solutions are often more natural and elegant than their iterative counterparts, they can come with a performance cost. The run-time system on a real computer, such as the PVM, must devote some overhead to recursive function calls. At program startup, the PVM reserves an area of memory named a **call stack**. For each call of a function, recursive or otherwise, the PVM must allocate on the call stack a small chunk of memory called a **stack frame**. In this type of storage, the system places the values of the arguments and the return address for each function call. Space for the function call's return value is also reserved in its stack frame. When a call returns or completes its execution, the return address is used to locate the next instruction in the caller's code, and the memory for the stack frame is deallocated. The stack frames for the process generated by **displayRange(1, 3)** are shown in **Figure 7-1**. The frames in the figure include storage for the function's arguments only.

Although this sounds like a complex process, the PVM handles it easily. However, when a function invokes hundreds or even thousands of recursive calls, the amount of extra resources required, both in processing time and in memory usage, can add up to a significant performance hit. When, because of a design error, the recursion is infinite, the stack frames are added until the PVM runs out of memory, which halts the program with an error message.

Figure 7-1 The stack frames for `displayRange(1, 3)`

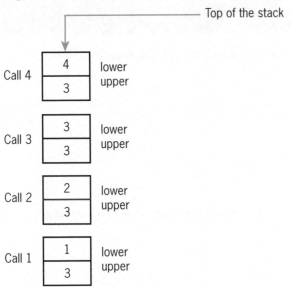

By contrast, the same problem can often be solved using a loop with a constant amount of memory, in the form of two or three variables. Because the amount of memory needed for the loop does not grow with the size of the problem's data set, the amount of processing time for managing this memory does not grow, either.

Despite these words of caution, we encourage you to consider developing recursive solutions when they seem natural, particularly when the problems themselves have a recursive structure. Testing can reveal performance bottlenecks that might lead you to change the design to an iterative one. Smart compilers can optimize some recursive functions by translating them to iterative machine code. Finally, as we will see later in this book, some problems with an iterative solution must still use an explicit stack-like data structure, so a recursive solution might be simpler and no less efficient.

Recursion is a powerful design technique that is used throughout computer science. We will return to it in later chapters.

Exercise 7-1

1. In what way is a recursive design different from top-down design?

2. The factorial of a positive integer **n**, **fact(n)**, is defined recursively as follows:

   fact(n) = 1, when n = 1
   fact(n) = n* fact(n − 1), otherwise

   Define a recursive function **fact** that returns the factorial of a given positive integer.

3. Describe the costs and benefits of defining and using a recursive function.

4. Explain what happens when the following recursive function is called with the value 4 as an argument:

   ```
   def example(n):
       if n > 0:
           print(n)
           example(n - 1)
   ```

(continues)

Exercise 7-1 (continued)

5. Explain what happens when the following recursive function is called with the value 4 as an argument:

```
def example(n):
    if n > 0:
        print(n)
        example(n)
    else:
        example(n - 1)
```

6. Explain what happens when the following recursive function is called with the values **"hello"** and 0 as arguments:

```
def example(aString, index):
    if index < len(aString):
        example(aString, index + 1)
        print(aString[index], end = "")
```

7. Explain what happens when the following recursive function is called with the values **"hello"** and 0 as arguments:

```
def example(aString, index):
    if index == len(aString):
        return ""
    else:
        return aString[index] + example(aString, index + 1)
```

Case Study 7-1 | Gathering Information from a File System

Modern file systems come with a graphical browser, such as Microsoft's Windows Explorer or Apple's Finder. These browsers allow the user to navigate to files or folders by selecting icons of folders, opening these by double-clicking, and selecting commands from a drop-down menu. Information on a folder or a file, such as the size and contents, is also easily obtained in several ways.

Users of terminal-based user interfaces (see Chapter 2) must rely on entering the appropriate commands at the terminal prompt to perform these functions. In this case study, we develop a simple terminal-based file system navigator that provides some information about the system. In the process, we will have an opportunity to exercise some skills in top-down design and recursive design.

Request

Write a program that allows the user to obtain information about the file system.

Analysis

File systems are tree-like structures, as shown in Figure 7-2.

Figure 7-2   **The structure of a file system**

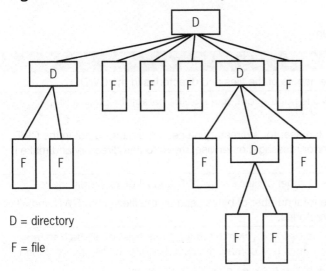

D = directory

F = file

At the top of the tree is the **root directory** (the term "directory" is a synonym for "folder," among users of terminal-based systems). Under the root are files and subdirectories. Each directory in the system except the root lies within another directory called its **parent**. For example, in Figure 7-2, the root directory contains four files and two subdirectories. On a UNIX-based file system (the system that underlies macOS), the **path** to a given file or directory in the system is a string that starts with the / (forward slash) symbol (the root), followed by the names of the directories traversed to reach the file or directory. The / (forward slash) symbol also separates each name in the path. Thus, the path to the file for this chapter on Ken's laptop might be the following:

/Users/KenLaptop/Book/Chapter7/Chapter7.docx

On a Windows-based file system, the \ symbol is used instead of the / symbol.

The program we will design in this case study is named **filesys.py**. It provides some basic browsing capability as well as options that allow you to search for a given filename and find statistics on the number of files and their size in a directory. At program startup, the current working directory (CWD) is the directory containing the Python program file. The program should display the path of the CWD, a menu of command options, and a prompt for a command, as shown in Figure 7-3.

Figure 7-3   **The command menu of the `filesys` program**

```
/Users/ken/
1    List the current directory
2    Move up
3    Move down
4    Number of files in the directory
5    Size of the directory in bytes
6    Search for a file name
7    Quit the program
Enter a number:
```

When the user enters a command number, the program runs the command, which may display further information, and the program displays the CWD and command menu again. An unrecognized command produces an error message, and command number 7 quits the program. Table 7-1 summarizes what the commands do.

Table 7-1 The commands in the `filesys` program

Command	What it Does
List the current working directory (CWD)	Prints the names of the files and directories in the CWD.
Move up	If the CWD is not the root, move to the parent directory and make it the CWD.
Move down	Prompts the user for a directory name. If the name is not in the CWD, print an error message; otherwise, move to this directory and make it the CWD.
Number of files in the directory	Prints the number of files in the CWD and all of its subdirectories.
Size of the directory in bytes	Prints the total number of bytes used by the files in the CWD and all of its subdirectories.
Search for a filename	Prompts the user for a search string. Prints a list of all the filenames (with their paths) that contain the search string, or "String not found."
Quit the program	Prints a signoff message and exits the program.

Design

You can structure the program according to two sets of tasks: those concerned with implementing a menu-driven command processor, and those concerned with executing the commands. The first group of operations includes the **main** function. In the following discussion, we work top-down and begin by examining the first group of operations.

As in many of the programs we have examined recently in this book, the **main** function contains a driver loop. This loop prints the CWD and the menu, calls other functions to input and run the commands, and breaks with a signoff message when the command is to quit. Here is the pseudocode:

```
function main()
    while True
        print(os.getcwd())
        print(MENU)
        command = acceptCommand()
        runCommand(command)
        if command == QUIT
            print("Have a nice day!")
            break
```

The function **os.getcwd** returns the path of the CWD. Note also that **MENU** and **QUIT** are module variables initialized to the appropriate strings before **main** is defined. The **acceptCommand** function loops until the user enters a number in the range of the valid commands. These commands are specified in a tuple named **COMMANDS** that is also initialized before the function is defined. The function thus always returns a valid command number.

The **runCommand** function expects a valid command number as an argument. The function uses a multiway selection statement to select and run the operation corresponding to the command number. When the result of an operation is returned, it is printed with the appropriate labeling.

That's it for the menu-driven command processor in the **main** function. Although there are other possible approaches, this design makes it easy to add new commands to the program.

The operations required to list the contents of the CWD, move up, and move down are simple and need no real design work. They involve the use of functions in the **os** and **os.path** modules to list the directory, change it, and test a string to see if it is the name of a directory. The implementation shows the details.

The other three operations all involve traversals of the directory structure in the CWD. During these traversals, every file and every subdirectory are visited. Directory structure is in fact recursive: each directory can contain files (base cases) and other directories (recursive steps). Thus, we can develop a recursive design for each operation.

The **countFiles** function expects the path of a directory as an argument and returns the number of files in this directory and its subdirectories. If there are no subdirectories in the argument directory, the function just counts the files and returns this value. If there is a subdirectory, the function moves down to it, counts the files (recursively) in it, adds the result to its total, and then moves back up to the parent directory. Here is the pseudocode:

```
function countFiles(path)
    count = 0
    lyst = os.listdir(path)
    for element in lyst
        if os.path.isfile(element)
            count += 1
        else:
            os.chdir(element)
            count += countFiles(os.getcwd())
            os.chdir("..")
    return count
```

The **countBytes** function expects a path as an argument and returns the total number of bytes in that directory and its subdirectories. Its design resembles **countFiles**.

The **findFiles** function accumulates a list of the filenames, including their paths, that contain a given target string, and returns this list. Its structure resembles the other two recursive functions, but the **findFiles** function builds a list rather than a number. When the function encounters a target file, its name is appended to the path, and then the result string is appended to the list of files. We use the module variable **os.sep** to obtain the appropriate slash symbol (/ or \) on the current file system. When the function encounters a directory, it moves to that directory, calls itself with the new CWD, and extends the files list with the resulting list. Here is the pseudocode:

```
function findFiles(target, path)
    files = []
    lyst = os.listdir(path)
    for element in lyst
        if os.path.isfile(element):
```

```
            if target in element:
                files.append(path + os.sep + element)
        else:
            os.chdir(element)
            files.extend(findFiles(target, os.getcwd()))
            os.chdir("..")
    return files
```

The trick with recursive design is to spot elements in a structure that can be treated as base cases (such as files) and other elements that can be treated as recursive steps (such as directories). The recursive algorithms for processing these structures flow naturally from these insights.

Implementation (Coding)

Near the beginning of the program code, we find the important variables, with the functions listed in a top-down order.

```
"""
Program: filesys.py
Author: Ken
Provides a menu-driven tool for navigating a file system
and gathering information on files.
"""

import os, os.path

QUIT = '7'
COMMANDS = ('1', '2', '3', '4', '5', '6', '7')
MENU = """1 List the current directory
2 Move up
3 Move down
4 Number of files in the directory
5 Size of the directory in bytes
6 Search for a filename
7 Quit the program"""

def main():
    while True:
        print(os.getcwd())
        print(MENU)
        command = acceptCommand()
        runCommand(command)
        if command == QUIT:
            print("Have a nice day!")
            break
```

```
def acceptCommand():
    """Inputs and returns a legitimate command number."""
    command = input("Enter a number: ")
    if command in COMMANDS:
        return command
    else:
        print("Error: command not recognized")
        return acceptCommand()

def runCommand(command):
    """Selects and runs a command."""
    if command == '1':
        listCurrentDir(os.getcwd())
    elif command == '2':
        moveUp()
    elif command == '3':
        moveDown(os.getcwd())
    elif command == '4':
        print("The total number of files is", \
              countFiles(os.getcwd()))
    elif command == '5':
        print("The total number of bytes is", \
              countBytes(os.getcwd()))
    elif command == '6':
        target = input("Enter the search string: ")
        fileList = findFiles(target, os.getcwd())
        if not fileList:
            print("String not found")
        else:
            for f in fileList:
                print(f)

def listCurrentDir(dirName):
    """Prints a list of the cwd's contents."""
    lyst = os.listdir(dirName)
    for element in lyst: print(element)

def moveUp():
    """Moves up to the parent directory."""
    os.chdir("..")

def moveDown(currentDir):
    """Moves down to the named subdirectory if it exists."""
    newDir = input("Enter the directory name: ")
```

```python
        if os.path.exists(currentDir + os.sep + newDir) and \
            os.path.isdir(newDir):
            os.chdir(newDir)
    else:
        print("ERROR: no such name")

def countFiles(path):
    """Returns the number of files in the cwd and
    all its subdirectories."""
    count = 0
    lyst = os.listdir(path)
    for element in lyst:
        if os.path.isfile(element):
            count += 1
        else:
            os.chdir(element)
            count += countFiles(os.getcwd())
            os.chdir("..")
    return count

def countBytes(path):
    """Returns the number of bytes in the cwd and
    all its subdirectories."""
    count = 0
    lyst = os.listdir(path)
    for element in lyst:
        if os.path.isfile(element):
            count += os.path.getsize(element)
        else:
            os.chdir(element)
            count += countBytes(os.getcwd())
            os.chdir("..")
    return count

def findFiles(target, path):
    """Returns a list of the filenames that contain
    the target string in the cwd and all its
    subdirectories."""
    files = []
    lyst = os.listdir(path)
    for element in lyst:
        if os.path.isfile(element):
            if target in element:
                files.append(path + os.sep + element)
```

```
        else:
            os.chdir(element)
            files.extend(findFiles(target, os.getcwd()))
            os.chdir("..")
    return files

if __name__ == "__main__":
    main()
```

7.2 Higher-Order Functions

Like any skill, a designer's knack for spotting the need for a function is developed with practice. As you gain experience in writing programs, you will learn to spot common and redundant patterns in the code. One pattern that occurs again and again is the application of a function to a set of values to produce some results. Here are some examples:

- The numbers in a text file must be converted to integers or floats after they are input.

- The first-person pronouns in a list of words must be changed to the corresponding second-person pronouns in the doctor program.

- Only scores above the average are kept in a list of grades.

- The sum of the squares of a list of numbers is computed.

In this section, we learn how to capture these patterns in a new abstraction called a **higher-order function**. For these patterns, a higher-order function expects a function and a set of data values as arguments. The argument function is applied to each data value, and a set of results or a single data value is returned. A higher-order function separates the task of transforming each data value from the logic of accumulating the results.

Functions as First-Class Data Objects

In Python, functions can be treated as **first-class data objects**. This means that they can be assigned to variables (as they are when they are defined), passed as arguments to other functions, returned as the values of other functions, and stored in data structures such as lists and dictionaries. The next session shows some of the simpler possibilities:

```
>>> abs                          # See what abs looks like
<built-in function abs>
>>> import math
>>> math.sqrt
<built-in function sqrt>
>>> f = abs                      # f is an alias for abs
>>> f                            # Evaluate f
<built-in function abs>
>>> f(-4)                        # Apply f to an argument
4
>>> funcs = [abs, math.sqrt]     # Put the functions in a list
>>> funcs
```

```
[<built-in function abs>, <built-in function sqrt>]
>>> funcs[1](2)                          # Apply math.sqrt to 2
1.4142135623730951
```

Passing a function as an argument to another function is no different from passing any other datum. The function argument is first evaluated, producing the function itself, and then the parameter name is bound to this value. The function can then be applied to its own argument with the usual syntax. Here is an example, which simply returns the result of an application of any single-argument function to a datum:

```
>>> def applyFunc(functionArg, dataArg):
        return functionArg(dataArg)
>>> applyFunc(abs, -4)
4
>>> applyFunc(math.sqrt, 2)
1.4142135623730951
```

Mapping

The first type of useful higher-order function to consider is called a **mapping**. This process applies a function to each value in a sequence (such as a list, a tuple, or a string) and returns a new sequence of the results. Python includes a **map** function for this purpose. Suppose we have a list named **words** that contains strings that represent integers. We want to replace each string with the corresponding integer value. The **map** function easily accomplishes this, as the next session shows:

```
>>> words = ["231", "20", "-45", "99"]
>>> map(int, words)                      # Convert all strings to ints
<map object at 0x14cbd90>
>>> words                                # Original list is not changed
['231', '20', '-45', '99']
>>> words = list(map(int, words))        # Reset variable to change it
>>> words
[231, 20, -45, 99]
```

Note that **map** builds and returns a new map object, which we feed to the **list** function to view the results. We could have written a **for** loop that does the same thing, but that would entail several lines of code instead of the single line of code required for the **map** function. Another reason to use the **map** function is that, in programs that use lists, we might need to perform this task many times. Relying on a **for** loop for each instance would entail multiple sections of redundant code. Moreover, the conversion to a list is only necessary for viewing the results; a map object can be passed directly to another **map** function to perform further transformations of the data.

Another good example of a mapping pattern is in the **changePerson** function of the **doctor** program. This function builds a new list of words with the pronouns replaced.

```
def changePerson(sentence):
    """Replaces first person pronouns with second person pronouns."""
    words = sentence.split( )
    replyWords = []
    for word in words:
        replyWords.append(replacements.get(word, word))
    return " ".join(replyWords)
```

We can simplify the logic by defining an auxiliary function that is then mapped onto the list of words, as follows:

```
def changePerson(sentence):
    """Replaces first person pronouns with second person pronouns."""
    def getWord(word):
        return replacements.get(word, word)
    return " ".join(map(getWord, sentence.split()))
```

Note that the definition of the function `getWord` is nested within the function `changePerson`. Furthermore, the map object is passed directly to the string method `join` without converting it to a list.

As you can see, the `map` function is extremely useful; any time we can eliminate a loop from a program, it's a win.

Filtering

A second type of higher-order function is called a **filtering**. In this process, a type of function called a **predicate** is applied to each value in a list. If the predicate returns `True`, the value passes the test and is added to a filter object (similar to a map object). Otherwise, the value is dropped from consideration. The process is a bit like pouring hot water into a filter basket with coffee. The good stuff to drink comes into the cup with the water, and the coffee grounds left behind can be thrown on the garden.

Python includes a `filter` function that is used in the next example to produce a list of the odd numbers in another list:

```
>>> def odd(n): return n % 2 == 1
>>> list(filter(odd, range(10)))
[1, 3, 5, 7, 9]
```

As with the function `map`, the result of the function `filter` can be passed directly to another call of `filter` or `map`. List processing often consists of several mappings and filterings of data, which can be expressed as a series of nested function calls.

Reducing

Our final example of a higher-order function is called a **reducing**. Here we take a list of values and repeatedly apply a function to accumulate a single data value. A summation is a good example of this process. The first value is added to the second value, then the sum is added to the third value, and so on, until the sum of all the values is produced.

The Python `functools` module includes a `reduce` function that expects a function of two arguments and a list of values. The `reduce` function returns the result of applying the function as just described. The following example shows `reduce` used twice—once to produce a sum and once to produce a product:

```
>>> from functools import reduce
>>> def add(x, y): return x + y
>>> def multiply(x, y): return x * y
>>> data = [1, 2, 3, 4]
>>> reduce(add, data)
10
>>> reduce(multiply, data)
24
```

Using `lambda` to Create Anonymous Functions

Although the use of higher-order functions can simplify code, it is somewhat onerous to have to define new functions to supply as arguments to the higher-order functions. For example, the functions **add** and **multiply** will never be used anywhere else in a program, because the operators + and * are already available. It would be convenient if we could define a function "on the fly," right at the point of the call of a higher-order function, especially if it is not needed anywhere else.

Python includes a mechanism called lambda that allows the programmer to create functions in this manner. A **lambda** is an anonymous function. It has no name of its own, but it contains the names of its arguments as well as a single expression. When the **lambda** is applied to its arguments, its expression is evaluated, and its value is returned.

The syntax of a **lambda** is very tight and restrictive:

```
lambda <argname-1, ..., argname-n>: <expression>
```

All of the code must appear on one line and, although it is sad, a **lambda** cannot include a selection statement, because selection statements are not expressions. Nonetheless, **lambda** has its virtues. We can now specify addition or multiplication on the fly, as the next session illustrates:

```
>>> data = [1, 2, 3, 4]
>>> reduce(lambda x, y: x + y, data)      # Produce the sum
10
>>> reduce(lambda x, y: x * y, data)      # Produce the product
24
```

The next example shows the use of **range**, **reduce**, and **lambda** to simplify the definition of the **summation** function discussed earlier in this chapter:

```
from functools import reduce
def summation(lower, upper):
    """Returns the sum of the numbers from lower through upper."""
    return reduce(lambda x, y: x + y,
                  range(lower, upper + 1))
```

Creating Jump Tables

This chapter's case study contains a menu-driven command processor. When the user selects a command from a menu, the program compares this command number to each number in a set of numbers until a match is found. A function corresponding to this number is then called to carry out the command. The function **runCommand** implemented this process with a long, multiway selection statement. With more than three options, such statements become tedious to read and hard to maintain. Adding or removing an option also becomes tricky and error-prone.

A simpler way to design a command processor is to use a data structure called a jump table. A jump table is a dictionary of functions keyed by command names. At program startup, the functions are defined, and then the jump table is loaded with the command names and their associated functions. The function **runCommand** uses its **command** argument to look up the function in the jump table and then calls this function. Here is the modified version of **runCommand**:

```
def runCommand(command):           # How simple can it get?
    jumpTable[command]()
```

Note that this function makes two important simplifying assumptions: the command string is a key in the jump table, and its associated function expects no arguments.

Let's assume that the functions **insert**, **replace**, and **remove** are keyed to the commands '1', '2', and '3', respectively. Then the setup of the jump table is straightforward:

```
# The functions named insert, replace, and remove
# are defined earlier
jumpTable = {}
jumpTable['1'] = insert
jumpTable['2'] = replace
jumpTable['3'] = remove
```

Maintenance of the command processor becomes a matter of data management, wherein we add or remove entries in the jump table and the menu.

Exercise 7-2

1. Write the code for a mapping that generates a list of the absolute values of the numbers in a list named **numbers**.

2. Write the code for a filtering that generates a list of the positive numbers in a list named **numbers**. You should use a **lambda** to create the auxiliary function.

3. Write the code for a reducing that creates a single string from a list of strings named **words**.

4. Modify the **summation** function presented in Section 7.1 so that it includes default arguments for a step value and a function. The step value is used to move to the next value in the range. The function is applied to each number visited, and the function's returned value is added to the running total. The default step value is 1, and the default function is **lambda** that returns its argument (essentially an identity function). An example call of this function is **summation(1, 100, 2, math.sqrt)**, which returns the sum of the square roots of every other number between 1 and 100. The function can also be called as usual, with just the bounds of the range.

5. Three versions of the **summation** function have been presented in this chapter. One uses a loop, one uses recursion, and one uses the **reduce** function. Discuss the costs and benefits of each version in terms of programmer time and computational resources required.

Fail-Safe Programming

The **map** and **filter** functions discussed in Section 7.2 seem straightforward to use: you just supply a function of one argument and a list as arguments to these functions, and they return to you a list of results. The two functions work well with empty lists or nonempty lists (a map or filter on an empty list returns an empty list). However, when using **map** and **filter**, the programmer must take care to ensure the following:

1. The function argument is a function of one argument.

2. In the case of **map**, the function argument must expect as its argument the same type of value as the values contained in the list. For example, you can map the **abs** function onto a list of integers but not onto a list of strings.

(continues)

3. In the case of **filter**, the function argument must be a predicate, or a function that returns a Boolean value. For example, the function **lambda x: x % 2 == 0** is a predicate that can be used with **filter**, but the function **abs**, which returns an **int**, is not.

The **functools.reduce** function requires even more care in its use. This function requires a function of two arguments and a list as arguments and returns a value of the same type as the items in the list. The programmer must also take care to ensure the following:

1. The arguments of the function argument and its return value are of the same type as the items in the list. For example, the function **lambda x, y: x * y** can be used to build the product of the numbers in a list of numbers, but it will not work with a list of strings.

2. When used with just the two required arguments, **functools.reduce** will not work with empty lists.

   To illustrate, here are three attempts to obtain the product of numbers in a list:

```
>>> from functools import reduce
>>> reduce(lambda x, y: x * y, [1, 2, 3])
6
>>> reduce(lambda x, y: x * y, [1])
1
>>> reduce(lambda x, y: x * y, [])
Traceback (most recent call last):
  File "<pyshell#11>", line 1, in <module>
    reduce(lambda x, y: x * y, [])
TypeError: reduce() of empty iterable with no initial value
```

The third attempt, with an empty list, generates an error, because the function has no values to work with. The second attempt, with a list of one item, at least returns that item as a default value. A quick examination of Python's help can remind the programmer of the proper use of this function, which can take a base value as an optional argument:

```
>>> help(reduce)
Help on built-in function reduce in module _functools:

reduce(...)
    reduce(function, iterable[, initial]) -> value

    Apply a function of two arguments cumulatively to the items of a sequence
    or iterable, from left to right, so as to reduce the iterable to a single
    value. For example, reduce(lambda x, y: x+y, [1, 2, 3, 4, 5]) calculates
    ((((1+2)+3)+4)+5). If initial is present, it is placed before the items
    of the iterable in the calculation, and serves as a default when the
    iterable is empty.
```

Whenever you begin to use a new programming resource whose behavior might be unfamiliar to you, it's a good idea to check the Python help for a better understanding.

Summary

- Recursive design is a special case of top-down design, in which a complex problem is decomposed into smaller problems of the same form. Thus, the original problem is solved by a single recursive function.

- A recursive function is a function that calls itself. A recursive function consists of at least two parts: a base case that ends the recursive process and a recursive step that continues it. These two parts are structured as alternative cases in a selection statement.

- The design of recursive algorithms and functions often follows the recursive character of a problem or a data structure.

- Although it is a natural and elegant problem-solving strategy, recursion can be computationally expensive. Recursive functions can require extra overhead in memory and processing time to manage the information used in recursive calls.

- An infinite recursion arises as the result of a design error. The programmer has not specified the base case or reduced the size of the problem in such a way that the termination of the process is reached.

- Functions are first-class data objects. They can be assigned to variables, stored in data structures, passed as arguments to other functions, and returned as the values of other functions.

- Higher-order functions can expect other functions as arguments and/or return functions as values.

- A mapping function expects a function and a list of values as arguments. The function argument is applied to each value in the list, and a map object containing the results is returned.

- A predicate is a Boolean function.

- A filtering function expects a predicate and a list of values as arguments. The values for which the predicate returns True are placed in a filter object and returned.

- A reducing function expects a function and a list of values as arguments. The function is applied to the values, and a single result is accumulated and returned.

- A jump table is a simple way to design a command processor. The table is a dictionary whose keys are command names and whose values are the associated functions. A function for a given command name is simply looked up in the table and called.

Key Terms

anonymous function	infinite recursion	recursive definition
base case	jump table	recursive design
call stack	lambda	recursive function
Fibonacci number	mapping	recursive step
filtering	parent	reducing
first-class data objects	path	root directory
higher-order function	predicate	stack frame
indirect recursion	recursive call	stack overflow error

Review Questions

1. The part of a recursive function that ends the recursive process is called the

   a. recursive step
   b. base case
   c. loop continuation condition
   d. loop update

2. The part of a recursive function that continues the recursive process is called the

   a. recursive step
   b. base case
   c. loop continuation condition
   d. loop update

3. A recursive function usually

   a. runs faster than the equivalent loop
   b. runs more slowly than the equivalent loop
   c. runs at the same speed as the equivalent loop
   d. uses the same amount of memory the equivalent loop

4. When a recursive function is called, the values of its arguments and its return address are placed in a

   a. list
   b. dictionary
   c. set
   d. stack frame

5. The keyword used to construct an anonymous function is

   a. `while`
   b. `if`
   c. `return`
   d. `lambda`

6. The function that creates a sequence of the values by applying another function to a sequence of arguments is named

   a. `filter`
   b. `map`
   c. `reduce`
   d. `range`

7. The expression `list(map(math.sqrt, [9, 25, 36]))` evaluates to

   a. 70
   b. [81, 625, 1296]
   c. [3.0, 5.0, 6.0]
   d. []

8. The expression `list(filter(lambda x: x > 50, [34, 65, 10, 100]))` evaluates to

   a. []
   b. [65, 100]
   c. [34, 65, 10, 100]
   d. [34, 10]

9. The expression `reduce(max, [34, 21, 99, 67, 10])` evaluates to

   a. 231
   b. 0
   c. 99
   d. 100

10. A data structure used to implement a jump table is a

    a. list
    b. tuple
    c. dictionary
    d. string

Programming Exercises

1. Convert Newton's method for approximating square roots in Programming Exercise 6.1 (in the file **newton.py**) to a recursive function named **newton**. (*Hint:* The estimate of the square root should be passed as a second argument to the function.) (LO: 7.1)

2. Restructure Newton's method (Case Study 3-2: Approximating Square Roots, Chapter 3) by decomposing it into three cooperating functions. The **newton** function should use the recursive strategy of Programming Exercise 7.1 (in the file **newton.py**). The task of testing for the limit is assigned to a function named **limitReached**, whereas the task of computing a new approximation is assigned to a function named **improveEstimate**. Each function expects the relevant arguments and returns an appropriate value. (LO: 7.1)

3. Add a command to this chapter's case study program (in the file **filesys.py**) that allows the user to view the contents of a file in the current working directory. When the command is selected, the program should call the function **viewFile** to display a list of filenames and a prompt for the name of the file to be viewed. Be sure to include error recovery. (LO: 7.1)

4. Write a recursive function that expects a pathname as an argument. The pathname can be either the name of a file or the name of a directory. If the pathname refers to a file, its name is displayed, followed by its contents. Otherwise, if the pathname refers to a directory, the function is applied to each name in the directory. Test this function in a new program (in the file **viewfiles.py**). (LO: 7.1)

5. Lee has discovered what he thinks is a clever recursive strategy for printing the elements in a sequence (string, tuple, or list). He reasons that he can get at the first element in a sequence using the 0 index, and he can obtain a sequence of the rest of the elements by slicing from index 1. This strategy is realized in a function that expects just the sequence as an argument. If the sequence is not empty, the first element in the sequence is printed and then a recursive call is executed. On each recursive call, the sequence argument is sliced using the range **1:**. Here is Lee's function definition:

```python
def printAll(seq):
    if seq:
        print(seq[0])
        printAll(seq[1:])
```

Write a script (in the file **testprintlist.py**) that tests this function and add code to trace the argument on each call. Does this function work as expected? If so, explain how it works, and describe any hidden costs in running it. (LO: 7.1)

6. Write a program (in the file **average.py**) that computes and prints the average of the numbers in a text file. You should make use of two higher-order functions to simplify the design. (LO: 7.2)

7. The grammar checker of Case Study 6-1: Recognizing Sentences in Chapter 6 (in the file **recognizer.py**) does not handle sentences with an arbitrary number of independent clauses. Use the modified grammar rule discussed in Section 7.1 to design, implement, and test a recursive **sentence** function that performs this task. (LO: 7.1)

8. Suppose that Python does not include the higher-order functions **map**, **filter**, and **reduce**. Define three corresponding functions, named **myMap**, **myFilter**, and **myReduce**, in a new module named **hof** (in the file **hof.py**). The **myMap** and **myFilter** functions expect a function of one argument and a list as arguments and return a list of the results. The **myReduce** function expects a function of two arguments and a nonempty list as arguments and returns a single value. Test your functions in a short tester program (in the file **testhof.py**) that compares their behavior to that of Python's own **map**, **filter**, and **reduce** functions. (LO: 7.2)

Debugging Exercise

Jill points out to Jack that English grammar allows a noun to be modified by zero or more adjectives. Examples are "The girl hit the ball," "The girl hit the red ball," and "The girl hit the little red ball." She asks Jack to design and implement a function to generate noun phrases based on the following grammar rules:

```
nounphrase = article [adjectivephrase] noun
adjectivephrase = adjective [adjectivephrase]
```

where an adjective phrase is one or more adjectives (remember that the [] brackets indicate an optional item in a grammar rule). Jack's code for the **nounPhrase** and **adjectivePhrase** functions follows:

```
#nounphrase = article [adjectivephrase] noun
def nounPhrase():
    """Builds and returns a noun phrase."""
    return random.choice(articles) + " " + \
            adjectivePhrase() + " " + random.choice(nouns)


#adjectivephrase = adjective [adjectivephrase]
def adjectivePhrase():
    """Builds and returns an adjective phrase."""
    return random.choice(adjective) + " " + adjectivePhrase()
```

When Jack tests the **nounPhrase** function, the PVM halts the program with a **RecursionError**. Explain why this error occurs and correct it.

Custom Multiply Recursive

Prompt

If we go back to elementary school, we remember multiplication is just repeated addition. That is, when you multiply a number by 2, you are adding it together such that you have two original numbers together. Multiplying a number by 3 means you add it to itself in such a way that you are adding 3 of that number together. Let us revisit a prior lab—manual multiplication. You will be rewriting the lab so that your solution is done recursively.

Hints

Remember, you will have a base case and a recursive case. Your base case might actually contain checks for two values, like 0 and 1. This is still considered your base case. Think about your base case as a rule that is always true, where we can start calculations. If you don't have a base case, then you need to split the problem up into a smaller one and have your function call itself again!

Examples

Your prior examples should still work the exact same way. You are only changing the internals of the algorithm NOT what the algorithm does.

Answer

See Chapter 7_Custom Multiplier Recursive.py

After Discussion

Because we use "range(0,x)" we first make sure that x is positive. If x is negative, we do some basic algebra:

```
-x * y = (-1)*x * y = x * (-1)*y = x * -y
```

This preserves the sign of x in the equation, while making the range() statement work as well. From here, we just perform repeated addition (if y is negative, it will be subtraction) the needed number of times. Python handles the rest!

As always, there are multiple solutions to this exercise.

## Chapter 8

Simple Graphics and Image Processing

Learning Objectives

After you complete this chapter, you will be able to:

8.1 Create two-dimensional simple graphics using RGB systems, recursive algorithms, and Turtle operations.

8.2 Process digital images using nested loops and image-manipulating operations.

Until about 35 years ago, computers processed numbers and text almost exclusively. Since then, the computational processing of images, video, and sound has become increasingly important. Computers have evolved from number crunchers and data processors to multimedia platforms deploying a wide array of applications on devices such as DVD players and smartphones.

All of these exciting tools and applications still rely on number crunching and data processing. However, because the supporting algorithms and data structures can be quite complex, they are often hidden from the average user. In this chapter, we explore some basic concepts related to two important areas of media computing: graphics and image processing. We also examine **object-based programming**, a type of programming that relies on objects and methods to control complexity and solve problems in these areas. (*Note*: Object-based programming, which involves just the use of objects, classes, and methods, is a simpler idea than object-oriented programming, a more advanced topic that we explore in Chapters 9 and 10.)

8.1 Simple Graphics

Graphics is the discipline that underlies the representation and display of geometric shapes in two- and three-dimensional space, as well as image processing. Python comes with a large array of resources that support graphics operations. However, these operations can be complex. To help you ease into the world of graphics, this section provides an introduction to a gentler set of graphics operations known as **Turtle graphics**. A Turtle graphics toolkit provides a simple and enjoyable way to draw pictures in a window and gives you an opportunity to run several methods with an object. In the next few sections, we use Python's `turtle` module to illustrate various features of object-based programming.

Overview of Turtle Graphics

Turtle graphics were originally developed as part of the children's programming language Logo, created by Seymour Papert and his colleagues at MIT in the late 1960s. The name is intended to suggest a way to think about the drawing process. Imagine a turtle crawling on a piece of paper with a pen tied to its tail. Commands direct the turtle as it moves across the paper and tell it to lift or lower its tail, turn some number of degrees left or right, and move a specified distance. Whenever the tail is down, the pen drags along the paper, leaving a trail. In this manner, it is possible to program the turtle to draw pictures ranging from simple to complex.

In the context of a computer, of course, the sheet of paper is a window on a display screen, and the turtle is an icon, such as an arrowhead. At any given moment in time, the turtle is located at a specific position in the window. This position is specified with (x, y) coordinates. The **coordinate system** for Turtle graphics is the standard Cartesian system, with the **origin** $(0, 0)$ at the center of a window. The turtle's initial position is the origin, which is also called the **home**. An equally important attribute of a turtle is its heading, or the direction in which it currently faces. The turtle's initial heading is 0 degrees, or due east on its map. The degrees of the heading increase as it turns to the left, so 90 degrees is due north.

In addition to its position and heading, a turtle also has several other attributes, as described in **Table 8-1**.

Table 8-1   Some attributes of a turtle

Heading	Specified in degrees, the heading or direction increases in value as the turtle turns to the left, or counterclockwise. Conversely, a negative quantity of degrees indicates a right, or clockwise, turn. The turtle is initially facing east, or 0 degrees. North is 90 degrees.
Color	Initially black, the color can be changed to any of more than 16 million other colors.
Width	This is the width of the line drawn when the turtle moves. The initial width is 1 pixel. (You'll learn more about pixels shortly.)
Down	This attribute, which can be either true or false, controls whether the turtle's pen is up or down. When true (i.e., when the pen is down), the turtle draws a line when it moves. When false (i.e., when the pen is up), the turtle can move without drawing a line.

Together, these attributes make up a turtle's **state**. The concept of state is an important one in object-based programming. Generally, an object's state is the set of values of its attributes at any given point in time.

The turtle's state determines how the turtle will behave when any operations are applied to it. For example, a moving turtle will draw if its pen is currently down, but it will simply move without drawing when its pen is currently up. Operations also change a turtle's state. For instance, moving a turtle changes its position but not its direction, pen width, or pen color.

Turtle Operations

In Chapter 5, you learned that every data value in Python is an **object**. The types of objects are called **classes**. Included in a class are the **methods** (or operations) that apply to objects of that class. Because a turtle is an object, its operations are also defined as methods. **Table 8-2** lists some of the methods belonging to the `Turtle` class. In this table, the variable `t` refers to a particular `Turtle` object. Don't be concerned if you don't understand all the terms used in the table. You'll learn more about these graphics concepts throughout this chapter.

The set of methods of a given class of objects is called its **interface**. This is another important idea in object-based programming. Programmers who use objects interact with them through their interfaces. Thus, an interface should contain only enough information to use an object of a given class. This information includes method headers and documentation

Table 8-2 The `Turtle` methods

Turtle Method	What it Does
`t = Turtle()`	Creates a new `Turtle` object and opens its window
`t.home()`	Moves `t` to the center of the window and then points `t` east
`t.up()`	Raises `t`'s pen from the drawing surface
`t.down()`	Lowers `t`'s pen to the drawing surface
`t.setheading(degrees)`	Points `t` in the indicated direction, which is specified in degrees; east is 0 degrees, north is 90 degrees, west is 180 degrees, and south is 270 degrees
`t.left(degrees)` `t.right(degrees)`	Rotates `t` to the left or the right, relative to its current heading, by the specified degrees
`t.goto(x, y)`	Moves `t` to the specified position
`t.forward(distance)`	Moves `t` the specified distance in the current direction
`t.pencolor(r, g, b)` `t.pencolor(string)`	Changes the pen color of `t` to the specified RGB value or to the specified string, such as `"red"`; returns the current color of `t` when the arguments are omitted
`t.fillcolor(r, g, b)` `t.fillcolor(string)`	Changes the fill color of `t` to the specified RGB value or to the specified string, such as `"red"`; returns the current fill color of `t` when the arguments are omitted.
`t.begin_fill()` `t.end_fill()`	Encloses a set of turtle commands that will draw a filled shape using the current fill color
`t.clear()`	Erases all of the turtle's drawings without changing the turtle's state
`t.width(pixels)`	Changes the width of `t` to the specified number of pixels; returns `t`'s current width when the argument is omitted
`t.hideturtle()` `t.showturtle()`	Makes the turtle invisible or visible
`t.position()`	Returns the current position `(x, y)` of `t`
`t.heading()`	Returns the current direction of `t`
`t.isdown()`	Returns `True` if `t`'s pen is down or `False` otherwise

about the method's arguments, values returned, and changes to the state of the associated objects. As you have seen in previous chapters, Python's docstring mechanism allows the programmer to view an interface for an entire class or an individual method by entering expressions of the form `help(<class name>)` or `help(<class name>.<method name>)` at a shell prompt. The expression `dir(<class name>)` lists the names of methods in a class's interface.

To illustrate the use of some methods with a `Turtle` object, let's define a function named `drawSquare`. This function expects as arguments a `Turtle` object, a pair of integers that indicate the coordinates of the square's upper-left corner, and an integer that designates the length of a side. The function begins by lifting the turtle up and moving it to the square's corner point. It then points the turtle due south—270 degrees—and places the turtle's pen down on the drawing surface. Finally, it moves the turtle the given length and turns it left by 90 degrees, four times. Here is the code for the `drawSquare` function:

```python
def drawSquare(t, x, y, length):
    """Draws a square with the given turtle t, an upper-left
    corner point (x, y), and a side's length."""
    t.up()
    t.goto(x, y)
    t.setheading(270)
    t.down()
```

```
for count in range(4):
    t.forward(length)
    t.left(90)
```

As you can see, this function exercises half a dozen methods in the turtle's interface. Almost all you need to know in many graphics applications are the interfaces of the appropriate objects and the geometry of the desired shapes.

Two other important classes used in Python's Turtle graphics system are **Screen**, which represents a turtle's associated window, and **Canvas**, which represents the area in which a turtle can move and draw lines. A canvas can be larger than its window, which displays just the area of the canvas visible to the human user. We will have more to say about these two objects later, but first let's examine how to create and manipulate a turtle in the IDLE shell.

Setting Up a turtle.cfg File and Running IDLE

Before you run a program or an experiment in IDLE with Python's **turtle** module, it will help to set up a configuration file. A Turtle graphics configuration file, which has the filename **turtle.cfg**, is a text file that contains the initial settings of several attributes of **Turtle**, **Screen**, and **Canvas** objects. Python creates default settings for these attributes, which you can find in the Python documentation. For example, the default window size is half of your computer monitor's width and three-fourths of its height, and the window's title is "Python Turtle Graphics." If you want an initial window size of 300 by 200 pixels instead, you can override the default size by including the specific dimensions in a configuration file. The attributes in the file used for most of our examples are as follows:

```
width = 300
height = 200
using_IDLE = True
colormode = 255
```

To create a file with these settings, open a text editor, enter the settings as shown, and save the file as **turtle.cfg** in your current working directory (the one where you are saving your Python script files or from which you launch IDLE). Or you can just use the file that comes with the examples used in this book.

Now you can launch IDLE in the usual way, and you should be able to run the Turtle graphics examples discussed in this section.

Object Instantiation and the `turtle` Module

Before you use some objects, like a **Turtle** object, you must create them. To be precise, you must create an **instance** of the object's class. The process of creating an object is called **instantiation**. In the programs you have seen so far in this book, Python automatically created objects such as numbers, strings, and lists when it encountered them as literals. The programmer must explicitly instantiate other classes of objects, including those that have no literals. The syntax for instantiating a class and assigning the resulting object to a variable is the following:

```
<variable name> = <class name>(<any arguments>)
```

The expression on the right side of the assignment, also called a **constructor**, resembles a function call. The constructor can receive any initial values for the new object's attributes or other information needed to create the object as arguments. As you might expect, if the arguments are optional, reasonable defaults are provided automatically. The constructor then manufactures and returns a new instance of the class.

The **Turtle** class is defined in the **turtle** module (note carefully the spelling of both names). The following code imports the **Turtle** class for use in a session:

```
>>> from turtle import Turtle
```

The next code segment creates and returns a **Turtle** object and opens a drawing window. The window is shown in **Figure 8-1**.

```
>>> t = Turtle()
```

As you can see, the turtle's icon is located at the home position (0, 0) in the center of the window, facing east and ready to draw. The user can resize the window in the usual manner.

Figure 8-1   Drawing window for a turtle

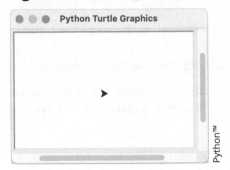

Let's continue with the turtle named **t** and tell it to draw the letter T, in black and red. It begins at the home position, accepts a new pen width of 2, turns 90 degrees left, and moves north 30 pixels to draw a black vertical line. Then it turns 90 degrees left again to face west, picks its pen up, and moves 10 pixels. The turtle next turns to face due east, changes its color from black to red, puts its pen down, and moves 20 pixels to draw a horizontal line. Finally, we hide the turtle. The session with the code follows.

Figure 8-2 shows screenshots of the window after each line segment is drawn.

Figure 8-2   Drawing vertical and horizontal lines for the letter T

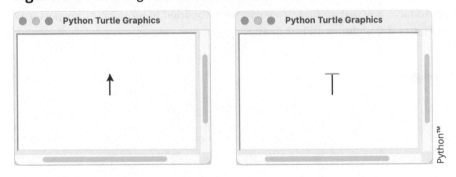

```
>>> t.width(2)          # For bolder lines
>>> t.left(90)          # Turn to face north
>>> t.forward(30)       # Draw a vertical line in black
>>> t.left(90)          # Turn to face west
>>> t.up()              # Prepare to move without drawing
>>> t.forward(10)       # Move to beginning of horizontal line
>>> t.setheading(0)     # Turn to face east
>>> t.pencolor("red")
>>> t.down()            # Prepare to draw
>>> t.forward(20)       # Draw a horizontal line in red
>>> t.hideturtle()      # Make the turtle invisible
```

To close a turtle's window, you click its close box. An attempt to manipulate a turtle whose window has been closed raises an exception.

Drawing Two-Dimensional Shapes

Many graphics applications use **vector graphics**, which includes the drawing of simple two-dimensional shapes, such as rectangles, triangles, pentagons, and circles. Earlier we defined a `drawSquare` function that draws a square with a given corner point and length, and we could do the same for other types of shapes as well. However, our design of the `drawSquare` function has two limitations:

1. The caller must provide the shape's location, such as a corner point, as an argument, even though the turtle itself could already provide this location
2. The shape is always oriented in the same way, even though the turtle itself could provide the orientation.

A more general method of drawing a square would receive just its length and the turtle as arguments and begin drawing from the turtle's current heading and position. Here is the code for the new function to draw squares, named `square`:

```
def square(t, length):
    """Draws a square with the given length."""
    for count in range(4):
        t.forward(length)
        t.left(90)
```

The same design strategy works for drawing any **regular polygon**. Here is a function to draw a hexagon:

```
def hexagon(t, length):
    """Draws a hexagon with the given length."""
    for count in range(6):
        t.forward(length)
        t.left(60)
```

Because these functions allow the shapes to have any orientation, they can be embedded in more complex patterns. For example, the radial pattern shown in **Figure 8-3** includes 10 hexagons.

Figure 8-3   A radial pattern with 10 hexagons

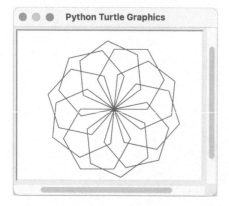

The code for a function to draw this type of pattern, named `radialHexagons`, expects a turtle, the number of hexagons, and the length of a side as arguments. Here is the code for the function:

```
def radialHexagons(t, n, length):
    """Draws a radial pattern of n hexagons with the given length."""
    for count in range(n):
        hexagon(t, length)
        t.left(360 / n)
```

To give these functions a test drive, you can define them in a module named **polygons**. Then, after launching IDLE from the same directory, you can run a session like the following:

```
>>> from polygons import *        # Import all the functions
>>> from turtle import Turtle
>>> t = Turtle()
>>> t.pencolor("blue")
>>> t.hideturtle()
>>> square(t, 50)                 # Embed a square in a hexagon
>>> hexagon(t, 50)
>>> t.clear()                     # Erase all drawings
>>> radialHexagons(t, 10, 50)   # Shown in Figure 8.3
```

You can define similar functions to draw radial patterns consisting of other shapes, such as squares or pentagons. However, the perceptive reader will note that the only change in the code for these functions would be the name of the function called to draw the shape within the loop. This observation suggests providing this function an additional argument of a more general function, which can draw a radial pattern using any regular polygon. Here is the code for this new function, named **radialPattern**, followed by a session using it with squares and hexagons:

```
def radialPattern(t, n, length, shape):
    """Draws a radial pattern of n shapes with the given length."""
    for count in range(n):
        shape(t, length)
        t.left(360 / n)

>>> from polygons import *
>>> from turtle import Turtle
>>> t = Turtle()
>>> radialPattern(t, n = 10, length = 50, shape = square)
>>> t.clear()
>>> radialPattern(t, n = 10, length = 50, shape = hexagon)
```

Note the use of keywords with the arguments to these two function calls. Keywords are not required, but they help the reader to see what the roles of the arguments are.

Examining an Object's Attributes

The **Turtle** methods shown in the examples thus far modify a **Turtle** object's attributes, such as its position, heading, and color. These methods are called **mutator methods**, meaning that they change the internal state of a **Turtle** object. Other methods, such as **position()**, simply return the values of a **Turtle** object's attributes without altering its state. These methods are called **accessor methods**. The next code segment shows some accessor methods in action:

```
>>> from turtle import Turtle
>>> t = Turtle()
>>> t.position()
(0.0, 0.0)
>>> t.heading()
0.0
>>> t.isdown()
True
```

Manipulating a Turtle's Screen

As mentioned earlier, a `Turtle` object is associated with instances of the classes `Screen` and `Canvas`, which represent the turtle's window and the drawing area underneath it. The `Screen` object's attributes include its width and height in pixels and its background color, among other things. You access a turtle's `Screen` object using the notation `t.screen`, and then call a `Screen` method on this object. The methods `window_width()` and `window_height()` can be used to locate the boundaries of a turtle's window. The following code resets the screen's background color, which is white by default, to orange, and prints the coordinates of the upper left and lower right corners of the window:

```
>>> from turtle import Turtle
>>> t = Turtle()
>>> t.screen.bgcolor("orange")
>>> x = t.screen.window_width() // 2
>>> y = t.screen.window_height() // 2
>>> print((-x, y), (x, -y))
```

Taking a Random Walk

Animals often appear to wander about randomly, but they often may be searching for food, shelter, or a mate. Other times they might be truly lost, disoriented, or just out for a stroll. Let's get a turtle to wander about randomly. A turtle engages in this harmless activity by repeatedly turning in a random direction and moving a given distance. The following script defines a function `randomWalk` that expects as arguments a `Turtle` object, the number of turns, and distance to move after each turn. The distance argument is optional and defaults to 20 pixels. When called in this script, the function performs 40 random turns with a distance of 30 pixels. **Figure 8-4** shows one resulting output.

```
from turtle import Turtle
import random

def randomWalk(t, turns, distance = 20):
    """Turns a random number of degrees and moves a given
    distance for a fixed number of turns."""
    for x in range(turns):
        degrees = random.randint(0, 270)
        if x % 2 == 0:
            t.left(degrees)
        else:
            t.right(degrees)
        t.forward(distance)

def main():
    t = Turtle()
    t.shape("turtle")
    randomWalk(t, 40, 30)

if __name__ == "__main__":
    main()
```

Figure 8-4   A random walk

Colors and the RGB System

The rectangular display area on a computer screen is made up of colored dots called picture elements or **pixels**. The smaller the pixel, the smoother the lines drawn with them will be. The size of a pixel is determined by the size and resolution of the display. For example, one common screen resolution is 1680 pixels by 1050 pixels, which, on a 20-inch monitor, produces a rectangular display area that is 17 inches by 10.5 inches. Setting the resolution to smaller values increases the size of the pixels, making the lines on the screen appear more ragged.

Each pixel represents a color. While the turtle's default color is black, you can easily change it to one of several other basic colors, such as red, yellow, or orange, by running the **pencolor** method with the corresponding string as an argument. To provide the full range of several million colors available on today's computers, we need a more powerful representation scheme. Among the various schemes for representing colors, the **RGB system** is a common one. The letters stand for the color components of red, green, and blue, to which the human retina is sensitive. These components are mixed together to form a unique color value. The computer represents these values as integers, and the display hardware translates this information to the colors you see. Each color component can range from 0 through 255. The value 255 represents the maximum saturation of a given color component, whereas the value 0 represents the total absence of that component. **Table 8-3** lists some example colors and their RGB values.

Table 8-3   Some example colors and their RGB values

Color	RGB Value
Black	(0, 0, 0)
Red	(255, 0, 0)
Green	(0, 255, 0)
Blue	(0, 0, 255)
Yellow	(255, 255, 0)
Gray	(127, 127, 127)
White	(255, 255, 255)

You might be wondering how many total RGB color values are at your disposal. That number would be equal to all the possible combinations of the three values, each of which has 256 possible values, or 256 * 256 * 256, which is 16,777,216 distinct color values. Although the human eye cannot discriminate between adjacent color values in this set, the RGB system is called a **true color** system.

Another way to consider color is from the perspective of the computer memory required to represent a pixel's color. In general, N bits of memory can represent $2N$ distinct data values. Conversely, N distinct data values require at least $\log_2 N$ bits of memory. In the old days, when memory was expensive and displays came in black and white, only a single bit of memory was required to represent the two color values (a bit of 0 turned off the light source at a given pixel position, leaving the pixel black, while a bit of 1 turned the light source on, leaving the pixel white). When displays capable of showing eight shades of gray came along, three bits of memory were required to represent each color value. Early color monitors might have supported the display of 256 colors, so eight bits were needed to represent each color value. Each color component of an RGB color requires eight bits, so the total number of bits needed to represent a distinct color value is 24. The total number of RGB colors, 2^{24}, happens to be 16,777,216.

Example: Filling Radial Patterns with Random Colors

The **Turtle** class includes the **pencolor** and **fillcolor** methods for changing the turtle's drawing and fill colors, respectively. These methods can accept integers for the three RGB components as arguments. The next script draws radial patterns of squares and hexagons with random fill colors at the corners of the turtle's window. The output is shown in **Figure 8-5**.

```
"""
File: randompatterns.py
Draws a radial pattern of squares in a random fill color
at each corner of the window.
"""

from turtle import Turtle
from polygons import *
import random

def drawPattern(t, x, y, count, length, shape):
    """Draws a radial pattern with a random
    fill color at the given position."""
    t.begin_fill()
    t.up()
    t.goto(x, y)
    t.setheading(0)
    t.down()
    t.fillcolor(random.randint(0, 255),
                random.randint(0, 255),
                random.randint(0, 255))
    radialPattern(t, count, length, shape)
    t.end_fill()

def main():
    t = Turtle()
    t.speed(0)
    t.hideturtle()
    # Number of shapes in radial pattern
    count = 10
    # Relative distances to corners of window from center
    width = t.screen.window_width() // 2
    height = t.screen.window_height() // 2
    # Length of the square
    length = 30
    # Inset distance from window boundary for squares
    inset = length * 2
    # Draw squares in upper-left corner
    drawPattern(t, -width + inset, height - inset, count,
            length, square)
```

```
    # Draw squares in lower-left corner
    drawPattern(t, -width + inset, inset - height, count,
                length, square)
    # Length of the hexagon
    length = 20
    # Inset distance from window boundary for hexagons
    inset = length * 3
    # Draw hexagons in upper-right corner
    drawPattern(t, width - inset, height - inset, count,
                length, hexagon)
    # Draw hexagons in lower-right corner
    drawPattern(t, width - inset, inset - height, count,
                length, hexagon)
if __name__ == "__main__":
    main()
```

Figure 8-5   Radial patterns with random fill colors

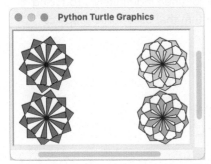

Exercise 8-1

1. Explain the importance of the interface of a class of objects.

2. What is object instantiation? What are the options at the programmer's disposal during this process?

3. Add a function named **circle** to the **polygons** module. This function expects the same arguments as the **square** and **hexagon** functions. The function should draw a circle. (*Hint*: The loop iterates 360 times.)

4. The functions that draw polygons in the **polygons** module have the same pattern, varying only in the number of sides (iterations of the loop). Factor this pattern into a more general function named **polygon**, which takes the number of sides as an additional argument.

5. Turtle graphics windows do not automatically expand in size. What do you suppose happens when a **Turtle** object attempts to move beyond a window boundary?

6. The **Turtle** class includes a method named **circle**. Import the **Turtle** class, run **help(Turtle. circle)**, and study the documentation. Then use this method to draw a filled circle and a half moon.

Case Study 8-1 | Recursive Patterns in Fractals

In this case study, we develop an algorithm that uses Turtle graphics to display a special kind of curve known as a **fractal object**. Fractals are highly repetitive or recursive patterns. A fractal object appears geometric, yet it cannot be described with ordinary Euclidean geometry. Strangely, a fractal curve is not one-dimensional, and a fractal surface is not two-dimensional. Instead, every fractal shape has its own fractal dimension. To understand what this means, let's start by considering the nature of an ordinary curve, which has a precise finite length between any two points. By contrast, a fractal curve has an indefinite length between any two points. The apparent length of a fractal curve depends on the level of detail in which it is viewed. As you zoom in on a segment of a fractal curve, you can see more and more details, and its length appears greater and greater. Consider a coastline, for example. Seen from a distance, it has many wiggles but a discernible length. Now put a piece of the coastline under magnification. It has many similar wiggles, and the discernible length increases. Self-similarity under magnification is the defining characteristic of fractals and is seen in the shapes of mountains, the branching patterns of tree limbs, and many other natural objects.

One example of a fractal curve is the **c-curve**. Figure 8-6 shows the first seven levels of c-curves and a level-10 c-curve. The level-0 c-curve is a simple line segment. The level-1 c-curve replaces the level-0 c-curve with two smaller level-0 c-curves that meet at right angles. The level-2 c-curve does the same thing for each of the two line segments in the level-1 c-curve. This pattern of subdivision can continue indefinitely, producing quite intricate shapes. In the remainder of this case study, we develop an algorithm that uses Turtle graphics to display a c-curve.

Request

Write a program that allows the user to draw a particular c-curve at varying levels.

Analysis

The proposed interface is shown in Figure 8-7. The program should prompt the user for the level of the c-curve. After this integer is entered, the program should display a Turtle graphics window in which it draws the c-curve.

Design

An N-level c-curve can be drawn with a recursive function. The function receives a **Turtle** object, the end points of a line segment, and the current level as arguments. At level 0, the function draws a simple line segment. Otherwise, a level N c-curve consists of two level $N - 1$ c-curves, constructed as follows:

Let xm be $(x1 + x2 + y1 - y2) // 2$

Let ym be $(x2 + y1 + y2 - x1) // 2$

The first level $N - 1$ c-curve uses the line segment $(x1, y1)$, (xm, ym), and level $N - 1$, so the function is called recursively with these arguments.

The second level $N - 1$ c-curve uses the line segment (xm, ym), $(x2, y2)$, and level $N - 1$, so the function is called recursively with these arguments.

For example, in a level-0 c-curve, let $(x1, y1)$ be $(50, -50)$ and $(x2, y2)$ be $(50, 50)$. Then, to obtain a level-1 c-curve, use the formulas for computing xm and ym to obtain (xm, ym), which is $(0, 0)$. Figure 8-8 shows a

Figure 8-6   C-curves of levels 0 through 6 and a c-curve of level 10

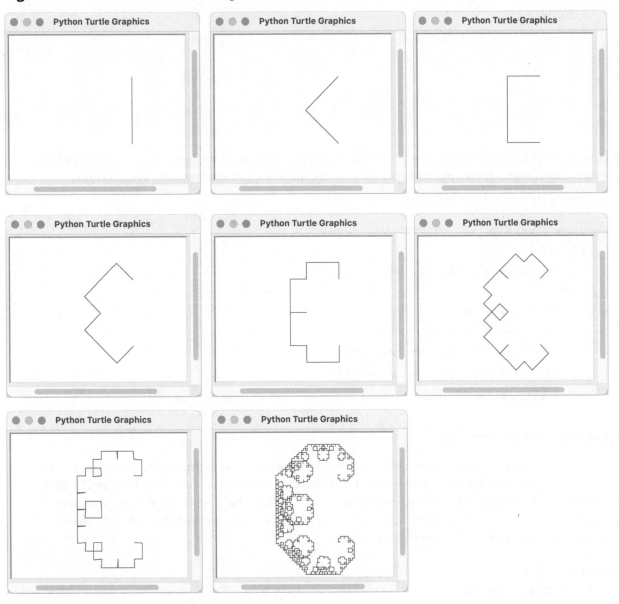

Figure 8-7   The interface for the c-curve program

Figure 8-8 A level-0 c-curve (solid) and a level-1 c-curve (dashed)

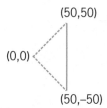

(50,50)

(0,0)

(50,–50)

solid line segment for the level-0 c-curve and two dashed line segments for the level-1 c-curve that result from these operations. In effect, the operations produce two shorter line segments that meet at right angles.

Here is the pseudocode for the recursive algorithm:

```
function cCurve(t, x1, y1, x2, y2, level)
    if level == 0:
        drawLine(x1, y1, x2, y2)
    else
        xm = (x1 + x2 + y1 - y2) // 2
        ym = (x2 + y1 + y2 - x1) // 2
        cCurve(t, x1, y1, xm, ym, level - 1)
        cCurve(t, xm, ym, x2, y2, level - 1)
```

The function **drawLine** uses the turtle to draw a line between two given endpoints.

Implementation (Coding)

The program includes the three function definitions of **cCurve**, **drawLine**, and **main**. Because **drawLine** is an auxiliary function, its definition is nested within the definition of **cCurve**. In addition to the **Turtle** class, the program imports the functions **tracer** and **update** from the **turtle** module. Because c-curves with large degrees can take a long time to draw, you can suspend the turtle's output until the entire shape has been internally generated. The pattern of code for doing this is

```
tracer(False)
<code to draw shapes>
update()


"""
Program file: ccurve.py
Author: Ken
This program prompts the user for the level of a c-curve
and draws a c-curve of that level.
"""


from turtle import Turtle, tracer, update


def cCurve(t, x1, y1, x2, y2, level):
    """Draws a c-curve of the given level."""
```

```
    def drawLine(x1, y1, x2, y2):
        """Draws a line segment between the endpoints."""
        t.up()
        t.goto(x1, y1)
        t.down()
        t.goto(x2, y2)
    if level == 0:
        drawLine(x1, y1, x2, y2)
    else:
        xm = (x1 + x2 + y1 - y2) // 2
        ym = (x2 + y1 + y2 - x1) // 2
        cCurve(t, x1, y1, xm, ym, level - 1)
        cCurve(t, xm, ym, x2, y2, level - 1)
def main():
    """Suspends drawing output if level > 8."""
    level = int(input("Enter the level (0 or greater): "))
    t = Turtle()
    if level > 8:
        tracer(False)
    t.pencolor("blue")
    t.hideturtle()
    cCurve(t, 50, -50, 50, 50, level)
    if level > 8:
        update()

if __name__ == "__main__":
    main()
```

8.2 Image Processing

Over the centuries, human beings have developed numerous technologies for representing the visual world, the most prominent being sculpture, painting, photography, and movies. The most recent form of this type of technology is digital image processing. This enormous field includes the principles and techniques for the following:

- The capture of images with devices such as flatbed scanners and digital cameras.

- The representation and storage of images in efficient file formats.

- Constructing the algorithms in image-manipulation programs such as Apple's Photos and iMovie apps.

In this section, we will focus on some of the basic concepts and principles used to solve problems in image processing.

Analog and Digital Information

Representing photographic images in a computer poses an interesting problem. As you have seen, computers must use digital information which consists of **discrete values**, such as individual integers, characters of text, or bits in a bit string. However, the information contained in images, sound, and much of the rest of the physical world is analog. **Analog information** contains a **continuous range** of values. You can get an intuitive sense of what this means by contrasting the behaviors of a digital clock and a traditional analog clock. A digital clock shows each second as a discrete number on the display. An analog clock displays the seconds as tick marks on a circle. The clock's second hand passes by these marks as it sweeps around the clock's face. This sweep reveals the analog nature of time: between any two tick marks on the analog clock, there is a continuous range of positions or moments of time through which the second hand passes. You can represent these moments as fractions of a second, but between any two such moments are others that are more precise (recall the concept of precision used with real numbers). The ticks representing seconds on the analog clock's face thus represent an attempt to **sample** moments of time as discrete values, whereas time itself is continuous, or analog.

Early recording and playback devices for images and sound were all analog devices. If you examine the surface of a vinyl record under a magnifying glass, you will notice grooves with regular wave patterns. These patterns directly reflect, or analogize, the continuous wave forms of the recorded sounds. Likewise, the chemical media on photographic film directly reflect the continuous color and intensity values of light reflected from the subjects of photographs.

Somehow, the continuous analog information in a real visual scene must be mapped into a set of discrete values. This conversion process also involves sampling, a technology we consider next.

Sampling and Digitizing Images

A visual scene projects an infinite set of color and intensity values onto a two-dimensional sensing medium, such as a human being's retina or a scanner's surface. If you sample enough of these values, the digital information can represent an image that is more or less indistinguishable to the human eye from the original scene.

Sampling devices measure discrete color values at distinct points on a two-dimensional **grid**. These values are pixels, which were introduced earlier in this chapter. In theory, the more pixels that are sampled, the more continuous and realistic the resulting image will appear. In practice, however, the human eye cannot discern objects that are closer together than 0.1 mm, so a sampling of 10 pixels per linear millimeter (250 pixels per inch and 62,500 pixels per square inch) would be plenty accurate. Thus, a 3-inch by 5-inch image would need

$$3 * 5 * 62,500 \, \text{pixels} \, / \, \text{inch}^2 = 937,500 \, \text{pixels}$$

which is approximately one megapixel. For most purposes, however, you can settle for a much lower sampling size and, thus, fewer pixels per square inch.

Image File Formats

Once an image has been sampled, it can be stored in one of many file formats. A **raw image file** saves all of the sampled information. This has a cost and a benefit: The benefit is that the display of a raw image will be the most true to life, but the cost is that the file size of the image can be quite large. Back in the days when disk storage was still expensive, computer scientists developed several schemes to compress the data of an image to minimize its file size. Although storage is now cheap, these formats are still quite economical for sending images across networks. Two of the most popular image file formats are JPEG (Joint Photographic Experts Group) and GIF (Graphic Interchange Format).

Various data-compression schemes are used to reduce the file size of a JPEG image. One scheme examines the colors of each pixel's neighbors in the grid. If any color values are the same, their positions rather than their values are stored, thus potentially saving many bits of storage. Before the image is displayed, the original color values are restored during the process of decompression. This scheme is called **lossless compression**, meaning that no information is lost. To save even more bits, another scheme analyzes larger regions of pixels and saves a color value that the pixels' colors approximate. This is called a **lossy scheme**, meaning that some of the original color information is lost. However, when the image is decompressed and displayed, the human eye usually is not able to detect the difference between the new colors and the original ones.

A GIF image relies on an entirely different compression scheme. The compression algorithm consists of two phases. In the first phase, the algorithm analyzes the color samples to build a table, or **color palette**, of up to 256 of the most prevalent colors. The algorithm then visits each sample in the grid and replaces it with the *key* of the closest color in the color palette. The resulting image file thus consists of at most 256 color values and the integer keys of the image's colors in the palette. This strategy can potentially save a huge number of bits of storage. The decompression algorithm uses the keys and the color palette to restore the grid of pixels for display. Although GIF uses a lossy compression scheme, it works very well for images with broad, flat areas of the same color, such as cartoons, backgrounds, and banners.

Image-Manipulation Operations

Image-manipulation programs either transform the information in the pixels or alter the arrangement of the pixels in the image. These programs also provide fairly low-level operations for transferring images to and from file storage. Among other things, these programs can do the following:

- Rotate an image

- Convert an image from color to grayscale

- Apply color filtering to an image

- Highlight a particular area in an image

- Blur all or part of an image

- Sharpen all or part of an image

- Control the brightness of an image

- Perform edge detection on an image

- Enlarge or reduce an image's size

- Apply color inversion to an image

- Morph an image into another image

You'll learn how to write Python code that can perform some of these manipulation tasks later in this chapter, and you will have a chance to practice others in the programming exercises.

The Properties of Images

When an image is loaded into a program such as a web browser, the software maps the bits from the image file into a rectangular area of colored pixels for display. The coordinates of the pixels in this two-dimensional grid range from (0, 0) at the upper-left corner of an image to (*width* – 1, *height* – 1) at the lower-right corner, where *width* and *height* are the image's dimensions in pixels. Thus, the **screen coordinate system** for the display of an image is somewhat different from the standard Cartesian coordinate system that we used with Turtle graphics, where the origin (0, 0) is at the center of the rectangular grid. The RGB color system introduced earlier in this chapter is a common way of representing the colors in images. For our purposes, then, an image consists of a width, a height, and a set of color values accessible by means of (*x*, *y*) coordinates. A color value consists of the tuple (*r*, *g*, *b*), where the variables refer to the integer values of its red, green, and blue components, respectively.

The `images` Module

To facilitate our discussion of image-processing algorithms, we now present a small module of high-level Python resources for image processing. This package of resources, which is named **images**, allows the programmer to load an image from a file, view the image in a window, examine and manipulate an image's RGB values, and save the image to a file. The **images** module is a nonstandard, open-source Python tool. You can find installation instructions in Appendix B, but placing the file **images.py** and some sample image files (in GIF format) in your current working directory will get you started.

The **images** module includes a class named **Image**. The **Image** class represents an image as a two-dimensional grid of RGB values. The methods for the **Image** class are listed in **Table 8-4**. In this table, the variable **i** refers to an instance of the **Image** class.

Table 8-4   The **Image** methods

Image Method	What it Does
`i = Image(filename)`	Loads and returns an image from a file with the given filename; raises an error if the filename is not found or the file is not a GIF file
`i = Image(width, height)`	Creates and returns a blank image with the given dimensions; the color of each pixel is transparent, and the filename is the empty string
`i.getWidth()`	Returns the width of i in pixels
`i.getHeight()`	Returns the height of i in pixels
`i.getPixel(x, y)`	Returns a tuple of integers representing the RGB values of the pixel at position (x, y)
`i.setPixel(x, y, (r, g, b))`	Replaces the RGB value at the position (x, y) with the RGB value given by the tuple `(r, g, b)`
`i.draw()`	Displays i in a window; the user must close the window to return control to the method's caller
`i.clone()`	Returns a copy of i
`i.save()`	Saves i under its current filename; if i does not yet have a filename, **save** does nothing
`i.save(filename)`	Saves i under **filename**; automatically adds a **.gif** extension if **filename** does not contain it

Before we discuss some standard image-processing algorithms, let's try out the resources of the **images** module. This version of the **images** module accepts only image files in GIF format. For the purposes of this exercise, we also assume that a GIF image of my cat, Smokey, has been saved in a file named **smokey.gif** in the current working directory (a program to convert your JPEG files to GIF format is mentioned in Appendix B). The following session with the interpreter does three things:

1. Imports the **Image** class from the **images** module
2. Instantiates this class using the file named **smokey.gif**
3. Draws the image

The resulting image display window is shown in **Figure 8-9**.

```
>>> from images import Image
>>> image = Image("smokey.gif")
>>> image.draw()
```

Figure 8-9   An image display window

Python raises an exception if it cannot locate the file in the current directory or if the file is not a GIF file. Note also that the user must close the window to return control to the caller of the method **draw**. If you are working in the shell, the shell prompt will reappear when you do this. The image can then be redrawn, after other operations are performed, by calling **draw** again.

Once an image has been created, you can examine its width and height, as follows:

```
>>> image.getWidth()
198
>>> image.getHeight()
149
```

Alternatively, you can print the image's string representation:

```
>>> print(image)
Filename: smokey.gif
Width: 198
Height: 149
```

The method **getPixel** returns a tuple of the RGB values at the given coordinates. The following session shows the information for the pixel at position (0, 0), which is at the image's upper-left corner.

```
>>> image.getPixel(0, 0)
(194, 221, 114)
```

Instead of loading an existing image from a file, the programmer can create a new, blank image. The programmer specifies the image's width and height; the resulting image consists of transparent pixels. Such images are useful for creating backgrounds for drawing simple shapes, or for creating new images that receive information from existing images.

The programmer can use the method **setPixel** to replace an RGB value at a given position in an image. The next session creates a new 150-by-150 image. The pixels along the three horizontal lines at the middle of the image are then replaced with new blue pixels. The images before and after this transformation are shown in **Figure 8-10**. The loop visits every pixel along the row of pixels whose *y* coordinate is the image's height divided by 2.

```
>>> image = Image(150, 150)
>>> image.draw()      # Close window to run next command
>>> blue = (0, 0, 255)
>>> y = image.getHeight() // 2
>>> for x in range(image.getWidth()):
        image.setPixel(x, y - 1, blue)
        image.setPixel(x, y, blue)
        image.setPixel(x, y + 1, blue)
>>> image.draw()
```

Figure 8-10   An image before and after replacing the pixels

Finally, you can save an image under its current filename or a different filename. Use the **save** operation to write an image back to an existing file using the current filename. The **save** operation can also receive a string argument for a new filename. The image is written to a file with that name, which then becomes the current filename. The following code saves the new image using the filename **horizontal.gif**:

```
>>> image.save("horizontal.gif")
```

If you omit the **.gif** extension in the filename, the method adds it automatically.

A Loop Pattern for Traversing a Grid

Most of the loops we have used in this book have had a linear loop structure—that is, they visit each item in a sequence of items, or they count through a sequence of numbers using a single loop control variable. By contrast, many image-processing algorithms use a nested loop structure to traverse a two-dimensional grid of pixels. **Figure 8-11** shows such a grid. Its height is 3 rows, numbered 0 through 2. Its width is 5 columns, numbered 0 through 4. Each data value in the grid is accessed with a pair of coordinates using the form (`<column>`, `<row>`). Thus, the datum in the middle of the grid, which is shaded, is at position (2, 1). The datum in the upper-left corner is at the origin of the grid, (0, 0).

Figure 8-11   A grid with three rows and five columns

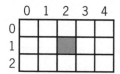

A nested loop structure to traverse a grid consists of two loops, an outer one and an inner one. Each loop has a different loop control variable. The outer loop iterates over one coordinate, while the inner loop iterates over the other coordinate. Here is a session that prints the pairs of coordinates visited when the outer loop traverses the *y* coordinates:

```
>>> width = 2
>>> height = 3
>>> for y in range(height):
        for x in range(width):
            print((x, y), end = " ")
        print()
(0, 0) (1, 0)
(0, 1) (1, 1)
(0, 2) (1, 2)
```

As you can see, this loop marches across a row in an imaginary 2-by-3 grid, prints the coordinates at each column in that row, and then moves on to the next row. The following template captures this pattern, which is called a row-major traversal. We use this template to develop many of the algorithms that follow.

```
for y in range(height):
    for x in range(width):
        <do something at position (x, y)>
```

The next code segment uses a nested **for** loop to fill a blank image in red:

```
image = Image(150, 150)
for y in range(image.getHeight()):
    for x in range(image.getWidth()):
        image.setPixel(x, y, (255, 0, 0))
```

A Word on Tuples

Many of the algorithms obtain a pixel from the image, apply some function to the pixel's RGB values, and reset the pixel with the results. Because a pixel's RGB values are stored in a tuple, manipulating them is quite easy. As you have already seen, Python allows the assignment of one tuple to another in such a manner that the elements of the source tuple can be bound to distinct variables in the destination tuple. For example, suppose you want to increase each of a pixel's RGB values by 10, thereby making the pixel brighter. You first call **getPixel** to retrieve a tuple and assign it to a tuple that contains three variables, as follows:

```
>>> image = Image("smokey.gif")
>>> (r, g, b) = image.getPixel(0, 0)
```

You can now see what the RGB values are by examining the following variables:

```
>>> r
194
>>> g
221
>>> b
114
```

The task is completed by building a new tuple with the results of the computations and resetting the pixel to that tuple:

```
>>> image.setPixel(0, 0, (r + 10, g + 10, b + 10))
```

You can use patterns like `(r, g, b)` almost anywhere except when defining parameters to a function. Instead, a function parameter must be a single name, and you must extract the components of the structure so named in the function's body. For example, the function **average** computes the average of the numbers in a triple, or 3-tuple, as follows:

```
>>> def average(triple):
        (a, b, c) = triple
        return (a + b + c) // 3
>>> average((40, 50, 60))
50
```

Armed with these basic operations, we can now examine some simple image-processing algorithms. Some of the algorithms visit every pixel in an image and modify its color in some manner. Other algorithms use the information from an image's pixels to build a new image. For consistency and ease of use, we represent each algorithm as a Python function that expects an image as an argument. Some functions return a new image, whereas others simply modify the argument image.

Converting an Image to Black and White

Perhaps the easiest transformation is to convert a color image to black and white. For each pixel, the algorithm computes the average of the red, green, and blue values. The algorithm then resets the pixel's color values to 0 (black) if the average is closer to 0, or to 255 (white) if the average is closer to 255. The code for the function **blackAndWhite** follows. **Figure 8-12** shows Smokey the cat before and after the transformation.

```
def blackAndWhite(image):
    """Converts the argument image to black and white."""
    blackPixel = (0, 0, 0)
    whitePixel = (255, 255, 255)
```

Figure 8-12 Converting a color image to black and white

```
for y in range(image.getHeight()):
    for x in range(image.getWidth()):
        (r, g, b) = image.getPixel(x, y)
        average = (r + g + b) // 3
        if average < 128:
            image.setPixel(x, y, blackPixel)
        else:
            image.setPixel(x, y, whitePixel)
```

Note that the second image appears rather stark, like a woodcut.

The function can be tested in a short script, as follows:

```
from images import Image
# Code for blackAndWhite's function definition goes here
def main(filename = "smokey.gif"):
    image = Image(filename)
    print("Close the image window to continue.")
    image.draw()
    blackAndWhite(image)
    print("Close the image window to quit.")
    image.draw()

if __name__ == "__main__":
    main()
```

Note that the **main** function includes an optional argument for the image filename. Its default should be the name of an image in the current working directory.

Converting an Image to Grayscale

Black-and-white photographs are not really just black and white; they also contain various shades of gray known as **grayscale**. Grayscale can be an economical color scheme, wherein the only color values might be 8, 16, or 256 shades of gray (including black and white at the extremes). Let's consider how to convert a color image to grayscale. As a first step, you might try replacing the color values of each pixel with their average, as follows:

```
average = (r + g + b) // 3
image.setPixel(x, y, (average, average, average))
```

Although this method is simple, it does not reflect the manner in which the different color components affect human perception. The human eye is actually more sensitive to green and red than it is to blue. As a result, the blue component appears darker than the other two components. A scheme that combines the three components needs to take these differences in luminance into account. A more accurate method would weight green more than red and red more than blue. Therefore, to obtain the new RGB values, instead of adding up the color values and dividing by 3, you should multiply each one by a weight factor and add the results. Psychologists have determined that the relative luminance proportions of green, red, and blue are .587, .299, and .114, respectively. Note that these values add up to 1. The next function, **grayscale**, uses this strategy, and **Figure 8-13** shows the results.

```python
def grayscale(image):
    """Converts the argument image to grayscale."""
    for y in range(image.getHeight()):
        for x in range(image.getWidth()):
        (r, g, b) = image.getPixel(x, y)
        r = int(r * 0.299)
        g = int(g * 0.587)
        b = int(b * 0.114)
        lum = r + g + b
        image.setPixel(x, y, (lum, lum, lum))
```

A comparison of the results of this algorithm with those of the simpler one using the crude averages is left as an exercise for you.

Figure 8-13   Converting a color image to grayscale

Copying an Image

The next few algorithms do not modify an existing image but instead use that image to generate a new image with the desired properties. One could create a new, blank image of the same height and width as the original, but it is often useful to start with an exact copy of the original image that retains the pixel information as well. The **Image** class includes a **clone** method for this purpose. The method **clone** builds and returns a new image with the same attributes as the original one, but with an empty string as the filename. The two images are thus structurally equivalent but not identical, as discussed in Chapter 5. This means that changes to the pixels in one image will have no impact on the pixels in the same positions in the other image. The following session demonstrates the use of the **clone** method:

```python
>>> from images import Image
>>> image = Image("smokey.gif")
>>> image.draw()
>>> newImage = image.clone()      # Create a copy of image
>>> newImage.draw()
>>> grayscale(newImage)           # Change in second window only
>>> newImage.draw()
>>> image.draw()                  # Verify no change to original
```

Blurring an Image

Occasionally, an image appears to contain rough, jagged edges. This condition, known as **pixilation**, can be mitigated by blurring the image's problem areas. **Blurring** makes these areas appear softer, but at the cost of losing some definition. We can now develop a simple algorithm to blur an entire image. This algorithm resets each pixel's color to the average of the colors of the four pixels that surround it. The function **blur** expects an image as an argument and returns a copy of that image with blurring. The function **blur** begins its traversal of the grid with position (1, 1) and ends with position (*width* – 2, *height* – 2). This means that the algorithm does not transform the pixels on the image's outer edges. We would like to avoid this, because otherwise the code would have to check for the grid's boundaries when it obtains information from a pixel's neighbors (the pixels on the boundaries have only two or three neighbors, rather than four). Here is the code for **blur**, followed by an explanation:

```
def blur(image):
    """Builds and returns a new image which is a
    blurred copy of the argument image."""
    def tripleSum(triple1, triple2):
#1
        (r1, g1, b1) = triple1
        (r2, g2, b2) = triple2
        return (r1 + r2, g1 + g2, b1 + b2)
    new = image.clone()
    for y in range(1, image.getHeight() - 1):
        for x in range(1, image.getWidth() - 1):
            oldP = image.getPixel(x, y)
            left = image.getPixel(x - 1, y)     # To left
            right = image.getPixel(x + 1, y)    # To right
            top = image.getPixel(x, y - 1)      # Above
            bottom = image.getPixel(x, y + 1)   # Below
            sums = reduce(tripleSum,
                        [oldP, left, right, top, bottom])
#2
            averages = tuple(map(lambda x: x // 5, sums))
#3
            new.setPixel(x, y, averages)
    return new
```

The code for **blur** includes some interesting design work. In the following explanation, the numbers noted appear to the right of the corresponding lines of code:

- At **#1**, the nested auxiliary function **tripleSum** is defined. This function expects two tuples of integers as arguments and returns a single tuple containing the sums of the values at each position.

- At **#2**, five tuples of RGB values are wrapped in a list and passed with the **tripleSum** function to the **reduce** function. This function repeatedly applies **tripleSum** to compute the sums of the tuples, until a single tuple containing the sums is returned.

- At **#3**, a **lambda** function is mapped onto the tuple of sums, and the result is converted to a tuple. The **lambda** function divides each sum by 5. Thus, you are left with a tuple of the average RGB values.

- Although this code is still rather complex, try writing it without **map** and **reduce**, and then compare the two versions.

Edge Detection

When artists paint pictures, they often sketch an outline of the subject in pencil or charcoal. They then fill in and color over the outline to complete the painting. **Edge detection** performs the inverse function on a color image: It removes the full colors to uncover the outlines of the objects represented in the image.

A simple edge-detection algorithm examines the neighbors below and to the left of each pixel in an image. If the luminance of the pixel differs from that of either of these two neighbors by a significant amount, you have detected an edge, and you set that pixel's color to black. Otherwise, you set the pixel's color to white.

The function **detectEdges** expects an image and an integer as parameters. The function returns a new black-and-white image that explicitly shows the edges in the original image. The integer parameter allows the user to experiment with various differences in luminance. **Figure 8-14** shows the image of Smokey the cat before and after detecting edges with luminance thresholds of 10 and 20. Here is the code for function **detectEdges**:

```python
def detectEdges(image, amount):
    """Builds and returns a new image in which the edges of
    the argument image are highlighted and the colors are
    reduced to black and white."""
    def average(triple):
        (r, g, b) = triple
        return (r + g + b) // 3
    blackPixel = (0, 0, 0)
    whitePixel = (255, 255, 255)
    new = image.clone()
    for y in range(image.getHeight() - 1):
        for x in range(1, image.getWidth()):
            oldPixel = image.getPixel(x, y)
            leftPixel = image.getPixel(x - 1, y)
            bottomPixel = image.getPixel(x, y + 1)
            oldLum = average(oldPixel)
            leftLum = average(leftPixel)
            bottomLum = average(bottomPixel)
            if abs(oldLum - leftLum) > amount or \
                abs(oldLum - bottomLum) > amount:
                new.setPixel(x, y, blackPixel)
            else:
                new.setPixel(x, y, whitePixel)
    return new
```

Figure 8-14   Edge detection: the original image, a luminance threshold of 10, and a luminance threshold of 20

 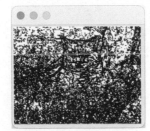 

Reducing the Image Size

The size and the quality of an image on a display medium, such as a computer monitor or a printed page, depend on two factors: the image's width and height in pixels and the display medium's **resolution**. Resolution is measured in pixels, or dots per inch (DPI). When the resolution of a monitor is increased, the images appear smaller, but their quality increases. Conversely, when the resolution is decreased, images become larger, but their quality degrades. Some devices, such as printers, provide good-quality image displays with small DPIs such as 72, whereas monitors tend to give better results with higher DPIs. You can set the resolution of an image itself before the image is captured. Scanners and digital cameras have controls that allow the user to specify the DPI values. A higher DPI causes the sampling device to take more samples (pixels) through the two-dimensional grid.

In this section, we ignore the issues raised by resolution and learn how to reduce the size of an image once it has been captured. (For the purposes of this discussion, the size of an image is its width and height in pixels.) Reducing an image's size can dramatically improve its performance characteristics, such as load time in a web page and space occupied on a storage medium. In general, if the height and width of an image are each reduced by a factor of N, the number of color values in the resulting image is reduced by a factor of N^2.

A size reduction usually preserves an image's **aspect ratio** (i.e., the ratio of its width to its height). A simple way to shrink an image is to create a new image whose width and height are a constant fraction of the original image's width and height. The algorithm then copies the color values of just some of the original image's pixels to the new image. For example, to reduce the size of an image by a factor of 2, you could copy the color values from every other row and every other column of the original image to the new image.

The Python function **shrink** exploits this strategy. The function expects the original image and a positive integer shrinkage factor as parameters. A shrinkage factor of 2 tells Python to shrink the image to half of its original dimensions, a factor of 3 tells Python to shrink the image to one-third of its original dimensions, and so forth. The algorithm uses the shrinkage factor to compute the size of the new image and then creates it. Because a one-to-one mapping of grid positions in the two images is not possible, separate variables are used to track the positions of the pixels in the original image and the new image. The loop traverses the larger image (the original) and skips positions by incrementing its coordinates by the shrinkage factor. The new image's coordinates are incremented by 1, as usual. The loop continuation conditions are also offset by the shrinkage factor to avoid range errors. Here is the code for the function **shrink**:

```python
def shrink(image, factor):
    """Builds and returns a new image which is a smaller
    copy of the argument image, by the factor argument."""
    width = image.getWidth()
    height = image.getHeight()
    new = Image(width // factor, height // factor)
    oldY = 0
    newY = 0
    while oldY < height - factor:
        oldX = 0
        newX = 0
        while oldX < width - factor:
            oldP = image.getPixel(oldX, oldY)
            new.setPixel(newX, newY, oldP)
            oldX += factor
            newX += 1
        oldY += factor
        newY += 1
    return new
```

Reducing an image's size throws away some of its pixel information. The greater the reduction, the greater the information loss. However, as the image becomes smaller, the human eye does not normally notice the loss of visual information, and therefore the quality of the image remains stable to perception.

The results are quite different when an image is enlarged. To increase the size of an image, you have to add pixels that were not there to begin with. In this case, you try to approximate the color values that pixels would receive if you took another sample of the subject at a higher resolution. This process can be very complex, because you also have to transform the existing pixels to blend in with the new ones that are added. Because the image gets larger, the human eye is in a better position to notice any degradation of quality when comparing it to the original. The development of a simple enlargement algorithm is left as an exercise for you.

Although we have covered only a tiny subset of the operations typically performed by an image-processing program, these operations and many more use the same underlying concepts and principles.

Exercise 8-2

1. Explain the advantages and disadvantages of lossless and lossy image file-compression schemes.

2. The size of an image is 1680 pixels by 1050 pixels. Assume that this image has been sampled using the RGB color system and placed into a raw image file. What is the minimum size of this file in megabytes? (*Hint*: There are 8 bits in a byte, 1024 bits in a kilobyte, and 1000 kilobytes in a megabyte.)

3. Describe the difference between Cartesian coordinates and screen coordinates.

4. Describe how a row-major traversal visits every position in a two-dimensional grid.

5. How would a column-major traversal of a grid work? Write a code segment that prints the positions visited by a column-major traversal of a 2-by-3 grid.

6. Explain why one would use the **clone** method with a given object.

7. Why does the **blur** function need to work with a copy of the original image?

Fail-Safe Programming

When you load an image from a file using the **images** module of Section 8.2, the **Image** constructor assumes that your image file is in GIF format. If you attempt to load an image file that is in another format, such as JPEG, Python raises an error. A robust program would recover from this error by detecting the format of the file, printing an error message, and gracefully allowing the user to continue. The application using the **Image** constructor can take a couple of steps in this direction:

1. If the input file's name does not have a **.gif** extension, add that to the file name. Thus, an input string named **"smokey"** would become **"smokey.gif"**. This step is similar to the step that the **save** method automatically performs when the application saves an image to a file.

2. After the application has a legitimate file name at its disposal, check the current working directory, using the **os.path.exists** function, to determine that this file exists. If that's not true, print an error message; otherwise, pass the file name on to the **Image** constructor.

These steps remedy the problems of a bad file name and a missing file. Unfortunately, the file itself might still not be in GIF format, even though its name appears to be totally respectable. You will learn how to handle this kind of error in Chapter 9.

Summary

- Object-based programming uses classes, objects, and methods to solve problems.

- A class specifies a set of attributes and methods for the objects of that class.

- The values of the attributes of a given object make up its state.

- A new object is obtained by instantiating its class. An object's attributes receive their initial values during instantiation.

- The behavior of an object depends on its current state and on the methods that manipulate this state.

- The set of a class's methods is called its interface. The interface is what a programmer needs to know to use objects of a class. The information in an interface usually includes the method headers and documentation about arguments, return values, and changes of state.

- Turtle graphics is a lightweight toolkit used to draw pictures in a Cartesian coordinate system. In this system, the `Turtle` object has a position, a color, a line width, a direction, and a state of being down or up with respect to a drawing window. The values of these attributes are used and changed when the `Turtle` object's methods are called.

- The RGB system represents a color value by mixing integer components that represent red, green, and blue intensities. There are 256 different values for each component, ranging from 0, indicating absence, to 255, indicating complete saturation. There are 2^{24} different combinations of RGB components for 16,777,216 unique colors.

- A grayscale system uses 8, 16, or 256 distinct shades of gray.

- Digital images are captured by sampling analog information from a light source, using a device such as a digital camera or a flatbed scanner. Each sampled color value is mapped to a discrete color value among those supported by the given color system.

- Digital images can be stored in several file formats. A raw image format preserves all of the sampled color information but occupies the most storage space. The JPEG format uses various data-compression schemes to reduce the file size while preserving fidelity to the original samples. Lossless schemes either preserve or reconstitute the original samples upon decompression. Lossy schemes lose some of the original sample information. The GIF format is a lossy scheme that uses a palette of up to 256 colors and stores the color information for the image as indexes into this palette.

- During the display of an image file, each color value is mapped onto a pixel in a two-dimensional grid. The positions in this grid correspond to the screen coordinate system, in which the upper-left corner is at (0, 0), and the lower-right corner is at (*width* – 1, *height* – 1).

- A nested loop structure is used to visit each position in a two-dimensional grid. In a row-major traversal, the outer loop of this structure moves down the rows using the *y*-coordinate, and the inner loop moves across the columns using the *x*-coordinate. Each column in a row is visited before moving to the next row. A column-major traversal reverses these settings.

- Image-manipulation algorithms either transform pixels at given positions or create a new image using the pixel information of a source image. Examples of the former type of operation are conversion to black and white and conversion to grayscale. Blurring, edge detection, and altering the image size are examples of the second type of operation.

Key Terms

accessor methods	grid	pixels
analog information	home	pixilation
aspect ratio	instance	raw image file
blurring	instantiation	resolution
c-curve	interface	regular polygon
classes	linear loop structure	RGB system
color filtering	lossless compression	row-major traversal
color palette	lossy scheme	sample
constructor	luminance	screen coordinate system
continuous range	methods	state
coordinate system	mutator methods	true color
discrete values	nested loop structure	Turtle graphics
edge detection	object	vector graphics
fractal object	object-based programming	
graphics	origin	

Review Questions

1. The interface of a class is the set of all its

   a. objects

   b. attributes

   c. methods

   d. functions

2. The state of an object consists of

   a. its class of origin

   b. the values of all of its attributes

   c. its physical structure

   d. its methods

3. Instantiation is a process that

   a. compares two objects for equality

   b. builds a string representation of an object

   c. creates a new object of a given class

   d. destroys an object

4. The `print` function

   a. creates a new object

   b. copies an existing object

   c. prints a string representation of an object

   d. compares two objects

5. The `clone` method

   a. creates a new object

   b. copies an existing object

   c. returns a string representation of an object

   d. returns a reference to the original object

6. The origin (0, 0) in a screen coordinate system is at the

   a. center of a window

   b. upper-left corner of a window

   c. upper-right corner of a window

   d. lower-left corner of a window

7. A row-major traversal of a two-dimensional grid visits all of the positions in a

   a. row before moving to the next row

   b. column before moving to the next column

   c. row from the last position to the first

   d. column from the last position to the first

8. In a system of 256 unique colors, the minimum number of bits needed to represent each color is

   a. 4

   b. 8

   c. 16

   d. 32

9. In the RGB system, where each color contains three components with 256 possible values each, the number of bits needed to represent each color is

   a. 8

   b. 24

   c. 256

   d. 512

10. The process whereby analog information is converted to digital information is called

   a. recording

   b. sampling

   c. filtering

   d. compressing

Programming Exercises

1. Define a function **drawCircle** (in the file **circle.py**). This function should expect a **Turtle** object, the coordinates of the circle's center point, and the circle's radius as arguments. The function should draw the specified circle. The algorithm should draw the circle's circumference by turning 3 degrees and moving a given distance 120 times. Calculate the distance moved with the formula $2.0 * \pi * radius / 120.0$. (LO: 8.1)

2. Modify this chapter's case study program (the c-curve, in the file **ccurve.py**) so that it draws the line segments using random colors. (LO: 8.1)

3. The *Koch snowflake* is a fractal shape. At level 0, the shape is an equilateral triangle. At level 1, each line segment is split into four equal parts, producing an equilateral bump in the middle of each segment. **Figure 8-15** shows these shapes at levels 0, 1, and 2. (LO: 8.1)

Figure 8-15   First three levels of a Koch snowflake

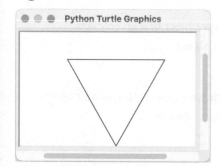 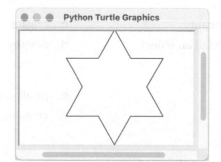 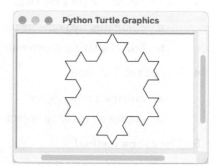

At the top level, the script uses a function **drawFractalLine** to draw three fractal lines. Each line is specified by a given distance, direction (angle), and level. The initial angles are 0, –120, and 120 degrees. The initial distance can be any size, such as 200 pixels. The function **drawFractalLine** is recursive. If the level is 0, then the turtle moves the given distance in the given direction. Otherwise, the function draws four fractal lines with one-third of the given distance, angles that produce the given effect, and the given level minus 1. Write a script (in the file **koch.py**) that draws the Koch snowflake.

4. The twentieth-century Dutch artist Piet Mondrian developed a style of abstract painting that exhibited simple recursive patterns. To generate such a pattern with a computer, one would begin with a filled rectangle in a random color and then repeatedly fill two unequal subdivisions with random colors, as shown in **Figure 8-16**. (LO: 8.1)

Figure 8-16   Generating a simple recursive pattern in the style of Piet Mondrian

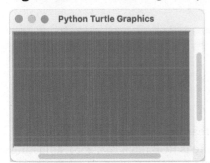 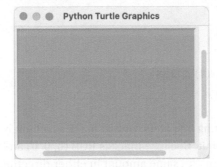 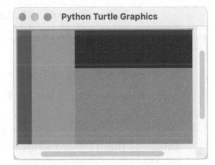

As you can see, the algorithm continues the process of subdivision until an "aesthetically right moment" is reached. In this version, the algorithm divides the current rectangle into portions representing one-third and two-thirds of its area and alternates these subdivisions along the horizontal and vertical axes. Design, implement, and test a script (in the file **mondrian.py**) that uses a recursive function to draw these patterns.

5. Define and test a function named **posterize** (in the file **posterize.py**). This function expects an image and a tuple of RGB values as arguments. The function modifies the image like the **blackAndWhite** function, but it uses the given RGB values instead of black. (LO: 8.2)

6. Define a second version of the **grayscale** function (in the file **grayscale.py**) that uses the allegedly crude method of simply averaging each RGB value. Test the function by comparing its results with those of the other version discussed in this chapter. (LO: 8.2)

7. Inverting an image makes it look like a photographic negative. Define and test a function named **invert** (in the file **invert.py**). This function expects an image as an argument and resets each RGB component to 255 minus that component. Be sure to test the function with images that have been converted to grayscale and black and white as well as color images. (LO: 8.2)

8. Old-fashioned photographs from the nineteenth century are not quite black and white and not quite color, but seem to have shades of gray, brown, and blue. This effect is known as **sepia**, as shown in **Figure 8-17**. (LO: 8.2)

Figure 8-17   Converting a color image to sepia

Write and test a function named **sepia** (in the file **sepia.py**) that converts a color image to sepia. This function should first call **grayscale** to convert the color image to grayscale. A code segment for transforming the grayscale values to achieve a sepia effect follows. Note that the value for green does not change.

```
(red, green, blue) = image.getPixel(x, y)
if red < 63:
    red = int(red * 1.1)
    blue = int(blue * 0.9)
elif red < 192:
    red = int(red * 1.15)
    blue = int(blue * 0.85)
else:
    red = min(int(red * 1.08), 255)
    blue = int(blue * 0.93)
```

9. Darkening an image requires adjusting its pixels toward black as a limit, whereas lightening an image requires adjusting them toward white as a limit. Because black is RGB (0, 0, 0) and white is RGB (255, 255, 255), adjusting the three RGB values of each pixel by the same amount in either direction will have the desired effect. Of course, the algorithms must avoid exceeding either limit during the adjustments. (LO: 8.2)

   Lightening and darkening are actually special cases of a process known as **color filtering**. A color filter is any RGB triple applied to an entire image. The filtering algorithm adjusts each pixel by the amounts specified in the triple. For example, you can increase the amount of red in an image by applying a color filter with a positive red value and green and blue values of 0. The filter (20, 0, 0) would make an image's overall color slightly redder. Alternatively, you can reduce the amount of red by applying a color filter with a negative red value. Once again, the algorithms must avoid exceeding the limits on the RGB values.

   Develop three algorithms for lightening, darkening, and color filtering as three related Python functions, **lighten**, **darken**, and **colorFilter** (in the file **colorfilter.py**). The first two functions should expect an image and a positive integer as arguments. The third function should expect an image and a tuple of integers (the RGB values) as arguments. The following session shows how these functions can be used with the images **image1**, **image2**, and **image3**, which are initially transparent:

```
>>> image1 = Image(100, 50)
>>> image2 = Image(100, 50)
>>> image3 = Image(100, 50)
>>> darken(image1, 128)                   # Converts to gray
>>> darken(image2, 64)                     # Converts to dark gray
>>> colorFilter(image3, (255, 0, 0))    # Converts to red
```

   Note that most of the code to change the image is in the function **colorFilter**. (LO: 8.2)

10. The edge-detection function described in this chapter returns a black-and-white image. Think of a similar way to transform color values so that the new image is still in its original colors but the outlines within it are merely sharpened. Then, define a function named **sharpen** (in the file **sharpen.py**) that performs this operation. The function should expect an image and two integers as arguments. One integer should represent the degree to which the image should be sharpened. The other integer should represent the threshold used to detect edges. (*Hint*: A pixel can be darkened by making its RGB values smaller.) (LO: 8.2)

Debugging Exercise

Jill is developing an image processing program that creates artworks with random colors. The inputs to the program are the width and height of a new image, and the name of a file to which the image should be saved. Here is the code for Jill's program:

```python
"""
File: randomart.py
Generates and saves images with random colors.
"""

from images import Image
import random

def main():
    """Generates and saves images with random colors.
    Inputs: The image's width, height,
    and output file name."""
    width = int(input("Enter the image's width: "))
    height = int(input("Enter the image's height: "))
    fileName = input("Enter the image's file name: ")

    image = Image(width, height)
    for y in range(image.getHeight()):
        for x in range(image.getWidth()):
            r = random.randint(0, 255)
            g = random.randint(0, 255)
            b = random.randint(0, 255)
            image.setPixel(x, y, (r, g, b))

    print("Close the image window to quit. ")
    image.draw()
    image.save(fileName)

if __name__ == "__main__":
    main()
```

When Jill runs the program, she enters her inputs and views the image before it's saved. But when she closes the window and the program attempts to save the image, Python raises an error that the image has too many colors, as shown in **Figure 8-18**.

Figure 8-18 Attempting to create and save artwork with random colors

```
●  ●  ●                        IDLE Shell 3.10.4
Python 3.10.4 (v3.10.4:9d38120e33, Mar 23 2022, 17:29:05) [Clang 13.0.0 (clang-1300.0.29.30)] on
darwin
Type "help", "copyright", "credits" or "license()" for more information.
>>>
================= RESTART: /Users/ken/pythonfiles/randomart.py =================
Enter the image's width: 200
Enter the image's height: 100
Enter the image's file name: myartwork.gif
Close the image window to quit.
Traceback (most recent call last):
  File "/Users/ken/pythonfiles/randomart.py", line 30, in <module>
    main()
  File "/Users/ken/pythonfiles/randomart.py", line 27, in main
    image.save(fileName)
  File "/Users/ken/pythonfiles/images.py", line 158, in save
    self.image.write(self.filename, format = "gif")
  File "/Library/Frameworks/Python.framework/Versions/3.10/lib/python3.10/tkinter/__init__.py",
line 4157, in write
    self.tk.call(args)
tkinter.TclError: too many colors
>>>
                                                                          Ln: 19  Col: 0
```

Explain why this error occurs and describe how it can be corrected. Jack reminds Jill that the GIF format supports at most 256 unique colors.

Turtle Operations

Prompt

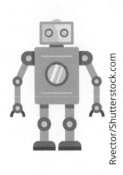

Rvector/Shutterstock.com

Ira Yapanda/Shutterstock.com

tele52/Shutterstock.com

With all of the major activities of the robot out of the way, you have been asked to begin the process of creating some diagrams and some analysis of some of the data points that we've been collecting from the robot's activities. To that end, we want to make use of some of the data points to create some potential future graphs and other shapes which can be used to analyze the movements and collection activities of the robot.

With that in mind, you're going to be drawing lines, arrows, circles, squares, and rectangles. You will create one of each of the following, show a screen shot of your environment, with the script having run and created the desired shape.

You will start with importing turtle, like so:

```
Python 3.8.2 Shell                                             —    □    ×
File  Edit  Shell  Debug  Options  Window  Help
Python 3.8.2 (tags/v3.8.2:7b3ab59, Feb 25 2020, 22:45:29) [MSC v.1916 32 bit (In
tel)] on win32
Type "help", "copyright", "credits" or "license()" for more information.
>>> from turtle import *
>>> myScreen = getscreen()
>>>
```

Now, using these tools, you will draw:

1. A square of whatever size you wish
2. An empty circle of whatever size you wish
3. A filled in circle of whatever size you wish
4. Change the screen color to red

Hints

In this lesson, you're going to be working with the turtle library. This library will allow you to call pre-defined methods that exist or were created, in the turtle library. You can then call these, after using the import statement, by supplying the required parameters, or arguments, inside the parenthesis of the function call. In the hints section, you'll find a glossary of commands that you can use to draw and create shapes using the turtle library. In addition, you'll also find some examples of how to use the commands via the screenshots included in this section.

Commands Glossary:

```
backward() - Moves the turtle backward by the desired amt.
begin_fill() - Starting point for a filled polygon
color() -- Changes the pen's color
dot() - Put a dot at the current position
down() - Puts down the Pen
end_fill() - Closes the polygon with the current fill color
fillcolor() - Changes the color used to fill a polygon
forward() - Moves the turtle forward by the desired amt
goto() - Moves to position x,y
heading() - Returns the heading
left() - Positions the turtle counterclockwise
pendown() - Puts down the pen
penup() - Picks up the pen
position() - Returns current position
right() - Turn clockwise
stamp() - Create an impression of a turtle shape at the current location
shape() - Shapes are 'arrow', 'classic', 'turtle' or 'circle'
Turtle() - Creates a new turtle object
up() - Picks up the pen
```

Drawing Examples:

Commands:

```
import turtle
skk = turtle.Turtle()


for i in range(4):
    skk.forward(50)
    skk.right(90)


turtle.done()
```

Output:

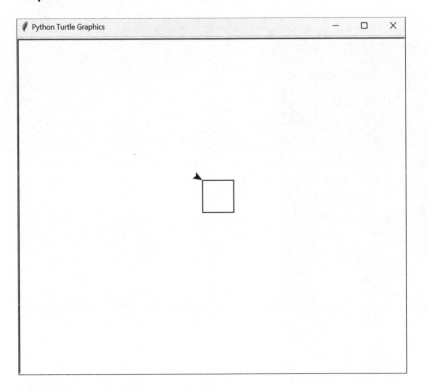

Commands:

```python
import turtle

# Set up the turtle screen
screen = turtle.Screen()
screen.bgcolor("yellow")

# Create a turtle object
circle = turtle.Turtle()
circle.color("red")
circle.speed(2)

# Draw the circle
circle.penup()
circle.goto(0, -100)
circle.pendown()
circle.begin_fill()
circle.circle(100)
circle.end_fill()

# Hide the turtle
circle.hideturtle()

# Exit the program when the screen is clicked
screen.exitonclick()
```

Output:

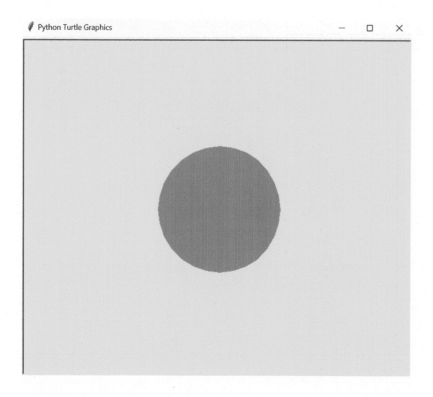

Answer

See Chapter 8_Turtle Operations.py

After Discussion

In this assignment, you've been exposed to some of the basic drawing components that can be used to create various shapes out of whatever data that is fed into it. With these shapes, any number of analysis and potentially other objectives can be fulfilled. Remember, with the shapes that you're drawing, the moves that are being made are completed using a built-in Python library, the turtle library, instead of having to create these shapes on your own—a truly custom application.

As your skills continue to grow, make sure that you explore the libraries that are available to you, as using these will drastically decrease the time needed to develop applications. Great job!

Collage Maker

Prompt

Rvector/Shutterstock.com

Ira Yapanda/Shutterstock.com

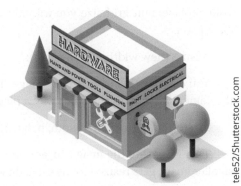

tele52/Shutterstock.com

You will be writing a program that generates a collage. The program will convert a supplied image into a collage of little images, and when you zoom out, you will see the original image!

This program will go pixel by pixel of an original input image, choose "the best" smaller image to replace it with, and output a new image made up entirely of smaller images. You could use many smaller pictures of your pet to output a larger image of your pet; you could use many smaller pictures of your individual family members to output an image of a family photo. The possibilities are endless! The smaller the images, and the more diverse they are in terms of colors, the better quality your output image can be.

Hints

Break your program down from large problems into little problems you can easily solve. You will probably want to create the following functions:

find_hamming_distance():

For this lab, we will use a very basic method of determining how different 2 color values are. The technique we will use is called a "hamming distance."

To calculate a hamming distance, you sum together the differences of each position of 2 arrays of data (or lists, tuples, etc.). For example, if you have 2 tuples, (0, 4) and (1, 6), the hamming distance would be $(1 - 0) + (6 - 4) = 1 + 2 = 3$. The hamming distance between "cat" and "bat" would be 1 ("c" changing to a "b" would be changing the "c" 1 position in the alphabet. "at" is the same as "at" so its difference would be 0). In this exercise, you will calculate hamming distances between each pixel in your source image, and the "average" (Red, Green, Blue) color tuple you determine for each smaller image in your collage.

get_average_color():

You will need to create a function to determine the "average" color of each of your smaller images. There are a variety of ways to do this, some of which apply more advanced statistical measurements. For this exercise, it is OK to calculate the statistical mean of each pixels' red, green, and blue values. Feel free to experiment here with a better algorithm!

find_best_hamming_distance():

After you calculate the "average" color of each pixel and save them off, you will need to search this array to find the best fit (the image with the smallest hamming distance to the pixel you are trying to replace).

The official documentation to the PIL.Image library is found here: https://pillow.readthedocs.io/en/stable/reference/Image.html. We will list a few helpful hints for using this library:

.width and .height:

Each image that is .open()'ed will contain these 2 attributes. Use the source image's width and height to determine your replacement grid size you will fill with smaller images, and use them to iterate over the source image to read each pixel.

.resize((new width, new height)):

You can use this to resize an image. This function might be helpful to resize your smaller images so they are all the same dimensions, the same way a pixel is the same width and height (1x1).

.paste(image_to_add, (width, height))

This will paste the image_to_add into the object it is invoked upon, with the offset at the tuple specified. If each smaller image gets resized to the same dimensions, then you can paste square by square into your output collage image.

.getpixel((width, height))

This will return a (Red, Green, Blue) tuple for the pixel found at the image's width, height coordinate.

Use "collage_maker_skel.py" as a starting point for this lab. Code is already included to generate basic smaller images in an "images/" folder of wherever you run the code from. The input image and output images are hardcoded, so make sure you check those values and change as needed.

Examples

Using the input image as the main collage image, and the default simple square images:

Input Image:

Output Image:

Notice, if you zoom in, each pixel was replaced with another image (the default images are solid colors, but you are free to find whatever you want to use).

Refer to "collage_maker_skel.py" for helper functions.

Answer

Refer to collage_maker.py

## Chapter 9

Graphical User Interfaces

Learning Objectives

After you complete this chapter, you will be able to:

9.1 Distinguish the appearance and behavior of GUI-based program from a terminal-based program

9.2 Define a new class using subclassing and inheritance to code a simple GUI-based program

9.3 Instantiate and lay out different types of window components in a window's frame

9.4 Define methods that handle events associated with window components

9.5 Perform input and output of text and numbers with entry fields

9.6 Define and use instance variables in classes

9.7 Use window components such as nested frames, popup dialogs, check boxes, and radio buttons to structure a GUI application

We are told not to judge a book by its cover. We look for its contents, not its appearance. However, users judge a software product by its user interface because they have no other way to access its functionality. With the exception of Chapter 8, in which we explored graphics and image processing, this book has focused on programs that present a terminal-based user interface. This type of user interface is perfectly adequate for some applications, and it is the simplest and easiest for beginning programmers to code. However, 99% of the world's computer users never see such a user interface. Instead, most interactive computer software employs a **graphical user interface (GUI)** (or its close relative, the touchscreen interface). A GUI displays text as well as small images (called icons) that represent objects such as folders, files of different types, command buttons, and drop-down menus. In addition to entering text at the keyboard, the user of a GUI can select some of these icons with a pointing device, such as a mouse, and move them around on the display. Commands can be activated by pressing the enter key or control keys, by pressing a command button, by selecting a drop-down menu item, or by double-clicking on some icons with the mouse. Put more simply, a GUI displays all information, including text, graphically to its users and allows them to manipulate this information directly with a pointing device.

In this chapter, you will learn how to develop GUIs. GUI-based programming requires you to use existing classes, objects, and their methods. You will also learn how to develop new classes of objects, such as application windows, by extending or repurposing existing classes. Rather than defining a new class of objects from scratch, you will create a customized version of an existing class by the mechanisms of subclassing and inheritance. GUI programming provides an engaging area for learning these techniques, which play a prominent role in modern software development.

9.1 The Behavior of Terminal-Based Programs and GUI-Based Programs

The transition to GUIs involves making a significant adjustment to your thinking. A GUI program is event driven, meaning that it is inactive until the user clicks a button or selects a menu option. In contrast, a terminal-based program maintains constant control over the interactions with the user. Put differently, a terminal-based program prompts users to enter successive inputs, whereas a GUI program puts users in charge, allowing them to enter inputs in any order and waiting for them to press a command button or select a menu option.

To make this difference clear, we begin by examining the look and behavior of two different versions of the same program from a user's point of view. This program, first introduced in Chapter 2, computes and displays a person's income tax given two inputs—the gross income and the number of dependents. The first version of the program includes a terminal-based user interface, whereas the second version uses a graphical user interface. Although both programs perform the same function, their behavior, look, and feel from a user's perspective are quite different.

The Terminal-Based Version

The terminal-based version of the program prompts the user for their gross income and number of dependents. After they enter their inputs, the program responds by computing and displaying their income tax. The program then terminates execution. A sample session with this program is shown in **Figure 9-1**.

Figure 9-1 A session with the terminal-based tax calculator program

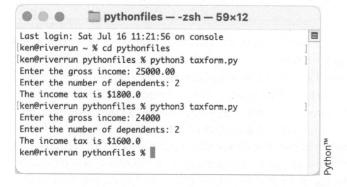

This terminal-based user interface has several obvious effects on its users:

- The user is constrained to reply to a definite sequence of prompts for inputs. Once an input is entered, there is no way to back up and change it.

- To obtain results for a different set of input data, the user must run the program again. At that point, all of the inputs must be re-entered.

Each of these effects poses a problem for users that can be solved by converting the interface to a GUI.

The GUI-Based Version

The GUI-based version of the program displays a **window** that contains various components, also called **widgets**. Some of these components look like text, while others provide visual cues as to their use. **Figure 9-2** shows snapshots of a sample session with this version of the program. The snapshot on the left shows the interface at program start-up, whereas the snapshot on the right shows the interface after the user has entered inputs and clicked the **Compute** button. This program was run on a Macintosh; on a Windows- or Linux-based PC, the windows look slightly different.

Figure 9-2   A GUI-based tax calculator program

The window in Figure 9-2 contains the following components:

- A **title bar** at the top of the window. This bar contains the title of the program, "Tax Calculator." It also contains three colored disks. Each disk is a **command button**. The user can use the mouse to click the left disk to quit the program, the middle disk to minimize the window, or the right disk to zoom the window. The user can also move the window around the screen by holding the left mouse button on the title bar and dragging the mouse.

- A set of **labels** along the left side of the window. These are text elements that describe the inputs and outputs. For example, "Gross income" is one label.

- A set of **entry fields** along the right side of the window. These are boxes within which the program can output text or receive it as input from the user. The first two entry fields will be used for inputs, while the last field will be used for the output. At program start-up, the fields contain default values, as shown in the window on the left side of Figure 9-2.

- A single command button labeled **Compute**. When the user presses this button with the mouse, the program responds by using the data in the two input fields to compute the income tax. This result is then displayed in the output field. Sample input data and the corresponding output are shown in the window on the right side of Figure 9-2.

- The user can also alter the size of the window by holding the mouse on its lower-right corner and dragging in any direction.

Although this review of features might seem tedious to anyone who regularly uses GUI-based programs, a careful inventory is necessary for the programmer who builds them. Also, a close study of these features reveals the following effects on users:

- The user is not constrained to enter inputs in a particular order. Before they press the **Compute** button, they can edit any of the data in the two input fields.

- Running different data sets does not require re-entering all of the data. The user can edit just one value and press the **Compute** button to observe different results.

When we compare the effects of the two interfaces on users, the GUI seems to be a definite improvement on the terminal-based user interface. The improvement is even more noticeable as the number of command options increases and the information to be presented grows in quantity and complexity.

Event-Driven Programming

Rather than guide the user through a series of prompts, a GUI-based program opens a window and waits for the user to manipulate window components with the mouse. These user-generated events, such as mouse clicks, trigger operations in the program to respond by pulling in inputs, processing them, and displaying results. This type of software system is event-driven, and the type of programming used to create it is called **event-driven programming**.

Like any complex program, an event-driven program is developed in several steps. In the analysis step, the types of window components and their arrangement in the window are determined. Because GUI-based programs are almost always object based, this becomes a matter of choosing among GUI component classes available in the programming language or inventing new ones if needed. Graphic designers and cognitive psychologists might be called in to assist in this phase if the analysts do not already possess this type of expertise. To a certain extent, the number, types, and arrangement of the window components depend on the nature of the information to be displayed and on the set of commands that will be available to the user for manipulating that information.

Let us return to the example of the tax calculator program to see how it might be structured as an event-driven program. The GUI in this program consists of the window and its components, including the labeled entry fields and the **Compute** button. The action triggered when this button is clicked is a method call. This method fetches the input values from the input fields and performs the computation. The result is then sent to the output field to be displayed.

Once the interactions among these resources have been determined, their coding can begin. This phase consists of several steps:

1. Define a new class to represent the main application window.
2. Instantiate the classes of window components needed for this application, such as labels, fields, and command buttons.
3. Position these components in the window.
4. Register a method with each window component in which an event relevant to the application might occur.
5. Define these methods to handle the events.
6. Define a `main` function that instantiates the window class and runs the appropriate method to launch the GUI.

In coding the program, you could initially skip Steps 4 and 5, which concern responding to user events. This would allow you to preview and refine the window and its layout, even though the command buttons and other GUI elements lack functionality.

In the sections that follow, we explore these elements of GUI-based, event-driven programming with examples in Python.

Exercise 9-1

1. Describe two fundamental differences between terminal-based user interfaces and GUIs.
2. Give an example of one application for which a terminal-based user interface is adequate and one example that lends itself best to a GUI.

9.2 Coding Simple GUI-Based Programs

In this section, we show some examples of simple GUI-based programs in Python. Python's standard `tkinter` module includes classes for windows and numerous types of window components, but its use can be challenging for beginners. Therefore, this book uses a custom, open-source module called `breezypythongui`, while occasionally relying upon some of the simpler resources of `tkinter`. You will find the code, documentation, and installation instructions for the `breezypythongui` module at **http://kennethalambert.com/breezypythongui/**. We will start with some short demo programs that illustrate some basic GUI components, and, in later sections, we will develop some examples with more significant functionality.

A Simple "Hello World" Program

Our first demo program defines a class for a main window that displays a greeting. **Figure 9-3** shows a screenshot of the window.

Figure 9-3   Displaying a label with text in a window

As in all of our GUI-based programs, a new window class **extends** the `EasyFrame` class. By "extends," we mean "repurposes" or "provides extra functionality for." The `EasyFrame` class provides the basic functionality for any window, such as the command buttons in the title bar. Our new class, named `LabelDemo`, provides additional functionality to the `EasyFrame` class. Here is the code for the program:

```
"""
File: labeldemo.py
"""

from breezypythongui import EasyFrame

class LabelDemo(EasyFrame):
    """Displays a greeting in a window."""
    def __init__(self):
        """Sets up the window and the label."""
        EasyFrame.__init__(self)
        self.addLabel(text = "Hello world!", row = 0, column = 0)

def main():
    """Instantiates and pops up the window."""
    LabelDemo().mainloop()

if __name__ == "__main__":
    main()
```

We will speak more generally about class definitions shortly. For now, note that this program performs the following steps:

1. Import the `EasyFrame` class from the `breezypythongui` module. This class is a subclass of `tkinter`'s `Frame` class, which represents a top-level window. In many GUI programs, this is the only import that you will need.

2. Define the `LabelDemo` class as a subclass of `EasyFrame`. The `LabelDemo` class describes the window's layout and functionality for this application.

3. Define an `__init__` method in the `LabelDemo` class. This method is automatically run when the window is created. The `__init__` method runs a method with the same name on the `EasyFrame` class and then sets up any window components to display in the window. In this case, the `addLabel` method is run on

the window itself. The **addLabel** method creates a window component, a label object with the text "Hello world!" and adds it to the window at the grid position (0, 0).

4. The last five lines of code define a **main** function and check to see if the Python code file is being run as a program. If this is true, the **main** function is called to create an instance of the **LabelDemo** class. The **mainloop** method is then run on this object. At this point, the window pops up for viewing. Note that **mainloop**, as the name implies, enters a loop. The Python Virtual Machine runs this loop behind the scenes. Its purpose is to wait for user events, as mentioned earlier. The loop terminates when the user clicks the window's close box.

Because Steps 1 and 4 typically have the same format in each program, they will be omitted from the text of many of the program examples that follow.

A Template for All GUI Programs

Writing the code to pop up a window that says "Hello world!" might seem like a lot of work. However, the good news is that the structure of a GUI program is always the same, no matter how complex the application becomes. Here is the template for this structure:

```
from breezypythongui import EasyFrame
Other imports
class ApplicationName(EasyFrame):
    The __init__ method definition
    Definitions of event handling methods
def main():
    ApplicationName().mainloop()
if __name__ == "__main__":
    main()
```

A GUI application window is always represented as a class that extends **EasyFrame**. The __init__ method initializes the window by setting its attributes and populating it with the appropriate GUI components. In our example, Python runs this method automatically when the constructor function **LabelDemo** is called. The event handling methods provide the responses of the application to user events (not relevant in this example program). The last lines of code, beginning with the definition of the **main** function, create an instance of the application window class and run the **mainloop** method on this instance. The window then pops up and waits for user events. Pressing the window's close button quits the program normally. If you have launched the program from an IDLE window, you can run it again after quitting by entering **main()** at the shell prompt.

The Syntax of Class and Method Definitions

Note that the syntax of class and method definitions is a bit like the syntax of function definitions. Each definition has a one-line header that begins with a keyword (**class** or **def**), followed by a body of code indented one level in the text.

A class header contains the name of the class, conventionally capitalized in Python, followed by a parenthesized list of one or more parent classes. The body of a class definition, nested one tab under the header, consists of one or more method definitions, which may appear in any order.

A method header looks very much like a function header, but a method always has at least one parameter, in the first position, named **self**. At call time, the PVM automatically assigns to this parameter a reference to the object on which the method is called; thus, you do not pass this object as an explicit argument at call time. For example, given the method header

```
def someMethod(self):
```

the method call

```
anObject.someMethod()
```

automatically assigns the object **anObject** to the **self** parameter for this method. The parameter **self** is used within class and method definitions to call other methods on the same object, or to access that object's instance variables or data, as will be explained shortly.

Subclassing and Inheritance as Abstraction Mechanisms

Our first example program defined a new class named **LabelDemo**. This class was defined as a subclass of the class **breezypythongui.EasyFrame**, which in turn is a subclass of the class **tkinter.Frame**. The subclass relationships among these classes are shown in the class diagram of **Figure 9-4**.

Figure 9-4   A class diagram for the label demo program

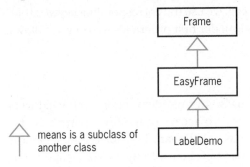

Note that the **EasyFrame** class is the parent of the **LabelDemo** class, and the **Frame** class is the parent of the **EasyFrame** class. This makes the **Frame** class the ancestor of the **LabelDemo** class. When you make a new class a subclass of another class, your new class inherits and thereby acquires the attributes and behavior defined by its parent class, and any of its ancestor classes, for free. Subclassing and inheritance are useful abstraction mechanisms since you do not have to reinvent the wheel when defining a new class of objects, just customize it a bit. For example, the **EasyFrame** class customizes the **Frame** class with methods to add window components to a window; the **LabelDemo** class customizes the **EasyFrame** method __init__ to set up a window with a specific window component.

As a rule of thumb, when you are defining a new class of objects, you should look around for a class that already supports some of the structure and behavior of such objects, and then subclass that class to provide exactly the service that you need.

> ## Exercise 9-2

1. Describe what usually happens in the __init__ method of a main window class.

2. Explain why it's a good idea to make a new class a subclass of an existing class.

9.3 Windows and Window Components

In this section, you will explore the details of windows and window components. In the process, you will learn how to choose appropriate classes of GUI objects, to access and modify their attributes, and to organize them to cooperate to perform the task at hand.

Windows and Their Attributes

A window has several attributes. The most important ones are its

- title (an empty string by default)

- width and height in pixels

- resizability (true by default)

- background color (white by default)

The attributes of our label demo program's window have default values. The background color is white, and the window is resizable. The window's initial dimensions are automatically established by shrink-wrapping the window around the label contained in it. We can override the window's default title, an empty string, by supplying another string as an optional `title` argument to the `EasyFrame` method `__init__`. Other options are to provide a custom initial width and height in pixels. Note that whenever we supply arguments to a method call, we use the corresponding keywords for clarity in the code. For example, you might override the dimensions and title of our first program's window as follows:

```
EasyFrame.__init__(self, width = 300, height = 200,
                   title = "Label Demo")
```

Another way to change a window's attributes is to reset them in the window's **attribute dictionary**. Each window or window component maintains a dictionary of its attributes and their values. To access or modify an attribute, the programmer uses the standard subscript notation with the attribute name as a dictionary key. For example, later in the label demo's `__init__` method, the window's background color can be set to yellow with the following statement:

```
self["background"] = "yellow"
```

Note that `self` in this case refers to the window itself.

The final way to change a window's attributes is to run a method included in the `EasyFrame` class. This class includes the four methods listed in **Table 9-1**.

Table 9-1 Methods to change a window's attributes

`EasyFrame` **Method**	**What it Does**
`setBackground(color)`	Sets the window's background color to `color`.
`setResizable(aBoolean)`	Makes the window resizable (`True`) or not (`False`).
`setSize(width, height)`	Sets the window's width and height in pixels.
`setTitle(title)`	Sets the window's title to `title`.

For example, later in the `LabelDemo` class's `__init__` method, the window's size can be permanently frozen with the following statement:

```
self.setResizable(False)
```

Window Layout

Window components are laid out in the window's two-dimensional **grid**. The grid's rows and columns are numbered from the position (0, 0) in the upper left corner of the window. A window component's row and column position in the grid is specified when the component is added to the window. For example, the next program (**layoutdemo.py**) labels the four quadrants of the window shown in **Figure 9-5**:

```
class LayoutDemo(EasyFrame):
    """Displays labels in the quadrants."""
```

```
def __init__(self):
    """Sets up the window and the labels."""
    EasyFrame.__init__(self)
    self.addLabel(text = "(0, 0)", row = 0, column = 0)
    self.addLabel(text = "(0, 1)", row = 0, column = 1)
    self.addLabel(text = "(1, 0)", row = 1, column = 0)
    self.addLabel(text = "(1, 1)", row = 1, column = 1)
```

Figure 9-5   Laying out labels in the window's grid

Because the window is shrink-wrapped around the four labels, they appear to be centered in their rows and columns. However, when the user stretches this window, the labels stick to the upper left or northwest corners of their grid positions.

Each type of window component has a default alignment within its grid position. Because labels frequently appear to the left of data entry fields, their default alignment is northwest. The programmer can override the default alignment by including the **sticky** attribute as a keyword argument when the label is added to the window. The values of **sticky** are the strings "N," "S," "E," and "W," or any combination thereof. The next code segment centers the four labels in their grid positions:

```
self.addLabel(text = "(0, 0)", row = 0, column = 0,
              sticky = "NSEW")
self.addLabel(text = "(0, 1)", row = 0, column = 1,
              sticky = "NSEW")
self.addLabel(text = "(1, 0)", row = 1, column = 0,
              sticky = "NSEW")
self.addLabel(text = "(1, 1)", row = 1, column = 1,
              sticky = "NSEW")
```

Now, when the user expands the window, the labels retain their alignments in the exact center of their grid positions.

One final aspect of window layout involves the spanning of a window component across several grid positions. For example, when a window has two components in the first row and only one component in the second row, the latter component might be centered in its row, thus occupying two grid positions. The programmer can force a horizontal and/or vertical spanning of grid positions by supplying the **rowspan** and **columnspan** keyword arguments when adding a component (like merging cells in a table or spreadsheet). The spanning does not take effect unless the alignment of the component is centered along that dimension, however. The next code segment adds the three labels shown in **Figure 9-6**. The window's grid cells are outlined in the figure.

```
self.addLabel(text = "(0, 0)", row = 0, column = 0,
              sticky = "NSEW")
self.addLabel(text = "(0, 1)", row = 0, column = 1,
              sticky = "NSEW")
self.addLabel(text = "(1, 0 and 1)", row = 1, column = 0,
              sticky = "NSEW", columnspan = 2)
```

Figure 9-6   Labels with center alignment and a column span of 2

Types of Window Components and Their Attributes

GUI programs use several types of window components, or widgets. These include labels, entry fields, text areas, command buttons, drop-down menus, sliding scales, scrolling list boxes, canvases, and many others. The `breezypythongui` module includes methods for adding each type of window component to a window. Each such method uses the form

```
self.addComponentType(<arguments>)
```

When this method is called, `breezypythongui`

- Creates an instance of the requested type of window component

- Initializes the component's attributes with default values or any values provided by the programmer

- Places the component in its grid position (the row and column are required arguments)

- Returns a reference to the component

The window components supported by `breezypythongui` are either of the standard `tkinter` types, such as `Label`, `Button`, and `Scale`, or subclasses thereof, such as `IntegerField`, `TextArea`, and `EasyCanvas`. A complete list is shown in **Table 9-2**. Parent classes are shown in parentheses.

Table 9-2   Window components in `breezypythongui`

Type of Window Component	Purpose
`Label`	Displays text or an image in the window
`IntegerField(Entry)`	A box for input or output of integers
`FloatField(Entry)`	A box for input or output of floating-point numbers
`TextField(Entry)`	A box for input or output of a single line of text
`TextArea(Text)`	A scrollable box for input or output of multiple lines of text
`EasyListbox(Listbox)`	A scrollable box for the display and selection of a list of items
`Button`	A clickable command area
`EasyCheckbutton(Checkbutton)`	A labeled checkbox
`Radiobutton`	A labeled disc that, when selected, deselects related radio buttons
`EasyRadiobuttonGroup(Frame)`	Organizes a set of radio buttons, allowing only one at a time to be selected
`EasyMenuBar(Frame)`	Organizes a set of menus
`EasyMenubutton(Menubutton)`	A menu of drop-down command options
`EasyMenuItem`	An option in a drop-down menu
`Scale`	A labeled slider bar for selecting a value from a range of values
`EasyComboBox`	Combines the features of a visible text field and a drop-down list box
`EasyCanvas(Canvas)`	A rectangular area for drawing shapes or images
`EasyPanel(Frame)`	A rectangular area with its own grid for organizing window components
`EasyDialog(simpleDialog.Dialog)`	A resource for defining special-purpose popup windows

As with windows, some of a window component's attributes can be set when the component is created or can be reset by accessing its attribute dictionary at a later time.

Displaying Images

To illustrate the use of attribute options for a label component, let's examine a program (**imagedemo.py**) that displays an image with a caption. The program's window is shown in **Figure 9-7**.

Figure 9-7   Displaying a captioned image

This program adds two labels to the window. One label displays the image, and the other label displays the caption. Unlike earlier examples, the program now keeps variable references to both labels for further processing.

The image label is first added to the window with an empty text string. The program then creates a **PhotoImage** object from an image file and sets the **image** attribute of the image label to this object. Note that the variable used to hold the reference to the image must be an instance variable (prefixed by **self**), rather than a temporary variable. The image file must be in GIF format. Finally, the program creates a **Font** object with a nonstandard font and resets the text label's **font** and **foreground** attributes to obtain the caption shown in Figure 9-7. The window is shrink-wrapped around the two labels, and its dimensions are fixed.

Here is the code for the program:

```
from breezypythongui import EasyFrame
from tkinter import PhotoImage
from tkinter.font import Font
class ImageDemo(EasyFrame):
    """Displays an image and a caption."""
    def __init__(self):
        """Sets up the window and the widgets."""
        EasyFrame.__init__(self, title = "Image Demo")
        self.setResizable(False);
        imageLabel = self.addLabel(text = "",
                                   row = 0, column = 0,
                                   sticky = "NSEW")
        textLabel = self.addLabel(text = "Smokey the cat",
                                  row = 1, column = 0,
                                  sticky = "NSEW")
        # Load the image and associate it with the image label.
        self.image = PhotoImage(file = "smokey.gif")
        imageLabel["image"] = self.image
```

```
# Set the font and color of the caption.
font = Font(family = "Verdana", size = 20,
            slant = "italic")
textLabel["font"] = font
textLabel["foreground"] = "blue"
```

Table 9-3 summarizes the `tkinter.Label` attributes used in this book.

Table 9-3   The `tkinter.Label` attributes

`Label` **Attribute**	**Type of Value**
`image`	A `PhotoImage` object (imported from `tkinter`); must be loaded from a GIF file
`text`	A string
`background`	A color; a label's background is the color of the rectangular area enclosing the text of the label
`foreground`	A color; a label's foreground is the color of its text
`font`	A `Font` object (imported from `tkinter.font`)

You are encouraged to browse the **breezypythongui** documentation for information on the different types of window components and their attributes. Python also has excellent documentation on the window components at **https://docs.python.org/3/library/tkinter.html#module-tkinter**. For an overview of fonts, see **https://en.wikipedia.org/wiki/Font**. Learning which fonts are available on your system requires some geekery with **tkinter**. A demo program, **fontdemo.py**, that lets you view these fonts is available in the example programs for this book.

In the next section, we show how to make GUI programs interactive by responding to user events.

Exercise 9-3

1. Write a code segment that centers the labels RED, WHITE, and BLUE vertically in a GUI window. The text of each label should have the color that it names, and the window's background color should be green. The background color of each label should also be green.

2. Run the demo program **fontdemo.py** to explore the font families available on your system. Then write a code segment that centers the labels COURIER, HELVETICA, and TIMES horizontally in a GUI window. The text of each label should be the name of the font family associated with the text. Substitute a different font family if necessary.

3. Write a code segment that uses a loop to create and place nine labels into a 3-by-3 grid. The text of each label should be its coordinates in the grid, starting with (0, 0) in the upper left corner. Each label should be centered in its grid cell. You should use a nested **for** loop in your code. Then modify and run the same program to display labels in an 8 by 10 grid.

4. Jill has a plan for a window layout with two rows of widgets. The first row contains two widgets, and the second row contains four widgets. Describe how she can align the widgets so that they are evenly spaced in each row.

5. Describe the procedure for setting up the display of an image in a window.

9.4 Command Buttons and Responding to Events

A command button is added to a window just like a label, by specifying its text and position in the grid. A button is centered in its grid position by default. The method `addButton` accomplishes all this and returns an object of type `tkinter.Button`. Like a label, a button can display an image, usually a small icon, instead of a string. A button also has a `state` attribute, which can be set to "normal" to enable the button (its default state) or "disabled" to disable it.

GUI programmers often lay out a window and run the application to check its look and feel before adding the code to respond to user events. Let's adopt this strategy for our next example. This program **(buttondemo.py)** displays a single label and two command buttons. The buttons allow the user to clear or restore the label. When the user clicks **Clear**, the label is erased, the **Clear** button is disabled, and the **Restore** button is enabled. When the user clicks **Restore**, the label is redisplayed, the **Restore** button is disabled, and the **Clear** button is enabled.

Figure 9-8 shows these two states of the window, followed by the code for the initial version of the program.

Figure 9-8   Using command buttons

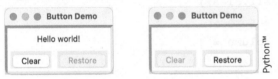

```
class ButtonDemo(EasyFrame):
    """Illustrates command buttons and user events."""
    def __init__(self):
        """Sets up the window, label, and buttons."""
        EasyFrame.__init__(self)
        # A single label in the first row.
        self.label = self.addLabel(text = "Hello world!",
                                   row = 0, column = 0,
                                   columnspan = 2,
                                   sticky = "NSEW")
        # Two command buttons in the second row.
        self.clearBtn = self.addButton(text = "Clear",
                                row = 1, column = 0)
        self.restoreBtn = self.addButton(text = "Restore",
                                row = 1, column = 1,
                                state = "disabled")
```

Note that the **Restore** button, which appears in gray in the window on the right, is initially disabled. When running the first version of the program, the user can click the **Clear** button, but to no effect.

To allow a program to respond to a button click, the programmer must set the button's `command` attribute. There are two ways to do this: either by supplying a keyword argument when the button is added to the window or, later, by assignment to the button's attribute dictionary. The value of the `command` attribute should be a method of no arguments, defined in the program's window class. The default value of this attribute is a method that does nothing.

The completed version of the example program supplies two methods, which are commonly called **event handlers**, for the program's two buttons. Each of these methods resets the label to the appropriate string and then enables and disables the relevant buttons.

```python
class ButtonDemo(EasyFrame):
    """Illustrates command buttons and user events."""
    def __init__(self):
        """Sets up the window, label, and buttons."""
        EasyFrame.__init__(self)
        # A single label in the first row.
        self.label = self.addLabel(text = "Hello world!",
                                   row = 0, column = 0,
                                   columnspan = 2,
                                   sticky = "NSEW")
        # Two command buttons in the second row, with event
        # handler methods supplied.
        self.clearBtn = self.addButton(text = "Clear",
                                       row = 1, column = 0,
                                       command = self.clear)
        self.restoreBtn = self.addButton(text = "Restore",
                                         row = 1, column = 1,
                                         state = "disabled",
                                         command = self.restore)

    # Methods to handle user events.
    def clear(self):
        """Resets the label to the empty string and updates
        the button states."""
        self.label["text"] = ""
        self.clearBtn["state"] = "disabled"
        self.restoreBtn["state"] = "normal"

    def restore(self):
        """Resets the label to 'Hello world!' and updates
        the button states."""
        self.label["text"] = "Hello world!"
        self.clearBtn["state"] = "normal"
        self.restoreBtn["state"] = "disabled"
```

Now, when the user clicks the **Clear** button, Python automatically runs the `clear` method on the window. Likewise, when the programmer clicks the **Restore** button, Python automatically runs the `restore` method on the window.

Exercise 9-4

1. Explain what happens when a user clicks a command button in a fully functioning GUI program.

2. Why is it a good idea to write and test the code for laying out a window's components before you add the methods that perform computations in response to events?

9.5 Input and Output with Entry Fields

An entry field is a box in which the user can position the mouse cursor and enter a number or a single line of text. This section explores the use of entry fields to allow a GUI program to take input text or numbers from a user and display text or numbers as output.

Text Fields

A text field is appropriate for entering or displaying a single-line string of characters. The programmer uses the method `addTextField` to add a text field to a window. The method returns an object of type `TextField`, which is a subclass of `tkinter.Entry`. Required arguments to `addTextField` are `text` (the string to be initially displayed), `row`, and `column`. Optional arguments are `rowspan`, `columnspan`, `sticky`, `width`, and `state`.

A text field is aligned by default to the northeast of its grid cell. A text field has a default width of 20 characters. This represents the maximum number of characters viewable in the box, but the user can continue typing or viewing them by moving the cursor key to the right.

The programmer can set a text field's `state` attribute to "readonly" to prevent the user from editing an output field.

The `TextField` method `getText` returns the string currently contained in a text field. Thus, it serves as an input operation. The method `setText` outputs its string argument to a text field.

Our example program (**textfielddemo.py**) converts a string to uppercase. The user enters text into the input field, clicks the **Convert** button, and views the result in the output field. The output field is read only, to prevent editing the result. **Figure 9-9** shows an interaction with the program's window, and the code follows.

Figure 9-9   Using text fields for input and output

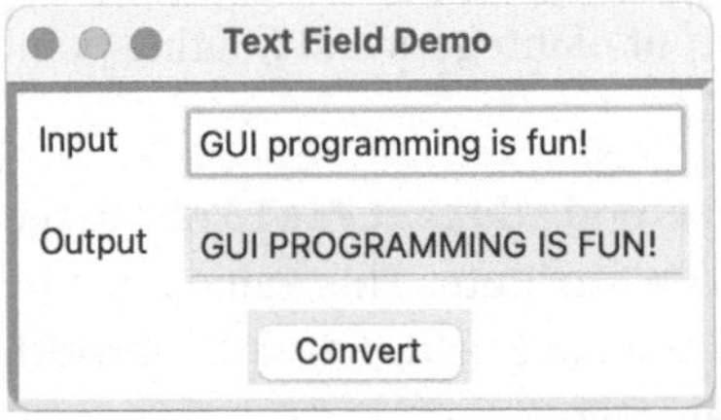

```
class TextFieldDemo(EasyFrame):
    """Converts an input string to uppercase and displays
    the result."""
    def __init__(self):
        """Sets up the window and widgets."""
        EasyFrame.__init__(self, title = "Text Field Demo")
        # Label and field for the input
        self.addLabel(text = "Input", row = 0, column = 0)
        self.inputField = self.addTextField(text = "",
                                            row = 0,
                                            column = 1)
        # Label and field for the output
        self.addLabel(text = "Output", row = 1, column = 0)
        self.outputField = self.addTextField(text = "",
                                             row = 1,
                                             column = 1,
                                             state = "readonly")
```

```
        # The command button
        self.addButton(text = "Convert", row = 2, column = 0,
                       columnspan = 2, command = self.convert)
    # The event handling method for the button
    def convert(self):
        """Inputs the string, converts it to uppercase,
        and outputs the result."""
        text = self.inputField.getText()
        result = text.upper()
        self.outputField.setText(result)
```

Note that the __init__ method contains about 80% of the program's code. This method is concerned with setting up the window components. The actual program logic is just the three lines of code in the **convert** method. This logic, which takes input data, computes a result, and outputs this result, is similar to the logic of the following ridiculously simple terminal-based program:

```
text = input("Input: ")
result = text.upper()
print("Output:", result)
```

Integer and Float Fields for Numeric Data

Although the programmer can use a text field for the input and output of numbers, the data must be converted to numbers after input and back to strings before output. To simplify the programmer's task, **breezypythongui** includes two types of data fields, called **IntegerField** and **FloatField**, for the input and output of integers and floating-point numbers, respectively.

The methods **addIntegerField** and **addFloatField** are similar in usage to the method **addTextField** discussed earlier. However, instead of an initial **text** attribute, the programmer supplies a **value** attribute. This value must be an integer for an integer field but can be either an integer or a floating-point number for a float field. The default width of an integer field is 10 characters, whereas the default width of a float field is 20 characters.

The method **addFloatField** allows an optional **precision** argument. Its value is an integer that specifies the precision of the number displayed in the field.

The methods **getNumber** and **setNumber** are used for the input and output of numbers with integer and float fields. The conversion between numbers and strings is performed automatically.

Our example program takes an input integer from a field, computes the square root of this value, and outputs the result, rounded to the nearest hundredth, to a second field. **Figure 9-10** shows an interaction with this program (**numberfielddemo.py**), and the code follows.

Figure 9-10   Using an integer field and a float field for input and output

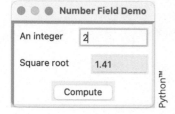

```python
class NumberFieldDemo(EasyFrame):
    """Computes and displays the square root of an
    input number."""
    def __init__(self):
        """Sets up the window and widgets."""
        EasyFrame.__init__(self, title = "Number Field Demo")
        # Label and field for the input
        self.addLabel(text = "An integer",
                      row = 0, column = 0)
        self.inputField = self.addIntegerField(value = 0,
                                               row = 0,
                                               column = 1,
                                               width = 10)

        # Label and field for the output
        self.addLabel(text = "Square root",
                      row = 1, column = 0)
        self.outputField = self.addFloatField(value = 0.0,
                                              row = 1,
                                              column = 1,
                                              width = 8,
                                              precision = 2,
                                              state = "readonly")

        # The command button
        self.addButton(text = "Compute", row = 2, column = 0,
                       columnspan = 2,
                       command = self.computeSqrt)
    # The event handling method for the button
    def computeSqrt(self):
        """Inputs the integer, computes the square root,
        and outputs the result."""
        number = self.inputField.getNumber()
        result = math.sqrt(number)
        self.outputField.setNumber(result)
```

The program as written will run correctly if the inputs are integers, and these integers are greater than or equal to 0. If the input text is not an integer or is a negative integer, Python raises an exception and, if the program is terminal based, it crashes (you learned about exceptions, like dividing by zero and using an index out of range, in earlier chapters). However, when a GUI-based program raises an exception, the GUI stays alive, allowing the user to edit the input and continue, but a stack trace appears in the terminal window. We later examine how to trap such errors and respond gracefully with error messages.

Exercise 9-5

1. Explain why you would not use a text field to perform input and output of numbers.

2. Write a line of code that adds a **FloatField** to a window, at position (1, 1) in the grid, with an initial value of 0.0, a width of 15, and a precision of 2.

3. What happens when you enter a number with a decimal point into an **IntegerField**?

4. When would you make a data field read-only, and how would you do this?

9.6 Defining and Using Instance Variables

Earlier we said that methods use the parameter **self** to call other methods in an object's class or to access that object's instance variables. An instance variable is used to store data belonging to an individual object. Together, the values of an object's instance variables make up its state. The state of a given window, for example, includes its title, background color, and dimensions, among other things. You have seen that a dictionary maintains these data within the window object. The window class's __init__ method establishes the initial state of a window object when it is created, and other methods within that class are run to access or modify this state (to make the window larger, change its title, or respond to an event). These basic elements of a window's state are defined and managed in the classes **breezypythongui.EasyFrame** and **tkinter.frame**.

When you customize an existing class, you can add to the state of its objects by including new instance variables. You define these new variables, which must begin with the name **self**, within the class's __init__ method. They then become visible to other methods throughout the class definition. An example will make this clear. A simple counter application is shown in **Figure 9-11**.

Figure 9-11   The GUI for a counter application

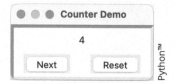

At start-up, the window displays a label of 0 and two buttons named **Next** and **Reset**. When the user clicks **Next**, the window increments the number in the label; when the user clicks **Reset**, the window resets the label to 0.

Clearly, the program must have some way to track the value of the counter, as it changes states after button clicks. We accomplish this by adding an instance variable to the window class in the __init__ method and updating this variable in the event-handling methods for the buttons. Here is the code for the **CounterDemo** class:

```
class CounterDemo(EasyFrame):
    """Illustrates the use of a counter with an
    instance variable."""
    def __init__(self):
```

```
"""Sets up the window, label, and buttons."""
EasyFrame.__init__(self, title = "Counter Demo")
self.setSize(200, 75)
# Instance variable to track the count.
self.count = 0
# A label to display the count in the first row.
self.label = self.addLabel(text = "0",
                           row = 0, column = 0,
                           sticky = "NSEW",
                           columnspan = 2)
# Two command buttons.
self.addButton(text = "Next",
               row = 1, column = 0,
               command = self.next)
self.addButton(text = "Reset",
               row = 1, column = 1,
               command = self.reset)

# Methods to handle user events.
def next(self):
    """Increments the count and updates the display."""
    self.count += 1
    self.label["text"] = str(self.count)

def reset(self):
    """Resets the count to 0 and updates the display."""
    self.count = 0
    self.label["text"] = str(self.count)
```

The separation of the code for setting up and managing the user interface from the code for computation and managing the data is a common design pattern seen in many GUI-based programs. We will explore this design pattern in more detail later in this book.

Exercise 9-6

1. What is meant by the state of an object, and how does the programmer access and manipulate it?

2. Explain the differences between instance variables and temporary variables. Focus on their visibility in a class definition, and on their roles in managing data for an object of that class.

3. Explain the purpose of the variable **self** in a Python class definition.

Case Study 9-1 | The Guessing Game Revisited

We now pause our survey of GUI components to develop a GUI for a significant application. Chapter 3 presented a guessing game with a terminal-based user interface. We now revise that program to replace the user interface with a GUI.

Request

Replace the terminal-based interface of the guessing game program with a GUI.

Analysis

The program retains the same functions but presents the user with a different look and feel. **Figure 9-12** shows a sequence of user interactions with the main window.

Figure 9-12 The GUI for a guessing game

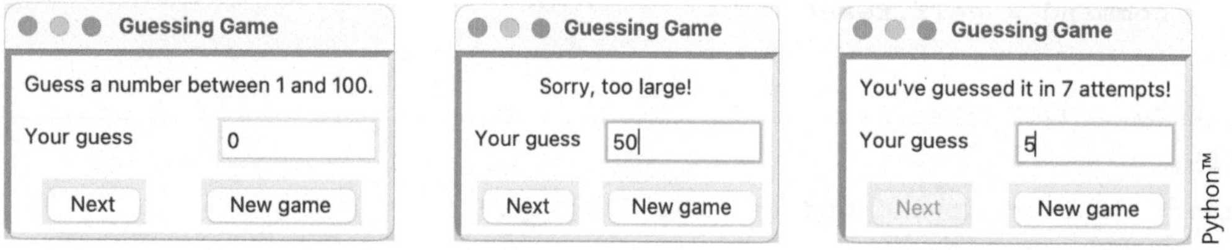

As you can see, the GUI includes a labeled entry field for the user's input guesses, a label for the computer's greeting and responses to the user, and two buttons, one for submitting a guess and another for obtaining a new game. The user plays the game as before, but they enter guesses into the entry field and press the **Next** button to move the game forward. When the game ends, that button is disabled, and the user can either click the **New game** button to start a new game or close the window to quit.

The program requires one new class, named **GuessingGame**, which extends the **EasyFrame** class.

Laying out the GUI

As in many GUI applications, it's possible to write the code to lay out the user interface before designing the logic (in this case, the game logic) of the application. You can think of this step as part of analysis, in which you create a working **prototype** without any real functionality to get an idea of the application's look and feel. Therefore, here is the code for this part of the process **(guessversion1.py)**, which can run without supporting any user interaction:

```
"""
File: guessversion1.py
A prototype that lays out the user interface for a GUI-based
guessing game.
"""
import random
from breezypythongui import EasyFrame
class GuessingGame(EasyFrame):
    """Plays a guessing game with the user."""
    def __init__(self):
```

```
        """Sets up the window, widgets, and data."""
        EasyFrame.__init__(self, title = "Guessing Game")
        # Initialize the instance variables for the data
        self.myNumber = random.randint(1, 100)
        self.count = 0
        # Create and add widgets to the window
        greeting = "Guess a number between 1 and 100."
        self.hintLabel = self.addLabel(text = greeting,
                                       row = 0, column = 0,
                                       sticky = "NSEW",
                                       columnspan = 2)
        self.addLabel(text = "Your guess", row = 1, column = 0)
        self.guessField = self.addIntegerField(0, row = 1, column = 1)
        # Buttons have no command attributes yet
        self.nextButton = self.addButton(text = "Next", row = 2,
                                         column = 0)
        self.newButton = self.addButton(text = "New game",
                                        row = 2, column = 1)

def main():
    """Instantiate and pop up the window."""
    GuessingGame().mainloop()


if __name__ == "__main__":
    main()
```

Note that the buttons are added without **command** attributes. Thus, when the user clicks on these buttons, no responses will be triggered. You will develop this functionality in the design phase of the process.

Design

The logic of the guessing game program after displaying the computer's greeting is to take user guesses as inputs and respond with hints if the guesses are incorrect. If the user guesses correctly, the process halts with a confirmation message and the number of guesses made. Here is a pseudocode algorithm for the game logic:

```
While True
    count += 1
    Input a guess
    If guess == myNumber
        Output "You've guessed it in", count, "attempts"
        Break
    Else if guess < myNumber
        Output "Sorry, too small"
    Else
        Output "Sorry, too large"
```

(continues)

As you can see, there is a main loop in which the user's inputs and the computer's hints drive the process forward until the user guesses correctly. These events will also drive the process forward in a GUI application, but the loop becomes the window's event-driven loop. That is, you will not need an explicit loop in your code; instead, you will embed the logic of the loop's body in an event-handling method. The pseudocode for this method follows:

```
Method nextGuess
    count += 1
    Input a guess
    If guess == myNumber
        Output "You've guessed it in", count, "attempts!"
        Disable the Next button
    Else if guess < myNumber
        Output "Sorry, too small!"
    Else
        Output "Sorry, too large!"
```

This method is triggered whenever the user clicks the **Next** button in the GUI. The inputs now come from the input field, and the outputs go to a label, both also in the GUI. Note that we disable the **Next** button to prevent further user input when a game has finished. The **break** statement is no longer necessary.

The other event in play occurs when the user clicks the **New game** button. In this case, a method is triggered to reset the contents of the GUI to their original state. Here is the pseudocode for this method:

```
Method newGame
    myNumber = a random number between 1 and 100
    count = 0
    Hint label = "Guess a number between 1 and 100."
    Guess field = 0
    Enable the Next button
```

Implementation

The prototype already has most of the code for laying out the GUI. You just have to add the code for the definitions of the two event-handling methods and set the **command** attributes of the two buttons to these methods when they are added to the window. Here is the code for the two new methods:

```python
def nextGuess(self):
    """Processes the user's next guess."""
    self.count += 1
    guess = self.guessField.getNumber()
    if guess == self.myNumber:
        self.hintLabel["text"] = "You've guessed it in " + \
                                 str(self.count) + " attempts!"
        self.nextButton["state"] = "disabled"
    elif guess < self.myNumber:
        self.hintLabel["text"] = "Sorry, too small!"
```

```
        else:
            self.hintLabel["text"] = "Sorry, too large!"

    def newGame(self):
        """Resets the data and GUI to their original states."""
        self.myNumber = random.randint(1, 100)
        self.count = 0
        greeting = "Guess a number between 1 and 100."
        self.hintLabel["text"] = greeting
        self.guessField.setNumber(0)
        self.nextButton["state"] = "normal"
```

Note the use of the temporary variables **guess** and **greeting** in these two methods. Because its use is restricted to the method in which it appears, a temporary variable should not begin with the prefix **self**. By contrast, variables that begin with the prefix **self**, such as **self.count**, **self.hintLabel**, and **self. guessField**, are instance variables, whose scope is the entire class definition. Their purpose is to retain the state of an object (here the instance of **GuessingGame**) between calls of methods. Put metaphorically, the window object does not have to remember the user's guess and the computer's greeting between method calls, but it does have to remember the computer's number, the count, the label, and the entry field. In general, you should try to minimize the use of instance variables, relying on temporaries or parameter names in your methods wherever possible.

Fail-Safe Programming

When errors arise in a GUI-based program, the program often responds by popping up a dialog window with an error message. Such errors are usually the result of invalid input data. The program detects the error, pops up the dialog to inform the user, and, when the user closes the dialog, continues to accept and check input data. In a terminal-based program, this process usually requires an explicit loop structure. In a GUI-based program, Python's implicit event-driven loop continues the process automatically. We now modify an earlier program example to show how this works.

You have seen examples of errors caused by attempting to divide by zero or using a list index that is out of bounds. Python raises an exception or runtime error when these events occur. The square root program raises an exception of type **ValueError** if the input datum is not an integer or is a negative integer. To recover gracefully from this event, we can modify the code of the program's **computeSqrt** method by embedding it in Python's **try-except** statement. The syntax of this statement is a bit like that of the **if-else** statement:

```
try:
    <statements that might raise an exception>
except <exception type>:
    <statements to recover from the exception>
```

In the **try** clause, our program attempts to input the data, compute the result, and output the result, as before. If an exception is raised anywhere in this process, control shifts immediately to the **except** clause. Here, in our example, the program pops up a message box with the appropriate error message. **Figure 9-13** shows an interaction with the program, and the modified code follows.

Figure 9-13　Responding to an input error with a message box

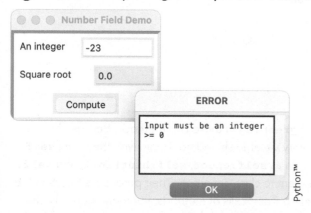

```
# The event handling method for the button
def computeSqrt(self):
    """Inputs the integer, computes the square root,
    and outputs the result. Handles input errors
    by displaying a message box."""
    try:
        number = self.inputField.getNumber()
        result = math.sqrt(number)
        self.outputField.setNumber(result)
    except ValueError:
        self.messageBox(title = "ERROR",
                        message = "Input must be an integer >= 0")
```

Python will raise the **ValueError** in the **getNumber** method, if the input datum is not an integer, or in the **math.sqrt** function, if the well-formed integer input is negative. In either case, the **except** clause traps the exception and allows the user to correct the input after closing the message box. A message box is a useful way to alert the user to any special event, even if it is not an input error.

9.7 Other Useful GUI Resources

Many simple GUI-based applications rely on the resources that we have presented thus far in this chapter. However, as applications become more complex and, in fact, begin to look like the ones we use on a daily basis, other resources must come into play. The layout of GUI components can be specified in more detail, and groups of components can be nested in multiple subframes in a window. Paragraphs of text can be displayed in scrolling text boxes. Lists of information can be presented for selection in scrolling list boxes, as check boxes, and as radio buttons. Finally, GUI-based programs can be configured to respond to various keyboard and mouse events.

In this section, we provide a brief overview of some of these advanced resources, so that you may use them to solve problems in the programming exercises.

Using Nested Frames to Organize Components

Suppose that a GUI requires a row of three command buttons beneath two columns of labels and text fields, as shown in **Figure 9-14**.

Figure 9-14   Widgets in uneven columns

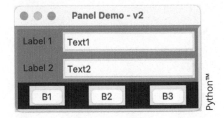

This grid appears to have two columns in two rows and three columns in a third row. The layout is not ragged, but if you look closely, the buttons in the bottom row are unevenly spaced. Because all of the widgets lie in the same grid, there is no way to center each button in its own column.

A more natural design decomposes the window into two nested frames, sometimes called **panels**. Each panel contains its own independent grid. The top panel contains a 2-by-2 grid of labels and entry fields, whereas the bottom panel contains a 1-by-3 grid of buttons. The **breezypythongui** method **addPanel** adds a panel to the window at a given row and column in the window's grid. This method returns an instance of the **EasyPanel** class, so you can add widgets to it just as if it were a top-level window. Because **EasyPanel** is a descendant of the **tkinter.Frame** class and has almost the same interface as the **EasyFrame** class, you can run many of the same methods on a panel object that you run on a top-level window object. The user interface for a new version of the program that organizes the widgets in two panels is shown in **Figure 9-15**. Note that we have added background colors gray and black to the panels for emphasis.

Figure 9-15   Using panels to organize widgets evenly

Here is the code for laying out the GUI shown in Figure 9-15:

```
class PanelDemo(EasyFrame):
    def __init__(self):
        # Create the main frame
        EasyFrame.__init__(self, "Panel Demo - v2")
        # Create the nested frame for the data panel
        dataPanel = self.addPanel(row = 0, column = 0,
                                  background = "gray")
```

```
                    # Create and add widgets to the data panel
                    dataPanel.addLabel(text = "Label 1", row = 0, column = 0,
                                       background = "gray")
                    dataPanel.addTextField(text = "Text1", row = 0, column = 1)
                    dataPanel.addLabel(text = "Label 2", row = 1, column = 0,
                                       background = "gray")
                    dataPanel.addTextField(text = "Text2", row = 1, column = 1)
                    # Create the nested frame for the button panel
                    buttonPanel = self.addPanel(row = 1, column = 0,
                                                background = "black")
                    # Create and add buttons to the button panel
                    buttonPanel.addButton(text = "B1", row = 0, column = 0)
                    buttonPanel.addButton(text = "B2", row = 0, column = 1)
                    buttonPanel.addButton(text = "B3", row = 0, column = 2)
```

As you can see from this code, the grids of the two panels are independent, as multiple widgets appear to be placed in the same rows and columns. When you design a complex interface like this one, be sure to draw a sketch of the panels with their grids, so you can determine the positions of the widgets and eliminate some guesswork.

Multiline Text Areas

Although text fields are useful for entering and displaying single lines of text, some applications need to display larger chunks of text with multiple lines. For instance, the message box introduced earlier displays a multiline message in a scrolling text area. In a manner similar to the editing window of a word processor, a text area widget allows the program to output and the user to input and edit multiple lines of text.

The method **addTextArea** adds a text area to the window. The required arguments are the initial text to display, the row, and the column. Optional arguments include a width and height in columns (characters) and rows (lines), with defaults of 80 and 5, respectively. The final optional argument is called **wrap**. This argument tells the text area what to do with a line of text when it reaches the right border of the viewable area. The default value of wrap is "none," which causes a line of text to continue invisibly beyond the right border. The other values are "word" and "char," which break a line at a word or a character, and then continue the text on the next line.

Figure 9-16   Displaying data in a multiline text area

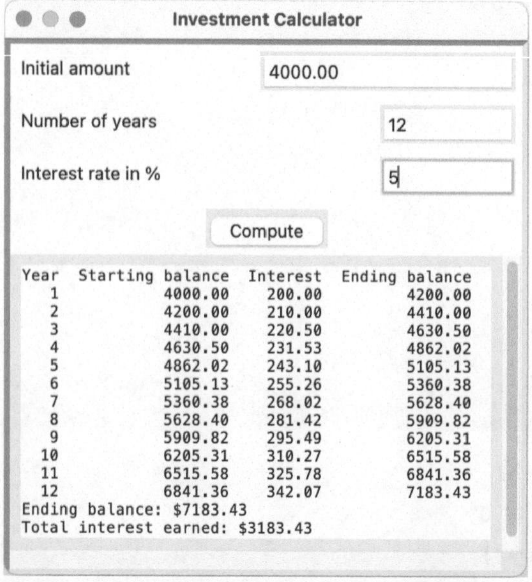

The **addTextArea** method returns an object of type **TextArea**, a subclass of **tkinter.Text**. This object recognizes three important methods: **getText**, **setText**, and **appendText**. The first two methods have the same effect as they do with a text field. The **appendText** method does not replace the text in the text area with its string argument, but instead appends this string to the end of the string currently displayed there. A text area can be disabled to prevent editing, but this disables its input and output methods as well. Therefore, before text is input or output, a disabled text area must be re-enabled.

You can use a text area to recast the user interface of the investment calculator program of Chapter 3. As shown in **Figure 9-16**, the GUI inputs the initial balance, the number of years, and the interest rate via entry fields. When the user clicks the **Compute** button, the program displays the table of results in a text area.

Here is the code for the window class:

```python
class TextAreaDemo(EasyFrame):
    """An investment calculator demonstrates the use of a
    multi-line text area."""
    def __init__(self):
        """Sets up the window and widgets."""
        EasyFrame.__init__(self, "Investment Calculator")
        self.addLabel(text = "Initial amount", row = 0, column = 0)
        self.addLabel(text = "Number of years", row = 1, column = 0)
        self.addLabel(text = "Interest rate in %", row = 2, column = 0)
        self.amount = self.addFloatField(value = 0.0, row = 0, column = 1)
        self.period = self.addIntegerField(value = 0, row = 1, column = 1)
        self.rate = self.addIntegerField(value = 0, row = 2, column = 1)
        self.outputArea = self.addTextArea("", row = 4, column = 0,
                                           columnspan = 2,
                                           width = 50, height = 15)
        self.compute = self.addButton(text = "Compute", row = 3, column = 0,
                                      columnspan = 2,
                                      command = self.compute)

    # Event handling method.
    def compute(self):
        """Computes the investment schedule based on the inputs
        and outputs the schedule."""
        # Obtain and validate the inputs
        startBalance = self.amount.getNumber()
        rate = self.rate.getNumber() / 100
        years = self.period.getNumber()
        if startBalance == 0 or rate == 0 or years == 0:
            return
        # Set the header for the table
        result = "%4s%18s%10s%16s\n" % ("Year",
                                        "Starting balance",
                                        "Interest",
                                        "Ending balance")
```

```
# Compute and append the results for each year
totalInterest = 0.0
for year in range(1, years + 1):
    interest = startBalance * rate
    endBalance = startBalance + interest
    result += "%4d%18.2f%10.2f%16.2f\n" % \
              (year, startBalance, interest, endBalance)
    startBalance = endBalance
    totalInterest += interest
# Append the totals for the period
result += "Ending balance: $%0.2f\n" % endBalance
result += "Total interest earned: $%0.2f\n" % totalInterest
# Output the result while preserving read-only status
self.outputArea["state"] = "normal"
self.outputArea.setText(result)
self.outputArea["state"] = "disabled"
```

File Dialogs

As anyone who has opened or saved a file on a modern computer knows, GUI-based programs allow the user to browse the computer's file system with **file dialogs**. **Figure 9-17** shows a file dialog asking for an input file on my computer.

Figure 9-17 A file dialog

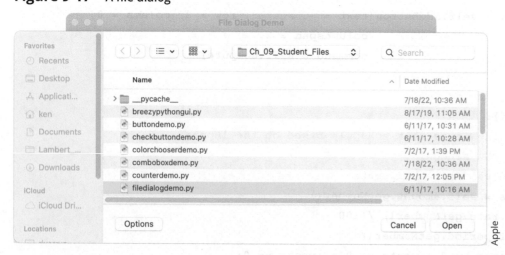

Python's `tkinter.filedialog` module includes two functions, `askopenfilename` and `asksaveasfilename`, to support file access in a GUI-based program. Each function pops up the standard file dialog for the user's particular computer system. If the user selects the dialog's **Cancel** button, the function returns the empty string. Otherwise, when the user selects the **Open** or **Save** button, the function returns the full pathname of the file that the user has selected (opening or saving) or entered as input (saving only) in the dialog. The program can then use the filename to open the file for input or output in the usual manner.

For purposes of this book, we use the following syntax with these two functions:

```
fList = [("Python files", "*.py"), ("Text files", "*.txt")]
filename = tkinter.filedialog.askopenfilename(parent = self,
                                              filetypes = fList)
filename = tkinter.filedialog.asksaveasfilename(parent = self)
```

Note that you can use the optional `filetypes` argument to mask the types of files available for input. In our example, we want the user to be able to open files with a **.py** or **.txt** extension, and no others. **Table 9-4** lists all of the optional arguments one can supply to the two file dialog functions.

Table 9-4   The optional arguments to the file dialog methods

Argument	Value
`defaultextension`	The extension to add to the filename, if not given by the user (ignored by the open dialog)
`filetypes`	A sequence of (label, pattern) tuples; specifies the file types available for input
`initialdir`	A string representing the directory in which to open the dialog
`initialfile`	A string representing the filename to display in the save dialog name field
`parent`	The dialog's parent window
`title`	A string to display in the dialog's title bar

You can use a file dialog and a text area to create a simple browser that allows the user to view text files. As shown in **Figure 9-18**, when the user clicks the **Open** button and chooses a file from the file dialog, the text of the file is input and displayed in the window's text area.

Figure 9-18   A simple file browser

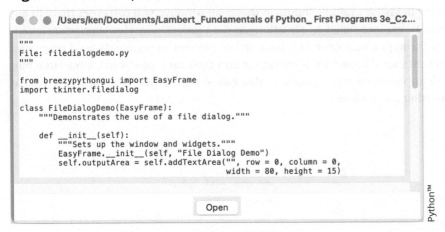

Here is the code for the window class:

```
from breezypythongui import EasyFrame
import tkinter.filedialog
class FileDialogDemo(EasyFrame):
    """Demonstrates the use of a file dialog."""

    def __init__(self):
        """Sets up the window and widgets."""

        EasyFrame.__init__(self, "File Dialog Demo")
```

```
            self.outputArea = self.addTextArea("", row = 0,
                                                column = 0,
                                                width = 80,
                                                height = 15)
            self.addButton(text = "Open", row = 1,
                           column = 0, command = self.openFile)


    # Event handling method.
    def openFile(self):
        """Pops up an open file dialog, and if a file is
        selected, displays its text in the text area and
        its pathname in the title bar."""
        fList = [("Python files", "*.py"),
                 ("Text files", "*.txt")]
        fileName = tkinter.filedialog.askopenfilename(parent = self,
                                                      filetypes = fList)
        if fileName != "":
            file = open(fileName, 'r')
            text = file.read()
            file.close()
            self.outputArea.setText(text)
            self.setTitle(fileName)
```

Obtaining Input with Prompter Boxes

You have seen the advantages of displaying fields for multiple inputs in the same window: you can enter them in any order and change just one or two of them to explore "what if" situations in data processing. However, occasionally you might want to guide the user rigidly through a sequence of inputs, in the manner of terminal-based programs. For example, at start-up a program might prompt the user for a username and then for a password, after launching the main window of the application. GUI applications use a popup dialog called a **prompter box** for this purpose. **Figure 9-19** shows a prompter box requesting a username.

Figure 9-19   Using a prompter box

The prompter box displays a title, a message for the prompt, an entry field for the user's input, and a button to submit the input. The entry field can have some optional initial text. You popup a prompter box by calling the **EasyFrame** method **prompterBox** with the appropriate arguments. When the user closes the dialog by clicking the **OK** button or the dialog's close disc, the method returns the contents of the entry field. The next code segment shows the window class that displays the prompter box in Figure 9-19. The program simply displays the user's input in a label.

```
class PrompterBoxDemo(EasyFrame):
    def __init__(self):
        """Sets up the window and widgets."""
        EasyFrame.__init__(self, title = "Prompter Box Demo",
                           width = 300, height = 100)
        self.label = self.addLabel(text = "", row = 0,
                                   column = 0, sticky = "NSEW")
        self.addButton(text = "Username", row = 1, column = 0,
                       command = self.getUserName)

    # Event handling method.
    def getUserName(self):
        text = self.prompterBox(title = "Input Dialog",
                                promptString = "Your username:")
        self.label["text"] = "Hi " + name + "!"
```

Check Buttons

A **check button** consists of a label and a box that a user can select or deselect with the mouse. Check buttons often represent a group of several options, any number of which may be selected at the same time. The application program can either respond immediately when a check button is manipulated or examine the state of the button at a later point in time.

As a simple example, let's assume that a restaurant serves chicken dinners with a standard set of sides. These include French fries, green beans, and applesauce. A customer can omit any of the sides from their order, and vegetarians will want to omit the chicken. The user selects these options via check buttons and clicks the **Place order** button to place their order. A message box then pops up with a summary of the order. **Figure 9-20** shows the user interface for the program **(checkbuttondemo.py)**.

Figure 9-20   Using check buttons

The method **addCheckbutton** expects a **text** argument (the button's label) and an optional **command** argument (a method to be triggered when the user checks or unchecks the button) and returns an object of type **EasyCheckbutton**. The **EasyCheckbutton** method **isChecked** returns **True** if the button is checked, or **False** otherwise. Here is the code for the demo program:

```
class CheckbuttonDemo(EasyFrame):
    """Allows the user to place a restaurant order from a set
    of options."""
    def __init__(self):
        """Sets up the window and widgets."""
        EasyFrame.__init__(self, "Check Button Demo")
        # Add four check buttons
        self.chickCB = self.addCheckbutton(text = "Chicken",
                                           row = 0, column = 0)
```

```
        self.taterCB = self.addCheckbutton(text = "French fries",
                                            row = 0, column = 1)
        self.beanCB = self.addCheckbutton(text = "Green beans",
                                            row = 1, column = 0)
        self.sauceCB = self.addCheckbutton(text = "Applesauce",
                                            row = 1, column = 1)
        # Add the command button
        self.addButton(text = "Place order", row = 2, column = 0,
                        columnspan = 2, command = self.placeOrder)


    # Event handling method.
    def placeOrder(self):
        """Display a message box with the order information."""
        message = ""
        if self.chickCB.isChecked():
            message += "Chicken\n\n"
        if self.taterCB.isChecked():
            message += "French fries\n\n"
        if self.beanCB.isChecked():
            message += "Green beans\n\n"
        if self.sauceCB.isChecked():
            message += "Applesauce\n"
        if message == "":
            message = "No food ordered!"
        self.messageBox(title = "Customer Order",
                        message = message)
```

Radio Buttons

Check buttons allow a user to select multiple options in any combination. When the user must be restricted to one selection only, the set of options can be presented as a group of **radio buttons**. Like a check button, a radio button consists of a label and a control widget. One of the buttons is normally selected by default at program start-up. When the user selects a different button in the same group, the previously selected button automatically deselects.

To illustrate the use of radio buttons, consider another restaurant scenario, where a customer has two choices of meats, potatoes, and vegetables, and must choose exactly one of each food type (our apologies to vegetarians). Three radio button groups can be set up to take this order, as shown in the program's user interface **(radiobuttondemo.py)** in **Figure 9-21**. The default options are chicken, French fries, and applesauce.

Figure 9-21 Using radio buttons

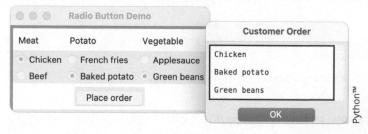

To add radio buttons to a window, the programmer first adds the radio button group to which these buttons will belong. The method `addRadiobuttonGroup` expects the grid coordinates as required arguments. Optional arguments are `orient` (whose default is "vertical"), `rowspan`, and `columnspan`. In the case of a vertically aligned button group, `rowspan` should be set to the number of buttons, and `columnspan` should be likewise set for a horizontally aligned group. The method returns an object of type `EasyRadiobuttonGroup`, which is a subclass of `tkinter.Frame`. This allows the programmer to place a custom background color in the region of the button group.

The `EasyRadiobuttonGroup` method `getSelectedButton` returns the currently selected radio button in a radio button group. The method `setSelectedButton` selects a radio button under program control. Once a radio button group is created, the programmer can add radio buttons to it with the `EasyRadiobuttonGroup` method `addRadiobutton`. This method expects a `text` argument (the button's label) and an optional `command` argument (a zero-argument method to be triggered when the button is selected). The method returns an object of type `tkinter.Radiobutton`.

Here is the code for the main window of the radio button demo program:

```
class RadiobuttonDemo(EasyFrame):
    """Allows the user to place a restaurant order from a set
    of options."""
    def __init__(self):
        """Sets up the window and widgets."""
        EasyFrame.__init__(self, "Radio Button Demo")
        # Add the label, button group, and buttons for meats
        self.addLabel(text = "Meat", row = 0, column = 0)
        self.meatGroup = self.addRadiobuttonGroup(row = 1,
                                                  column = 0,
                                                  rowspan = 2)
        defaultRB = self.meatGroup.addRadiobutton(text = "Chicken")
        self.meatGroup.setSelectedButton(defaultRB)
        self.meatGroup.addRadiobutton(text = "Beef")
        # Add the label, button group, and buttons for potatoes
        self.addLabel(text = "Potato", row = 0, column = 1)
        self.taterGroup = self.addRadiobuttonGroup(row = 1,
                                                   column = 1,
                                                   rowspan = 2)
        defaultRB = self.taterGroup.addRadiobutton(text = "French fries")
        self.taterGroup.setSelectedButton(defaultRB)
        self.taterGroup.addRadiobutton(text = "Baked potato")
        # Add the label, button group, and buttons for veggies
        self.addLabel(text = "Vegetable", row = 0, column = 2)
        self.vegGroup = self.addRadiobuttonGroup(row = 1,
                                                 column = 2,
                                                 rowspan = 2)
        defaultRB = self.vegGroup.addRadiobutton(text = "Applesauce")
        self.vegGroup.setSelectedButton(defaultRB)
        self.vegGroup.addRadiobutton(text = "Green beans")
        self.addButton(text = "Place order", row = 3, column = 0,
                       columnspan = 3, command = self.placeOrder)
```

```
# Event handler method.
def placeOrder(self):
    """Display a message box with the order information."""
    message = ""
    message += self.meatGroup.getSelectedButton()["text"] + "\n\n"
    message += self.taterGroup.getSelectedButton()["text"] + "\n\n"
    message += self.vegGroup.getSelectedButton()["text"]
    self.messageBox(title = "Customer Order",
                    message = message)
```

Note that the code for the `placeOrder` method is now simpler than in the check button demo, because exactly one button in each radio button group must be selected.

Keyboard Events

GUI-based programs can also respond to various keyboard events. Perhaps the most common event is pressing the enter or return key when the mouse cursor has become the insertion point in an entry field. This event might signal the end of an input and a request for processing.

You can associate a keyboard event and an event-handling method with a widget by calling the `bind` method. This method expects a string containing a key event as its first argument, and the method to be triggered as its second argument. The string for the return key event is `"<Return>"`. The event-handling method should have a single parameter named `event`. This parameter will automatically be bound to the event object that triggered the method.

Let's revisit the square root program to allow the user to compute a result by pressing the return key while the insertion point is in the input field. You bind the keyboard return event to a handler for the `inputField` widget as follows:

```
self.inputField.bind("<Return>",
                     lambda event: self.computeSqrt())
```

You cannot use the `computeSqrt` method directly as the event handler, because `computeSqrt` does not have a parameter for the event. Instead, you package a call of `computeSqrt` within a `lambda` function that accepts the event as an argument and ignores it. You can set event handlers for the keyboard return event for other fields in a similar manner.

Working with Colors

You have seen that you can set the background color of a window and most widgets using the string values of common colors, such as "red" and "blue." However, in Chapter 8, you learned that there are millions of colors available to the programmer who uses the RGB scheme. You saw that Turtle graphics and image processing use a triple with the form (R, G, B) to represent a color in this scheme. Each integer in the triple represents the saturation level of red, green, and blue in the given color. To work with colors in a GUI-based application, you must be aware of two other ways of representing RGB values in Python. Python represents an RGB value as a string containing a six-digit hexadecimal number of the form "0x*RRGGBB*" where the pairs of digits indicate the values of red, green, and blue in hex. The `tkinter` module also accepts the simpler representation "#*RRGGBB*" for hexadecimal values. We call this representation a **hex string**. **Table 9-5** lists some basic Python color values in ordinary, RGB triple, and hex string notations.

Table 9-5   Some basic colors and their rgb values

Ordinary Value	RGB Triple	Hex String
"black"	(0, 0, 0)	"#000000"
"red"	(255, 0, 0)	"#ff0000"
"green"	(0, 255, 0)	"#00ff00"
"blue"	(0, 0, 255)	"#0000ff"
"gray"	(127, 127, 127)	"#7f7f7f"
"white"	(255, 255, 255)	"#ffffff"

For example, to set the background color of a window to a less intense shade of red than the maximum value denoted by "red," you might run the statement

```
self["background"] = "#DD0000"
```

Now suppose you want to use a random color in a GUI. You must find a way to map a triple of three random integers, (R, G, B), to a hex string. Note that each integer in the (R, G, B) notation maps to two hex digits in the corresponding hex string. You could use one of the conversion algorithms discussed in Chapter 4 to perform these conversions, but Python's built-in **hex** function already does that:

```
>>> hex(255)
'0xff'
>>> hex(8)
'0x8'
```

To obtain just the hex digits, you would slice away the `'0x'` prefix as follows:

```
>>> hex(255)[2:]
'ff'
>>> hex(8)[2:]
'8'
```

To handle the case of a single digit, you would pad the string to the left by prepending a `'0'`, as follows:

```
>>> hexDigits = hex(8)[2:]
>>> if len(digits) == 1:
    hexDigits = '0' + hexDigits
>>> hexDigits
'08'
```

Because such conversions might occur frequently, let's define a function, named **rgbToHexString**, that expects a triple of integers as arguments and returns the corresponding hex string. Here is the code (in **rgb.py**):

```
def rgbToHexString(rgbTriple):
    """Converts the rgbTriple (R, G, B) to a hex string
    of the form #RRGGBB."""
    hexString = ""
    for i in rgbTriple: # Iterate through the triple
        twoDigits = hex(i)[2:]
        if len(twoDigits) == 1:
            twoDigits = '0' + twoDigits
        hexString += twoDigits
    return '#' + hexString
```

You are now in a position to easily create colors from RGB triples, including random ones, for a GUI application, as follows:

```
>>> rgbToHexString((255, 255, 255))
'#ffffff'
>>> rgbToHexString((10, 8, 32))
'#0a0820'
>>> from random import randint
>>> triple = (randint(0, 255), randint(0, 255), randint(0, 255))
>>> triple
(107,104,145)
>>> rgbToHexString(triple)
'#6b6891'
```

Using a Color Chooser

Most graphics software packages allow the user to pick a color with a standard color chooser. This is a dialog that presents a color wheel from which the user can choose a color with the mouse. Python's **tkinter.colorchooser** module includes an **askcolor** function for this purpose. **Figure 9-22** shows screenshots of a demo program (**colorchooserdemo.py**) that uses this resource. The window displays the current color in a **canvas** widget (a rectangular area that supports graphics operations). When the user clicks the **Choose color** button in the main window, a color chooser dialog pops up. When the user clicks **OK** to close the dialog, the main window updates its fields and canvas with the information about the chosen color.

Figure 9-22   Using a color chooser

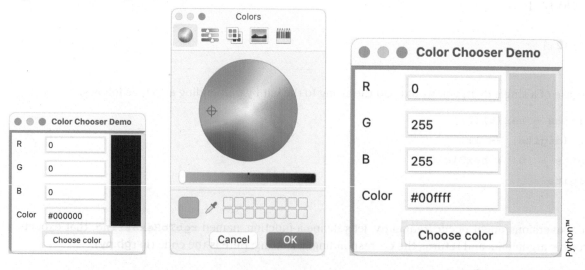

The **tkinter.colorchooser.askcolor** function returns a tuple of two elements. If the user has clicked **OK** in the dialog, the first element in the tuple is a nested tuple containing the three RGB values, and the second element is the hex string value of the color. If the user has clicked **Cancel** in the dialog, both elements in the tuple are **None**. Because the RGB values are returned as floating-point numbers, the demo program converts them to integers for display. Here is the code for the main window:

```
import tkinter.colorchooser
class ColorPicker(EasyFrame):
    """Displays the results of picking a color."""
```

```python
    def __init__(self):
        """Sets up the window and widgets."""
        EasyFrame.__init__(self,
                           title = "Color Chooser Demo")
        # Labels and output fields
        self.addLabel('R', row = 0, column = 0)
        self.addLabel('G', row = 1, column = 0)
        self.addLabel('B', row = 2, column = 0)
        self.addLabel("Color", row = 3, column = 0)
        self.r = self.addIntegerField(value = 0,
                                      row = 0, column = 1)
        self.g = self.addIntegerField(value = 0,
                                      row = 1, column = 1)
        self.b = self.addIntegerField(value = 0,
                                      row = 2, column = 1)
        self.hex = self.addTextField(text = "#000000",
                                     row = 3, column = 1,
                                     width = 10)
        # Canvas with an initial black background
        self.canvas = self.addCanvas(row = 0, column = 2,
                                     rowspan = 4,
                                     width = 50,
                                     background = "#000000")
        # Command button
        self.addButton(text = "Choose color", row = 4,
                       column = 0, columnspan = 3,
                       command = self.chooseColor)

    # Event handling method
    def chooseColor(self):
        """Pops up a color chooser and outputs the results."""
        colorTuple = tkinter.colorchooser.askcolor()
        if not colorTuple[0]: return
        ((r, g, b), hexString) = colorTuple
        self.r.setNumber(int(r))
        self.g.setNumber(int(g))
        self.b.setNumber(int(b))
        self.hex.setText(hexString)
        self.canvas["background"] = hexString
```

This concludes our introduction to GUI programming. You are now ready to program applications like the ones you use on a daily basis. Although it might seem like we have covered many features of GUIs, we have only scratched the surface. For a discussion on the use of other window components, such as canvases for graphics, sliding scales, and scrolling list boxes, as well as responding to different types of mouse events, consult the **breezypythongui** website at **https://kennethalambert.com/breezypythongui/**.

Summary

- GUI-based programs display information using graphical components in a window. They allow a user to manipulate information by manipulating GUI components with a mouse.

- A GUI-based program responds to user events by running methods to perform various tasks.

- The `tkinter` and `breezypythongui` modules include classes, functions, and constants used in GUI programming.

- A GUI-based program is structured as a main window class. This class extends the `EasyFrame` class. The `__init__` method in the main window class creates and lays out the window components. The main window class also includes the definitions of any event-handling methods.

- Examples of window components are labels (either text or images), command buttons, entry fields, multiline text areas, and check buttons.

- Popup dialog boxes are used to display messages and to prompt the user for inputs.

- Window components can be arranged within a grid in a window. The grid's attributes can be set to allow components to expand or align in any direction.

- Complex layouts can be decomposed into several panels of components.

- Each component has attributes for the foreground color and background color. Colors are represented using the RGB system in hexadecimal format.

- The text of a label has a font attribute that allows the programmer to specify the family, size, and other attributes of a font.

- The `command` attribute of a button can be set to a method that handles a button click.

- Keyboard events can be associated with event handler methods for window components by using the `bind` method.

Key Terms

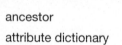

ancestor	file dialogs	prompter box
attribute dictionary	grid	prototype
canvas	graphical user interface (GUI)	radio buttons
check button	hex string	state
class diagram	inheritance	subclass
command button	instance variable	subclassing
entry fields	labels	title bar
event-driven programming	label object	widgets
event handler	panels	window
extends	parent	

Review Questions

1. In contrast to a terminal-based program, a GUI-based program

    a. completely controls the order in which the user enters inputs

    b. can allow the user to enter inputs in any order

    c. permits just text-based inputs

    d. permits just text-based outputs

2. The main window class in a GUI-based program is a subclass of

    a. `TextArea`

    b. `EasyFrame`

    c. `Window`

    d. `Menu`

3. The attribute used to attach an event-handling method to a button is named

    a. `row`

    b. `column`

    c. `command`

    d. `text`

4. GUIs represent color values using

    a. RGB triples of integers

    b. hex strings

    c. the names of the colors

    d. instances of the class `Color`

5. Multiline text is displayed in a

    a. text field

    b. text area

    c. label

    d. title bar of a window

6. The window component that allows a user to move the text visible beneath a `TextArea` widget is a

    a. list box

    b. label

    c. scroll bar

    d. button

7. The `sticky` attribute

    a. controls the alignment of a window component in its grid cell

    b. makes it difficult for a window component to be moved

    c. connects window components to each other

    d. automatically places the mouse pointer on a window component

8. A window component that supports selecting one option only is the

    a. check button

    b. radio button

    c. text field

    d. text area

9. A rectangular subarea with its own grid for organizing widgets is a

    a. canvas

    b. panel

    c. list box

    d. combo box

10. The rows and columns in a grid layout are numbered starting from

    a. (0, 0)

    b. (1, 1)

    c. (1, 0)

    d. (0, 1)

Programming Exercises

1. Write a GUI-based program in the file **taxformwithgui.py** that implements the tax calculator program shown in Figure 9-2. (LO: 9.2, 9.3, 9.4, 9.5)

2. Write a GUI-based program in the file **bouncywithgui.py** that implements the `bouncy` program discussed in Programming Exercise 4 of Chapter 3. (LO: 9.2, 9.3, 9.4, 9.5)

3. Write a GUI-based program in the file **temperatureconverter.py** that allows the user to convert temperature values between degrees Fahrenheit and degrees Celsius. The interface should have labeled entry fields for these two values. These components should be arranged in a grid where the labels occupy the first row and the corresponding fields occupy the second row. At start-up, the Fahrenheit field should contain 32.0, and the Celsius field should contain 0.0. The third row in the window contains two command buttons, labeled >>>> and <<<<. When the user presses the first button, the program should use the data in the Fahrenheit field to compute the Celsius value, which should then be output to the Celsius field. The second button should perform the inverse function. (LO: 9.2, 9.3, 9.4, 9.5, 9.6)

4. Modify the temperature conversion program in the file **temperatureconverterwithkey.py** so that it responds to the user's press of the return or enter key. If the user presses this key when the insertion point is in a given field, the action that uses that field for input is triggered. (LO: 9.2, 9.3, 9.4, 9.5, 9.6)

5. Write a GUI-based program in the file **guesswithgui.py** that plays a guess-the-number game in which the roles of the computer and the user are the reverse of what they are in the Case Study of this chapter. In this version of the game, the computer guesses a number between 1 and 100 and the user provides the responses. The window should display the computer's guesses with a label. The user enters a hint in response, by selecting one of a set of command buttons labeled **Too small, Too large**, and **Correct**. When the game is over, you should disable these buttons and wait for the user to click **New game**, as before. (LO: 9.2, 9.3, 9.4, 9.5, 9.6, 9.7)

6. Add radio button options for filing status to the tax calculator program of Project 1 (in the file **taxformwithgui.py**). The user selects one of these options to determine the tax rate. The Single option's rate is 20%. The Married option is 15%. The Divorced option is 10%. The default option is Single. (LO: 9.7)

7. The TidBit Computer Store (Chapter 3, Programming Exercise 10) has a credit plan for computer purchases. Inputs are the annual interest rate and the purchase price. Monthly payments are 5% of the listed purchase price, minus the down payment, which must be 10% of the purchase price. Write a GUI-based program in the file **tidbitwithgui.py** that displays labeled fields for the inputs and a text area for the output. The program should display a table, with appropriate headers, of a payment schedule for the lifetime of the loan. Each row of the table should contain the following items:

   - The month number (beginning with 1)

   - The current total balance owed

   - The interest owed for that month

   - The amount of principal owed for that month

   - The payment for that month

   - The balance remaining after payment

   The amount of interest for a month is equal to balance * rate / 12. The amount of principal for a month is equal to the monthly payment minus the interest owed. Your program should include separate classes for the model and the view. The model should include a method that expects the two inputs as arguments and returns a formatted string for output by the GUI. (LO: 9.2, 9.3, 9.4, 9.5, 9.6, 9.7)

8. Write a GUI-based program in the file **texteditor.py** that allows the user to open, edit, and save text files. The GUI should include a labeled entry field for the filename and a multiline text widget for the text of the file. The user should be able to scroll through the text by manipulating a vertical scrollbar. Include command buttons labeled **Open**, **Save**, and **New** that allow the user to open, save, and create new files. The `New` command should then clear the text widget and the entry widget. (LO: 9.2, 9.3, 9.4, 9.6, 9.7)

9. Write a GUI-based program in the file **imagebrowser.py** that implements an image browser for your computer's file system. The look, feel, and program logic should be like those of the simple text file bowser developed in this chapter. The file dialog should filter for GIF image files and create and open a `PhotoImage` when a file is accessed. (LO: 9.2, 9.3, 9.4, 9.6, 9.7)

Debugging Exercise

Jack is responsible for designing and laying out a GUI for the game of chess. A chessboard is an 8 by 8 grid of squares of alternating colors, where no two adjacent squares have the same color. A prototype of the desired interface is shown on the left in **Figure 9-23**, along with the result of Jack's design effort thus far on the right.

Figure 9-23   Two versions of a chessboard

Python™

Obviously, there is an error somewhere in Jack's code. Describe this error and suggest a remedy. Here is Jack's code (in the file **chessboard.py**):

```
"""
File: chessboard.py
Displays an 8 by 8 grid of black and white squares of a chessboard.
"""

from breezypythongui import EasyFrame

class Chessboard(EasyFrame):

    def __init__(self):
        """Sets up the window and the panels."""
        EasyFrame.__init__(self, title = "Chess",
                           width = 200, height = 100)
```

```python
        color = "white"
        for row in range(8):
            for column in range(8):
                if color == "black":
                    color = "white"
                else:
                    color = "black"
                self.addPanel(row = row, column = column,
                              background = color)

def main():
    """Instantiate and pop up the window."""
    Chessboard().mainloop()

if __name__ == "__main__":
    main()
```

## Chapter 10

Design with Classes

Learning Objectives

After you complete this chapter, you will be able to:

10.1 Determine the attributes and behavior of a class of objects, choose the appropriate data structures to represent the attributes, and list the methods, including their parameters and return types, that realize this behavior.

10.2 Define classes to model different types of objects and include operations that compare them, transfer them to and from external storage, and provide their string representations.

10.3 Define a class for a two-dimensional grid data structure.

10.4 Exploit inheritance and polymorphism when developing classes.

This book has covered the use of many software tools in computational problem solving. The most important of these tools are the abstraction mechanisms for simplifying designs and controlling the complexity of solutions. Abstraction mechanisms include functions, modules, objects, and classes. In each case, we have begun with an external view of a resource, showing what it does and how it can be used. For example, to use a function in the built-in **math** module, you import it, run **help** to learn how to use the function correctly, and then include it appropriately in your code. You follow the same procedures for built-in data structures such as strings and lists, and for library resources such as the **Turtle** and **Image** classes covered in Chapter 8. From a user's perspective, you shouldn't be concerned with how a resource performs its task. The beauty and utility of an abstraction is that it frees you from the need to be concerned with such details.

Unfortunately, not all useful abstractions are built in. You will sometimes need to custom design an abstraction to suit the needs of a specialized application or suite of applications you are developing. You did exactly that while learning how to program GUIs in Chapter 9. There you learned how to customize an existing class by creating custom subclasses to represent windows for various applications. However, in defining a new subclass, you are still working within the helpful confines of already established abstractions, and merely extending them by adding new features and behavior.

The next step is to learn how to design and implement new classes from scratch. When designing your own abstraction, you must take a different view from that of users and concern yourself with the inner workings of a resource. In this chapter, we will take a more detailed internal view of objects and classes than we did in Chapter 9, showing how to design, implement, and test another useful abstraction mechanism—the class. You will learn how to take a real-world problem situation and model its structure and behavior with entirely new classes of objects.

Programming languages that allow the programmer to define new classes of objects are called **object-oriented languages**. These languages also support a style of programming called **object-oriented programming**. Unlike object-based programming, which simply uses ready-made objects and classes within a framework of functions and algorithmic code, object-oriented programming sustains an effort to conceive and build entire software systems from cooperating classes. We begin this chapter by exploring the definitions of a few classes. We then discuss how cooperating classes can be organized into complex software systems. This strategy is rather different from the strategy of procedural design with functions discussed in Chapters 6 and 7. The advantages and disadvantages of each design strategy will become clear as we proceed.

10.1 Getting Inside Objects and Classes

Programmers who use objects and classes know several things:

- The interface or set of methods that can be used with a class of objects
- The attributes of an object that describe its state from the user's point of view
- How to instantiate a class to obtain an object

Like functions, objects are abstractions. A function packages an algorithm in a single operation that can be called by name. An object packages a set of data values—its **state**—and a set of operations—its methods—in a single entity that can be referenced with a name. This makes an object a more complex abstraction than a function. To get inside a function, you must view the code contained in its definition. To get inside an object, you must view the code contained in its class. A class definition is like a blueprint for each of the objects of that class. This blueprint contains

- Definitions of all of the methods that its objects recognize
- Descriptions of the data structures used to maintain the state of an object, or its attributes, from the implementer's point of view

To illustrate these ideas, we now present a simple class definition for a course-management application, followed by a discussion of the basic concepts involved.

A First Example: The `Student` Class

A course-management application represents information about students in a course. Each student has a name and a list of test scores. We can use these as the attributes of a class named **Student**. The **Student** class should allow the user to view a student's name, view a test score at a given position (counting from 1), reset a test score at a given position, view the highest test score, view the average test score, and obtain a string representation of the student's information. When a **Student** object is created, the user supplies the student's name and the number of test scores. Each score is initially presumed to be 0.

The interface or set of methods of the **Student** class is described in **Table 10-1**. Assuming that the **Student** class is defined in a file named **student.py**, the next session shows how it could be used:

```
>>> from student import Student
>>> s = Student("Maria", 5)
>>> print(s)
Name: Maria
Scores: 0 0 0 0 0
>>> s.setScore(1, 100)
```

```
>>> print(s)
Name: Maria
Scores: 100 0 0 0 0
>>> s.getHighScore()
100
>>> s.getAverageScore()
20
>>> s.getScore(1)
100
>>> s.getName()
'Maria'
```

Table 10-1 The interface of the `Student` class

`Student` **Method**	**What it Does**
`s = Student(name, number)`	Returns a `Student` object with the given `name` and `number` of scores; each score is initially 0
`s.getName()`	Returns the student's name
`s.getScore(i)`	Returns the student's ith score; i must range from 1 through the number of scores
`s.setScore(i, score)`	Resets the student's ith score to `score`; i must range from 1 through the number of scores
`s.getAverageScore()`	Returns the student's average score
`s.getHighScore()`	Returns the student's highest score
`s.__str()__`	Same as `str(s)`; returns a string representation of the student's information

As you learned in Chapter 9, the syntax of a simple class definition is the following:

```
class <class name>(<parent class name>):
  <method definition-1>
  ...
  <method definition-n>
```

The class definition syntax has two parts: a class header and a set of method definitions that follow the class header. The class header consists of the class name and the parent class name.

The class name is a Python identifier. Although built-in type names are not capitalized, Python programmers typically capitalize their own class names to distinguish them from variable names.

The parent class name refers to another class. All Python classes, including the built-in ones, are organized in a tree-like **class hierarchy**. At the top, or root, of this tree is the most abstract class, named **object**, which is built in. Each class immediately below another class in the hierarchy is referred to as a **subclass**, whereas the class immediately above it, if there is one, is called its **parent class**. If the parenthesized parent class name is omitted from the class definition, the new class is automatically made a subclass of **object**. In the example class definitions shown in this book, we explicitly include the parent class names. More will be said about the relationships among classes in the hierarchy later in this chapter.

The code for the **Student** class follows, and its structure is explained in the next few subsections:

```
"""
File: student.py
Resources to manage a student's name and test scores.
"""
```

```python
class Student(object):
    """Represents a student."""

    def __init__(self, name, number):
        """Constructor creates a Student with the given
        name and number of scores and sets all scores
        to 0."""
        self.name = name
        self.scores = []
        for count in range(number):
            self.scores.append(0)

    def getName(self):
        """Returns the student's name."""
        return self.name

    def setScore(self, i, score):
        """Resets the ith score, counting from 1."""
        self.scores[i - 1] = score

    def getScore(self, i):
        """Returns the ith score, counting from 1."""
        return self.scores[i - 1]

    def getAverageScore(self):
        """Returns the average score."""
        return sum(self.scores) / len(self.scores)

    def getHighScore(self):
        """Returns the highest score."""
        return max(self.scores)

    def __str__(self):
        """Returns the string representation of the
        student."""
        return "Name: " + self.name + "\nScores: " + \
            " ".join(map(str, self.scores))
```

Docstrings

The first thing to note is the positioning of the docstrings in our code. They can occur at three levels. The first level is that of the module. Its purpose should be familiar to you by now. The second level is just after the class header. Because there might be more than one class defined in a module, each class can have a docstring that describes its purpose. The third level is located after each method header. Docstrings at this level serve the same role as they do for function definitions. When you enter **help(Student)** at a shell prompt, the interpreter prints the documentation for the class and all of its methods.

Method Definitions

All of the method definitions are indented below the class header. Because methods are a bit like functions, the syntax of their definitions is similar. As you learned in Chapter 9, each method definition must include a first parameter named **self**, even if that method seems to expect no arguments when called. When a method is called with an object, the interpreter binds the parameter **self** to that object so that the method's code can refer to the object by name. Thus, for example, the code

```
s.getScore(4)
```

binds the parameter **self** in the method **getScore** to the **Student** object referenced by the variable **s**. The code for **getScore** can then use **self** to access that individual object's test scores.

Otherwise, methods behave just like functions. They can have required and/or optional arguments, and they can return values. They can create and use temporary variables. A method automatically returns the value **None** when it includes no **return** statement.

The __init__ Method and Instance Variables

Most classes include a special method named __init__. Here is the code for this method in the **Student** class:

```
def __init__(self, name, number):
    """All scores are initially 0."""
    self.name = name
    self.scores = []
    for count in range(number):
        self.scores.append(0)
```

Note that __init__ must begin and end with two consecutive underscores. This method is also called the class's **constructor**, because it is run automatically when a user instantiates the class. Thus, when the code segment

```
s = Student("Juan", 5)
```

is run, Python automatically runs the constructor or __init__ method of the **Student** class. The purpose of the constructor is to initialize an individual object's attributes. In addition to **self**, the **Student** constructor expects two arguments that provide the initial values for these attributes. From this point on, when we refer to a class's constructor, we mean its __init__ method.

The attributes of an object are represented as **instance variables**. Each individual object has its own set of instance variables. These variables serve as storage for its state. The scope of an instance variable (including **self**) is the entire class definition. Thus, all of the class's methods are in a position to reference the instance variables. The lifetime of an instance variable is the lifetime of the enclosing object. An object's lifetime will be discussed in more detail later in this chapter.

Within the class definition, the names of instance variables must begin with **self**. For example, in the definition of the **Student** class, the instance variables **self.name** and **self.scores** are initialized to a string and a list, respectively.

The __str__ Method

Many built-in Python classes usually include an __str__ method. This method builds and returns a string representation of an object's state. When the **str** function is called with an object, that object's __str__ method is automatically invoked to obtain the string that **str** returns. For example, the function call **str(s)** is equivalent to the method call **s.__str__()** but is simpler to write. The function call **print(s)** also automatically runs **str(s)** to obtain the object's string representation for output. Here is the code for the __str__ method in the **Student** class:

```
def __str__(self) :
    """Returns the string representation of the student."""
    return "Name: " + self.name + "\nScores: " + \
           " ".join(map(str, self.scores))
```

The programmer can return any information that would be relevant to the users of a class. Perhaps the most important use of __str__ is in debugging, when you often need to observe the state of an object after running another method.

Accessors and Mutators

Methods that allow a user to observe but not change the state of an object are called **accessors**. Methods that allow a user to modify an object's state are called **mutators**. The **Student** class has just one mutator method. It allows the user to reset a test score at a given position. The remaining methods are accessors. Here is the code for the mutator method **setScore**:

```
def setScore(self, i, score):
    """Resets the ith score, counting from 1."""
    self.scores[i - 1] = score
```

In general, the fewer the number of changes that can occur to an object, the easier it is to use it correctly. That is one reason Python strings are immutable. In the case of the **Student** class, if there is no need to modify an attribute, such as a student's name, we do not include a method to do that.

The Lifetime of Objects

Earlier, we said that the lifetime of an object's instance variables is the lifetime of that object. What determines the span of an object's life? We know that an object comes into being when its class is instantiated. When does an object die? In Python, an object becomes a candidate for the graveyard when the program that created it can no longer refer to it. For example, the next session creates two references to the same **Student** object:

```
>>> s = Student("Sam", 10)
>>> cscilll = [s]
>>> cscilll
[<__main__.Student instance at 0xllba2b0>]
>>> s
<__main__.Student instance at 0xllba2b0>
```

The strange-looking code in angle brackets is what Python displays when it prints this type of object in the IDLE shell. As long as one of these references survives, the **Student** object can remain alive. Continuing this session, we now sever both references to the **Student** object:

```
>>> s = None
>>> cscilll.pop()
<__main__.Student instance at 0xllba2b0>
>>> print(s)
None
>>> cscilll
[]
```

The **Student** object still exists, but the Python virtual machine will eventually recycle its storage during a process called **garbage collection**. For all intents and purposes, this object has expired, and its storage will eventually be used to create other objects.

Rules of Thumb for Defining a Simple Class

We conclude this section by listing several rules of thumb for designing and implementing a simple class:

1. Before writing a line of code, think about the behavior and attributes of the objects of the new class. What actions does an object perform, and how, from the external perspective of a user, do these actions access or modify the object's state?

2. Choose an appropriate class name and develop a short list of the methods available to users. This interface should include appropriate method names and parameter names, as well as brief descriptions of what the methods do. Avoid describing how the methods perform their tasks.

3. Write a short script that appears to use the new class in an appropriate way. The script should instantiate the class and run all of its methods. Of course, you will not be able to execute this script until you have completed the next few steps, but it will help to clarify the interface of your class and serve as an initial test bed for it.

4. Choose the appropriate data structures to represent the attributes of the class. These will be either built-in types such as integers, strings, and lists, or other programmer-defined classes.

5. Fill in the class template with a constructor (an __init__ method) and an __str__ method. Remember that the constructor initializes an object's instance variables, whereas __str__ builds a string from this information. As soon as you have defined these two methods, you can test your class by instantiating it and printing the resulting object.

6. Complete and test the remaining methods incrementally, working in a bottom-up manner. If one method depends on another, complete the second method first.

7. Remember to document your code. Include a docstring for the module, the class, and each method. Do not add docstrings as an afterthought. Write them as soon as you write a class header or a method header. Be sure to examine the results by running **help** with the class name.

Exercise 10-1

1. What are instance variables, and what role does the name **self** play in the context of a class definition?

2. Explain what a constructor does.

3. Explain what the __str__ method does and why it is a useful method to include in a class.

4. The **Student** class has no mutator method that allows a user to change a student's name. Define a method **setName** that allows a user to change a student's name.

5. The method **getAge** expects no arguments and returns the value of an instance variable named **self.age**. Write the code for the definition of this method.

6. How is the lifetime of an object determined? What happens to an object when it dies?

Case Study 10-1 | Playing the Game of Craps

College students are known to study hard and play hard. In this case study, we develop some classes that cooperate to allow students to play and study the behavior of the game of craps.

Request

Write a program that allows the user to play and study the game of craps.

Analysis

A player in the game of craps rolls a pair of dice. If the sum of the values on this initial roll is 2, 3, or 12, the player loses. If the sum is 7 or 11, the player wins. Otherwise, the player continues to roll until the sum is 7, indicating a loss, or the sum equals the initial sum, indicating a win.

During analysis, you decide which classes of objects will be used to model the behavior of the objects in the problem domain. The classes often become evident when you consider the nouns used in the problem description. In this case, the two most significant nouns in our description of a game of craps are "player" and "dice." Thus, the classes will be named **Player** and **Die** (the singular of "dice").

Analysis also specifies the roles and responsibilities of each class. You can describe these in terms of the behavior of each object in the program. A **Die** object can be rolled and its value examined. That's about it. A **Player** object can play a complete game of craps. During the course of this game, the player keeps track of the rolls of the dice. After a game is over, the player can be asked for a history of the rolls and for the game's outcome. The player can then play another game, and so on.

A terminal-based user interface for this program prompts the user for the number of games to play. The program plays that number of games and generates and displays statistics about the results for that round of games. These results, our "study" of the game, include the number of wins, losses, rolls per win, rolls per loss, and winning percentage for the given number of games played.

The program includes two functions, **playOneGame** and **playManyGames**, for convenient testing in the IDLE shell. Here is a sample session with these functions:

```
>>> playOneGame()
(2, 2) 4
(2, 1) 3
(4, 6) 10
(6, 5) 11
(4, 1) 5
(5, 6) 11
(3, 5) 8
(3, 1) 4
You win!
>>> playManyGames(100)
The total number of wins is 49
The total number of losses is 51
The average number of rolls per win is 3.37
```

```
The average number of rolls per loss is 4.20
The winning percentage is 0.490
```

Design

During design, you choose the appropriate data structures for the instance variables of each class and develop its methods using pseudocode, if necessary. You can work from class interfaces provided by analysis or develop the interfaces as the first step of design. The interfaces of the `Die` and `Player` classes are listed in **Table 10-2**.

Table 10-2   The interfaces of the `Die` and `Player` classes

`Player` Method	What it Does
`p = Player()`	Returns a new player object
`p.play()`	Plays the game and returns `True` if there is a win, `False` otherwise
`p.getNumberOfRolls()`	Returns the number of rolls
`p.__str__()`	Same as `str(p)`; returns a formatted string representation of the rolls
`Die` Method	**What it Does**
`d = Die()`	Returns a new die object whose initial value is 1
`d.roll()`	Resets the die's value to a random number between 1 and 6
`d.getValue()`	Returns the die's value
`d.__str__()`	Same as `str(d)`; returns the string representation of the die's value

A `Die` object has a single attribute, an integer ranging in value from 1 through 6. At instantiation, the instance variable `self.value` is initialized to 1. The method `roll` modifies this value by resetting it to a random number from 1 to 6. The method `getValue` returns this value. The method `__str__` returns its string representation. The `Die` class can be coded immediately without further design work.

A `Player` object has three attributes, a pair of dice and a history of rolls in its most recent game. We represent each roll as a tuple of two integers and the set of rolls as a list of these tuples. At instantiation, the instance variable `self.rolls` is set to an empty list.

The method `__str__` converts the list of rolls to a formatted string that contains a roll and the sum from that roll on each line.

The `play` method implements the logic of playing a game and tracking its results. Here is the pseudocode:

```
Create a new list of rolls
Roll the dice and add their values to the rolls list
If sum of the initial roll is 2, 3, or 12
    return false
Else if the sum of the initial roll is 7 or 11
    return true
While true
    Roll the dice and add their values to the rolls list
    If the sum of the roll is 7
        return false
    Else if the sum of the roll equals the initial sum,
        return true
```

(continues)

Note that the rolls list, which is an instance variable, is reset to an empty list on each play. That allows the same player to play multiple games.

The script that defines the **Player** and **Die** classes also includes two functions. The role of these functions is to interact with the human user by playing the games and displaying their results. The **playManyGames** function expects the number of games as an argument, creates a single **Player** object, plays the games and gathers data on the results, processes these data, and displays the required information. We also include a simpler function **playOneGame** that plays just one game and displays the results.

Implementation (Coding)

The **Die** class is defined in a file named **die.py**. The **Player** class and the top-level functions are defined in a file named **craps.py**. Here is the code for the two modules:

```
"""
File: die.py
This module defines the Die class.
"""


from random import randint


class Die(object):
    """This class represents a six-sided die."""

    def __init__(self):
        """Sets the initial face of the die."""
        self.value = 1

    def roll(self):
        """Resets the die's value to a random number
        between 1 and 6."""
        self.value = randint(1, 6)

    def getvalue(self):
        """Returns the current face of the die."""
        return self.value

    def __str__(self):
        """Returns the string rep of the die."""
        return str(self.value)

"""
File: craps.py
This module studies and plays the game of craps.
"""
```

```
from die import Die
class Player(object):

    def __init__(self):
        """Has a pair of dice and an empty rolls list."""
        self.die1 = Die()
        self.die2 = Die()
        self.rolls = []

    def __str__(self):
        """Returns the string rep of the history of
        rolls."""
        result = ""
        for (v1, v2) in self.rolls:
            result = result + str((v1, v2)) + " " + \
                        str(v1 + v2) + "\n"
        return result

    def getNumberOfRolls(self):
        """Returns the number of the rolls in one game."""
        return len(self.rolls)

    def play(self):
        """Plays a game, saves the rolls for that game,
        and returns True for a win and False for a loss."""
        self.rolls = []
        self.die1.roll()
        self.die2.roll()
        (v1, v2) = (self.die1.getvalue(),
                        self.die2.getvalue())
        self.rolls.append((v1, v2) )
        initialSum = v1 + v2
        if initialSum in (2, 3, 12):
            return False
        elif initialSum in (7, 11):
            return True
        while True:
            self.die1.roll()
            self.die2.roll()
            (v1, v2) = (self.die1.getvalue(),
                            self.die2.getvalue())
            self.rolls.append((v1, v2))
            laterSum = v1 + v2
```

(continues)

```
                if laterSum == 7:
                    return False
                elif laterSum == initialSum:
                    return True

# Functions that interact with the user to play the games
def playOneGame():
    """Plays a single game and prints the results."""
    player = Player()
    youWin = player.play()
    print(player)
    if youWin:
        print("You win!")
    else:
        print("You lose!")

def playManyGames(number):
    """Plays a number of games and prints statistics."""
    wins = 0
    losses = 0
    winRolls = 0
    lossRolls = 0
    player = Player()
    for count in range(number):
        hasWon = player.play()
        rolls = player.getNumberOfRolls()
        if hasWon:
            wins += 1
            winRolls += rolls
        else:
            losses += 1
            lossRolls += rolls
    print("The total number of wins is", wins)
    print("The total number of losses is", losses)
    print("The average number of rolls per win is %0.2f" % \
            (winRolls / wins))
  print("The average number of rolls per loss is %0.2f" % \
      (lossRolls / losses))
  print("The winning percentage is %0.3f" % \
      (wins / number))

def main():
    """Plays a number of games and prints statistics."""
```

```
        number = int(input("Enter the number of games: "))
        playManyGames(number)


if __name__ == "__main__":
    main()
```

A GUI for Dice Games

Gambling is gambling, but it's more fun on a computer if you can visualize the dice. You can deploy the skills you picked up in Chapter 9 to create the graphical user interface shown in **Figure 10-1**.

Figure 10-1   Displaying images of dice

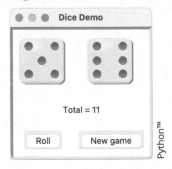

The code for this version of the interface loads and displays images of dice from a folder of GIF files. It is a good idea to rough out the GUI before incorporating the game logic. Here is the code for laying out the window and rolling two dice:

```
"""
File: dicedemo.py
Pops up a window that allows the user to roll the dice.
"""


from breezypythongui import EasyFrame
from tkinter import PhotoImage
from die import Die

class DiceDemo(EasyFrame):

    def __init__(self):
        """Creates the dice, and sets up the Images and
        labels for the two dice to be displayed,
        the state label, and the two command buttons."""
        EasyFrame.__init__(self, title = "Dice Demo")
        self.setSize(220, 200)
        self.die1 = Die()
        self.die2 = Die()
```

(continues)

```python
            self.dieLabel1 = self.addLabel("", row = 0,
                                             column = 0,
                                             sticky = "NSEW")
            self.dieLabel2 = self.addLabel("", row = 0,
                                             column = 1,
                                             sticky = "NSEW",
                                             columnspan = 2)
            self.stateLabel = self.addLabel("", row = 1,
                                             column = 0,
                                             sticky = "NSEW",
                                             columnspan = 2)
            self.addButton(row = 2,column = 0, text = "Roll",
                        command = self.nextRoll)
            self.addButton(text = "New game", row = 2,
                        column = 1,
                        command = self.newGame)
            self.refreshImages()

    def nextRoll(self):
        """Rolls the dice and updates the view with
        the results."""
        self.die1.roll()
        self.die2.roll()
        total = self.die1.getValue() + self.die2.getValue()
        self.stateLabel["text"] = "Total = " + str(total)
        self.refreshImages()

    def newGame(self):
        """Create new dice and updates the view."""
        self.die1 = Die()
        self.die2 = Die()
        self.stateLabel["text"] = ""
        self.refreshImages()

    def refreshImages(self):
        """Updates the images in the window."""
        fileName1 = "DICE/" + str(self.die1) + ".gif"
        fileName2 = "DICE/" + str(self.die2) + ".gif"
        self.image1 = PhotoImage(file = fileName1)
        self.dieImageLabel1["image"] = self.image1
        self.image2 = PhotoImage(file = fileName2)
        self.dieImageLabel2["image"] = self.image2
```

```
def main():
    """Instantiate and pop up the window."""
    DiceDemo().mainloop()


if __name__ == "__main__":
    main()
```

The completion of a GUI-based craps game is left as an exercise.

10.2 Data-Modeling Examples

As you have seen, objects and classes are useful for modeling objects in the real world. In this section, we explore several other examples.

Rational Numbers

We begin with numbers. A **rational number** consists of two integer parts, a numerator and a denominator, and is written using the format *numerator / denominator*. Examples are 1/2, 1/3, and so forth. Operations on rational numbers include arithmetic and comparisons. Python has no built-in type for rational numbers. Let us develop a new class named **Rational** to support this type of data.

The interface of the **Rational** class includes a constructor for creating a rational number, an **str** function for obtaining a string representation, and accessors for the numerator and denominator. We will also show how to include methods for arithmetic and comparisons. Here is a sample session to illustrate the use of the new class:

```
>>> oneHalf = Rational(1, 2)
>>> oneSixth = Rational(1, 6)
>>> print(oneHalf)
1/2
>>> print(oneHalf + oneSixth)
2/3
>>> oneHalf == oneSixth
False
>>> oneHalf > oneSixth
True
```

Note that this session uses the built-in operators +, ==, and < with objects of the new class, **Rational**. Python allows the programmer to **overload** many of the built-in operators for use with new data types.

We develop this class in two steps. First, we take care of the internal representation of a rational number and also its string representation. The constructor expects the numerator and denominator as arguments and sets two instance variables to this information. This method then reduces the rational number to its lowest terms. To reduce a rational number to its lowest terms, you first compute the greatest common divisor (GCD) of the numerator and the denominator, using Euclid's algorithm, as described in Programming Exercise 8 of Chapter 3. You then divide the numerator and the denominator by this GCD. These tasks are assigned to two other **Rational** methods, **_reduce** and **_gcd**. Because these methods are not intended to be in the class's interface, their names begin with the _ symbol. Performing the reduction step in the constructor guarantees that it will not have to be done in any other operation. Here is the code for the first step:

```
"""
File: rational.py
Resources to manipulate rational numbers.
"""

class Rational(object):
    """Represents a rational number."""

    def __init__(self, numer, denom) :
        """Constructor creates a number with the given
        numerator and denominator and reduces it to lowest
        terms."""
        self.numer = numer
        self.denom = denom
        self._reduce()

    def numerator(self):
        """Returns the numerator."""
        return self.numer

    def denominator(self):
        """Returns the denominator."""
        return self.denom

    def __str__(self):
        """Returns the string representation of the
        number."""
        return str(self.numer) + "/" + str(self.denom)

    def _reduce(self):
        """Helper to reduce the number to lowest terms."""
        divisor = self._gcd(self.numer, self.denom)
        self.numer = self.numer // divisor
        self.denom = self.denom // divisor

    def _gcd(self, a, b):
        """Euclid's algorithm for greatest common
        divisor (hacker's version)."""
        (a, b) = (max(a, b), min(a, b))
        while b > 0:
            (a, b) = (b, a % b)
        return a

    # Methods for arithmetic and comparisons go here
```

You can now test the class by instantiating numbers and printing them. Note that this class only supports positive rational numbers. When you are satisfied that the data are being represented correctly, you can move on to the next step.

Rational Number Arithmetic and Operator Overloading

We now add methods to perform arithmetic with rational numbers. Recall that the earlier session used the built-in operators for arithmetic. For a built-in type such as `int` or `float`, each arithmetic operator corresponds to a special method name. You will see many of these methods by entering `dir(int)` or `dir(str)` at a shell prompt, and they are listed in **Table 10-3**. The object on which the method is called corresponds to the left operand, whereas the method's second parameter corresponds to the right operand. Thus, for example, the code `x + y` is actually shorthand for the code `x.__add__(y)`.

Table 10-3   Built-in arithmetic operators and their corresponding methods

Operator	Method Name
+	__add__
-	__sub__
*	__mul__
/	__div__
%	__mod__

To overload an arithmetic operator, you just define a new method using the appropriate method name. The code for each method applies a rule of rational number arithmetic. The rules are listed in **Table 10-4**.

Table 10-4   Rules for rational number arithmetic

Type of Operation	Rule
Addition	$n_1/d_1 + n_2/d_2 = (n_1 d_2 + n_2 d_1) / d_1 d_2$
Subtraction	$n_1/d_1 - n_2/d_2 = (n_1 d_2 - n_2 d_1) / d_1 d_2$
Multiplication	$n_1/d_1 * n_2/d_2 = n_1 n_2 / d_1 d_2$
Division	$n_1/d_1 / n_2/d_2 = n_1 d_2 / d_1 n_2$

Each method builds and returns a new rational number that represents the result of the operation. Here is the code for the addition operation:

```
def __add__(self, other):
    """Returns the sum of the numbers.
    self is the left operand and other is
    the right operand."""
    newNumer = self.numer * other.denom + \
               other.numer * self.denom
    newDenom = self.denom * other.denom
    return Rational(newNumer, newDenom)
```

Note that the parameter `self` is viewed as the left operand of the operator, whereas the parameter `other` is viewed as the right operand. The instance variables of the rational number named `other` are accessed in the same manner as the instance variables of the rational number named `self`. Note also that this method, like the other methods for rational arithmetic, returns a rational number. Arithmetic operations on numbers are said to be **closed under combination**, meaning that these operations usually return values of the same types as their arguments, allowing the user to combine the operations in arbitrarily complex expressions.

Another example of an abstraction mechanism is **operator overloading**. In this case, programmers can use operators with single, standard meanings even though the underlying operations vary from data type to data type.

Comparison Methods

You can compare integers and floating-point numbers using the operators `==`, `!=`, `<`, `>`, `<=`, and `>=`. When the Python interpreter encounters one of these operators, it uses a corresponding method defined in the **float** or **int** class. Each of these methods expects two arguments. The first argument, `self`, represents the operand to the left of the operator, and the second argument represents the other operand. **Table 10-5** lists the comparison operators and the corresponding methods.

Table 10-5   The comparison operators and methods

Operator	Meaning	Method
==	Equals	__eq__
!=	Not equals	__ne__
<	Less than	__lt__
<=	Less than or equal	__le__
>	Greater than	__gt__
>=	Greater than or equal	__ge__

To use the comparison operators with a new class of objects, such as rational numbers, the class must include these methods with the appropriate comparison logic. However, once the implementer of the class has defined methods for `==`, `<`, and `>=`, the remaining methods are automatically provided.

Let's implement `<` here and wait on `==` until the next section. The simplest way to compare two rational numbers is to compare the product of the extremes and the product of the means. The extremes are the first numerator and the second denominator, whereas the means are the second numerator and the first denominator. Thus, the comparison 1/6 < 2/3 translates to 1 * 3 < 2 * 6. The implementation of the `__lt__` method for rational numbers uses this strategy, as follows:

```
def __lt__(self, other):
    """Compares two rational numbers, self and other,
    using <."""
    extremes = self.numer * other.denom
    means = other.numer * self.denom
    return extremes < means
```

When objects of a new class are comparable, it's a good idea to include the comparison methods in that class. Then, other built-in methods, such as the **sort** method for lists, will be able to use your objects appropriately.

Equality and the __eq__ Method

Equality is a different kind of relationship from the other types of comparisons. Not all objects are comparable using less than or greater than, but any two objects can be compared for equality or inequality. For example, when the variable `twoThirds` refers to a rational number, it does not make sense to say `twoThirds < "hi there"`, but it does make sense to say `twoThirds != "hi there"` (true, they aren't the same). Put another way, the first expression should generate a semantic error, whereas the second expression should return **True**.

The Python interpreter picks out equality from the other comparisons by looking for an `__eq__` method when it encounters the `==` and `!=` operators. As you'll recall from Chapter 5, Python includes an implementation of this method for objects like lists and dictionaries as well as the numeric types. However, unless you include an implementation of this method for a new class, Python relies upon the implementation of `__eq__` in the `object` class, which uses the `is` operator. This implementation returns **True** only if the two operands refer to the exact same object (object identity). This criterion of equality is too narrow for many objects, such as rational numbers, where you might want two distinct objects that both represent the same number to be considered equal.

To remedy this problem, you must include an `__eq__` method in a new class. This method supports equality tests with any types of objects. Here is the code for this method in the **Rational** class:

```python
def __eq__(self, other):
    """Tests self and other for equality."""
    if self is other:                   # Object identity?
        return True
    elif type(self) != type(other):  # Types do not match?
        return False
    else:
        return self.numer == other.numer and \
               self.denom == other.denom
```

Note that the method first tests the two operands for object identity using Python's `is` operator. The `is` operator returns **True** if `self` and `other` refer to the exact same object. If the two objects are distinct, the method then uses Python's `type` function to determine whether or not they are of the same type. If they are not of the same type, they cannot be equal. Finally, if the two operands are of the same type, the second one must be a rational number, so it is safe to access the components of both operands to compare them for equality in the last alternative.

As a rule of thumb, you should include an `__eq__` method in any class where a comparison for equality uses a criterion other than object identity. You should also include comparison methods for `<` and `>=` when the objects are comparable using less than or greater than.

The `__repr__` Method for Printing an Object in IDLE

You may have noticed that when you enter a simple variable refence to a new type of object in the IDLE shell, Python prints a strange notation in angle brackets. This notation is different from the object's string representation as defined in its `__str__` method, which Python's `print` function automatically uses when you call `print` with the object as an argument. The next session illustrates this difference with some instances of the **Rational** class:

```python
>>> oneThird = Rational(1, 3)
>>> oneEighth = Rational(1, 8)
>>> print(oneThird)      # print calls str(oneThird)
1/3
>>> oneThird             # No automatic call of str here
<__main__.Rational object at 0x103ea7880>
>>> print(oneThird + oneEighth)
11/24
>>> oneThird + oneEighth
<__main__.Rational object at 0x103ea6f50>
```

This difference is not normally a problem for most uses of objects, but in cases of interaction with new types of numbers like `Rational`, it would be helpful to see their commonly used string representations in IDLE without having to call the `print` function to obtain it. You can do this by adding a method named `__repr__` to the class definition (the name is an acronym for "read/evaluate/print," which refers to the process that IDLE executes when you enter a Python expression in its environment). This method simply returns the result of calling `str` with `self`, as follows:

```
def __repr__(self):
    """Returns the string rep for IDLE's printing."""
    return str(self)
```

The interaction in IDLE with rational numbers now more closely resembles that with floats and integers:

```
>>> oneThird = Rational(1, 3)
>>> oneEighth = Rational(1, 8)
>>> oneThird              # It's automatic now!
1/3
>>> oneThird + oneEighth
11/24
>>> oneThird + Rational(1, 2) + oneEighth # 1/3 + 1/2 + 1/8
23/24
```

Savings Accounts and Class Variables

Turning to the world of finance, banking systems are easily modeled with classes. For example, a savings account allows owners to make deposits and withdrawals. These accounts also compute interest periodically. A simplified version of a savings account includes an owner's name, PIN, and balance as attributes. The interface for a `SavingsAccount` class is listed in **Table 10-6**.

Table 10-6 The interface for `SavingsAccount`

`SavingsAccount` **Method**	**What it Does**
`a = SavingsAccount(name, pin, balance = 0.0)`	Returns a new account with the given name, PIN, and balance
`a.deposit(amount)`	Deposits the given amount to the account's balance
`a.withdraw(amount)`	Withdraws the given amount from the account's balance
`a.getBalance()`	Returns the account's balance
`a.getName()`	Returns the account's name
`a.getPin()`	Returns the account's PIN
`a.computeInterest()`	Computes the account's interest and deposits it
`a.__str__()`	Same as `str(a)`; returns the string representation of the account

When the interest is computed, a rate is applied to the balance. If you assume that the rate is the same for all accounts, then it does not have to be an instance variable. Instead, you can use a **class variable**. A class variable is visible to all instances of a class and does not vary from instance to instance. While it normally behaves like a constant, in some situations a class variable can be modified. But when it is, the change takes effect for the entire class.

To introduce a class variable, we place the assignment statement that initializes it between the class header and the first method definition. For clarity, class variables are written in uppercase only. The code for **SavingsAccount** shows the definition and use of the class variable **RATE**:

```python
"""
File: savingsaccount.py
This module defines the SavingsAccount class.
"""


class SavingsAccount(object):
    """This class represents a savings account
    with the owner's name, PIN, and balance."""

    RATE = 0.02      # Single rate for all accounts

    def __init__(self, name, pin, balance = 0.0):
        self.name = name
        self.pin = pin
        self.balance = balance

    def __str__(self):
        """Returns the string rep."""
        result = 'Name:      ' + self.name + '\n'
        result += 'PIN:       ' + self.pin + '\n'
        result += 'Balance:   ' + str(self.balance)
        return result

    def getBalance(self):
        """Returns the current balance."""
        return self.balance

    def getName(self):
        """Returns the current name."""
        return self.name

    def getPin(self):
        """Returns the current pin."""
        return self.pin

    def deposit(self, amount):
        """Deposits the given amount and returns None."""
        self.balance += amount
        return None

    def withdraw(self, amount):
        """Withdraws the given amount.
```

```
        Returns None if successful, or an
        error message if unsuccessful."""
        if amount < 0:
            return "Amount must be >= 0"
        elif self.balance < amount:
            return "Insufficient funds"
        else:
            self.balance -= amount
            return None


    def computeInterest(self):
        """Computes, deposits, and returns the interest."""
        interest = self.balance * SavingsAccount.RATE
        self.deposit(interest)
        return interest
```

When you reference a class variable, you must prefix it with the class name and a dot, as in **SavingsAccount. RATE**. Class variables are visible both inside a class definition and to external users of the class.

In general, you should use class variables only for symbolic constants or to maintain data held in common by all objects of a class. For data that are owned by individual objects, you must use instance variables instead.

Putting the Accounts into a Bank

Savings accounts make the most sense in the context of a bank. A very simple bank allows a user to add new accounts, remove accounts, get existing accounts, and compute interest on all accounts. A **Bank** class thus has these four basic operations (**add**, **remove**, **get**, and **computeInterest**) and a constructor. This class, of course, also includes the usual **str** function for development and debugging. We assume that **Bank** is defined in a file named **bank.py**. Here is a sample session that uses a **Bank** object and some **SavingsAccount** objects. The interface for **Bank** is listed in **Table 10-7**.

Table 10-7   The interface for the **Bank** class

Bank **Method**	**What it Does**
`b = Bank()`	Returns a bank
`b.add(account)`	Adds the given account to the bank
`b.remove(name, pin)`	Removes the account with the given **name** and **pin** from the bank and returns the account; if the account is not in the bank, returns **None**
`b.get(name, pin)`	Returns the account associated with the **name** and **pin** if it's in the bank; otherwise, returns **None**
`b.computeInterest()`	Computes the interest on each account, deposits it in that account, and returns the total interest
`b.__str__()`	Same as `str(b)`; returns a string representation of the bank (all the accounts)

```
>>> from bank import Bank
>>> from savingsaccount import SavingsAccount
>>> bank = Bank()
>>> bank.add(SavingsAccount("Wilma", "1001", 4000.00))
>>> bank.add(SavingsAccount("Fred", "1002", 1000.00))
```

```
>>> print(bank)
Name:     Fred
PIN:      1002
Balance:  1000.00
Name:     Wilma
PIN:      1001
Balance:  4000.00
>>> account = bank.get("Wilma", "1000")
>>> print(account)
None
>>> account = bank.get("Wilma", "1001")
>>> print(account)
Name:     Wilma
PIN:      1001
Balance:  4000.00
>>> account.deposit(25.00)
>>> print(account)
Name:     Wilma
PIN:      1001
Balance:  4025.00
>>> print(bank)
Name:     Fred
PIN:      1002
Balance:  1000.00
Name:     Wilma
PIN:      1001
Balance:  4025.00
```

To keep the design simple, the bank maintains the accounts in no particular order. Thus, you can choose a dictionary keyed by owners' credentials to represent the collection of accounts. Access and removal then depend on an owner's credentials. Here is the code for the **Bank** class:

```
"""
File: bank.py
This module defines the Bank class.
"""

from savingsaccount import SavingsAccount

class Bank(object):

    def __init__(self):
        self.accounts = {}

    def __str__(self):
        """Return the string rep of the entire bank."""
```

```
        return '\n'.join(map(str, self.accounts.values()))

    def makeKey(self, name, pin):

        """Makes and returns a key from name and pin."""

        return name + "/" + pin

    def add(self, account):
        """Inserts an account with name and pin as a key."""
        key = self.makeKey(account.getName(),
                           account.getPin())
        self.accounts[key] = account

    def remove(self, name, pin):
        """Removes the account from the bank and
        and returns it, or None if the account does
        not exist."""
        key = self.makeKey(name, pin)
        return self.accounts.pop(key, None)

    def get(self, name, pin):
        """Returns the account from the bank,
        or returns None if the account does
        not exist."""
        key = self.makeKey(name, pin)
        return self.accounts.get(key, None)

    def computeInterest(self):
        """Computes interest for each account and
        returns the total."""
        total = 0.0
        for account in self.accounts.values():
            total += account.computeInterest()
        return total
```

Note the use of the value **None** in the methods **remove** and **get**. In this context, **None** indicates to the user that the given account is not in the bank. Note also that the module names for the **Bank** and **SavingsAccount** classes are **bank** and **savingsaccount**, respectively. This naming convention is standard practice among Python programmers and helps them to remember where classes are located for import.

Using `pickle` for Permanent Storage of Objects

Chapter 4 discussed saving data in permanent storage with text files. Now suppose you want to save new types of objects to files. For example, it would be a wise idea to back up the information for a savings account to a file whenever that account is modified. You can convert any object to text for storage, but the mapping of complex objects to text and back again can be tedious and cause maintenance headaches. Fortunately, Python includes a module that allows the programmer to save and load objects using a process called **pickling**. The term comes from the process of converting cucumbers to pickles for preservation in jars. However, in the case of computational objects, you can metaphorically get the cucumbers back from the pickle jar again. You can pickle an object before it is saved to a file, and then unpickle it as it is loaded from a file into a program. Python takes care of all of the conversion details automatically. You start by importing the `pickle` module. Files are opened for input and output and closed in the usual manner, except that the flags `"rb"` and `"wb"` are used instead of 'r' and 'w', respectively. To save an object, you use the function `pickle.dump`. Its first argument is the object to be "dumped," or saved to a file, and its second argument is the file object.

You can use the `pickle` module to save the accounts in a bank to a file. You start by defining a **Bank** method named **save**. The method includes an optional argument for the filename. You assume that the **Bank** object also has an instance variable for the filename. For a new, empty bank, this variable's value is initially **None**. Whenever the bank is saved to a file, this variable becomes the current filename. When the method's filename argument is not provided, the method uses the bank's current filename if there is one. This is similar to using the **Save** option in a **File** menu. When the filename argument is provided, it is used to save the bank to a different file. This is similar to the **Save As** option in a **File** menu. Here is the code:

```python
import pickle


def save(self, fileName = None):
    """Saves pickled accounts to a file. The parameter
    allows the user to change filenames."""
    if fileName:
        self.fileName = fileName
    else:
        return
    fileObj = open(self. fileName, "wb")
    for account in self.accounts.values():
        pickle.dump(account, fileObj)
    fileObj.close()
```

Input of Objects and the `try-except` Statement

You can load pickled objects into a program from a file using the function `pickle.load`. If the end of the file has been reached, this function raises an exception. This complicates the input process, because we have no apparent way to detect the end of the file before the exception is raised. However, Python's `try-except` statement comes to our rescue. As you learned in Chapter 9, this statement allows an exception to be caught and the program to recover. The syntax of a simple `try-except` statement is the following:

```python
try:
    <statements>
except <exception type>:
    <statements>
```

When this statement is run, the statements within the **try** clause are executed. If one of these statements raises an exception, control is immediately transferred to the **except** clause. If the type of exception raised matches the type in this clause, its statements are executed. Otherwise, control is transferred to the caller of the **try-except** statement and further up the chain of calls, until the exception is successfully handled or the program halts with an error message. If the statements in the **try** clause raise no exceptions, the **except** clause is skipped, and control proceeds to the end of the **try-except** statement.

We can now construct an input file loop that continues to load objects until the end of the file is encountered. When this happens, an **EOFError** is raised. The **except** clause then closes the file and breaks out of the loop. We also add a new instance variable to track the bank's filename for saving the bank to a file. Here is the code for a **Bank** method **__init__** that can take some initial accounts from an input file. This method now either creates a new, empty bank if the filename is not present, or loads accounts from a file into a **Bank** object.

```python
def __init__(self, fileName = None):
    """Creates a new dictionary to hold the accounts.
    If a filename is provided, loads the accounts from
    a file of pickled accounts."""
    self.accounts = {}
    self.fileName = fileName
    if fileName:
        fileObj = open(fileName, "rb")
        while True:
            try:
                account = pickle.load(fileObj)
                self.add(account)
            except EOFError:
                fileObj.close()
                break
```

Playing Cards

Many games, such as poker, blackjack, and solitaire, use playing cards. Modeling playing cards provides a nice illustration of the design of cooperating classes. A standard deck of cards has 52 cards. There are four suits: spades, hearts, diamonds, and clubs. Each suit contains 13 cards. Each card also has a rank, which is a number used to sort the cards and determine the count in a hand. The literal numbers are 2 through 10. An ace counts as the number 1 or some other number, depending on the game being played. The face cards, jack, queen, and king, often count as 11, 12, and 13, respectively.

A **Card** class and a **Deck** class would be useful resources for game-playing programs. A **Card** object has two instance attributes, a rank and a suit. The **Card** class has two class attributes, the set of all suits and the set of all ranks. You can represent these two sets of attributes as instance variables and class variables in the **Card** class.

Because the attributes are only accessed and never modified, we do not include any methods other than an **__str__** method for the string representation. The **__init__** method expects an integer rank and a string suit as arguments and returns a new card with that rank and suit. The next session shows the use of the **Card** class:

```
>>> threeOfSpades = Card(3, "Spades")
>>> jackOfSpades = Card(11, "Spades")
>>> print(jackOfSpades)
Jack of Spades
>>> threeOfSpades.rank < jackOfSpades.rank
True
>>> print(jackOfSpades.rank, jackOfSpades.suit)
11 Spades
```

Note that you can directly access the rank and suit of a **Card** object by using a dot followed by the instance variable names. A card is little more than a container of two data values. Here is the code for the **Card** class:

```python
class Card(object):
    """ A card object with a suit and rank."""

    RANKS = tuple(range(1, 14))     # Ranks 1..13
    SUITS = ("Spades", "Diamonds", "Hearts", "Clubs")

    def __init__(self, rank, suit):
        """Creates a card with the given rank and suit."""
        self.rank = rank
        self.suit = suit

    def __str__(self) :
        """Returns the string representation of a card."""
        if self.rank == 1:
            rank = "Ace"
        elif self.rank == 11:
            rank = "Jack"
        elif self.rank == 12:
            rank = "Queen"
        elif self.rank == 13:
            rank = "King"
        else:
            rank = self.rank
        return str(rank) + " of " + self.suit
```

Unlike an individual card, a deck has significant behavior that can be specified in an interface. One can shuffle the deck, deal a card, and determine the number of cards left in it. **Table 10-8** lists the methods of a **Deck** class and what they do. Here is a sample session that tries out a deck:

Table 10-8 The interface for the **Deck** class

Deck Method	What it Does
d = Deck()	Returns a deck
d.__len__()	Same as len(d); returns the number of cards currently in the deck
d.shuffle()	Shuffles the cards in the deck
d.deal()	If the deck is not empty, removes and returns the topmost card; otherwise, returns None
d.__str__()	Same as str(d); returns a string representation of the deck (all the cards in it)

```python
>>> deck = Deck()
>>> print(deck)
<the print reps of 52 cards, in order of suit and rank>
>>> deck.shuffle()
>>> len(deck)
52
>>> while len(deck) > 0:
```

```
        card = deck.deal()
        print(card)
<the print reps of 52 randomly ordered cards>
>>> len(deck)
0
```

During instantiation, all 52 unique cards are created and inserted in sorted order into a deck's internal list of cards. The **Deck** constructor makes use of the class variables **RANKS** and **SUITS** in the **Card** class to order the new cards appropriately. The **shuffle** method simply passes the list of cards to **random.shuffle**. The **deal** method removes and returns the first card in the list, if there is one, or returns the value **None** otherwise. The **len** function, like the **str** function, calls a method (in this case, __**len**__) that returns the length of the list of cards. Here is the code for **Deck**:

```
import random


# The definition of the Card class goes here


class Deck(object):
    """ A deck containing 52 cards."""

    def __init__(self):
        """Creates a full deck of cards."""
        self.cards = []
        for suit in Card.SUITS:
            for rank in Card.RANKS:
                c = Card(rank, suit)
                self.cards.append(c)

    def shuffle(self):
        """Shuffles the cards."""
        random.shuffle(self.cards)

    def deal(self):
        """Removes and returns the top card or None
        if the deck is empty."""
        if len(self) == 0:
            return None
        else:
            return self.cards.pop(0)

    def __len__(self):
        """Returns the number of cards left in the deck."""
        return len(self.cards)

    def __str__(self):
        """Returns the string representation of a deck."""
        result = ""
```

```
for c in self.cards:
    result = result + str(c) + '\n'
return result
```

Exercise 10-2

1. Although the use of a PIN to identify a person's bank account is simple, it's not very realistic. Real banks typically assign a unique 12-digit number to each account and use this as well as the customer's PIN during a login at an ATM. Suggest how to rework the banking system discussed in this section to use this information.

2. What is a class variable? When should the programmer define a class variable rather than an instance variable?

3. Describe how the arithmetic operators can be overloaded to work with a new class of numbers.

4. Define a method for the **Bank** class that returns the total assets in the bank (the sum of all account balances).

5. Describe the benefits of pickling objects for file storage.

6. Why would you use a **try-except** statement in a program?

7. Two playing cards can be compared by rank. For example, an ace is less than a 2. When **c1** and **c2** are cards, **c1.rank < c2.rank** expresses this relationship. Explain how a method could be added to the **Card** class to simplify this expression to **c1 < c2**.

Case Study 10-2 | An ATM

In this case study, we develop a simple ATM program that uses the **Bank** and **SavingsAccount** classes discussed in the previous section.

Request

Write a program that simulates a simple ATM.

Analysis

Our ATM user logs in with a name and a personal identification number, or PIN. If either string is unrecognized, an error message is displayed. Otherwise, the user can repeatedly select options to get the balance, make a deposit, and make a withdrawal. A final option allows the user to log out. **Figure 10-2** shows the sample interface for this application.

Figure 10-2 The user interface for the ATM program

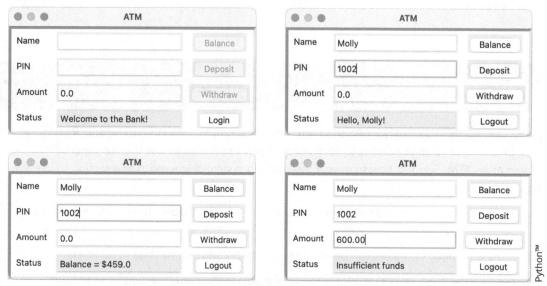

The data model classes for the program are the **Bank** and **SavingsAccount** classes developed earlier in this chapter. To support user interaction, we also develop a new class called **ATM**. The **class diagram** in **Figure 10-3** shows the relationships among these classes.

Figure 10-3 A Unified Modeling Language diagram for the ATM program showing the program's classes

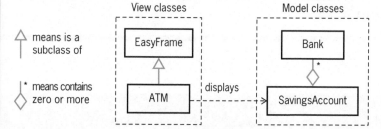

As you learned in Chapter 9, in a class diagram the name of each class appears in a box. The lines or edges connecting the boxes show the relationships. Note that these edges are labeled or contain arrows. This information describes the number of accounts in a bank (zero or more) and the dependency of one class on another (the direction of an arrow). Class diagrams of this type are part of a graphical notation called the **Unified Modeling Language**, or UML. UML is used to describe and document the analysis and design of complex software systems.

In general, it is a good idea to divide the code for most interactive applications into at least two sets of classes. One set of classes, which we call the **view**, handles the program's interactions with human users, including the input and output operations. The other set of classes, called the **model**, represents and manages the data used by the application. In the current case study, the **Bank** and **SavingsAccount** classes belong to the model, whereas the **ATM** class belongs to the view. One of the benefits of this separation of responsibilities is that you can write different views for the same data model, such as a terminal-based view and a GUI-based view, without changing a line of code in the data model. Alternatively, you can write different representations of the data model without altering a line of code in the views. In some of the case studies that follow, we apply this framework, called the **model/view pattern**, to structure the code.

Design

The **ATM** class maintains two instance variables. Their values are the following:

- A **Bank** object

- The **SavingsAccount** of the currently logged-in user

At program start-up, a **Bank** object is loaded from a file. An **ATM** object is then created for this bank. The ATM's **mainloop** method is then called. This method enters an event-driven loop that waits for user events. If a user's name and PIN match those of an account, the ATM's **account** variable is set to the user's account and the buttons for manipulating the account are enabled. The selection of an option triggers an event-handling method to process that option. **Table 10-9** lists the methods in the **ATM** class.

Table 10-9   The interface for the **ATM** class

ATM Method	What it Does
ATM(bank)	Returns a new ATM object based on the data model bank
login()	Allows the user to log in
logout()	Allows the user to log out
getBalance()	Displays the user's balance
deposit()	Allows the user to make a deposit
withdraw()	Allows the user to make a withdrawal and displays any error messages

The **ATM** constructor receives a **Bank** object as an argument and saves a reference to it in an instance variable. It also sets its **account** variable to **None**.

Implementation (Coding)

The data model classes **Bank** and **SavingsAccount** are already available in **bank.py** and **savingsaccount.py**. The code for the GUI, in **atm.py**, includes definitions of a main window class named **ATM** and a **main** function. We discuss this function and several of the **ATM** methods without presenting the complete implementation here.

Before you can run this program, you need to create a bank. For testing purposes, we include in the **Bank** class a simple function named **createBank** that creates and returns a **Bank** object with a number of dummy accounts. Alternatively, the program can load a bank object that has been saved in a file, as discussed earlier.

The **main** function creates a bank and passes this object to the constructor of the **ATM** class. The **ATM** object's **mainloop** method is then run to pop up the window. Here is the code for the imports and the **main** function:

```
"""
File: atm.py
This module defines the ATM class, which provides a window
for bank customers to perform deposits, withdrawals, and check balances.
"""


from breezypythongui import EasyFrame
from bank import Bank, createBank


# Code for the ATM class goes here (in atm.py)
```

(continues)

```
def main(fileName = None):
    """Creates the bank with the optional file name,
    wraps the window around it, and opens the window.
    Saves the bank when the window closes."""
    if not fileName:
        bank = createBank(5)
    else:
        bank = Bank(fileName)
    print(bank) # For testing only
    atm = ATM(bank)
    atm.mainloop()
    # Could save the bank to a file here.


if __name__ == "__main__":
    main()
```

Note that when you launch this as a standalone program, you open the ATM on a bank with five dummy accounts; but if you run **main** with a **filename** argument in the IDLE shell, you open the ATM on a bank created from a saved bank file.

The **__init__** method of **ATM** receives a **Bank** object as an argument and saves a reference to it in an instance variable. This step connects the view (**ATM**) to the model (**Bank**) for the application. The **ATM** object also keeps a reference to the currently open account, which has an initial value of **None**. Here is the code for this method, which omits the straightforward, but rather lengthy and tedious, step of adding the widgets to the window:

```
class ATM(EasyFrame):
    """Represents an ATM window.
    The window tracks the bank and the current account.
    The current account is None at startup and logout.
    """

    def __init__(self, bank):
        """Initialize the window and establish
        the data model."""
        EasyFrame.__init__(self, title = "ATM")
        # Create references to the data model.
        self.bank = bank
        self.account = None
        # Create and add the widgets to the window.
        # Detailed code available in atm.py


        # Event handling methods go here
```

The event handling method to log the user in takes the username and pin from the input fields and attempts to retrieve an account with these credentials from the bank. If this step is successful, the **account** variable will refer to this account, a greeting will be displayed in the status area, and the buttons to manipulate the account will be enabled. Otherwise, the program displays an error message in the status area. Here is the code for the method **login**:

```python
def login(self):
    """Attempts to login the customer. If successful,
    enables the buttons, including logout."""
    name = self.nameField.getText()
    pin = self.pinField.getText()
    self.account = self.bank.get(name, pin)
    if self.account:
        self.statusField.setText("Hello, " + name + "!")
        self.balanceButton["state"] = "normal"
        self.depositButton["state"] = "normal"
        self.withdrawButton["state"] = "normal"
        self.loginButton["text"] = "Logout"
        self.loginButton["command"] = self.logout
    else:
        self.statusField.setText("Name and pin not found!")
```

Note that if a login succeeds, the **text** and **command** attributes of the button named **loginButton** are set to the information for logging out. This allows the login and logout functions to be assigned to a single button, as if it were an on/off switch, thereby simplifying the user interface.

The **logout** method clears the view and restores it to its initial state, where it can await another customer, as follows:

```python
def logout(self):
    """Logs the customer out, clears the fields,
    disables the buttons, and enables login."""
    self.account = None
    self.nameField.setText("")
    self.pinField.setText("")
    self.amountField.setNumber(0.0)
    self.statusField.setText("Welcome to the Bank!")
    self.balanceButton["state"] = "disabled"
    self.depositButton["state"] = "disabled"
    self.withdrawButton["state"] = "disabled"
    self.loginButton["text"] = "Login"
    self.loginButton["command"] = self.login
```

The remaining three methods cannot be run unless a user has logged in and the account object is currently available. Each method operates on the **ATM** object's **account** variable. The **getBalance** method asks the account for its balance and displays it in the status field:

```python
def getBalance(self):
    """Displays the current balance in the
    status field."""
```

```
balance = self.account.getBalance()
self.statusField.setText("Balance: $" + str(balance))
```

Here you can clearly see the model/view design pattern in action: the user's button click triggers the **getBalance** method, which obtains data from the **SavingsAccount** object (the model), and updates the **TextField** object (the view) with those data.

The **withdraw** method exhibits a similar pattern, but it obtains input from the view and handles possible error conditions as well:

```
def withdraw(self):
    """Attempts a withdrawal. If not successful,
    displays error message in statusfield;
    otherwise, announces success."""
    amount = ammountField.getNumber()
    message = self.account.withdraw(amount)
    if message: # Check for an error message
        self.statusField.setText(message)
    else:
        self.statusField.setText("Withdrawal successful!")
```

Note that the logic of error checking (an amount greater than the funds available) and the logic of the withdrawal itself are the responsibilities of the **SavingsAccount** object (the model), not of the **ATM** object (the view).

10.3 Building a New Data Structure: The Two-Dimensional Grid

Like most programming languages, Python includes several basic types of data structures, such as strings, lists, tuples, and dictionaries. Each type of data structure has a specific way of organizing the data contained therein: strings, lists, and tuples are sequences of items ordered by position, whereas dictionaries are sets of key/value pairs in no particular order. Another useful data structure is a two-dimensional grid. A grid organizes items by position in rows and columns. You have worked with grids to organize

- pixels in images (Chapter 8)
- widgets in window layouts (Chapter 9)

In Chapter 4, we mentioned that a sophisticated data encryption algorithm uses an invertible matrix, which is also a type of grid. In this section, we develop a new class called **Grid** for applications that require grids.

The Interface of the **Grid** Class

The first step in building a new class is to describe the kind of object it models. You focus on the object's attributes and behavior. A grid is basically a container where you organize items by row and column. You can visualize a grid as a rectangular structure with rows and columns. The rows are numbered from 0 to the number of rows minus 1. The columns are numbered from 0 to the number of columns minus 1. Unlike a list, a grid has a height (number of rows) and a width (number of columns), rather than a length.

The constructor or operation to create a grid allows you to specify the width, the height, and an optional initial fill value for all of the positions. The default fill value is **None**. You access or replace an item at a given position by specifying the row and column of that position, using the notation

```
grid[<row>][<column>]
```

To assist in operations such as traversals, a grid provides operations to obtain its height and its width. A search operation returns the position, expressed as (*<row>*, *<column>*) of a given item, or the value **None** if the item is not present in the grid. Finally, an operation builds and returns a two-dimensional string representation of the grid. A sample session shows how these operations might be used:

```
>>> from grid import Grid
>>> grid = Grid(rows = 3, columns = 4, fillValue = 0)
>>> print(grid)
0 0 0 0
0 0 0 0
0 0 0 0
>>> grid[1][2] = 5
>>> print(grid)
0 0 0 0
0 0 5 0
0 0 0 0
>>> print(grid.find(5))
(1,2)
>>> print(grid.find(6))
None
>>> for row in range(grid.getHeight()):
        for column in range(grid.getWidth()):
            grid[row][column] = (row, column)
>>> print(grid)
(0,0)  (0,1)  (0,2)  (0,3)
(1,0)  (1,1)  (1,2)  (1,3)
(2,0)  (2,1)  (2,2)  (2,3)
```

Using these requirements, we can provide the interface for the **Grid** class shown in **Table 10-10**.

Table 10-10   The interface for the **Grid** class

Grid Method	What it Does
g = Grid(rows, columns, fillValue = None)	Returns a new **Grid** object
g.getHeight()	Returns the number of rows
g.getWidth()	Returns the number of columns
g.__str__()	Same as str(g); returns the string representation
g.__getitem__(row)[column]	Same as g.[row][column]
g.find(value)	Returns (row, column) if value is found, or None otherwise

The Implementation of the `Grid` Class: Instance Variables for the Data

The implementation of a class provides the code for the methods in its interface, as well as the instance variables needed to track the data contained in objects of that class. Because none of these resources can be inherited from a parent class, the `Grid` class will be a subclass of `object`.

The next step is to choose the data structures that will represent the two-dimensional structure within a `Grid` object. A list of lists seems like a wise choice, because most of the grid's operations can easily map to list operations. A single instance variable named `self.data` holds the top-level list of rows, and each item within this list will be a list of the columns in that row. The method `getHeight` returns the length of the top-level list, while the method `getWidth` returns the length of the list at position 0 within the top-level list. Note that because the grid is rectangular, all of the nested lists are of the same length. The expression `self.data[row][column]` drills into the list at position `row` within the top-level list and then accesses the item at position `column` in the nested list.

The other two methods to treat in this step are `__init__`, which initializes the instance variables, and `__str__`, which allows you to view the data during testing. Here is the code for a working prototype of the `Grid` class with the four methods discussed thus far:

```python
class Grid(object):
    """Represents a two-dimensional grid."""

    def __init__(self, rows, columns, fillValue = None):
        """Sets up the data."""
        self.data = []
        for row in range(rows):
            dataInRow = []
            for column in range(columns):
                dataInRow.append(fillValue)
            self.data.append(dataInRow)

    def getHeight(self):
        """Returns the number of rows."""
        return len(self.data)

    def getWidth(self):
        """Returns the number of columns."""
        return len(self.data[0])

    def __str__(self):
        """Returns a string representation of the grid."""
        result = ""
        for row in range(self.getHeight()):
            for col in range(self.getWidth()):
                result += str(self.data[row][col]) + " "
            result += "\n"
        return result
```

The Implementation of the `Grid` Class: Subscript and Search

The remaining methods implement the subscript and the search operations on a grid.

The subscript operator is used to access an item at a grid position or to replace it there. In the case of access, the subscript appears within an expression, as in `grid[1][2]`. In this case, when Python sees the `[]` following an object, it looks for a method named `__getitem__` in the object's class. This method expects an index as an argument and returns the item at that index in the underlying data structure. In the case of the `Grid` class, this method returns a nested list at the given index in the top-level list. This list represents a row of data in the grid. Python then uses the second subscript on this list to obtain the item at the given column in this row. Here is the code for this method:

```
def __getitem__(self, index):
    """Supports two-dimensional indexing with [][].
    Index represents a row number."""
    return self.data[index]
```

This method also handles the case when the subscript appears on the left side of an assignment statement, during a replacement of an item at a given position in a grid, as in

```
grid[1][2] = 5
```

The search operation named `find` must loop through the grid's list of lists until it finds the target item or runs out of items to examine. The code for the implementation uses the familiar grid traversal pattern that you learned in Chapters 8 and 9:

```
def find(self, value):
    """Returns (row, column) if value is found,
    or None otherwise."""
    for row in range(self.getHeight()):
        for column in range(self.getWidth()):
            if self[row][column] == value:
                return (row, column)
    return None
```

Note how this method uses the subscripts with `self` rather than `self.data`. Here we take advantage of the fact that the subscripts now work with grids as well as lists.

Exercise 10-3

1. Define a function `gridSum` that computes and returns the sum of the numbers in its grid argument.

2. Define a function `gridMax` that returns the largest value in its grid argument.

3. Define a function `diagonal` that builds and returns a list containing the values that appear in the positions that form a diagonal in its grid argument, running from the upper left position to the lower right position. You may assume that the height and the width of the grid are the same.

4. Define an `__eq__` method for the `Grid` class. This method returns `True` if the two grids have the same dimensions and the same values at the corresponding positions. Don't forget to test for identity and the same types first.

Case Study 10-3 | Data Encryption with a Block Cipher

In Chapter 4, we developed code to encrypt text with a Caesar cipher. We mentioned that a linear encryption method like this one is easy to crack, but that a method that uses a block cipher is harder to crack. In this case study, we use the `Grid` class to develop an encryption program that employs a block cipher.

Request

Write a program that uses a block cipher to encrypt text.

Analysis

A block cipher encryption method uses a two-dimensional grid of the characters, also called a **matrix**, to convert the plaintext to the ciphertext. The algorithm converts consecutive pairs of characters in the plaintext to pairs of characters in the ciphertext. For each pair of characters, it locates the positions of those characters in the matrix. If the two characters are in the same row or column, it simply swaps the positions of these characters and adds them to the ciphertext. Otherwise, it locates the two characters at the opposite corners of a rectangle in the matrix and adds these two characters to the ciphertext. **Figure 10-4** shows a snapshot of this process.

This interface allows the user to step through the encryption process. When the user clicks the `Encrypt` button, the program locates the next pair of plaintext characters in the matrix and marks them with gray boxes. It then marks the ciphertext characters at the opposite corners, if they exist, with pink boxes. The window on the left in Figure 10-4 shows two sets of marked characters, whereas the window on the right shows gray marks only. In the first case, the characters in pink are added to the ciphertext; in the second case, the characters in gray are reversed before this addition.

Figure 10-4   Encrypting text with a block cipher

Note that the characters are in random order in the matrix, and that the program allows the user to reset the grid to a new randomly ordered set of characters when the encryption is finished.

Although the GUI shown in Figure 10-4 is available in the example programs for this book, we develop a simpler terminal-based version here. The following session illustrates its features:

```
>>> main()
Enter the plaintext: Ken Lambert
Encrypting ...
    Plain text: Ken Lambert
Cipher text: .n1UM@8Gs/t
Decrypting ...
    Cipher text: .n1UM@8Gs/t
Plain text: Ken Lambert
>>> main("Weather: cloudy tomorrow")
Encrypting ...
    Plain text: Weather: cloudy tomorrow
Cipher text: q-taPgfQ@solWQgUTa];rr;T
Decrypting ...
    Cipher text: q-taPgfQ@solWQgUTa];rr;T
Plain text: Weather: cloudy tomorrow
```

Note that the **main** function defaults to a prompt for user input if an argument is not supplied. Otherwise, **main** uses its argument as the plaintext.

Design and Implementation

The first step in this design is to define a function that builds the matrix for the block cipher. This function, **makeMatrix**, fills a list with the characters from ASCII 32 through ASCII 127. These are the printable characters in this set (except for the newline and tab characters). The function then shuffles the list to randomize the characters. It next creates a new 8-by-12 **Grid** object and copies the characters from the list to the grid. Finally, the grid is returned. Here is the code for the **makeMatrix** function:

```python
from grid import Grid
import random

def makeMatrix():
    """Builds and returns an encryption matrix."""
    listOfChars = []
    for asciiValue in range(32, 128):
        listOfChars.append(chr(asciiValue))
    random.shuffle(listOfChars)
    matrix = Grid(8, 12)
    i = 0
    for row in range(matrix.getHeight()):
        for column in range(matrix.getWidth()):
            matrix[row][column] = listOfChars[i]
            i += 1
    return matrix
```

The next step is the design of the **encrypt** function. This function expects the plaintext and a matrix as arguments and returns the ciphertext. The function guides the process of moving through consecutive

(continues)

pairs of characters in the plaintext and adding the corresponding pairs of characters to the ciphertext under construction. Because the process of converting a pair of characters is rather complicated, we delegate it to a helper function named **encryptPair**. The **encrypt** function also handles the oddball case of a plaintext with an odd number of characters. In that case, the function simply adds the last plaintext character to the ciphertext. Here is the code for the **encrypt** function:

```
def encrypt(plainText, matrix):
    """Uses matrix to encrypt plainText,
    and returns cipherText."""
    cypherText = ""
    limit = len(plainText)
    # Adjust for an odd number of characters
    if limit % 2 == 1:
        limit -= 1
    # Use the matrix to encrypt pairs of characters
    i = 0
    while i < limit:
        cypherText += encryptPair(plainText, i, matrix)
        i += 2
    # Add the last character if length was odd
    if limit < len(plainText):
        cypherText += plainText[limit]
    return cypherText
```

The **encryptPair** function expects the plaintext, the current character position, and the matrix as arguments and returns a string containing a two-character ciphertext. The function first searches the matrix for the characters at the current and next positions in the plaintext. The function then uses the results, two pairs of grid coordinates, to generate the pair of characters in the ciphertext. In one case, where the two rows or the two columns in the coordinates are the same, the function just swaps the positions of the plaintext characters. In the other case, it retrieves the ciphertext characters from the opposite corners of the rectangle formed by the positions of the plaintext characters in the matrix. Here is the code for the **encryptPair** function:

```
def encryptPair(plainText, i, matrix):
    """Returns the cipherText of the pair of
    characters at i and i + 1 in plainText."""
    # Locate the characters in the matrix
    (row1, col1) = matrix.find(plainText[i])
    (row2, col2) = matrix.find(plainText[i + 1])
    # Swap them if they are in the same row or column
    if row1 == row2 or col1 == col2:
        return plainText[i + 1] + plainText[i]
    # Otherwise, use the characters at the opposite
    # corners of the rectangle in the matrix
    else:
        ch1 = matrix[row2][col1]
```

```
        ch2 = matrix[row1][col2]
    return ch1 + ch2
```

The good news is that the algorithm to decrypt a ciphertext with a block cipher is the same as the algorithm to encrypt a plaintext with the same block cipher. Therefore, the **decrypt** function simply calls **encrypt** with the ciphertext and matrix as arguments:

```
def decrypt(cipherText, matrix):
    """Uses matrix to decrypt cipherText,
    and returns plainText."""
    return encrypt(cipherText, matrix)
```

One limitation of our design is that it works only for one-line strings of text. A more general method would add all 128 ASCII values, including the newline and tab characters, to the matrix. Then you would be able to encrypt and decrypt entire text files.

10.4 Structuring Classes with Inheritance and Polymorphism

Object-based programming involves the use of objects, classes, and methods to solve problems. Object-oriented programming requires the programmer to master the following additional concepts:

1. **Data encapsulation.** Restricting the manipulation of an object's state by external users to a set of method calls.
2. **Inheritance.** Allowing a class to automatically reuse and extend the code of similar but more general classes.
3. **Polymorphism.** Allowing several different classes to use the same general method names.

Although Python is considered an object-oriented language, its syntax does not enforce data encapsulation. As you have seen, in the case of simple container objects, like playing cards, with little special behavior, it is handy to be able to access the objects' data without a method call.

Unlike data encapsulation, inheritance and polymorphism are built into Python's syntax. In this section we examine how they can be exploited to structure code.

Inheritance Hierarchies and Modeling

Objects in the natural world and objects in the world of artifacts can be classified using inheritance hierarchies. A simplified hierarchy of natural objects is depicted in **Figure 10-5**.

Figure 10-5 A simplified hierarchy of objects in the natural world

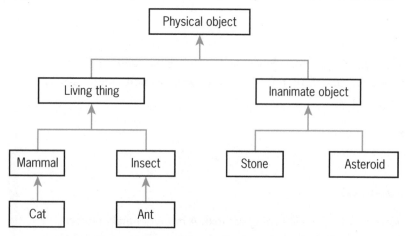

At the top of a hierarchy is the most general class of objects. This class defines features that are common to every object in the hierarchy. For example, every physical object has a mass. Classes just below this one have these features as well as additional ones. Thus, a living thing has a mass and can also grow and die. The path from a given class back up to the topmost one goes through all of that given class's ancestors. Each class below the topmost one inherits attributes and behaviors from its ancestors and extends these with additional attributes and behavior.

An object-oriented software system models this pattern of inheritance and extension in real-world systems by defining classes that extend other classes. In Python, all classes automatically extend the built-in **object** class, which is the most general class possible. However, as you learned in Chapter 9, it is possible to extend any existing class using the syntax:

```
class <new class name>(<existing parent class name>):
```

Thus, for example, **PhysicalObject** would extend **object**, **LivingThing** would extend **PhysicalObject**, and so on.

The real advantage of inheritance in a software system is that each new subclass acquires all of the instance variables and methods of its ancestor classes for free. Like function definitions and class definitions, inheritance hierarchies provide an abstraction mechanism that allows the programmer to avoid reinventing the wheel or writing redundant code, as you clearly saw in Chapter 8. To review how inheritance works in Python, we explore two more examples.

Example 1: A Restricted Savings Account

So far, our examples have focused on ordinary savings accounts. Banks also provide customers with restricted savings accounts. These are like ordinary savings accounts in most ways, but with some special features, such as allowing only a certain number of deposits or withdrawals a month. Let's assume that a savings account has a name, a PIN, and a balance. You can make deposits and withdrawals and access the account's attributes. Let's also assume that this restricted savings account permits only three withdrawals per month. The next session shows an interaction with a **RestrictedSavingsAccount** that permits up to three withdrawals:

```
>>> account = RestrictedSavingsAccount("Ken", "1001", 500.00)
>>> print(account)
Name:      Ken
PIN:       1001
Balance:   500.0
>>> account.getBalance()
500.0
>>> for count in range(3):
```

```
        account.withdraw(100)
>>> account.withdraw(50)
'No more withdrawals this month'
>>> account.resetCounter()
>>> account.withdraw(50)
```

The fourth withdrawal has no effect on the account, and it returns an error message. A new method named `resetCounter` is called to enable withdrawals for the next month.

If `RestrictedSavingsAccount` is defined as a subclass of `SavingsAccount`, every method but `withdraw` can simply be inherited and used without changes. The `withdraw` method is redefined in `RestrictedSavingsAccount` to return an error message if the number of withdrawals has exceeded the maximum. The maximum will be maintained in a new class variable, and the monthly count of withdrawals will be tracked in a new instance variable. Finally, a new method, `resetCounter`, is included to reset the number of withdrawals to 0 at the end of each month. Here is the code for the `RestrictedSavingsAccount` class, followed by a brief explanation:

```
"""
File: restrictedsavingsaccount.py
This module defines the RestrictedSavingsAccount class.
"""

from savingsaccount import SavingsAccount

class RestrictedSavingsAccount(SavingsAccount):
    """This class represents a restricted
    savings account."""

    MAX_WITHDRAWALS = 3

    def __init__(self, name, pin, balance = 0.0):
        """Same attributes as SavingsAccount, but with
        a counter for withdrawals."""
        SavingsAccount.__init__(self, name, pin, balance)
        self.counter = 0

    def withdraw(self, amount):
        """Restricts number of withdrawals to MAX_WITHDRAWALS."""
        if self.counter == RestrictedSavingsAccount.MAX_WITHDRAWALS:
            return "No more withdrawals this month"
        else:
            message = SavingsAccount.withdraw(self, amount)
        if message == None:
            self.counter += 1
        return message

    def resetCounter(self):
        """Resets the withdrawal count."""
        self.counter = 0
```

The `RestrictedSavingsAccount` class includes a new class variable not found in `SavingsAccount`. This variable, called `MAX_WITHDRAWALS`, is used to restrict the number of withdrawals that are permitted per month.

The `RestrictedSavingsAccount` constructor first calls the constructor in the `SavingsAccount` class to initialize the instance variables for the name, PIN, and balance defined there. The syntax uses the class name before the dot, and explicitly includes `self` as the first argument. The general form of the syntax for calling a method in the parent class from within a method with the same name in a subclass follows:

```
<parent class name>.<method name>(self, <other arguments>)
```

Continuing in `RestrictedSavingsAccount`'s constructor, the new instance variable `counter` is then set to 0. The rule of thumb to remember when writing the constructor for a subclass is that each class is responsible for initializing its own instance variables. Thus, the constructor of the parent class should always be called to do this.

The `withdraw` method is redefined in `RestrictedSavingsAccount` to override the definition of the same method in `SavingsAccount`. You allow a withdrawal only when the counter's value is less than the maximum, and you increment the counter only after a withdrawal is successful. Note that this version of the method calls the same method in the parent or **superclass** to perform the actual withdrawal. The syntax for this is the same as is used in the constructor.

Finally, the new method `resetCounter` is included to allow the user to continue withdrawals in the next month.

Example 2: The Dealer and a Player in the Game of Blackjack

The card game of blackjack is played with at least two players, one of whom is also a dealer. The object of the game is to receive cards from the deck and play to a count of 21 without going over 21. A card's point equals its rank, but all face cards are 10 points, and an ace can count as either 1 or 11 points as needed. At the beginning of the game, the dealer and the player each receive two cards from the deck. The player can see both of their cards and just one of the dealer's cards initially. The player then "hits" or takes one card at a time until their total exceeds 21 (a "bust" or loss), or they "pass" (stop taking cards). When the player passes, the dealer reveals their other card and must keep taking cards until their total is greater than or equal to 17. If the dealer's final total is greater than 21, they also lose. Otherwise, the player with the higher point total wins, or else there is a tie.

A computer program that plays this game can use a `Dealer` object and a `Player` object. The dealer's moves are completely automatic, whereas the player's moves (decisions to pass or hit) are partly controlled by a human user. A third object belonging to the `Blackjack` class sets up the game and manages the interactions with the user. The `Deck` and `Card` classes developed earlier are also included. A class diagram of the system is shown in **Figure 10-6**.

Figure 10-6   The classes in the blackjack game application

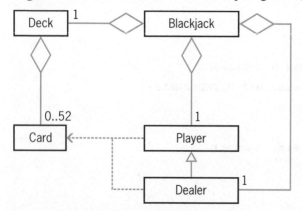

Here is a sample run of the program:

```
>>> from blackjack import Blackjack
>>> game = Blackjack()
```

```
>>> game.play()
Player:
2 of Spades, 5 of Spades
7 points Dealer:
5 of Hearts
Do you want a hit? [y/n]: y
Player:
2 of Spades, 5 of Spades, King of Hearts
17 points
Do you want a hit? [y/n]: n
Dealer:
5 of Hearts, Queen of Hearts, 7 of Diamonds
22 points
Dealer busts and you win
```

When a **Player** object is created, it receives two cards. A **Player** object can be hit with another card, can be asked for the points in its hand, and can be asked for its string representation. Here is the code for the **Player** class, followed by a brief explanation:

```python
from cards import Deck, Card

class Player(object):
    """This class represents a player in
    a blackjack game."""

    def __init__(self, cards):
        self.cards = cards

    def __str__(self):
        """Returns string rep of cards and points."""
        result = ", ".join(map(str, self.cards))
        result += "\n " + str(self.getPoints()) + " points"
        return result

    def hit(self, card):
        self.cards.append(card)

    def getPoints(self) :
        """Returns the number of points in the hand."""
        count = 0
        for card in self.cards:
            if card.rank > 9:
                count += 10
            elif card.rank == 1:
                count += 11
            else:
```

```
            count += card.rank
        # Deduct 10 if Ace is available and needed as 1
        for card in self.cards:
            if count <= 21:
                break
            elif card.rank == 1:
                count -= 10
        return count

    def hasBlackjack(self):
        """Dealt 21 or not."""
        return len(self.cards) == 2 and self.getPoints() == 21
```

The problem of computing the points in a player's hand is complicated by the fact that an ace can count as either 1 or 11. The getPoints method solves this problem by first totaling the points using an Ace as 11. If this initial count is greater than 21, then there is a need to count an ace, if there is one, as a 1. The second loop accomplishes this by counting such aces as long as they are available and needed. The other methods require no comment.

A **Dealer** object also maintains a hand of cards and recognizes the same methods as a **Player** object. However, the dealer's behavior is a bit more specialized. For example, the dealer at first shows just one card, and the dealer repeatedly hits until 17 points are reached or exceeded. Thus, as Figure 10-6 shows, **Dealer** is best defined as a subclass of **Player**. Here is the code for the **Dealer** class, followed by a brief explanation:

```
class Dealer(Player) :
    """Like a Player, but with some restrictions."""

    def __init__(self, cards):
        """Initial state: show one card only."""
        Player.__init__(self, cards)
        self.showOneCard = True

    def __str__(self) :
        """Return just one card if not hit yet."""
        if self.showOneCard:
            return str(self.cards[0])
        else:
            return Player.__str__(self)

    def hit(self, deck):
        """Add cards while points < 17,
        then allow all to be shown."""
        self.showOneCard = False
        while self.getPoints() < 17:
            self.cards.append(deck.deal())
```

Dealer maintains an extra instance variable, **showOneCard**, which restricts the number of cards in the string representation to one card at start-up. As soon as the dealer hits, this variable is set to **False**, so all of the cards will be included in the string from then on. The `hit` method actually receives a deck rather than a single card as an argument, so cards may repeatedly be dealt and added to the dealer's list at the close of the game.

The `Blackjack` class coordinates the interactions among the `Deck` object, the `Player` object, the `Dealer` object, and the human user. Here is the code:

```python
class Blackjack(object):

    def __init__(self):
        self.deck = Deck()
        self.deck.shuffle()
        # Pass the player and the dealer two cards each
        self.player = Player([self.deck.deal(),
                              self.deck.deal()])
        self.dealer = Dealer([self.deck.deal(),
                              self.deck.deal()])

    def play(self):
        print("Player:\n", self.player)
        print("Dealer:\n", self.dealer)
        # Player hits until user says NO
        while True:
            choice = input("Do you want a hit? [y/n]: ")
            if choice in ("Y", "y"):
                self.player.hit(self.deck.deal())
                points = self.player.getPoints()
                print("Player:\n", self.player)
                if points >= 21:
                    break
            else:
                break
        playerPoints = self.player.getPoints()
        if playerPoints > 21:
            print("You bust and lose")
        else:
            # Dealer's turn to hit
            self.dealer.hit(self.deck)
            print("Dealer:\n", self.dealer)
            dealerPoints = self.dealer.getPoints()
            # Determine the outcome
            if dealerPoints > 21:
                print("Dealer busts and you win")
            elif dealerPoints > playerPoints:
                print("Dealer wins")
            elif dealerPoints < playerPoints and \
                 playerPoints <= 21:
```

```
        print("You win")
    elif dealerPoints == playerPoints:
        if self. player.hasBlackjack() and \
           not self.dealer.hasBlackjack():
            print("You win")
        elif not self.player.hasBlackjack() and \
             self.dealer.hasBlackjack():
            print("Dealer wins")
        else:
            print("There is a tie")
```

Polymorphic Methods

As we have seen in our two examples, a subclass inherits data and methods from its parent class. We would not bother subclassing unless the two classes shared a substantial amount of **abstract behavior**. By this term, we mean that the classes have similar sets of methods or operations. A subclass usually adds something extra, such as a new method or a data attribute, to the ensemble provided by its superclass. A new data attribute is included in both of our examples, and a new method is included in the first one.

In some cases, the two classes have the same interface, or set of methods available to external users. In these cases, one or more methods in a subclass override the definitions of the same methods in the superclass to provide specialized versions of the abstract behavior. Like any object-oriented language, Python supports this capability with **polymorphic methods**. The term *polymorphic* means "many bodies," and it applies to two methods that have the same header but have different definitions in different classes. Two examples are the **withdraw** method in the bank account hierarchy and the **hit** method in the blackjack player hierarchy. The **__str__** method is a good example of a polymorphic method that appears throughout Python's system of classes.

Like other abstraction mechanisms, polymorphic methods make code easier to understand and use, because the programmer does not have to remember so many different names.

The Costs and Benefits of Object-Oriented Programming

Whenever you learn a new style of programming, you sooner or later become acquainted with its costs and benefits. To hasten this process, we conclude this section by comparing several programming styles, all of which have been used in this book.

The approach with which this book began is called **imperative programming**. Code in this style consists of input and output statements, assignment statements, and control statements for selection and iteration. The name derives from the idea that a program consists of a set of commands to the computer, which responds by performing such actions as manipulating data values in memory. This style is appropriate for writing short code sequences that accomplish simple tasks, such as solving the problems that were introduced in Chapters 1 through 5 of this book.

However, as problems become more complex, the imperative programming style does not scale well. In particular, the number of interactions among statements that manipulate the same data variables quickly grows beyond the point of comprehension of a human programmer who is trying to verify or maintain the code.

As we saw in Chapters 6 and 7, you can mitigate some of this complexity by embedding sequences of imperative code in function definitions or subprograms. It then becomes possible to decompose complex problems into simpler subproblems that can be solved by these subprograms. In other words, the use of subprograms reduces the number of program components that one must keep track of. Moreover, when each subprogram has its own temporary variables and receives data from the surrounding program by means of explicit parameters, the number of possible dependencies and interactions among program components also decreases. The use of cooperating subprograms to solve problems is called **procedural programming**.

Although procedural programming takes a step in the direction of controlling program complexity, it simply masks and ultimately recapitulates the problems of imperative programming at a higher level of abstraction. When many subprograms share and modify a common data pool, as they did in some of our early examples, it becomes difficult once again for the programmer to keep track of all of the interactions among the subprograms during verification and maintenance.

One cause of this problem is the use of the assignment statement to modify data. Some computer scientists have developed a style of programming that dispenses with assignment altogether. This radically different approach, called **functional programming**, views a program as a set of cooperating functions. A function in this sense is a highly restricted subprogram. Its sole purpose is to transform the data in its arguments into other data, its returned value. Because assignment does not exist in this approach, functions perform computations by either evaluating expressions or calling other functions. Selection is handled by a conditional expression, which is like an `if-else` statement that returns a value, and iteration is implemented by recursion. By restricting how functions can use data, this simple model of computation dramatically reduces the conceptual complexity of programs. However, some argue that this style of programming does not conveniently model situations where data objects must change their state.

Object-oriented programming attempts to control the complexity of a program while still modeling data that change their state. This style divides up the data into relatively small units called objects. Each object is then responsible for managing its own data. If an object needs help with its own tasks, it can call upon another object or use methods defined in its superclass. The main goal is to divide responsibilities among small, relatively independent or loosely coupled components. Cooperating objects, when they are well designed, decrease the likelihood that a system will break when changes are made within a component.

Although object-oriented programming has become quite popular, it can be overused and abused. Many small and medium-sized problems can still be solved effectively, simply, and—most important—quickly using any of the other three styles of programming mentioned here, either individually or in combination. The solutions of problems, such as numerical computations, often seem contrived when they are cast in terms of objects and classes. For other problems, the use of objects is easy to grasp, but their implementation in the form of classes reflects a complex model of computation with daunting syntax and semantics. Finally, hidden and unpleasant interactions can lurk in poorly designed inheritance hierarchies that resemble those afflicting the most brittle procedural programs.

To conclude, whatever programming style or combination of styles you choose to solve a problem, good design and common sense are essential.

Exercises 10-4

1. What are the benefits of having class **B** extend or inherit from class **A**?

2. Describe what the `__init__` method should do in a class that extends another class.

3. Class **B** extends class **A**. Class **B** defines an `__str__` method that returns the string representation of its instance variables. Class **B** defines a single instance variable named **age**, which is an integer. Write the code to define the `__str__` method for class **B**. This method should return the combined string information from both classes. Label the data for **age** with the string `"Age: "`.

Fail-Safe Programming

When working with functions and methods in programs, you have seen that some of them place restrictions on the arguments that you provide to them. For example, the function **math.sqrt** expects a number greater than or equal to 0 as an argument. When you violate this requirement with an argument that is not a number or is less than 0, Python raises an exception, as shown in the next session:

```
>>> import math
>>> help(math.sqrt)
Help on built-in function sqrt in module math:

sqrt(x, /)
    Return the square root of x.

>>> math.sqrt(-1)
Traceback (most recent call last):
  File "<pyshell#2>", line 1, in <module>
    math.sqrt(-1)
ValueError: math domain error
```

As you can see, Python does not let this error go undetected but halts the program with a useful error message. Now that you are developing new classes with many methods, you can provide the same type of error handling when your client programmers violate restrictions on arguments, if there are any. Consider the following session with an instance of the **Student** class developed earlier in this chapter:

```
>>> from student import Student
>>> s = Student("Ken", 5)
>>> print(s)
Name: Ken
Scores: 0 0 0 0 0
>>> s.setScore(6, -35)
Traceback (most recent call last):
  File "<pyshell#4>", line 1, in <module>
    s.setScore(6, -35)
  File "/Users/ken/pythonfiles/student.py", line 22, in setScore
    self.scores[i - 1] = score
IndexError: list assignment index out of range.
```

The programmer has provided a position, 6, that does not exist in this student's set of scores. Python raises an exception when the code for **setScore** attempts to access position 6 in a list whose length is 5, but the error message is not as informative as it could be. Also, the score, –35, is not a typical score, but this error goes undetected.

The first step to make the error handling more useful is to specify, in the method's docstring, the **preconditions** on the method's arguments. Preconditions specify what must be true so that the method (or function) can provide a guaranteed outcome.

The second step is to verify that each argument obeys its precondition and to raise an exception if one of them does not. Python includes a **raise** statement for this purpose, whose form for this usage is

```
raise RuntimeError(<message>)
```

Here is a new version of the method **setScore** that does this for its two arguments:

```
def setScore(self, i, score):
    """Resets the ith score, counting from 1.
    Preconditions: 1 <= i <= number of scores.
                   0 <= score <= 100
    """
    # Check preconditions and respond if necessary
    if i < 0 or i > len(self.scores):
        raise RuntimeError("i must be >= 0 and <= " + \
                           str(len(self.scores)))
    if score < 0 or score > 100:
        raise RuntimeError("score must be >= 0 and <= 100")
    # Now safe to reset the ith score
    self.scores[i - 1] = score
```

Now the programmer can receive a more informative error message when an error does occur:

```
>>> from student import Student
>>> s = Student("Ken", 5)
>>> s.setScore(6, 100)
Traceback (most recent call last):
  File "<pyshell#2>", line 1, in <module>
    s.setScore(6, 100)
  File "/Users/ken/pythonfiles/student.py", line 26, in setScore
    raise RuntimeError("i must be >= 0 and <= " + \
RuntimeError: i must be >= 0 and <= 5
```

Summary

- A simple class definition consists of a header and a set of method definitions. Several related classes can be defined in the same module. Each element, a module, a class, and a method, can have a separate docstring associated with it.

- In addition to methods, a class can also include instance variables. These represent the data attributes of the class. Each instance or object of a class has its own chunk of memory storage for the values of its instance variables.

- The constructor or `__init__` method is called when a class is instantiated. This method initializes the instance variables. The method can expect required and/or optional arguments to allow the users of the class to provide initial values for the instance variables.

- A method contains a header and a body. The first parameter of a method is always the reserved word `self`. This parameter is bound to the object with which the method is called, so that the code within the method can reference that particular object.

- An instance variable is introduced and referenced like any other variable, but it is always prefixed with `self`. The scope of an instance variable is the body of the enclosing class definition, whereas its lifetime is the lifetime of the object associated with it.

- Some standard operators can be overloaded for use with new classes of objects. One overloads an operator by defining a method that has the corresponding name.

- When a program can no longer reference an object, it is considered dead, and the garbage collector recycles its storage.

- A class variable is a name for a value that all instances of a class share in common. It is created and initialized when a class is defined and must be accessed by using the class name, a dot, and the variable name.

- Pickling is the process of converting an object to a form that can be saved to permanent file storage. Unpickling is the inverse process.

- The `try-except` statement is used to catch and handle exceptions that might be raised in a set of statements.

- The three most important features of object-oriented programming are encapsulation, inheritance, and polymorphism. All three features simplify programs and make them more maintainable.

- Encapsulation restricts access to an object's data to users of the methods of its class. This helps to prevent indiscriminate changes to an object's data.

- Inheritance allows one class to pick up the attributes and behavior of another class for free. The subclass may also extend its parent class by adding data and/or methods or modifying the same methods. Inheritance is a major means of reusing code.

- Polymorphism allows methods in several different classes to have the same headers. This reduces the need to learn new names for standard operations.

- A data model is a set of classes that are responsible for managing the data of a program. A view is a set of classes that are responsible for presenting information to a human user and handling user inputs. The model/view pattern structures software systems using these two sets of components.

Key Terms

abstract behavior	Data encapsulation	matrix
accessors	functional programming	model
class diagram	garbage collection	model/view pattern
class hierarchy	imperative programming	mutators
class variable	Inheritance	object-oriented languages
closed under combination	inheritance hierarchies	object-oriented programming
constructor	instance variables	operator overloading

overload	preconditions	superclass
parent class	procedural programming	two-dimensional grid
pickling	rational number	Unified Modeling Language
polymorphic methods	state	view
Polymorphism	subclass	

Review Questions

1. An instance variable refers to a data value that

    a. is owned by a particular instance of a class and no other

    b. is shared in common and can be accessed by all instances of a given class

    c. is visible just within the method where it is introduced

    d. cannot be modified outside the scope of the class where it is defined

2. The name used to refer to the current instance of a class within the class definition is

    a. `this`

    b. `other`

    c. `self`

    d. `super`

3. The purpose of the `__init__` method in a class definition is to

    a. build and return a string representation of the instance variables

    b. set the instance variables to initial values

    c. return storage for variables to the PVM

    d. display an object's print representation in IDLE

4. A method definition

    a. can have zero or more parameter names

    b. always must have at least one parameter name, called `self`

    c. must have at least two parameter names

    d. must include a `return` statement

5. The scope of an instance variable is

    a. the statements in the body of the method where it is introduced

    b. the entire class in which it is introduced, as well as any module in which an object that owns the variable is referenced

    c. the entire module where it is introduced

    d. undefined

6. An object's lifetime ends

    a. several hours after it is created

    b. when it can no longer be referenced anywhere in a program

    c. when its data storage is recycled by the garbage collector

    d. not ever

7. A class variable is used for data that

    a. all instances of a class have in common

    b. each instance owns separately

    c. belong to a module

    d. are strings only

8. Class **B** is a subclass of class **A**. The __init__ methods in both classes expect no arguments. The call of class **A**'s __init__ method in class **B** is

    a. `A.__init__()`

    b. `A.__init__(self)`

    c. `__init__()`

    d. `__init__(self)`

9. The easiest way to save objects to permanent storage is to

    a. convert them to strings and save this text to a text file

    b. pickle them using the `pickle` function `dump`

    c. use Python's `write` method

    d. use a text file

10. A polymorphic method

    a. has a single header but different bodies in different classes

    b. creates harmony in a software system

    c. has the same name as other methods but has a different number of parameters

    d. makes object-oriented software systems more complex than they need to be

Programming Exercises

1. Add three methods to the **Student** class (in the file **student.py**) that compare two **Student** objects. One method should test for equality. A second method should test for less than. The third method should test for greater than or equal to. In each case, the method returns the result of the comparison of the two students' names. Include a **main** function that tests all of the comparison operators. (LO: 10.2)

2. This exercise assumes that you have completed Programming Exercise 1. Place several **Student** objects containing different names into a list and shuffle it. Then run the **sort** method with this list and display all of the students' information. (LO: 10.1, 10.2)

3. The **str** method of the **Bank** class (in the file **bank.py**) returns a string containing the accounts in random order. Design and implement a change that causes the accounts to be placed in the string by order of name. (*Hint*: You will also have to define some methods in the **SavingsAccount** class, in the file **savingsaccount.py**.) (LO: 10.1, 10.2)

4. The ATM program (in the file **atm.py**) allows a user an indefinite number of attempts to log in. Fix the program so that it displays a popup message that the police will be called after a user has had three successive failures. The program should also disable the login button when this happens. (LO: 10.1)

5. The Doctor program described in Chapter 5 combines the data model of a doctor and the operations for handling user interaction. Restructure this program according to the model/view pattern so that these areas of responsibility are assigned to separate sets of classes. The program (in the file **doctor.py**) should include a **Doctor** class with an interface that allows one to obtain a greeting, a signoff message, and a reply to a patient's string. The rest of the program, in a separate main program module, handles the user's interactions with the **Doctor** object. You may develop either a terminal-based user interface (also in **doctor.py**) or a GUI (in **doctorgui.py**). (LO: 10.1, 10.2)

6. The **play** method in the **Player** class of the craps game plays an entire game without interaction with the user. Revise the **Player** class (in the file **craps.py**) so that its user can make individual rolls of the dice and view the results after each roll. The **Player** class no longer accumulates a list of rolls but saves the string representation of each roll after it is made. Add new methods **rollDice**, **getRollsCount**, **isWinner**, and **isLoser** to the

Player class. The last three methods allow the user to obtain the number of rolls and to determine whether there is a winner or a loser. The last two methods are associated with new Boolean instance variables. Two other instance variables track the number of rolls and the string representation of the most recent roll. Another instance variable tracks whether or not the first roll has occurred. At instantiation, the **roll**, **rollsCount**, **atStartup**, **winner**, and **loser** variables are set to their appropriate initial values. All game logic is now in the **rollDice** method. This method rolls the dice once, updates the state of the **Player** object, and returns a tuple of the values of the dice for that roll. Include in the module the **playOneGame** and **playManyGames** functions, suitably updated for the new interface to the **Player** class. (LO: 10.1, 10.2)

7. Convert the **DiceDemo** program discussed in this chapter to a completed craps game application, using the **Player** data model class you developed in Programming Exercise 6. A screen shot of a possible window is shown in **Figure 10-7**. (LO: 10.1, 10.2)

Figure 10-7   A GUI-based craps game

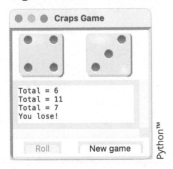

8. In many card games, cards are either face up or face down. Add a new instance variable named **faceup** to the **Card** class (in the file **cards.py**) to track this attribute of a card. Its default value is **False**. Then add a **turn** method to turn the card over. This method resets the **faceup** variable to its logical negation. (LO: 10.1, 10.2)

9. Computer card games are more fun if you can see the images of the cards in a window, as shown in the screen shot in **Figure 10-8**.

Figure 10-8   Viewing images of playing cards

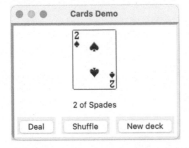

Assume that the 52 images for a deck of cards are in a DECK folder, with the file naming scheme **<rank number><suit letter>.gif**. Thus, for example, the image for the Ace of Hearts is in a file named **1h.gif**, and the image for the King of Spades is in a file named **13s.gif**. Furthermore, there is an image file named **b.gif** for the backside image of all the cards. This will be the card's image if its **faceup** variable is **False**. Using the **DiceDemo** program as a role model, write a GUI program (in the files **cardsgui.py** and **cards.py**) that allows you to deal and view cards from a deck. Be sure to define a helper method that takes a **Card** object as an argument and returns its associated image, and remember to turn the cards as you deal them. (LO: 10.1, 10.2)

10. Geometric shapes can be modeled as classes. Develop classes for line segments, circles, and rectangles. Each shape object should contain a **Turtle** object and a color that allow the shape to be drawn in a Turtle graphics

window (see Chapter 8 for details). Factor the code for these features (instance variables and methods) into an abstract **Shape** class (in the file **shapes.py**). The **Circle**, **Rectangle**, and **Line** classes are all subclasses of **Shape**. These subclasses include other information about the specific types of shapes, such as a radius or a corner point and a **draw** method. Write a script (in the file **testshapes.py**) that uses several instances of the different shape classes to draw a house and a stick figure. (LO: 10.1, 10.2, 10.4)

Debugging Exercise

Jack is testing the **Student** class developed earlier in this chapter. He creates an instance of this class with 0 scores and receives an error message when he attempts to view the average score:

```
>>> s = Student("Jack", 0)
>>> print(s)
Name: Jack
Scores:
>>> s.getAverageScoreScore()
Traceback (most recent call last):
  File "<pyshell#8>", line 1, in <module>
    s.getAverageScore()
  File "/Users/ken/pythonfiles/student.py", line 42, in getAverageScoreScore
    return sum(self.scores) / len(self.scores)
ZeroDivisionError: division by zero
```

Explain the error detected during this test and describe a way to prevent it from happening.

Economy Game

Prompt

In STEM we often need to process lots of data to try out how a model may work. We are going to create a very simple retirement model to play with.

We have provided overall market data from 1926 to 2022. Measuring a market or economy is a very difficult task beyond the scope of this textbook; we will be creating a very simple model using simplified data.

You will create an Economy class (we have started it for you in the skeleton). You will start with a dictionary containing a year and the percent change the market moved in that year. For example, in 2008 our market changed −37%. You will have 2 accounts to track, 1 being a savings account that does not earn any interest, and the other being your market account that changes at the end of each year per the market data provided. Every year you will add a preset amount to your savings account, and you will come up with several simple algorithms to decide grammatically if you should invest that year or not. Investing sets your savings account to zero. For the sake of this exercise, you can know how the market moved that year before you choose to buy or not.

You should come up with at least three strategies to buy or not. Some suggestions include 1) buy every year, 2) buy years that are down, and 3) buy years that are up.

If you do not buy, your savings account will grow and you will have more to buy into the market next time. Modify the economy class to allow a subset of years. (For example, our data set contains 96 years of data. Allow your model to only take into account a variable amount of years, based on some parameter.)

After completing this exercise, which strategy worked best? Did changing the years change the winning strategy?

Starting Skeleton

Use economy_game_skel.py to start. Fill in the TODOs.

Examples

With the data set, from 1988 to 2022, we found the best investment method would have been CONDITION_BUY_EVERY_YEAR. With an annual savings rate of 2000, we would have ended with $483,632.04.

Answer

Refer to Chapter 10_Economy Game.py for one possible solution

After Discussion

Our main function checks to make sure starting data is available and then runs 5 instances of our Economy class, with dates 1988 to 2022, each one with a different strategy.

The networth() method simply adds up our savings account wealth without market wealth. We abstract this simple math in 1 function so if we ever expand our code (to say support the bond, real estate, cryptocurrency, or precious metals markets) we only need to change 1 function, as opposed to every place net worth is calculated. Our print_finish_info() contains the format specifier for displaying a float as 2 digits. Our run() simply iterates through the preset range of years, ticking by year by year. The last helper function, csv_to_dict(), uses the csv module and loads a comma separated value dataset into a Python dictionary that our program can use.

Our Economy's __init__() requires that the creator specify the algorithm for purchasing or not. We have default start and end years (our entire data set). Notice how the default value of −1 causes our __init__() to determine the range of the data at run time, and these values are not hard coded into our program. This allows us to change our data without having to modify our code.

Our Economy's new_year() simply runs through the given year: adds what is saved per year into the savings account, changes current market holdings (lose or make money), and then invests or not based on the algorithm supplied at creation.

Our Economy's should_buy() is a series of if statements. The algorithms themselves are simple here, a few lines at most. There is no reason they could not be incredibly complex, calling out to external statistical libraries or pulling in other data sources!

## Chapter 11

Data Analysis and Visualization

Learning Objectives

After you complete this chapter, you will be able to:

11.1 Use functions to analyze a set of data and determine relationships among them.

11.2 Visualize a set of data and choose an appropriate type of graph, plot, or chart for doing so.

11.3 Load data sets with multiple columns and rows from files, clean these data sets, perform analyses on them, and visualize them.

In the overview of data processing, you have encountered applications that work with various types of data, including numbers, text, images, and structures that organize the data in useful ways. Some of these applications, such as the Flesch Score program discussed in Chapter 4, the concordance program introduced in Chapter 5, and the sentence recognizer program developed in Chapter 10, perform what might be called **data analysis**. A data analysis application attempts to discover patterns in data to provide support for decisions that must be made in many different personal and institutional settings, such as commerce, government, science, education, and leisure activity. Examples include the following:

- A movie or music subscription service analyzing customers' browsing and rental choices to provide recommendations for further viewing or listening

- A bank analyzing account activity for signs of fraud

- A government agency analyzing reports of virus infections to determine where to focus treatment resources

- A university analyzing high school student grade reports to determine eligibility for admission.

The results of these analyses may be passed on to human beings to take action directly or on to other computer programs for further processing. An important component of data analysis is the **visualization** of data and the patterns contained therein. This can take the form of plots, graphs, charts, and animations that reveal or focus on relevant relationships among the data.

Several terms refer to fields of study and processes related to data analysis that you should be aware of:

- **Data set**—This term refers to the data gathered from sources of interest, such as student test scores, medical records, customer purchases, websites visited, user mouse movements, and even user eye movements. A data set is usually "raw" and requires structuring, filtering, and "cleaning" to become useful for analysis.

- **Big data**—This term refers to the scale of data sets that are used in many applications. These data sets can be enormous. The size of a data set gathered by a large corporation, such as Alphabet (the parent company of Google) or Meta (the parent company of Facebook), might be measured not in gigabytes (a billion bytes) or terabytes (a thousand gigabytes) but in petabytes (1 million gigabytes) or exabytes (1 million terabytes).

- **Data warehouse**—This term refers to an organization's store of data, as represented in digitized form. Organizations own or rent physical space for data warehouses in giant server farms, such as Amazon Web Services.

- **Database**—This term refers to the organization of data in a highly structured form that can support search by query or further analysis.

- **Data mining**—This term refers to the process of extracting useful patterns from a raw data set for further analysis. Data mining uses some preliminary analysis to turn raw data into something like a structured database.

- **Machine learning**—This term refers to the capacity of an algorithm to improve its analysis by training on data sets of increasing size. For instance, the Genius Playlist feature on Apple Music can automatically create a playlist of music tracks that are similar to those you listen to, rank highly, or have recommended to you based on other factors.

- **Analytics**—This term is used synonymously with data analysis.

- **Data science**—A field of study that incorporates computer science and statistics to develop algorithms and data structures for data analysis.

The concepts and techniques used in machine learning and in analyzing very large data sets form the subject of courses in data science and statistics. This chapter introduces some basic algorithms and data structures for performing analyses on data sets and visualizing the results. It examines some simple functions for analysis, the preparation of raw data sets for analysis, and some tools for visualizing relationships discovered by analysis.

11.1 Some Basic Functions for Analyzing a Data Set

As mentioned earlier, the data sets analyzed in real-world settings are huge, consisting of billons of values, and the analyses performed are often quite complex. To give you a sense of the kinds of analyses that can be performed, the discussion in this section is confined to a few simple functions that operate on a small set of values.

Consider the set of test scores belonging to the **Student** class developed in Chapter 10. This class already includes methods for viewing the student's average score (also called the **mean**) and highest score. If you add a method to view the minimum score, you can perform such tasks as computing the student's final grade as the average of the student's scores after dropping the lowest grade.

Other operations might also be useful in assessing a student's test performance. For example, a data set that has a few very large values or a few very small values might tend to skew the data set's mean value in one direction or another. In that case, one might examine the **median** value, which is the value at the middle position of the data set after it has been sorted. The median income of a population, which might have a few very wealthy individuals and the vast majority with low incomes, is for this reason usually reported rather than the average income.

Another useful property of a data set is its **mode**, which is the value that occurs most often within it. Variations on this feature of the distribution of values are the **bimodal distribution** (where two distinct values appear most frequently) and the **multimodal distribution** (where there are more than two front-running values).

A data set whose average value is not skewed by a preponderance of large or small values exhibits a **normal distribution** of values. The **standard deviation** of the values in a data set is a measure of its "normality": values in a data set with a low standard deviation tend to cluster around the average value, whereas some values in a data set with a high standard deviation lie much further from the average value. Before examining how these functions are computed, they are summarized in **Table 11-1**. Assume that the argument to the function in each case is a nonempty list.

Table 11-1   Some commonly used functions in data analysis

Function	What it Does	Example Usage	
`max`	Returns the largest value	`>>> max([1, 2, 3, 4])` `4`	
`min`	Returns the smallest value	`>>> min([1, 2, 3, 4])` `1`	
`mean`	Returns the average value	`>>> mean([1, 2, 3, 4])` `2.5`	

`median`	Returns the value at the middle position if the size of the data set is odd, or the mean of the two values in the middle if the size of the data set is even	`>>> median([1, 2, 3, 4, 5])`
		`3.0`
		`>>> median([1, 2, 3, 4])`
		`2.5`	

`mode`	Returns the unique value that appears most frequently	`>>> mode([1, 2, 3, 3, 5])` `3`	
`modes`	Returns the set of unique values that appear most frequently	`>>> modes([2, 2, 3, 3, 5])` `[2, 3]`	

`std`	Returns a measure of the closeness of the values to the mean	`>> std([1,2,3,4])`
		`1.118033988749895`
		`>> std([100,2,3,4])`
		`42.00818372650738`	

Computing the Maximum, Minimum, and Mean

Python includes the standard functions **max** and **min** for viewing the maximum or minimum value in a list. The function **mean** can be easily defined to return the sum of a list's values divided by its length, as follows:

```
def mean(lyst):
    """Precondition: lyst is non-empty.
    Returns the arithmetic mean of numbers in lyst."""
    if len(lyst) == 0:
        raise RuntimeError("List must be non-empty. ")
    return sum(lyst) / len(lyst)
```

Computing the Median

The median value in a list is the one that would be in the middle position if the list were sorted. This position is exactly determined by dividing the length of the list by 2 if the list has an odd number of positions; otherwise, the median value is the mean of the values at the end of the first half of the list and at the beginning of its second half. Because the list's values might be in random order, you must first sort them before returning the value at the appropriate position. To avoid modifying the argument list, you first obtain a copy of it before sorting the copy. Here is the code for the function **median**:

```
def median(lyst):
    """Precondition: lyst is non-empty.
    Returns the median of numbers in lyst."""
    if len(lyst) == 0:
        raise RuntimeError("List must be non-empty. ")
    copy = list(lyst)   # Construct a copy of lyst
    copy.sort()
    midpoint = len(lyst) // 2
    if len(lyst) % 2 == 1:
        return copy[midpoint]
    else:
        return mean([copy[midpoint - 1], copy[midpoint]])
```

Although the code for **median** is more complex than that for **mean**, you have called upon other functions, such as **list** and **mean**, to simplify your task as much as possible.

Computing the Mode and Modes

The mode of a list of values is the one that appears most often. If two or more unique values appear most often, you might still be interested in knowing what they are. Thus, you can provide two functions: **mode**, which returns a single value, and **modes**, which returns a list of values.

You implemented an algorithm for finding a single mode in Chapter 5. The strategy is to build a dictionary keyed by the unique values in the list, associated with the frequencies of each such value. The mode is then the key whose associated frequency is the maximum one. Because a dictionary of frequencies is needed for both functions now under development, first define a function named **frequencies**, which might have other uses as well. Here is the code for this function:

```
def frequencies(lyst):
    """Returns a dictionary of numbers and their
    frequencies in lyst."""
    theDictionary = {}
    for number in lyst:
        count = theDictionary.get(number, 0)
        theDictionary[number] = count + 1
    return theDictionary
```

The function **mode** now selects the maximum frequency from the values in the dictionary and returns the first associated key:

```
def mode(lyst):
    """Precondition: lyst is non-empty.
    Returns the mode of the numbers in lyst."""
    if len(lyst) == 0:
        raise RuntimeError("List must be non-empty. ")
    theDictionary = frequencies(lyst)
```

```
    theMaximum = max(theDictionary.values())
    for key in theDictionary:
        if theDictionary[key] == theMaximum:
            result = key
            break
    return result
```

To obtain a list of multiple values whose frequencies are equal to the maximum one, the **modes** function uses the same strategy as **mode**, but adds each key having the maximum frequency to a list of keys:

```
def modes(lyst):
    """Precondition: lyst is non-empty.
    Returns a list of the modes of the numbers in lyst."""
    if len(lyst) == 0:
        raise RuntimeError("List must be non-empty. ")
    theDictionary = frequencies(lyst)
    theMaximum = max(theDictionary.values())
    result = []
    for key in theDictionary:
        if theDictionary[key] == theMaximum:
            result.append(key)
    return result
```

Computing the Standard Deviation

The standard deviation of a list of numbers is a measure of their closeness or distance from the mean of these numbers. This value is computed by the following:

1. Computing the mean of the numbers.
2. Subtracting this mean from each number.
3. Squaring each difference from step 2.
4. Computing the mean of the squares from step 3.
5. Computing the square root of the mean from step 4.

For example, take the list [1, 2, 3, 4], whose standard deviation is 1.118033988749895, as shown in Table 11-1. Here are the five steps to compute the standard deviation for this particular data set:

1. The mean of [1, 2, 3, 4] is 2.5.
2. The subtractions of the mean are (1 – 2.5), (2 – 2.5), (3 – 2.5), and (4 – 2.5), producing the differences –1.5, –0.5, 0.5, and 1.5.
3. The squares of the differences are 2.25, 0.25, 0.25, and 2.25.
4. The mean of these squares is 1.25.
5. The square root of this mean is 1.118033988749895.

As you implement these design steps in Python, you should be eager to employ function calls wherever possible, thereby avoiding the complexity of loops and selection statements. A quick examination of the design reveals two calls of the **mean** function and a call of Python's **math.sqrt** function. The remaining steps apply functions to lists of numbers to produce lists of results. In one case, the function subtracts the mean from a value, and in the other case, the function takes the square of a value. Both tasks are implemented quite easily using Python's **map** function, where the results of the first mapping provide the argument to the second mapping. Using these simplifications, the five steps in the design can be accomplished in just four lines of code:

```python
def std(lyst):
    """Precondition: lyst is non-empty.
    Returns the standard deviation of the numbers in lyst."""
    if len(lyst) == 0:
        raise RuntimeError("List must be non-empty. ")
    # Step 1
    average = mean(lyst)
    # Step 2
    differences = map(lambda x: x - average, lyst)
    # Step 3
    squares = list(map(lambda x: x ** 2, differences))
    # Steps 4 and 5
    return math.sqrt(mean(squares))
```

Using the NumPy Library

Our discussion of the various functions for analyzing data sets has gone into some detail about their use and how they work. While our implementations work correctly on data sets of numbers, they are not necessarily the best versions to use with very large data sets. As you will see in Chapter 13, for example, the **sort** method used by our version of the **median** function performs impractically poorly with very large data sets. A much faster algorithm for computing the median is available. Furthermore, even if you had chosen the fastest algorithm for each function, our versions would still run more slowly than those available in standard libraries, which have been compiled to machine code.

To mitigate these problems, you can import some of these functions from NumPy, a popular library for numerical analysis. The functions **mean**, **median**, and **std** in NumPy use the fastest available algorithms. The next session shows their use with an example data set from Table 11-1:

```python
>>> import numpy as np
>>> lyst = [1, 2, 3, 4]
>>> np.mean(lyst)
2.5
>>> np.median(lyst)
2.5
>>> np.std(lyst)
1.118033988749895
```

Note the syntax of the special form of the **import** statement, in which you create a more easily written abbreviation of the module name:

```python
import <module name> as <abbreviated name>
```

In general, it's a good idea to use a library function whenever it's available, and it's also a good idea to prefix calls of your imported function with its module name or an abbreviation. You can find documentation and installation instructions for NumPy at **https://numpy.org/**.

Exercise 11-1

1. The **variance** of a data set is defined to be the mean of the squares of the numbers in a list minus the square of the mean of those numbers. Define a Python function that computes and returns this value. (You may use the **mean** function defined earlier.)

2. The **percentile** of a value is the fraction of its data set whose values fall below the magnitude of that value. For example, to rise into the 90th percentile means that at least 90% of the other values lie below the given value (assuming they are in descending order). Describe a strategy for computing the percentile of a given value in a list of values.

3. Why do most of the data analysis functions have a precondition?

4. Explain the difference between the median and the mean of a data set. Explain why you might select one function rather than the other.

Case Study 11-1 │ Analyzing Student Test Scores

To put our data analysis functions to work, let's update the **Student** class developed in Chapter 10 so that clients (instructors or students) can find patterns in a student's test scores.

Request

Add some data analysis functions that will allow clients to view the mean, median, mode, and standard deviation of a student's test scores.

Analysis

A graphical user interface provides a view of the student's name and test scores, as well as labeled fields for the display of the results of data analysis. At program startup, a default **Student** object with 10 grades of 0 is created and displayed in a window. At that point, the user can select a command from a set of four command buttons:

1. *Edit* a score at a given position in the list of scores.

2. *Add* a new score to the list, increasing its size by 1.

3. *Delete* a score from a given position in the list, decreasing its size by 1.

4. *Randomize* the list of scores with a set of randomly generated values.

When the user successfully completes any of these tasks, the program automatically recomputes the analytical results and updates the view. The proposed interface is shown in **Figure 11-1**.

Figure 11-1 The user interface of the student test scores analysis program

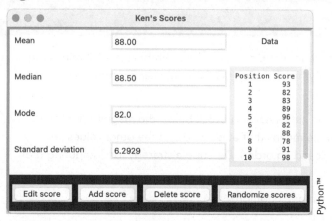

Design

Use the model/view design pattern introduced in Chapter 10 to structure the program. The model class is of course **Student**, and the view classes include the window class **StudentView** as well as several prompter and pop-up message boxes. In addition, the program includes a separate module named **studentapp** that launches the application by creating instances of the model and view. The relationships among these resources are shown in the class diagram in **Figure 11-2**.

Figure 11-2 The resources in the student test scores analysis program

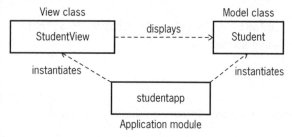

You will develop the design of the model class **Student** first. The interface or set of methods of this class is listed in **Table 11-2**.

Table 11-2 The interface of the **Student** class

Student Method	What it Does
s = Student(name, numScores)	Returns a new **Student** object with the given name and number of test scores; the scores are initially 0
s.__str__()	Same as str(s); returns a formatted string representation of the student
s.numScores()	Returns the number of scores
s.getScore(i)	Returns the score at position i, counting from 1
s.setScore(i, score)	Replaces the score at position i, counting from 1
s.addScore(score)	Adds a new score to the end of the list
s.deleteScore(i)	Removes the score at position i, counting from 1
s.randomizeScores(numScores, lower, upper)	Replaces all scores with the given number of scores, chosen at random from values from lower to upper
s.getMean()	Returns the mean of the scores
s.getMedian()	Returns the median of the scores
s.getMode()	Returns the mode of the scores
s.getStd()	Returns the standard deviation of the scores

Some of these operations already belong to the **Student** class of Chapter 10, so you can simply add the new methods to it and revise any existing methods as needed.

Implementation (Coding) of the **Student** Class

The **Student** class retains the same instance variables and constructor that were presented in Chapter 10. Modify the __str__ method to return a formatted string suitable for display in the application's view:

```
def __str__(self):
    """Returns the string representation of the student scores."""
    result = "Position Score\n"
    i = 1
    for score in self.scores:
        result += "%4d     %3d\n" % (i, score)
    return result
```

The **Student** method **randomizeScores**, which creates a new set of random scores for analysis, utilizes a new general-purpose function that creates a list of randomly generated integers. This function, named **getRandomList**, is defined in the **stats** module (along with the analysis functions developed earlier in this chapter). The function has three required parameters, specifying the number of numbers to be generated and the lower and upper bounds of the range of numbers. An optional parameter allows the caller to ask for a set of unique numbers or a set of numbers with possible duplicates (the default). Here are a couple of calls of the function, with unique and duplicate numbers:

```
>>> getRandomList(10, 1, 10)        # With duplicates
[1, 9, 2, 10, 1, 2, 5, 9, 10, 8]
>>> getRandomList(10, 1, 10, unique = True)
[5, 1, 8, 7, 2, 4, 3, 9, 10, 6]
```

Here is the code for the function and the **Student** method that uses it:

```
# In the file stats.py
def getRandomList(size, lower, upper, unique = False):
    """Returns a list of randomly generate numbers
    within the given bounds."""
    theList = []
    for count in range(size):
        number = random.randint(lower, upper)
        if unique:
            while number in theList:
                number = random.randint(lower, upper)
        theList.append(number)
    return theList
# In the file student.py
def randomizeScores(self, size, lower, upper):
    """Resets the scores to a list of randomly
    generated scores."""
    self.scores = stats.getRandomList(size, lower, upper)
```

(continues)

The methods to add a new score and delete an existing score simply call the `list` methods **append** and **pop**, respectively. The data analysis methods **mean**, **median**, **std**, and **mode** just call the corresponding **numpy** methods or, in the case of **mode**, call the function developed earlier in this chapter. All are left as exercises for you.

Design and Implementation (Coding) of `StudentView` and `studentapp`

The layout of the GUI shown in Figure 11-1 shows labels, fields, a text area, and command buttons. The constructor for **StudentView** creates these window components and lays them out in the usual manner. When the application's **main** function calls the constructor to create the window, it can pass the **Student** object as an argument, which permits the constructor to refresh the window with this student's data at program startup. Here is the code for the module **studentapp**, which creates the model, connects it to the view, and starts the application:

```
"""
File: studentapp.py
The application for editing and analyzing student scores.
"""

from student import Student
from studentview import StudentView

def main():
    """Creates the model and view and starts the app."""
    model = Student("Ken", 10)
    StudentView(model)

if __name__ == "__main__":
    main()
```

Here is the code for the constructor of **StudentView**:

```
"""
File: studentview.py
The view for editing and analyzing student scores.
"""

from breezypythongui import EasyFrame

class StudentView(EasyFrame):

    def __init__(self, model):
        """Creates and lays out window components
        to view and manipulate the model's data."""
        EasyFrame.__init__(self)
        self.setSize(500, 200)
        self.model = model
```

```
      self.addLabel("Mean", row = 0, column = 0)
      self.addLabel("Median", row = 1, column = 0)
      self.addLabel("Mode", row = 2, column = 0)
      self.addLabel("Standard deviation", row = 3,
                                          column = 0)
      self.meanFld = self.addFloatField(value = 0.0,
                                        row = 0, column = 1,
                                        precision = 2)
      self.medianFld = self.addFloatField(value = 0.0,
                                          row = 1, column = 1,
                                          precision = 2)
      self.modeFld = self.addFloatField(value = 0.0,
                                        row = 2, column = 1
                                        precision = 2)
      self.stdFld = self.addFloatField(value = 0.0,
                                       row = 3, column = 1
                                       precision = 4)
      self.addLabel("Data", row = 0, column = 2,
                    sticky = "NEW")
      self.scoreArea = self.addTextArea(text = "",
                                        row = 1,
                                        column = 2,
                                        width = 12,
                                        rowspan = 3)
      # Create a panel for the buttons to center them
      # in 4 columns
      bp = self.addPanel(row = 4, column = 0,
                         columnspan = 3,
                         background = "black")
      bp.addButton(text = "Edit score",
                   row = 0, column = 0,
                   command = self.editScore)
      bp.addButton(text = "Add score",
                   row = 0, column = 1,
                   command = self.addScore)
      bp.addButton(text = "Delete score",
                   row = 0, column = 2,
                   command = self.deleteScore)
      bp.addButton(text = "Randomize scores",
                   row = 0, column = 3,
                   command = self.randomizeScores)
      # Place the model's contents in the view
      self.refreshData()
   # Event-handling methods go here
```

(continues)

Note that after laying out the window components, the constructor calls the method **refreshData**. This method sets the fields and text area to the data belonging to the **Student** object, including the initial results of analysis. Whenever the user modifies the scores by editing, adding, deleting, or randomizing them, **refreshData** is then called to update the view with the new data and results. Here is the definition of this method:

```
def refreshData(self):
    """Updates the view with the contents of the model."""
    self.setTitle(self.model.getName() + "'s Scores")
    self.meanFld.setNumber(self.model.getMean())
    self.medianFld.setNumber(self.model.getMedian())
    self.modeFld.setNumber(self.model.getMode())
    self.stdFld.setNumber(self.model.getStd())
    self.scoreArea.setText(str(self.model))
```

Each command button is associated with an event-handling method. For example, the **Delete score** button allows the user to remove a score at a given position. **Figure 11-3** shows this process for dropping a student's lowest score (78).

Figure 11-3   Deleting a score from a student's scores

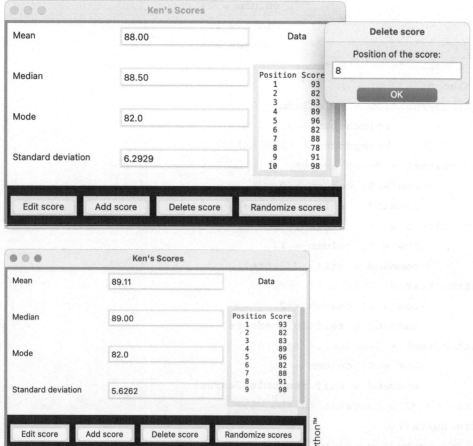

Note that after the score is dropped, the set of scores and the results of the analysis are refreshed with any changes.

To handle this task, the view's **deleteScore** method pops up a prompter box for the position of the score to be removed. This input is converted to an integer and passed to the model's **deleteScore** method. Finally, the view is refreshed to show the modified data set and its analysis. Here is the code for the **StudentView** method **deleteScore**:

```
def deleteScore(self):
    """Obtains the position of a score from the user,
    deletes the score at that position from the model,
    and updates the view."""
    position = self.prompterBox(title = "Delete score",
                                promptString = "Position of the score:")
    self.model.deleteScore(int(position))
    self.refreshData()
```

Note that you have not included code to detect errors in the user input, such as a position that might be out of range. Prompter boxes can also be used to obtain the number of scores, the lowest score, and the highest score from the user when the **Randomize scores** button is selected. The completion of this task and the rest of the application is left as an exercise for you.

11.2 Visualizing a Data Set

"A picture is worth a thousand words," and when it comes to discerning patterns and relationships among data in a data set, this adage certainly rings true. For example, consider the data on consumer prices gathered by the U.S. Bureau of Labor Statistics (available at **https://www.bls.gov/charts/consumer-price-index/**). These data track the rate of price increases (and inflation) at various levels of detail, and when visualized in graphical form can give the viewer a sense of the impact of rising prices on American consumers. **Figure 11-4** shows three bar charts from this site that illustrate a pattern of price increases at various levels of detail, during an inflationary "spike" that peaked in the month of July 2022.

Data visualization generally involves the graphical representation of data in such a form as to assist in their analysis. Some visualizations, such as a map of the connections on the Internet, can be quite complex and sophisticated, and they can include animations and embedded links to other visual elements. This section introduces the concept of data visualization by examining several standard types of graphical representation, including pie charts, bar charts, line and scatter plots, and histograms.

Figure 11-4   The rate of increase in U.S. food prices in July 2022

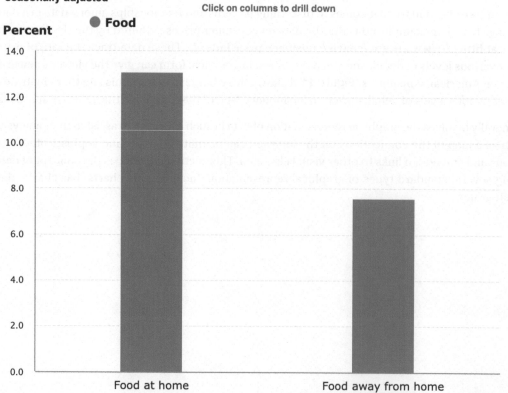

12-month percentage change, Consumer Price Index, selected categories, July 2022, not seasonally adjusted

Click on columns to drill down

Major categories

Percent

12-month percentage change, Consumer Price Index, selected categories, July 2022, not seasonally adjusted

Click on columns to drill down

● **Food**

Percent

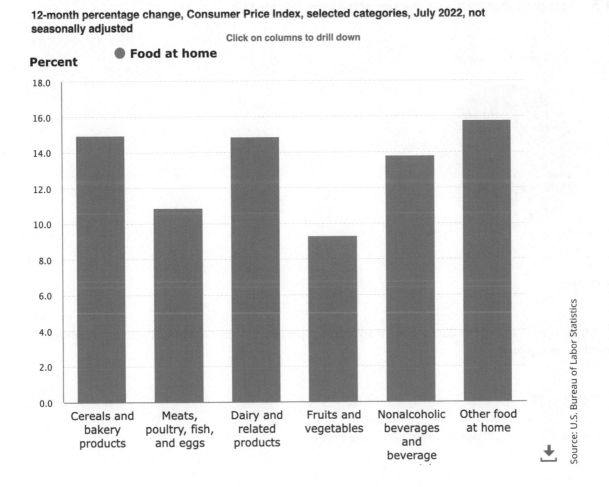

12-month percentage change, Consumer Price Index, selected categories, July 2022, not seasonally adjusted

Click on columns to drill down

● **Food at home**

Source: U.S. Bureau of Labor Statistics

Pie Charts

A **pie chart** visually represents a data set in terms of "slices," each of which shows the relative percentage of a data set's item in a whole circular "pie." For example, consider the list of rough estimates of a person's living expenses shown in **Table 11-3**.

Table 11-3   A rough estimate of living expenses

Item	Expense
Rent	$1200
Food	$700
Healthcare	$500
Transportation	$300
Utilities	$600
Entertainment	$200

The percentage of the cost of each item in the table is depicted quite vividly in the pie chart of **Figure 11-5**.

Figure 11-5   A pie chart showing the relative cost of the items in Table 11-3

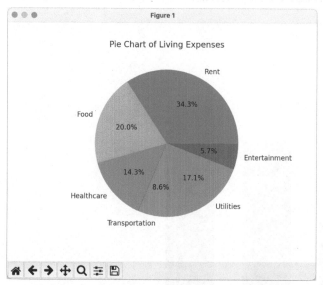

A short Python script created the data set and displayed the pie chart for this example. Here is the code for the script, followed by an explanation:

```
"""
File: piechart.py

Displays a pie chart of monthly living expenses.
"""

import matplotlib.pyplot as plt

# Prepare the data
expenses = {"Rent":1200, "Food":700, "Healthcare":500,
            "Transportation":300, "Utilities":600,
            "Entertainment":200}
labels = list(expenses.keys())
slices = list(expenses.values())

# Set up and show the pie chart
plt.pie(slices, labels = labels, autopct = "%1.1f%%")
plt.title("Pie Chart of Living Expenses")
plt.show()
```

The script begins by importing the module `matplotlib.pyplot` and abbreviating its name to `plt`. This module, available at **https://matplotlib.org/**, includes resources for creating all the visualizations shown in this section.

The rest of the script consists of two parts:

1. Preparing the data set.
2. Setting up and showing the pie chart.

To prepare the data set, transfer the data from Table 11-3 to a Python dictionary. You then extract lists of labels and slices from the keys and values of this dictionary. These lists will be used to create a pie chart with labeled slices in the next part.

The function `matplotlib.pyplot.pie` creates the pie chart. The function expects one required argument, a list of slices, in this case, the six expense items in **Table 11-4**. You also supply optional arguments for the slices' labels and the precision of the percentage values displayed within the slices. Other useful optional arguments are listed in Table 11-4.

Table 11-4 Some optional arguments for the `matplotlib.pyplot.pie` function

Argument Keyword	Default Value
`colors`	A list of standard colors that fill the pie slices
`explode`	A list of distances from the center point for each slice; 0 is the default distance for all slices
`rotatelabels`	`False` by default; `True` causes the labels to align with the angles of their slices
`shadow`	Places a 3D shadow around part of the pie; `False` by default
`startangle`	0 or due east by default; the angle at which the first slice in the set of values is drawn; angles increase in a counterclockwise direction

The `colors` argument can include any of a set of commonly used values, such as "red," "blue," and "green," or their abbreviations "r," "g," and "b." ("k" is short for "black.") Any color in the full range of RGB colors can be expressed using the hex string notation introduced in Chapter 9 (for example, the string `"#ff0000"` would be the brightest red).

The `explode` argument is used to pull one or more slices out from the pie chart's center for emphasis. Note that the lists provided for `colors` and `explode` must have the same length as the number of slices.

You can find a full discussion of all the optional arguments by running `help` on the `matplotlib.pyplot.pie` function.

Bar Charts

A **bar chart** visually represents a data set in terms of rectangular shapes or bars, each of which directly measures the magnitude of a data value. For example, consider the enrollments for Ken's three courses listed in **Table 11-5**.

Table 11-5 Enrollments in Ken's courses

Course Code	Course Title	Enrollment
CSCI112	Data Structures	40
CSCI312	Programming Language Design	32
PHIL258	Seminar on Freud and Philosophy	19

A bar chart displays a bar for each enrollment value in a two-dimensional grid. If the bars are displayed in a vertical orientation, the enrollment values appear along the *y*-axis, while the course codes labeling the bars appear along the *x*-axis, as shown in **Figure 11-6**.

Figure 11-6   A vertical bar chart showing the enrollments in Ken's courses

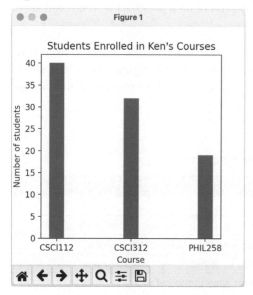

Here is the code for the setup and display of the vertical bar chart shown in Figure 11.6, followed by an explanation:

```
"""
File: barchartvertical.py

Displays enrollments in three courses
in a vertical bar chart.
"""

import matplotlib.pyplot as plt

# Prepare the data
data = {"CSCI112":40, "CSCI312":32, "PHIL258":19}
courses = list(data.keys())
enrollments = list(data.values())

# Set up and show the horizontal bar chart
plt.figure(figsize = (4, 4))
plt.bar(courses, enrollments, width = 0.2)
plt.title("Students Enrolled in Ken's Courses")
plt.xlabel("Course")
plt.ylabel("Number of students")
plt.show()
```

The data set is prepared for this program in a similar manner to the pie chart program discussed earlier. In this case, **enrollments** names a list of numbers whose values will appear along the chart's vertical axis, while **courses** names a list of the course codes associated with the enrollment numbers, to be displayed along the horizontal axis beneath each bar. These two values are passed as required arguments to the **bar** function to create the vertical bar chart. You also override the default **width** argument (.8) of the bars. The bar function has many other optional arguments, which you can consult by running Python's **help** function. For example, one can override the default **color** argument to assign the same color to all the bars or a different color to each one. Note also that the `figure` function is called before the bar chart is created to set the initial dimensions of the chart (4 inches by 4 inches).

Alternatively, one might orient the bars horizontally. In that case, the enrollment values would appear along the *x*-axis and the course names would appear along the *y*-axis. A horizontal bar chart might be preferred when the labels for the data, such as the course titles listed in Table 11-5, are too long to appear side by side on the *x*-axis. **Figure 11-7** illustrates this change in bar orientation.

Figure 11-7   A horizonal bar chart showing the enrollments in Ken's courses

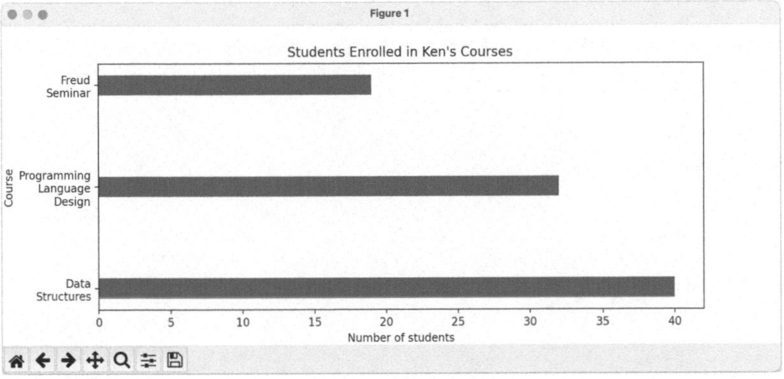

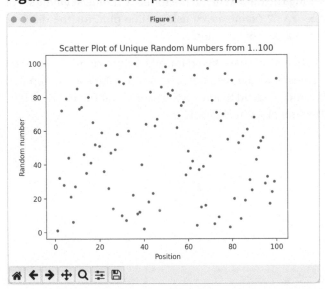

To create a horizontal bar chart, you call the `barh` function instead of the `bar` function, and you override its `height` argument instead of its `width` argument. You might also have to increase the width supplied to the `figure` function before creating the chart. The code for displaying a horizontal bar chart like the one shown in Figure 11-7 is left as an exercise for you.

Scatter Plots

A **scatter plot** visually represents a data set as a collection of points or dots in a two-dimensional grid. The magnitude of each data value appears along the *y*-axis, and its position in the data set appears along the *x*-axis. **Figure 11-8** shows a scatter plot of the unique numbers from 1 through 100, scattered at random positions.

Figure 11-8   A scatter plot of the unique numbers from 1 through 100, generated randomly

Scatter plots help us to recognize patterns, such as randomness in this case, or the clustering of data around certain parameters.

The code for our sample program creates the set of unique random numbers by calling the `getRandomList` function introduced earlier. The program also creates a list of the positions in the usual manner. The `scatter` function is then called to create the scatter plot with these two required arguments, as well as an optional `color` and `marker` shape. Here is the code for the script that produces the scatter plot in Figure 11-8:

```
"""
File: scatterplot.py

Displays unique random numbers between 1 and 100, in the
order in which they are generated, in a scatter plot.
"""

import matplotlib.pyplot as plt
import stats

# Prepare the data
positions = list(range(1, 101))
numbers = stats.getRandomList(100, 1, 100, unique = True)

# Set up and show the scatter plot
plt.scatter(positions, numbers,
            color = "purple", marker = '.')
plt.title("Scatter Plot of Unique Random Numbers from 1..100")
plt.xlabel("Position")
plt.ylabel("Random number")
plt.show()
```

Line Plots

A line plot is like a scatter plot but connects the dots representing the data at given positions with line segments. For example, let's plot the values of the expressions `x * 2` and `x ** 2` (same as x^2) using a line plot, for the discrete values of `x` 1 through 5. **Figure 11-9** shows these relationships in a pair of line plots.

Because there are two functions to plot, you'll need to create and prepare two data sets before running the `plot` function with each set. The two data sets share the same *x*-values, and the respective sets of *y*-values are computed ahead of time. The script provides a separate color for each line and a legend to inform the user about the relationships being plotted. Here is the code for the script that produced the line plots in Figure 11-9:

```
"""
File: lineplot.py

Displays values of y = x * 2 and y = x ** 2,
for x = 1..5, in line plots.
"""
```

```
import matplotlib.pyplot as plt
# Prepare the data
xValues = list(range(1, 6))
doubles = list(map(lambda x: x * 2, xValues))
squares = list(map(lambda x: x ** 2, xValues))

# Set up and show the line plots
plt.plot(xValues, doubles, label = "y = x * 2",
        color = "blue", marker = 'o')
plt.plot(xValues, squares, label = "y = x ** 2",
        color = "red", marker = 'o')
plt.xticks(xValues)
plt.title("Line Plots of Doubles and Squares of Discrete Values 1..5")
plt.xlabel("x axis")
plt.ylabel("y axis")
plt.legend()
plt.show()
```

Figure 11-9   Line plots of $y = x * 2$ and $y = x ** 2$, for $x =$ the integers 1 through 5

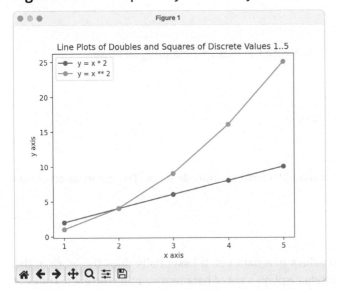

The information in the legend is provided by the `label` argument for each call of the `plot` function. The `xticks` function is also called to restrict the labels on the x-axis to discrete integers.

The data dots in this example could have been plotted just as easily in two scatter plots. One of the virtues of line plots is that they are capable of plotting functions across a continuous range of x-values in their domains. Our example shows results for just five discrete x-values, but for many functions, there are actually an infinite number of real x-values between any two discrete bounds. Plotting along a continuous range of x-values yields the smooth curves that you see in plots of many mathematical functions, without the discrete dots, as shown in **Figure 11-10**.

To achieve this effect, deploy NumPy's `linspace` function to generate a continuous range of x-values, as follows:

```
import numpy as np
xValues = np.linspace(1, 5)
```

Figure 11-10 Line plots of $y = x * 2$ and $y = x ** 2$, for x = continuous range from 1 through 5

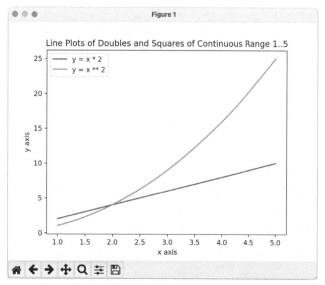

The y-values for each function are then computed as functions of the x-values:

```
doubles = xValues * 2
squares = xValues ** 2
```

These data are then used with the plot function, as before, but with the marker defaulting to **None**:

```
plt.plot(xValues, doubles, label = "y = x * 2",
        color = "blue")
plt.plot(xValues, squares, label = "y = x ** 2",
        color = "red")
```

Like line plots, bar plots can also visualize multiple sets of data by creating multiple plots. The exploration of this capability is left as an exercise for you.

Histograms

A **histogram** visually represents the relative frequencies of values in a data set. It essentially does the work of the `frequencies` function developed earlier in this chapter, and then displays a set of bars representing the magnitudes of these frequencies. The bars can be aligned either vertically or horizontally, and they are labeled with the unique values in the data set. **Figure 11-11** shows a vertical histogram of a data set containing 50 random integer scores from 95 through 100.

The code to generate this histogram is quite simple:

```
"""
File: histogram.py

Displays frequencies of 50 random scores between 95 and 100
in a histogram.
"""

import matplotlib.pyplot as plt
import stats
```

```
# Prepare the data
scores = stats.getRandomList(50, 95, 100)

# Set up and show the histogram
plt.hist(scores, width = .2)
plt.title("Frequencies of 50 random scores between 95 and 100.")
plt.xlabel("Score")
plt.ylabel("Frequency")
plt.show()
```

Histograms can be a bit tricky to format, but you can consult Python's **help** function if you run into snags.

Figure 11-11   A histogram of 50 random scores from 95 to 100

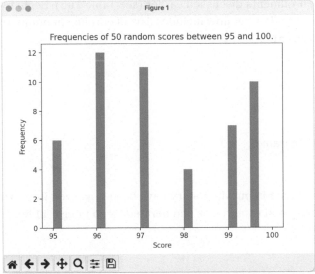

Exercise 11-2

1. Describe the difference between a scatter plot and a line plot.

2. Describe the difference between a bar chart and a histogram.

3. Describe how one would plot several data sets in the same line plot.

4. When is it appropriate to visualize a data set using a pie chart?

5. Jill wants to create a histogram of a concordance, which represents the frequencies of words in a text file. Should she align the histogram vertically or horizontally, and why?

11.3 Working with More Complex Data Sets

The data sets examined thus far in this chapter have had a simple structure. They have been lists of labels and values or a dictionary. In either case, their contents conceptually form a labeled column of data. Many real-world data sets are much more complex: they are structured as two-dimensional tables with multiple rows and columns. Their data values can be entered into spreadsheets or databases, which already have special functions for performing analyses of data in given rows and columns. These structured data can be saved in a special type of text file in **CSV format** for export to other data analysis programs. (CSV stands for comma-separated values.) Although they are structured, data sets obtained from CSV files can still be in "raw" form, containing missing, incorrect, or improperly formatted values in some rows. Thus, you must engage in a process of examining and "cleaning" these values before the data set can be analyzed. This section explores the use of Python's `pandas` library to load data sets from CSV files and to clean them before performing analyses and visualizations.

Creating a Data Set with `pandas`

The `pandas` library, available at **https://pandas.pydata.org/**, provides resources for manipulating structured data sets. In `pandas`, a data set is represented as a data frame. Like the `Grid` type discussed in Chapter 10, a data frame consists of a set of columns and rows, but it includes many operations that support data analysis. Once a data set is loaded into a data frame, individual columns or rows can be selected for further processing, including cleaning, analysis, and visualization.

You can easily explore some basic `pandas` operations interactively in the IDLE shell. Let's examine the way in which `pandas` organizes and handles the simple data set of course enrollments discussed earlier (see Table 11-5). Begin by importing the `pandas` module and then preparing the data set. The data set now includes lists of enrollment numbers and course codes, keyed by the labels **"Course"** and **"Enrollment"**.

```
>>> import pandas as pd
>>> data = {"Course":["CSCI112", "CSCI312", "PHIL258"],
            "Enrollment":[40, 32, 19]}
```

You then ask `pandas` to further organize these data in a data frame:

```
>>> frame = pd.DataFrame(data)
```

When you print the data frame, you can see that the lists of data in our dictionary have been organized into two columns, where each column is headed by a key in the dictionary and each row is enumerated by an integer index:

```
>>> print(frame)
    Course  Enrollment
0   CSCI112         40
1   CSCI312         32
2   PHIL258         19
```

Visualizing Data with `pandas` and `matplotlib.pyplot`

You can visualize the data in a `pandas` data frame in any of the styles considered earlier, such as line plots, bar plots, scatter plots, and histograms, among many others. For example, you can quickly show a line plot on our simple course enrollment data frame as follows:

```
>>> import pandas as pd
>>> import matplotlib.pyplot as plt
>>> data = {"Course":["CSCI112", "CSCI312", "PHIL258"],
            "Enrollment":[40, 32, 19]}
>>> frame = pd.DataFrame(data)
>>> frame.plot(marker = 'o', xlabel = "Course",
               ylabel = "Enrollment")
>>> plt.show()
```

Note that the `DataFrame.plot` method expects similar arguments to the `matplotlib.pyplot.plot` function examined earlier. As happened with the earlier line plot, the enrollment numbers appear along the *y*-axis of the plot. However, the integer index values of the data frame's rows now appear along the *x*-axis, rather than the course code labels. To correct this, you can reframe the data set by supplying a list of the course code labels as an optional **index** argument before plotting:

```
>>> frame = pd.DataFrame(data, index = data["Course"])
```

This operation replaces the integer indexes labeling the frame's rows with the course code labels, as shown when the frame is printed:

```
>>> print(frame)
          Course   Enrollment
CSCI112   CSCI112          40
CSCI312   CSCI312          32
PHIL258   PHIL258          19
```

The **plot** method now labels the *x*-axis coordinates with the course codes rather than the integer index positions of the rows. The two plots just discussed are shown in **Figure 11-12**.

Figure 11-12   Line plots of a data frame without and with labeled indexes

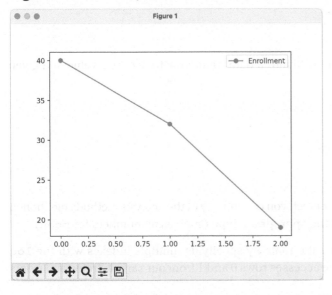
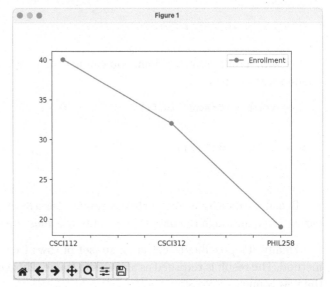

You are encouraged to explore the other methods for visualizing data frames, such as **bar**, **barh**, **scatter**, and **hist**, in the **pandas** documentation.

Accessing Columns and Rows in a Data Frame

Processing a data frame often involves accessing individual rows or columns of data. For example, you might want to find the mean, median, and/or standard deviation of a column of data, such as the set of enrollment numbers in our simple example. The code for this is surprisingly simple:

```
>>> enrollmentCol = frame["Enrollment"]
>>> print("Mean enrollment:", enrollmentCol.mean())
Mean enrollment: 30.333333333333332
>>> print("Median enrollment:", enrollmentCol.median())
Median enrollment: 32.0
>>> print("Standard deviation:", enrollmentCol.std())
Standard deviation: 10.598742063723098
```

Each column in a **pandas** data frame is represented as a **series**, which is similar to a sequence of values but supports many standard statistical analysis methods. Here is what a **Series** object and one of its values look like when printed:

```
>>> print(enrollmentCol)
0      40
1      32
2      19
Name: Enrollment, dtype: int64
>>> print(enrollmentCol[1])
32
```

The rows of a **pandas** data frame are likewise represented as **Series** objects. To access an individual row, you run the **loc** method with a subscript on the data frame. The subscript should be an integer value if the frame's index consists of integers (the default) or a label if the index labels are supplied when the frame is created. If the frame's index consists of labels, you can instead run the **iloc** method with an integer subscript to access a given row. For example, the following code segment accesses and prints a row in the course enrollments frame with an integer index:

```
>>> print(frame.loc[1])
Course          CSCI312
Enrollment           32
Name: 1, dtype: object
```

As with a data frame column, you can use a subscript to drill into a data frame row to access a value at a given column within a row:

```
>>> row1 = frame.loc[1]

>>> print(row1[1])      # Alternatively, frame.loc[1][1]
32
```

Because a data frame row is also represented as a **Series** object, you can run any of the analysis methods mentioned earlier on it, although the data values in the row must be of the appropriate type (such as all numbers for **mean**).

Finally, it's possible to extract a subset of rows from a data frame by specifying multiple indexes with the **loc** method. The result is returned as a new data frame. This code accesses rows 0 and 1 from our sample frame and prints the new frame:

```
>>> twoRows = frame.loc[[0, 1]]
>>> print(twoRows)
    Course   Enrollment
0   CSCI112          40
1   CSCI312          32
```

Creating a Data Frame from a CSV File

Simple data sets for experimentation with **pandas** are easy to create by hand, but real-world data sets are typically imported from files. There are thousands of available data sets on the web, and many can be downloaded in either spreadsheet or CSV format. The CSV is a standard format for transferring data between data analysis applications. A CSV file is a text file in which each row of data begins on a new line, and the values in each row are separated by commas.

Let's consider a still relatively small data set maintained by the U.S. Bureau of Labor Statistics. This data set, available at **https://www.bls.gov/data/home.htm**, tracks the price of bread in the United States and was downloaded for the period from January 2012 to the peak of an inflationary spike in July 2022. When opened in a text editor like TextEdit or WordPad, the file shows some prefatory information followed by the actual data. As you can see in

Figure 11-13, the columns of data are separated by commas and headed by labels for the year and the names of the 12 months.

Figure 11-13 The contents of a CSV file for a data set of bread prices

```
SeriesReport-20220828113454_1d0680.csv
"CPI Average Price Data, U.S. city average (AP)",,,,,,,,,,,,
Original Data Value,,,,,,,,,,,,
,,,,,,,,,,,,
Series Id:,APU0000702111,,,,,,,,,,,
Series Title:,"Bread, white, pan, per lb. (453.6 gm) in U.S. city average, average price, not
seasonally adjusted",,,,,,,,,,,
Area:,U.S. city average,,,,,,,,,,,
Item:,"Bread, white, pan, per lb. (453.6 gm)",,,,,,,,,,,
Years:,2012 to 2022,,,,,,,,,,,
,,,,,,,,,,,,
Year,Jan,Feb,Mar,Apr,May,Jun,Jul,Aug,Sep,Oct,Nov,Dec
2012,1.423,1.442,1.395,1.426,1.412,1.403,1.427,1.407,1.401,1.422,1.418,1.436
2013,1.422,1.411,1.412,1.409,1.401,1.439,1.434,1.408,1.419,1.358,1.382,1.385
2014,1.365,1.388,1.359,1.388,1.401,1.400,1.413,1.396,1.405,1.414,1.420,1.466
2015,1.479,1.435,1.440,1.454,1.463,1.467,1.447,1.420,1.432,1.418,1.409,1.428
2016,1.425,1.407,1.416,1.406,1.382,1.333,1.349,1.341,1.329,1.343,1.362,1.362
2017,1.351,1.358,1.329,1.328,1.327,1.335,1.327,1.348,1.349,1.328,1.295,1.316
2018,1.281,1.265,1.309,1.281,1.293,1.279,1.293,1.302,1.288,1.277,1.274,1.290
2019,1.274,1.282,1.261,1.285,1.289,1.280,1.281,1.275,1.296,1.325,1.361,1.363
2020,1.351,1.375,1.374,1.406,1.412,1.474,1.485,1.495,1.492,1.503,1.515,1.538
2021,1.546,1.537,1.526,1.510,1.511,1.510,1.491,1.467,1.580,1.526,1.547,1.532
2022,1.555,1.578,1.607,1.612,1.606,1.691,1.715,,,,,
```

Python™

Before loading the data from this file into a **pandas** data frame, you will need to delete the prefatory information at the beginning of the file, down to the row of column headings just mentioned. (You can use a text editor for this step.) After saving your changes to a new file named **breadprices.csv**, you can now load the entire CSV file into a **pandas** data frame as follows:

```
>>> import pandas as pd
>>> frame = pd.read_csv("breadprices.csv")
>>> print(frame)
    Year    Jan    Feb    Mar    Apr    May    Jun    Jul    Aug    Sep    Oct    Nov    Dec
0   2012  1.423  1.442  1.395  1.426  1.412  1.403  1.427  1.407  1.401  1.422  1.418  1.436
1   2013  1.422  1.411  1.412  1.409  1.401  1.439  1.434  1.408  1.419  1.358  1.382  1.385
2   2014  1.365  1.388  1.359  1.388  1.401  1.400  1.413  1.396  1.405  1.414  1.420  1.466
3   2015  1.479  1.435  1.440  1.454  1.463  1.467  1.447  1.420  1.432  1.418  1.409  1.428
4   2016  1.425  1.407  1.416  1.406  1.382  1.333  1.349  1.341  1.329  1.343  1.362  1.362
5   2017  1.351  1.358  1.329  1.328  1.327  1.335  1.327  1.348  1.349  1.328  1.295  1.316
6   2018  1.281  1.265  1.309  1.281  1.293  1.279  1.293  1.302  1.288  1.277  1.274  1.290
7   2019  1.274  1.282  1.261  1.285  1.289  1.280  1.281  1.275  1.296  1.325  1.361  1.363
8   2020  1.351  1.375  1.374  1.406  1.412  1.474  1.485  1.495  1.492  1.503  1.515  1.538
9   2021  1.546  1.537  1.526  1.510  1.511  1.510  1.491  1.467  1.580  1.526  1.547  1.532
10  2022  1.555  1.578  1.607  1.612  1.606  1.691  1.715    NaN    NaN    NaN    NaN    NaN
```

This appears to be a data set that you can now work with. Before you can do so, however, note the data values labeled **NaN** in the rightmost five columns of row 10. This symbol stands for "Not a Number," or the **null value**, indicating that a number was not yet available for these months in 2022 (because the file was downloaded in August of that year). Before you can analyze these data, you must clean the data set.

Cleaning the Data in a Data Frame

There are a couple of ways to clean a data set with null values:

1. Delete the rows containing them. In very large data sets, several missing rows might not affect the analyses significantly.
2. Replace each null value with a single value that serves as a filler, to keep the row in play. This could be a value reasonably close to the other values in the row, such as the mean or median of those values.

To execute the strategy of option 1, deleting the rows with null values, you can run the following code:

```
>>> frame.dropna(inplace = True)
```

The **dropna** method deletes all the rows with null values in the data frame on which it is run. If you want to delete these rows from a copy of the data frame and not the original, you can omit the optional **inplace** argument, which is **False** by default. In that case, the **dropna** method returns a working copy of the data frame with the rows deleted, leaving the original data frame intact:

```
>>> theCopy = frame.dropna()
```

In the case of the example data set, row 10 would disappear from the data frame.

If this seems too drastic a move, especially in the case of smaller data sets like the example, you can execute the second strategy. In this case, you might replace each null value with the mean of the existing values in its row. However, because the datum in the first column, labeled "Year," should not be part of this calculation for the given row, you must first delete this column from the data frame before computing the mean of the values in the row. The following code segment achieves the desired result in three steps:

```
>>> frame.drop(columns = "Year", inplace = True)
>>> newValue = frame.loc[10].mean()
>>> frame.fillna(newValue, inplace = True)
```

To see if this strategy worked correctly, run the **tail** method on the data frame to display just the last five rows:

```
>>> print(frame.tail())
       Jan    Feb    Mar    Apr   ...       Sep       Oct       Nov       Dec
6     1.281  1.265  1.309  1.281  ...  1.288000  1.277000  1.274000  1.290000
7     1.274  1.282  1.261  1.285  ...  1.296000  1.325000  1.361000  1.363000
8     1.351  1.375  1.374  1.406  ...  1.492000  1.503000  1.515000  1.538000
9     1.546  1.537  1.526  1.510  ...  1.580000  1.526000  1.547000  1.532000
10    1.555  1.578  1.607  1.612  ...  1.623429  1.623429  1.623429  1.623429

[5 rows x 12 columns]
```

Alternatively, if you want to retain the "Years" column in the original data frame, you could delete it from a copy, compute the mean value of the last row in the copy, and replace the null values with this mean value in the original.

pandas includes several options for loading CSV files, such as replacing the integer indexes of the data frame with a given column of data in the file, as well as methods for saving data frames to files. You are encouraged to peruse the documentation for further details.

Accessing Other Attributes of a Data Frame

For larger, more complex data sets, you may want to know the number of rows or the number of columns or be able to iterate through them. For example, to create a list of the average bread prices for each year in our bread prices data frame, you would need to visit each row in the frame, compute its mean, and append it to a list. The **len** function returns the number of rows in a data frame, so a simple range-based **for** loop will do the trick for a data frame of any size:

```
averagesList = []
for row in range(len(frame)):
    averagesList.append(frame.iloc[row].mean())
```

Note that you use `iloc` rather than `loc` to access a row at a given position just in case the frame has been created with labels rather than integers as row indexes.

Two other important attributes of a data frame are named `index` and `columns`. Each attribute is an object of type `Index`, which represents a sequence of values over which you can iterate with a `for` loop. For example, the next code segment prints the values of the row indexes and the column labels of the bread prices data set:

```
for row in frame.index:
    print(row, end = ' ')
print()
for col in frame.columns:
    print(col, end = ' ')
print()
0 1 2 3 4 5 6 7 8 9 10
Year Jan Feb Mar Apr May Jun Jul Aug Sep Oct Nov Dec
```

Table 11-6 summarizes some important `DataFrame` methods, where `df` is a `DataFrame` object.

Table 11-6 Some useful `dataframe` attributes and methods

DataFrame Attribute or Method	What it Does
`df.index`	An `Index` object representing the sequence of row labels in `df`
`df.columns`	An `Index` object representing the sequence of column labels in `df`
`len(df)`	Returns the number of rows in `df`
`len(df.columns)`	Returns the number of columns in `df`
`df.loc[position]`	Returns the row (a `Series` object) at `position`, which can be either an integer or a label, in `df`
`df.iloc[position]`	Returns the row (a `Series` object) at `position`, which must be an integer, in `df`
`df.[columnLabel]`	Returns the column (a `Series` object) at `columnLabel` in `df`
`df.insert(position, columnLabel, value)`	Inserts a column into `df` at the integer `position`, with heading `columnLabel` and `list` or `Series` object `value`
`df.drop(index = rowPosition)`	Removes the row at `rowPosition` from `df`
`df.drop(columns = columnLabel)`	Removes the column at `columnLabel` from `df`
`df.pop(label)`	Removes and returns the column (a `Series` object) from `df`
`df.dropna(inplace = False)`	Drops the rows containing null values. If `inplace` is `True`, modifies `df`; otherwise, modifies and returns a copy of `df`
`df.fillna(newValue, inplace = False)`	Replaces the null values with `newValue`; if `inplace` is `True`, modifies `df`; otherwise, modifies and returns a copy of `df`

Exercise 11-3

1. Explain the difference between a data frame and a series.

2. Give two reasons why a data set might have to be cleaned and describe the techniques used to clean it.

3. What is a CSV file, and how does it map data to a data frame?

Case Study 11-2 | Analyzing Basketball Statistics

The statistics for basketball players at the high school, college, and professional levels are available on many websites. These data include minutes played, shots attempted and made, free throws attempted and made, rebounds, assists, and points scored, among many other categories of data, for each game over the course of a season or a career. Data analysis uses these data sets to support decisions about recruiting, salary contracts, trades, and end-of-season awards. To give you a taste of what is involved, this case study examines the data for a month of one player's performance.

Request

Write a program that allows the user to view the statistics of a basketball player and compute the mean, median, and standard deviation of various factors, such as free throw percentage, field goal percentage, and rebounds, over the course of a period of games.

Analysis

A GUI-based program takes its input from a CSV file and displays the contents of a data frame in a text area. The user can select a column of data, such as FG% (field goal percentage) from a radio button group to compute and display the mean, median, and standard deviation of the data in that column. The proposed user interface is shown in **Figure 11-14**.

Figure 11-14 The user interface for the basketball statistics analyzer

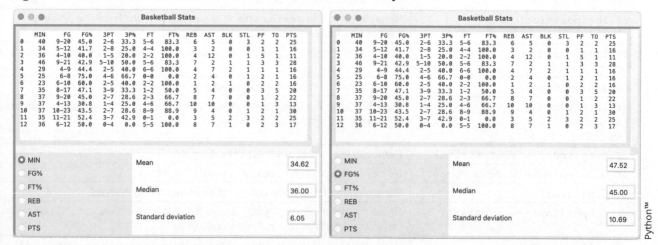

The original data set for our example was taken from the ESPN website at **https://www.espn.com/nba/player/gamelog/_/id/2566769/malcolm-brogdon**, which shows the NBA player Malcolm Brogdon's statistics for games played during the month of November 2021. Because the dates of the games on the website are listed from most recent to least recent, a short Python script (available in the file **reverselines.py**) was run to reverse the order of the lines of text after the header line in the CSV file.

Design

The program's application module, **hoopstatsapp**, loads the data model for this program from a CSV file into an instance of **DataFrame** at program startup. The model is then passed to the view, an instance of the class **HoopsStatsView**, which opens the window shown in Figure 11.14.

Most of the design work for **HoopStatsView** consists in laying out the window components, which are arranged in three areas of the window:

- A scrollable text area to hold the statistics, in the top half of the window

- A group of radio buttons labeled with the column headings of the statistics, in the lower left corner of the window

- A panel of labels and fields for the display of the analysis results, in the lower right corner of the window

The single event handling method, named **analyze**, is triggered at program startup and when the user selects a radio button. This surprisingly simple method first retrieves the text of the selected button and uses that text to fetch the associated column from the data frame. The results of running the **mean**, **median**, and **std** methods on that column are then displayed in the corresponding fields.

Implementation (Coding) of `hoopstatsapp`

The structure of the application module is familiar, with the addition of some file input to create the model:

```
"""
File: hoopstatsapp.py

The application for analyzing basketball stats.
"""

from hoopstatsview import HoopStatsView
import pandas as pd

def main():
    """Creates the data frame and view and starts the app."""
    frame = pd.read_csv("brogdonstats.csv")
    HoopStatsView(frame)

if __name__ == "__main__":
    main()
```

Implementation (Coding) of `HoopStatsView`

Most of the code for the view class sits in the __**init**__ method, which must lay out many components and organize them in panels. We include for this method just the layout of the text area and radio buttons; the layout of the labels and numeric fields is suppressed for brevity:

```
"""
File: hoopsstatsview.py
The view for viewing and analyzing basketball player statistics.
"""

from breezypythongui import EasyFrame
import pandas as pd
```

(continues)

```
class HoopStatsView(EasyFrame):

    def __init__(self, frame):
        """Creates and lays out window components
        to view and manipulate the model's data."""
        EasyFrame.__init__(self, title = "Basketball Stats")
        self.setSize(600, 400)
        self.frame = frame
        self.dataArea = self.addTextArea(text = self.frame.to_string(),
                                         row = 0,
                                         column = 0,
                                         columnspan = 2,
                                         height = 15)
        # Create a panel for the radio buttons
        self.radioGroup = self.addRadiobuttonGroup(row = 1,
                                                   column = 0)
        defaultRB = self.radioGroup.addRadiobutton(text = "MIN",
                                                   command = self.analyze)
        self.radioGroup.setSelectedButton(defaultRB)
        self.radioGroup.addRadiobutton(text = "FG%",
                                       command = self.analyze)
        self.radioGroup.addRadiobutton(text = "FT%",
                                       command = self.analyze)
        self.radioGroup.addRadiobutton(text = "REB",
                                       command = self.analyze)
        self.radioGroup.addRadiobutton(text = "AST",
                                       command = self.analyze)
        self.radioGroup.addRadiobutton(text = "PTS",
                                       command = self.analyze)
        # Create a panel for the output fields and add them here

        self.analyze()
```

Note several points:

1. Radio buttons are provided for some but not all of the columns of data; adding the remaining buttons is easy and is left as an exercise for you.

2. The radio button labeled **"MIN"** (for Minutes Played) is specified as the default radio button, meaning that it will be selected and the analysis results for column labeled **"MIN"** will be displayed when the window opens.

3. The event-handling method **analyze** is added as the **command** attribute of each radio button. This method will be triggered when a radio button is selected.

4. The **analyze** method is called as the last step in the **__init__** method, to perform the initial analysis before the window opens.

The implementation of the **analyze** method follows directly from its design:

```
# Event-handling method
def analyze(self):
    """Updates the view with the results of analysis."""
    columnLabel = self.radioGroup.getSelectedButton()["text"]
    column = self.frame[columnLabel]
    self.meanFld.setNumber(column.mean())
    self.medianFld.setNumber(column.median())
    self.stdFld.setNumber(column.std())
```

The complete code for this case study, in the files **hoopstatsapp.py**, **hoopstatsview.py**, and **reverselines.py**, as well as the CSV files **rawbrogdonstats.csv** and **brogdonstats.csv**, are available in the Data Files for this book.

Fail-Safe Programming

This chapter has presented the basic tools and techniques for acquiring data sets, cleaning them, preforming analyses, and visualizing results. However, it has barely touched the tip of the iceberg on this enormous field of study and application.

The operations of commerce and government are increasingly driven by data acquisition and analysis. Your mouse movements, gestures, voice, images, and geolocation can be used to track your past and present behavior, and sophisticated algorithms can be applied to these data to predict your future behavior. Needless to say, major legal and ethical issues are raised in collecting and analyzing data. Governments can use data analysis for search and rescue operations or to detect fraud. Governments can also use data analysis to disrupt legitimate political opposition. Businesses can use data analysis to improve search and suggest related services or resources that might enhance your life. Businesses can also use data analysis to nudge you to purchase things you don't need. You are encouraged to explore these issues further by consulting the selected readings in Appendix E.

Summary

- Data analysis discovers patterns and relationships in a set of data to support decisions or further processing.

- Data visualization displays patterns and relationships among data using graphical plots or charts.

- The mean, median, mode, and standard deviation are functions that provide information about patterns or relationships in a data set.

- A CSV file provides a useful way of sharing data among data analysis applications.

- The data frame and the series are useful structures for organizing data sets for analysis.

Key Terms

analytics	data visualization	normal distribution
bar chart	data warehouse	null value
big data	database	percentile
bimodal distribution	histogram	pie chart
CSV format	line plot	scatter plot
data analysis	machine learning	series
data frame	mean	standard deviation
data mining	median	variance
data set	mode	visualization
data science	multimodal distribution	

Review Questions

1. The mean of a given set of numbers refers to the

    a. average of the numbers.

    b. number that lies at the midpoint when the numbers are sorted.

    c. number that appears most frequently.

    d. average distance of the numbers from the mean.

2. The median of a given set of numbers refers to the

    a. average of the numbers.

    b. number that lies at the midpoint when the numbers are sorted.

    c. number that appears most frequently.

    d. average distance of the numbers from the mean.

3. The mode of a given set of numbers refers to the

    a. average of the numbers.

    b. number that lies at the midpoint when the numbers are sorted.

    c. number that appears most frequently.

    d. average distance of the numbers from the mean.

4. The standard deviation of a given set of numbers refers to the

   a. average of the numbers.

   b. number that lies at the midpoint when the numbers are sorted.

   c. number that appears most frequently.

   d. average distance of the numbers from the mean.

5. A scatter plot is useful for visualizing

   a. clusters of data.

   b. increasing or decreasing trends of data.

   c. values plotted along a continuous range.

   d. relative percentages of groups of data in a whole.

6. A pie chart is useful for visualizing

   a. clusters of data.

   b. increasing or decreasing trends of data.

   c. values plotted along a continuous range.

   d. relative percentages of groups of data in a whole.

7. A histogram is useful for visualizing

   a. clusters of data.

   b. increasing or decreasing trends of data.

   c. relative frequencies of data.

   d. relative percentages of groups of data in a whole.

8. A data frame is a structure that represents

   a. rows and columns in a multidimensional table of data.

   b. a single row or column of data.

   c. the boundary of a set of data in a graphical display.

   d. a snapshot of data in a list.

9. A series is a structure that represents

   a. rows and columns in a multidimensional table of data.

   b. a single row or column of data.

   c. the boundary of a set of data in a graphical display.

   d. a snapshot of data in a list.

10. The term CSV in the expression CSV file stands for

    a. comma-separated values.

    b. comma-spliced values.

    c. content-stored version.

    d. a popular pharmacy.

Programming Exercises

1. Complete the implementation of the **Student** class from the Analyzing Student Test Scores case study. Include a short tester program in a file named **studenttest.py** that exercises the new methods. (LO: 11.1)

2. This exercise assumes that you have completed Programming Exercise 1. Complete the implementation of the **StudentView** class from the Analyzing Student Test Scores case study. (LO: 11.1)

3. Add a command button named **Plot scores** to the user interface for the Analyzing Student Test Scores case study. When the user selects this button, the program displays a line plot of the student's test scores. You should plot the positions along the *x*-axis and the scores along the *y*-axis. (LO: 11.2)

4. Write a program in a file named **histogram.py** that displays the histogram depicted in Figure 11-7. (LO: 11.2)

5. Visit the website of the U.S. Bureau of Labor Statistics at **https://www.bls.gov/data/home.htm** and download the data for the average price of bread, as shown earlier in this chapter (there will be data for more recent years added since these words were written). Write a program in a file named **breadprice.py** that loads the data set and cleans it as you did earlier in this chapter. Then include code to display a line plot of the average price for each year in the table. (LO: 11.1, 11.2, 11.3)

6. The columns labeled FG, 3PT, and FT of the data set in the Analyzing Basketball Statistics case study do not show a single integer value but instead show values with the format `<makes-attempts>`, which is not suitable for the kind of data analysis performed on the other columns. For example, analysts might like to view the mean of free throws attempted as well as mean of the free throw percentage. You can correct this problem with a cleaning step that, for each such column:

   - removes it from the data frame

   - creates two new columns from this series, where the first column includes the numbers of makes and the second column includes the number of attempts

   - inserts the new pairs of columns into the data frame at the appropriate positions, with the appropriate column headings (for example, FTM and FTA)

   Define a function named `cleanStats` in the file **hoopstatsapp.py**. This function expects a data frame as an argument and returns the frame cleaned according to the steps listed previously. You should call this function after the frame is loaded from the CSV file and before it is passed to the `HoopStatsView` constructor. (LO: 11.2, 11.3)

7. This exercise assumes that you have completed Programming Exercise 6. Add radio buttons for the remaining columns of data to the program window of the Analyzing Basketball Statistics case study. (LO: 11.3)

8. Add a line plot feature to the program of the Analyzing Basketball Statistics case study. When the user selects a radio button, the data for a column are analyzed and the program displays the results as before, but the program also pops up a line plot of the selected column of data. The line plot's *y*-axis should be labeled with the name of the column heading. (LO: 11.2, 11.3)

Sorting and Filtering Data

Prompt

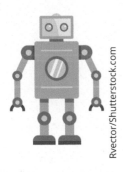

Rvector/Shutterstock.com

Ira Yapanda/Shutterstock.com

tele52/Shutterstock.com

All of the data that our robot Herby collects throughout the course of his collection of items and how it is done is an important component of the continued refinement of his processes and of the way in which our ERP and shipping processes work and function. As we are always on the lookout for better ways to serve our customers and increase profit margins, a more efficient and effective robotic staff will help in making that happen.

An important component of creating a more efficient set of processes is doing some thorough analysis, searing, sorting, and filtering of the data based on various criteria. Applications that are intelligent and can help to assist in finding patterns are a huge part of finding more efficient and effective ways to create data.

You've now been asked to perform some custom data analysis and create some scripting components that will search, sort, and aggregate the data to find those patterns. In this script, you will have the data set to import into your database and you will perform the following actions:

1. Average transaction product totals
2. Sorting transaction totals from highest to lowest using a bubble sort and using Python sorted function

Hints

With all of the skills that you've built over the course of this set of modules and assignments so far, you've worked with data types, branching logic, iteration, files, and libraries. You've been able to build out some console applications. These console applications could be used to automate any number of company activities and allow employees to focus on truly creative type work. One other skill that is important to work with is the ability to sort and filter data. There are a number of basic setup type of sorts, whether that is a bubble sort, which can be used to work with data and massage it into the required format, you'll notice that there are both basic iteration examples and also built-in functions that will help you to sort your data. Consider the following:

Examples

Sorting Example:

```
a = (2, 22, 4)
z = sorted(z)
print("Your list is "+z)
a = ("z", "c", "d", "b", "h", "f", "h", "k")
z = sorted(a, reverse=True)
print("Your list is "+z)
```

Average Example:

```
def getAverage(nums):
    numTot = 0
    for z in nums:
        numTot = numTot + z
    totAvg = numTot / len(nums)
    return totAvg
print("The average sale is", avgDSet([21,27,7,28,3]))
```

Answer

See assignment11Source.py

After Discussion

In this assignment, you've been asked to work with some basic data analysis and sorting. Organizations can become very successful with these classification of applications. While there are many off-the-shelf solutions that can be used to work with data, there are also many custom applications that can be used specifically for a department, specific data types, or organizations. The analysis that is performed can help companies to fine-tune their operations and to allocate resources, personnel, and budgetary needs. The work that you do with creating applications which can potentially pull data from multiple locations, combine, and sort/filter the data to produce the necessary output is extremely important.

## Chapter 12

Multithreading, Networks, and Client/ Server Programming

Learning Objectives

When you complete this chapter, you will be able to:

12.1 Describe the purpose of a thread, code an algorithm to run as a thread, and use conditions to solve a simple synchronization problem with threads.

12.2 Use conditions to support thread-safe access to shared data.

12.3 Create a simple client/server application on a network that uses threads to efficiently handle client requests.

So far in this book you have explored ways of solving problems by using multiple cooperating algorithms and data structures. Another commonly used strategy for problem solving involves the use of multiple **threads**. Threads describe processes that can run concurrently to solve a problem. They can also be organized in a system of **clients** and **servers**. For example, a web browser runs in a client thread and allows a user to view web pages that are sent by a web server, which runs in a server thread. Client and server threads can run concurrently on a single computer or can be distributed across several computers that are linked in a **network**. The technique of using multiple threads in a program is known as **multithreading**. This chapter offers an introduction to multithreading, networks, and client/server programming. Just enough material is provided to get you started with these topics; more complete surveys are available in advanced computer science courses.

12.1 Threads and Processes

You are aware that an algorithm describes a computational process that runs to completion. You may think of a **process** as a running algorithm or a program in execution. You are also aware that a process consumes resources, such as CPU (central processing unit) cycles and memory. Until now, you have associated an algorithm or a program with a single process and have assumed that this process runs on a single CPU. However, your program's process is not the only one that runs on your computer. Other processes could be the computer's operating system (which is always active), its web browser, and its email application, in addition to many subprocesses that support these top-level processes. A single program may also describe several processes that can run concurrently on your computer or on several networked computers. The following historical summary shows how this is the case.

Time-sharing operating systems: In the late 1950s and early 1960s, computer scientists developed the first time-sharing operating systems. These systems allow several programs to run concurrently on a single computer. Instead of giving their programs to a human scheduler to run one after the other on a single machine, users log in to the computer via remote terminals. They then run their programs. They have the illusion, if the system performs well, of having sole possession of the machine's resources (CPU, disk drives, printer, etc.). Behind the scenes, the operating system creates separate processes for these programs. The system gives each process a turn at the CPU and other resources, and it performs all the work of scheduling. When a process is about to be swapped out of the CPU, the system saves its state (the values of variables currently in play and the call stack for any active subroutines) and then restores the state of the process about to execute. If this procedure, called a **context switch**, happens rapidly, the illusion of concurrency is maintained. Time-sharing systems are still in widespread use in the form of web servers, email servers, print servers, and other kinds of servers on networked systems.

Multiprocessing systems: The early time-sharing systems allowed a single user to run one program and then return to the operating system to run another program before the first program is finished. The concept of a single user running several programs simultaneously was extended to desktop microcomputers in the late 1980s, when these machines became more powerful. For example, the Macintosh MultiFinder allowed a user to run a word processor, a spreadsheet, and the Finder (the file browser) concurrently and to switch focus from one application to another by selecting an application's window. Users of stand-alone computing devices now take this capability for granted. A related development was the ability of a program to start another program by "forking," or creating a new process. For example, a word processor might create another process to print a document in the background or run a real-time spell checker while the user is staring at the editor window thinking about the next words to type.

Networked or distributed systems: The late 1980s and early 1990s saw the rise of networked systems. At that time, the processes associated with a single program or with several programs began to be distributed across several CPUs linked by high-speed communication lines. Thus, for example, the web browser that appears to be running on your machine is actually making requests as a client to a web server application that runs on a multiuser machine at a remote location on the Internet. The problems of scheduling and running processes are more complex on a networked system, but the basic ideas are the same.

Parallel systems: As CPUs became less expensive and smaller, it became feasible to run a single program on several CPUs at once. **Parallel computing** is the discipline of building the hardware architectures, operating systems, and specialized algorithms for running a program on a cluster of processors. The multicore technology now found in all computers, from desktops to tablets to smartphones to watches, can be used to run a single program or multiple programs on several processors simultaneously.

Threads

Most modern computers, whether they are networked or stand-alone machines, represent some processes as threads. For example, a web browser uses one thread to load an image from the Internet while using another thread to format and display text. The Python virtual machine runs several threads that you have already used without realizing it. For example, the IDLE editor runs as a separate thread, as does your main Python application program. The garbage collector that recycles objects in your Python programs runs as a separate thread in the Python virtual machine. The event-driven loop in a GUI-based program runs in its own thread when you open the application's window.

In Python, a thread is an object like any other in that it can hold data, be stored in data structures, and be passed as arguments to methods. However, some code defined in a thread can also be executed as a process. To execute this code, a thread's class must implement a **run** method.

During its lifetime, a thread can be in various states. **Figure 12-1** shows some of the states in the lifetime of a Python thread. In this diagram, the box labeled "The ready queue" is a data structure, whereas the box labeled "The CPU" is a hardware resource. The thread states are the labeled ovals.

Figure 12-1   States in the life of a thread

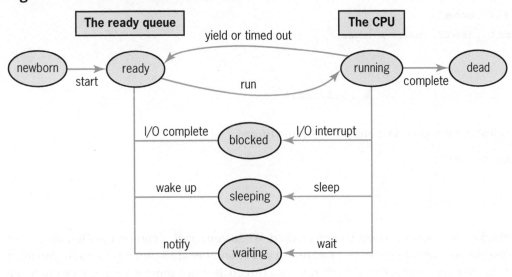

After it is created, a thread remains newborn and inactive until someone runs its **start** method. Running this method also makes the thread "ready" and places a reference to it in the **ready queue**. A queue is a data structure that enforces first-come, first-served access to a single resource. The resource in this case is the CPU, which can execute the instructions of just one thread at a time. A newly started thread's **run** method is also activated. However, before its first instruction can be executed, the thread must wait its turn in the ready queue for access to the CPU. After the thread gets access to the CPU and executes some instructions in its **run** method, the thread can lose access to the CPU in several ways:

- **Time-out**: Most computers running Python programs automatically time-out a running thread every few milliseconds. The process of automatically timing-out, also known as **time slicing**, has the effect of pausing the running thread's execution and sending it to the rear of the ready queue. The thread at the front of the ready queue is then given access to the CPU.

- **Sleep**: A thread can be put to sleep for a given number of milliseconds. When the thread wakes up, it goes to the rear of the ready queue.

- **Block**: A thread can wait for some event, such as user input, to occur. When a blocked thread is notified that an event has occurred, it goes to the rear of the ready queue.

- **Wait**: A thread can voluntarily relinquish the CPU to wait for some condition to become true. A waiting thread can be notified when the condition becomes true and move again to the rear of the ready queue.

When a thread gives up the CPU, the computer saves its state (the values of its instance variables and data on its call stack), so that when the thread returns to the CPU, its **run** method can pick up where it left off. As mentioned earlier, the process of saving or restoring a thread's state is called a context switch.

When a thread's **run** method has executed its last instruction, the thread dies as a process but continues to exist as an object. A thread object can also die if it raises an exception that is not handled.

Python's **threading** module includes resources for creating threads and managing multithreaded applications. The most common way to create a thread is to define a class that extends the class **threading.Thread**. The new class should include a **run** method that executes the algorithm in the new thread. The **start** method places a thread at the rear of the ready queue. The next code segment defines a simple thread class that prints its name.

```
from threading import Thread


class MyThread (Thread):
    """A thread that prints its name."""

    def __init__(self, name):
        Thread.__init__(self, name = name)


    def run(self):
        print("Hello, my name is %s" % self.name)
```

The session that follows instantiates this class and starts up the thread.

```
>>> process = MyThread("Ken")
>>> process.start()
Hello, my name is Ken
```

The thread's **start** method automatically invokes its **run** method. When you run this code in the IDLE shell, your new thread runs to completion but does not appear to quit and return you to another shell prompt. To do so, you must press Control-C to interrupt the process. Because IDLE itself runs in a thread, it is not generally a good idea to test a multithreaded application in that environment. From now on, you will launch Python programs containing threads from the operating system's terminal prompt rather than from an IDLE window. Here is the code for a **main** function that starts up a thread and runs to a normal termination at the terminal:

```
def main():
    MyThread("Ken").start()


if __name__ == "__main__":
    main()
```

The **Thread** class maintains the instance variable **name** for the thread's name. **Table 12-1** lists some important **Thread** methods.

Table 12-1   Some **thread** methods

Thread Method	**What it Does**
__init__(name = None)	Initializes the thread's name
run()	Executes when the thread acquires the CPU
start()	Makes the new thread ready; raises an exception if run more than once
isAlive()	Returns **True** if the thread is alive or **False** otherwise

Other important resources used with threads include the function **time.sleep** and the class **threading. Condition**. Next, consider some example programs that illustrate the use of these resources.

Sleeping Threads

As a first example, you develop a program that allows the user to start several threads. Each thread does not do much when started; it simply prints a message, goes to sleep for a random number of seconds, and then prints a message and terminates on waking up. The program allows the user to specify the number of threads to run and the maximum sleep time. When a thread is started, it prints a message identifying itself and its sleep time and then goes to sleep. When a thread wakes up, it prints another message identifying itself. A session with this program is shown in **Figure 12-2**.

Note the following points about the example in Figure 12-2:

Figure 12-2   A run of the sleeping threads program

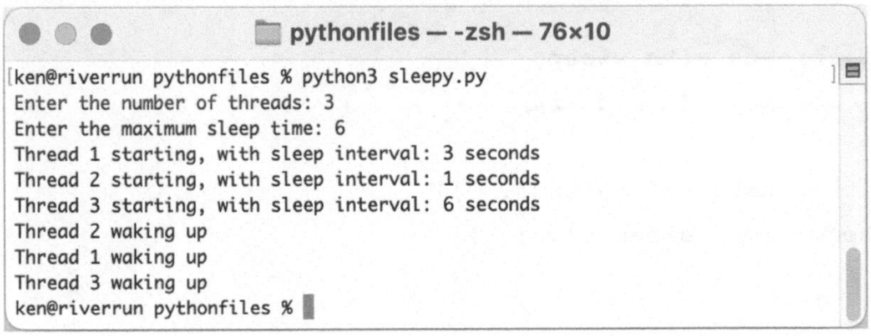

```
[ken@riverrun pythonfiles % python3 sleepy.py
Enter the number of threads: 3
Enter the maximum sleep time: 6
Thread 1 starting, with sleep interval: 3 seconds
Thread 2 starting, with sleep interval: 1 seconds
Thread 3 starting, with sleep interval: 6 seconds
Thread 2 waking up
Thread 1 waking up
Thread 3 waking up
ken@riverrun pythonfiles %
```

- When a thread goes to sleep, the next thread has an opportunity to acquire the CPU and display its information in the view.

- Threads with random sleep times do not necessarily wake up in the order in which they were started. The size of the sleep interval determines this order. In Figure 12-2, thread 2 has the shortest sleep time, so it wakes up first. Thread 1 wakes up before thread 3, because thread 3 has the longest sleep time.

The program consists of the class **SleepyThread**, a subclass of **Thread**, and a **main** function. When called within a thread's **run** method, the function **time.sleep** puts that thread to sleep for the specified number of seconds. Here is the code:

```
"""
File: sleepy.py
Illustrates concurrency with multiple threads.
"""

import random, time
from threading import Thread

class SleepyThread(Thread):
    """Represents a sleepy thread."""

    def __init__(self, number, sleepMax):
        """Create a thread with the given name
        and a random sleep interval less than the
        maximum."""
        Thread.__init__(self, name = "Thread " + str(number))
        self.sleepInterval = random.randint(1, sleepMax)

    def run(self):
        """Print the thread's name and sleep interval
```

```
            and sleep for that interval. Print the name
            again at wake-up."""
            print("%s starting, with sleep interval: %d seconds" % \
                    (self.name, self.sleepInterval))
            time.sleep(self.sleepInterval)
            print("%s waking up" % self.name)

def main():
    """Create the user's number of threads with sleep
    intervals less than the user's maximum. Then start
    the threads."""
    numThreads = int(input("Enter the number of threads: "))
    sleepMax = int(input("Enter the maximum sleep time: "))
    threadList = []
    for count in range(numThreads):
        threadList.append(SleepyThread(count + 1, sleepMax))
    for thread in threadList: thread.start()

if __name__ == "__main__":
    main()
```

Producer, Consumer, and Synchronization

In the previous example, the threads ran independently and did not interact. However, in many applications, threads interact by sharing data. One such interaction is the **producer/consumer relationship**. Think of an assembly line in a factory. Worker A, at the beginning of the line, produces an item that is then ready for access by the next person on the line, Worker B. In this case, Worker A is the producer, and Worker B is the consumer. Worker B then becomes the producer, processing the item in some way until it is ready for Worker C, and so on.

Three requirements must be met for the assembly line to function properly:

1. A producer must produce each item before a consumer consumes it.

2. Each item must be consumed before the producer produces the next item.

3. A consumer must consume each item just once.

Let us now consider a computer simulation of the producer/consumer relationship. In its simplest form, the relationship has only two threads: a producer and a consumer. They share a single data cell that contains an integer. The producer sleeps for a random interval, writes an integer to the shared cell, and generates the next integer to be written, until the integer reaches an upper bound. The consumer sleeps for a random interval and reads the integer from the shared cell, until the integer reaches the upper bound. **Figure 12-3** shows two runs of this program. The user enters the number of accesses (data items produced and consumed). The output announces that the producer and consumer threads have started up and shows when each thread accesses the shared data.

Figure 12-3 Two runs of the producer/consumer program

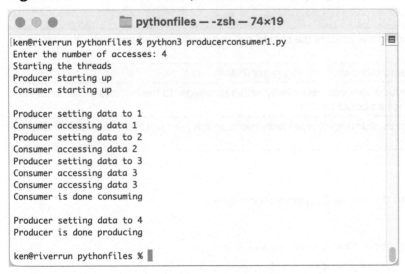

```
[ken@riverrun pythonfiles % python3 producerconsumer1.py
Enter the number of accesses: 4
Starting the threads
Producer starting up
Consumer starting up

Producer setting data to 1
Consumer accessing data 1
Producer setting data to 2
Consumer accessing data 2
Producer setting data to 3
Consumer accessing data 3
Consumer accessing data 3
Consumer is done consuming

Producer setting data to 4
Producer is done producing

ken@riverrun pythonfiles %
```

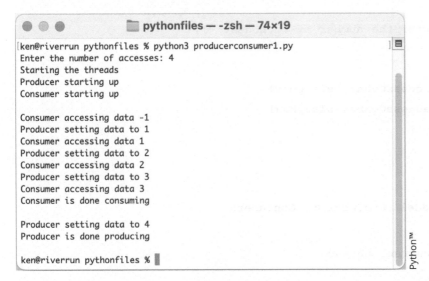

```
[ken@riverrun pythonfiles % python3 producerconsumer1.py
Enter the number of accesses: 4
Starting the threads
Producer starting up
Consumer starting up

Consumer accessing data -1
Producer setting data to 1
Consumer accessing data 1
Producer setting data to 2
Consumer accessing data 2
Producer setting data to 3
Consumer accessing data 3
Consumer is done consuming

Producer setting data to 4
Producer is done producing

ken@riverrun pythonfiles %
```

In the first run of the program, the producer happens to update the shared data each time before the consumer accesses it. However, some bad things happen in the second run of the program:

1. The consumer accesses the shared cell before the producer has written its first datum.
2. The producer and consumer then appear to access the shared cell in the proper order, with the data values 1 through 3 each being produced before it is consumed.
3. After the producer writes its final value, 4, there is no consumer thread alive to consume it, because this thread wasted an access at the beginning of the process.

Although the producer always produces all of its data, the consumer can access data that are not there, can miss data, and can access the same data more than once. These are known as **synchronization problems**. Before understanding why they occur, you should learn the essential parts of the program itself (**producerconsumer1.py**), which consists of the four resources in **Table 12-2**.

Table 12-2 The classes and `main` function in the producer/consumer program

Class or Function	Role and Responsibility
`main`	Manages the user interface; creates the shared cell and producer and consumer threads and starts the threads
`SharedCell`	Represents the shared data, which is an integer (initially −1)
`Producer`	Represents the producer process; repeatedly writes an integer to the cell and increments the integer until it reaches an upper bound
`Consumer`	Represents the consumer process; repeatedly reads an integer from the cell, until it reaches an upper bound

The code for the **main** function is similar to the one in the previous example:

```python
def main():
    """Get the number of accesses from the user, create a
    shared cell, and create and start up a producer and a
    consumer."""
    accessCount = int(input("Enter the number of accesses: "))
    sleepMax = 4
    cell = SharedCell()
    producer = Producer(cell, accessCount, sleepMax)
    consumer = Consumer(cell, accessCount, sleepMax)
    print("Starting the threads")
    producer.start()
    consumer.start()
```

Here is the code for the classes **SharedCell**, **Producer**, and **Consumer**:

```python
import time, random
from threading import Thread, current_thread


class SharedCell(object):
    """Shared data for the producer/consumer problem."""

    def __init__(self):
        """Data undefined at startup."""
        self.data = -1

    def setData(self, data):
        """Producer's method to write to shared data."""
        print("%s setting data to %d" % \
            (current_thread().name, data))
        self.data = data

    def getData(self):
        """Consumer's method to read from shared data."""
```

```
        print("%s accessing data %d" % \
              (current_thread().name, self.data))
        return self.data

class Producer(Thread):
    """A producer of data in a shared cell."""

    def __init__(self, cell, accessCount, sleepMax):
        """Create a producer with the given shared cell,
        number of accesses, and maximum sleep interval."""
        Thread.__init__(self, name = "Producer")
        self.accessCount = accessCount
        self.cell = cell
        self.sleepMax = sleepMax

    def run(self):
        """Announce start-up, sleep and write to shared
        cell the given number of times, and announce
        completion."""
        print("%s starting up" % self.name)
        for count in range(self.accessCount):
            time.sleep(random.randint(1, self.sleepMax))
            self.cell.setData(count + 1)
        print("%s is done producing\n" % self.name)

class Consumer(Thread):
    """A consumer of data in a shared cell."""

    def __init__(self, cell, accessCount, sleepMax):
        """Create a consumer with the given shared cell,
        number of accesses, and maximum sleep interval."""
        Thread.__init__(self, name = "Consumer")
        self.accessCount = accessCount
        self.cell = cell
        self.sleepMax = sleepMax

    def run(self):
        """Announce start-up, sleep, and read from shared
        cell the given number of times, and announce completion."""
        print("%s starting up" % self.name)
        for count in range(self.accessCount):
            time.sleep(random.randint(1, self.sleepMax))
            value = self.cell.getData()
        print("%s is done consuming\n" % self.name)
```

The cause of the synchronization problems is not hard to spot in this code. On each pass through their main loops, the threads sleep for a random interval of time. Thus, if the consumer thread has a shorter interval than the producer thread on a given cycle, the consumer wakes up sooner and accesses the shared cell before the producer has a chance to write the next datum (including the initial datum). Conversely, if the producer thread wakes up sooner, it accesses the shared data and writes the next datum before the consumer has a chance to read the previous datum.

To solve this problem, you need to synchronize the actions of the producer and consumer threads. In addition to holding data, the shared cell must be in one of two states: writeable or not writeable. The cell is writeable if it has not yet been written to (at start-up) or if it has just been read from. The cell is not writeable if it has just been written to. These two conditions can now control the callers of the **setData** and **getData** methods in the **SharedCell** class as follows:

1. While the cell is writeable, the caller of **getData** (the consumer) must wait or suspend activity, until the producer writes a datum. When this happens, the cell becomes not writeable, the other thread (the producer) is notified to resume activity, and the data are returned (to the consumer).

2. While the cell is not writeable, the caller of **setData** (the producer) must wait or suspend activity, until the consumer reads a datum. When this happens, the cell becomes writeable, the other thread (the consumer) is notified to resume activity, and the data are modified (by the producer).

To implement these restrictions, the **SharedCell** class now includes two additional instance variables:

1. A Boolean flag named **writeable**. If this flag is **True**, only writing to the cell is allowed; if it is **False**, only reading from the cell is allowed.

2. An instance of the **threading.Condition** class. This object allows each thread to block until the Boolean flag is in the appropriate state to write to or read from the cell.

A **Condition** object is like a lock on a resource. When a thread acquires this lock, no other thread can access the resource, even if the acquiring thread is timed out. After a thread successfully acquires the lock, it can do its work or relinquish the lock in one of two ways:

1. By calling the condition's **wait** method. This method causes the thread to block until it is notified that it can continue its work.

2. By calling the condition's **release** method. This method unlocks the resource and allows it to be acquired by other threads.

When other threads attempt to acquire a locked resource, they block until the lock is released or a thread holding the lock calls the condition's **notify** method. To summarize, the pattern for a thread accessing a resource with a lock is the following:

```
Run acquire on the condition
While it's not OK to do the work
    Run wait on the condition
Do the work with the resource
Run notify on the condition
Run release on the condition
```

Computer scientists call the step labeled **Do the work with the resource** a critical section. The code in a critical section must be run in a thread-safe manner, meaning that the thread executing this code must be able to finish it before another thread accesses the same resource. **Table 12-3** lists the methods of the **Condition** class.

Table 12-3 The methods of the `Condition` class

Condition Method	What it Does
`acquire()`	Attempts to acquire the lock; blocks if the lock is already taken
`release()`	Relinquishes the lock, leaving it to be acquired by others
`wait()`	Releases the lock, blocks the current thread until another thread calls `notify` or `notifyAll` on the same condition, and then reacquires the lock; if multiple threads are waiting, the `notify` method wakes up only one of the threads, while `notifyAll` always wakes up all of the threads
`notify()`	Lets the next thread waiting on the lock know that it's available
`notifyAll()`	Lets all threads waiting on the lock know that it's available

Here is the code that shows the addition of synchronization to the **SharedCell** class (**producerconsumer2.py**):

```python
import time, random
from threading import Thread, current_thread, Condition

class SharedCell(object):
    """Shared data that sequences writing before reading."""

    def __init__(self):
        """Can produce but not consume at startup."""
        self.data = -1
        self.writeable = True
        self.condition = Condition()

    def setData(self, data):
        """Second caller must wait until someone has
        consumed the data before resetting it."""
        self.condition.acquire()
        while not self.writeable:
            self.condition.wait()
        print("%s setting data to %d" % \
              (current_thread().name, data))
        self.data = data
        self.writeable = False
        self.condition.notify()
        self.condition.release()

    def getData(self):
        """Caller must wait until someone has produced the
        data before accessing it."""
        self.condition.acquire()
        while self.writeable:
```

```
        self.condition.wait()
    print("%s accessing data %d" % \
          (current_thread().name, self.data))
    self.writeable = True
    self.condition.notify()
    self.condition.release()
    return self.data
```

Exercise 12-1

1. Describe the purpose of a thread's **run** method.

2. What is time slicing?

3. What is a synchronization problem?

4. What is the difference between a sleeping thread and a waiting thread?

5. Give a real-world example of the producer-consumer problem.

12.2 The Readers and Writers Problem

In many applications, threads may share data as readers and writers in a looser manner than producers and consumers. Unlike producers and consumers, readers and writers may access the shared data in any order, and there may be multiple readers and writers. For example, different threads may access a database, either in primary memory or secondary file storage, to access or modify the state of the data. In this situation, also known as the **readers and writers problem**:

- readers access the data to observe it

- writers access the data to modify it

- only one writer can be writing at a given time, and that writer must be able to finish before other writers or readers can begin writing or reading

- multiple readers can read the shared data concurrently without waiting for each other to finish, but all active readers must finish before a writer starts writing

Reader and writer threads must be synchronized around the shared data to avoid having a reader or writer access the data at an inappropriate moment. For example, although it's okay for two readers to access the shared data at the same time, you would not want two writers to do so. Moreover, you would not want a writer and a reader to access the shared data at the same time.

Some Python data structures, such as lists and dictionaries, are already thread-safe because they provide automatic support for synchronizing multiple readers and writers. Thus, in the case of a dictionary, Python guarantees that multiple threads may access the data to read from it (using any of the operations such as **get**, the subscript, or **len**). But if a thread is writing to a dictionary (using the subscript or **pop**), no other thread may read or write until the current writer completes its operation.

By contrast, many other objects, including those that might be contained in a list or a dictionary, are not themselves thread-safe. Examples include many of the new types of objects you defined in Chapter 10, such as **SavingsAccount** objects. In these cases, you would need to include extra machinery to ensure thread-safety, when using such objects in a multithreaded program.

A solution to the readers and writers problem is to encase the shared data in a shared cell object, with a locking mechanism to synchronize access for multiple readers and writers. The retooled shared cell class (in **sharedcell.py**) can be used in any application to synchronize readers and writers. The interface for this resource is listed in **Table 12-4**.

Table 12-4 `SharedCell` methods

`SharedCell` **Method**	**What it Does**
`SharedCell(data)`	Constructor; creates a shared cell containing `data`.
`read(readerFunction)`	Applies `readerFunction` to the cell's shared data in a critical section. `readerFunction` must be a function of one argument, which is of the same type as the shared data. The function's code should only observe, not modify, the data. Returns the result of this function.
`write(writerFunction)`	Applies `writerFunction` to the cell's shared data in a critical section. `writerFunction` must be a function of one argument, which is of the same type as the shared data. The function's code can observe or modify the data. Returns the result of this function.

Using the `SharedCell` Class

To see how a shared cell is used, suppose that readers and writers must access a common **SavingsAccount** object of the type discussed in Chapter 10. Readers can use the **getBalance** method to observe the account's balance, while writers can use the **deposit**, **withdraw**, or **computeInterest** methods to make changes to the account's balance. But they must use these methods in a thread-safe manner, and that's where the **SharedCell** resource comes into play. Assume that you create a shared cell containing a **SavingsAccount** object for multiple readers and writers, as follows:

```
account = SavingsAccount(name = "Ken", balance = 100.00)
cell = SharedCell(account)
```

Then at some point, a reader could run the code

```
print("The account balance is ",
        cell.read(lambda account: account.getBalance()))
```

to display the account's balance. A writer could run the code

```
amount = 200.00
cell.write(lambda account: account.deposit(amount))
```

to deposit $200.00 into the account.

Note the use of Python's **lambda** expression, introduced in Chapter 7. The syntax of the **lambda** expressions used here is

```
lambda <parameter name>: <expression>
```

When Python sees a **lambda** expression, it creates a function to be applied later. When this function is called, in the **read** or **write** method, the function's single parameter becomes the data object encased in the shared cell. The **lambda**'s expression is then evaluated in a critical section. This expression should contain an operation on the encased object. The operation's value is then returned. Although the construction and use of **lambda** expressions might seem challenging at first, they provide a clean and powerful way to structure the shared cell abstraction for any readers and writers.

Implementing the Interface of the `SharedCell` Class

Two locks or conditions are needed to synchronize multiple readers and writers: one on which the readers wait and the other on which the writers wait. Two other data values belong to the shared cell's state: a Boolean value to indicate whether a writer is currently writing, and a counter to track the number of readers currently reading (remember that only one writer can be writing, but many readers can be concurrently reading).

Consequently, the instance variables of a `SharedCell` object include the shared data object named `data`, two conditions named `okToRead` and `okToWrite`, a Boolean variable named `writing`, and an integer variable named `readerCount`. Here is the code for the `__init__` method:

```
class SharedCell(object):
    """Synchronizes readers and writers around shared data,
    to support thread-safe reading and writing."""

    def __init__(self, data):
        """Sets up the conditions and the count of
        active readers."""
        self.data = data
        self.writing = False
        self.readerCount = 0
        self.okToRead = Condition()
        self.okToWrite = Condition()
```

Note that the user of a shared cell object will pass the shared data to the cell when it is instantiated. This will allow the shared cell to be used for any kind of data that you want to make thread-safe for reading and writing.

The next step is to develop the code for accessing the shared cell for reading and writing. Recall that the `SharedCell` class for the producer-consumer problem includes the methods `setData` and `getData` for the use of the producer and consumer threads, respectively. For the readers and writers problem, there are two analogous methods, named `read` and `write`, for the use of reader and writer threads, respectively (see Table 12-4). You'll also recall that the methods `getData` and `setData` have a similar structure. They each aim to acquire access to a single lock on the shared data, run a critical section of code, and then release the lock. The design of the methods `read` and `write` also has a similar pattern, even though they are concerned with two locks, as shown in the following pseudocode:

```
Acquire access to the two locks on the shared data
Perform actions on the data in the critical section
Release access to the two locks on the shared data
```

Because readers and writers have different mechanisms for acquiring and releasing the locks, package this code in the helper methods `beginRead`, `endRead`, `beginWrite`, and `endWrite`. Likewise, the code to be executed in the critical section will vary with the application, as one can read or write in many different ways. Therefore, package this code in a function that gets passed as an argument to the `read` and `write` methods. This function expects one argument, a data object of the type encased within the shared cell. The code of the function runs an accessor method on its argument for a reader or runs a mutator method on this argument for a writer. In either case, the `read` or `write` method returns the result. Here is the code for the `SharedCell` methods `read` and `write`:

```
def read(self, readerFunction):
    """Observe the data in the shared cell."""
    self.beginRead()
    # Enter the reader's critical section
    result = readerFunction(self.data)
    # Exit the reader's critical section
```

```
    self.endRead()
    return result

def write(self, writerFunction):
    """Modify the data in the shared cell."""
    self.beginWrite()
    # Enter the writer's critical section
    result = writerFunction(self.data)
    # Exit the writer's critical section
    self.endWrite()
    return result
```

The beauty of these operations is their abstract and general character: they will work with any type of data you want to share among threads, and with any operations that can observe (read) or modify (write) the shared data.

Implementing the Helper Methods of the `SharedCell` Class

Our final task is to tackle the implementation of the methods that acquire and release the locks for reading and writing. As in the producer–consumer problem, a thread will be either executing in the CPU (the current thread), active on the ready queue (ready), or asleep or waiting on a condition (blocked). When multiple threads wait on a condition, they go onto a queue associated with that condition. Python's `Condition` class has an instance variable, named `_waiters`, which refers to a condition's queue. Armed with this information, you can now consider the code for the methods `beginRead` and `endRead`, which acquire and release access to the critical section for readers.

In `beginRead`, the reader thread must wait on its condition if a writer is currently writing or writers are waiting on their condition. Otherwise, the reader is free to increment the count of active readers, notify the next reader waiting on its condition, and enter the critical section. Here is the code for method `beginRead`:

```
def beginRead(self):
    """Waits until a writer is not writing or the writers
    condition queue is empty. Then increments the reader
    count and notifies the next waiting reader."""
    self.okToRead.acquire()
    self.okToWrite.acquire()
    while self.writing or len(self.okToWrite._waiters) > 0:
        self.okToRead.wait()
    self.readerCount += 1
    self.okToRead.notify()
```

When a reader is finished in its critical section, the method `endRead` decrements the count of active readers. It then notifies the next waiting writer, if there are no active readers:

```
def endRead(self):
    """Notifies a waiting writer if there are
    no active readers."""
    self.readerCount -= 1
    if self.readerCount == 0:
        self.okToWrite.notify()
    self.okToWrite.release()
    self.okToRead.release()
```

Note that `beginRead` acquires both locks and `endRead` releases both locks.

The methods `beginWrite` and `endWrite` show a similar pattern. A writer can enter its critical section if there is no current writer and there are no active readers. When leaving its critical section, a writer notifies the next reader waiting on its condition, if there are any such readers. Otherwise, it notifies the next waiting writer. Here is the code for these two methods:

```python
def beginWrite(self):
    """Can write only when someone else is not
    writing and there are no readers ready."""
    self.okToWrite.acquire()
    self.okToRead.acquire()
    while self.writing or self.readerCount != 0:
        self.okToWrite.wait()
    self.writing = True


def endWrite(self):
    """Notify the next waiting writer if the readers
    condition queue is empty. Otherwise, notify the
    next waiting reader."""
    self.writing = False
    if len(self.okToRead._waiters) > 0:
        self.okToRead.notify()
    else:
        self.okToWrite.notify()
    self.okToRead.release()
    self.okToWrite.release()
```

Testing the `SharedCell` Class with a `Counter` Object

Figure 12-4 shows a run of a tester program that creates a shared cell on a `Counter` object.

Figure 12-4　A run of the readers and writers program

```
[ken@riverrun pythonfiles % python3 readersandwriters.py
Creating reader threads.
Creating writer threads.
Starting the threads.
Reader1 starting up
Reader2 starting up
Reader3 starting up
Reader4 starting up
Writer1 starting up
Writer2 starting up
Reader1 is done getting 0
Reader2 is done getting 0
Reader3 is done getting 0
Writer1 is done incrementing to 1
Reader4 is done getting 1
Writer2 is done incrementing to 2
ken@riverrun pythonfiles %
```

At start-up, the program wraps a shared cell around a new `Counter` object. The program then starts several reader and writer threads that access the shared cell. The readers print the current value of the counter, whereas the writers increment and print the updated value. As in the producer–consumer example, threads begin by sleeping a random interval, so they arrive at the shared cell in a random order. As you can see, all of the threads obtain access to the shared counter, and the counter retains its integrity throughout the process. The coding of this program, which is similar in structure to the producer-consumer program, is left as an exercise for you.

Defining a Thread-Safe Class

This chapter mentioned earlier that Python data structures such as lists and dictionaries are thread-safe, but the data objects contained therein might not be. For example, the dictionary that contains the accounts in the **Bank** class of Chapter 10 is thread-safe, but the individual accounts, of type **SavingsAccount**, are not. How can you use the technology of the shared cell to fix this problem?

The solution is to apply a design pattern known as the **decorator pattern**. In this strategy, you define a new class that has the same interface or set of methods as the class that it "decorates." Thus, programmers can substitute objects of this new class wherever they have used objects of the decorated class. **Figure 12-5** shows the decorator relationship between two classes, **ThreadSafeSavingsAccount** and the class it decorates, **SavingsAccount**.

Figure 12-5   Using the decorator pattern

The new class encases an object of the decorated class, as well as other information necessary to accomplish its decoration. When the programmer calls a method on an object of the new class, the object behaves just as it did before, but with extra functionality—in this case, thread-safety. The beauty of this solution is that none of the code in the application must change, except for the name of the class being decorated. For example, applications that create instances of **SavingsAccount** need only change this name to **ThreadSafeSavingsAccount**, and they can make thread-safe accounts available to multiple readers and writers.

The code for the **ThreadSafeSavingsAccount** class (**threadsafesavingsaccount.py**) contains a **SharedCell** object, which in turn contains a **SavingsAccount** object. The constructor for **ThreadSafeSavingsAccount** creates a new **SavingsAccount** object and passes this to a new **SharedCell** object, as follows:

```
from savingsaccount import SavingsAccount
from sharedcell import SharedCell


class ThreadSafeSavingsAccount(object):
    """This class represents a thread-safe savings account
    with the owner's name, PIN, and balance."""

    def __init__(self, name, pin, balance = 0.0):
        """Wrap a new account in a shared cell for
        thread-safety."""
        account = SavingsAccount(name, pin, balance)
        self.cell = SharedCell(account)
```

The other methods in **ThreadSafeSavingsAccount** observe or modify the data in the account by running the **read** or **write** methods on the shared cell. For example, here is the code for the **getBalance** and **deposit** methods:

```
def getBalance(self):
    """Returns the current balance."""
    return self.cell.read(lambda account: account.getBalance())
```

```
def deposit(self, amount):
    """If the amount is valid, adds it
    to the balance and returns None;
    otherwise, returns an error message."""
    return self.cell.write(lambda account: account.deposit(amount))
```

The remaining methods in **ThreadSafeSavingsAccount** follow a similar pattern. The only change you need to make in the **bank** module is where you create accounts to test the module. For example, the function **createBank** now adds the new type of account with the statement

```
bank.add(ThreadSafeSavingsAccount(name, str(pinNumber),
                                  balance))
```

Exercise 12-2

1. Give two real-world examples of the readers and writers problem.

2. State two ways in which the readers and writers problem is different from the producer–consumer problem.

3. Describe how you would make the **Student** class from Chapter 10 thread-safe for readers and writers.

4. Define a new class called **PCCell**. This class provides an abstraction of a shared cell for the producer–consumer problem. The design pattern should be similar for the one presented for the shared cell for readers and writers, but it should use the mechanism specific to the producer–consumer situation.

12.3 Networks, Clients, and Servers

Clients and servers are applications or processes that can run locally on a single computer or remotely across a network of computers. As explained in the following sections, the resources required for this type of application are IP addresses, sockets, and threads.

IP Addresses

Every computer on a network has a unique identifier called an **IP address** (IP stands for Internet Protocol). This address can be specified either as an **IP number** or as an **IP name**. An IP number typically has the form *ddd.ddd.ddd.ddd*, where each *d* is a digit. The number of digits to the right or the left of a decimal point may vary but does not exceed three. For example, the IP number of the author's office computer might be 137.112.194.77. Because IP numbers can be difficult to remember, people customarily use an IP name to specify an IP address. For example, the IP name of the author's computer might be **lambertk**.

Python's **socket** module includes two functions that can look up these items of information. These functions are listed in **Table 12-5**, followed by a short session showing their use.

Table 12-5   **socket** functions for IP addresses

Socket Function	What it Does
gethostname()	Returns the IP name of the host computer running the Python interpreter; raises an exception if the computer does not have an IP address
gethostbyname(ipName)	Returns the IP number of the computer whose IP name is ipName; raises an exception if ipName cannot be found

```
>>> from socket import *
>>> gethostname()
'riverrun.home'
>>> gethostbyname(gethostname())
'193.169.1.209'
>>> gethostbyname("Ken")
Traceback (most recent call last):
  File "<pyshell#3>", line 1, in <module>
    gethostbyname("Ken")
socket.gaierror: [Errno 8] nodename nor servname provided, or not known
```

Note that these functions raise exceptions if they cannot locate the information. To handle this problem, one can embed these function calls in a **try-except** statement. The next code segment recovers from an unknown IP address error by printing the exception's error message:

```
try:
    print(gethostbyname("Ken"))
except Exception as exception:
    print(exception)
```

When developing a network application, the programmer can first try it out on a local host—that is, on a standalone computer that may or may not be connected to the Internet. The computer's IP name in this case is **"localhost"**, a name that is standard for any computer. The IP number of a computer that acts as a local host is distinct from its IP number as an Internet host, as shown in the next session:

```
>>> gethostbyname(gethostname())
'196.128.1.159'
>>> gethostbyname("localhost")
'127.0.0.1'
```

When the programmer is satisfied that the application is working correctly on a local host, the application can then be deployed on the Internet host simply by changing the IP address. The discussion that follows uses a local host to develop network applications.

Ports, Servers, and Clients

Clients connect to servers via objects known as ports. A port serves as a channel through which several clients can exchange data with the same server or with different servers. Ports are usually specified by numbers. Some ports are dedicated to special servers or tasks. For example, almost every computer reserves port number 13 for the day/time server, which allows clients to obtain the date and time. Port number 80 is reserved for a web server, and so forth. Most computers also have hundreds or even thousands of free ports available for use by any network applications.

Sockets and a Day/Time Client Script

You can write a Python script that is a client to a server. To do this, you need to use a socket. A socket is an object that serves as a communication link between a single server process and a single client process. You can create and open several sockets on the same port of a host computer. **Figure 12-6** shows the relationships between a host computer, ports, servers, clients, and sockets.

Figure 12-6   Setup of day/time host and clients

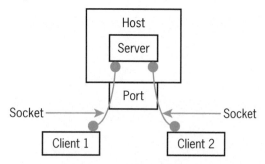

A Python day/time client script uses the **socket** module introduced earlier. This script does the following:

- Creates a socket object
- Opens the socket on a free port of the local host; use a large number, 6000, for this port
- Reads and decodes the day/time from the socket
- Displays the day/time

Here is a Python script that performs these tasks:

```python
"""
Client for obtaining the day and time.
"""
from socket import *
from codecs import decode
HOST = "localhost"
PORT = 6000
BUFSIZE = 1024
ADDRESS = (HOST, PORT)
server = socket(AF_INET, SOCK_STREAM)
server.connect(ADDRESS)
dayAndTime = decode(server.recv(BUFSIZE), "ascii")
print(dayAndTime)
server.close()
```

Although you cannot run this script until you write and launch the server program, **Figure 12-7** shows the client's anticipated output.

Figure 12-7   The user interface of the day/time client script

```
● ● ●              📁 pythonfiles — -zsh — 80×7
Last login: Sat Oct  1 10:55:59 on ttys000                    ▤
[ken@riverrun ~ % cd pythonfiles                            ]
[ken@riverrun pythonfiles % python3 timeclient.py           ]
Sat Oct  1 10:57:51 2022
Have a nice day!
ken@riverrun pythonfiles % ▮
```

As you can see, a Python socket is fairly easy to set up and use. A socket resembles a file object, in that the programmer opens it, receives data from it, and closes it when finished. We now explain these steps in the client script in more detail.

The script creates a socket by running the function **socket** in the **socket** module. This function returns a new socket object, when given a socket family and a socket type as arguments. The family **AF_INET** and the type **SOCK_STREAM**, both **socket** module constants, are used in all of the following examples.

To connect the socket to a host computer, you run the socket's **connect** method. This method expects as an argument a tuple containing the host's IP address and a port number. In this case, these values are **"localhost"** and 6000, respectively. These two values should be the same as the ones used in the server script.

To obtain information sent by the server, the client script runs the socket's **recv** method. This method expects as an argument the maximum size in bytes of the data to be read from the socket. The **recv** method returns an object of type **bytes**. You convert this to a string by calling the **codecs** function **decode**, with the encoding **"ascii"** as the second argument.

After the client script has printed the string read from the socket, the script closes the connection to the server by running the socket's **close** method.

A Day/Time Server Script

You can also write a day/time server script in Python to handle requests from many clients. **Figure 12-8** shows the interaction between a day/time server and two clients in a series of screenshots. In the first shot, the day/time server script is launched in a terminal window and is waiting for a connection. In the second shot, two successive clients are launched in a separate terminal window (you can open several terminal windows at once). They have connected to the server and have received the day/time. The third shot shows the updates to the server's window after it has served these two clients. Note that the two clients terminate execution after they print their results, whereas the server appears to continue waiting for another client.

Figure 12-8   A day/time server and two clients

```
● ● ●          📁 pythonfiles — Python timeserver1.py — 80×6
Last login: Sat Oct  1 10:57:40 on ttys001
[ken@riverrun ~ % cd pythonfiles                                        ]
[ken@riverrun pythonfiles % python3 timeserver1.py                      ]
Waiting for connection . . .
▊
```

```
● ● ●          📁 pythonfiles — -zsh — 80×10
Last login: Sat Oct  1 11:01:59 on ttys000
[ken@riverrun ~ % cd pythonfiles                                        ]
[ken@riverrun pythonfiles % python3 timeclient.py                       ]
Sat Oct  1 11:03:46 2022
Have a nice day!
[ken@riverrun pythonfiles % python3 timeclient.py                       ]
Sat Oct  1 11:03:50 2022
Have a nice day!
ken@riverrun pythonfiles % ▊
```

```
● ● ●          📁 pythonfiles — Python timeserver1.py — 80×10
Last login: Sat Oct  1 10:57:40 on ttys001
[ken@riverrun ~ % cd pythonfiles                                        ]
[ken@riverrun pythonfiles % python3 timeserver1.py                      ]
Waiting for connection . . .
... connected from:  ('127.0.0.1', 49848)
Waiting for connection . . .
... connected from:  ('127.0.0.1', 49849)
Waiting for connection . . .
▊
```

Python™

A Python day/time server script also uses the resources of the **socket** module. The basic sequence of operations for a simple day/time server script is the following:

```
Create a socket and open it on port 6000 of the local host
While true
    Wait for a connection from a client
    When the connection is made,
    send the date to the client
```

The script also displays information about the host, the port, and the client. Here is the code, followed by a brief explanation:

```
"""
Server for providing the day and time.
"""
from socket import *
from time import ctime
HOST = "localhost"
PORT = 6000
ADDRESS = (HOST, PORT)
server = socket(AF_INET, SOCK_STREAM)
server.bind(ADDRESS)
server.listen(5)
while True:
    print("Waiting for connection ...")
    (client, address) = server.accept()
    print("... connected from: ", address)
    client.send(bytes(ctime() + "\nHave a nice day!",
                "ascii"))
    client.close()
```

The server script uses the same information to create a socket object as the client script presented earlier. In particular, the IP address and port number must be *exactly* the same as they are in the client's code.

However, connecting the socket to the host and to the port so as to become a server socket is done differently. First, the socket is bound to this address by running its **bind** method. Second, the socket then is made to listen for up to five requests at a time from clients by running its **listen** method. If you want the server to handle more concurrent requests before rejecting additional ones, you can increase this number.

After the script enters its main loop, it prints a message indicating that it is waiting for a connection. The socket's **accept** method then pauses execution of the script, in a manner similar to Python's **input** function, to wait for a request from a client.

When a client connects to this server, **accept** returns a tuple containing the client's socket and its address information. The script binds the variables **client** and **address** to these values and uses them in the next steps.

The script prints the client's address and then sends the current day/time to the client by running the **send** method with the client's socket. The **send** method expects a **bytes** object as an argument. You create a **bytes** object from a string by calling the built-in **bytes** function, with the string and an encoding, in this case, **"ascii"**, as arguments. The Python function **time.ctime** returns a string representing the day/time.

Finally, the script closes the connection to the client by running the client socket's `close` method. The script then returns in its infinite loop to accept another client connection.

A Two-Way Chat Script

The communication between the day/time server and its client is one-way. The client simply receives a message from the server and then quits. In a two-way chat, the client connects to the server, and the two programs engage in a continuous communication until one of them, usually the client, decides to quit.

Once again, there are two distinct Python scripts, one for the server and one for the client. The setup of a two-way chat server is similar to that of the day/time server discussed earlier. The server script creates a socket with a given IP address and port and then enters an infinite loop to accept and handle clients. When a client connects to the server, the server sends the client a greeting.

Instead of closing the client's socket and listening for another client connection, the server then enters a second, nested loop. This loop engages the server in a continuous conversation with the client. The server receives a message from the client. If the message is an empty string, the server displays a message that the client has disconnected, closes the client's socket, and breaks out of the nested loop. Otherwise, the server prints the client's message and prompts the user for a reply to send to the client.

Here is the code for the two loops in the server script:

```
CODE = "ascii"
while True:
    print("Waiting for connection ...")
    client, address = server.accept()
    print("... connected from: ", address)
    client.send(bytes("Welcome to my chat room!", CODE))
    while True:
        message = decode(client.recv(BUFSIZE), CODE)
        if not message:
            print("Client disconnected")
            client.close()
            break
        else:
            print(message)
            client.send(bytes(input("> "), CODE)
```

The client script for the two-way chat sets up a socket in a similar manner to the day/time client. After the client has connected to the server, it receives and displays the server's initial greeting message.

Instead of closing the server's socket, the client then enters a loop to engage in a continuous conversation with the server. This loop mirrors the loop that is running in the server script. The client's loop prompts the user for a message to send to the server. If this string is empty, the loop breaks. Otherwise, the client sends the message to the server's socket and receives the server's reply. If this reply is the empty string, the loop also breaks. Otherwise, the server's reply is displayed. The server's socket is closed after the loop has terminated. Here is the code for the part of the client script following the client's connection to the server:

```
print(decode(server.recv(BUFSIZE), CODE))
while True:
    message = input("> ")
```

```
    if not message:
        break
    server.send(bytes(message, CODE))
    reply = decode(server.recv(BUFSIZE), CODE)
    if not reply:
        print("Server disconnected")
        break
    print(reply)
server.close()
```

As you can see, it is important to synchronize the sending and the receiving of messages between the client and the server. If you get this right, the conversation can proceed, usually without a hitch.

Handling Multiple Clients Concurrently

The client/server programs discussed thus far are rather simple and limited. First, the server handles a client's request and then returns to wait for another client. In the case of the day/time server, the processing of each request happens so quickly that clients will never notice a delay. However, when a server provides extensive processing, other clients will have to wait until the currently connected client is finished.

To solve the problem of giving many clients timely access to the server, you relieve the server of the task of handling the client's request and assign it instead to a separate client-handler thread. Thus, the server simply listens for client connections and dispatches these to new client-handler objects. The structure of this system is shown in **Figure 12-9**.

Figure 12-9   A day/time server with a client handler

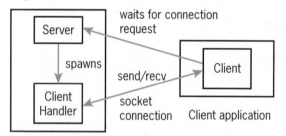

The use of separate server and client handler objects accomplishes two things in this design:

1. The details of fielding a request for service are separated from the details of performing that service, making the design of each task simpler and more maintainable.
2. Because the server object and the client handler objects run in separate threads, their processes can run concurrently. This means that new clients will not have to wait for service until a connected client has been served (think of a busy server running for Google or Amazon, with hundreds of millions of clients being served simultaneously).

Returning to the day/time server script, you will now add a client handler to improve efficiency. This handler is an instance of a new class, **TimeClientHandler**, which is defined in its own module. This class extends the **Thread** class. Its constructor receives the client's socket from the server and assigns it to an instance variable. The **run** method includes the code to send the date to the client and close its socket. Here is the code for the **TimeClientHandler** class:

```
"""
File: timeclienthandler.py
Client handler for providing the day and time.
"""

from time import ctime
from threading import Thread

class TimeClientHandler(Thread):
    """Handles a client request."""

    def __init__(self, client):
        Thread.__init__(self)
        self.client = client

    def run(self):
        self.client.send(bytes(ctime() + \
                        "\nHave a nice day!",
                        "ascii"))
        self.client.close()
```

The code for the server's script now imports the **TimeClientHandler** class. The server creates a socket and listens for requests, as before. However, when a request comes in, the server creates a client socket and passes it to a new instance of **TimeClientHandler** for processing. The server then immediately returns to listen for new requests. Here is the code for the modified day/time server:

```
"""
File: timeserver2.py
Server for providing the day and time. Uses client
handlers to handle clients' requests.
"""
from socket import socket
from timeClienthandler import TimeClientHandler

HOST = "localhost"
PORT = 6000
ADDRESS = (HOST, PORT)
server = socket(AF_INET, SOCK_STREAM)
server.bind(ADDRESS)
server.listen(5)
# The server now just waits for connections from clients
# and hands sockets off to client handlers
while True:
    print("Waiting for connection ... ")
    client, address = server.accept()
    print("... connected from: ", address)
```

```
handler = TimeClientHandler(client)
handler.start()
```

The code for the day/time client's script does not change at all. Moreover, to create a new server for different kind of service, you just define a new type of client handler and use it in the code for the server just presented.

Exercise 12-3

1. Explain the roles that ports and IP addresses play in a client/server program.

2. What is a local host, and how is it used to develop networked applications?

3. Why is it a good idea for a server to create threads to handle clients' requests?

4. Describe how a menu-driven command processor of the type developed for an ATM application in Chapter 10 could be run on a network.

5. The ATM application discussed in Chapter 10 has a single user. Will there be a synchronization problem if you deploy that application with threads for multiple users? Justify your answer.

6. The servers discussed in this section all contain infinite loops. Thus, the applications running them cannot do anything else while the server is waiting for a client's request, and they cannot even gracefully be shut down. Suggest a way to restructure these applications so that the applications can do other things, including performing a graceful shutdown.

Case Study 12-1 | Setting Up Conversations between Doctors and Patients

Now that you have modified the day/time server to handle multiple clients, can you also modify the two-way chat program to support chats among multiple clients? Let's consider first the problem of supporting multiple two-way chats. You don't want to involve the server in the chat, much less the human user who is running the server. Can you first set up a chat between a human user and an automated agent? The doctor program developed in the Nondirective Psychotherapy Case Study 5-2 in Chapter 5 is a good example of an automated agent or **bot** that chats with its client, who is a human user.

Request

Write a program that allows multiple clients to be served by doctors who provide nondirective psychotherapy.

Analysis

A doctor server program listens for requests from clients for doctors. Upon receiving a request, the server dispatches the client's socket to a new handler thread. This thread creates a new **Doctor** object (see Programming Exercise 5 in Chapter 10) and then manages the conversation between the doctor and the client. The server returns to field more requests from clients for sessions with their doctors. **Figure 12-10** shows the structure of this program.

Figure 12-10   The structure of a client/server program for patients and doctors

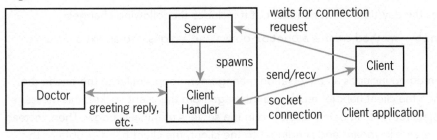

The user interface for the server script is terminal-based, as you have seen in other examples. The client script provides a GUI for clients, as shown in **Figure 12-11**. The GUI provides widgets for the user's inputs and the doctor's replies, and a button to connect or disconnect to the server.

Figure 12-11   The user interface of clients in the doctor program

Design and Implementation

The design of the server script is the same as that of the multithreaded day/time server, but it now uses a **DoctorClientHandler** class to be developed shortly.

In the code that follows, assume that a **Doctor** class is defined in the module **doctor.py**. This class includes two methods. The method **greeting** returns a string representing the doctor's welcome. The method **reply** expects the patient's string as an argument and returns the doctor's response string.

The client handler resembles the day/time client handler, but it includes the following changes:

- The client handler's **__init__** method creates a **Doctor** object and assigns it to an extra instance variable.

- The client handler's **run** method includes a conversation management loop similar to the one in the chat server. However, when the client handler receives a message from the client socket, this message is sent to the **Doctor** object rather than being displayed in the server's terminal window. Then, instead of taking input from the server's keyboard and sending it to the client, the client handler obtains this reply from the **Doctor** object.

Here is the code for the client handler:

```
"""
File: doctorclienthandler.py
Client handler for a therapy session. Handles multiple clients concurrently.
"""

from codecs import decode
from threading import Thread
from doctor import Doctor

BUFSIZE = 1024
CODE = "ascii"

class DoctorClientHandler(Thread):
    """Handles a session between a doctor and a patient."""

    def __init__(self, client):
        Thread.__init__(self)
        self.client = client
        self.dr = Doctor()

    def run(self):
        self.client.send(bytes(self.dr.greeting(), CODE)
        while True:
            message = decode(self.client.recv(BUFSIZE), CODE)
            if not message:
                print("Client disconnected")
                self.client.close()
                break
            else:
                self.client.send(bytes(self.dr.reply(message),
                                       CODE)
```

The **doctorclient** module includes the code for the GUI and the code for managing the connection to the server. When the user clicks the **Connect** button, the program connects to the server, as in previous examples. It then receives and displays the doctor's greeting and waits for the user's input. The user replies by entering text in an input field and clicking the **Send** button. The user signals the end of a session by clicking the **Disconnect** button, which closes the server's socket.

Here is the code for the client, which includes the class **DoctorClient:**

```python
"""
File: doctorclient.py
GUI-based view for client for nondirective psychotherapy.
"""

from socket import *
from codecs import decode
from breezypythongui import EasyFrame

HOST = "localhost"
PORT = 6000
BUFSIZE = 1024
ADDRESS = (HOST, PORT)
CODE = "ascii"

class DoctorClient(EasyFrame):
    """Represents the client's window."""

    COLOR = "#CCEEFF"        # Light blue

    def __init__(self):
        """Initialize the window and widgets."""
        EasyFrame.__init__(self, title = "Doctor",
                           background = DoctorClient.COLOR)
        # Add the labels, fields, and buttons
        self.drLabel = self.addLabel("Want to connect?",
                                     row = 0, column = 0,
                                     columnspan = 2,
                                     background = DoctorClient.COLOR)
        self.ptField = self.addTextField(text = "",
                                         row = 1,
                                         column = 0,
                                         columnspan = 2,
                                         width = 50)
        self.sendBtn = self.addButton(row = 2, column = 0,
                                      text = "Send",
                                      command = self.sendReply,
                                      state = "disabled")
```

```python
        self.connectBtn = self.addButton(row = 2,
                                         column = 1,
                                         text = "Connect",
                                         command = self.connect)
        # Support the return key in the input field
        self.ptField.bind("<Return>",
                         lambda event: self.sendReply())

    def sendReply(self):
        """Sends patient input to doctor, receives
        and outputs the doctor's reply."""
        ptInput = self.ptField.getText()
        if ptInput != "":
            self.server.send(bytes(ptInput, CODE))
            drReply = decode(self.server.recv(BUFSIZE),
                            CODE)
            if not drReply:
                self.messageBox(message = "Doctor disconnected")
                self.disconnect()
            else:
                self.drLabel["text"] = drReply
                self.ptField.setText("")

    def connect(self):
        """Starts a new session with the doctor."""
        self.server = socket(AF_INET, SOCK_STREAM)
        self.server.connect(ADDRESS)
        self.drLabel["text"] = decode(self.server.recv(BUFSIZE),
                                     CODE)
        self.connectBtn["text"] = "Disconnect"
        self.connectBtn["command"] = self.disconnect
        self.sendBtn["state"] = "normal"

    def disconnect(self):
        """Ends the session with the doctor."""
        self.server.close()
        self.ptField.setText("")
        self.drLabel["text"] = "Want to connect?"
        self.connectBtn["text"] = "Connect"
        self.connectBtn["command"] = self.connect
        self.sendBtn["state"] = "disabled"
```

```
def main():
    """Instantiate and pop up the window."""
    DoctorClient().mainloop()


if __name__ == "__main__":
    main()
```

You might have noticed that each client interacts with its own **Doctor** object. Thus, no synchronization problems arise when a patient's replies are added to the doctor's history list, because the client threads do not access any shared data.

However, in other applications, such as the ATM developed in Chapter 10, concurrent users would be accessing shared data. In the case of the ATM application, the server would create the common **Bank** object and pass it to the client handlers. Because this object holds the accounts in a dictionary and dictionaries are thread-safe, additions or removals of accounts pose no synchronization problems. However, the **SavingsAccount** objects within the **Bank** object's dictionary are not themselves thread-safe, and thus they could cause synchronization problems when two or more users access a joint account. The solution is to provide a lock and condition mechanism for a **SavingsAccount** object to allow concurrent access to readers and writers of that shared object. You will work with shared data in client server applications in the programming exercises.

Fail-Safe Programming

Programs that connect to a network, either as servers or as clients, face challenges that a program running on a standalone computer does not. You have already seen that a client or server application can fail to connect to a host computer's IP address. The cause of this failure could be

- an incorrect IP address
- the computer with that IP address is not running the server application
- the computer with that IP address is not running at all

In addition, even after a successful network connection has been made, the computer hosting the client or the server could go down at any time, or the client or server program could crash, thereby causing any connections to be lost. Finally, Internet service to the server or client can be lost, due to weather conditions or other technical issues with the service provider. Many of these types of errors can be caught and dealt with at runtime, thus allowing network-based programs to recover gracefully.

To make a client/server application more robust, you must focus on the points where the client or server attempts to access the network connection and include code that can recover from failures. The use of a **try-except** statement to handle the initial failure to connect was discussed earlier. Other pressure points in a network application include attempts to send to or receive from a socket after the connection is made. The forms of these two operations for text-based input and output in the examples are

```
aSocket.send(bytes(outputData, "ascii"))
inputData = decode(aSocket.recv(BUFSIZE), "ascii")
```

If **aSocket** no longer refers to a live connection in either of these statements, an exception will be raised. Instead of embedding every instance of such statements in **try-except** statements, you can package them in a pair of functions for robust network input and output, as you did with keyboard input in earlier chapters.

The function for network output, called **robustSend**, expects a socket and an output string as arguments and returns a tuple containing two values. If the operation is successful, the tuple contains the Boolean value **True** and the value **None**; otherwise, if an exception occurs, the tuple contains the Boolean value **False** and the **Exception** object generated by Python. Here is an example use of this function:

```
(success, exception) = robustSend(aSocket,
                             "How are you today?")
if not success:
    print("Connection failed:", str(exception))
```

Here is the code for the function **robustSend**:

```
def robustSend(aSocket, outputData):
    """Attempts to send outputData to aSocket.
    Returns (True, None) if successful, or
    (False, anException) otherwise. """
    try:
        aSocket.send(bytes(outputData, "ascii"))
        return (True, None)
    except Exception as anException:
        return (False, anException)
```

The function for robust network input, named **robustRecv**, expects a socket and a buffer size as arguments and returns a tuple of three values. These values are **True**, **None**, and the input string if the operation is successful, or **False**, the **Exception** object, and **None** if the operation fails. The definition of the function **robustRecv** is left as an exercise for you.

Summary

- Threads allow the work of a single program to be distributed among several computational processes. These processes may be run concurrently on the same computer or may collaborate by running on separate computers.

- A thread can have several states during its lifetime, such as newborn, ready, executing (in the CPU), sleeping, and waiting. A ready queue schedules the threads for access to the CPU in first-come, first-served order.

- After a thread is started, it goes to the end of the ready queue to be scheduled for a turn in the CPU.

- A thread may give up the CPU when it is timed-out, goes to sleep, waits on a condition, or finishes its **run** method.

- When a thread wakes up, is timed-out, or is notified that it can stop waiting, it returns to the rear of the ready queue.

- Thread synchronization problems can occur when two or more threads share data. These threads can be synchronized by waiting on conditions that control access to the data.

- Each computer on a network has a unique IP address that allows other computers to locate it. An IP address contains an IP number but can also be labeled with an IP name.

- Servers and clients can communicate on a network by means of sockets. A socket is created with a port number and an IP address of the server on the client's computer and on the server's computer.

- Clients and servers communicate by sending and receiving bytes through their socket connections. A string is converted to bytes before being sent, and the bytes are converted to a string after receipt.

- A server can handle several clients concurrently by assigning each client request to a separate handler thread.

Key Terms

Block	lock	ready queue
bot	Multiprocessing systems	servers
clients	multithreading	Sleep
context switch	network	socket
critical section	Networked or distributed systems	synchronization problem
decorator pattern	Parallel computing	threads
Internet host	Parallel systems	thread-safe
IP address	ports	Time-out
IP name	process	Time-sharing operating system
IP number	producer/consumer relationship	time slicing
local host	readers and writers problem	Wait

Review Questions

1. Multiple threads can run on the same desktop computer by means of
   - **a.** time-sharing
   - **b.** multiprocessing
   - **c.** distributed computing
   - **d.** multiple windows

2. A `Thread` object moves to the ready queue when
   - **a.** its `wait` method is called
   - **b.** its `sleep` method is called
   - **c.** its `start` method is called
   - **d.** its `__init__` method is called

3. The method that executes a thread's code is called
   - **a.** the `start` method
   - **b.** the `run` method
   - **c.** the `execute` method
   - **d.** the `__init__` method

4. A lock on a resource is provided by an instance of the
   - **a.** `Thread` class
   - **b.** `Condition` class
   - **c.** `Lock` class
   - **d.** `Vault` class

5. If multiple threads share data, they can have

    a. total cooperation

    b. synchronization problems

    c. equal access to the data

    d. independent access to the data

6. The object that uniquely identifies a host computer on a network is a(n)

    a. port

    b. socket

    c. IP address

    d. thread

7. The object that allows several clients to access a server on a host computer is a(n)

    a. port

    b. socket

    c. IP address

    d. thread

8. The object that effects a connection between an individual client and a server is a(n)

    a. port

    b. socket

    c. IP address

    d. thread

9. The data that are transmitted between client and server are

    a. of any type

    b. strings

    c. bytes

    d. lists

10. The best way for a server to handle requests from multiple clients is to

    a. directly handle each client's request.

    b. create a separate client-handler thread for each client.

    c. refuse requests to connect after the first request.

    d. handle the requests in random order.

Programming Exercises

1. Redo the producer/consumer program (in the file **pc.py**) so that it allows multiple consumers. Each consumer must be able to consume the same data before the producer produces more data. (LO: 12.1)

2. Sometimes servers are down, so clients cannot connect to them. Python raises an exception of type `ConnectionRefusedError` in a client program when a network connection is refused. Add code to the day/time client program (in the file **timeclient.py**) to catch and recover from this kind of exception. (LO: 12.3)

3. Modify the code in the day/time server application (in the file **timeserver.py**) so that the user on the server side can shut the server down. That user should be able to press the return or enter key at the terminal to do this. (LO: 12.3)

4. Modify the doctor application discussed in this chapter so that it tracks clients by name and history. A `Doctor` object has its own history list of a patient's inputs for generating replies that refer to earlier conversations, as discussed in Chapter 5. A `Doctor` object (in the file **doctor.py**) is now associated with a patient's name. The client application (in the file **doctorclient.py**) takes this name as input and sends it to the client handler (in the file **doctorclienthandler.py**) when the patient connects. The client handler checks for a pickled file with the patient's name as its filename (`"<patient name>.dat"`). If that file exists, it will contain the patient's history, and the client handler loads the file to create the `Doctor` object. Otherwise, the patient is visiting the doctor for the first time, so the client handler creates a brand-new `Doctor` object. When the client disconnects, the client handler pickles the `Doctor` object in a file with the patient's name. (LO: 12.1, 12.3)

5. Design, implement, and test a network application that maintains an online phone book. The data model for the phone book (in the file **phonebook.py**) is saved in a file on the server's computer. A client (in the file **phonebookclient.py**) should be able to look up a person's phone number or add a name and number to the phone book. The server (in the file **phonebookserver.py**) should handle multiple clients without delays. Unlike the doctor program, there should be just one phone book that all clients share. The server creates this object at start-up and passes it to the client handlers (in the file **phonebookclienthandler.py**). (LO: 12.1, 12.3)

6. Convert the ATM application presented in Chapter 10 to a networked application. The client (in the file **atmclient.py**) manages the user interface, whereas the server (in the file **atmserver.py**) and client handler (in the file **atmclienthandler.py**) manage connecting to and the transactions with the bank (in the file **bank.py**). Do not be concerned about synchronization problems in this exercise. (LO: 12.1, 12.3)

7. Write the tester program (in the file **readersandwriters.py**) for readers and writers of a shared `Counter` object. A sample run is shown in Figure 12-4. (LO: 12.1, 12.2)

8. Add synchronization to the ATM program of Programming Exercise 6. You will need to give concurrent readers access to a single account as long as a writer is not writing to it, and give a single writer access, as long as other writers and readers are not accessing the account. *Hint*: Just complete the `ThreadSafeSavingsAccount` class discussed in this chapter (in the file **threadsafesavingsaccount.py**) and use it to create account objects in the `Bank` class. (LO: 12.1, 12.2, 12.3)

9. Jack has been working on the shared cell classes for the producer–consumer problem and the readers and writers problem, and he notices some serious redundancy in the code. The `read` and `write` methods are the same in both classes, and both classes include the same instance variable for the data. Jill, his team manager, advises him to place this redundant code in a parent class named `SharedCell` (in the file **sharedcell.py**) Then two subclasses, named `PCSharedCell` (in the file **pcsharedcell.py**) and `RWSharedCell` (in the file **rwsharedcell.py**), can inherit this code and define the methods `beginRead`, `endRead`, `beginWrite`, and `endWrite` to enforce their specific synchronization protocols. Also, the `__init__` method in each subclass first calls the `__init__` method in the `SharedCell` class to set up the data, and then adds the condition(s) and other instance variables for its specific situation. Jack has called in sick, so you must complete this hierarchy of classes and redo the demo programs (in the files **producerconsumer.py** and **readersandwriters.py**) so that they use them. (LO: 12.1, 12.2)

10. A crude multiclient chat room allows two or more users to converse by sending and receiving messages. On the client side (in the file **chatclient.py**), a user connects to the chat room, as in the ATM application, by clicking a **Connect** button. At that point, a transcript of the conversation thus far appears in a text area. At any time, the user can send a message to the chat room by entering it as input and clicking a **Send** button. When the user sends a message, the chat room returns another transcript of the entire conversation to display in the text area. The user disconnects by clicking the **Disconnect** button.

   On the server side, there are five resources: a server, a client handler, a transcript, a thread-safe transcript, and a shared cell. Their roles are much the same as they are in the ATM application of Programming Exercise 8. The server (in the file **chatserver.py**) creates a thread-safe transcript (in the file **threadsafetranscript**.py) at start-up, listens for client connections, and passes a client's socket and the thread-safe transcript to a client handler (in the file **chatclienthandler.py**) when a client connects. The client handler receives the client's name from the client socket, adds this name and the connection time to the thread-safe transcript, sends the thread-safe transcript's string to the client, and waits for a reply. When the client's reply comes in, the client handler adds the client's name and time to it, adds the result to the thread-safe transcript, and sends the thread-safe transcript's string back to the client. When the client disconnects, her name and a message to that effect are added to the thread-safe transcript.

   The `SharedCell` class includes the usual `read` and `write` methods for a readers and writers protocol, and the `SharedTranscript` and `Transcript` classes include an `add` method and an `__str__` method. The `add` method adds a string to a list of strings, while `__str__` returns the `join` of this list, separated by newlines. (LO: 12.1, 12.2, 12.3)

Debugging Exercise

Jill is developing a client/server program. Her server script launches without a problem, but she receives the following error message when she launches the client's script:

```
Traceback (most recent call last):
  File "/Users/jill/pythonfiles/client.py", line 15, in <module>
    server.connect(ADDRESS)         # Connect it to a host
ConnectionRefusedError: [Errno 61] Connection refused
```

Here are the code segments in her server and client scripts that are responsible for setting up the connection:

```python
"""
File: server.py
"""

from socket import *
from codecs import decode


HOST = "localhost"
PORT = 6000
ADDRESS = (HOST, PORT)


server = socket(AF_INET, SOCK_STREAM)
server.bind(ADDRESS)


"""
File: client.py
"""

from socket import *
from codecs import decode


HOST = "localhost"
PORT = 5000
BUFSIZE = 1024
ADDRESS = (HOST, PORT)


server = socket(AF_INET, SOCK_STREAM)   # Create a socket
server.connect(ADDRESS)                 # Connect it to a host
```

Explain why the error occurs in Jill's program and suggest a way to correct this error.

Sudoku

Prompt

Sudokus are a popular number-based puzzle with a simple set of rules. Typically they come as a 9×9 grid square with multiple values filled in. In order for such a puzzle to be solved it:

1. Must use the digits 1–9 (inclusive) only once per row.
2. Must use the digits 1–9 (inclusive) only once per column.
3. Must use the digits 1–9 (inclusive) only once per smaller grid square. In a 9×9 sudoku puzzle you would have 9 3×3 subgrid squares.

Your goal will be to write a function that returns True or False based on whether the given input is a valid solved sudoku grid board or not. You may store the sudoku board in any Python data structure you might like, however we suggest you use a multidimensional list. We have provided you with multiple valid boards as well as multiple invalid boards for your testing and experimentation.

An additional requirement is that each of the conditions listed above be checked in parallel. Each should be kicked off as its own thread.

Hints

> When writing multithreaded code, get a single-threaded version working first. Then go back and add threads.

> Break this down into smaller pieces. You can write multiple functions, each one validating or doing one very specific thing.

Examples

```
valid_boards = [
  [
      [5, 3, 4, 6, 7, 8, 9, 1, 2],
      [6, 7, 2, 1, 9, 5, 3, 4, 8],
      [1, 9, 8, 3, 4, 2, 5, 6, 7],
      [8, 5, 9, 7, 6, 1, 4, 2, 3],
      [4, 2, 6, 8, 5, 3, 7, 9, 1],
      [7, 1, 3, 9, 2, 4, 8, 5, 6],
      [9, 6, 1, 5, 3, 7, 2, 8, 4],
      [2, 8, 7, 4, 1, 9, 6, 3, 5],
      [3, 4, 5, 2, 8, 6, 1, 7, 9],
  ],
```

```
    [
        [5, 3, 4, 6, 7, 8, 9, 1, 2],
        [6, 7, 2, 1, 9, 5, 3, 4, 8],
        [1, 9, 8, 3, 4, 2, 5, 6, 7],
        [8, 5, 9, 7, 6, 1, 4, 2, 3],
        [4, 2, 6, 8, 5, 3, 7, 9, 1],
        [7, 1, 3, 9, 2, 4, 8, 5, 6],
        [9, 6, 1, 5, 3, 7, 2, 8, 4],
        [2, 8, 7, 4, 1, 9, 6, 3, 5],
        [3, 4, 5, 2, 8, 6, 1, 7, 9],
    ],
    [
        [5, 3, 4, 6, 7, 8, 9, 1, 2],
        [6, 7, 2, 1, 9, 5, 3, 4, 8],
        [1, 9, 8, 3, 4, 2, 5, 6, 7],
        [8, 5, 9, 7, 6, 1, 4, 2, 3],
        [4, 2, 6, 8, 5, 3, 7, 9, 1],
        [7, 1, 3, 9, 2, 4, 8, 5, 6],
        [9, 6, 1, 5, 3, 7, 2, 8, 4],
        [2, 8, 7, 4, 1, 9, 6, 3, 5],
        [3, 4, 5, 2, 8, 6, 1, 7, 9],
    ],
]

invalid_boards = [
    [
        [3, 5, 4, 6, 7, 8, 9, 1, 2], #non-unique elements in same col
        [6, 7, 2, 1, 9, 5, 3, 4, 8],
        [1, 9, 8, 3, 4, 2, 5, 6, 7],
        [8, 5, 9, 7, 6, 1, 4, 2, 3],
        [4, 2, 6, 8, 5, 3, 7, 9, 1],
        [7, 1, 3, 9, 2, 4, 8, 5, 6],
        [9, 6, 1, 5, 3, 7, 2, 8, 4],
        [2, 8, 7, 4, 1, 9, 6, 3, 5],
        [3, 4, 5, 2, 8, 6, 1, 7, 9],
    ],
    [
        [5, 3, 4, 6, 7, 8, 9, 1, 2],
        [6, 7, 2, 1, 9, 5, 3, 4, 8],
        [1, 9, 8, 3, 4, 2, 5, 6, 7],
        [8, 5, 9, 9, 6, 1, 4, 2, 3], #non unique elements in same row
        [4, 2, 6, 8, 5, 3, 7, 9, 1],
        [7, 1, 3, 9, 2, 4, 8, 5, 6],
        [9, 6, 1, 5, 3, 7, 2, 8, 4],
        [2, 8, 7, 4, 1, 9, 6, 3, 5],
        [3, 4, 5, 2, 8, 6, 1, 7, 9],
    ],
```

```
    [
        [5, 3, 4, 6, 7, 8, 9, 1, 2],
        [6, 7, 2, 1, 9, 5, 3, 4, 8],
        [1, 9, 8, 3, 4, 2, 5, 6, 3],
        [8, 5, 9, 9, 6, 1, 4, 7, 7],    #non unique elements in same square
        [4, 2, 6, 8, 5, 3, 7, 9, 1],
        [7, 1, 3, 9, 2, 4, 8, 5, 6],
        [9, 6, 1, 5, 3, 7, 2, 8, 4],
        [2, 8, 7, 4, 1, 9, 6, 3, 5],
        [3, 4, 5, 2, 8, 6, 1, 7, 9],
    ],
    [
        [5, 3, 4, 6, 7, 8, 9, 1, 2],
        [6, 7, 2, 1, 9, 5, 3, 4, 8],
        [1, 9, 8, 3, 4, 2, 5, 6, 7],
        [8, 5, 9, 7, 6, 1, 4, 2, 3],
        [4, 2, 6, 8, 5, 3, 7, 9, 1],
        [7, 1, 3, 9, 2, 4, 8, 5],       #missing an element
        [9, 6, 1, 5, 3, 7, 2, 8, 4],
        [2, 8, 7, 4, 1, 9, 6, 3, 5],
        [3, 4, 5, 2, 8, 6, 1, 7, 9],
    ],
]
```

Answer

See sudoku.py for a possible solution

After Discussion

Our main function runs through our two sample lists, making sure the valid sudokus are found to be valid, and our invalid sudokus are found to be invalid. This time we are printing out [PASSED] instead of True/False, validating that True is returned when we expect it, and False is returned when we expect it.

The driving function in this program is is_valid_sudoku(), which makes calls to several smaller functions via kicking them off as threads. Because the board itself is only read from, and never written to, the board is not something we need to worry about making thread safe.

Before we kick off threads to check rows, columns, and squares, we need to do some bounds checking. We have not learned exception handling, so we need to be extra sure that we are dealing with known sizes of rows and columns! In our case, every dimension should be 9. When is_equal_rows_and_cols() returns True, we know we are dealing with a game board with a 9×9 board.

The three functions kicked off in threads each check one of the criteria for being a valid sudoku. One checks that each row contains only the digits 1 through 9, inclusive, and that each digit is used once. Another builds a new list from a given column index and then makes sure that it is valid. The 3rd function builds lists from the small 3×3 squares, and makes sure they too are valid.

If you time this code (which is beyond the scope of this module), you may see that multithreading gave only a little performance increase, or even took longer than a single-threaded version of this. The reasons behind this are for a deeper dive into how Python works at a later time.

## Chapter 13

Searching, Sorting, and Complexity Analysis

Learning Objectives

When you complete this chapter, you will be able to:

13.1 Measure the performance of an algorithm by obtaining running times and instruction counts with different data sets.

13.2 Analyze an algorithm's performance by determining its order of complexity using big-O notation.

13.3 Distinguish between the improvements obtained by tweaking an algorithm and by reducing its order of complexity.

13.4 Design, implement, and analyze sort algorithms.

13.5 Deploy recursive strategies to implement faster sort algorithms.

13.6 Recognize algorithms with exponential running times.

Earlier in this book, you learned about several criteria for assessing the quality of an algorithm. The most essential criterion is correctness, but readability and ease of maintenance are also important. This chapter examines another important criterion of the quality of algorithms—run-time performance.

Algorithms describe processes that run on real computers with finite resources. Processes consume two resources: processing time and space or memory. When run with the same problems or data sets, processes that consume less of these two resources are of higher quality than processes that consume more, and so are the corresponding algorithms. This chapter introduces tools for complexity analysis—for assessing the run-time performance or efficiency of algorithms. You will also apply these tools to search algorithms and sort algorithms.

13.1 Measuring the Efficiency of Algorithms

Some algorithms consume an amount of time or memory that is below a threshold of tolerance. For example, most users are happy with any algorithm that loads a file in less than one second. For such users, any algorithm that meets this requirement is as good as any other. Other algorithms take an amount of time that is totally impractical (say, thousands of years) with large data sets. You can't use these algorithms and you need to find others, if they exist, that perform better.

When choosing algorithms, you often have to settle for a space/time tradeoff. An algorithm can be designed to gain faster run times at the cost of using extra space (memory), or the other way around. Some users might be willing to pay for more memory to get a faster algorithm, whereas others would rather settle for a slower algorithm that economizes on memory. Primary memory is now quite inexpensive for desktop and laptop computers, but not yet for some miniature devices.

In any case, because efficiency is a desirable feature of algorithms, it is important to pay attention to the potential of some algorithms for poor performance. In this section, we consider several ways to measure the efficiency of algorithms.

Measuring the Run Time of an Algorithm

One way to measure the time cost of an algorithm is to use the computer's clock to obtain an actual run time. This process, called benchmarking or profiling, starts by determining the time for several different data sets of the same size and then calculates the average time. Next, similar data are gathered for larger and larger data sets. After several tests, enough data are available to predict how the algorithm will behave for a data set of any size.

Consider a simple, if unrealistic, example. The following program implements an algorithm that counts from 1 to a given number. Thus, the problem size is the number. You start with the number 10,000,000, time the algorithm, and output the running time to the terminal window. You then double the size of this number and repeat this process. After five such increases, there is a set of results from which you can generalize. Here is the code for the tester program:

```
"""
File: timing1.py
Prints the running times for problem sizes that double,
using a single loop.
"""

import time
problemSize = 10000000
print("%12s16s" % ("Problem Size", "Seconds"))
for count in range(5):
    start = time.time()
    # The start of the algorithm
    work = 1
    for x in range(problemSize):
        work += 1
        work -= 1
    # The end of the algorithm
    elapsed = time.time() - start
    print("%12d%16.3f" % (problemSize, elapsed))
    problemSize *= 2
```

The tester program uses the `time()` function in the `time` module to track the running time. This function returns the number of seconds that have elapsed between the current time on the computer's clock and January 1, 1970 (also called "The Epoch"). Thus, the difference between the results of two calls of `time.time()` represents the elapsed time in seconds. Note also that the program does a constant amount of work in the form of two extended assignment statements on each pass through the loop. This work consumes enough time on each pass through the loop so that the total running time is significant, but it has no other impact on the results. **Figure 13-1** shows the output of the program.

Figure 13-1   The output of the tester program

Problem Size	Seconds
10000000	3.8
20000000	7.591
40000000	15.352
80000000	30.697
160000000	61.631

A quick glance at the results reveals that the running time more or less doubles when the size of the problem doubles. Consequently, you might predict that the running time for a problem of size 32,000,000 would be approximately 124 seconds.

As another example, consider the following change in the tester program's algorithm:

```
for j in range(problemSize):
    for k in range(problemSize):
        work += 1
        work -= 1
```

In this version, the extended assignments have been moved into a nested loop. This loop iterates through the size of the problem within another loop that also iterates through the size of the problem. This program was left running overnight. By morning it had processed only the first data set, 1,000,000. The program was then terminated and run again with a smaller problem size of 1000. **Figure 13-2** shows the results.

Figure 13-2   The output of the second tester program with a nested loop and initial problem size of 1000

Problem Size	Seconds
1000	0.387
2000	1.581
4000	6.463
8000	25.702
16000	102.666

Note that when the problem size doubles, the number of seconds of running time more or less quadruples. At this rate, it would take 175 days to process the largest number in the previous data set!

This method permits accurate predictions of the running times of many algorithms. However, there are two major problems with this technique:

1. Different hardware platforms have different processing speeds, so the running times of an algorithm differ from machine to machine. Also, the running time of a program varies with the type of operating system that lies between it and the hardware. Finally, different programming languages and compilers produce code

whose performance varies. For example, an algorithm coded in C usually runs slightly faster than the same algorithm in Python byte code. Therefore, predictions of performance generated from the results of timing on one hardware or software platform generally cannot be used to predict potential performance on other platforms.

2. It is impractical to determine the running time for some algorithms with very large data sets. For some algorithms, it doesn't matter how fast the compiled code or the hardware processor is. They are impractical to run with very large data sets on any computer.

Although timing algorithms may in some cases be a helpful form of testing, you also want an estimate of the efficiency of an algorithm that is independent of a particular hardware or software platform. As you will learn in the next section, such an estimate tells how well or how poorly the algorithm would perform on any platform.

Counting Instructions

Another technique used to estimate the efficiency of an algorithm is to count the instructions executed with different problem sizes. These counts provide a good predictor of the amount of abstract work performed by an algorithm, no matter what platform the algorithm runs on. Keep in mind, however, that when you count instructions, you are counting the instructions in the high-level code in which the algorithm is written, not instructions in the executable machine language program.

When analyzing an algorithm in this way, you distinguish between two classes of instructions:

1. Instructions that execute the same number of times regardless of the problem size
2. Instructions whose execution count varies with the problem size

For now, you ignore instructions in the first class, because they do not figure significantly in this kind of analysis. The instructions in the second class normally are found in loops or recursive functions. In the case of loops, you also zero in on instructions performed in any nested loops or, more simply, just the number of iterations that a nested loop performs. For example, let's wire the algorithm of the previous program to track and display the number of iterations the inner loop executes with the different data sets:

```
"""
File: counting.py
Prints the number of iterations for problem sizes
that double, using a nested loop.
"""
problemSize = 1000
print("%12s%15s" % ("Problem Size", "Iterations"))
for count in range(5):
    number = 0
    # The start of the algorithm
    work = 1
    for j in range(problemSize):
        for k in range(problemSize):
            number += 1
            work += 1
            work -= 1
    # The end of the algorithm
    print("%12d%15d" % (problemSize, number))
    problemSize *= 2
```

As you can see from the results, the number of iterations is the square of the problem size (**Figure 13-3**).

Figure 13-3   The output of a tester program that counts iterations

```
Problem Size     Iterations
        1000        1000000
        2000        4000000
        4000       16000000
        8000       64000000
       16000      256000000
```

Here is a similar program that tracks the number of calls of a recursive Fibonacci function, as introduced in Chapter 7, for several problem sizes. Note that the function now has an optional second argument, which is a **Counter** object, as discussed in Chapter 10. Each time the function is called at the top level, a new **Counter** object is created and passed to it. On that call and each recursive call, the function's counter object is incremented.

```python
"""
File: countfib.py
Prints the number of calls of a recursive Fibonacci
function with problem sizes that double.
"""

from counter import Counter
def fib(n, counter = None):
    """Count the number of calls of the Fibonacci function."""
    if counter: counter.increment()
    if n < 3:
        return 1
    else:
        return fib(n - 1, counter) + fib(n - 2, counter)
problemSize = 2
print("%12s%15s" % ("Problem Size", "Calls"))
for count in range(5):
    counter = Counter()
    # The start of the algorithm
    fib(problemSize, counter)
    # The end of the algorithm
    print("%12d%15s" % (problemSize, counter))
    problemSize *= 2
```

The output of this program is shown in **Figure 13-4**.

As the problem size doubles, the instruction count (number of recursive calls) grows slowly at first and then quite rapidly. At first, the instruction count is less than the square of the problem size. However, the instruction count for a problem size of 16, 1973, is significantly larger than 256, the square of 16.

The problem with tracking counts in this way is that, with some algorithms, the computer still cannot run fast enough to show the counts for very large problem sizes. Counting instructions is the right idea, but you need to turn to logic and mathematical reasoning for a complete method of analysis. The only tools we need for this type of analysis are paper and pencil.

Figure 13-4 The output of a tester program that runs the Fibonacci function

```
Problem Size        Calls
           2            1
           4            5
           8           41
          16         1973
          32      4356617
```

Exercise 13-1

1. Write a tester program that counts and displays the number of iterations of the following loop:

   ```
   while problemSize > 0:
       problemSize = problemSize // 2
   ```

2. Run the program you created in Exercise 13-1 using problem sizes of 1000, 2000, 4000, 10,000, and 100,000. As the problem size doubles or increases by a factor of 10, what happens to the number of iterations?

3. The difference between the results of two calls of the **time** function **time()** is an elapsed time. Because the operating system might use the CPU for part of this time, the elapsed time might not reflect the actual time that a Python code segment uses the CPU. Browse the Python documentation for an alternative way of recording the processing time and describe how this would be done.

13.2 Complexity Analysis

In this section, you will develop a method of determining the efficiency of algorithms that allows you to rate them independently of platform-dependent timings or impractical instruction counts. This method, called complexity analysis, entails reading the algorithm and using pencil and paper to work out some simple algebra.

Orders of Complexity

Consider the two counting loops discussed earlier. The first loop executes n times for a problem of size n. The second loop contains a nested loop that iterates n^2 times. The amount of work done by these two algorithms is similar for small values of n, but is very different for large values of n. **Figure 13-5** and **Table 13-1** illustrate this divergence. Note that in this context, "work" usually means the number of iterations of the most deeply nested loop.

The performances of these algorithms differ by what you call an order of complexity. The performance of the first algorithm is linear, in that its work grows in direct proportion to the size of the problem (problem size of 10, work of 10; 20 and 20, etc.). The behavior of the second algorithm is quadratic, in that its work grows as a function of the square of the problem size (problem size of 10, work of 100). As you can see from the graph and the table, algorithms with linear behavior do less work than algorithms with quadratic behavior for most problem sizes n. In fact, as the problem size gets larger, the performance of an algorithm with the higher order of complexity becomes worse more quickly.

Several other orders of complexity are commonly used in the analysis of algorithms. An algorithm has constant performance if it requires the same number of operations for any problem size. List indexing is a good example of a constant-time algorithm. This is clearly the best kind of performance to have.

Figure 13-5   A graph of the amounts of work done in the tester programs

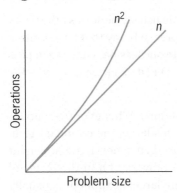

Table 13-1   The amounts of work in the tester programs

Problem Size	Work of the First Algorithm	Work of the Second Algorithm
2	2	4
10	10	100
1000	1000	1,000,000

Another order of complexity that is better than linear but worse than constant is called **logarithmic**. The amount of work of a logarithmic algorithm is proportional to the $\log_2$ of the problem size. Thus, when the problem doubles in size, the amount of work only increases by 1 (that is, just add 1).

The work of a **polynomial time algorithm** grows at a rate of n^k, where k is a constant greater than 1. Examples are n^2, n^3, and n^{10}.

Although n^3 is worse in some sense than n^2, they are both of the polynomial order and are better than the next higher order of complexity. An order of complexity that is worse than polynomial is called **exponential**. An example rate of growth of this order is 2^n. Exponential algorithms are impractical to run with large problem sizes. The most common orders of complexity used in the analysis of algorithms are summarized in **Figure 13-6** and **Table 13-2**.

Figure 13-6   A graph of some sample orders of complexity

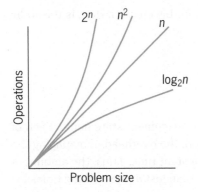

Table 13-2   Some sample orders of complexity

N	Logarithmic ($\log_2 n$)	Linear (n)	Quadratic (n^2)	Exponential (2^n)
100	7	100	10,000	Off the charts
1000	10	1000	1,000,000	Off the charts
1,000,000	20	1,000,0000	1,000,000,000,000	Really off the charts

Big-O Notation

An algorithm rarely performs a number of operations exactly equal to n, n^2, or k^n. An algorithm usually performs other work in the body of a loop, above the loop, and below the loop. For example, you might more precisely say that an algorithm performs $2n + 3$ or $2n^2$ operations. In the case of a nested loop, the inner loop might execute one less pass after each pass through the outer loop. Consequently, the total number of iterations would equal $n + (n-1) + (n-2) + \ldots + 1$, or $\frac{1}{2}n^2 - \frac{1}{2}n$, rather than n^2.

The amount of work in an algorithm typically is the sum of several terms in a polynomial. Whenever the amount of work is expressed as a polynomial, you focus on one term as **dominant**. As n becomes large, the dominant term becomes so large that the amount of work represented by the other terms can be ignored. In general, the dominant term of a given polynomial is the term with the largest power of n. For example, the powers of n in the terms of $3n^2 + 5n - 10$ are 2, 1, and 0, respectively, so the dominant term is $3n^2$. The term with the largest exponent is usually the leftmost one.

Let's consider another example. In the polynomial $\frac{1}{2}n^2 - \frac{1}{2}n$, you focus on the quadratic term, $\frac{1}{2}n^2$, in effect dropping the linear term, $\frac{1}{2}n$, from consideration. You can also drop the coefficient $\frac{1}{2}$ because the ratio between $\frac{1}{2}n^2$ and n^2 does not change as n grows. For example, if you double the problem size, the run times of algorithms that are $\frac{1}{2}n^2$ and n^2 both increase by a factor of 4. This type of analysis is sometimes called **asymptotic analysis** because the value of a polynomial asymptotically approaches or approximates the value of its largest term as n becomes very large.

One notation that computer scientists use to express the efficiency or computational complexity of an algorithm is called **big-O notation**. "O" stands for "on the order of," a reference to the order of complexity of the work of the algorithm. Hence, for example, the order of complexity of a linear-time algorithm is $O(n)$. Big-O notation formalizes our discussion of orders of complexity.

The Role of the Constant of Proportionality

The **constant of proportionality** involves the terms and coefficients that are usually ignored during big-O analysis. However, when these items are large, they may have an impact on the algorithm, particularly for small and medium-sized data sets. For example, the difference between n and $n/2$ when n is $1,000,000$ is significant to anyone needing money. In the example algorithms discussed so far, the instructions that execute within a loop are part of the constant of proportionality, as are the instructions that initialize the variables before the loops are entered. When analyzing an algorithm, you must be careful to determine that any instructions do not hide a loop that depends on a variable problem size. If that is the case, then the analysis must move down into the nested loop.

Let's determine the constant of proportionality for the first algorithm discussed in this chapter. Here is the code:

```
work = 1
for x in range(problemSize):
    work += 1
    work -= 1
```

Note that, aside from the loop itself, there are three lines of code, each of them assignment statements. Each of these three statements runs in constant time. Let's also assume that on each iteration, the overhead of managing the loop, which is hidden in the loop header, runs two more instructions that require constant time. Thus, the amount of abstract work performed by this algorithm is $4n + 1$. Although this number is greater than just n, the running times for the two amounts of work, n and $4n + 1$, increase at the same rate.

Measuring the Memory Used by an Algorithm

A complete analysis of the resources used by an algorithm includes the amount of memory required. Once again, you focus on rates of potential growth. Some algorithms require the same amount of memory to solve a problem of any size. Other algorithms require more memory as the problem size gets larger.

For example, consider the recursive **summation** function, as defined in Chapter 7:

```
def summation(lower, upper):
    """Returns the sum of the numbers from lower through
    upper."""
    if lower > upper:
        return 0
    else:
        return lower + summation(lower + 1, upper)
```

As mentioned in Chapter 7, each recursive call requires a new chunk of memory for a stack frame on the system call stack. A call of **summation(1, 6)** requires six such stack frames, and a call of **summation(1, n)** requires n of them. You therefore can conclude that the rate of growth of memory for the recursive **summation** function is linear. By contrast, the version of **summation** that uses a loop, also discussed in Chapter 7, requires just one stack frame, for the top-level call, and so there is no growth of memory required as the problem size increases.

Exercise 13-2

1. Assume that each of the following expressions indicates the number of operations performed by an algorithm for a problem size of n. Point out the dominant term of each algorithm, and use big-O notation to classify it.

   a. $2n - 4n^2 + 5n$
   b. $3n^2 + 6$
   c. $n^3 + n^2 - n$

2. For problem size n, algorithms A and B perform n^2 and $\frac{1}{2}n^2 + \frac{1}{2}n$ instructions, respectively. Which algorithm does more work? Are there particular problem sizes for which one algorithm performs significantly better than the other? Are there particular problem sizes for which both algorithms perform approximately the same amount of work?

3. At what point does an n^4 algorithm begin to perform better than a 2^n algorithm?

13.3 Search Algorithms

Searching and sorting have widespread application, so much effort is devoted to discovering the fastest search and sort algorithms. The analysis of the performance of these algorithms is critical. Here are several algorithms that can be used for searching and sorting lists. In what follows, the design of an algorithm is discussed, its implementation as a Python function is shown, and, finally, an analysis of the algorithm's computational complexity is provided. To keep things simple, each function processes a list of integers. Lists of different sizes can be passed as parameters to the functions. The functions are defined in a single module that is used in the case study later in this chapter.

Search for a Minimum

Python's **min** function returns the minimum or smallest item in a list. To study the complexity of this algorithm, let's develop an alternative version that returns the *position* of the minimum item. The algorithm assumes that the list is not empty and that the items are in arbitrary order. The algorithm begins by treating the first position as that of the minimum item. It then searches to the right for an item that is smaller and, if it is found, resets the position of the minimum item to the current position. When the algorithm reaches the end of the list, it returns the position of the minimum item. Here is the code for the algorithm, in function `ourMin`:

```python
def ourMin(lyst):
    """Returns the position of the minimum item."""
    minpos = 0
    current = 1
    while current < len(lyst):
        if lyst[current] < lyst[minpos]:
            minpos = current
        current += 1
    return minpos
```

As you can see, there are three instructions outside the loop that execute the same number of times regardless of the size of the list. Therefore, we can discount them. Within the loop, you find three more instructions. Of these, the comparison in the `if` statement and the increment of `current` execute once on each pass through the loop. There are no nested or hidden loops in these instructions. This algorithm must visit every item in the list to guarantee that it has located the position of the minimum item. Consequently, the algorithm must make $n - 1$ comparisons for a list of size n. Therefore, the algorithm's complexity is $O(n)$.

Sequential Search of a List

Python's `in` operator is implemented as a method named `__contains__` in the `list` class. This method searches for a particular item (called the target item) within a list of arbitrarily arranged items. In such a list, the only way to search for a target item is to begin with the item at the first position and compare it to the target. If the items are equal, the method returns `True`. Otherwise, the method moves on to the next position and compares items again. If the method arrives at the last position and still cannot find the target, it returns `False`. This kind of search is called a **sequential search** or a **linear search**. A more useful search function would return the index of a target if it's found, or −1 otherwise. Here is the Python code for a sequential search function:

```python
def sequentialSearch(target, lyst):
    """Returns the position of the target item if found,
    or -1 otherwise."""
    position = 0
    while position < len(lyst):
        if target == lyst[position]:
            return position
        position += 1
    return -1
```

Note that the loop in `sequentialSearch`, unlike the loop in `ourMin`, may end early because of the nested `return` statement. This makes the analysis of a sequential search a bit different from the analysis of a search for a minimum, as we shall see in the next subsection.

Best-Case, Worst-Case, and Average-Case Performance

The performance of some algorithms depends on the placement of the data that are processed. The sequential search algorithm does less work to find a target at the beginning of a list than at the end of the list. For such algorithms, you can determine the best-case performance, the worst-case performance, and the average performance. A thorough analysis of an algorithm's complexity divides its behavior into these three types of cases:

1. *Best case:* Under what circumstances does an algorithm do the least amount of work? What is the algorithm's complexity in this best case?
2. *Worst case:* Under what circumstances does an algorithm do the most amount of work? What is the algorithm's complexity in this worst case?
3. *Average case:* Under what circumstances does an algorithm do a typical amount of work? What is the algorithm's complexity in this typical case?

In general, you worry more about average and worst-case performances than about best-case performances.

Our analysis of a sequential search considers three cases:

1. In the worst case, the target item is at the end of the list or not in the list at all. Then the algorithm must visit every item and perform n iterations for a list of size n. Therefore, the worst-case complexity of a sequential search is $O(n)$.
2. In the best case, the algorithm finds the target at the first position, after making one iteration, for an $O(1)$ complexity.
3. To determine the average case, you add the number of iterations required to find the target at each possible position and divide the sum by n. Hence, the algorithm performs $(n + n - 1 + n - 2 + \ldots + 1) / n$, or $(n + 1) / 2$ iterations. For very large n, the constant factor of $/2$ is insignificant, so the average complexity is still $O(n)$.

Clearly, the best-case performance of a sequential search is rare when compared with the average and worst-case performances, which are essentially the same.

Binary Search of a List

A sequential search is necessary for data that are not arranged in any special order. When searching sorted data, you can use a **binary search**.

To understand how a binary search works, think about what happens when you look up a term in this book's index (assuming you have the print edition). The terms in an index are already sorted, so you don't do a sequential search. Instead, you estimate the term's alphabetical position in the index and open the index pages as close to that position as possible. You then determine if the target term lies, alphabetically, on an earlier page or later page, and flip back or forward through the pages as necessary. You repeat this process until you find the term or conclude that it's not in the index.

Now let's consider an example of a binary search of a list in Python. To begin, let's assume that the items in the list are sorted in ascending order (as they are in an index). The search algorithm goes directly to the middle position in the list and compares the item at that position to the target. If there is a match, the algorithm returns the position. Otherwise, if the target is less than the current item, the algorithm searches the portion of the list before the middle position. If the target is greater than the current item, the algorithm searches the portion of the list after the middle position. The search process stops when the target is found or the current beginning position is greater than the current ending position.

Here is the code for the binary search function:

```
def binarySearch(target, lyst):
    """Returns the position of the target item if found,
    or -1 otherwise."""
    left = 0
    right = len(lyst) - 1
    while left <= right:
        midpoint = (left + right) // 2
        if target == lyst[midpoint]:
            return midpoint
        elif target < lyst[midpoint]:
            right = midpoint - 1        # Search to left
        else:
            left = midpoint + 1         # Search to right
    return -1
```

There is just one loop with no nested or hidden loops. Once again, the worst case occurs when the target is not in the list. How many times does the loop run in the worst case? This is equal to the number of times the size of the list can be divided by 2 until the quotient is 1. For a list of size n, you essentially perform the reduction $n / 2 / 2 \ldots / 2$ until the result is 1. Let k be the number of times we divide n by 2. To solve for k, you have $n/2^k = 1$, and $n = 2^k$, and $k = \log_2 n$. Thus, the worst-case complexity of binary search is $O(\log_2 n)$.

Figure 13-7 shows the portions of the list being searched in a binary search with a list of 9 items and a target item, 10, that is not in the list. The items compared to the target are shaded. Note that none of the items in the left half of the original list are visited.

The binary search for the target item 10 requires four comparisons, whereas a linear search would have required 10 comparisons. This algorithm actually appears to perform better as the problem size gets larger. Our list of 9 items requires at most 4 comparisons, whereas a list of 1,000,000 items requires at most only 20 comparisons!

Binary search is certainly more efficient than sequential search. However, the kind of search algorithm we choose depends on the organization of the data in the list. There is some additional overall cost to a binary search, which has to do with keeping the list in sorted order. In the next section, we examine several strategies for sorting a list and analyze their complexity.

Figure 13-7 The items of a list visited during a binary search for 10

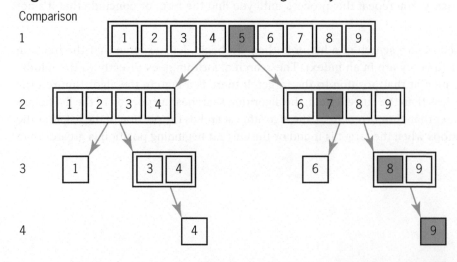

> ## Exercise 13-3

1. Suppose that a list contains the values

   20 44 48 55 62 66 74 88 93 99

   at index positions 0 through 9. Trace the values of the variables **left**, **right**, and **midpoint** in a binary search of this list for the target value 90. Repeat for the target value 44.

2. The method you usually use to look up an entry in a phone book is not exactly the same as a binary search because, when using a phone book, you don't always go to the midpoint of the sublist being searched. Instead, you estimate the position of the target based on the alphabetical position of the first letter of the person's last name. For example, when you are looking up a number for "Smith," you first look toward the middle of the second half of the phone book instead of in the middle of the entire book. Suggest a modification of the binary search algorithm that emulates this strategy for a list of names. Is its computational complexity any better than that of the standard binary search?

13.4 Basic Sort Algorithms

You have just seen how a sorted list is a critical precondition of a log *n* search algorithm. Lists whose items are in random order cannot be searched in this manner; you need to run a sort algorithm on such lists at some point to guarantee optimal searches. Python's **sort** method accomplishes this, but how does it work, and how fast does it run? Computer scientists have devised many ingenious strategies for sorting a list of items. In this section, you will examine some algorithms that are easy to write but are inefficient, and you will consider some faster but more complicated algorithms in the next section.

Each of the Python sort functions that you develop operates on a list of integers and uses a **swap** function to exchange the positions of two items in the list. Here is the code for that function:

```python
def swap(lyst, i, j):
    """Exchanges the items at positions i and j."""
    # You could say lyst[i], lyst[j] = lyst[j], lyst[i]
    # but the following code shows what is really going on
    temp = lyst[i]
    lyst[i] = lyst[j]
    lyst[j] = temp
```

Selection Sort

Perhaps the simplest strategy is to search the entire list for the position of the smallest item. If that position does not equal the first position, the algorithm swaps the items at those positions. It then returns to the second position and repeats this process, swapping the smallest item with the item at the second position, if necessary. When the algorithm reaches the last position in this overall process, the list is sorted. The algorithm is called **selection sort** because each pass through the main loop selects a single item to be moved. **Table 13-3** shows the states of a list of five items after each search and swap pass of selection sort. The two items just swapped on each pass have asterisks next to them, and the sorted portion of the list is shaded.

Table 13-3 A trace of the data during a selection sort (passes through outer loop)

Unsorted List	After 1st Pass	After 2nd Pass	After 3rd Pass	After 4th Pass
5	1*	1	1	1
3	3	2*	2	2
1	5*	5	3*	3
2	2	3*	5*	4*
4	4	4	4	5*

Here is the Python function for a selection sort:

```python
def selectionSort(lyst):
    """Sorts the items in lyst in ascending order."""
    i = 0
    while i < len(lyst) - 1:       # Do n - 1 searches
        minIndex = i               # for the smallest item
        j = i + 1
        while j < len(lyst):       # Start a search
            if lyst[j] < lyst[minIndex]:
                minIndex = j
            j += 1
        if minIndex != i:          # Swap if necessary
            swap(lyst, minIndex, i)
        i += 1
```

This function includes a nested loop. For a list of size n, the outer loop executes $n - 1$ times. On the first pass through the outer loop, the inner loop executes $n - 1$ times. On the second pass through the outer loop, the inner loop executes $n - 2$ times. On the last pass through the outer loop, the inner loop executes once. Consequently, the total number of comparisons for a list of size n is the following:

$$(n-1)+(n-2)+...+1=$$
$$n(n-1)/2=$$
$$\tfrac{1}{2}n^2 - \tfrac{1}{2}n$$

For large n, you can pick the term with the largest degree and drop the coefficient, so selection sort is $O(n^2)$ in all cases. For large data sets, the cost of swapping items might also be significant. Because data items are swapped only in the outer loop, this additional cost for selection sort is linear in the worst and average cases.

Bubble Sort

Another sort algorithm that is relatively easy to conceive and code is called a **bubble sort**. Its strategy is to start at the beginning of the list and compare pairs of data items as it moves down to the end. Each time the items in the pair are out of order, the algorithm swaps them. This process has the effect of bubbling the largest items to the end of the list. The algorithm then repeats the process from the beginning of the list and goes to the next-to-last item, and so on, until it begins with the last item. At that point, the list is sorted.

Table 13-4 shows a trace of a single bubbling process through a list of five items. This process makes four passes through a nested loop to bubble the largest item down to the end of the list. Once again, the items just swapped are marked with asterisks, and the sorted portion is shaded.

Table 13-4   A trace of the data during a bubble sort (passes through inner loop)

Unsorted List	After 1st Pass	After 2nd Pass	After 3rd Pass	After 4th Pass
5	4*	4	4	4
4	5*	2*	2	2
2	2	5*	1*	1
1	1	1	5*	3*
3	3	3	3	5*

Here is the Python function for a bubble sort:

```python
def bubbleSort(lyst):
    """Sorts the items in lyst in ascending order."""
    n = len(lyst)
    while n > 1:                        # Do n - 1 bubbles
        i = 1                           # Start each bubble
        while i < n:
            if lyst[i] < lyst[i - 1]:   # Exchange if needed
                swap(lyst, i, i - 1)
            i += 1
        n -= 1
```

As with the selection sort, a bubble sort has a nested loop. The sorted portion of the list now grows from the end of the list up to the beginning, but the performance of the bubble sort is quite similar to the behavior of the selection sort: the inner loop executes $\frac{1}{2}n^2 - \frac{1}{2}n$ times for a list of size n. Thus, bubble sort is $O(n^2)$. Like selection sort, bubble sort won't perform any swaps if the list is already sorted. However, bubble sort's worst-case behavior for exchanges is greater than linear. The proof of this is left as an exercise for you.

You can make a minor adjustment to the bubble sort to improve its best-case performance to linear. If no swaps occur during a pass through the main loop, then the list is sorted. This can happen on any pass, and in the best case will happen on the first pass. You can track the presence of swapping with a Boolean flag and return from the function when the inner loop does not set this flag. Here is the modified bubble sort function:

```python
def bubbleSort(lyst):
    """Sorts the items in lyst in ascending order."""
    n = len(lyst)
    while n > 1:                        # Do n - 1 bubbles
        swapped = False                 # Start each bubble
        i = 1
        while i < n:
            if lyst[i] < lyst[i - 1]:   # Exchange if needed
                swap(lyst, i, i - 1)
                swapped = True
            i += 1
        if not swapped: return          # Exit if no swaps
        n -= 1
```

Note that this modification only improves best-case behavior. On the average, the behavior of bubble sort is still $O(n^2)$.

Insertion Sort

Our modified bubble sort performs better than a selection sort for lists that are already sorted. But our modified bubble sort can still perform poorly if only a few items are out of order in the list. Another algorithm, called an **insertion sort**, attempts to exploit the partial ordering of the list in a different way. The strategy is as follows:

- On the ith pass through the list, where i ranges from 1 to $n-1$, the ith item should be inserted into its proper place among the first i items in the list.

- After the ith pass, the first i items should be in sorted order.

- This process is analogous to the way in which many people organize playing cards in their hands. That is, if you hold the first $i-1$ cards in order, you pick the ith card and compare it to these cards until its proper spot is found.

- As with our other sort algorithms, insertion sort consists of two loops. The outer loop traverses the positions from 1 to $n-1$. For each position i in this loop, you save the item and start the inner loop at position $i-1$. For each position j in this loop, you move the item to position $j+1$ until you find the insertion point for the saved (ith) item.

Here is the code for the **insertionSort** function:

```
def insertionSort(lyst):
    """Sorts the items in lyst in ascending order."""
    i = 1
    while i < len(lyst):
        itemToInsert = lyst[i]
        j = i - 1
        while j >= 0:
            if itemToInsert < lyst[j]:
                lyst[j + 1] = lyst[j]
                j -= 1
            else:
                break
        lyst[j + 1] = itemToInsert
        i += 1
```

Table 13-5 shows the states of a list of five items after each pass through the outer loop of an insertion sort. The item to be inserted on the next pass is marked with an arrow; after it is inserted, this item is marked with an asterisk.

Table 13-5 A trace of the data during an insertion sort (passes through outer loop)

Unsorted List	After 1st Pass	After 2nd Pass	After 3rd Pass	After 4th Pass
2	2	1*	1	1
5 ←	5 (no insertion)	2	2	2
1	1 ←	5	4*	3*
4	4	4 ←	5	4
3	3	3	3 ←	5

Once again, analysis focuses on the nested loop. The outer loop executes $n-1$ times. In the worst case, when all of the data are out of order, the inner loop iterates once on the first pass through the outer loop, twice on the second pass, and so on, for a total of $\frac{1}{2}n^2 - \frac{1}{2}n$ times. Therefore, the worst-case behavior of insertion sort is $O(n^2)$.

The more items in the list that are in order, the better insertion sort gets until, in the best case of a sorted list, the sort's behavior is linear. In the average case, however, insertion sort is still quadratic.

Best-Case, Worst-Case, and Average-Case Performance Revisited

As mentioned earlier, for many algorithms, a single measure of complexity cannot be applied to all cases. Sometimes an algorithm's behavior improves or gets worse when it encounters a particular arrangement of data. For example, the bubble sort algorithm can terminate as soon as the list becomes sorted. If the input list is already sorted, the bubble sort requires approximately n comparisons. In many other cases, however, bubble sort requires approximately n^2 comparisons. Clearly, a more detailed analysis may be needed to make programmers aware of these special cases. Let's apply this kind of analysis to the search for a minimum algorithm and to the smarter version of the bubble sort algorithm.

Because the search for a minimum algorithm must visit each number in the list, unless it is sorted, the algorithm is always linear. Therefore, its best-case, worst-case, and average-case performances are $O(n)$.

The smarter version of bubble sort can terminate as soon as the list becomes sorted. In the best case, this happens when the input list is already sorted. Therefore, bubble sort's best-case performance is $O(n)$. However, this case is rare (1 out of $n!$). In the worst case, even this version of bubble sort will have to bubble each item down to its proper position in the list. The algorithm's worst-case performance is clearly $O(n^2)$. Bubble sort's average-case performance is closer to $O(n^2)$ than to $O(n)$, although the demonstration of this fact is a bit more involved than it is for sequential search.

There are algorithms whose best-case and average-case performances are similar, but whose performance can degrade to a worst case. Whether you are choosing an algorithm or developing a new one, it is important to be aware of these distinctions.

Exercise 13-4

1. Which configuration of data in a list causes the smallest number of exchanges in a selection sort? Which configuration of data causes the largest number of exchanges?

2. Explain the role that the number of data exchanges plays in the analysis of selection sort and bubble sort. What role, if any, does the size of the data objects play?

3. Explain why the modified bubble sort still exhibits $O(n^2)$ behavior on the average.

4. Explain why insertion sort works well on partially sorted lists.

13.5 Faster Sorting

The three sort algorithms considered so far have $O(n^2)$ running times. There are several variations on these sort algorithms, some of which are marginally faster, but they, too, are $O(n^2)$ in the worst and average cases. However, you can take advantage of some better algorithms that are $O(n \log n)$. The secret to these better algorithms is a divide-and-conquer strategy. That is, each algorithm finds a way of breaking the list into smaller sublists. These sublists are then sorted recursively. Ideally, if the number of these subdivisions is $\log(n)$ and the amount of work needed to rearrange the data on each subdivision is n, then the total complexity of such a sort algorithm is $O(n \log n)$. In **Table 13-6**, you can see that the growth rate of work of an $O(n \log n)$ algorithm is much slower than that of an $O(n^2)$ algorithm.

Table 13-6   Comparing n Log n and n^2

n	n Log n	n^2
512	4,608	262,144
1,024	10,240	1,048,576
2,048	22,458	4,194,304
8,192	106,496	67,108,864
16,384	229,376	268,435,456
32,768	491,520	1,073,741,824

In this section, you will examine two recursive sort algorithms that break the n^2 barrier: quicksort and merge sort.

Quicksort

Here is an outline of the strategy used in the `quicksort` algorithm:

1. Begin by selecting the item at the list's midpoint. You call this item the pivot. (Later, we discuss alternative ways to choose the pivot.)
2. Partition items in the list so that all items less than the pivot are moved to the left of the pivot, and the rest are moved to its right. The final position of the pivot itself varies, depending on the actual items involved. For instance, the pivot ends up being rightmost in the list if it is the largest item and leftmost if it is the smallest. But wherever the pivot ends up, that is its final position in the fully sorted list.
3. Divide and conquer. Reapply the process recursively to the sublists formed by splitting the list at the pivot. One sublist consists of all items to the left of the pivot (now the smaller ones), and the other sublist has all items to the right (now the larger ones).
4. The process terminates each time it encounters a sublist with fewer than two items.

Partitioning

From the programmer's perspective, the most complicated part of the algorithm is the operation of partitioning the items in a sublist. There are two principal ways of doing this. What follows is an informal description of the easier method as it applies to any sublist:

1. Swap the pivot with the last item in the sublist.
2. Establish a boundary between the items known to be less than the pivot and the rest of the items. Initially, this boundary is positioned immediately before the first item.
3. Starting with the first item in the sublist, scan across the sublist. Every time an item less than the pivot is encountered, swap it with the first item after the boundary and advance the boundary.
4. Finish by swapping the pivot with the first item after the boundary.

Table 13-7 lists these steps as applied to the numbers 12 19 17 18 14 11 15 13 16. In Step 1, the pivot is established and swapped with the last item. In Step 2, the boundary is established before the first item. In Steps 3–6, the sublist is scanned for items less than the pivot; these are swapped with the first item after the boundary, and the boundary is advanced. Notice that items to the left of the boundary are less than the pivot at all times. Finally, in Step 7, the pivot is swapped with the first item after the boundary, and the sublist has been successfully partitioned.

After a sublist has been partitioned, you reapply the process to its left and right sublists (12 11 13 and 16 19 15 17 18) and so on until the sublists have lengths of at most one.

Complexity Analysis of Quicksort

Now, here is an informal analysis of the quicksort's complexity. During the first partition operation, you scan all of the items from the beginning of the list to its end. Consequently, the amount of work during this operation is proportional to n, the list's length.

Table 13-7   Partitioning a sublist in quicksort

1	Let the sublist consist of the numbers shown with a pivot of 14.	12 19 17 18 14 11 15 13 16
	Swap the pivot with the last item.	12 19 17 18 16 11 15 13 14
2	Establish the boundary before the first item.	: 12 19 17 18 16 11 15 13 14
3	Scan for the first item less than the pivot.	: 12 19 17 18 16 11 15 13 14
	Swap this item with the first item after the boundary. In this example, the item gets swapped with itself.	: 12 19 17 18 16 11 15 13 14
		12 : 19 17 18 16 11 15 13 14
	Advance the boundary.	
4	Scan for the next item less than the pivot.	12 : 19 17 18 16 11 15 13 14
	Swap this item with the first item after the boundary.	12 : 11 17 18 16 19 15 13 14
	Advance the boundary.	12 11 : 17 18 16 19 15 13 14
5	Scan for the next item less than the pivot.	12 11 : 17 18 16 19 15 13 14
	Swap this item with the first item after the boundary.	12 11 : 13 18 16 19 15 17 14
	Advance the boundary.	12 11 13 : 18 16 19 15 17 14
6	Scan for the next item less than the pivot; however, there is not one.	12 11 13 : 18 16 19 15 17 14
7	Interchange the pivot with the first item after the boundary. At this point, all items less than the pivot are to the pivot's left and the rest are to its right.	12 11 13 : 14 16 19 15 17 18

The amount of work after this partition is proportional to the left sublist's length plus the right sublist's length, which together yield $n - 1$. And when these sublists are divided, there are four pieces whose combined length is approximately n, so the combined work is proportional to n yet again. As the list is divided into more pieces, the total work remains proportional to n.

To complete the analysis, we need to determine how many times the lists are partitioned. We will make the optimistic assumption that, each time, the dividing line between the new sublists turns out to be as close to the center of the current sublist as possible. In practice, this is not usually the case. You already know from the discussion of the binary search algorithm that when you divide a list in half repeatedly, you arrive at a single element in about $\log_2 n$ steps. Thus, the algorithm is $O(n \log n)$ in the best-case performance.

For the worst-case performance, consider the case of a list that is already sorted. If the pivot element chosen is the first element, then there are $n - 1$ elements to its right on the first partition, $n - 2$ elements to its right on the second partition, and so on, as shown in **Figure 13-8**.

Although no elements are exchanged, the total number of partitions is $n - 1$, and the total number of comparisons performed is $\frac{1}{2}n^2 - \frac{1}{2}n$, the same number as in selection sort and bubble sort. Thus, in the worst case, the quicksort algorithm is $O(n^2)$.

If quicksort is implemented as a recursive algorithm, analysis must also consider memory usage for the call stack. Each recursive call requires a constant amount of memory for a stack frame, and there are two recursive calls after each partition. Therefore, memory usage is $O(\log n)$ in the best case and $O(n)$ in the worst case.

Although the worst-case performance of quicksort is rare, programmers certainly prefer to avoid it. Choosing the pivot at the first or last position is not a wise strategy. Other methods of choosing the pivot, such as selecting a random position or choosing the median of the first, middle, and last elements, can help to approximate $O(n \log n)$ performance in the average case.

Implementation of Quicksort

The quicksort algorithm is most easily coded using a recursive approach. The following script defines a top-level `quicksort` function for the client, a recursive `quicksortHelper` function to hide the extra arguments for the end points of a sublist, and a `partition` function. The script runs quicksort on a list of 20 randomly ordered integers.

Figure 13-8 A worst-case scenario for quicksort (arrows indicate pivot elements)

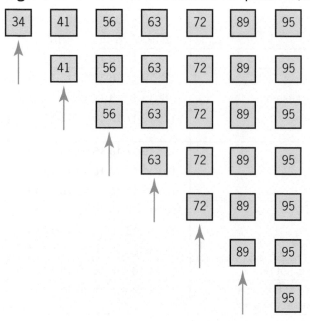

```
def quicksort(lyst):
    """Sorts the items in lyst in ascending order."""
    quicksortHelper(lyst, 0, len(lyst) - 1)


def quicksortHelper(lyst, left, right):
    """Partition lyst, then sort the left segment and
    sort the right segment."""
    if left < right:
        pivotLocation = partition(lyst, left, right)
        quicksortHelper(lyst, left, pivotLocation - 1)
        quicksortHelper(lyst, pivotLocation + 1, right)

def partition(lyst, left, right):
    """Shifts items less than the pivot to its left,
    and items greater than the pivot to its right,
    and returns the position of the pivot."""
    # Find the pivot and exchange it with the last item
    middle = (left + right) // 2
    pivot = lyst[middle]
    lyst[middle] = lyst[right]
    lyst[right] = pivot
    # Set boundary point to first position
    boundary = left
```

```
    # Move items less than pivot to the left
    for index in range(left, right):
        if lyst[index] < pivot:
            swap(lyst, index, boundary)
            boundary += 1
    # Exchange the pivot item and the boundary item
    swap(lyst, right, boundary)
    return boundary


# swap is defined as before

import random
def main(size = 20, sort = quicksort):
    """Sort a randomly ordered list and print
    before and after."""
    lyst = list(range(1, size + 1))
    random.shuffle(lyst)
    print(lyst)
    sort(lyst)
    print(lyst)

if __name__ == "__main__":
    main()
```

Merge Sort

Another algorithm called **merge sort** employs a recursive, divide-and-conquer strategy to break the $O(n^2)$ barrier. Here is an informal summary of the algorithm:

- Compute the middle position of a list and recursively sort its left and right sublists (divide and conquer).

- Merge the two sorted sublists back into a single sorted list.

- Stop the process when sublists can no longer be subdivided.

    Three Python functions collaborate in this top-level design strategy:

- **mergeSort**—The function called by users.

- **mergeSortHelper**—A helper function that hides the extra parameters required by recursive calls.

- **merge**—A function that implements the merging process.

Implementing the Merging Process

The merging process uses a temporary list of the same size as the list being sorted. This list is called the **copyBuffer**. To avoid the overhead of allocating and deallocating the **copyBuffer** each time **merge** is called, the buffer is allocated once in **mergeSort** and subsequently passed as an argument to **mergeSortHelper** and **merge**. Each time `mergeSortHelper` is called, it needs to know the bounds of the sublist with which it is working. These bounds are provided by two other parameters, `low` and `high`. Here is the code for `mergeSort`:

```
def mergeSort(lyst):
    # lyst              list being sorted
    # copyBuffer        temporary space needed during merge
    copyBuffer = list(lyst)
    mergeSortHelper(lyst, copyBuffer, 0, len(lyst) - 1)
```

After checking that it has been passed a sublist of at least two items, `mergeSortHelper` computes the midpoint of the sublist, recursively sorts the portions below and above the midpoint, and calls `merge` to merge the results. Here is the code for `mergeSortHelper`:

```
def mergeSortHelper(lyst, copyBuffer, low, high):
    # lyst              list being sorted
    # copyBuffer        temporary space needed during merge
    # low, high         bounds of sublist
    # middle            midpoint of sublist
    if low < high:
        middle = (low + high) // 2
        mergeSortHelper(lyst, copyBuffer, low, middle)
        mergeSortHelper(lyst, copyBuffer, middle + 1, high)
        merge(lyst, copyBuffer, low, middle, high)
```

Figure 13-9 shows the sublists generated during recursive calls to **mergeSortHelper**, starting from a list of eight items.

Figure 13-9 Sublists generated during calls of `mergeSortHelper`

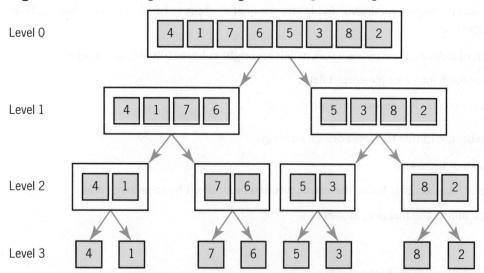

Note that, in this example, the sublists are evenly subdivided at each level, and there are 2^k sublists to be merged at level k. Had the length of the initial list not been a power of two, then an exactly even subdivision would not have been achieved at each level, and the last level would not have contained a full complement of sublists. **Figure 13-10** traces the process of merging the sublists generated in Figure 13-9.

Figure 13-10   Merging the sublists during a merge sort

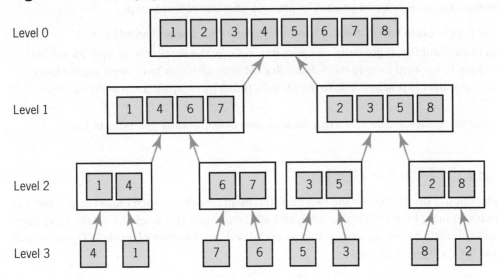

Finally, here is the code for the **merge** function:

```
def merge(lyst, copyBuffer, low, middle, high):
    # lyst             list that is being sorted
    # copyBuffer       temp space needed during the merge process
    # low              beginning of first sorted sublist
    # middle           end of first sorted sublist
    # middle + 1       beginning of second sorted sublist
    # high             end of second sorted sublist
    # Initialize i1 and i2 to the first items in each sublist
    i1 = low
    i2 = middle + 1
    # Interleave items from the sublists into the
    # copyBuffer in such a way that order is maintained.
    for i in range(low, high + 1):
        if i1 > middle:
            copyBuffer[i] = lyst[i2]        # First sublist exhausted
            i2 += 1
        elif i2 > high:
            copyBuffer[i] = lyst[i1]        # Second sublist exhausted
            i1 += 1
        elif lyst[i1] < lyst[i2]:
            copyBuffer[i] = lyst[i1]        # Item in first sublist <
            i1 += 1
        else:
            copyBuffer[i] = lyst[i2]        # Item in second sublist <
            i2 += 1
    for i in range(low, high + 1):          # Copy sorted items back to
        lyst[i] = copyBuffer[i]             # proper positions in lyst
```

The `merge` function combines two sorted sublists into a larger sorted sublist. The first sublist lies between `low` and `middle` and the second between `middle + 1` and `high`. The process consists of three steps:

1. Set up index pointers to the first items in each sublist. These are at positions `low` and `middle + 1`.

2. Starting with the first item in each sublist, repeatedly compare items. Copy the smaller item from its sublist to the copy buffer and advance to the next item in the sublist. Repeat until all items have been copied from both sublists. If the end of one sublist is reached before the other's, finish by copying the remaining items from the other sublist.

3. Copy the portion of `copyBuffer` between `low` and `high` back to the corresponding positions in list.

Complexity Analysis of Merge Sort

The running time of the `merge` function is dominated by the two `for` statements, each of which loops (*high* – *low* + 1) times. Consequently, the function's running time is O(*high* – *low*), and all the merges at a single level take O(*n*) time. Because `mergeSortHelper` splits sublists as evenly as possible at each level, the number of levels is O(log *n*), and the running time for this function is O(*n* log *n*) in all cases.

The merge sort has two space requirements that depend on the list's size. First, O(log *n*) space is required on the call stack to support recursive calls. Second, O(*n*) space is used by the copy buffer.

Exercise 13-5

1. Describe the strategy of quicksort and explain why it can reduce the time complexity of sorting from O(n^2) to O(*n* log *n*).

2. Why is quicksort not O(*n* log *n*) in all cases? Describe the worst-case situation for quicksort and give a list of 10 integers, 1–10, that would produce this behavior.

3. The partition operation in quicksort chooses the item at the midpoint as the pivot. Describe two other strategies for selecting a pivot value.

4. Jill has a bright idea: When the length of a sublist in quicksort is less than a certain number—say, 30 items—run an insertion sort to process that sublist. Explain why this is a bright idea.

5. Why is merge sort an O(*n* log *n*) algorithm in the worst case?

13.6 An Exponential Algorithm: Recursive Fibonacci

Earlier in this chapter, you ran the recursive Fibonacci function to obtain a count of the recursive calls with various problem sizes. You saw that the number of calls seemed to grow much faster than the square of the problem size. Here is the code for the function once again:

```
def fib(n):
    """Returns the nth Fibonacci number."""
    if n < 3:
        return 1
    else:
        return fib(n - 1) + fib(n - 2)
```

Another way to illustrate this rapid growth of work is to display a **call tree** for the function for a given problem size. **Figure 13-11** shows the calls involved when you use the recursive function to compute the sixth Fibonacci number. To keep the diagram reasonably compact, you write **(6)** instead of **fib(6)**.

Figure 13-11   A call tree for **fib(6)**

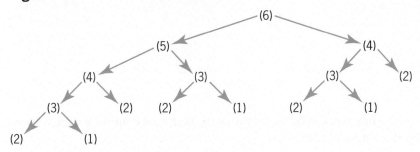

Note that **fib(4)** requires only 4 recursive calls, which seems linear, but **fib(6)** requires 2 calls of **fib(4)**, among a total of 14 recursive calls. It gets much worse as the problem size grows, with possibly many repetitions of the same subtrees in the call tree.

Exactly how bad is this behavior, then? If the call tree were fully balanced, with the bottom two levels of calls completely filled in, a call with an argument of 6 would generate $2 + 4 + 8 + 16 = 30$ recursive calls. Note that the number of calls at each filled level is twice that of the level above it. Hence, the number of recursive calls generally is $2^{n-1} - 2$ in fully balanced call trees, where n is the argument at the top or root of the call tree. This is clearly the behavior of an exponential, $O(k^n)$ algorithm. Although the bottom two levels of the call tree for recursive Fibonacci are not completely filled in, its call tree is close enough in shape to a fully balanced tree to rank recursive Fibonacci as an exponential algorithm. The constant k for recursive Fibonacci is approximately 1.63.

Exponential algorithms are generally impractical to run with any but very small problem sizes. Although recursive Fibonacci is elegant in its design, there is a less beautiful but much faster version that uses a loop to run in linear time (see the next section).

Alternatively, recursive functions that are called repeatedly with the same arguments, such as the Fibonacci function, can be made more efficient by a technique called **memoization**. According to this technique, the program maintains a dictionary of the values for each argument used with the function. Before the function recursively computes a value for a given argument, it checks the dictionary to see if that argument already has a value. If so, that value is simply returned. If not, the computation proceeds, and the argument and value are added to the dictionary afterward.

Computer scientists devote much effort to the development of fast algorithms. As a rule, any reduction in the order of magnitude of complexity, say, from $O(n^2)$ to $O(n)$, is preferable to a "tweak" of code that reduces the constant of proportionality.

Converting Fibonacci to a Linear Algorithm

Although the recursive Fibonacci function reflects the simplicity and elegance of the recursive definition of the Fibonacci sequence, the run-time performance of this function is unacceptable. A different algorithm improves on this performance by several orders of magnitude and, in fact, reduces the complexity to linear time. In this section, we develop this alternative algorithm and assess its performance.

Recall that the first two numbers in the Fibonacci sequence are 1s, and each number after that is the sum of the previous two numbers. Thus, the new algorithm starts a loop if n is at least the third Fibonacci number. This number will be at least the sum of the first two $(1 + 1 = 2)$. The loop computes this sum and then performs two replacements: the first number becomes the second one, and the second one becomes the sum just computed. The loop counts from 3 through n.

The sum at the end of the loop is the *n*th Fibonacci number. Here is the pseudocode for this algorithm:

```
Set sum to 1
Set first to 1
Set second to 1
Set count to 3
While count <= n
    Set sum to first + second
    Set first to second
    Set second to sum
    Increment count
```

The Python function `fib` now uses a loop. The function can be tested within the script used for the earlier version. Here is the code for the function, followed by the output of the script:

```
def fib(n, counter = None):
    """Count the number of iterations in the Fibonacci
    function."""
    theSum = 1
    first = 1
    second = 1
    count = 3
    while count <= n:
        if counter: counter.increment()
        theSum = first + second
        first = second
        second = theSum
        count += 1
    return theSum
```

```
Problem Size     Iterations
      2               0
      4               2
      8               6
     16              14
     32              30
```

As you can see, the performance of the new version of the function has improved to linear. Removing recursion by converting a recursive algorithm to one based on a loop can sometimes reduce its run-time complexity.

Case Study 13-1 | An Algorithm Profiler

Profiling is the process of measuring an algorithm's performance by counting instructions and/or timing execution. In this case study, you will develop a program to profile sort algorithms.

Request

Write a program that allows a programmer to profile different sort algorithms.

Analysis

The profiler should allow programmers to run a sort algorithm on a list of numbers. The profiler can track the algorithm's running time, the number of comparisons, and the number of exchanges. In addition, when the algorithm exchanges two values, the profiler can print a trace of the list. Programmers can provide their own list of numbers to the profiler or ask the profiler to generate a list of randomly ordered numbers of a given size. Programmers can also ask for a list of unique numbers or a list that contains duplicate values. For ease of use, the profiler allows programmers to specify most of these features as options before the algorithm is run. The default behavior is to run the algorithm on a randomly ordered list of 10 unique numbers where the running time, comparisons, and exchanges are tracked.

The profiler is an instance of the class **Profiler**. Programmers profile a **sort** function by running the profiler's **test** method with the function as the first argument and any of the options mentioned earlier. The next session shows several test runs of the profiler with the selection sort algorithm and different options:

```
>>> from profiler import Profiler
>>> from algorithms import selectionSort
>>> p = Profiler()
>>> p.test(selectionSort)       # Default behavior
Problem size: 10
Elapsed time: 0.0
Comparisons: 45
Exchanges: 7
>>> p.test(selectionSort, size = 5, trace = True)
[4, 2, 3, 5, 1]
[1, 2, 3, 5, 4]
Problem size: 5
Elapsed time: 0.117
Comparisons: 10
Exchanges: 2
>>> p.test(selectionSort, size = 100)
Problem size: 100
Elapsed time: 0.044
Comparisons: 4950
Exchanges: 97
>>> p.test(selectionSort, size = 1000)
Problem size: 1000
Elapsed time: 1.628
Comparisons: 499500
Exchanges:995
>>> p.test(selectionSort, size = 10000,
           exch = False, comp = False)
Problem size: 10000
Elapsed time: 111.077
```

The programmer configures a sort algorithm to be profiled as follows:

1. Define a sort function and include an optional second parameter, a **Profiler** object, in the sort function's header.

2. In the sort algorithm's code, run the methods **comparison** and **exchange** with the **Profiler** object where relevant, to count comparisons and exchanges.

3. The interface for the **Profiler** class is listed in **Table 13-8**.

Table 13-8 The interface for the Profiler class

Profiler **Method**	**What it Does**
p.test(function, lyst = None, size = 10, unique = True, comp = True, exch = True, trace = False)	Runs function with the given settings and prints the results
p.comparison( )	Increments the number of comparisons if that option has been specified
p.exchange( )	Increments the number of exchanges if that option has been specified
p.__str__( )	Returns a string representation of the results, depending on the options

Design

The programmer uses two modules:

1. **profiler**—This module defines the **Profiler** class.

2. **algorithms**—This module defines the sort functions, as configured for profiling.

The sort functions have the same design as those discussed earlier in this chapter, except that they receive a **Profiler** object as an additional parameter. The **Profiler** methods **comparison** and **exchange** are run with this object whenever a sort function performs a comparison or an exchange of data values, respectively. In fact, any list-processing algorithm can be added to this module and profiled just by including a **Profiler** parameter and running its two methods when comparisons and/or exchanges are made.

As shown in the earlier session, one imports the **Profiler** class and the **algorithms** module into a Python shell and performs the testing at the shell prompt. The profiler's **test** method sets up the **Profiler** object, runs the function to be profiled, and prints the results.

Implementation (Coding)

Here is a partial implementation of the **algorithms** module. We omit most of the sort algorithms developed earlier in this chapter, but include one, **selectionSort**, to show how the statistics are updated.

```
"""
File: algorithms.py
Algorithms configured for profiling.
"""


def selectionSort(lyst, profiler = None):
    """Sorts the items in lyst in ascending order."""
    i = 0
```

```
        while i < len(lyst) - 1:
            minIndex = i
            j = i + 1
            while j < len(lyst):
                if profiler: profiler.comparison()
                if lyst[j] < lyst[minIndex]:
                    minIndex = j
                j += 1
            if minIndex != i:
                swap(lyst, minIndex, i, profiler)
            i += 1

def swap(lyst, i, j, profiler = None):
    """Exchanges the elements at positions i and j."""
    if profiler: profiler.exchange()
    temp = lyst[i]
    lyst[i] = lyst[j]
    lyst[j] = temp

# Testing code can go here, optionally
```

The **Profiler** class includes the four methods listed in the interface as well as some helper methods for managing the clock.

```
"""
File: profiler.py
Defines a class for profiling sort algorithms.
A Profiler object tracks the list, the number of comparisons and exchanges,
and the running time. The Profiler can also print a trace and can create a
list of unique or duplicate numbers.
Example use:
from profiler import Profiler
from algorithms import selectionSort
p = Profiler()
p.test(selectionSort, size = 15, comp = True,
exch = True, trace = True)
"""

import time
import random

class Profiler(object):
    def test(self, function, lyst = None, size = 10,
             unique = True, comp = True, exch = True,
             trace = False):
```

(continues)

```python
        """
        function: the algorithm being profiled
        lyst: allows the caller to use her list
        size: the size of the list, 10 by default
        unique: if True, list contains unique integers
        comp: if True, count comparisons
        exch: if True, count exchanges
        trace: if True, print the list after each exchange
        Run the function with the given
        attributes and print its profile results.
        """
        self.comp = comp
        self.exch = exch
        self.trace = trace
        if lyst != None:
            self.lyst = lyst
        elif unique:
            self.lyst = list(range(1, size + 1))
            random.shuffle(self.lyst)
        else:
            self.lyst = []
            for count in range(size):
                self.lyst.append(random.randint(1, size))
        self.exchCount = 0
        self.cmpCount = 0
        self.startClock()
        function(self.lyst, self)
        self.stopClock()
        print(self)

    def exchange(self):
        """Counts exchanges if on."""
        if self.exch:
            self.exchCount += 1
        if self.trace:
            print(self.lyst)

    def comparison(self):
        """Counts comparisons if on."""
        if self.comp:
            self.cmpCount += 1

    def startClock(self):
        """Record the starting time."""
        self.start = time.time()
```

```
def stopClock(self):
    """Stops the clock and computes the elapsed time
    in seconds, to the nearest millisecond."""
    self.elapsedTime = round(time.time() - self.start, 3)
def __str__(self):
    """Returns the results as a string."""
    result = "Problem size: "
    result += str(len(self.lyst)) + "\n"
    result += "Elapsed time: "
    result += str(self.elapsedTime) + "\n"
    if self.comp:
        result += "Comparisons: "
        result += str(self.cmpCount) + "\n"
    if self.exch:
        result += "Exchanges: "
        result += str(self.exchCount) + "\n"
    return result
```

Summary

- Different algorithms for solving the same problem can be ranked according to the time and memory resources that they require. Generally, algorithms that require less running time and less memory are considered better than those that require more of these resources. However, there is often a tradeoff between the two types of resources. Running time can occasionally be improved at the cost of using more memory, or memory usage can be improved at the cost of slower running times.

- The running time of an algorithm can be measured empirically using the computer's clock. However, these times will vary with the hardware and the types of programming language used.

- Counting instructions provides another empirical measurement of the amount of work that an algorithm does. Instruction counts can show increases or decreases in the rate of growth of an algorithm's work, independently of hardware and software platforms.

- The rate of growth of an algorithm's work can be expressed as a function of the size of its problem instances. Complexity analysis examines the algorithm's code to derive these expressions. Such an expression enables the programmer to predict how well or poorly an algorithm will perform on any computer.

- Big-O notation is a common way of expressing an algorithm's run-time behavior. This notation uses the form $O(f(n))$, where n is the size of the algorithm's problem and $f(n)$ is a function expressing the amount of work done to solve it.

- Common expressions of run-time behavior are $O(\log_2 n)$ (logarithmic), $O(n)$ (linear), $O(n^2)$ (quadratic), and $O(k^n)$ (exponential).

- An algorithm can have different best-case, worst-case, and average-case behaviors. For example, bubble sort and insertion sort are linear in the best case, but they are quadratic in the average and worst cases.

- In general, it is better to try to reduce the order of an algorithm's complexity than it is to try to enhance performance by tweaking the code.

- A binary search is substantially faster than a linear search. However, the data in the search space for a binary search must be in sorted order.

- The $n \log n$ sort algorithms use a recursive, divide-and-conquer strategy to break the n^2 barrier. Quicksort rearranges items around a pivot item and recursively sorts the sublists on either side of the pivot. Merge sort splits a list, recursively sorts each half, and merges the results.

- Exponential algorithms are primarily of theoretical interest and are impractical to run with large problem sizes.

Key Terms

asymptotic analysis	constant of proportionality	memoization
benchmarking	dominant	order of complexity
big-O notation	exponential	polynomial time algorithm
binary search	insertion sort	profiling
bubble sort	linear	quadratic
call tree	linear search	selection sort
complexity analysis	logarithmic	sequential search

Review Questions

1. Timing an algorithm with different problem sizes

   a. can give you a general idea of the algorithm's run-time behavior.

   b. can give you an idea of the algorithm's run-time behavior on a particular hardware platform.

   c. can give you an idea of the algorithm's run-time behavior on a particular software platform.

   d. provides no indication of the algorithm's run-time behavior.

2. Counting instructions

   a. provides the same data on different hardware and software platforms.

   b. can demonstrate the impracticality of exponential algorithms with large problem sizes.

   c. is impractical.

   d. provides no indication of the algorithm's run-time behavior.

3. The expressions $O(n)$, $O(n^2)$, and $O(k^n)$ are, respectively,

   a. exponential, linear, and quadratic.

   b. linear, quadratic, and exponential.

   c. logarithmic, linear, and quadratic.

   d. constant, linear, and quadratic.

4. A binary search

   a. assumes that the data are arranged in no particular order.

   b. assumes that the data are sorted.

   c. assumes that the data values are unique.

   d. assumes that the data do not recognize the comparison operators.

5. A selection sort makes at most

    a. n^3 exchanges of data items.

    b. n^2 exchanges of data items.

    c. n exchanges of data items.

    d. one exchange of data items.

6. The best-case behavior of insertion sort and modified bubble sort is

    a. constant

    b. linear

    c. quadratic

    d. exponential

7. An example of an algorithm whose best-case, average-case, and worst-case behaviors are the same is

    a. sequential search

    b. insertion sort

    c. selection sort

    d. quicksort

8. Generally speaking, it is better to

    a. tweak an algorithm to shave a few seconds of running time.

    b. choose an algorithm with the lowest order of computational complexity.

    c. choose a recursive algorithm over an algorithm that uses a loop.

    d. make no changes to an algorithm to improve its efficiency.

9. The recursive Fibonacci function makes approximately

    a. n recursive calls for problems of a large size n.

    b. n^2 recursive calls for problems of a large size n.

    c. n^3 recursive calls for problems of a large size n.

    d. 2^n recursive calls for problems of a large size n.

10. Each level in a completely filled binary call tree has

    a. four times as many calls as the level above it.

    b. three times as many calls as the level above it.

    c. twice as many calls as the level above it.

    d. the same number of calls as the level above it.

Programming Exercises

1. A sequential search of a sorted list can halt when the target is less than a given element in the list. Define a modified version of the **sequentialSearch** function that uses this algorithm (in the file **search.py**), and state the computational complexity, using big-O notation, of its best-, worst-, and average-case performances. (LO: 13.2, 13.3)

2. The list method **reverse** reverses the elements in the list. Define a function named **reverse** (in the file **reverse.py**) that reverses the elements in its list argument (without using the method **reverse**!). Try to make this function as efficient as possible and state its computational complexity using big-O notation. (LO: 13.2)

3. Python's **pow** function returns the result of raising a number to a given power. Define a function **expo** (in the file **expo.py**) that performs this task and state its computational complexity using big-O notation. The first argument of this function is the number, and the second argument is the exponent (nonnegative numbers only). You may use either a loop or a recursive function in your implementation. *Caution*: Do not use Python's ****** operator or **pow** function in this exercise! (LO: 13.2)

4. An alternative strategy for the **expo** function uses the following recursive definition:

```
expo(number, exponent)

    = 1, when exponent = 0

    = number * expo(number, exponent - 1), when exponent is odd

    = (expo(number, exponent // 2))², when exponent is even
```

Define a recursive function `expo` (in the file **expo.py**) that uses this strategy and state its computational complexity using big-O notation. (LO: 13.2, 13.3)

5. Python's `list` method `sort` includes the keyword argument `reverse`, whose default value is `False`. The programmer can override this value to sort a list in descending order. Modify the `selectionSort` function (in the file **sort.py**) discussed in this chapter so that it allows the programmer to supply this additional argument to redirect the sort. (LO: 13.4)

6. Modify the recursive Fibonacci function (in the file **fib.py**) to employ the memoization technique discussed in this chapter. The function creates a dictionary and then defines a nested recursive helper function. The base case is the same as before. However, before making a recursive call, the helper function looks up the value for the function's current argument in the dictionary (use the method `get`, with `None` as the default value). If the value exists, the function returns it. Otherwise, after the helper function adds the results of its two recursive calls, it saves the sum in the dictionary with the current argument of the function as the key. Also use the **Counter** object discussed in this chapter to count the number of recursive calls of the helper function. (LO: 13.2, 13.6)

7. Profile the performance of the memoized version of the Fibonacci function defined in Programming Exercise 6. The function (in the file **fib.py**) should count the number of recursive calls. State its computational complexity using big-O notation and justify your answer. (LO: 13.1, 13.2, 13.6)

8. The function `makeRandomList` creates and returns a list of numbers of a given size (its argument). The numbers in the list are unique and range from 1 through the size. They are placed in random order. Here is the code for the function:

```
def makeRandomList(size):
    lyst = []
    for count in range(size):
        while True:
            number = random.randint(1, size)
            if not number in lyst:
                lyst.append(number)
                break
    return lyst
```

You may assume that **range**, **randint**, and **append** are constant time functions. You may also assume that `random.randint` more rarely returns duplicate numbers as the range between its arguments increases. State the computational complexity of this function using big-O notation and justify your answer. (LO: 13.2, 13.6)

9. A computer supports the calls of recursive functions using a structure called the call stack. Generally speaking, the computer reserves a constant amount of memory for each call of a function. Thus, the memory used by a recursive function can be subjected to complexity analysis. State the computational complexity of the memory used by the recursive factorial and Fibonacci functions, as defined in Chapter 7. (LO: 13.2, 13.6)

10. The function that draws c-curves, and which was discussed in Chapter 8, has two recursive calls. Here is the code:

```
def cCurve(t, x1, y1, x2, y2, level):
    def drawLine(x1, y1, x2, y2):
        """Draws a line segment between the endpoints."""
        t.up()
        t.goto(x1, y1)
        t.down()
        t.goto(x2, y2)
```

```
if level == 0:
    drawLine(x1, y1, x2, y2)
else:
    xm = (x1 + x2 + y1 - y2) // 2
    ym = (x2 + y1 + y2 - x1) // 2
    cCurve(t, x1, y1, xm, ym, level - 1)
    cCurve(t, xm, ym, x2, y2, level - 1)
```

You can assume that the function **drawLine** runs in constant time. State the computational complexity of the **cCurve** function, in terms of the level, using big-O notation. Also, draw a call tree for a call of this function with a level of 3. (LO: 13.2, 13. 6))

13

Alphabetizing

Prompt

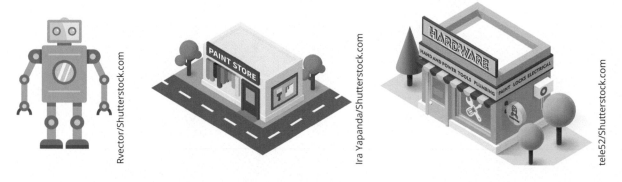

Rvector/Shutterstock.com

Ira Yapanda/Shutterstock.com

tele52/Shutterstock.com

Herby now is tasked with alphabetizing every item in the warehouse. He wants to get the best, most efficient algorithm to do so. He wants to alphabetize without the prebuilt sort() function. And he wants to create two methods and figure out which one is more efficient.

He will perform the following actions:

1. Generate a list of a thousand strings of letters, as it is more simple than generating words.
2. Create an alphabetization algorithm based on bubble sort.
3. Create a second alphabetization algorithm based on binary.
4. Compare the two with cProfile.
5. Make a conclusion about the fitness of each algorithm to work.

Hints

Understand that when you read a list of strings, you must iterate through the first letter first, and upon finding matching first letter, compare the second letters and the third letter. Understand that the complexity of alphabetizing strings is a little greater than the complexity of ordering numbers, and that therefore a more efficient algorithm is necessary.

Example

Lists of random strings (in lieu of words) can be generated thusly:

```
for _ in range(1000):
    length = random.randint(5, 10)  # Random length between 5 and 10
```

```
    random_string = ''.join(random.choices('abcdefghijklmnopqrstuvwxyzABCDEFGHIJKLM
NOPQRSTUVWXYZ', k=length))
    letter_strings.append(random_string)
```

I used insertion sort and merge sort. Insertion can be thought of in this manner:

```
for i in range(1, len(arr)):
    key = arr[i]
    j = i - 1

    while j >= 0 and arr[j] > key:
        arr[j + 1] = arr[j]
        j -= 1
```

While Merge sort can look at the middle and both halves

```
mid = len(arr) // 2
 left = arr[:mid]
 right = arr[mid:]

 left = merge_sort(left)
 right = merge_sort(right)
```

To analyze outputs, cProfile.run() is ideal.

Answer

See Chapter 13_Alphabetizing.py

After Discussion

In this assignment, you've analyzed the quality of a couple alphabetizing algorithms. While Big O-notation might seem intimidating at first, you should understand the value of keeping your code at the lowest possible levels of complexity for larger and larger tasks. You should understand how quickly smaller calculations can balloon into more time and processing power.

Implementing this knowledge can help you create code that runs faster and more efficiently.

Python Resources

Table A-1 provides information on an excellent website where programmers can find complete documentation for the Python Application Programming Interface (API) and download Python and other resources.

Table A-1 Online python documentation

Description	URL	Explanation
Python's top-level webpage	**https://www.python.org/**	This page contains news about events in the Python world and links to documentation, Python-related products, program examples, and free downloads of resources.
Downloads	**https://www.python.org/download/**	This page allows you to select the version of Python that matches your computer and to begin the download process.
Documentation and training	**https://www.python.org/doc/**	This page allows you to browse the documentation for the Python API, tutorials, and other training aids. You can also download many of these items to your computer for offline reference.

The following sections discuss some situations that involve downloading files or information from the Web.

Installing Python on Your Computer

As of this writing, the current version of Python is 3.10.4. This version likely will not come preinstalled on a Windows computer. You must download the Windows installer from **https://www.python.org/download/**. The installer might run automatically, or you might have to double-click an icon for the installer to launch it. The installer automatically puts Python into a folder and inserts various command options on the **All Programs** menu. Note that administrators installing Python for all users on Windows need to be logged in as Administrator.

Macintosh users running macOS will need to update the version of Python that comes preinstalled on their systems (Python 2 comes preinstalled, but you don't want to use that as it is not the current version). A macOS installer can be downloaded for this purpose and behaves in a manner similar to that of the Windows installer.

Unix and Linux users also might need to upgrade the version of Python that comes preinstalled on their systems. In these cases, they have to download a compressed Python source code "tarball" from the same site and install it.

Most users will also want to place aliases of the important Python commands, such as the one that launches IDLE, on their desktops, docks, or trays.

Using the Terminal Command Prompt, IDLE, and Other IDEs

To launch an interactive session with Python's shell from a terminal command prompt, open a terminal window, and enter **python3** at the prompt. To end the session on Unix machines (including macOS), press the Control+D key combination at the session prompt. To end a session on Windows, press Control+Z, and then press Enter.

Before you run a Python script from a terminal command prompt, the script file must be in the current working directory, or the system path must be set to the file's directory. You should consult your system's documentation on how to set a path. To run a script, enter **python3**, followed by a space, followed by the name of the script's file (including the **.py** extension), followed by any command-line arguments that the script expects.

On Windows, you can also launch a Python script by double-clicking the script's file icon. On Macintosh, Unix, and Linux systems, you must first configure the system to launch Python when files of this type are launched. The **File/Get Info** option on a Macintosh, for example, allows you to do this. You can also configure your system to launch Python using the simpler **python** command rather than **python3**.

You can also launch an interactive session with a Python shell by launching IDLE (as of this writing, the specific command to run is **idle3**). There are many advantages to using an IDLE shell rather than a terminal-based shell, such as color-coded program elements, menu options for editing code and consulting documentation, and the ability to repeat commands.

IDLE also helps you manage program development with multiple editor windows. You can run code from these windows and easily move code among them. Although this book does not discuss it, a debugging tool is also available within IDLE.

Installing the `images` and `breezypythongui` Libraries

The **`images`** library is a nonstandard, open-source Python module developed to support easy image processing. The image library supports the processing of GIF images only. The source code for the library, in the file **images.py**, is available on the author's website at **https://kennethalambert.com/python/**, or from your instructor.

The **`breezypythongui`** library is a nonstandard, open-source Python module developed to support easy GUI programming. The source code for the library, in the file **breezypythongui.py**, is available on the author's website at **https://kennethalambert.com/breezypythongui/**, or from your instructor. You will also find complete documentation and a tutorial for the use of this library at the author's website.

To install a Python library, you place the source file for the library in the current working directory. Then, when you launch a Python script from this directory or load it from an IDLE window into a shell, Python can locate the library resources that are imported by that script.

Appendix C

The API for Image Processing

The **images** image-processing library is based on Python's standard **tkinter** library. The Application Programming Interface (API) for the **images** library follows.

The **images** module includes a single class named **Image**. Each **Image** object represents an image. The programmer can supply the filename of an image on disk when **Image** is instantiated. The resulting **Image** object contains pixels loaded from an image file on disk. If a filename is not specified, a height and width must be specified. The resulting **Image** object contains the specified number of pixels with a single default color.

When the programmer imports the **Image** class and instantiates it, no window opens. At that point, the programmer can run various methods with this **Image** object to access or modify its pixels, as well as save the image to a file. At any point in your code, you may run the **draw** method with an **Image** object. At this point, a window will open and display the image. The program then waits for you to close the window before allowing you, either in the shell or in a script, to continue running more code.

The positions of pixels in an image are the same as screen coordinates for display in a window. That is, the origin (0, 0) is in the upper-left corner of the image, and its (width, height) is in the lower-right corner.

Images can be manipulated either interactively within a Python shell or from a Python script. It is recommended that the shell or script be launched from a system terminal rather than from IDLE.

Image objects cannot be viewed in multiple windows at the same time from the same script. If you want to view two or more **Image** objects simultaneously, you can create separate scripts for them and launch the scripts in separate terminal windows.

As mentioned earlier, the **images** module supports the use of GIF files only. Here is a list of the **Image** methods:

- **Image(filename)**: Loads an image from the file named **filename** and returns an **Image** object that represents this image. The file must exist in the current working directory.

- **Image(width, height)**: Returns an **Image** object of the specified width and height with a single default color.

- **getWidth()**: Returns the width of the image in pixels.

- **getHeight()**: Returns the height of the image in pixels.

- `getPixel(x, y)`: Returns the pixel at the specified coordinates. A pixel is of the form (r, g, b), where the letters are integers representing the red, green, and blue values of a color in the RGB system.

- `setPixel(x, y, (r, g, b))`: Resets the pixel at position (x, y) to the color value represented by (r, g, b). The coordinates must be in the range of the image's coordinates, and the RGB values must range from 0 through 255.

- `draw()`: Opens a window and displays the image. The user must close the window to continue the program.

- `save()`: Saves the image to its current file, if it has one. Otherwise, it does nothing.

- `save(filename)`: Saves the image with the given `filename` and makes it the current filename. This is similar to the **Save As** option in most **File** menus.

Transition from Python to Java and C++

Although Python is an excellent teaching language and has widespread use in the industry, Java and the C/C++ family of languages remain the most widespread languages used in higher education and real-world settings. Computer science students must become proficient in these languages, both to continue in their course work and to prepare for careers in the field.

Fortunately, the transition from Python to Java or C++ is not difficult. Although the syntactic structures of Python and these other languages are somewhat different, the languages support the same programming styles. For an overview of all the essential differences between Python, Java, and C++, visit the author's website at **https://kennethalambert.com/python/**.

Suggestions for Further Reading

John Battelle, *The Search: How Google and Its Rivals Rewrote the Rules of Business and Transformed Our Culture* (New York: Portfolio Trade, 2006).

Tim Berners-Lee, *Weaving the Web: The Original Design and Ultimate Destiny of the World Wide Web* (New York: HarperCollins, 2000).

Brian Christian, *The Alignment Problem: Machine Learning and Human Values* (New York: W. W. Norton & Company, 2020).

Jonathan Crary, *Scorched Earth: Beyond the Digital Age to a Post-capitalist World* (New York: Verso, 2022).

Paul Graham, *Hackers and Painters: Big Ideas from the Computer Age* (Sebastopol, CA: O'Reilly, 2004).

Katie Hafner and Matthew Lyon, *Where Wizards Stay Up Late: The Origins of the Internet* (New York: Simon and Schuster, 1996).

Michael E. Hobart and Zachary S. Schiffman, *Information Ages: Literacy, Numeracy, and the Computer Revolution* (Baltimore: The Johns Hopkins University Press, 1998).

Georges Ifrah, *The Universal History of Computing: From the Abacus to the Quantum Computer* (New York: John Wiley & Sons, Inc., 2001).

Walter Issacson, *Steve Jobs* (New York: Simon & Schuster, 2011).

John Markoff, *What the Doormouse Said: How the Sixties Counterculture Shaped the Personal Computer Industry* (New York: Viking, 2005).

Antonio García Martínez, *Chaos Monkeys: Obscene Fortune and Random Failure in Silicon Valley* (New York: HarperCollins, 2016).

Liza Mundy, *Code Girls: The Untold Story of the American Women Code Breakers of World War II* (New York: Hachette Book Group, 2017).

Cathy O'Neil, *Weapons of Math Destruction: How Big Data Increases Inequality and Threatens Democracy* (New York: Crown, 2016).

Edward Snowden, *Permanent Record* (New York: Metropolitan Books, 2019).

Curtis White, *We, Robots: Staying Human in the Age of Big Data* (Brooklyn, NY: Melville House, 2016).

Shoshana Zuboff, *The Age of Surveillance Capitalism: The Fight for a Human Future at the New Frontier of Power* (New York: Public Affairs, 2019).

Glossary

A

abacus   An early computing device that allowed users to perform simple calculations by moving beads along wires.

absolute pathname   A pathname that begins with the file system's root directory. *See also* pathname.

abstract behavior   Operations that multiple classes have in common.

abstraction   A simplified view of a task or data structure that ignores complex detail.

accessor methods   A method used to examine an attribute of an object without changing it.

accessors   A method used to examine an attribute of an object without changing it.

algorithm   A finite sequence of instructions that, when applied to a problem, will solve it.

aliases   A situation in which two or more names in a program can refer to the same memory location. An alias can cause subtle side effects.

analog information   Information that contains a continuous range of values.

analysis   The phase of the software life cycle in which the programmer describes what the program will do.

analytics   *See* data analysis.

ancestor   Any class that is either a parent of a class or lies on a path in the class hierarchy above that parent.

anonymous function   A function without a name, constructed in Python using `lambda`.

applications software   Programs that allow human users to accomplish specialized tasks, such as word processing or database management. Also called applications or apps.

argument   A value or expression passed in a function or method call.

arithmetic expression   A sequence of operands and operators that computes a value.

artificial intelligence   A field of computer science whose goal is to build machines that can perform tasks that require human intelligence.

ASCII set   The American Standard Code for Information Interchange ordering for a character set.

aspect ratio   The ratio of width to height of an image.

assembler   A program that translates an assembly language program to machine code.

assembly languages   A computer language that allows the programmer to express operations and memory addresses with mnemonic symbols.

assignment statement   A method of giving values to variables.

association lists   *See* dictionary.

association   A pair of items consisting of a key and a value.

asymptotic analysis   The view of a polynomial wherein its value approaches or approximates that of its dominant term, as the size of the problem gets very large.

attribute dictionary   A data structure that holds the values of the attributes of a window or widget within a window.

augmented assignment operations   Assignment operations that perform a designated operation, such as addition, before storing the result in a variable.

B

bar chart   A visualization that displays data quantities in the form of vertical or horizontal bars.

base 10 number system   *See* decimal number system.

base 2 number system   *See* binary number system.

base case   The condition in a recursive algorithm that is tested to halt the recursive process.

batch processing   The scheduling of multiple programs so that they run in sequence on the same computer.

benchmarking   The process of determining the running time and memory cost of an algorithm by gathering data on actual running times and memory usage.

big data   The gathering and analysis of massive amounts of data.

big-O notation   A notation expressing the rate of growth of the work of an algorithm as a function of the size of a problem.

bimodal distribution   The property of a data set in which there are two values whose frequency predominates.

binary digits   A digit, either 0 or 1, in the binary number system. Program instructions are stored in memory using a sequence of binary digits. *See also* bits.

binary number system   A number system that represents base 2 numbers, using the digits 1 and 0.

binary search   A type of search in which approximately half of the data are ignored after each unsuccessful comparison to the target value, leading to a worst-case logarithmic running time.

bit shift   The process of moving the bits in a bit string to the left or to the right, wrapping them around the end of the string as necessary.

bit string   A string containing the binary digits 0 and 1.

bit-mapped display screen   A type of display screen that supports the display of graphics and images.

bits   Binary digits.

block cipher   An encryption method that replaces characters with other characters located in a two-dimensional grid of characters.

block   The making of a thread inactive until some event occurs.

blurring   The process of making the edges of a shape less ragged by softening them.

body   The code segment nested within a loop, selection statement, function definition, method definition, or class definition.

Boolean data type   A data type whose values are `True` and `False`.

Boolean expression   An expression whose value is either true or false. *See also* simple Boolean expression and compound Boolean expression.

Boolean function   A function that returns the value `True` of `False`.

bot   An automated software agent.

bottom-up testing   The process of testing more basic program components before one tests the components that depend on them.

`break` **statement**   A control statement that exits a loop.

bubble sort   A sort algorithm that repeatedly swaps elements that are out of order in a list until they are in their sorted positions.

buffer   An area of computer memory used to transmit data to and from external storage.

byte code   The kind of object code generated by a Python compiler and interpreted by a Python virtual machine. Byte code is platform independent.

C

Caesar cipher   An encryption method that replaces characters with other characters a given distance away in the character set.

call stack   The area of computer memory reserved for managing data associated with function and method calls.

call tree   A diagram that traces the calls of a recursive function, which is useful in illustrating the work done by a function with two or more embedded recursive calls.

canvas   A rectangular area of a window within which geometric shapes, images, and text can be drawn.

card reader   A device that inputs information from punched cards into the memory of a computer.

cathode ray tube (CRT) screen   The first type of display device used to show computer output to users.

c-curve   A fractal shape that resembles the letter C.

central processing unit (CPU)   A major hardware component that consists of the arithmetic/logic unit and the control unit. Also sometimes called a **processor**.

character sets   Lists of characters available for data and program statements.

check button A window component with a label and a control that the user can select or deselect, and which can be selected concurrently with other check buttons in the window.

cipher text The output of an encryption process.

class diagram A graphical notation that describes the relationships among the classes in a software system.

class hierarchy An arrangement of classes that shows the subclass/superclass/inheritance relationships among them.

class variable A variable that is visible to all instances of a class and is accessed by specifying the class name.

classes Types of objects with state and behavior.

client An agent that requests and receives some service.

Client/server applications A type of application that allows many agents to receive service from one provider.

closed under combination The property of operations on a data type whereby the operand data types and the result data type are the same type.

cloud computing The use of server farms to provide data and applications to devices via wireless technology. *See also* server farm.

color filtering The process of applying a triple of color values to modify the color of each pixel in an image.

color palette A table of colors used to save memory in representing a digital image.

command button A window component that allows the user to execute a command by pressing or clicking it with the mouse.

compiler A computer program that automatically converts instructions in a high-level language to machine language.

complexity analysis The process of determining the running time and memory cost of an algorithm by reading the code, which results in a mathematical formula expressing this cost for any computer.

compound Boolean expression Refers to the complete expression when logical connectives and negation are used to generate Boolean values. *See also* Boolean expression and simple Boolean expression.

computing agent The entity that executes instructions in an algorithm.

concurrent processing The simultaneous performance of two or more tasks.

condition A Boolean expression used to control the flow of a computation.

condition-controlled loop A type of loop whose continuation depends on the value of a Boolean expression.

conditional iteration A type of loop that continues as long as a condition is true.

constant of proportionality Terms and coefficients that are usually ignored in complexity analysis.

constructor A method that is run when an object is instantiated, usually to initialize that object's instance variables. This method is named __init__ in Python.

context switch The process whereby a thread's state is saved or restored when it relinquishes or gains access to the CPU.

continuation condition A Boolean expression that is checked to determine whether or not to continue iterating within a loop. If this expression is true, iteration continues.

continuous range A range containing an infinite number of values between two values.

control statements Statements that allow the computer to repeat or select an action.

coordinate system A grid that allows a programmer to specify positions of points in a plane or of pixels on a computer screen.

correct A program that produces the expected outputs for all legitimate inputs.

count-controlled loops Loops that stop when a counter variable reaches a specified limit.

critical section Code that must be able to finish execution before another thread can access the same resource.

CSV format Short for comma-separated values, a file format in which rows of data values appears on separate lines and the data in each line are separated by commas.

current working directory The directory to which a running program is attached, in which a file can be accessed directly by its name.

customer request A broad statement of a problem to be solved by a computer.

D

data   The symbols that are used to represent information in a form suitable for storage, processing, and communication.

data analysis   The discovery of patterns in data sets to support decisions or further data processing.

data encapsulation   Restricting access to an object's data to method calls on that object.

data encryption   The process of transforming data so that others cannot use it.

data frame   A structure in which data are organized in labeled rows and columns, with high-level functions to assist in data analysis.

data mining   The extraction of useful patterns from raw data sets for further analysis.

data science   A field of study that incorporates computer science and statistics to develop algorithms and data structures for data analysis.

data set   Data gathered from sources of interest, usually requiring cleaning and structuring before being subjected to analysis.

data structure   A compound unit consisting of several data values.

data type   A set of values and operations on those values.

data visualization   The use of graphics, images, and animations to present patterns discovered in data sets.

data warehouse   A store of data in digital form.

database   The organization of data in highly structured form to support queries or analysis.

decimal notation   The use of the digits 0 through 9 to represent numbers in base 10.

decimal number system   A number system that represents base 10 numbers, using the digits 0 through 9.

decorator pattern   A design pattern in which a new class adds functionality to an existing class but keeps the same interface.

decrypts   Translates encrypted data to a form that can be used.

default arguments   A special type of argument that is automatically provided if the caller does not supply one.

default behavior   Behavior that is expected and provided under normal circumstances.

defining   Giving a variable a value for the first time.

definite iteration   The process of repeating a given action a preset number of times.

design   The phase of the software life cycle in which the programmer describes how the program will accomplish its tasks.

design error   An error such that a program runs, but unexpected results are produced. Also referred to as a logic error. *See also* syntax error.

dictionary   A collection that allows the programmer to access values by specifying keys.

digital cloud   A storage technology that allows users to store and access their data from remote locations, usually wirelessly.

discrete values   Values, such as integers, in a range between which there are no other values.

docstring   A sequence of characters enclosed in triple quotation marks (""") that Python uses to document program components such as modules, classes, methods, and functions.

dominant   The term in a formula which grows the fastest as the size of a problem increases.

driver   A method used to test other methods.

E

edge detection   The process of discovering boundaries between shapes in an image.

elements   A data value that is contained in a collection, such as a list.

empty string   A string that contains no characters.

end-of-line comments   Parts of a single line of text in a program that are not executed but serve as documentation for readers.

entries   *See* association.

entry fields   Rectangular boxes that support the input and output of a single line of text.

entry-control loop   A type of loop whose continuation condition is tested at the beginning of the loop.

escape sequence   A sequence of two characters in a string, the first of which is /. The sequence stands for another character, such as the tab or newline.

event handlers   A method that is triggered when an event occurs.

event-driven programming   The programming of operations that handle events.

executed To carry out the instructions of a program.

exponential A function expressing a rate of growth of work that is the square of the size of a problem.

expressions Descriptions of a computation that produces a value.

extends The process whereby a given class becomes a subclass of another class, thereby inheriting its attributes and behavior.

extension The characters following the period in a filename, indicating the type of file.

F

fail-safe programming The discipline of creating programs that avoid, trap, and recover from illegitimate inputs or exceptional conditions in their environments.

Fibonacci number One of a series of numbers generated by taking the sum of the previous two numbers in the series. The series begins with the numbers 1, 1, and 2.

field width The number of columns used for the output of text.

file dialogs A type of dialog that allows the user to browse the file system to open or save files.

file system Software that organizes data on secondary storage media.

filtering The successive application of a Boolean function to a sequence of arguments that returns a sequence of the arguments that make this function return True.

first-class data objects Data objects that can be passed as arguments to functions and returned as their values.

floating-point A data type that represents real numbers in a computer program.

for loop A structured loop consisting of an initializer expression, a termination expression, an update expression, and a statement.

format operator The operator %, when used with a format string and a set of one or more data values, returns a string with the given format.

format string A special syntax within a string that allows the programmer to specify the number of columns within which data are placed in a string.

fractal object A type of mathematical object that maintains self-sameness when viewed at greater levels of detail.

function A chunk of code that can be treated as a unit and called to perform a task.

functional programming A programming style that views a program as a set of cooperating functions, where a function maps data into new data and no function modifies the state of a variable or data structure.

G

garbage collection The automatic process of reclaiming memory when the data of a program no longer need it.

general method A method that solves a class of problems, not just one individual problem.

grammar The set of rules for constructing sentences in a language.

graphical user interface (GUI) A means of communication between human beings and computers that uses a pointing device for input and a bitmapped screen for output. The bitmap displays images of windows and window objects such as buttons, text fields, and drop-down menus. The user interacts with the interface by using the mouse to directly manipulate the window objects. *See also* window component.

graphics The set of techniques for creating and manipulating images and geometric shapes.

grid A data structure in which the items are accessed by specifying at least two index positions, one that refers to the item's row and another that refers to the item's column.

H

hardware The computing machine and its support devices.

header The first line in loop, selection statement, function definition, method definition, or class definition.

hex string A string with the format *#RRGGBB*, where each letter is a hexadecimal digit, to represent information about an RGB color value in Python.

hexadecimal Base 16, using the digits 0 through 9 and A through F.

higher-order function A function that expects another function as an argument and/or returns another function as a value.

high-level programming languages   Programming languages whose vocabulary and sentence structure are fairly close to those of English.

histogram   A form of visualization in which the relative frequencies of data in a data set are displayed.

home   The initial position of the turtle in a Turtle graphics application.

hypermedia   A data structure that allows the user to access different kinds of information (text, images, sound, video, applications) by traversing links.

I

`if` **statement**   A type of control statement that prevents a program from performing an action if the condition is false.

`if-else` **statement**   A selection statement that allows a program to perform alternative actions based on a condition.

immutable data structure   A data structure in which one cannot insert, remove, or revise the values contained therein.

imperative programming   A programming style that views a program as a set of statements that issue commands to a computer, especially to modify variables with assignment.

implementation   The phase of the software life cycle in which the program is coded in a programming language.

incremental   The process of completing a rough draft of a step in a process before moving on the to next step.

indefinite iteration   The process of repeating a given action until a condition stops the repetition.

index   The relative position of a component of a linear data structure or collection.

indirect recursion   A recursive process that results when one function calls another, causing at some point a second call to the first function.

infinite loop   A loop in which the controlling condition is not changed in such a manner to allow the loop to terminate.

infinite precision   The characteristic of a real number that its fractional part can extend for an indefinite number of digits.

infinite recursion   In a running program, the state that occurs when a recursive method cannot reach a stopping state.

information processing   The transformation of one piece of information into another piece of information.

inheritance   The process by which a subclass can reuse attributes and behavior defined in a superclass. *See also* subclass and superclass.

inheritance hierarchies   *See* class hierarchy.

initializing   Giving a variable a value for the first time.

input   Data obtained by a program from the external world during execution.

input/output devices   Devices that allow information to be transmitted between the central processing unit of a computer and the external world.

insertion sort   A sort algorithm that repeatedly inserts the ith element into its proper place in the first i items in the list.

instance   A computational object bearing the attributes and behavior specified by a class.

instance variables   Storage for data in an instance of a class.

instantiation   The process whereby an object is created.

integers   Positive or negative whole numbers, or the number 0. The magnitude of an integer is limited by a computer's memory.

integrated circuit   The arrangement of computer hardware components in a single, miniaturized unit.

Integration   The phase of the software development life cycle during which program components are brought together and tested.

interface   A formal statement of how communication occurs between the user of a module (class or method) and its implementer.

Internet host   The property of a computer that allows it to receive connections from other computers on the Internet.

Internet of things (IOT)   The embedding of computer chips in physical objects, allowing them to send and receive digital information.

interpreter   A program that translates and executes another program.

invertible matrix   A data structure used in a block cipher.

IP address   The unique location of an individual computer on the Internet.

IP name   A representation of an IP address that uses letters and periods.

IP number   A representation of an IP address that uses digits and periods.

items   A data value that is contained in a collection, such as a list.

iteration   *See* loop.

iterative   Circling back to an earlier stage in a process before moving forward.

J

jump table   A dictionary that associates command names with functions that are invoked when those functions are looked up in the table.

K

keypunch machine   An early input device that allowed the user to enter programs and data onto punched cards.

keys   Items that are associated with a value and which are used to locate that value in a dictionary.

keyword arguments   The association of parameter names with default values in a function or method header, which allows the caller to omit the arguments in those parameters' positions or to override the default values of those arguments when the function or method is called.

L

label object   A window object that displays text or an image, usually to describe the roles of other window objects.

labels   *See* label object.

lambda   The mechanism by which an anonymous function is created.

lifetime   The time during which a data object or method call exists.

line plot   A visualization that displays data as points in a two-dimensional graph, where the values are connected by line segments.

linear   A function expressing a rate of growth of work in direct proportion to the size of a problem.

linear loop structure   A loop that does not contain a nested loop.

linear search   A type of search that examines each value in a sequence, until a target value is found or the end of the sequence is reached.

list   A collection of data values that are ordered by position.

literal   An element of a language that evaluates to itself, such as 34 or "hi there."

loader   A software program that copies program code and data from secondary memory into primary memory before program execution begins.

local host   The property of a computer that allows it to receive connections from clients that are running on it as a standalone computer, not necessarily connected to the Internet.

lock   A software object that restricts access to a resource to one thread at a time.

logarithmic   A function expressing a rate of growth of work that is the $\log_2$ of the size of a problem.

logic error   A type of error that cannot be detected by the computer at compile time or run time, but usually shows up in the form of unexpected output.

logical negation   The use of the logical operator `not` with a Boolean expression, returning `True` if the expression is false, and `False` if the expression is true.

logical operator   Any of the logical connective operators `and`, `or`, or `not`.

loop body   The action(s) performed on each iteration through a loop.

loop control variable   A variable that is checked within the continuation condition of a loop.

loop header   Information at the beginning of a loop that includes the conditions for continuing the iteration process.

loops   Statements that repeatedly execute a set of statements.

lossless compression   A compression scheme in which no information is lost.

lossy scheme   A compression scheme in which information is lost.

luminance   A property of light and its effect on the human retina that makes the retina more sensitive to some colors than to others.

M

machine code   The language used directly by the computer in all its calculations and processing.

machine learning   The capacity of an algorithm to improve its analysis by training on data sets of increasing size.

magnetic storage media   Any media that allow data to be stored as patterns in a magnetic field.

main module   The module where program codes begins to execute at program startup.

mainframe computers   Large computers typically used by major companies and universities.

maintenance   The phase of the software life cyle in which errors are repaired and changes and improvements are made.

mapping   The successive application of a function to a sequence of arguments that returns a sequence of results.

matrix   A data structure in which the items are accessed by specifying two or more indices.

mean   The average of a set of data values.

median   The data value that would be at the midpoint of a sorted set of data values.

median   The item in a set of data values wherein half of the data values are greater than and half of the data values are less than said item.

memoization   A technique to improve the efficiency of a recursive algorithm, in which the result of each recursive call is saved to a cache memory, so that this result need not be recomputed on subsequent recursive calls with the same arguments.

memory   The ordered sequence of storage cells that can be accessed by address. Instructions and variables of an executing program are temporarily held here.

merge sort   A sort algorithm in which a list of data is repeatedly subdivided on each recursive call, and the contents of the sublists are merged as the recursion unwinds, resulting in O(*nlogn*) running time.

method names   Names used to identify or reference methods.

methods   Chunks of code that can be treated as a unit and invoked by name. A method is called with an object or class.

methods   Operations that are called by name and run on or associated with objects.

microprocessor   A processor that incorporates the entire central processing unit on a single integrated chip.

mixed-mode arithmetic   Expressions containing data of different types; the values of these expressions will be of either type, depending on the rules for evaluating them.

mode string   A string argument to the open function, such as `'r'` or `'w'`, that indicates whether the file is being opened for input or output.

mode   The data value or values that appear(s) most often in a data set.

model   A computational representation of a object or system of objects and their relationships that occur in a problem domain.

model/view pattern   A design pattern in which the roles and responsibilities of the system are cleanly divided between data management (model) and user interface display (view).

module variables   Variables defined within a module whose scope is the entire module *See also* scope.

modules   Independent program components that can contain variables, functions, and classes.

Moore's Law   A hypothesis that states that the processing speed and storage capacity of computers will increase by a factor of 2 every 18 months.

multimodal distribution   The property of a data set in which there are more than two values whose frequency predominates.

multiprocessing systems   Operating systems that run several processes concurrently on the same computer.

multithreading   The use of several threads or processes to structure the running of a program.

multiway selection statement   A type of control statement that includes two or more conditions and possible courses of action.

mutator   A method used to change the value of an attribute of an object.

N

namespace   The set of all of a program's variables and their values.

natural ordering   The placement of data items relative to each other by some internal criteria, such as numeric value or alphabetical value.

nested loop structure   A loop as one of the statements in the body of another loop.

networked or distributed systems   Applications that run by assigning tasks to different computers on a network.

network   A collection of resources that are linked together for communication.

newline character   A special character ('\n') used to indicate the end of a line of characters in a string or a file stream.

normal distribution   A data set whose average value is not skewed by a preponderance of large or small values.

null value   A value that is missing in a row of values in a data set.

numeric data types   Data types that represent numbers.

O

object   A data value that has an internal state and a set of operations for manipulating that state.

object identity   The property of an object that it is the same thing at different points in time, even though the values of its attributes might change.

object-based programming   The construction of software systems that use objects.

object-oriented languages   Languages that support object-oriented programming. *See* object-oriented programming.

object-oriented programming   The construction of software systems that define classes and rely on data encapsulation, inheritance, and polymorphism.

octal   Base 8.

off-by-one error   Usually seen with loops, this error shows up as a result that is one less or one greater than the expected value.

one-way selection statement   *See* `if` statement.

operating system   A large program that allows the user to communicate with the hardware and performs various management tasks.

operator overloading   The process of using the same operator symbol or identifier to refer to many different functions. *See also* polymorphism.

optical storage media   Devices such as CDs and DVDs that store data permanently and from which the data are accessed by using laser technology.

optional arguments   Arguments to a function or method that may be omitted.

order of complexity   A mathematical formula which expresses running time or memory usage as a function of the size of the problem.

origin   The point (0,0) in a coordinate system.

output   Information that is produced by a program and sent to the external world.

overload   The process of adding new definitions of built-in operators.

P

panels   Rectangular window components with their own grids that are useful for organizing other window components.

parallel computing   The assignment of tasks in an application to multiple CPUs, either on a single (multicore) computer or on multiple computers connected in a network.

parallel systems   Software systems that support the assignment of tasks to multiple CPUs.

parameters   Names that appear in the header of function or method definition that are assigned the values of arguments when the method or function is called.

parent   In the file system, a directory that contains a subdirectory, so that their relationship is that of parent to child.

parent class   The immediate superclass of a class.

pass   The execution of a set of statements with a loop.

path   A string constructed to describe the sequence of directory names that leads from a current position in a file system to a given file or subdirectory.

pathname   A chain of directory names that allows the computer to access a file on a file system.

pattern matching   The use of a data structure containing variables to access data within another structure.

percentile   The fraction of a data set whose values fall below the magnitude of a given value.

personal digital assistant (PDA)   A handheld device that allows the user to perform some simple tasks.

pickling   The process of converting objects for storage in files.

pie chart   A visualization that displays relative percentages of data as slices in a whole.

pixels   Picture elements or dots of color used to display images on a computer screen.

pixilation   The ragged appearance of the edges of a shape caused by low-resolution images.

plaintext   The source text or input for an encryption process.

polymorphic methods   Methods that have the same headers but are defined in different classes.

polymorphism   The property of one operator symbol or method identifier having many meanings. *See also* overloading.

polynomial time algorithm   A function expressing a rate of growth of work that is n^k, where n is the size of the problem and k is a constant greater than 1.

ports   Channels through which several clients can exchange data with the same server.

positional notation   The type of representation used in based number systems, in which the position of each digit denotes a power in the system's base.

positional value   The value resulting from multiplying the digit at a given position by the number's base raised to that position.

precedence rules   Rules that govern the order in which operators are applied in expressions.

preconditions   Statements that specify what must be true so that a method or function can provide a guaranteed outcome.

predicate   A function that returns a Boolean value.

primary memory   A device that provides temporary storage for data and programs for fast access by a computer's central processing unit. *See also* random access memory.

problem decomposition   The process of breaking a problem into subproblems.

problem instances   Individual problems that belong to a class of problems.

procedural programming   A programming style that decomposes the tasks of imperative programming into subtasks to be handled by subprograms. *See also* imperative programming.

process   A running algorithm or program in execution.

processor   The hardware components that perform computation and control the flow of execution.

producer/consumer relationship   The sharing of data in which one thread or process modifies the data before other threads or processes access that data.

profiling   *See* benchmarking.

program comments   Text in a program that is not executed as code, but informs the reader about what the code does.

program libraries   Software tools or resources used in applications.

programming languages   A formal language that computer scientists use to give instructions to the computer.

programs   A set of instructions that tells the machine (the hardware) what to do.

prompter box   A popup dialog box that accepts input from the user.

prototype   A trimmed-down version of a class or software system that still functions and allows the programmer to study its essential features.

pseudocode   A stylized half-English, half-code language written in English but suggesting program code.

Python Shell   An interactive program that allows the programmer to enter Python code and receive immediate feedback.

Python virtual machine (PVM)   A program that interprets Python byte codes and executes them.

Q

quadratic   A function expressing a rate of growth of work that is the square of the size of a problem.

R

radio buttons   Window components with a label and a control that a user can select, which have the effect of deselecting the other radio buttons in the same radio button group.

random access memory (RAM)   Memory where a program and data are loaded for execution. Same as primary memory.

random numbers   Numbers chosen from a given sequence to simulate randomness in a computer application.

rational number   A number consisting of a numerator and a denominator, written using the format *numerator/denominator*.

raw image file   The data captured directly of an image with a recording device, before any data compression is applied.

readers and writers problem   A situation in which multiple readers and writers can have access to shared data, in any order.

ready queue   A data structure used to schedule processes or threads for CPU access.

recursive call   The call of a function that already has a call waiting in the current chain of function calls.

recursive definition   A set of statements in which at least one statement is defined in terms of itself.

recursive design   The process of decomposing a problem into subproblems of exactly the same form that can be solved by the same algorithm.

recursive function   A function that calls itself.

recursive step   A step in the recursive process that solves a similar problem of smaller size and eventually leads to a termination of the process.

reducing   The application of a function to a sequence of its arguments to produce a single value.

regular polygon   A figure of three or more sides, each of which is the same length.

relative pathname   A pathname that begins just above or below the current working directory. *See also* pathname.

required arguments   Arguments that must be supplied by the programmer when a function or method is called.

resolution   The number of pixels per unit of distance (usually an inch) in an image.

responsibility-driven design   The assignment of roles and responsibilities to different actors in a program.

returning a value   The process whereby a function or method makes the value that it computes available to its caller.

RGB system   The representation of color values using red, green, and blue components.

robust   A program that avoids, traps, and recovers from illegitimate inputs or exceptional conditions in its environment.

root directory   The directory at the top or beginning of a file system.

row-major traversal   The process whereby each cell in a row is visited before any cells in the following row.

run-time system   Software that supports the execution of a program.

S

sample   The process of selecting a discrete color value from a continuous range of color values.

scatter plot   A visualization that displays data as points in a two-dimensional graph.

scientific notation   The representation of a floating-point number that uses a decimal point and an exponent to express its value.

scope   The area of program text in which the value of a variable is visible.

screen coordinate system   A coordinate system used by most programming languages in which the origin is in the upper-left corner of the screen, window, or panel, and the *y* values increase toward the bottom of the drawing area.

secondary memory   A device such as a hard drive or flash stick where data can be backed up or stored permanently.

selection sort   A sort algorithm that repeatedly swaps the smallest element in the unsorted portion of a list with the element at the beginning of the unsorted portion.

selection statements   Control statements that select some particular logical path based on the value of an expression. Also referred to as conditional statements.

semantic error   A type of error that occurs when the computer cannot carry out the instruction specified.

semantics   The rules for interpreting the meaning of a program in a language.

semiconductor storage media   Devices, such as flash sticks, that use solid state circuitry to store data permanently.

sentinel   (or **sentinel value**) A special value that indicates the end of a set of data or of a process.

sequential search   *See* linear search.

series   A sequence of values in a row or column of a data frame.

server   An agent that receives requests and provides a service.

server farms   A collection of computers which can store massive amounts of data for many users.

servers   A computational object that provides a service from another computational object, usually over a network.

shell   A program that allows users to enter and run Python program expressions and statements interactively.

short-circuit evaluation   The process by which a compound Boolean expression halts evaluation and returns the value of the first subexpression that evaluates to true, in the case of **or**, or false, in the case of **and**.

side effect A change in a variable that is the result of some action taken in a program, usually from within a method.

simple Boolean expressions The values `True` or `False`, the call of a function that returns `True` or `False`, or a comparison of two values. *See also* Boolean expression and compound Boolean expression.

sleep The making of a thread inactive for a designated period of time.

slicing An operation that returns a subsection of a linear collection, for example, a sublist or a substring.

sniffing software Programs that allow the user to spy on data transmissions over a network.

socket An object that serves as a communication link between a single server process and a single client process.

software development The discipline of systematically planning, coding, and testing a complex program.

software development life cycle The process of development, maintenance, and demise of a software system. Phases include analysis, design, coding, testing/verification, maintenance, and obsolescence.

software engineering The construction of large software systems using a disciplined method of requirements analysis, design, coding, and testing that involves the coordination of a team of specialized developers.

software Programs that make the machine (the hardware) do something, such as word processing, database management, or games.

solid-state device An electronic device, typically based on a transistor, which has no moving parts.

source code The program text as viewed by the human being who creates or reads it, prior to compilation.

stack frame An area of computer memory that keeps track of a function or method call's parameters, local values, return value, and the caller's return address.

stack overflow error A situation that occurs when the computer runs out of memory to allocate for its call stack. This situation usually arises during an infinite recursion.

standard deviation A measure of the distribution of values in a data set.

state The current values of an object's attributes.

step value The amount by which a counter is incremented or decremented in a count-controlled loop.

stepwise refinement The process of repeatedly subdividing tasks into subtasks until each subtask is easily accomplished. *See also* top-down design.

string A sequence of zero or more characters enclosed in quote marks.

strongly typed programming language A language in which the types of operands are checked prior to applying an operator to them, and which disallows such applications, either at run time or at compile time, when operands are not of the appropriate type.

structural equivalence A criterion of equality between two distinct objects in which one or more of their attributes are equal.

structure chart A diagram that shows the relationships among functions and the passage of data among them in a program's design.

subclass A class that inherits attributes and behaviors from another class.

subclassing The process of making a new class a subclass of an existing class.

subscript operator The symbols [and], which enclose an integer or range of integers, that allow a program to access a character or a substring at a given position or range of positions in a string.

substrings Strings that represent a segment of another string.

summation The accumulation of the sum of a sequence of numbers.

superclass The class from which a subclass inherits attributes and behavior. *See also* inheritance and subclass.

symbolic constants Names that receive a value at program start up and whose value cannot be changed.

synchronization problems A type of problem arising from the execution of threads or processes that share memory.

syntax The form or structure of a sentence in a programming language.

syntax errors Errors in spelling, punctuation, or placement of certain key symbols in a program. *See also* design error.

system software The programs that allow users to write and execute other programs, including operating systems such as Windows and macOS.

T

table *See* dictionary.

tabular format The presentation of output in columns of data that are either left-aligned or right-aligned.

temporary variables Variable that are introduced in the body of a function or method for the use of that subroutine only.

terminal-based interface A user interface that allows the user to enter input from a keyboard and view output as text in a window.

termination condition A Boolean expression that is checked to determine whether or not to stop iterating within a loop. If this expression is true, iteration stops.

test suite A set of test cases that exercise the capabilities of a software component.

text editor A program that allows the user to enter text, such as a program, and save it in a file.

text file A file that contains characters and is readable and writable by text editors.

threads A type of process that can run concurrently with other processes.

thread-safe The property of a data structure in which threads are automatically provided synchronized access.

time slicing A means of scheduling threads or processes wherein each process receives a definite amount of CPU time before returning to the ready queue.

time-out The notification of a thread to relinquish the CPU after a designated interval of time.

time-sharing operating systems Computer systems that can run multiple programs in such a manner that users have the illusion that they are running simultaneously.

title bar The top border of a window that can contain a title and can be dragged with a mouse.

top-down design A method for coding by which the programmer starts with a top-level task and implements subtasks. Each subtask is then subdivided into smaller subtasks. This process is repeated until each remaining subtask is easily coded. *See also* stepwise refinement.

touchscreen interface A user interface that allows the user to enter input by tapping or gesturing while touching its screen.

transistor A device with no moving parts that can hold an electromagnetic signal and that is used to build computer circuitry for memory and a processor.

translator A program that converts a program written in one language to an equivalent program in another language.

true color The use of enough color values that the human eye cannot distinguish adjacent colors on the scale.

truth table A means of listing all of the possible values of a Boolean expression.

tuple A linear, immutable collection.

turtle graphics A set of resources that manipulate a pen in a graphics window.

two-dimensional grid A data structure whose items can be accessed by specifying two indices, a row and a column.

two-way selection statement See `if-else` statement.

type conversion function A function that takes one type of data as an argument and returns the same data represented in another type.

U

unicode set A character set that uses 16 bits to represent over 65,000 possible characters. These include the ASCII character set as well as symbols and ideograms in many international languages. *See also* ASCII character set.

Unified Modeling Language A graphical notation for describing a software system in various phases of development.

user interfaces Software and hardware devices that present information to human users and receive input data or commands from them.

V

values Items that are associated with a key and are located by a key in a dictionary.

variable A memory location, referenced by an identifier, whose value can be changed during execution of a program.

variable identifier A name that refers to a memory location, whose value can be changed during execution of a program.

variable references The process whereby the computer looks up and returns the values of variables.

variance The mean of the squares of the numbers in a data set minus the square of the mean of those numbers.

vector graphics The drawing of simple two-dimensional shapes.

view The set of resources that are responsible for displaying data in a program and interacting with the user.

virtual assistant A computing device that responds to user's commands, usually via voice.

virtual machine A software tool that behaves like a high-level computer.

virtual reality A technology that allows a user to interact with a computer-generated environment, usually simulating movement in three dimensions.

visualization The use of plots, charts, graphs, and animations to reveal or focus attention on patterns in a data set.

vocabulary The set of words in a language.

W

Wait The making of a thread inactive until a condition becomes true.

waterfall model A series of steps in which a software system trickles down from analysis to design to implementation. *See also* software development life cycle.

web applications A program that runs on a remote server but uses clients' Web browsers to deliver them services.

web browser Software that makes requests for Web pages, receives them from a Web server, and renders them on a display.

web client Software on a computer that makes requests for resources and receives them from the Web.

web servers Software on a computer that responds to requests for resources and makes them available on the Web.

while loop A pretest loop that examines a Boolean expression before causing a statement to be executed.

widgets Computational objects that display an image, such as a button or a text field, in a window and support interaction with the user.

window A rectangular area of a computer screen that can contain window objects. Windows typically can be resized, minimized, maximized, zoomed, or closed.

Index

Note: Boldface type indicates key terms

Special Characters

\ (backslash), 36, 43, 111
* (asterisk), 37, 443, 444, 446
" (double quotation mark), 36
= (equal sign), 38, 69
/ (forward slash), 110
% (percent sign), 63
+ (plus sign), 37, 45, 130
' (single quotation mark), 36

A

abacus, 7–9
absolute pathname, 110
abstract behavior, 342
abstraction, 11, 38, 160, 161, 191, 199, 296, 312, 336, 342, 343, 403
abstraction mechanisms, 160, 161, 185, 259, 295, 312, 336, 342
   subclassing and inheritance as, 259
accept method, 412
accessor methods, 217, 404
accessors, 300, 309
addButton method, 265
addCheckbutton method, 283
addFloatField, 268
addRadiobuttonGroup method, 285
addTextArea method, 279
Advanced Research Projects Agency Network
   (ARPANET), 13, 14
algorithms, 2–3, 8, 431–436
   counting instructions, 434–436
   efficiency of, 431–436
   exponential, 454–456
   information processing related, 3
   linear, 455–456
   memory used by, 438–439
   profiler case study, 456–461
   quicksort, 448
   run time of, 432–434
   search, 439–442
   sort, 443–447
aliases, 132

aliasing, 132–133
Allen, Paul, 13
Alto, 13
analog information, 226
analysis, 30
Analytical Engine, 8
analytics, 354
analyze methods, 383
ancestor, 259
ancestors, 336
and operator, 73
anonymous function, 202
Apollo Space Mission, 12
append method, 129–131, 134
appendText method, 279
applications software, 6
approximating square roots case study, 81–83
apps, 6
argument function, 199
arguments, 19, 45–46, 137
arithmetic expressions, 41–43
arithmetic operations, 42, 311
artificial intelligence, 11
ASCII set, 40
aspect ratio, 236
assembler, 11
assembly languages, 11
assignment, 34–38
assignment statement, 37–38
associated software technologies, 15
association, 142
association lists, 142
asymptotic analysis, 438
Atanasoff–Berry Computer (ABC), 10
Atanasoff, John, 10
ATM case study, 323–328
attribute dictionary, 260
augmented assignment operations, 60
average-case performance, 441, 447

B

Babbage, Charles, 8, 9
Backus, John, 11
Bank class, 316–318
bar charts, 369–371

493